MARXISM AND LAW

MARXISM AND LAW

EDITED BY
PIERS BEIRNE
University of Connecticut
RICHARD QUINNEY
Brown University

JOHN WILEY & SONS
New York / Chichester / Brisbane / Toronto / Singapore

Library of Congress Cataloging in Publication Data:

Main entry under title:

Marxism and law.

Includes bibliographical references and indexes.
1. Law and socialism—Addresses, essays,
lectures. I. Beirne, Piers. II. Quinney, Richard.
K357.Z9M37   340'.11   81-15927
ISBN 0-471-08758-0   AACR2

Printed in the United States of America

10 9 8 7 6 5 4 3 2 1

Faced with working class struggle on the political plane, law organizes the structure of the compromise equilibrium permanently imposed on the dominant classes by the dominated. It also regulates the forms in which physical repression is exercised: indeed, we need to stress the fact that this juridical system, these 'formal' and 'abstract' liberties are also conquests of the popular masses. In this sense and this alone does modern law set the limits of the exercise of power and of intervention by the state apparatuses.

Nicos Poulantzas, State, Power, Socialism

PREFACE

Marxism and Law is designed to provide readers with a wide yet coherent range of contemporary Marxist writings on law. Our primary audience is intended to be students in the sociology of law, but we hope that this book will be useful to upper-level undergraduate and graduate students in any discipline that makes the sociality of law a problematic object of inquiry. We sincerely thank the many students and colleagues who have offered us their suggestions for the structure and contents of this collection. We believe that students will find the scope and quality of the authors' arguments demanding, provocative, and exciting. We are especially indebted to the generosity and time given us by Rick Abel, Bill Chambliss, Randy Garber, Alan Hunt, Peter Manning, Steve Spitzer, Mark Tushnet, and Steven Vago. Carol Luitjens our editor at Wiley was most helpful. It is the authors who have contributed to *Marxism and Law* to whom we owe our deepest appreciation. Their scholarship has greatly advanced our understanding of law.

Piers Beirne
Richard Quinney
October, 1981

ABOUT THE AUTHORS

PIERS BEIRNE was born in London in 1949 and received his Ph.D. from the University of Durham in 1974. He is the author of *Fair Rent and Legal Fiction* (1977), and with Robert Sharlet edited and introduced *Pashukanis: Selected Writings on Marxism and Law* (1980, tr. Peter Maggs). After a year at the University of Wisconsin-Madison, he has taught sociology at the University of Connecticut since 1977.

JAMES BRADY is assistant professor at the University of Massachusetts, Boston, where he teaches courses on comparative law, the CIA, the Vietnam War, and imperialism. He has two books forthcoming on justice and society in China, Cuba, and the United States. As a Marxist activist, he is involved in movements for prisoners' rights, opposition to nuclear power and militarism, and local community-organizing efforts to combat crime and racism. He lives in a socialist collective in Boston.

MAUREEN CAIN is currently a free-lance sociologist with visiting appointments at the London School of Economics and the University of Surrey, and is editor of the *International Journal of the Sociology of Law*. She is the author of *Society and the Policeman's Role* (1973) and, with Alan Hunt, edited and introduced *Marx and Engels on Law* (1979).

ALAN D. FREEMAN has been a professor of law at the University of Minnesota Law School since 1971. He teaches constitutional law, property law, land-use regulation, civil rights, and law and Marxism, and also researches and publishes articles in these fields. He is a member of the National Lawyers Guild and is active in the Conference on Critical Legal Studies.

PETER GABEL is a member of the organizing committee of the Conference on Critical Legal Studies, and is co-president of New College of California, a democratically-run college and law school in San Francisco, where he teaches contracts and law and political theory. He has published several articles on legal theory, and is currently preparing a book-length manuscript entitled "The Denial of Desire and the Psychoanalytic Foundations of Belief in Authority."

EUGENE D. GENOVESE was editor of the now-defunct quarterly *Marxist Perspectives*. He is a Fellow of the American Academy of Arts and Sciences and past president of the Organization of American Historians. A professor of history at the University of Rochester, his most recent book is *From Rebellion to Revolution: Afro-American Slave Revolts in the Making of the Modern World.*

CHARLES W. GRAU gained a J.D. from the University of Wisconsin–Madison in 1977. He is currently Senior Research Attorney at the American Judicature Society in Chicago, for whom he has edited several publications.

DOUGLAS HAY is the author of several articles, and is currently working on English and Quebec criminal law and crime of the eighteenth century. In 1980 he was a visiting professor at Yale Law School, and now teaches at the Memorial University of Newfoundland.

ALAN HUNT holds degrees in law and sociology and is on the editorial board of *Marxism Today.* Assistant Dean of Law at Middlesex Polytechnic, he is the author of *The Sociological Movement in Law, Marx and Engels on Law* (with Maureen Cain) and editor of *Marxism and Democracy.*

KARL E. KLARE is professor of law at Northeastern University School of Law. With Dick Howard, he edited *The Unknown Dimension: European Marxism Since Lenin.* A member of the organizing committee of the Conference on Critical Legal Studies, his current work is on the intellectual and social history of labor law in the United States from 1935 to 1980.

SOL PICCIOTTO lectures in law at Warwick University. Active in the Conference of Socialist Economists as an editor of its journal *Capital and Class,* and as convenor of its Law and State working group, he has had some experience of political struggles involving law and working with local trade union and community groups.

NICOS POULANTZAS was born in Athens in 1936 and taught sociology at the University of Vincennes until his untimely death in 1979. One of the greatest exponents of Marxist political theory, his most important works include *Political Power and Social Classes, Fascism and Dictatorship, Classes in Contemporary Capitalism, Crisis of the Dictatorships—Portugal, Spain, Greece* and *State, Power, Socialism.*

RICHARD QUINNEY received his Ph.D. from the University of Wisconsin in 1962. His many radical contributions to the study of crime and law include *The Social Reality of Crime, Critique of Legal Order,* and *Class, State, and Crime.* Recently, in the continuing project to develop a critically reflective sociology, Quinney published *Providence: The Reconstruction of Social and Moral Order,* an integration of Marxism and prophetic theology. Currently he is investigating the grounding of contemporary social theory in the metaphysics of social existence.

STEVE REDHEAD has been a student at the Universities of Manchester and Warwick. He is currently Senior Lecturer in Law at Manchester Polytechnic. He is presently researching the forms of legal regulation of professional football in Britain.

JANET RIFKIN is associate professor in the Legal Studies Program at the University of Massachusetts/Amherst. She currently serves as ombudsperson at the University of Massachusetts, and works on a project examining the limits of the adversary model of conflict resolution.

BOAVENTURA de SOUSA SANTOS is professor of sociology at the School of Economics, University of Coimbra. He has studied at Coimbra, Yale, and in West Germany. His research in the sociology of law has concentrated on questions of popular justice, legal pluralism, and the sociology of legal rhetoric.

ANDREW T. SCULL is associate professor at the University of California/San Diego. He is the author of *Decarceration: Community Treatment of the Deviant—A Radical View, Museums of Madness: The Social Organization of Insanity in Nineteenth Century England,* and has edited *Mad-Doctors, Madhouses, and Mad-men.*

ROBERT SHARLET is professor of political science at Union College in Schenectady. Co-editor of *The Soviet Union Since Stalin* (1980), with Piers Beirne he edited *Pashukanis: Selected Writings on Marxism and Law* (1980, tr. Peter Maggs). The author of numerous articles on Soviet Law, with Beirne and Maggs he is now working on *Stuchka: Selected Writings on Marxism and Law,* funded by the National Endowment for the Humanities.

STEVEN SPITZER is associate professor of sociology at Suffolk University in Boston. Most of his recent work involves an attempt to develop and apply a historical and comparative perspective on the transformation of social control in capitalist societies. At present he is completing a historical study of private policing and capitalist development in America.

COLIN SUMNER is a law graduate who moved into criminology and sociology. He has taught sociology at the University of Wales (Aberystwyth) and now lectures at Cambridge University, specializing in social theory, philosophy of social science, and the sociology of crime and deviance. Author of *Reading Ideologies* (1979), he has just completed a book on crime and justice in the underdeveloped world.

E. P. THOMPSON was professor of social history at Warwick University, and now is active in the antinuclear movement. His many books include *The Making of the English Working Class, Whigs and Hunters: The Origin of the Black Act, William Morris, Romantic to Revolutionary, The Poverty of Theory,* and *Writing by Candlelight.*

CONTENTS

EDITORS' INTRODUCTION

THEMES AND ISSUES

Several factors prompted us to collaborate as editors of the collection of essays in *Marxism and Law*. Both of us have encountered, within different institutional and geographical settings, similar difficulties as teachers in compiling and distributing to students the materials for our courses associated with Marxist analyses of law. To begin with, the published writings of the authors of classical Marxism have never been noted for their easy access or unambiguous interpretation. Now this in itself does not incur any special problem. But clear exposition of the content of Marx's and Engels' numerous references to law is made most cumbersome when these are scattered throughout the entire corpus of their work.

It has long been true that important references to state and law, in the writings, speeches, and notebooks of Marx and Engels, have been assiduously woven together and circulated in inexpensive editions (on the state, on revisionism, on anarchism, etc.) by Progress Publishers of Moscow. But because of the uncritical and turgid manner in which these were introduced, the peculiar information contained in the *Notes* at the end of each volume, and the suspicions inevitably aroused by passages omitted or excised, they provided more of a catechismic than a pedagogic asset. Material not found in the Progress volumes could perhaps still be located between other covers. But the arguments in them invariably occurred in the spirit of other debates, in other languages, and for different purposes. This situation was considerably eased in 1979 with the overdue appearance of *Marx and Engels on Law,* a comprehensive collection of Marx's and Engels' original writings on law that was capably edited and introduced by Cain and Hunt.[1] Students will find the Cain and Hunt volume doubly useful; as a reliable source for distinguishing Marx's and Engels' theoretical analyses *of* law from their sometimes contradictory polemic *against* law, and as a background to many of the issues raised in *Marxism and Law*.

Not since the pioneering efforts of the commodity-exchange school of law—which flourished in the USSR from the early 1920s until its violent suppression in the

---

[1]Maureen Cain and Alan Hunt, Eds., *Marx and Engels on Law* (London: Academic Press, 1979). Rather different accounts of Marx's and Engels' view of law that we also recommend are Gary Young, "Marx on Bourgeois Law," in S. Spitzer, Ed., *Research in Law and Sociology* (Conn.: JAI Press, 1979), Vol. 2, pp. 133–168; and Paul Phillips, *Marx and Engels on Law and Laws* (Oxford: Martin Robertson, 1980).

mid-1930s—has the need for a theory of law held such strategic importance within Marxism as now. The 1980s are likely to be a period when several of the most exacting questions that confront the whole socialist movement have reference points that have already become central categories in the Marxist analysis of law. The history and consequences of mechanistic determinism, and the dull legacy bequeathed by Bolshevik economism; the uneasy metaphor of base and superstructure; the ontological status of individualism within the discourse of human rights; the problem of the right to national and cultural self-determination; the significance of the demand for the retention of civil liberties—in each of these issues a necessary component is an urgent concern with the limits and contradictions of social regulation through law, with the historical specificity of certain forms of law. These issues propel us, cumulatively and rudely, to a region that by earlier generations was almost deemed sacrosanct. The very concept of socialism itself, and the forms of social regulation most appropriate to it, are fast becoming the object of open and rigorous debate.[2]

To our knowledge *Marxism and Law* is the only collection of contemporary Marxist writings on law. Several of the essays we solicited especially for it. Many of the essays can be found only in little-known journals or periodicals with low circulation confined to one side of the Atlantic. We hope that all of the essays in *Marxism and Law* can now be widely disseminated and discussed, and that they will be useful to students and scholars who are developing a Marxist perspective in the study of law. In nearly all cases, and without regard to intellectual error or insight, we have tried to resist the obvious pressures to abbreviate the text of the essays. Not to have done this would have been to violate the integrity of the authors' original intentions. Necessary textual abbreviations are indicated by the conventional symbol (. . .).

Students should be aware of several points about *Marxism and Law* before they embark on its contents. The book, first, does not presume to provide a general Marxist theory of law. Such a grandiose project is nowadays notoriously difficult to reconcile with the pressing need for specific empirico-historical analyses of law—analyses that have lately been thrust onto the agenda of socialist politics. Second, there are still some very important areas of inquiry that are absent from Marxist analyses of law, and this is reflected in the pages of *Marxism and Law*. There is still a notable dearth of studies that deal with socialist feminism, with the comparative analysis of legal systems (especially in the technologically undeveloped parts of the world), and with the substantive branches of law relating to property, contract, and tort.[3]

For those students who wish to focus only on Marxist analyses of law we believe, in our recent experience, that *Marxism and Law* can profitably be used in conjunction with a book such as Cain and Hunt's *Marx and Engels on Law*. For those with broader intentions, *Marxism and Law* could be used as a supplement to, or a dialogue with, books such as Donald Black's *The Behavior of Law*, Roberto Unger's *Law in Modern Society*, or Friedman and Macaulay's *Law and the Behavioral Sci-*

[2]For example, Paul Hirst, "Law, Socialism and Rights," in Pat Carlen and Mike Collison, Eds., *Radical Issues in Criminology* (Oxford: Martin Robertson, 1980), pp. 58–105.

[3]Some of these deficiencies are to be remedied in a book forthcoming from the Conference on Critical Legal Studies.

ences.[4] We have not included suggestions for further reading in *Marxism and Law*. Given the extensive bibliographies at the end of most of the essays, this would be inappropriate. Students will, however, find a brief introduction to the development of Marxist analyses of law in this Editors' Introduction; this contains fairly lengthy bibliographical footnotes. The five chapters in *Marxism and Law* were constructed according to what we take to be the major systemic relations of law. Each chapter is prefaced by our summaries of the essays in them, and brief indications of the issues that they raise.

SOCIAL THEORY AND LAW

One of the modest virtues of much contemporary Marxism is the desire to transcend the intellectual vice imposed by formal disciplinary boundaries. It is therefore inexcusable that the concepts of Marxist theory are often presented to students as an isolated and closed world, or as Jean-Paul Sartre was keen to put it, as an already totalized knowledge positing its own self-sufficiency. Familiarity does, indeed, breed content. There are, we stress, invaluable lessons to be gleaned from various non-Marxist traditions that some, regrettably, continue to designate carte blanche as bourgeois social theory.

Accordingly, this first chapter introduces students to the major sociological traditions within whose terms much of the general renewal of interest in law has been couched. By immersing the reader in what from the outset may appear as the very abstract world of classical social theory, we do not wish to give the impression that there exists a real dislocation between theoretical and empirical enquiry; on the contrary, theoretical and empirical investigations of any phenomena are equally necessary, dialectical moments of the same enterprise. But in a discipline that for 50 years has been defined by the objectives of social engineering, we sometimes forget that all empirical enquiry embodies and is guided by theoretical principles.

The four essays in Chapter 1 were selected because they are explicitly directed to the different theoretical principles invoked to identify the hallmarks of western law. These essays address, respectively, the concept of law within the writings of Durkheim, Weber, Marx and Engels, and modern sociology.

Students may eventually decide that various questions posed, for example, by Max Weber in Germany at the beginning of this century and by Evgeny Pashukanis in the USSR 25 years later, are not entirely dissimilar. Both Weber and Pashukanis predicated their analysis of bourgeois law on the acceptance of the juristic notion of the individual legal subject as the volitional bearer of rights and obligations. Why, they entreat us, is social regulation under capitalism typically conducted through law? Why *law,* rather than through custom or naked violence? What are the presuppositions for, and the unintended consequences of, an atomized social world that is engendered, defined, coded, and regulated through the prism of the abstract and universal postulates of law? Certain aspects of these questions comprise a terrain of which Marxist theory has tended to be singularly neglectful. We cede this terrain at our peril.

[4]Donald Black, *The Behavior of Law* (New York: Academic Press, 1976); Roberto Unger, *Law in Modern Society: Toward a Criticism of Social Theory* (New York: Free Press; 1976); Lawrence M. Friedman and Stewart Macaulay, *Law and the Behavioral Sciences* (New York: Bobbs-Merrill, 1977), 2nd ed.

LAW AND CLASS

Two features of legal regulation have unduly preoccupied Marxist analysis in the last decade. First, there have been many studies devoted to the enactment and differential, repressive enforcement of criminal law. Sometimes this has manifested itself in detailed analysis of the internal workings of institutions within systems of criminal justice. All too rarely have these studies attempted to lay bare the historical specificity of particular notions of justice itself.[5] The criminalization of social action is an important yet, we maintain, only the most visible facet of social regulation through law. Second, and fewer in number, have been studies that focus on the narrow, economistic relations between labor and capital.[6] In both these areas there has been an unfortunate tendency to conceive of law simply as a state apparatus that mechanically reflects the interests of economically dominant classes. Legislation that, for whatever reason, is contrary to the immediacy of these interests then tends to be explained—or explained away—in terms of its functional contribution to the long-run stability of the social formation as a whole.

The four readings in Chapter 2 indicate that a somewhat different view should be had of the relation between law and social classes. Law is not simply an instrument or bludgeon of capital. "Nothing characterises the spirit of capital better," Marx wrote in *Capital,* "than the history of English factory legislation."[7] But Marx at once adds that the legal limitation and regulation of the working day was wrung step by step from Parliament in the course of a protracted civil war.[8] Law must therefore be seen as a crucial arena of political struggle in which certain gains and losses can be made by all contending classes. As E. P. Thompson has reminded us:

> . . . if we suppose that law is no more a mystifying and pompous way in which class power is registered and executed, then we need not waste our labour studying its history and forms. One Act would be much the same as another. . . .[9]

But what inherent limits does the "rule of law"—the doctrinal separation between politics and civil society—set to the achievements of working class political action? As in each of the other chapters, we have tried to temper the tendency for unwarranted generalization with a selection of essays that are sensitive to the need for empirical and historical illustration.

[5]Two notable exceptions are Allen W. Wood, "The Marxian Critique of Justice," *Philosophy and Public Affairs,* 2 1972), 244–282; M. Cohen et al., Eds., *Marx, Justice and History* (Princeton, N.J.: Princeton University Press, 1980).

[6]The reader should refer to Colin Sumner, *Reading Ideologies: An Investigation into the Marxist Theory of Ideology and Law* (London: Academic Press, 1979), pp. 253–256.

[7]Karl Marx, *Capital,* Vol. I, (London: Penguin, 1976), at p. 390; quoted in Phillip Corrigan and Derek Sayer, "How the Law Rules: Variations on Some Themes in Karl Marx," in Alan Hunt, Ed., *Law, State and Economy* (London: Croom Helm, 1981).

[8]Margaret Somers (Department of Sociology, Harvard University) has written to us suggesting the massive historical problem that this leaves unexplained the failures of the equally class-conscious Chartist anti-Poor Law movements.

[9]E. P. Thompson, *Whigs and Hunters* (New York: Pantheon Books, 1975), p. 267. The concluding section of this book, from which this quotation is taken, is reprinted on pp. 130–137 of *Marxism and Law.*

LAW AND STATE

In different ways, following on the lead of Picciotto's essay in the preceding chapter, the essays in Chapter 3 begin to pose the considerably untheorized problem of the relation between law and state. Is the legal system always and only a state apparatus? Does legal doctrine have no autonomous, internal logic of development?[10] The institutions of law clearly act to coordinate and unify the very state institutions that constitutional doctrine declares ought to be separate in a democracy. The legal system therefore occupies a uniquely central position in relation to the state.

But how can law operate as the central factor of cohesion *between* state apparatuses and, without glaring and transparent contradiction, occur in the same moment as a component *of* the state? We are still very far from successfully addressing this question. To answer it we must, bluntly, confront the processes by which law is able to legitimate itself. As Pat Carlen has recently suggested, this confrontation involves both a contradiction and a recognition: "a contradiction of law's claims at the level of theory; and a recognition of law's claims and effects at the level of ideology."[11]

LAW AND IDEOLOGY

In Chapter 4 we are concerned with the way in which the sets of ideas and beliefs contained in legal doctrine propagate and reproduce certain forms of social relationships. The concept of ideology, both within the tradition of Marxism and that of the sociology of knowledge established largely by Karl Mannheim, has always been notoriously difficult to fathom. Within Marxist philosophy the concept has been variously understood to refer to systems of thought that serve class interests, to false or socially determined consciousness, and to the epistemologically grounded distinction between essences and the distorted character of surface appearances. Marx's own view (at least in sections of *Capital*) was that if the outward appearance and the essence of things directly coincided then science would be superfluous. Without such a view, of course, the analysis of any system of thought becomes an exercise only in a thoroughgoing Protagorean relativism.[12]

Discussion of the concept of ideology in this chapter is far removed from the very abstract debates in which its proper meaning and significance have been discussed. The four essays are generally concerned to show that the actual content of legislation embodies diverse ideological forms and practices. At the level of doctrine law is an authoritative form of injunction or prohibition. It is the intersection point, enforced by political power, of competing and sometimes mutually incompatible ideologies.

---

[10]This question is implicitly a focus in two essays by Mark Tushnet. See his "Perspectives on the Development of American Law: A Critical Review of Friedman's *A History of American Law*," *Wisconsin Law Review* (1977), 81–109; and "Truth, Justice and the American Way: An Interpretation of Public Law Scholarship in the Seventies," *Texas Law Review*, 57, no. 8 (1979), 1307–1359.

[11]Pat Carlen, "Radical Criminology, Penal Politics and the Rule of Law," pp. 7–24 in Pat Carlen and Mike Collison (1980), op. cit. supra n. 2, at p. 12.

[12]Good recent accounts of Marxist (and other) concepts of ideology may be found in Nicholas Abercrombie, *Class, Structure and Knowledge*, (New York: New York University Press, 1980); Joe McCarney, *The Real World of Ideology* (Brighton, Sussex: Harvester Press, 1980).

Law as injunction or prohibition cannot be exhausted simply as myth. The essays in this chapter explore the often invisible domination of legal thought through analyses of legal reasoning, legally sanctioned racism, and patriarchy.

LAW AND SOCIALIST CONSTRUCTION

The struggle for civil liberties and rights within the various forms of bourgeois democratic rule harbors the most serious dilemmas. As the preceding chapters make abundantly clear, the very limits of formal political struggle are defined by pregiven notions of justice, legal procedure, and fair play. Marx and Engels were often careful to warn, however, that it is usually the most backward sections of the socialist movement that articulate their revolutionary demands in legal terms. Yet it is also true that significant inroads may be confirmed and implemented through law. What relevance does this dilemma imply, after the initial destruction of bourgeois property, for the political struggle to construct and consolidate socialism? As Lenin once dryly noted, legality is not an empty sack that can be filled with a new class content immediately after the revolution. We must examine far more sensitively, and vigorously, what needs to be destroyed/created in the process of the building of socialism, with what consequences and for whom.

This concluding chapter raises some of the tremendous dilemmas and problems unavoidably sustained during the transitional period of socialism, the period between capitalism and communism. In his *Critique of the Gotha Programme,* Marx informs us that equal right (the "rule of law") is a bourgeois notion that merely reproduces the inequality of unequal labor; equal right is a "defect"[13] that cannot be crossed until the higher phase of communism. The first two essays in Chapter 5 show how the writings of Pashukanis and E. P. Thompson bear on the problems of the role of law in socialist construction. The two final essays discuss very different attempts to use law during the phase of socialist transition—in China, Portugal, and Brazil.

MARXIST THEORIES OF LAW: AN INTRODUCTION

The decade since the political and intellectual unrest of the late 1960s has produced a body of Marxist theory—much of it documented in *Marxism and Law*—broadly directed to the nature of legal regulation in social formations dominated by capitalist (and occasionally, collectivist) property.[14] In the English language this theory is most prominently expressed in organizations such as the Conference of Socialist Economists, the National Deviancy Conference, the Centre for Contemporary Cultural Studies, the Crime and Social Justice network, the Conference on Critical Legal Studies, and the Critique of Law Editorial Collective.[15] To trace the historical origins

[13]Karl Marx, *Critique of the Gotha Programme,* pp. 315–331 in *Marx Engels Selected Works*, one volume, London: Lawrence and Wishart, 1970), at p. 320.

[14]Some sections of this introduction may be found in Piers Beirne, "Empiricism and the Critique of Marxism on Law and Crime," *Social Problems*, 26, no. 4 (April 1979), 373–385; and Piers Beirne, "Some More on Empiricism in the Study of Law: A Reply to Jacobs," *Social Problems*, 27, no. 4 (April 1980), 471–475.

[15]A history of the Conference of Socialist Economists is provided in Hugo Radice, "A Short History of the CSE," *Capital and Class*, (spring 1980), 43–49. The most recent work of the CSE (law and the state

of the theoretical movement that has coalesced in these organizations, we must outline the development of the "new deviancy theory." This theory, which culminated in the publication of Taylor, Walton, and Young's *The New Criminology* in 1973, exercised a parallel and originally symbiotic relation with those Marxist accounts of legal regulations which at that time did not have criminal law as their primary focus.[16]

FROM CRIMINOLOGY TO MARXISM

The intellectual origins of contemporary Marxist analyses of law seem primarily to have lain in a politically motivated amalgam of certain concepts nurtured within criminology, deviance, and the conflict tradition in sociology. In outlining what is a plausible but incomplete history of this development Galliher has observed that:

> ... the popularity of the labeling perspective, with its emphasis on societal reaction and created deviance seems to have provided the conditions in the discipline for the swift re-emergence of the conflict orientation once it was triggered by the political milieu.... The conflict perspective stressing powerful interest groups' control of the law, police, and courts, in turn created the intellectual basis for the emergence of Marxism in criminology in the 1970's.[17]

Indeed, given the almost wholesale obsession with criminal law at this time, how could Marxist analyses of other branches of law have proceeded otherwise? There was no substantive precedent, at least in the English-language literature, for such analyses. Some relevant Marxist writings did exist elsewhere, such as the contributions made by Bonger, Renner, Gramsci, and Lukács, and numerous works on commodity exchange and criminal law by Stuchka, Pashukanis, Berman, and Krylenko in the USSR in the 1920s. But these remained, and remain, largely untranslated and hence effectively unavailable to an English-language audience. Moreover, there was an undercurrent of suspicion that many of these pioneering efforts were closer to European social democracy than to Marxism. And no strict precedent appeared to

---

group), in conjunction with the National Deviancy Conference, is Bob Fine, Richard Kinsey, John Lea, Sol Picciotto, and Jock Young, Eds., *Capitalism and the Rule of Law*, (London: Hutchinson, 1979). The National Deviancy Conference was first held in 1968 in York, England, and now meets only sporadically. Its most recent publication is *Permissiveness and Control* (London: Macmillan, 1980). The most well-known work from the University of Birmingham's Centre for Contemporary Cultural Studies is Stuart Hall, C. Critcher, T. Jefferson, J. Clarke, and B. Roberts, *Policing the Crisis* (London: Macmillan, 1978). The Crime and Social Justice network is a collective within the Center for the Study of Labor and Economic Crisis, in Berkeley. The Conference on Critical Legal Studies is a national organization of lawyers, teachers, students, social scientists, and others committed to the development of a critical theoretical perspective on law, legal practice, and legal education. It may be reached through its secretary, Mark Tushnet, Law School, University of Wisconsin-Madison, Madison, Wisconsin 53706, USA. The most recent work of the Critique of Law Editorial Collective is *Critique of Law: A Marxist Analysis* (1978), U.N.S.W. Critique of Law Society. It may be reached through Gill Boehringer, School of Law, Macquarie University, Balaclava Road, North Ryde, N.S.W. 2113, Australia.

[16]For one account of the theoretical journey from criminology to Marxism, students are advised to read Jock Young, "Left Idealism, Reformism and Beyond: From New Criminology to Marxism," pp. 11–28 in Bob Fine et al. (1979), op. cit. supra n. 15.

[17]John F. Galliher, "The Life and Death of Liberal Criminology," *Contemporary Crises*, 2, no. 2 (July 1978), 245–263. A similar argument is made in William V. Pelfrey, *The Evolution of Criminology* (Anderson Publishing, 1980), at p. 54.

exist in Marx's fragmented and unsatisfactory discourse on bourgeois law, even though some measure of inspiration has been afforded by his early confrontation with Hegel's *Rechtsphilosophie* and his humanist project for emancipation in such tracts as *On the Jewish Question*.

There is, therefore, obvious merit in the suggestion that the Marxist analyses of law and crime that emerged in the late 1960s had their origin in mainstream criminology and sociology. Strong candidates for their immediate intellectual ancestry, as some authors have observed, are labeling and conflict theories. Nor is this history inconvenienced by the fact that these latter theories received disciplinary prominence and academic respectability in the early 1960s. In that labeling and conflict theories were antiestablishment, cynical and bent on demystifying the legal order, it is clear that their surface structures were vehicles for carrying a political message not wholly incongruous with the one embraced by Marxism at that time. But we should by now have reason to be cautious. If this description is accurate, we are faced with the interesting paradox of a Marxism reared in the womb of theoretical structures to which it was, and is, ostensibly largely opposed.

In the intellectual history of social theory it is usually the case that the dominant problematic in a discipline is not reconstituted by a successor erected on novel or antagonistic sets of epistemological principles. It is far more common for the old problematic simply to be endowed with a different content, or for it to be shifted from one focus to another. It had become increasingly apparent that traditional or positivist[18] criminology was hopelessly unable to account for the new forms of social dissent that mushroomed in the 1960s. For 20 years it had virtually ignored the implications of Sutherland's work on white collar or corporate crime.[19] Sutherland's insights neither fostered nor permitted examination of the relationship between the legal system and social classes, but it did unequivocally reveal that crime was more evenly distributed throughout the social structure than criminologists then generally admitted. Positivist criminology was not only unable to explain the crimes committed by government and corporate enterprise. Incredibly, it had no competent explanation of the violence surrounding the civil rights, antiwar, and minority movements. In an influential argument Horowitz and Liebowitz demonstrated that the traditional distinction between social problems and the political system was rapidly becoming obsolete.[20] Behavior that in the past has been perceived and defined as social deviance was now assuming patterned ideological and organizational contours. Labeling theory, which came in many guises, was seen by its main protagonists if not as a coherent theory then as a palliative to a traditional criminology excessively imbued with positivism, correctionalism, and conservatism.

[18]The term positivism is rarely used in any precise epistemological sense, and tends to be popularly reserved as a derogatory label for those with whom one disagrees. The best analyses of positivism in criminology remain Chapter I of David Matza, *Delinquency and Drift* (New York: John Wiley, 1964); and Stanley Cohen, "Criminology and the Sociology of Deviance in Britain: A Recent History and a Current Report," in Paul Rock and Mary MacIntosh, Eds., *Deviance and Social Control* (London: Tavistock, 1974), pp. 1–40.

[19]See, especially, Edwin Sutherland, "White Collar Criminality," *American Sociological Review*, 5, no. I (1940) 5–12; *White Collar Crime* (New York: Dryden Press, 1949).

[20]Irving L. Horowitz and Martin Liebowitz, "Social Deviance and Political Marginality," *Social Problems*, 15, no. 3 (1968), 280–296.

Beginning with Howard Becker's noted statement in *Outsiders*[21] that deviance is not a quality of the action the person commits, but rather a result of the application by a social audience of rules and sanctions to an "offender," labeling theory promised to unravel the manner in which the boundaries between social dissent and more traditional forms of deviance were becoming blurred. What institutional processes coded certain forms of action, and not others, as deviant? Works by Becker[22] Matza,[23] and Lemert[24] roughly indicated the limits within which labeling theory would develop as a reaction to the excesses of positivist criminology. The focus of concern shifted from the characteristics of offenders to the social processes whereby an actor was labeled as deviant, stigmatized, and subsequently compelled into further deviation. Where positivist criminology saw its pregiven conceptual object as crime defined by statute and common law, labeling theory began by making the very notion of crime subjectively questionable.

Criminologists (or sociologists of deviance, as the new radicals now labeled themselves) were now forced to question the assumptions by which certain interactive meanings became routinized and enshrined with the institutional sanctity of legal authority. What was the social construction of the reality in which society created deviance? How was this reality negotiated? Positivist criminology had emphasized different versions of control theory whose common and basic unit (anthropological man) was subject to overwhelming social and ecological constraint. Labeling theory, although never successfully challenging the philosophical assumptions of constraint, and conscious of the dangers involved in the classical concept of free will, instead stressed the integrity and rationality of the subjective values of the outsider and the underdog. This entailed the simple methodological injunction that "offender" and "victim" were to be reversed. Where earlier research had tended to concentrate on property crimes and crimes of violence, the new problematic was filled with a concern for victimless and often esoteric "crimes." This required that sociologists suspend their personal values in order (empathetically) to understand the value systems under investigation. This method of naturalism, to use Matza's term, was thought to be "free from the philosophical preconceptions of the researcher . . . (it) is the philosophical view that strives *to remain true to the nature of the phenomenon under study or scrutiny.*"[25]

Where positivist criminology had dissolved the "causes" of crime into a plethora of multicausation and statistical correlations, labeling theory appeared to dispense with all mechanistic notions of causation. But this dispensation was deceptive. What was the logical form of explanation posited by labeling theory of secondary deviation if it was not based on the very mechanistic causation that labeling theorists detected and despised in positivist criminology? Secondary deviation merely turned out to be a sophisticated version of conventional theses that tried to explain recidivism. And

[21]Howard S. Becker, *Outsiders* (Glencoe: Free Press, 1963), at p. 9.

[22]Ibid., and *The Other Side* (Glencoe: Free Press, 1964).

[23]David Matza, *Delinquency and Drift* (New York: John Wiley, 1964); and *Becoming Deviant* (New Jersey: Prentice-Hall, 1969).

[24]Edwin M. Lemert, *Social Action and Legal Change: Revolution within the Juvenile Court* (Chicago: Aldine, 1970).

[25]David Matza, *Becoming Deviant* (1969), op. cit. supra n. 23, at p. 5, emphasis in the original.

the key concept of societal reaction occupied a causative status within labeling theory similar to that occupied, for example, by parental income, divorce, and education in traditional criminology.

Labeling theory left itself open to three other charges. Ethnomethodologists complained that it did not sufficiently explore the processes and meanings of social interaction at the microlevel. Even more damning was the charge that it was constructed on a sea of indiscriminate relativism. No useful advances could be made from a theory that made bedfellows of the prostitute and the pimp, organized crime and the stuttering habits of North Pacific coastal Indians. Marxists complained that labeling theory's focus on the interactive process between rule definers, rule breakers, and social audience was not carried through to its implicit conclusion—the mutual interpenetration of polity and economy. In 1970, in *The Coming Crisis of Western Sociology*, Alvin Gouldner concluded that ''Becker's school''

> . . . thus views the underdog as someone who is being mismanaged, not as someone who suffers and fights back. Here the deviant is sly but not defiant; he is tricky but not courageous; he sneers but does not accuse; he ''makes out'' without making a scene. Insofar as this school of theory has a critical edge to it, this is directed at the caretaking institutions who do the mopping-up job, rather than at the master institutions that produce the deviant's suffering.[26]

Labeling theory graciously gave the deviant a voice. But this voice was unable to articulate the lengthy social distance between ''caretaking'' and ''master'' institutions. Nor had it grasped that the social engineering policies of these institutions did not always occur in a complete vacuum. Sometimes these policies were explicable only in the context of the structural relations between social classes and state power. The great bulk of that tradition epitomized, in different ways, by Robert Merton's ''Social Structure and Anomie''[27] and Albert Cohen's *Delinquent Boys*[28] did, it was true, employ the concept of social class. But it used this concept very differently from the way it has normally been utilized in Marxist analysis, as a complex matrix constitutive of the social and technical relationships of production and exchange. Instead, it tended to assign to the concept of social class the rather loose meanings attributed to it during the post-1945 debates—within non-Marxist discourse—on functionalism, social stratification, and the imputed convergence of industrial societies.

It was conflict theory, drawing on the spirit of Weber, Simmel, C. Wright Mills, and Dahrendorf, that was quickly to supply an elemental theoretical vocabulary to fill this lacuna. Conflict theorists appear to have worked deductively from some highly contentious premises, and inductively from accounts of the origin and operation of particular pieces of legislation, to the type of statement recently embodied in the conclusion that ''the more there are differences in economic resources and economic power, the more one can expect that criminal codes will be administered

[26]Alvin W. Gouldner, *The Coming Crisis of Western Sociology* (New York: Basic Books, 1970).

[27]Robert K. Merton, ''Social Structure and Anomie,'' *American Sociological Review*, 3, no. 5 (1938), 672–682.

[28]Albert K. Cohen, *Delinquent Boys: The Culture of the Gang* (Chicago: Free Press, 1955).

in a way that pleases monied elites."[29] They began from the viewpoint that social life had certain invariant, universal features. A statement from Quinney's *The Social Reality of Crime,* first published in 1970, captures this viewpoint well: "In any society conflicts between persons, social units, or cultural elements are inevitable, the normal consequences of social life . . . *power* is the basic characteristic of social organization."[30] In Randall Collins's popular text *Conflict Sociology* we are informed that "for conflict theory the basic insight is that human beings are sociable but conflict-prone animals."[31]

An impressive body of research soon accumulated that strongly indicated that all legislation was typically the product of conflicts of interest.[32] All law was held to be created and coded according to the narrow interests of dominant social classes. Rarely, however, were these "interests" identified apart from the observation that law necessarily served them. This rigid causal chain was then extended to the argument that "when sanctions are imposed, the most severe sanctions will be imposed on persons in the lowest social class."[33] The historical problem with these arguments, when taken together, is that the truth of the former has often had implications incompatible with the truth of the latter. The "rule of law," if it is to gain the bare minimum of voluntary compliance, must appear to be just. There is much evidence to demonstrate that dominant social classes are unable to manipulate legal institutions and legal doctrine consistently, without contradiction and without political opposition. Such straightforward manipulation is, indeed, precluded by the tremendous diversity of political forms—the relation between social classes and state power—that may be associated with the processes of capital accumulation. The different political forms (caesarism, republicanism, fascism, democracy, etc.) have vastly different effects on the ability of particular social classes to manipulate state power. This reproduction of capitalist social relations *regularly* involves instances where capital itself is regulated, where certain working class interests are secured at the expense of capital. Only intellectual sophistry could assert that legislation raising the level of minimum wages, or reducing the length of the working day, represents something less than a positive gain for labor. We insist that the analysis of law must have empirical and historical specificity, and that this cannot be accomplished in terms of a rigid or unilinear causality. Each case must be examined empirically and on its own merits, and understood in its proper historical context.

The conflict theorists were rarely precise in delineating quite in what power and

[29]David Jacobs, "Inequality and the Legal Order: An Ecological Test of the Conflict Model," *Social Problems,* (1978), 515–525, at p. 516.

[30]Richard Quinney, *The Social Reality of Crime* (Boston: Little Brown, 1970), at pp. 8, 11.

[31]Randall Collins, *Conflict Sociology* (New York: Academic Press, 1975), at p. 59.

[32]The most influential of the conflict studies of law have been Jerome Hall, *Theft, Law and Society;* (Indianapolis: Bobbs-Merrill, 1952); William J. Chambliss, "A Sociological Analysis of the Law of Vagrancy," *Social Problems,* 12, no. 1, (1964), 67–77; Austin Turk, "Conflict and Criminality," *American Sociological Review,* 31, no. 3, (1966), 338–352; Pamela A. Roby, "Politics and Criminal Law: Revision of the New York State Penal Law on Prostitution," *Social Problems,* 17, no. 1 (1969) 83–109; Richard Quinney, *The Problem of Crime* (New York: Dodd Mead, 1970); and *The Social Reality of Crime* (1970), op. cit. supra n. 30; William J. Chambliss and Robert Seidman, *Law, Order, and Power* (Reading, Mass.: Addison-Wesley, 1971).

[33]William J. Chambliss and Robert Seidman (1971), op. cit. supra n. 26, at p. 475.

conflict consisted, how power manifested itself, how conflict was resolved, and why it was resolved at all. What in fact needed to be explained, given the surprising longevity of capitalist forms despite their endemic and pervasive contradictions, was precisely the absence of any sustained working class challenge to the legitimacy of capital itself. What were the conditions in which widespread ideological consensus was generated and prevailed?

This is not to underestimate the valuable legacy bequeathed by both labeling and conflict theories to the analysis of law. Primarily, this legacy lay in their attempt to infuse an intellectually impoverished discipline with many of the central questions raised earlier by classical social theory. But we must disagree with those who argue that the newly acquired institutional positions of labeling and conflict theories created an elective affinity with Marxist analysis. These positions could not have provided sufficient antecedent intellectual conditions for the application of Marxism to law. Labeling and conflict theories constituted part of the polemical climate but contained few, if any, intellectual premises for the emergence of Marxism in this area of social regulation.

Conflict theory was generally so vague in its basic assumptions, and so wide-ranging in its scope, that it always threatened to incorporate or co-opt a variety of perspectives, including what then passed for Marxist analysis of law, within the compass of its structure. But at the very moment when labeling and conflict accounts of law attained dominance among the liberal practitioners of the sociology of crime and deviance—and were found inadequate—there occurred an enormous re-surgence of interest in Marxist theory.[34] At first this was produced in the context of worldwide accumulation crises (the end of the German economic miracle, for example), the resounding defeats suffered by the socialist movement in the confusion of the 1960s, and open dissension within socialist and communist parties. Especially in Germany, France, and Italy, several of the most prominent European communist parties proceeded to debate the reasons for their successive political failures, their tactical and strategic mistakes in their national environs, and their continued ideolog-ical subservience to Stalinism after Stalin's death. These debates arose in the abstract realm of speculative philosophy. They then rapidly spread to the practical questions of political economy and the problem of the relation between state institutions and social classes.

Above all it was the work of Louis Althusser, in France, that first stimulated the attention of those Marxists concerned with the study of law. In *Reading Capital,* written with Etienne Balibar and translated into English in 1970, we rediscover Marx's notion that "the economic structure of the capitalist mode of production from the immediate process of production to circulation and the distribution of the social product, presupposes the existence of a *legal system;* the basic elements of which are

---

[34]This often manifested itself as a crude antinomy between Marxism and all other forms of social theory. Marxism *versus* social theory was a keynote of the times. Students should consult further Irving M. Zeitlin, *Ideology and the Development of Sociological Theory* (Englewood-Cliffs, N.J.: Prentice-Hall, (1968); Robin Blackburn, Ed., *Ideology in Social Science* (London: Fontana, 1972); Alvin W. Gouldner, *For Sociology* (London: Allen Lane, 1973); Martin Shaw, *Marxism and Social Science* (London: Pluto Press, 1975).

the *law of property* and the *law of contract.*"[35] A year later Althusser's "Ideology and Ideological State Apparatuses"[36] was made available to English-language audiences. The basis of this article was the seminal—if not entirely original—claim that the distinction between the public and private realms of social life was a distinction formulated by and internal to bourgeois law. The state was therefore every element that contributed to the cohesion of a social formation. In the Althusserian scheme, law occupies a unique role as a state apparatus in that it simultaneously discharges both ideological and repressive functions. Legal ideology lies at the heart of bourgeois individualism ("interpellating the subject"), and the primacy of the juridical subject contributes to the partial neutralization of the class struggle.[37] In other words, for Althusser law is a condition of existence of the capitalist mode of production. Law has its own ("relatively autonomous") logic of internal development. No longer could it be reduced to the level of a mere superstructural and passive reflection of economic and other relations.

Sociologists of law were slow in responding to Althusser's notion that law played a pervasive ideological role throughout the many levels of bourgeois social relations. In truth, this tardiness was partly because Althusser's intervention aroused more pressing debates on the status of humanism within Marxist philosophy, on the distinctions to be made between ideology and science within epistemology, and on the political status of intellectuals in the class struggle. Insulated from the major strands of social theory until the late 1960s, and baffled by the verbose terminology in which the exchanges on Marxist epistemology were now couched, sociologists of law tended to retain the notion that Marxism differed from other social theories not in its theoretical structure but only in that its political purpose was more radical.[38] The immediate result was a politicized approach to the study of criminal law and crime whereby Marxism was inserted into the traditional concerns of labeling and conflict theories. All the phenomena associated with criminal behavior and criminal law

[35]Louis Althusser and Etienne Balibar, *Reading Capital* (London: New Left Books, 1970), at p. 230. For a lucid summary of the Althusserian notion of ideology, students are recommended to read Nicholas Abercrombie, *Class, Structure and Knowledge* (New York: New York University Press, 1980), esp. pp. 92-113.

[36]Louis Althusser, "Ideology and Ideological State Apparatuses," pp. 127-86 *Lenin and Philosophy and Other Essays* (1971), (New York: Monthly Review Press, 1971), pp. 127-186. It should be noted that the major weakness of Althusser's argument in this essay, as Laclau has best shown, is that the state is portrayed simply as a functional quality that pervades all the levels of a social formation; this obscures the crucial distinction between class power and state power. See Ernesto Laclau, *Politics and Ideology in Marxist Theory* (London: New Left Books, 1977), pp. 51-79.

[37]Louis Althusser, *Essays in Self-Criticism* (London: New Left Books, 1976).

[38]Summaries of the theoretical condition of the sociology of law after 1970 may be found in Malcolm Feeley, "The Concept of Laws in Social Science: A Critique and Notes on an Expanded View," *Law and Society Review,* 10 (1976), 497-495; Alan Hunt, "Perspectives in the Sociology of Law," pp. 22-44 in Pat Carlen, Ed., *The Sociology of Law* (1976), *Sociological Review Monograph* no. 23, University of Keele; Lynn McDonald, *The Sociology of Law and Order* (Boulder: Westview Press, 1976), esp. pp. 100-137; Piers Beirne, *Fair Rent and Legal Fiction* (London: Macmillan, 1977), esp. pp. 1-50; David M. Trubek, "Complexity and Contradiction in the Legal Order: Balbus and the Challenge of Critical Social thought about Law," *Law and Society Review,* no. 3, (1977), 529-569. Strong criticism of Trubek is made in Peter d'Errico, "A Critique of 'Critical Social Thought about Law' and Some Comments on Decoding Capitalist Culture," unpublished ms., University of Massachusetts/Amherst; Alan Hunt, *The Sociological Movement in Law* (London: Macmillan, 1978).

were now to be understood from the vantage points of the mode of production, class struggle, and the state. The criminal justice system was now viewed as a state apparatus that existed simply to promote the functional requirements of the capitalist class. These endeavors did not produce a radical or Marxist criminology but a radical criminologist.[39]

A second wave of inspiration arrived with the controversy that surrounded the important contributions of Taylor, Walton, and Young's *The New Criminology* in 1973, and their edited collection, *Critical Criminology*, in 1975. Produced from within the National Deviancy Conference, *The New Criminology* was intended by its three authors to advance a "fully social theory of deviance."[40] This project was grounded in a rejection of positivism and an acceptance of the humanist and utopian bases of the writings of Marx and Engels. In the authors' own words:

> A full-blown Marxist theory of deviance, or at least a theory of deviance deriving from a Marxism so described, would be concerned to develop explanations of the ways in which particular sets of social relationships and means of production, give rise to attempts by the economically and politically powerful to order society in particular ways. It would ask with greater emphasis the question that Howard Becker poses (and does not face), namely, who makes the rules, and why?[41]

Taylor, Walton, and Young's attempt to extend Becker's question "who makes the rules, and why?" was an undoubted advance on earlier formulations. To paraphrase one nineteenth-century sage, we all at once became "new criminologists." In the Foreword to *The New Criminology*, Alvin Gouldner applauded that the three authors "have very keenly understood that a mere 'application' of Marxism to crime and deviance studies would be an exemplification of the very uncritical posture which is, at bottom, the position to which they are most relentlessly opposed."[42] Gouldner's praise turned out to be somewhat premature. The first salvo directed at the Marxism avowedly at the heart of *The New Criminology* had already been fired by Paul Hirst, a year earlier, in his article "Marx and Engels on Law, Crime and Morality."[43] In this article Hirst leveled the charge that

---

[39]Zenon Bankowski, Geoff Mungham, and Peter Young, "Radical Criminology or Radical Criminologist?" *Contemporary Crises*, 1, no. 1, (1977), 37–51.

[40]Ian Taylor, Paul Walton, and Jock Young, *The New Criminology* (London: Routledge and Kegan Paul, (1973), at p. 269.

[41]Ibid., p. 220.

[42]Ibid., p. xii. The seven formal requirements of Taylor, Walton, and Young's "fully social theory of deviance" are set out in pp. 270–278 of their book.

[43]Paul Q. Hirst, "Marx and Engels on Law, Crime and Morality," *Economy and Society*, 1, no. 1, (1972), 28–56. Other appraisals of *The New Criminology* have appeared in S. K. Mugsford, "Marxism and Criminology: A Comment on the Symposium Review of '*The New Criminology*'," *Sociological Quarterly*, (autumn 1974), 591–596; Elliott Currie, "Beyond Criminology: A Review of *The New Criminology*," *Issues in Criminology*, 9, no. 1 (1974), 123–157; Colin Sumner, "Marxism and Deviancy Theory," in Paul Wiles, Ed., *The Sociology of Crime and Delinquency in Britain* (London: Martin Robertson, 1976), Vol. 2, pp. 159–174; David Greenberg, "On One-Dimensional Marxist Criminology," *Theory and Society*, 3 (1976), 610–621; John F. Galliher, "The Life and Death of Liberal Criminology," *Contemporary Crises*, 2, no. 3 (1978), 245–263; David Downes, "Promise and Performance in British Criminology," *British Journal of Sociology*, 29, no. 4, (1978), 483–505; Robert Brown, "The New Criminology," in Eugene Kamenka et al., Eds., *Law and Society* (New York: St. Martin's Press, 1978), pp. 81–107; and several of the essays in James A. Inciardi, Ed., *Radical Criminology: The Coming Crises* (Beverly Hills: Sage Publications, 1980).

... Marxism has a quite different view of crime and "deviancy" from that of the radicals; a view that abolishes this field as a coherent object of study. There is no "Marxist theory of deviance".... The objects of Marxist theory are specified by its own concepts: the mode of production, the class struggle, the state, ideology, etc. Any attempt to apply Marxism to this pre-given field of sociology is therefore a more or less "revisionist" activity in respect of Marxism.[44]

Hirst's polemical criticisms were, in their turn, taken to task for leading toward a closure of theoretical development[45] and for suggesting that Marxism has a finite set or range of concepts.[46] With a twist of irony that would have delighted Max Weber, one consequence of these heated exchanges was the very opposite of that intended by Hirst. There at once ensued a veritable explosion of interest among Marxists in the study of law, crime, and deviance. If the Marxist study of deviance was not fully laid to rest, the Marxist study of law was by now brought to life. Within the space of a very short period of time there appeared summaries of Marx's and Engels' writings on law,[47] the rediscovery of the writings of the Austrian Karl Renner,[48] the popularity of the Russian commodity exchange school of law,[49] the renewed importance of Marxist historiography,[50] and studies of punishment and discipline.[51]

[44]Paul Q. Hirst, "Marx and Engels on Law, Crime and Morality," *Economy and Society*, 1, no. 1 (1972), 28–56. This article was reprinted in Ian Taylor, Paul Walton, and Jock Young, Eds., *Critical Criminology* (1975), pp. 203–232. Readers should also see the exchange in *Critical Criminology* between Ian Taylor and Paul Walton, "Radical Deviancy Theory and Marxism: A Reply to Paul Q. Hirst's 'Marx and Engels on Law, Crime and Morality', and Paul Q. Hirst, "Radical Deviancy Theory and Marxism: A Reply to Taylor and Walton."

[45]Colin Sumner, "Marxism and Deviancy Theory," in Paul Wiles, Ed., *The Sociology of Crime and Delinquency in Britain* (London: Martin Robertson, 1976), Vol. 2, pp. 159–174, at p. 269.

[46]Alan Hunt, "The Radical Critique of Law: Assessment," *International Journal of the Sociology of Law*, 8, no. 1 (1980), 33–46, at p. 43.

[47]For example, Maureen Cain, "The Main Themes of Marx's and Engels' Sociology of Law," *British Journal of Law and Society*, 1, no. 2 (1974), 136–168; Piers Beirne, "Marxism and the Sociology of Law: Theory or Practice?" *British Journal of Law and Society*, 2, no. 1 (1975) 78–81; Maureen Cain and Alan Hunt (1979), op. cit. supra n. 1; Paul Phillips (1980), op. cit. supra n. 1.

[48]Karl Renner's major treatise was first translated into English as K. Renner, *The Institutions of Private Law and their Social Functions* (London: Routledge & Kegan Paul, (1949), edited and with an introduction by O. Kahn-Freund. Recent appraisals of Renner's work may be found in Jim McManus, "The Emergence and Non-emergence of Legislation," *British Journal of Law and Society*, 5, no. 2 (1978), 185–201; Paul Q. Hirst, *On Law and Ideology* (London: Macmillan, 1979), in Chapter 5).

[49]For a brief introduction to the commodity exchange school of law readers should consult Piers Beirne and Robert Sharlet, Eds., *Pashukanis: Selected Writings on Marxism and Law* (London: Academic Press, 1980), translated by Peter B. Maggs, esp. editors' introduction pp. 1–36, reprinted in pp. 307–327 of *Marxism and Law*. The most complete but as yet unpublished account of this school remains Robert Sharlet, "Pashukanis and the Commodity Exchange Theory of Law," Ph.D. diss., 1968, Indiana University.

[50]Readers should here especially refer to the work of E. P. Thompson. See his *Whigs and Hunters: The Origins of the Black Act* (New York: Pantheon Books, 1975); "The Crime of Anonymity," in Douglas Hay, Peter Linebaugh, John G. Rule, E. P. Thompson, and Cal Winslow, *Albion's Fatal Tree* (1975), (New York: Pantheon Books, 1975), pp. 255–308; "The State and Civil Liberties," in E. P. Thompson, *Writing by Candlelight* (London: Merlin Press, 1980), pp. 91–256.

[51]David M. Gordon, "Capitalism, Class and Crime in America," *Crime and Delinquency*, 19 (April), 163–186; Richard Quinney, *Critique of Legal Order: Crime Control in Capitalist Society* (Boston: Little, Brown, 1974); Tony Platt, "The Prospects for a Radical Criminology in the United States," *Crime and Social Justice*, 1, (1974), 2–10; Barry Krisberg, *Crime and Privilege: Toward a New Criminology* (Englewood-Cliffs, N.J.: Prentice-Hall, 1975); Steven Spitzer, "Toward a Marxian Theory of Deviance," *Social Problems*, 22, no. 5 (1975), 638–651; Richard Quinney, *Class, State, and Crime* (New York:

THE DICHOTOMY OF INSTRUMENTALISM AND STRUCTURALISM

The Marxist analysis of how both civil and criminal law rules was suddenly thrust onto the center of the stage. We must stress that the Marxist study of law that has developed in the last few years has not been a monolithic enterprise consisting of a single theoretical perspective. This is nowhere more apparent than in the initial, and ultimately mistaken, division between instrumentalist and structuralist approaches to law.[52]

Instrumentalism in the study of law has tended to derive its source of support from a narrow reading of polemical statements by Marx and Engels, such as the famous phrase in *The Communist Manifesto* of 1847–1848 that "the executive of the modern state is but a committee for managing the common affairs of the whole bourgeoisie."[53] Beginning with a simplistic notion that economic relations always have primacy ("in the last instance"), that the processes of the superstructure are determined by the requirements of the economic base, instrumentalists have argued that political institutions (state, law, courts, armies, police, and prisons) are tools that can be manipulated at will by the capitalist class as a whole. In this manner several empirical studies[54] have tried to prove that the economic power that resides in the ownership or control of the means of production (industrial, financial, commercial, and land capitals) can be transformed into personal political influence on the legislative process. It is argued that this transformation is typically materialized in lobbying, campaign financing, intermarriage within the dominant power bloc, and by the direct corruption of the judiciary and of state and federal legislatures.

In a limited sense it must be admitted that instrumental Marxism has performed the useful iconoclastic function of disclosing some of the social fictions enshrined in doctrines such as the "rule of law," "equality before the law," and the "separation of powers." But the danger involved in such demystification, as Fraser has shown, is that it is likely to achieve little more than a moralistic inversion of the categories already present in legal doctrine itself.[55] What is good becomes bad, what is right becomes wrong. As Andrew Fraser puts it:

Longman, 1977). The notion of punishment as a form of discipline derives principally from Michel Foucault, *Discipline and Punish* (London: Allen Lane, 1978). For critical commentaries on Foucault see Bob Fine, "Struggles against Discipline: The Theory and Politics of Michel Foucault," *Capital and Class*, 9, (1979), 75–96; John Lea, "Discipline and Capitalist Development," pp. 76–89 in Bob Fine et al. (1979), op. cit. supra n. 9; Dario Melossi, "Institutions of Social Control and Capitalist Organization of Work," pp. 90–99, ibid.; Jeff Minson, "Strategies for Socialists? Foucault's Conception of Power," *Economy and Society*, 9, no. 1 (1980), 1–43.

[52]This division has, of course, an ancient history in the annals of political theory. The Miliband/Poulantzas debates best exemplify their modern form. These appear in Nicos Poulantzas, "The Problem of the Capitalist State," *New Left Review*, 58 (1969), 67–78; Ralph Miliband, "The Capitalist State: A Reply to Nicos Poulantzas," *New Left Review*, 59 (1970), 53–60; Ralph Miliband, "Poulantzas and the Capitalist State," *New Left Review*, 82 (1973), 83–92; Nicos Poulantzas, "The Capitalist State: A Reply to Miliband and Laclau," *New Left Review*, 95 (1976), 63–83.

[53]Karl Marx and Friedrich Engels, "The Communist Manifesto," in vol. I of *Marx/Engels Selected Works* (Moscow: Progress Publishers, 1973), Vol. 1, pp. 98–137, at pp. 110–111.

[54]For example, Gabriel Kolko, *Wealth and Power in America* (New York: Praeger, 1962); Ralph Miliband, *The State in Capitalist Society* (New York: Basic Books, 1969); William G. Domhoff, *The Higher Circles* (New York: Random House, 1970).

[55]Two attempts to destruct pregiven definitions of crime and justice are Herman and Julia Schwendinger, "Social Class and the Definition of Crime," *Crime and Social Justice*, 7 (1977), 4–13; Dean H.

The disguised victory of bourgeois legal theory has already become manifest among radical lawyers in North America whose theoretical radicalism is contained and exhausted in a perception of the law as an elaborate confidence trick. . . . The law, in other words . . . is dismissed as an elaborate structure of myths, the function of which is to obscure the underlying reality of bitter struggle between social classes.[56]

In Fraser's sense, therefore, instrumental Marxism and voluntaristic pluralism are polar opposites of the same continuum. No doubt all of the transformative factors mentioned above do actually occur; yet it is most unlikely that they can occur with sufficient frequency to enable them to be regarded as the normal path by which economic interests are intercalated with political processes and institutions. Instrumental Marxism and conflict theory are united by the very logic of their premises. Both retain a reductionist notion of the state that must be continually embarrassed by empirical evidence. Dominant classes are typically unable to manipulate state apparatuses (which? when? where?) at will and despite all political opposition. Do legislative and judicial institutions have no degree of autonomy, no internal histories? Is all legislation, and are the activities of all personnel within the legal system, always to be explained by the convenient *deus ex machina* of the interests of dominant classes? Karl Klare has summarized the complex process by which the expanded activities of the state confuse the instrumentalist picture of private economic interests determining the complete scope of public power:

> The state in advanced capitalism systematically and pervasively intervenes in, and indeed, reshapes the sphere of private economic and social activity. The process of capital accumulation is now dependent upon and contoured by state policy. . . . The state sets the ground rules of most economic transactions, directly regulates the class struggle through labor laws, through its actions determines the size of the "social wage," provides the infrastructure of capital accumulation, manages the tempo of business activity and economic growth, takes measures directly and indirectly to maintain effective demand, and itself participates in the market as a massive business actor and employer.[57]

Some authors have suggested that legislation does much more than make the process of capital accumulation dependent upon and contoured by state policy. This is because the distinction between economic and legal relations faces the logical difficulty that economic property is itself defined by legal concepts such as ownership, use, and possession. Both E. P. Thompson and Bernard Edelman, in very different ways, have written that law somehow *defines* the relations of production. Thompson has correctly insisted, in a misdirected polemic against a structuralist straw man, that it is impossible to distinguish the eighteenth-century activity of farming and quarrying in England, for example, from the rights to a certain strip of land or a particular quarry. "Law," says Thompson, "is deeply imbricated within the very basis of productive relations."[58] In his *The Legalisation of the Working Class,*

Clarke, "Marxism, Justice and the Justice Model," *Contemporary Crises*, 2, no. 1 (1978), 27–62. See also Gary Young, "Justice and Capitalist Production: Marx and Bourgeois Ideology," *Canadian Journal of Philosophy*, viii, no. 3 (1978), 421–455.

[56]Andrew Fraser, "Legal Theory and Legal Practice," *Arena*, nos. 44, 45 (1976), 123–156, at p. 128.

[57]Karl Klare, "Law-making as Praxis," *Telos* (1979), no. 40, 123–135.

[58]E. P. Thompson (1975), op. cit. supra n. 9, at p. 261.

Edelman has argued that the power of capital to dominate labor is secured and constituted juridically. The working class fact of class struggle through strike action is transformed and assimilated—through courts' subservience to bourgeois legal doctrine—to the "right" to strike. Class struggle becomes, according to Edelman, in a phrase strongly reminiscent of Dahrendorf's *Class and Class Conflict in an Industrial Society,* "a permanent regulation of disputes."[59]

From the viewpoint that law is deeply imbricated within the very basis of productive relations it is but a short step to the notion that law cuts across class boundaries, that law and state have a measure of autonomy from the demands of any or all social classes. Law not only defines economic relations, but it must be seen to define them neutrally. The specific factors which determine the "relative" autonomy of state apparatuses from economic relations has as yet been unconvincingly theorized. At times this autonomy is posited as an illusory, surface phenomenon that corresponds to the fiction embedded in the doctrine of the separation of powers. At other times it is held to be real and necessary in order for the state to fulfill its primary role as the factor of cohesion between the different levels in a given social formation. The message of structuralist analyses of state and law is predicated on the notion that all state apparatuses are subject to the complex functional constraints of the structural ensemble of capitalist social relations. The schematic sphere within which the state operates is limited economically,[60] politically,[61] and ideologically.[62] All state apparatuses confront both internal and external constraints. Internal constraints are produced by specialized belief systems, recruitment patterns, and organizational requirements. Isaac Balbus, for example, has described the relative autonomy of courts in Chicago, Detroit, and Los Angeles when faced with black ghetto revolts in the 1960s.[63] Any given court response to collective violence in these cities was likely to be a function of the delicate balance that court authorities are forced to achieve among their compelling and competing interests in order, formal rationality, and organizational maintenance. Internal constraints do not, of course, apply only to courts. Every state agency has its own internal logic of organizational and administrative rationality.

There is also a broad range of external constraints imposed on the state as it fulfills its twin functions of accumulation and the generation of mass loyalty. In the discharge of these functions, the state must systematically regulate the antagonistic relations between capital and labor in the sphere of direct production, between monopoly capital and small capital, between capital based in different geographic areas, between small capital and the working class, and between skilled and un-

[59]Bernard Edelman, *La Legalisation de la classe ouvriere* (Paris: Christian Bourgeois Editeur, 1978). Three extracts from this book have been translated into English in *Economy and Society,* 9, no. 1 (1980), 50-64, introduced by Elizabeth Kingdom.

[60]James O'Connor, *The Fiscal Crisis of the State* (New York: Basic Books, 1973).

[61]Nicos Poulantzas, *Political Power and Social Classes* (London: New Left Books, 1973). A recent assessment of Poulantzas's contribution to the socialist movement is Stuart Hall, "The Legacy of Nicos Poulantzas," *New Left Review,* 119 (1980), 60-69.

[62]Louis Althusser (1971), op. cit. supra n. 36; see also the comments in Alan Hunt, "Law, State and Class Struggle," *Marxism Today,* 20, no. 6 (1976), 178-187; S. Hall et al. (1978), op. cit. supra n. 15, esp. pp. 201-217.

[63]Isaac D. Balbus, *The Dialectics of Legal Repression* (New York: Russell Sage, 1973).

skilled labor. O'Connor has put forward the thesis that the state routinely incurs two competing and often contradictory expenses in the regulation of these inter- and intraclass antagonisms. On the one hand, it incurs costs designed to reproduce the process of capital accumulation and stimulate the rate of profit. On the other, it incurs costs needed to legitimate and harmonize the social and moral orders. In the expenditure of these costs, O'Connor argues, the state must appear ''independent or 'distant' from the particular interests of capital. . . . The basic problem is to win mass loyalty to insure legitimacy; too intimate a relation between capital and state normally is unacceptable or inadmissable to the ordinary person.''[64]

CLASS STRUGGLE AND THE LIMITS OF LAW

Some very tentative conclusions may be drawn from these analyses, and certain problems must be noted about them. In the long run, the capitalist state is a *capitalist* state because it expresses the political interests of capital. This fact, therefore, defines the negative limits of the thesis of the relative autonomy of the political from the economic. But there is no a priori reason why dominant economic classes should also always be dominant in the formal political sphere. In replying to criticisms from Miliband and Laclau that his *Political Power and Social Classes* was guilty of structuralist formalism and abstractionism, Poulantzas argued that the merit of his later *Classes in Contemporary Capitalism* was that it examined concrete relations between class struggles and state forms.[65] ''. . . the degree, the extent, the forms, etc. (*how relative*, and *how is it* relative) of the relative autonomy of the State can only be examined . . . with reference to a given capitalist State, and to the precise conjuncture of the corresponding class struggle. . . .''[66] For Poulantzas, therefore, if there is a clear coincidence between the interests of dominant economic classes and state policies, this is not because the bourgeoisie automatically wields state power, not because the state is composed of members of the bourgeoisie, but because of the objective relation exercised by the state in the capitalist mode of production. Within the Marxist theory of the state there are objective limits to state policy that the state, as a capitalist state, cannot transcend.

It may in the end be true, as Douglas Hay's essay in Chapter 2 of *Marxism and Law* indicates, that the benevolence of rich to poor is ultimately upheld by the sanction of the gallows and the rhetoric of the death sentence. But structuralist analyses of state and law have provided us with plausible reasons for why the content of legislation is not always in the immediate interests of capital. In the short run, the state often routinely enacts and pursues policies that are unambiguously opposed to the private interests of sections of capital. Obvious examples of such policies are antitrust laws, green belt and zoning ordinances, corporation taxes, and the compulsory determination of minimum wage and maximum interest levels. Sufficient conditions for the realization of these policies are the exercise of state legitimation functions or successful political struggle by dominated classes. We should, therefore, expect empirical

---

[64]James O'Connor (1973), op. cit. supra n. 54, at p. 70.

[65]Nicos Poulantzas (1976), op. cit. supra n. 46, at pp. 70–77.

[66]Ibid., p. 72. A similarly open-ended perspective lies at the basis of Mark Tushnet, ''Perspectives on the Development of American Law: A Critical Review of Friedman's *A History of American Law*,'' *Wisconsin Law Review* (1977), 81–109.

and historical analysis to reveal that the content of legislation will not always operate in the objective interests of capital. Some laws are directly the product of class struggles and reproduce the political power of combatants in them. Some laws favor specific classes, some laws cut across all class boundaries. Some laws have little or nothing overtly to do with class struggles.

By the mid-1970s it had become apparent that in at least one respect instrumentalist and structuralist accounts of state and law shared something in common. This was largely seen as a common failure, in that their theorization of political power was from the beginning based on a false separation of the political from the economic. In their introductory essay to the "state derivation" debate in the Federal Republic of Germany, John Holloway and Sol Picciotto remind us of the severe limitations in the dichotomy represented by Miliband and Poulantzas.[67] They argue that Miliband, on the one hand, confronts bourgeois political theory on its own empirical terrain and shows that it has misunderstood or misrepresented the facts. Having done this, Miliband then arrives at a theoretical impasse. They suggest that this impasse is a necessary consequence of working within terrain presently defined by bourgeois political theory and legal doctrine. In striving to avoid the errors of reductionism, on the other hand, Poulantzas identifies each of the regions of the capitalist social formation as relatively autonomous. This avenue is clearly preferable. But, in advancing it, Poulantzas loses sight of the historical connection between contradictions in the process of capital accumulation and the particular forms assumed by state and law.[68] The contributions to political theory by Miliband and Poulantzas, if taken together as a dichotomy, therefore provided a serious obstacle to the development of a Marxist theory of law. Neither of them had explicitly examined the problem of why the institutions of state and law appeared to predominate among the various forms of social regulation under capitalism.

By the late 1970s a third line of analysis was introduced in response to this problem. The importance of this new direction had originally been emphasized in the Russian writings emanating from the commodity exchange school of law in the 1920s. This school had flourished in the USSR between the advent of the New Economic Policy and the enactment of the 1936 Constitution, had long been familiar to American comparativists, and was first drawn on extensively by Marxists in France and Germany.[69] Almost from the first the commodity exchange theory of law was largely defined by questions raised in Evgeny Pashukanis' *The General Theory of Law and Marxism*. In this book, written at the outset of the New Economic Policy and published in 1924, Pashukanis addressed himself to the question of the historical specificity of state and law as follows:

> Class domination, both in its organized and unorganized form, is much broader than the area which can be designated as the official authority of state power. The domination of the

[67]John Holloway and Sol Picciotto, "Towards a Materialist Theory of the State," in Holloway and Picciotto, Eds., *State and Capital: A Marxist Debate* (London: Edward Arnold, 1978), pp. 1–31.
[68]Ibid, p. 5.
[69]See Nicos Poulantzas, "L'Examen Marxiste de l'État et du Droit Actuels et la Question de l'Alternative," *Les Tempes Moderne* (August/September 1964), 274–302; Hubert Rottleuthner, Ed., *Probleme der marxistischen Rechtstheorie* (Frankfurt am Main: Suhrkamp, 1975).

bourgeoisie is expressed in the dependence of the government upon the banks and capitalist groupings, in the dependence of each individual worker upon his employer . . . why does the dominance of a class not become that which it is, i.e. the actual subordination of one part of the population to another, but instead assumes the form of official state authority?[70]

In answering this question Pashukanis was chiefly concerned to rebut the view that law is a system of rules whose content must be understood primarily in terms of the demands and interests of dominant classes. If law is viewed as a system of rules that responds mechanically to the interests of dominant classes, then it cannot be distinguished from any other social relations that involve norms or rules. Not all rules are legal rules. For Pashukanis the starting point in a Marxist theory of law must be the precise determination of the conditions in which the regulation of social relations assumes a *legal* character.

Pashukanis' major thesis in *The General Theory of Law and Marxism* is that law is fundamentally a bourgeois form of social regulation. The fetishized form of legal rights and obligations becomes universal only with the development of the generalized commodity exchange that accompanies capitalist commodity production. Law is bourgeois because it reflects the form of this exchange. The logic of legal concepts corresponds with the logic of the social relationships of commodity exchange, and it is here—and not in the instrumental demands of domination, submission, or naked power—that the origin of law is to be sought. The subject of law is none other than the abstract commodity owner elevated to the heavens.

The argument that legal regulation is inherently bourgeois anticipates Pashukanis's second thesis that there can never be a proletarian or socialist law. Pashukanis was, of course, able to find some limited textual authority for this thesis—in Engels' vague assertions about law withering away under socialism, and about communist social regulation being a mere administration of things; and in Marx's famous dictum in *The Critique of the Gotha Programme* that the narrow horizons of bourgeois law can only be transcended at the stage of developed communism. But the basis of this authority amounts to little more than utopian or wishful thinking. What, then, are the characteristics of social regulation during the socialist transition? In answering this question, Pashukanis distinguished between legal norms and technical rules. The former derive from conflicts of private economic interests. Technical rules express only the administrative aspects of planned economic regulation and derive from the unity of the socialist purpose. Socialism is seen as the triumph of the socialist elements of the planned economy over the remnants of capitalist production and exchange. As socialism progressively displaces capitalism, so, correspondingly, technical rules displace legal norms.

In arriving at this terrain we are once again driven back to the thorny problems of

---

[70]Evgeny Pashukanis, "The General Theory of Law and Marxism," pp. 40-131 in Piers Beirne and Robert Sharlet (1980), op. cit. supra n. 49, at pp. 92, 94. Pashukanis's work has been subjected to intense criticism in recent literature—that it is merely a sophisticated version of economic reductionism, that it succumbs to formalism, that it is an anarchist theory motivated only by a complete rejection of all law. See, for example, Roger Cotterrell, "Law and Marxism: Review of Pashukanis," *Ideology and Consciousness*, no. 6 (1979), 111-119; Peter Binns, "Law and Marxism—Review Article," *Capital and Class*, 10 (1980), 100-113; Paul Hirst (1980), op. cit. supra n. 2.

class struggle and the rule of law. Whatever the merits of Pashukanis' strictures on the bourgeois nature of law, his commodity exchange theory leads to a dangerous nihilism. If all law is inherently bourgeois, if law is only the classical worldview of the bourgeoisie, then the attempt to transform social relations through, in, and by legal struggle is always either reformist or self-defeating. But this is certainly a mistaken position with disastrous consequences. Pashukanis' complete rejection of law contributed, with but a tinge of irony, to an anarchic climate whose outcome was the thoroughly antidemocratic exercise of political power by the Bolshevik party. Socialist construction was displaced by Stalin's jurisprudence of terror. In certain circumstances law and organized terror may be identical. But this is not always so. As Jock Young has warned, under those conditions where the regulation of social order is reproduced by law, we must distinguish between "law used as a means of defence for the working class at the ebb of struggle, law used as part of a working class offensive, law in a revolutionary situation and law in the transition to communism."[71] A concern with these distinctions is the major theme of *Marxism and Law.*

[71] Jock Young in Bob Fine et al. (1979), op. cit. supra n. 15, at pp. 27–28. See also the last chapter in Ralph Miliband, *Marxism and Politics* (Oxford: Oxford University Press, 1977).

CHAPTER ONE

SOCIAL THEORY AND LAW

This first set of readings offers students a broad overview of the major intellectual traditions within which much of the recent sociological interest in law has been couched. The four essays in this chapter are explicitly directed to the different theoretical principles used to identify the hallmarks of modern Western law.

In classical social theory Emile Durkheim (1858–1917) and Max Weber (1864–1920) may be seen as the founders of a distinctively sociological approach to the understanding of law. The intellectual milieu in which they were writing was a Europe fraught with acute epistemological debates over the logic of social scientific inquiry, the political stance of the committed social theorist and the problem of the intrusion of values, therefore, into the scientific enterprise. Against the rising militancy of national workers' movements, these debates took place, frequently, within the context of discovering the conditions for moral regeneration and national stability. Both Durkheim and Weber were studious observers of the complex role of legal systems and legal thought in the regulation of early capitalism. They tended to see law as a precondition and an effect of capitalist development. And both were concerned to distinguish law from other forms of social regulation such as religious taboo, mores, convention, and naked coercion.

In "Emile Durkheim: Towards a Sociology of Law," Alan Hunt shows that Durkheim displays a persistent interest in law throughout his life's work. What endures in Durkheim's analysis is the proposition that the type of law in any given culture is intimately linked with the general form of its social structure and division of labor. For Durkheim, law is the best and most visible example of a "social fact." Within a great historical and evolutionary framework, Durkheim provides us with tremendous insight into the changing forms of contract, property, and criminal legislation. But Hunt also shows that the omissions in Durkheim's analysis of law are perhaps as significant as his insights. Durkheim's treatment of law ultimately rests on an invariant and unquestioned assumption that it is simply a mechanism of functional integration. We find, therefore, insufficient consideration in his work for the relations between law and power, law and domination, and law and state.

The very considerations that Durkheim ignored Max Weber, in certain respects, was keen to emphasize. The intercalation of law, domination, and state lies at the heart of Weber's theory of the unique characteristics of Western Law. In "Ideology and Rationality in Max Weber's Sociology of Law," Piers Beirne situates Weber's theory of law within the context of debates in social philosophy and jurisprudence in late nineteenth-century Germany. These debates were themselves often addressed to material crises in the Germany economy and polity. What were the conditions for the emergence of the expression of the German popular will? With more clarity than any other theorist, Weber offers us an elaborate and systematic model of the reasons why specific forms of legal system and legal thought were conducive to and necessary for the development of Western capitalism.

Weber's gloomy vision was of a morally bankrupt present in which the individual is everywhere trapped within the iron cage of bureaucratic rationality. The future he sees as but a quantitative extension of capitalism's need for rational planning and accounting. Weber's response to the unintended consequences of capitalist development involved a condemnation of the irrationalities of capital, but, in the end, this condemnation also involved his fundamental resignation to the historical permanence of capital.

It is now well-established that there is no coherent or systematic theory of law in the voluminous writings of Marx and Engels. This is documented in the next reading, Maureen Cain's "The Main Themes of Marx' and Engels' Sociology of Law." Cain's essay was perhaps the first English-language summary of Marx's and Engels' view of law, and although subsequent discussion has moved considerably beyond it, we believe that it is still the most accessible introduction for a student audience. Cain shows us that Marx's and Engels' analysis of law tends to be subsumed within their wider understanding of the forces and relations of production—the social organization of the means of life—and generally occurs in the context of their theory of the state and their sociology of knowledge. In so doing, she suggests that their views exerted a significant influence on Durkheim and Weber.

Cain shows that for Marx and Engels, law—which they never clearly define—primarily acts as an ideological mechanism. Because law informs us that we are all in principle equal, that we all have the power to vote and to enter freely into contracts, for example, the reality of political domination is obscured and the exercise of real power is legitimated. She then exemplifies the general thesis that Marx and Engels held a dialectical notion of the relation between law and class interests. On the one hand, law serves the overall interests of ruling classes; on the other, and flowing from an understanding of the English Factory Acts, a politically conscious working class can gain concessions in the legal arena if it exploits differences within the ruling class.

The fourth selection in this chapter is Alan Hunt's "Dichotomy and Contradiction in the Sociology of Law." Hunt offers us the prognosis that there is a fundamental unity between the major concerns of contemporary Marxist and non-Marxist theories of law. This unity manifests itself in the extent to which both traditions are impaled on a dichotomy that inhibits their further advance. The general form of this dichotomy, his argument continues, is between theories of law based on coercion and theories of law based on consent. But Hunt is careful to warn that this unity is not a convergence between what are otherwise two very different traditions. Rather, the unity stems from a parallelism of interest between them.

Hunt supports this thesis by arguing that the dichotomy of coercion/consent lies at the heart of the apparently incompatible writings of Unger, Black, and Trubek. For Unger, it appears in the tension between collective values and bureaucratic welfare tyranny; for Black, in the hypothetical antinomies of more/less law, undifferentiated/ differentiated society, and simple/modern society; and for Trubek, it is found in a sophisticated version of the Realist concern with the gap between the ideals of law in the books and the actual performance of law in practice. Readers may wish to return to the second half of Hunt's essay after they have completed the other chapters of *Marxism and Law* Hunt's argument is powerful and compelling: "for very different reasons recent Marxist theories, in reaction to positions which had previously held sway within Marxism, have also been anxious to give emphasis to the consensual facet of law."

EMILE DURKHEIM: TOWARDS A SOCIOLOGY OF LAW

ALAN HUNT

Durkheim left behind him no general treatise on sociology. The titles of his major works indicate the very considerable range of subjects with which he dealt. Yet despite the diversity of his subject matter there exists a substantial unity to his thought. This unity is derived from his overriding and continuing concern with the nature and source of social cohesion or social integration. Running through all his works is a concern with the question: what is it about human society with its ever more complex interrelationships, structures and institutions which ensures not only its continuity and cohesion, but also its transformations? He manifests a persistent desire to account for the reality of the complex and arbitrary actions of individuals pursuing narrowly conceived individual ends but which nevertheless become welded into an entity which exhibits characteristics of stability and continuity. Simply, Durkheim's concern is with what holds society together; his object of inquiry is the social order.[1]

The explanation that he provides of the fascinating reality of "society" changes considerably over the duration of his intellectual life yet the fundamental question which he poses remains the same. Durkheim's work manifests the continuing affirmation of the primacy of the "social."

Man is man only because he lives in society.[2]

It is within society that the reality of human existence is to be found.

> Collective life is not born from individual life, but it is, on the contrary, the second which is born of the first.[3]

This affirmation of the primacy of the social leads him to adopt a consistently anti-individualist approach. Much of his first major work *Division of Labour* is given over explicitly to an attack upon Spencer, but it is one that we may read as a general critique of all individualist thought. He insisted that it was impossible to explain the evolution of human society by reference for example to the desire of men for "progress" since these apparently isolated, private ends are in fact social products.

Alongside his emphasis upon the social stands the prevailing positivism of Durkheim's thought. Positivism marked an important stage in the development of the social sciences and its major

---

[1]To stress his concern with the social order does not imply that such a concern is necessarily static. For this reason Giddens is wrong in identifying the association of Durkheim with a theory of social order as a myth; see Giddens, Anthony. "Four myths in the history of social thought" 1 *Economy and Society* 357–85 (1972).

Source: From Alan Hunt, *The Sociological Movement in Law* (Philadelphia: Temple University Press, 1978), pp. 61–74, 85–92. Reprinted by permission.

[2]Durkheim, E., *Professional Ethics and Civic Morals* (London, 1957), p. 60. Hereafter referred to as *Professional Ethics.*

[3]Durkheim. E., *The Division of Labour in Society* (Glencoe, Ill., 1964). First published in 1893. Hereafter referred to as *Division of Labour.*

premise is the very assertion that it is possible, that is logically or methodologically, to speak of social *science*. What was asserted was the possibility of scientific study of society. Espousing the cause of scientific method he insists upon the social sciences basing themselves upon the study of data that has an objective reality, that exists independent of the consciousness of the observer. Yet a social scientist who interprets this restriction as encompassing only material subjects would render it extremely difficult to say anything meaningful about social reality. Some of the more extreme variants of positivism have taken this approach and sought to explain social phenomena in ecological or biological terms. Indeed Durkheim's early work, with its emphasis upon morphological factors exhibits certain of these characteristics; for example the use of the forms of "density" in accounting for the evolution of the division of labour exhibits a marked degree of naturalism.

However the characteristic of people as conscious, sentient beings largely invalidates all approaches which take no cognisance of this element. Yet once conceded that any understanding of human society requires the recognition of human consciousness and self-consciousness it is but a short step to a purely subjective, and hence introspective, analysis. Durkheim insists upon the possibility of defining a subject matter for sociology which encompasses non-material "reality," yet which at the same time meets the criteria of scientific objectivity. In so doing he makes what is perhaps his most distinctive and enduring contribution to sociological positivism. His positivism is contained within the injunction: "The first and most fundamental rule is: consider social facts as things.[4] This methodological prescription is of such importance to his subsequent treatment of legal phenomena that it is necessary to elaborate upon it more fully. A social fact is to be distinguished by two features, its autonomous existence and its coercive power. Thus he defines

social facts as "ways of acting, thinking, and feeling, external to the individual, and endowed with a power of coercion, by reason of which they control him."[5] The coercive character of social facts is to be found in the fact that their violation is met with sanctions, or at least resistance. Law constitutes a paramount example of a "social fact" since it manifests both externality and constraint and, as will be demonstrated, explains in large measure the attention that Durkheim gives to law.[6]

Durkheim's methodology is based upon an epistemology that asserts that in studying a social phenomenon we must search for its "observable manifestations."[7] This leads him to adopt the proposition that it is necessary in order to study some social phenomena to approach them indirectly through some visible intermediary. The importance of this methodological device will become apparent when we discuss the role that the analysis of legal phenomena played in *Division of Labour*[8] For Durkheim law was a "visible symbol" and this in large measure accounts for the attention which he devoted to its study.

One further important implication of his concept of "social fact" is that it provides him with a mechanism for bridging the gulf that divides the natural and social sciences. It provides him with a means of coping with the "subjective" in social action. He defines the major manifestations of the subjective or mental element, namely values, sentiments and opinions, as "social facts" and hence capable of objective, scientific treatment on the grounds that they exercise constraint upon social behaviour. Durkheim, consistent with his anti-individualism, focuses attention on the collective aspects of these "social facts." He endows shared values, sentiments, and opinions with an autonomous existence that is independent of the individual bearer; they are "collective representations."

---

[4]Durkheim, E., *The Rules of Sociological Method* (Glencoe, Ill., 1964), p. 14, hereafter referred to as *Rules*.

[5]Durkheim, E., *ibid.*, p. 3.
[6]See pp. 67–8 of this chapter.
[7]Durkheim, E., *Rules*, p. 123.
[8]See pp. 66–74 of this chapter.

Society is not a mere sum of individuals. Rather the system formed by their association represents a specific reality which has its own characteristics.[9]

If society exists in its own right, independent of the individuals who constitute it, so too do the ideas and values. Thus he introduces his famous concept "conscience collective."[10] He also relies heavily on the notion of "collective representations." Apart from stressing their general importance in his sociology, two particular aspects of these concepts need to be emphasised.

Firstly they manifest what may be characterised as the reification of society by Durkheim. Starting with the positivistic premises indicated above he succeeds in reifying society, but he goes considerably beyond this; not only does society have an autonomous existence but it also has an independent power over individuals.

> The individual finds himself in the presence of a force which is superior to him and before which he bows.[11]

> Society commands us because it is exterior and superior to us.[12]

In his later works the reification of society becomes transformed into a tendency to deify the state. He produces a brand of statism in which the citizen is enjoined to fulfil a duty of obedience to the state as the embodiment of society.[13] Yet his statism is not a return to conceptions of an absolutist state; it bears much closer resemblances to Weber's authoritarian version of democracy;

the state is presented as a specialised agency "qualified to think and act instead of and on behalf of society."[14]

Secondly we find that his treatment of the "conscience collective" reveals itself with increasingly metaphysical trappings. He posits an existential reality that only just falls short of a "group mind" concept:

> The group thinks, feels and acts quite differently from the way in which its members would were they isolated.[15]

He frequently uses formulations such as "the diffuse soul of society,"[16] "society thinks of itself,"[17] "collective thinking."[18] Yet at the same time he recognises the dependence of the collective upon the individual. The result is that he ends up with the distinctly ambiguous formulation "it is the aggregate which thinks, feels, wishes even though it can neither wish, feel nor act except through individual minds."[19]

The reaction against individualism, especially against the economic individualism of classical political economy, leads him to identify the essence of the social in the existence of an ideological community.

> In short, social life is nothing but the moral milieu that surrounds the individual—or to be more accurate, it is the sum of the moral milieus that surround the individual. By calling them moral we mean that they are made up of ideas.[20]

Durkheim sets out with a strongly naturalistic position and in many instances comes close to materialism, but his attempt to pin down a social essence brings him to an unambiguously idealist

---

[9]Durkheim, E., *Division of Labour*, p. 103.

[10]There have been controversies over the translation of the expression; its meaning lies somewhere between "collective conscience" and "collective consciousness." In order to avoid ambiguity the original form of "conscience collective" will be retained.

[11]Durkheim, E., *Rules*, p. 123.

[12]Durkheim, E., "The determination of moral facts" in E. Durkheim, *Sociology and Philosophy* (Glencoe, Ill., 1953), p. 57.

[13]In Durkheim, E., *Moral Education* (Glencoe, Ill., 1961) he argues that education should be used as an agency for installing the appropriate reverential attitudes towards the state.

[14]Durkheim, E., *Professional Ethics*, p. 48.

[15]Durkheim, E., *Rules*, p. 104.

[16]Durkheim, E., *Division of Labour*, pp. 84–5.

[17]Durkheim, E., *Rules*, p. xiix.

[18]Durkheim, E., *ibid.*, p. li.

[19]Durkheim, E., "Individual and collective representations" in *Sociology and Philosophy*, p. 26.

[20]Durkheim, E., "Sociology and its scientific field" in Wolff (ed.), *Essays on Sociology and Philosophy by Emile Durkheim* (New York, 1964), p. 367.

position. Society exists only by virtue of the reality of common values, ideas and beliefs.

The general development of his thought, which has a marked bearing upon his treatment of law, departs from the more conventional positivism of *Division of Labour*. In this work he posits social solidarity as a product of changes in the morphological basis of society with the form of social solidarity thereby produced being reflected in the "conscience collective," whereas, in his later works, the "conscience collective" has achieved much greater autonomy and causal determinacy. Indeed it has *itself* become the foundation of social solidarity. Embodied in *The Elementary Forms of Religious Life*[21] and in *Moral Education*[22] is the quest for a new secular morality which will provide the foundation of social cohesion in the void resulting from the decline of religion in modern society.

It is this concern with social order and the means of securing social stability within modern society that has led a number of writers to stress the inherent conservatism of Durkheim's thought.[23] But this label of conservatism fails to capture the contradictory character of his position. He remained politically committed to "modern society" founded upon an advanced division of labour and individualism. However the conditions for securing and advancing modern society always remained problematic and he was led to analyse the conditions of stability against the joint assault of anomie and the forced division of labour. It is the programme he put forward to ensure social integration, occupational groups as the bearers of the new secular morality, that links him to nineteenth century French conservatism.[24]

Another characteristic of his sociology is a persistent "primitivist" reductionism; that is, the adoption of the view that, if the social scientist is able to study a social phenomenon as it exists in a primitive or simple society, his search for the essence or fundamentals of the phenomenon will be aided by the fact that it is likely to exist in such a form as to be more directly observable. The central or permanent characteristics will exhibit themselves unencumbered by the subsequent encrustations that arise in a complex society. This orientation explains his interest in primitive legal systems. Such a method of study lays itself open to serious objections. It rests on the assumption that the "advanced" form of a social phenomenon is merely a more complex variant of its "simple" predecessor. Such a thesis founders on the primary weakness of functionalism that implies the existence of a set of core or universal functions. While Durkheim avoids the worst reductionism of functionalism he cannot avoid an essentialism which rests upon a view of society as an ideological community existing as a system of shared values.[25]

DURKHEIM'S SOCIOLOGICAL ANALYSIS OF LAW

Introduction

Durkheim's interest in law is perhaps best characterised as tangential or indirect. He is not specifically interested in law for its own sake in the same way that he is for example interested in religion. He does not set out to develop a sociol-

[21]Durkheim, E., *The Elementary Forms of Religious Life: A Study in Religious Sociology* (London, 1915). Hereafter referred to as *Elementary Forms*. First published in French, 1912.

[22]Durkheim, E., *Moral Education: A Study in the Theory and Application of the Sociology of Education* (Glencoe, Ill., 1961).

[23]See in particular Coser, L. A., "Durkheim's conservatism and its implications for his sociological theory" in Wolff (ed.) *Emile Durkheim 1858–1917* (Columbus, 1960) and Nisbet, R. A., "Conservatism and sociology 58 *American Journal of Sociology* 167–75 (1952), and his *Emile Durkheim* (Englewood Cliffs, N.J., 1965); albeit in a more qualified form Lukes also emphasises the conservatism of Durkheim's social and political thought: Lukes, Steven, *Emile Durkheim: His Life and Work* (London, 1973).

[24]It is equally incorrect to deduce a "radical" position from his commitment to the abolition of inheritance as do Taylor, Walton and Young, *The New Criminology* (London, 1973) pp. 87–88.

[25]See Therborn, G., *Science, Class and Society* (London, 1976), Chapter 5, and Hirst, Paul, *Durkheim, Bernard and Epistemology* (London, 1973).

ogy of law. Yet it must not be thought that his treatment of law can be regarded as an unimportant or residual aspect of his work. His discussion is tangential in that he sees law as a prime example of the concretisation or objectification of social norms and values. Law is the example par excellence of the "social fact." Most of the illustrations he uses in *Rules* of the social fact are drawn from law. For Durkheim law is a visible symbol of all that is essentially social.

His consideration of law and legal phenomena is spread widely throughout his writings. Of particular importance is the study of the relationship between law and social solidarity in *Division of Labour*. In his methodological treatise *Rules* he relies heavily on law to provide examples and analogies to support the framework of his method. In a number of places he gives considerable attention to the institution of contract particularly in *Professional Ethics*. The nature of crime is a recurring theme to be found in *Division of Labour, Rules* and *Suicide*[26] and receives specific and detailed treatment in "Two laws of penal evolution."[27] In addition the journal *Année Sociologique*, which he founded and edited, dealt with law, legal institutions and legal sociology right up to the outbreak of the First World War.[28]

Yet despite the considerable volume of Durkheim's writing on law it cannot be said to amount to a "sociology of law." His concern is not with elaborating a general framework or method for the sociological analysis of law; rather he used law to advance his more general sociological interests. However his interest in law resulted in the school that formed around him developing a considerable interest in the study of

law as a social process. The work of George Davy, Marcel Mauss and Maurice Hauriou was very much influenced by Durkheim. Many of his formulations and methods of presenting questions constitute an important background to subsequent debates and discussions. The two most obvious examples are the anthropological debate about "primitive law,"[29] and the criminological discussion about the nature of crime.

Law and Social Solidarity

Law plays an important role in Durkheim's first major work *The Division of Labour in Society*. In this book he sets out to explore the nature and origins of "social solidarity" and the transformations it undergoes. In undertaking this study Durkheim was reacting explicitly against methodological individualism (particularly in its utilitarian form) and the notion that social "progress" could be accounted for in terms of the pursuit of individual self-interest.

He was engaged in a debate with French socialism. Zeitlin is wrong in characterising this as being a "debate with the ghost of Marx."[30] What is true of Weber as a consequence of the influence of Marxism upon German social democracy is not true in the case of French where Marxism had only very limited influence during this period on French socialism. We find a whole number of points in *Division of Labour* and elsewhere at which he advances positions that almost have a Marxist flavour. The parallel with Marx is the desire to penetrate beneath consciousness to seek for structural or "profound" causes. Beyond this the parallels are few. Politically Durkheim's general commitment to a meritocratic industrial capitalism separated him from Marx and led him to decry "the sad conflict of classes."[31] Thus Dur-

[26]Durkheim, E., *Suicide: A Study in Sociology* (Glencoe, Ill., 1951) hereafter referred to as *Suicide*.

[27]Durkheim, E., "Two laws of penal evolution." Originally appeared in *Année Sociologique* in 1899–1900. An English translation has appeared in 2(3) *Economy and Society* 285–308 (1973). Hereafter referred to as "Two laws."

[28]See detailed analysis of the contents of *Année Sociologique* in Alpert, H., *Emile Durkheim and his Sociology* (New York, 1961) pp. 217–24.

[29]The continuing debate has at one time or another involved such writers as Malinowski, Hogbin, Hoebel, Gluckman and Bohannan and owes much to the stimulus of Durkheim's ideas.

[30]Zeitlin, Irving, *Ideology and the Development of Sociological Theory* (Englewood Cliffs, N.J., 1968).

[31]Durkheim, E., 44 *Revue Philosophique* 200 5; quoted Lukes (1973), p. 232.

kheim's notion of "forced division of labour" bears close similarities with Marx's notion of "class struggle." Yet there is the profound difference; for Marx this was a natural and inevitable consequence of the division of labour, but for Durkheim it is an abnormal or pathological form to which he devoted little subsequent attention.

Whereas Marx pursued the analysis of the division of labour in terms of the development and transformation of social relations in the production of material life, Durkheim attributed some causal significance to certain morphological factors. Although these factors subsequently disappeared from his sociology the advance in the division of labour is in the first instance related to the increased "moral density," that is to the increase in population and its greater concentration manifesting itself in a higher level of interaction outside of kinship systems.

Durkheim advances the thesis that human society produces two distinct forms of social solidarity, namely "mechanical" and "organic solidarity." His types of solidarity are polar types. Yet he also sees them as part of an evolutionary continuum marking the distinction between primitive society, with a minimal division of labour, and advanced society, with a more extensive division of labour. At the same time he insists that any particular society in this evolutionary process contains within it elements of both forms of solidarity.

Mechanical solidarity is characteristic of simple societies with only a very limited division of labour. Society is characterised by a prevailing "sameness" or "likeness." The members are completely enveloped in the similitude of activities and as a consequence share the same values and ideals. This uniformity of values and ideas constitutes the "conscience collective." Under mechanical solidarity "collectivism" is highly developed and valued and "individualism" is only weakly present and usually suppressed.

Organic solidarity is characterised by the existence of an advanced division of labour. The society thus formed is marked by "interdependence" in which the economic and social activity of the society is highly specialised and in which complex patterns of mutual dependence exist. "Sameness" thus gives way to "differentiation." The "conscience collective" weakens and is replaced by differential moralities forming around different occupational categories, constituting what Durkheim called "occupational morality."[32] In his later works he presents these occupational moralities as playing a major role in providing the basis for the secular morality that is necessary for the maintenance of social cohesion after the eclipse of morality derived from religion. Collectivism declines and is replaced by individualism which is able to flourish amidst increased social tolerance resulting from the growth of "mutual indifference."[33]

Durkheim recognised that his types of social solidarity were extremely broad and did not lend themselves to exact observation. It was in his view necessary to find some more precise and measurable external symbol.

This visible symbol is law.[34]

Indeed social life, especially where it exists durably, tends inevitably to assume a definite form and to organise itself, and law is nothing else than this very organisation in so far as it has greater stability and precision. . . . We can thus be certain of finding reflected in law all the essential varieties of social solidarity.[35]

He provides us with the following general formulation of the relation between law and social solidarity.

Since law reproduces the principal forms of social solidarity, we have only to classify the different types of law to find therefrom the different types of social solidarity which correspond to it.[36]

[32]Durkheim, E., *Division of Labour*, p. 227.
[33]Durkheim, E., *ibid.*, p. 299.
[34]Durkheim, E., *ibid.*, p. 64.
[35]Durkheim, E., *ibid.*, pp. 64-5.
[36]Durkheim, E., *ibid.*, p. 68.

In his defence of his doctoral examination of *Division of Labour* he claimed that he had discovered a constant index of the division of labour in the legal system and that this relation was explored through "purely scientific method."[37]

Before turning to his classification of the different types of law it is worth noting that apart from this explicit utilisation of law as a tool for the observation of the central reality of social cohesion, his general method lends itself to a "legalistic" formulation. His picture of society is that of the individual confronted by a system of exterior rules which exercise constraint upon his behaviour.

After asserting the general relationship between law and social solidarity he indicates his method of enquiry.

> To proceed scientifically, we must find some characteristic which while being essential to juridical phenomena, varies as they vary.[38]

The key variable that he selects is that of "sanctions." He argues that law exhibits two main types of sanctions. These he calls "repressive" and "restitutive" sanctions and on this basis he speaks of "repressive" and "restitutive law."

Repressive law is characterised by the fact that its sanctions may be subsumed under the concept of punishment. It is synonomous with the more conventional designation criminal law (although he also includes within the concept certain elements of administrative law and what he loosely calls state law). Repressive law is associated with the existence of strong and enduring social sentiments; its violation gives rise to sanctions that impinge upon the fortune, liberty and life of the individual and also upon his honour. Since repressive law is diffuse its existence is not dependent upon the existence of any special judicial machinery but rather he sees it being enforced by the collective as a whole. In order to expound his concept of repressive law he embarks upon a protracted discussion of the nature of crime and punishment to which it will be necessary to return.[39] Restitutive law, "consists only of *the return of things as they were*, in the reestablishment of troubled relations to their normal state."[40] This category embraces all civil law, procedural law and most of administrative and constitutional law. We see that, while there are close parallels, he departs from the more conventional distinctions between civil and criminal law and between public and private law. This he does explicitly, for example, he rejects the utility of the distinction between public and private law. "We believe that all law is public, because all law is social."[41]

Restitutive law is concerned with the adjustment of social relations which arise from the differentiation of social labour. They are therefore not a product of the "conscience collective," and hence do not involve the same strong sentiments. Thus there is no disgrace or loss of honour associated with the imposition of restitutive sanctions.

He further subdivides his classification of restitutive relations in that he distinguishes between negative and positive relations. Negative relations are concerned with "abstention"; they reflect a form of social self-limitation and are particularly concerned with the relations between persons and things. Thus property law is negative and so also is tort law in that it is concerned not with the provision of any positive rights, but rather it consists of injunctions about "not harming."[42]

Positive relations differ in that they arise from cooperation and reflect that cooperation which is a necessary consequence of the division of labour.

> The contract is, *par excellence*, the juridical expression of cooperation.[43]

---

[37]Reported in Lukes, *Emile Durkheim*, p. 297.

[38]Durkheim, E., *ibid.*, p. 69.

[39]See "The theory of crime," pp. 74–85 deleted from Hunt's original manuscript, P. Beirne and R. Quinney, eds.

[40]Durkheim, E., *op cit.*, p. 69 (Durkheim's emphasis).

[41]Durkheim, E., *ibid.*, p. 127.

[42]Durkheim, E., *ibid.*, p. 119.

[43]Durkheim, E., *ibid.*, p. 123.

Also added to this category are domestic and commercial law and further both procedural and administrative on the basis that they also reflect cooperation in that these aspects of law serve to fix the respective roles played by the parties in the social process.

The increased complexity and subdivision of restitutive law is consistent with his view that it corresponds to a higher stage of the division of labour. Both the substantive content and the machinery for its enforcement take on more specialised characteristics. He regards the development of restitutive law as being part of a process towards a "law of positive cooperation."

His application of the repressive-restitutive law dichotomy suggests a very direct, in fact a quantifiable, application. The method suggested is that "it will suffice, in order to measure the part of the division of labour, to compare the number of juridical rules which express it with the total volume of law."[44]

He is here presenting a model in which the two forms of social solidarity exist as ideal types; the particular position which any given society has reached lies on a continuum between the polar types. This position is to be determined by calculating the relative percentage or volume of repressive and restitutive law. He himself nowhere carries out this exercise. Neither does he provide any further methodological advice for such an undertaking. It is not a very clear instruction to the researcher to ask him to count the "number of juridical rules." Hidden within this superficially straightforward exercise are endless methodological problems; in particular it would be necessary to ensure that an efficient operational definition of law was found which allowed phenomena to be measured at the same level. For example many statutes contain a relatively small number of "general" rules, but a much larger number of sections which stand in relation to that general rule are definitional, qualifying, limiting, etc. If one wished to count merely general rules it would be necessary to have available some criteria by which they could be extracted. Alpert, one of Durkheim's most consistent admirers, has attempted such an undertaking; basing himself on Durkheim's descriptive evidence he produces a table in which he tabulates the percentage composition of restitutive and repressive rules within a number of legal systems. The result is a typology of the stages of legal evolution which correspond broadly with Durkheim's stages of social evolution. But the connection is only of the most general character and the method does not constitute the precise method that Durkheim would appear to suggest.[45]

Durkheim posits a mirror image relationship between law and social solidarity. This rests upon the unsubstantiated assumption that law embodies the content of all normative systems and necessarily denies the possibility of conflict between legal norms and other normative systems; and such conflict could only be regarded as temporary and abnormal. It therefore follows that the use of law as an empirical index of social solidarity is a dubious undertaking.

Durkheim's evolutionary thesis of transition from repressive to restitutive law may also be assessed at the empirical level. To what extent does his model account for the known facts of the evolution of law? A cautionary note is necessary: the breadth of Durkheim's thesis invites an excursion into the wider debate about the evolution of law and legal systems. Attractive though such an invitation is, it is beyond the scope of the present concerns.

For convenience we may isolate three aspects of his thesis. Firstly to enquire whether it is valid to describe primitive law as "repressive." Secondly to assess whether the law of advanced societies marks a transition to restitutive law; and finally whether this is associated with a relative decline of repressive law.

His characterisation of primitive law as repressive has been at the centre of the anthropological debate about the nature of primitive law. We may

---

[44]Durkheim, E., *ibid.,* p. 68.

[45]Alpert, *op. cit.,* p. 197.

deliberately avoid entering the debate about whether or not primitive societies can usefully and meaningfully be said to have "law" before the emergence of legal institutions as such. If primitive societies have no "law" then there can be no question of it being repressive. If however we admit the legitimacy of the concept "primitive law," then it is clear that the overwhelming weight of currently available evidence runs against Durkheim. What may be termed the "classical debate" in the anthropology of law involving Malinowski,[46] Hogbin,[47] Radcliffe-Brown[48] and Hoebel[49] went very much against Durkheim. The closest to Durkheim was Radcliffe-Brown with his emphasis on a distinction between "public" and "private" delicts.[50] The more recent contributions of such anthropologists as Gluckman,[51] Bohannan[52] and Pospisil,[53] while being anxious to stress the diversity of forms of primitive legal systems, offer no more support to Durkheim. Diamond has attempted to collate a large quantity of existing evidence; he argues that in the early stages of development repressive law was restricted to a very small number of offences such as incest. The general characteristic of early law is that of a regulated or semi-regulated system of private vengeance or feuding.[54]

Alpert attempted to rework Durkheim's empir-ical evidence and therefore relied exclusively on societies actually mentioned by Durkheim.[55] These show some support for Durkheim's thesis, but it is important to note that the majority of these societies are ones which exhibit fairly well developed state institutions. The evidence accumulated by Diamond[56] and the argument advanced by Seagle[57] indicates that the rise of repressive law can be associated with the emergence of economic class divisions and state forms after earlier pre-state stages of development which exhibit predominantly non-repressive forms of social regulation. This evidence cannot be regarded as providing any support for Durkheim since he himself repudiated any direct connection between stratification, the state and repressive law. He vastly overstates the role of repressive law in primitive societies.

The study of Schwartz and Miller brought together available anthropological data and subjected it to fairly sophisticated analytical techniques.[58] They argued that the form of primitive law and the nature of the sanctions relied upon were not very useful criteria. They contended that a comparison of legal development with institutional developments was more revealing and showed that forms of mediation and conciliation were characteristic of societies with the lowest division of labour. Again this evidence sharply contradicts the Durkheimian thesis. It may safely be concluded that the balance of evidence points to the fact that Durkheim was quite simply wrong in his characterisation of primitive law.

His contention that advanced societies exhibit restitutive law is less directly open to contention. There has occurred a very substantial advance in the volume and social significance of law relying on restitutive sanctions. The growth of restitutive law has taken the form of the development of new areas of legal regulation that were absent or

[46] See in particular Malinowski, B., *Crime and Custom in Savage Society* (London, 1 1961).

[47] Hogbin, H. I., *Law and order in Polynesia* (London, 1934).

[48] Radcliffe-Brown, A. R., "Primitive law," vol. 9 *Encyclopaedia of the Social Sciences*.

[49] Llewellyn, K. N. and Hoebel, E. A., *The Cheyenne Way* (Norman, 1941) and Hoebel, E. A., *The Law of Primitive Man* (Cambridge, Mass., 1961).

[50] Radcliffe-Brown, A. R., *op. cit.*

[51] See in particular, Gluckman, Max, *The Judicial Process Amongst the Barotse* (Manchester, 1955).

[52] Bohannan, P. J., *Justice and Judgement Among the Tiv* (London, 1957).

[53] Pospisil, L., *Anthropology of Law: A Comparative Theory* (New York, 1971).

[54] Diamond, A. S., *The Evolution of Law and Order* (London, 1951) and his more recent version *Primitive Law, Past and Present* (London, 1972).

[55] Alpert, *op. cit.*

[56] Diamond, *op. cit.*

[57] Seagle, William, *The Quest for Law* (New York, 1941).

[58] Schwartz, R. D. and Miller, J. C., "Legal evolution and societal complexity" 70 *American Journal of Sociology* 159-69 (1964).

underdeveloped in earlier stages. The most fundamental area of development is that which derives from the growth of property and its penetration into every sphere of social activity in more complex forms. The major expression of this development has been the expansion of contractual law, but it should be noted that this method of exposition focuses attention upon developments in substantive law. Yet his major contention relates to the changing form of legal sanctions. He posits a solution to the problem of the relation between form and substance at a very high level of generality by asserting an integration between form and substance with respect to changing types of social solidarity. What such an analysis leaves both unasked and unanswered is the nature of the process of mediation between form and substance, the way in which changes in specific social relations find legal expression which do not necessarily manifest a congruence between form and substance. Durkheim's thesis on the advance of restitutive law fails to provide an analysis of significant problems central to a theory of legal evolution; it is the omissions and the unasked questions that persist after an acceptance of the bare bones contention of the advance of restitutive law.

It is straightforward to point to a growth of restitutive law. It is less clear whether he saw this as an independent development or whether he sought to suggest that restitutive law actually replaced repressive law, that is whether a particular form of social activity is at one stage regulated by repressive law and at a higher stage of development becomes subject predominantly to restitutive law. If this construction is to be placed upon his thesis it is certain that he provides little or no supporting evidence. Examples can be found, perhaps the most important being the general abolition of penal sanctions for civil debt, but there does not appear to be sufficient evidence to support a general pattern of substitution of penal by restitutive sanctions.

At the most general level his theory posits a general advance of restitutive law and a parallel decline of repressive law. The general character

of legal documents in advanced capitalist societies does certainly indicate an increase in the volume of restitutive law, but it is less obvious that repressive law has retreated. Changes in the forms and severity of sanctions have taken place and certain traditional offences have declined or ceased to exist. Yet an extension of the number and range of offences carrying repressive, or at least non-restitutive, sanctions can be pointed to. The analysis and classification of these new offences give rise to some important questions which affect the Durkheimian analysis.

In some areas there has occurred an increase in the number of "pure" criminal offences, the most important area being that associated with the increasing complexity of property in capitalist societies which has resulted in an increase in offences concerned with the dishonest or fraudulent dealing with property. Similarly as a result of the extension of state activity and intervention in social and economic life a wide range of new offences have been created. The most important area of expansion has been with respect to what have been termed "public welfare offences" or "regulatory offences."[59] This wide-ranging and constantly expanding category of offences are repressive in the sense that they make use of some, if not all, of the sanctions associated with repressive law. Yet these offences diverge significantly from the Durkheimian definition of crime. Their breach is generally not met with collective repudiation nor is there the loss of honour that he saw as the hallmark of criminality. It may be noted in passing that, particularly with respect to "public welfare offences," but also more generally with respect to the majority of minor offences, the prevailing form of sanction has come to be that of the monetary fine which again departs in important respects from the ideal type of a repressive sanction. It may be that the pure type of punishment is no longer loss of liberty but is increasingly economic in character.

[59]See, for example, Friedmann, Wolfgang, *Law in a Changing Society* (London, 1964) and Sayre, F., "Public welfare offences" 33 *Columbia L. R.* 55 (1933).

While many of the developments referred to have only fully asserted themselves in recent decades it is significant that these changes were strongly indicated by the turn of the century. They serve to establish the fact that the simple dichotomous characterisation of legal evolution is not merely incorrect in significant respects but also that it misses many of the distinctive features of modern legal evolution. Yet despire these criticisms it remains true that the thesis retains, rather in the same way as does Maine's status-contract dictum, a certain compelling force. The service of such forceful and polemical theses is that they serve to concentrate and focus the ongoing analysis of legal development. But like all such tight and polar formulations they also serve to obscure other fundamental features of the processes under examination.

What is most surprising about the thesis of the transition from mechanical to organic solidarity is the extent to which it totally fails to give any recognisable account of the broad sweep of the historical process. He is not alone amongst social theorists in seeking to explore the conditions that gave rise to "modern society." He was only slightly less obsessed than Weber by the "uniqueness of the West,"[60] but what is absent or repressed by Durkheim is any conception of intermediate stages between primitive and modern society. He was much less concerned than either Marx or Weber with the historical genesis of capitalist or industrial society; the conception of a specific process of transition is submerged under the more evolutionist notion of an advancing division of labour. The omission of transitional forms of society it will be argued has serious consequences for his treatment of the state.

The above considerations indicate that the particular relationship which Durkheim posited between law and social solidarity cannot be maintained. Yet at the same time it may be argued that while we are entitled to reject the specific thesis that he presents we would be foolish not to recognise that there remains a rather more general and enduring contribution in his analysis. What endures is the proposition that the type of law that exists within a particular society is intimately wedded to the form of its social structure. In societies with a low level of division of labour law is marked by its universalism, that is it deals with social relations that are encountered in common either in fact or potentially by all members of society. In societies marked by a high degree of differentiation law itself reflects this differentiation and specialisation. Yet if this is all that remains of Durkheim's thesis it must be freely admitted that he does little more than assert the social character of law and indicate that there is some developmental relation between the type of law and other features of the social system.

Taylor, Walton and Young see Durkheim as advancing a "fully social theory."[61] His superiority over the psychologistic theories that have dominated traditional criminology is not in dispute. However they seem unaware that the form taken by Durkheim's "fully social theory" is one which leads directly towards holism. Since the whole (society) is more than the sum of its parts (individuals) the distinctive attributes of society are not present in its parts; hence society is seen not only as the source of its distinct characteristics, but also to be its own spontaneous cause.

As has previously been noted he tends to retreat from his dualistic model of social evolution in his later works, but it is never abandoned. He no longer utilises the distinction between mechanical and organic solidarity. Instead he concentrates upon the changing function and character of the "conscience collective" as the source of social cohesion. He also drops his insistence upon law as the key index of social solidarity. He no longer places such emphasis upon the coercive character of social control. In its place

---

[60]Like Weber, Durkheim's treatment of modern society is never that of an apologist: his theory is never simply a ligitimating ideology. Indeed the persistence of the influence of both lies precisely in the fact that they do not treat capitalist society as unproblematic; had they done so their views would have soon been discarded as pure ideology.

[61]Taylor, Walton and Young. *The New Criminology* (London, 1973) Chapter 3.

he increasingly emphasises that morality and religion constitute the decisive methods for the realisation of social solidarity. The "social fact" or "is" of solidarity induced through exterior constraint is replaced by the "ought" of moral obligation. . . .

*   *   *

CONTRACT

Durkheim returns on a number of occasions to the discussion of the nature and function of contract. In both *The Division of Labour* and in *Rules* his treatment is essentially polemical. His treatment is characteristically Durkheimian; he takes a phenomenon which as conventionally viewed seems to imply a fairly obvious and direct explanation, but he promptly seeks to demonstrate that a true understanding of the phenomenon is to be found in some diametrically opposed analysis. Contract bears all the characteristics of the pre-eminently individualist act as the expression of individual free will. But he is insistent that contracts are inherently social rather than individual in character.

In *Division of Labour* great importance is attached to contract because of the central role that it has played in the individualist, and particularly utilitarian, social theory. Indeed it is necessary to recognise the major role that the concept "contract" played in nineteenth century thought, in economics, philosophy, sociology and in jurisprudence. His attacks are in particular directed against Spencer and, by implication, Maine.[62]

For Durkheim contract is essentially social.

> A contract is not sufficient unto itself, but is possible only thanks to the regulation of the contract which is originally social.[63]

Instead of the conventional two-party analysis he insists on a three-party model with the third party, namely society, laying down in advance the per-

mitted framework of contractual activity. His insistence is upon the social institution of contract, what he describes as "the non-contractual elements of contract."

> If the contract has power to bind, it is society which gives this power to it. . . . Moreover it lends this obligatory force only to contracts which have in themselves a social value.[64]

So far his treatment of contract has not gone beyond his characteristic assertion of the social character of the institution. He draws support for this view from the extent to which the social character of contract is winning wider recognition both in legal practice and in juristic thought in particular through the growth of such concepts as duress and undue influence and, of particular importance, the rapid advance of the doctrine of "public policy."

His next step is also fairly unexceptional; he relates contract to the advance of the division of labour.

> Contractual relations necessarily develop with the division of labour, since the latter is not possible without interchange and the contract is the juridical form of exchange.[65]

The more contentious aspect of his elaboration is to be found in *Professional Ethics*. Here he is at his most challenging, if not necessarily at his most convincing. He draws together apparently disparate elements of social reality and spans the epochs of social evolution in order to produce a very distinctive account of the historical evolution of contract. So crucial a role has contract played in social thought that it appears today to exist as a "natural institution," a permanent and inevitable component of human society. But he is anxious to show that it is a relatively recent innovation. If its primary social function is as a means of acquisition of property, he argues that the earliest form of such acquisition was through inher-

---

[62]Durkheim was clearly familiar with Maine's work and refers explicitly to him in footnotes on a number of occasions.

[63]Durkheim, E., *Division of Labour*, p. 215.

[64]Durkheim, E., *ibid.,* p. 114.

[65]Durkheim, E., *ibid.,* p. 381.

itance. This he sees as giving way before the advance of contract. He is particularly vehement against the institution of inheritance. His attack upon it was his only enduring link with the socialists; its abolition he demanded as a precondition of the realisation of a meritocratic society.

He posits the evolution of contract as passing through two distinct stages. Using terminology very similar to that used by Maine he labels this transition as the change from "status-contract" to "will-contract."

> On the one hand we have relations in due form according to law, having as their origin the status of persons or of things, or of the modifications so far latent in this status; on the other, relations according to law having as their origin wills that are in agreement to modify their status.[66]

The earlier form of contract, based on status, is religious in origin, the parties or the subject matter being endowed with a sacred character. It is this sacredness which provides the basis of the obligatory nature of the undertaking. His central concern is to explain how the transition to "will contract" takes place. The essence of the problem is to determine what it is that makes agreement between two wills binding. The crucial role is played by ritual.[67] Ritual may surround the parties to the contract, for example the sharing of a meal, shaking hands or drinking from the same cup, or it may surround the subject matter, for example the ritualistic character of transfer of realty in many societies. Such ritual gives a sacred character to the act of exchange. The decisive step is to endow the undertaking *itself* with a sacred and hence binding character. Thereby the declaration of will is given an exteriority; a ritual form of promise emerges, for example the universal appearance of the oath and other magico-sacred formulas. The undertaking is thus marked by "sacred formalism"; the next step is for "juridical formalism" to replace sacred formalism.

Here the symbolic act becomes the substitute for the actual transference of property.

> The symbolism represents only a decadence that comes when the primary meaning of the custom is lost. Customs begin by being active causes, and not symbols, of social relations.[68]

The truly consensual contract arises only when the ritual and symbolic element declines in importance and finally disappears. He recognises that factors such as the quantitative increase in the number of transactions plays some part in his process, but it is significant that he explicitly resists a "determinist" position.

> The mere fact that an institution is required does not mean it will appear at a given moment out of the void. There must be something to make it of, that is, current ideas must allow it to come about and existing institutions must not oppose it but, rather, supply the material needed to shape it. So it is not enough for the consensual contract to be demanded by the advance of economic life: the public mind, too, had to be ready to conceive it as possible.[69]

In order to assess his thesis it is necessary to recognise that the analysis fits fairly consistently with, for example, the historical development of contract in English law. However his overzealous efforts to avoid "determinism" tends to leave the theory somewhat nebulous. A crucial feature for a consistent sociological theory of contract must start from the study of the type of exchange relations which have in fact manifested themselves as a consequence of the development of economic activity. An understanding of the economic form and content is a necessary pre-condition for an explanation of the role of ritual and formalism in the evolution of contract. Durkheim tends simply to presume that exchange is a natural and invariant consequence of the division of labour. Whereas in reality the transition from simple barter to developed capitalistic exchange spans major changes which necessarily had some im-

[66]Durkheim, E., *Professional Ethics*, p. 177.
[67]It should be noted that the notion of ritual played a central part in his theory of the evolution of religion.
[68]Durkheim, E., *ibid.*, p. 189.
[69]Durkheim, E., *ibid.*, p. 191.

pact upon the legal expression of these transactions.

The consensual contract, which Durkheim sees as reflecting a growing secularisation of society, rests no longer on the words used; the obligation becomes based on the intentions of the parties. The words as such are not formally binding; they are evidence of intention.

The consensual contract amounts to a revolutionary innovation in the law[70]

So crucial a role has it played that a wide range of social relations have been subsumed under a contractual form. Of particular importance is the employer-employee relationship; to view such a relationship in purely contractual terms has major ideological implications and Durkheim stresses the unfree basis upon which this exercise of "free will" is based.

The consensual contract did not mark the end of the evolution of contract; Durkheim posits a new stage, that of a "contract of equity" which reflects an increasing awareness of social interest in not only the nature but the consequences of contractual activity. This process is reflected in the extension of the factors vitiating contracts, the emergence of the doctrine of public policy and the general movement towards increasing social intervention addressed towards the objective of "just contracts." Such a thesis has close resemblance to Pound's insistence upon the emergence of a new stage of the "socialisation of law."

Durkheim's model of the ideal society is of a system of socially just contracts as opposed to freewill contracts. This development he sees impeded by the pernicious institution of inheritance. This he sees as the cause although it is more correct to argue that it is a reflection of social inequality. Thus while rejecting the social doctrine of individualistic utilitarianism his projected society rests firmly upon contractual foundations, but with the proviso that such contracts must first pass the test of being socially just.

[70]Durkheim, E., *ibid.,* p. 203.

PROPERTY

Closely related to the discussion of contract is the analysis which Durkheim provides of the nature of property and property rights. His treatment is less fully developed than that concerning contract.[71] The treatment is predominantly philosophical rather than historical or evolutionary. The failure to treat the question developmentally is a major weakness and stems from his overriding ideological concerns.

In developing a theory of property Durkheim has two enemies to combat. One is the "labour theory of property" which he attributes both to the classical political theorists, in particular to Locke, and to the socialists. His dismissal of this approach is somewhat cursory and rests on the proposition that since the market value of certain objects, for example works of art, cannot be accounted for in terms of the labour time embodied in their production it is therefore impossible to utilise the labour theory in accounting for the institution of property. Secondly he rejects the Kantian theory of property which attributes property rights to acts of individual will based upon a notion of "first appropriation" which is unacceptable since it makes the whole theory rest upon the accidental or arbitrary event of "first appropriation."[72]

For Durkheim the allocation of property is an inherently social activity. "It is the society that does the allocation of property."[73] In order to provide an account that avoids the two rejected theories he characteristically locates the source of property relations in collective beliefs and values and in particular in religious values. It is "the opinion of each society which makes certain objects susceptible to appropriation, and others not."[74] The essence of religion is that it sets certain things, the sacred, aside as having particular

[71]Durkehim, E., *ibid.,* pp. 121–70.

[72]This same proposition, though from different philosophical antecedents, is to be found at the root of Locke's theory of property.

[73]Durkheim, E., *Professional Ethics,* p. 215.

[74]Durkheim, E., *ibid.,* p. 138.

attributes or qualities; once endowed the sacred object is shrouded with inviolability. Both the sacred and property have this common characteristic of inviolability and therefore he concludes must have a common origin.

> The origins of property are to be found in the nature of certain religious beliefs. Since the effects are identical, they can in all likelihood be attributed to similar causes.[75]

He is suggesting here that since they have a similar characteristic, consistent with his previously elaborated methodological position which has already been criticised, there must necessarily be a causal connection between the two phenomena.

In elaborating a theory of the religious origins of property he argues that initially sacredness is conferred upon special individuals, namely priests, and that they are able to transfer this inviolability to sacred objects. Gradually it is the object rather than the person who is regarded as sacred and hence inviolable.

> Human property is but sacred and divine property put into the hands of men by means of a number of ritual ceremonies.[76]

He finds support for his theory in the practical inalienability of property in many tribal and feudal societies and in the taboos that surround such things as marker stones demarcating property in land.

Durkheim's dualistic model of society, although he no longer uses the labels mechanical and organic, is reflected in his account of the transition from communal to individual property. The first step is the granting to certain individuals of a superior status manifested in the emergence of the patriarchal family. The sacred character is no longer invested in the land itself, but is placed in the hands of the head of the family. The second stage is the development of movable property which comes to have an increasingly important economic role and which is now endowed with the same sacred character as realty. Personalty is a "weak reflection, an attenuated form[77] of real property. Real property is historically primary and personal property is granted as a concession by the collectivity.

His theory of property has none of the power and persuasiveness of his analysis of the evolution of contract. His basic method is weak and no supporting evidence is produced. Stone correctly describes it as "an exotic variation of the metaphysical theory of property."[78] Any analysis of the evolution of property must have as its starting point a consideration of the economic function that various types of property play in the wider economic and social process. Attention must therefore be placed not only on the important role of land in early societies, but must take specific account of the particular forms of property in land related to the variety of forms of production that emerge under definite social and economic circumstances.

DURKHEIM: A SYSTEMATIC SOCIOLOGY OF LAW?

Durkheim was undoubtedly one of the "founding fathers" of modern sociology; can the same claim be made for his contribution to the emergence of a sociology of law? Gurvitch for example speaks of him as having "developed a systematic legal sociology."[79] To assess this judgment it is not possible artificially to extract or lift Durkheim's "sociology of law" from the totality of his sociological enterprise. It has been central to the argument developed in this chapter that his treatment of law flows directly from the total enterprise.

The fundamental significance of Durkheim's work is that he created the intellectual space within which modern sociology has developed. Starting from his critique of political economy

[75]Durkheim, E., *ibid.,* pp. 143–4.
[76]Durkheim, E., *Professional Ethics,* p. 160.
[77]Durkheim, E., *ibid.,* p. 167.
[78]Stone, Julius, "Review of *Division of Labour*" 47 *Harvard Law Review* 1451 (1934).
[79]Gurvitch, G., *The Sociology of Law* (New York, 1942), p. 83.

and moral philosophy he carved out an area of intellectual enquiry which has become the preserve of a distinct form of intellectual activity that carries the label "sociology." It was Durkheim more than any other who prescribed the boundaries or parameter of sociology; he provided or designated the space which twentieth century sociology has occupied. This intellectual territory is to be sharply differentiated from that occupied by Marxist theory and it is the reason which first and foremost renders the current preoccupation of comparison between sociology and Marxism a largely misdirected activity.[80]

The territory of sociology is occupied for Durkheim by a central problematic of the individual—society relationship. It is specified in *Division of Labour:* "This work has its origins in the question of the relations of the individual to social solidarity. Why does the individual, while becoming more autonomous, depend more upon society? How can he be at once more individual and more solidary?[81] It is this central problematic which leads Durkheim ⚑ the concern with social integration and stamps the specific orientation upon his sociology which Parsons describes as "The remarkable ability to see relations among fields usually treated as unconnected was possible only because Durkheim consistently kept in mind the fact that he was dealing with the problem of integration of a single system."[82] The specific form which the social integration perspective takes, in terms both of Durkheim's analysis and his prescriptions, is with the normative process as the fundamental ingredient of social integration; it is a quest for the ideological community as the basis of the conception of what are taken to be the distinctive characteristics of modern Western society, namely industrial society and political democracy.

It is within this context that the contention strenuously advanced by Anthony Giddens that Durkheim should not be branded as a theorist of social order or of conservatism can be assessed. Giddens is correct in so far as he is reacting against a persistent vice of modern sociology to classify all sociological theory as either "consensus" or "conflict theory."[83] However the counter-reaction cannot simply deny what has become the conventional wisdom. Were Durkheim simply a theorist of a non-problematic integrationist theory his influence on sociological thought would have rapidly faded. It is precisely because Durkheim presents the stability and integration of industrial society as problematic that gives stature and significance to his sociological theory. It is for this reason that his concept of anomie, and to a lesser extent that of the forced division of labour, is the medium through which the problematic character of contemporary society is conveyed. But, having made clear that Durkheim cannot be passed off as a pure integrationist, it needs to be insisted that his general perspective is precisely that of functional integration which operates primarily at the level of normative systems.

It is this dominant strand which directly informs his treatment of legal phenomena. His treatment of law rests upon an invariant and unquestioned assumption of law as a functionally integrative mechanism. It is central to the posited invariant relationship between law and social solidarity. Law is presented at one and the same time as the reflex and as an index of social solidarity. This orientation determines the specific character of his treatment of law. The spring of social cohesion rises from the collective sentiments, attitudes and values which are the product of social forces that operate upon individuals. Social cohesion is thus rooted in the normative system of society. Then law, along with morality, are presented

---

[80]This argument about the relationship between sociology and Marxism is developed by Hirst, Paul, *Social Evolution and Sociological Categories* (London, 1976) and by Therborn, Goran, *Science, Class and Society* (London, 1975).

[81]Durkheim, F., *Division of Labour*, p. 37.

[82]Parsons, Talcott, "Durkheim's contribution to the theory of integration of social systems" in Wolff (ed.), *op cit.*, p. 151.

[83]A recent and extreme example of this tendency is to be found in McDonald, Lynn, *The Sociology of Law and Order* (London, 1976) which classifies every thinker from Plato to the present day around a consensus conflict dichotomy.

both as embodiments of and as agents of social harmony.

This orientation has a number of quite specific consequences for his sociology of law. There is no space within his conceptual framework for a thorough analysis of social disharmony or conflict as an ever-present constituent of social relations. The nearest he can approach is either to regard conflict as pathological (forced division of labour) or as a consequence of social malfunction (anomie). As a result his sociology of law is marked by a number of important absences or gaps. Absent are the law-power relation, the law-domination relation and the law-state relation.

The direct relation posited between law and social solidarity amounts to a simple reductionism and as a consequence law whilst "functional" can have no autonomy or even relative autonomy; it cannot be considered as an active causal force since the theoretical framework within which it is placed prescribes that it passively reflects transformations in the forms of sociality. Similarly the emphasis upon the normative as the central reality of human sociality expresses itself in concern for the normative content of law and as a consequence little or no attention is given to the institutional forms of legal systems.

The discussion of law in Durkheim's sociology arises in the first instance, as we have seen tangentially, as a methodological device for the analysis of the forms of social solidarity. This has generally led commentators to attach little significance to his specific treatment of law.[84] But

this ignores the extent to which law has an important location within his general sociology. Law is a major institutionalised expression, embodiment and vehicle of the ideological community. Its forms of existence and surrounding ideology are a veritable celebration of social cohesion at the level of the total society. In this form there is an important continuity with the social control perspective of law as a specialised form thereof encountered in Poundian sociological jurisprudence and American realism.

The central feature of Durkheim's sociology of law is contained in the focus upon the relationship between law and social solidarity. Extracting this from its specifically Durkheimian form it amounts to a definition of the object of the sociology of law as being that of the interrelation of law and the forms of social relations. This constitutes a necessary and persistent focus for sociological treatment of law, but it is little more than a minimum condition for a sociology of law. It does not constitute a specific direction or thrust of enquiry. Considered in conjunction with those elements which it has been argued are missing from Durkheim's treatment of law, it can be concluded that his work cannot be taken as constituting either the beginning or as a crucial point of development for the sociology of law. Yet the persistent sociologism of Durkheim ensures that his work will remain a significant point of reference, but this very characteristic requires that it is a position that must be encountered in the development of a sociology of law.

---

[84]One exception is Alpert who places much stress on Durkheim's persistent concern with law and legal phenomena: Alpert, H., *Emile Durkheim and his Sociology* (New York, 1961).

IDEOLOGY AND RATIONALITY IN MAX WEBER'S SOCIOLOGY OF LAW

PIERS BEIRNE

An historical phenomenon completely understood and reduced to an item of knowledge is, in relation to the man who knows it, dead; for he has found out its madness, its injustice, its blind passion.

Nietzsche

INTRODUCTION

The intellectual history of sociological approaches to order and domination has, schematically, been marked by the attitudes of two competing versions of Kantianism. It is axiomatic to the argument which follows that the inability of modern social theory adequately to resolve this competition has occasioned a fundamental dilemma. This dilemma is the traditional one of social philosophy, namely, selection of the appropriate relation between the knowing subject and society, the object of knowledge. Such has been the historical force of this dilemma that the sociologist who addresses himself to it confronts the paradox that the conceptual categories used to unravel it presuppose much of the validity of what he is trying to resolve.

The recognition of the subject/object dilemma was immanent in the methodology which informed Max Weber's account of the origins and

reproduction of modern Western capitalism. A German obituary invoked that Weber's *verstehende soziologie* "was just as objective as any other form of causal explanation in spite of its element of subjectivity... no sociologist... has stated more adequately his position on the sociological dilemma of the subjective-objective" (Abel, 1965, p. 194).

Weber's methodology aspired to a conceptual precision, and in overtly avoiding the sins of historicism and rationalism, it promised to capture the varieties of human existence in the pathos of Western culture. His knowledge of global socio-cultural phenomena was truly encyclopaedic. Weber is almost unique, in the sociological tradition, in having developed a systematic sociology of law which appears both internally consistent and consonant with his wider sociological landscape. "There is no better analysis," Poulantzas (1973, p. 212) somewhat ambiguously remarks, "of this dominance of the juridico-political in capitalist ideology than Max Weber's." The argument which follows stems from the belief that the sociology of law is currently in a period of crisis, a crisis produced more by the influence of Weberianism than by specific texts, and a crisis from which it seems impossible to emerge without exploring Weber's own contribution to it. Such a venture minimally requires an outline of the key epistemological issues which Weber was to meet at the outset of his career as an academic lawyer.

Source: From *Research in Law and Sociology,* Volume 2 (1979), pages 103–131, S. Spitzer, ed., JAI Press, Greenwich, CT. Copyright © 1979 by JAI Press Inc. Reprinted by permission.

I. THE PRODUCTION OF WEBER'S METHODOLOGY

A. GERMAN PHILOSOPHICAL IDEALISM

The predominate source of intellectual inspiration in Bismarckian Germany had been the powerful heritage of philosophical idealism in its rejection of Cartesian determinism. Kant's solution to Humean epistemological skepticism was the preference for a radical dualism between the subjective and objective components of the "I," and between the domains of mind and matter. Analysis of an object was held to begin with the subject as it experienced and conceptualized the object. This implied that knowledge of reality— the "thing-in-itself"—was unobtainable, and that the analysis of mind or matter required a methodology specific to each.

For Kant, the phenomenal world could only be grasped by means of the formal generalizations found in Newtonian mechanics and natural science. But to extrapolate this model to the analysis of human action, or "culture," would be to ignore the rich uniqueness of human action. Man was therefore cast as a two-dimensional agent. On the one hand, his phenomenal nature was open to logical and formal analysis but, on the other, his sentient, purposive character as free agent could only be ascertained by a philosophy of history which explicated causal relationships between specific social actors.

However, in two respects Kantian dualism embodied far more than this radical distinction. Firstly, it combined both idealism and rationalism in that human action was in the final analysis seen as dependent on inexorable supra-historical natural laws and categorical imperatives. "When the play of freedom of the human will is examined on the great scale of universal history," Kant (1959, p. 23) asserted, "a regular march may be discovered in its moments . . . what appears to be tangled in the case of individuals, will be recognized in the history of the whole species as a continually advancing, though slow, development." This development was particularly slow in Kantian Germany, and envious but abstract

glances were directed towards the successes of the French bourgeoisie in 1789. In certain respects, Kantian idealism may aptly be characterized as a secular form of Protestantism in that, at the level of speculative philosophy, it sought to express the political interests of the nascent Prussian bourgeoisie. Kant's second departure lay in his solution to the disjunction between the relative positions of the German polity and economy. What was needed was a more rational reflection on the political immaturity of the German state. "The problem of the erection of the state, hard as it may seem," says Kant (1971, first supplement), "may be solved even for a people of devils, if only they be endowed with Reason." The categorical imperatives underlying the legal structure of the *Rechsstaat* were both cause and effect of the social contract produced by rational reflection; but this reflection was then present in embryonic form only.

Hegel later attempted to subvert Kantian dualism by arguing that subject and object are in a continuous process of self-transformation. Objectivity is constructed by consciousness, and the development of the objective world is throughout interwoven with the development of consciousness. The phenomenal and the social worlds are now to be understood as manifestations of a *Weltgeist,* the Absolute Idea. Absolute self-consciousness is God, and the objective meaning in history resides in the development of the Idea.

To Hegel, it was philosophy which had produced the French Revolution, but a revolution which uncritically accepted certain strains of social contract theory prevalent in the Enlightenment. For Hegel, the corollary of accepting the doctrine of methodological individualism was *ab initio* to ensure that the will of the nation state was subordinated to particular wills. His opposition to the Enlightenment can therefore be explained by his insistence that the individual can only realize his true particularity in the social whole. Only the expression and logic of the whole can produce genuine freedom for the individual. Indeed, it is this injunction which in turn explains Hegel's abhorrence of Robespierre's dictature: as a manifestation of ethical idealism, it sought to press particular demands for justice in contradistinction to the requirements for universal liberation.

Once Hegel had demonstrated that Kantian dualism was in error, that matter was merely an alienated form of spirit, then all that remained was to reveal the forces underlying the process and movement of history. The full implications of Hegel's ambivalent conservatism were revealed in his political philosophy, and it is to this aspect of his idealism that we must limit this section of the inquiry. The centerpiece of this drama was his *Rechtsphilosophie,* which was written in mid-1820. He sets the tone for the book as a whole when, in the preface, he identifies the state as Reason as it actualizes itself in the element of self-consciousness. Law is par excellence the shibboleth which marks out the enemies of the people.[1] He asserts that "what is rational is actual, and what is actual is rational!" (Hegel, 1973, p. 10). "Actual" in its Hegelian sense must not, however, be confused with its modern, empiricist usage. For Hegel, an event can only become actual when its character has been transformed by situating it within the social whole. But for Hegel, not all existence is actual, since the attribute of actuality only belongs to that which is necessary. Thus, the outmoded French monarchy was "unreal," whilst the revolution of 1789 was "real." Although Hegel is consciously doing only what all social philosophers must do, namely, demarcating as real and necessary that which he so evaluates, his immediate failure is due to his refusal to recognize the contradiction between the rational that was already actual, and the irrational which did still exist (see further Ilting, 1971, p. 109).

The argument takes a more sinister turn. Hegel was faced with a dilemma: individual freedom consists in the ownership of private property, and

yet it was manifestly obvious that in civil society—"civil society" refers to the sphere of material interests governed by the Hobbesian notion of *bellum omnium contra omnes*—this necessitates antagonism between individual property owners. The materialization of freedom therefore requires the submersion of a multitude of particular wills in a universal will. Civil society can only find its truth in the universal and it is the task of the state to reconcile the dialectical opposition between the particular and the universal. "The State," says Hegel, "is the Divine Idea as it exists on Earth" (1956, p. 39). The main function of the state executive is ensuring the observation of legality, and the real spirit of the executive lies in its bureaucratic hierarchy. Hegel was, however, extremely reticent to outline how such a state was to be realized, which is all the more remarkable since he was so precise in outlining its structure.

To summarize, Hegel's methodology implied that the phenomenal world emanates from and is subsumed under the Idea. The contradiction between the particular (the individual) and the universal (Society) is actually reconciled as they merge in the predicate of a state and its legislation which both protects free will yet simultaneously manages to express the universal will. Kant's proposition that subject (observer) and object (observed) are radically distinct thus becomes transformed by Hegel to the notion that subject (the Idea) and object (Society) are finally indissoluble, but that the historical subject is logically prior to the historical object.

German philosophy after Hegel met with something which a good tragedy is supposed not to meet, a dull ending. In the decade after his death, the system which Hegel had advanced exercised an unparalleled influence within German philosophy. What criticism there was of it inevitably took place within the compass of its structure. Out interest lies in its effect on methodological issues within philosophy and jurisprudence.

The immediate philosophical controversy centered around different interpretations of

---

[1]This early critical vein is undoubtedly aimed against the prefascist backlash which occurred in Germany after the failures of the 1813–1815 war with France. It was leveled particularly at those liberals and conservatives who rejected the notion that the state embodied practical reason.

Hegel's opening gambit in the *Rechtsphilosophie:* those Young Hegelians who asserted "What is actual, is rational" tended to a philosophy embedded in political conservatism. Those who asserted "what is rational, is actual" voiced their arguments from the perspective of religious liberalism. The first group tried to adapt philosophy to the exigencies of the real world, changing philosophy so that it conformed to the world. The second group (the Left Hegelians) saw the gap between philosophy and the real world and attempted to bridge it, so that by changing reality, reality would conform to philosophy. But the effect of each group was precisely the opposite of that intended. The first group merely upheld the status quo, and thus had an effect on reality but not on philosophy. The second group, in seeking to transform the world through the medium of philosophy, instead made philosophy an instrument of political action. This, however, changes the character of philosophy, but not the character of the world (see further, Marx, 1975).

Although challenged by Young Hegelians such as Strauss and Bauer, the Hegelian system remained generally intact. It was Ludwig Feuerbach who indicated the point of rupture. Feuerbach marshalled his criticism of Hegel with three assertions. Firstly, he pointed out that Hegel had failed to remember what he had accused other philosophers of forgetting: that all philosophy is a creature of its time and must therefore surrender its claim to absolute truth. Second, the Hegelian system was held to be a logical structure, but one which nevertheless had metaphysical and self-evident premises. In deducing existence from essence, the ideal from the real, and in showing how the Idea gradually unfolded its predicates—in doing all this, Hegel merely succeeded in elaborating his initial assumptions. Finally, Feuerbach argued that Hegel had grossly distorted the character of cognition by situating man's consciousness in the other-world of philosophy. Man himself must be the center of the universe. For Feuerbach, therefore, the subject (man) is logically prior to the object (community), and historical progress consists in the realization

of man's communal species-being as he becomes conscious of his alienation.

Engels (1970, p. 592) later described the effect of these criticisms on the Young Hegelians:

> With one blow it pulverized the contradictions, in that without circumlocutions, it placed materialism on the throne again . . . the "system" was exploded and cast aside . . . we all at once became Feuerbachians. How enthusiastically Marx greeted the new inception.

B. MATERIALIST PHILOSOPHY

In 1845, Marx characterized the partial nature of the Young Hegelians' criticism of Hegel as an advance which "consisted in subsuming the allegedly dominant metaphysical, political, juridical, moral and other conceptions under the class of religious or theological conceptions" (Marx and Engels, 1974, p. 40). He saw that the main impasse in German philosophy was the distance which existed between philosophical idealism and the material reality of Germany, a contradiction which Hegel had attempted to resolve by the fiction of the Absolute Idea. The initial problem for Marx was quite clearly how to transform philosophy into an instrument of practical change. "The *practice* of philosophy is itself *theoretical,*" Marx (1975, p. 85) bemoaned, "and it is the *critique* that measures the individual existence by the essence."

Marx was deeply impressed by the attraction of Feuerbach's transformative method, but he argued that Feuerbach had emphasized nature and individual man to the detriment of politics.[2] For our purposes, Marx's criticism of Hegel and his radical departure from Feuerbachian humanism may be reduced to three assertions: (1) the Hegelian dialectic occurs only within abstract philosophy, never in concrete historical space and as

---

[2]Feuerbach's transformative method essentially involved the simple reversal of the Hegelian dialectic within an anthropological problematic. In his 1843 "Theses on the Reform of Philosophy," Feuerbach asserted that "The true relation of thought to Being is this: Being is subject, thought is predicate. Thought springs from Being, but Being does not spring from thought."

such cannot comprehend that the final reality is man's practical activities; (2) Hegel's concept of the negation of the negation, whilst implying a criticism of what exists, is a static rather than a dynamic notion which tends to represent class, state, and bureaucracy as eternal institutions; (3) capitalist society (private property) will inevitably be transformed to a higher existence (socialism) through the activity of its only real subject (the proletariat). For Marx, the subject/object dilemma is a false one and there is a necessary relation between theory and practice such that subject and object are in a continuous process of self-transformation through praxis.

Marx's theory of state and law was never fully developed. The vulgar account of this embryo was the one which began with the instrumental definition in the *Communist Manifesto*: "the executive of the modern state is but a committee for managing the common affairs of the whole bourgeoisie" (Marx and Engels, 1973). This crude definition ignores three crucial factors. Firstly, the *executive* is only one section of the state apparatus, and as Marx was later to demonstrate in three articles on French politics, antagonism between different sections of this apparatus is a salient dynamic in the relations between social classes under capitalist modes of production. Second, the definition tends to blur conflict between different fractions of capital. In what is much more than a semantic defence, this confusion could partly be avoided if the words "common" and "whole" are emphasized. Third, it appears on this level as a static and non-dialectical account which underplays the state's origin in civil society, and which overplays its permanence.

For Marx and Engels, the state is an historical phenomenon which contributes to the ideological and political coherence of a social formation, which has definite roots in the social contradictions which arise from commodity production, but which nevertheless exerts a reflexive influence on the class relations which flow from production. The state is both a crucial part of civil society and yet increasingly assumes a relative

independence from it. But this "independence" obscures the state's real function as an illusory form in which class struggles are contested. Following Hegel, and paralleling the famous section on commodity fetishism in the first volume of *Capital*. Marx thus designates the state as a phenomenal form of capitalist society. In a letter of 1865 to J. B. Schweitzer, Marx (1969, p. 25) insisted on the distinction between phenomenal and real relations: the question of what constitutes bourgeois property was "only answerable by a critical analysis of political economy, embracing those property relations as a whole, not in their *legal* expression as *relations* of *volition* but in their real form, that is *as relations of production*." The break with Kantian dualism, and with idealism in general, could not be cleaner. The very distinction between essence and appearance embodies the notion that Kant's "thing-in-itself" can now be known.

C. SOCIAL ACTIONISM

German Jurisprudence.   As the nineteenth century entered its final quarter, two centers of dispute provided the initial nourishment for Weber's early career as an academic lawyer. The first was endemic to German jurisprudence and tended to be relatively immune from the more sophisticated issues which were debated in the *Geisteswissenschaften* concerning the appropriate values and duties of the social theorist. In many respects, the conceptual proclivities of jurisprudence in nineteenth century Germany may be accounted for by the incoherence of the German polity. By 1850, the agricultural and industrial economies were in a period of rapid growth, but with an economically successful bourgeoisie confronted by a reform-oriented proletariat. The immediate obstacle to the continued prosperity of the bourgeoisie was the pre-capitalist character of the political structure, which was dominated both by the presence of the landed aristocracy and the absence in the three hundred municipalities which comprised Germany, including Prussia, of a democratic political constitution (see further Droz and Ayçoberry, 1964).

This situation readily lent itself, as it had previously in medieval Italy, seventeenth century Holland, and eighteenth century France, to the intellectual and political importance of the Romanist lawyer. Rheinstein has correctly stressed that

> where a country is a political, social, and quite particularly, an economic unit, it requires a certain minimum of legal uniformity . . . . Where legal uniformity is achieved neither by a national legislature nor by a national supreme court the task of achieving at least some measure of legal uniformity must be undertaken by some other agency, and that very role was undertaken on the European continent by the scholars of the university law schools (Rheinstein, in Weber, 1954, p. 1i).

Ever since Thiabaut's proposal in 1814 for the codification of popular legislation, German jurisprudence had been faced with the persistent problem of how the formal qualities of Roman law could be adapted to the peculiar condition and needs of the unique German national spirit (*Volksgeist*).

Von Savigny replied to Thiabaut asserting that no amount of skillful codification could avoid the real origin of law in custom. The adaptation of Roman law to Germanic custom would crush the necessary creative qualities demanded by natural law and by Reason. Codification was a possibility, Savigny continued, only when the political condition of the *Volksgeist* permitted it. And Savigny detected that the *Volksgeist* was unprepared for such a major step. The introduction of a formal code, whose dictates were to be universally applicable, would "sanctify contradictions, ambiguities, omissions and confusions . . . and insulate the law from its source in popular consciousness."[3]

The main champion of codification was Rudolf Stammler, a legal philosopher who was primarily concerned to rebut a crude form of economic determinism which he incorrectly attributed to Marx. He therefore argued that there was nothing in the universal propositions of a formal code which inherently predisposed it to favor one section of a human community rather than another. The problem was rather how to bridge the gap between the Kantian notion of free will and the reality of a modern community. The solution to this, thought Stammler, lay in asserting that justice was an absolute concept but one which could successfully be applied to the members of a community which was based on the harmony of particular interests. If any discrepancy existed between the political condition of the *Volksgeist* and the harmony of individual and communal interests, then it was preferable for the *Volksgeist* to be mediated by the imperatives of a formal code.

The different responses to Thiabaut's original proposal—the first draft of the Pandectist Civil Code was prepared in 1887, and finally implemented in 1900—were thus agreed on the acceptance of the Kantian notion that law was "practical" and "rational" and the Hegelian notion that law was the manifestation of the *Volksgeist*.

But there was another vital notion in which German jurists necessarily concurred—irrespective of allegiance to any of the four juristic tendencies then flourishing—and this was the Romanist legal conception of the social actor (see further Kelly, 1977). Arising from the reactionary effect of notions of private property based on membership in the *gens,* this construct had been developed when the economic requirements of Roman trade and "the imperatives of the political economy of empire forced a reformulation of legal categories by which, in a Kantian sense, personhood might be conceptually established" (Kelly, 1977, p. 12). At the core of the construct of legal personhood was the image of the individual citizen as property owner, free contractor in the exchange of commodities, and the repository of rights and duties. Roman law was instigated in pre-Christian Germany, and the scope of its authority was subsequently enhanced by theologi-

[3]A good introduction to this period is provided in J. Stone, *The Province and Function of Law*, Cambridge, Mass: Harvard University Press, 1950, especially pp. 317-27 and pp. 421-48.

cal conceptions of free will found in canon law. Surviving the onslaught of the Reformation, the concept of legal personhood formed the very basis of juristic thought and entrenched a *Weltanschauung* which resided "in the initial presumption, creation and categorization of the individual subject as the focal point of discourse" (Kelly, 1977, p. 13) With this tradition, it is not difficult to understand why it was that in Germany in the late nineteenth century, social actionism was to become the dominant tendency in history and sociology. It is worth noting, at this point, that Max Weber was trained as a Romanist lawyer and was to write his first book on the significance which Roman agrarian history exercised on the German legal system.

The Methodenstreit.   The methodological issues within philosophy and social theory were formally of a very different nature to those in jurisprudence, and they crystallized in the *Methodenstreit* debate which focused on Dilthey, Rickert, and Windelband. The institutional forum of this debate was the *Verein für Sozialpolitik,* a body of social philosophers united both by their desire to cultivate the humane disciplines (*Geisteswissenschaften*) and by their spiritual aversion to French positivism and English social utilitarianism. The evident contradiction between the Hegelian notion of the state as the neutral embodiment of the universal interest and the particular demands for social reform made by representatives of the new economic classes prompted members of the *Verein* to reassess some very basic epistemological questions.

Dilthey (quoted in Hawthorn, 1976, p. 143) argued that the most pressing need was to establish "an empirical science of the human mind . . . to get to know the laws which govern social, intellectual and moral phenomena." In response to Dilthey's intention to construct this science as an amalgam of philosophy and psychology, Windelband asserted that it was impossible to build a study of social action on the principles of two disciplines which had been founded on contradictory objectives: philosophy tried to under-

stand the particular only insofar as the particular had a referent for the general, whilst psychology was interested in the particular *sui generis.* The hybrid proposed by Dilthey was therefore exposed as an absurdity. Rickert also took issue with Dilthey, basing his attack on the familiar notion that a science of human action was *a priori* to be excluded if its intention was the formulation of universal laws and scientific causality. For Rickert, the world of social reality was irreducible because the cultural world was infinite. Knowledge of the social world must always therefore be partial. An observer's delineation of the "value-relevant" and the "valued" was held to be dependent upon specific cultural circumstances, so that "there are as many historical truths as there are different spheres of culture" (Dilthey, quoted in Hawthorn, 1976, p. 146).

II.   WEBER'S METHODOLOGY

One of the most important protagonists in these debates was Max Weber. Weber agreed, in his inaugural lecture as professor of economics at Freiburg in 1895, that he was a member of the bourgeois class and had been raised in its ideals and aspirations. His central interest, from the beginning, was to explain the unique factors which had produced modern Western capitalism. His most famous work on this question, *The Protestant Ethic and the Spirit of Capitalism,* first appeared in the Verein's journal in 1905, and a deceptive summary of his broad intentions is contained in its concluding statement:

> It is, of course, not my aim to substitute for a one-sided materialistic an equally one-sided spiritualistic causal interpretation of culture and history. Each is equally possible, but each, if it does not serve as the preparation, but as the conclusion of an investigation, accomplishes equally little in the interest of historical truth (Weber, 1948, p. 183).

Weber's thesis in *The Protestant Ethic* was that to a significant extent, the origins of Western capitalism were to be found in the secular ethos of Protestantism, and in particular in the rationalist conceptions of the Calvinist belief system. For Weber, the Calvinist stress on worldly asceticism tended to be undermined by the consequences of a postulate which Calvin had borrowed from Luther, the concept of the "Calling." This concept entailed that each person had been pre-destined by God to go either to Heaven or to Hell. One could never be certain of one's ultimate destination, but worldly success was indicative of the grace needed to enter Heaven. Asceticism and puritanism were therefore engaged in a dynamic whereby the fruits of labor could not be exchanged for hedonistic purposes. Such fruits had in effect to be reinvested in industry. To be more accurate, it was the psychological results of such theological beliefs which produced the unintended consequence of a Christian culture bathed in an orgy of material decadence. Material acquisitions were a necessary *consequence* of the belief in hard work associated with the uncertainty of the Calling, yet they were also *unintended* since they contradicted the moral imperatives associated with puritanism.

For Weber, a major effect of the advance of rationalization—the belief that the world can be mastered through the calculative axioms of formal logic—was a universal disenchantment with the world. Rationalization remained of uncertain parenthood, but appeared to originate in the "totalizing" and "systematizing" accounts of modern religious prophets who attempted to reduce all phenomena to deductive explanation. Rationalization therefore enabled man to demystify religious beliefs, but the result was a disenchantment in which all systems of universal culture were systematically destroyed. Each person in the modern world now has their own God, and their own system of values. Marianne Weber (1975, p. 136) has recalled that Weber therefore wanted to cultivate and support, in this chaotic universe, "what appears to us as *valuable* in man: his personal responsibility, his basic drive towards higher things." Wright (1974/75, p. 102) has concluded that his plea, when translated to the demand for responsible, effective leadership, "becomes a program for stabilizing and strengthening capitalist hegemony." But it is more immediately possible to argue, as Horkheimer (1947, p. 6), for example, has done, that Weber's pessimism with regard to the possibility of rational insight "is itself a stepping-stone in the renunciation of philosophy and science as regards their aspiration of defining man's goals."

Following both Kant and Rickert, Weber accordingly attests that an observer can only know the partial knowledge which his own value system directs him to study. Values therefore intrude into the method and the object of study. "There is no absolutely 'objective' scientific analysis of culture . . . or of social phenomena," declared Weber (1949, p. 72) in *Objectivity in Social Science and Social Policy,* "independent of special and 'one-sided' viewpoints according to which expressly or tacitly, consciously or unconsciously, they are selected, analyzed, and organized for expository purposes." Science is itself determined by historical cultures and necessarily includes pre-scientific choices. An observer must be quite candid about his own vlaues, distancing them as much as possible from his object of study. The more an observer distinguishes between the evaluative and the analytical-logical parts of his work, the more his observations are "objective." Social science cannot reveal the ethical merits of competing values, but in uncovering the intelligibility of actions in terms of the dominant values to which they are oriented, it is able to demonstrate whether a particular course of action is likely to achieve the relevant value. Social science in this vein could, for example, aid man to see the historical disjunction between the formal intent of the Calvinist belief system and its substantive consequences once acted upon.

Having ostensibly demonstrated the possibility of a social science, Weber's next step was to outline the conceptual premises of such an endeavor. The starting point of sociological analysis must lie, he (1968, p. 13) argues," in the particular acts of individual persons, since these alone can be treated as agents in a course of subjectively understandable action." This proposition reflects both the objective corollaries of individuated disenchantment—in the sense that Weber recognized that the social world comprises an infinity of subjective meanings—and also his belief, therefore, in the ultimate relativity of knowledge.

Action, for Weber, is "social" behavior "insofar as its subjective meaning takes account of the behavior of others and is thereby oriented in its course" (1968, p. 4). Since knowledge of essence is impossible, Weber argues that the analysis of all types of action must be pursued through an heuristic and formally precise fiction, borrowed from Jellinek, and which he terms the "ideal type." Action may be traditional, affectual, value-oriented, or rational. Rational action is delineated by a correct and appropriate balance between means and foreseeable consequences, and is the most susceptible to rational proof. Weber's notion of "meaningfully oriented conduct" operates at two interlocking levels. On the one hand, it refers exclusively to the actor's own subjective definition of his situation; on the other, it refers to the theoretically conceived pure type of subjective meaning attributed to the hypothetical actor or actors, in a given hypothetical situation, by the observer. The latter level therefore refers to the degree of conformity between observed action and the sociologist's abstract or ideal typical model of such action.

Superficially, all appears harmonious. Weber has astutely avoided the serious errors which accompany both positivism and historicism, whilst managing to reject the immanentist postulates of the *Volksgeist* tradition. But in one respect we already have cause for suspicion. Weber's formal rejection of philosophical idealism belies the fact that his construct of the ideal type in practice embodies at least some of its assumptions. Further, although ideal types can possibly assist in the production of systematic frameworks of generalizations, they are nevertheless "nowhere applicable, (and) cannot play any real part in the deduction of empirically testable consequences" (Papineau, 1976, p. 146).

Weber's next step was to demonstrate how social structures articulate with individual social ac-

tion. To say that an actor's conduct is "meaningfully oriented" to that of another is to allow that each is entitled to expect a degree of conformity on the part of the other. This is the case irrespective of the content or quality of the action or value to which it refers. Regularities in social action are identical with—as opposed to contingent on—social structures, where "courses of actions . . . are repeated by the actor or (simultaneously) occur among numerous actors since the subjective meaning of the action is the same for each of them" (Weber, 1968, p. 29). Reciprocated patterns of action may be based on such diverse factors as custom or tradition, but the most permanent and stable forms of social action are those where the subjective meaning is attached to a belief in a legitimate order. Only where the possibility of reciprocal action is "probable" will social structures persist; it is in this sense that behavior becomes causally adequate. If an actor is cognizant of such probability, and correctly evaluates the rational means to achieve the intended value, then behavior becomes meaningfully adequate. It is the sociologist's use of the ideal type—a device which is able to generalize about social behavior whilst also uncovering the unique character of each social act—which differentiates the method of sociology from other disciplines.

Weber's relationship with Marx and Marxist theory was both uneasy and ill-defined. Talcott Parsons (1969, p. 6) has surmised that Weber "soon recoiled from the Marxian position as he became convinced of the indispensability of an important role of 'ideas' in the explanation of great historical processes." But this implies that Marx himself never accorded any causative role to "ideas" in historical development, and it ignores Weber's own lifelong admiration for certain aspects of the Marxist tradition. Indeed, as late as 1918, Weber (1973, p. 25) said of the *Communist Manifesto* that "however much one may reject its crucial thesis, and *I* do that, (it) is in its way a scientific achievement of the first order." For Marx, dialectical materialism invoked the likelihood of a collective subject (the proletariat) relentlessly transforming its conditions of existence to a new and higher phase of social development. But Weber's concept of disenchantment, whereby the social world was seen to be composed of an infinite universe of subjective meaning, precluded the emergence of such a force. On one level, Weber must be seen as attempting to discredit any monocausal type of explanation, whether this appeared under the banner of materialism or idealism. The only direct application which this had to Marxism was an attack on the vulgar Marxism of the Second International and the authoritarian tendencies which he detected, for example, in the Bolshevik Marxism of Munich in 1918. Weber was therefore keen to demonstrate that the emergence of social structures was caused neither by technological determinism nor by a simple complex of values. All elements could be causative agents, and there was no *a priori* factor which could attain the status of a "determinant in the last instance." However, as Razzell (1977, p. 34) has pointed out, "this infinite causal regress is clearly a very unsatisfactory mode of explanation, for in the last resort it explains both everything and nothing." On another level, and one at which it is in retrospect much easier to see Weber engaged in a broad refutation of Marx, Weber himself, in his early methodology but not in his subsequent intellectual practice, concentrated his attention on one side of his causal chain. This at once requires us to ask *how* Weber identified this multi-causal chain, and to do this we must return to his vision of rationality as the historical premise of capitalist development, and irrationality as its unintended fate.

Weber held that it was the unique conjunction of the eternal desire for monetary gain and the rational methods of discipline which constituted the hallmark of Western capitalism. What differentiated the pre-capitalist merchant from the modern entrepreneur was the key process of rationalization, a process which permeated such diverse objects as music and law. Economic rationality, for Weber, was predicated on the instruments of private enterprise and free wage labor. Like Marx, Weber drew a connection between this "rational" economic basis on the one hand, and social and political institutions on the other:

> This all important economic fact: the "separation" of the worker from the material means of production, destruction, administration, academic research, and finance in general, is the common basis of the modern state, in its political, cultural and military sphere, and of the private capitalist economy. In both cases, the disposition over these means is in the hands of the power whom the *bureaucratic apparatus* . . . directly obeys or to whom it is available in case of need. This apparatus is nowadays equally typical of all those organizations; its existence and function are inseparably cause and effect of this concentration of the means of operation—in fact, the apparatus is its very form. Increasing public ownership in the economic sphere today unavoidably means increasing bureaucratization (Weber, 1968, p. 1394).

Weber would therefore seem to have extricated a crucial theme of domination under *capitalist* modes of production, namely, the interpenetration of economy and bureaucracy and their combined effects on the individual worker. Bureaucratic domination involves a formalistic impersonality without hatred or passion, and hence without affection or enthusiasm. For Weber, bureaucracy was essentially impervious to the organizational type of economy in which it resided. But his assignation of the specific locus of domination is open to serious dispute, the source of which stems from his committed separation of the economic, social, and political worlds. How, for example, are "economics"— the economics of the rational entrepreneur—to be distinguished from the social relations of production? Marx himself was often ambiguous in positing the economic mode of production as the motive force of the social formation, but Weber erred in the opposite direction. Weber's stance flows from the notion that the capitalist economy, however loosely identified, does not begin with concrete relationships of work and labor, is not constitutive of capital-labor relations, but rather comprises a constellation of interest and status groups where objective class relations are *a priori* excluded. Weber's position is that the economy, from the differing perspectives of the entrepreneur, the worker, *and Weber himself as observer,* is an individual matter. In denying the possibility of a universal subject transforming its conditions of existence through political struggle. Weber ironically and pessimistically sides with the vulgar Marxists whom he so vehemently attacked. Economic development is seen in economic terms.

This is not, however, to deny that Weber saw domination and bureaucracy as inevitable features of capitalist organization. Indeed, the two-edged process of rationalization specifically incorporated this trend. The tension between formal and substantive rationality incurred a necessary conflict between democracy and bureaucracy, and in the bureaucratic process means become irrationally and unintentionally elevated to the status of ends. Weber therefore indicts capitalist organization as an "iron cage" and capitalist entrepreneurs are chided as "specialists without vision and sensualists without heart." The ideals of the charismatic hero are forsaken for the mundane concerns of the trader. As a prophet of spiritual and cultural doom, Weber views the march of socialism as an almost inevitable extension of capitalism's need for rational planning, the transition from one mode of production to another as an advance in which quantity presides over quality. Weber intimately extrapolated the "alienation" of the factory system to all cultural institutions in a moribund Germany which "at his most pessimistic moments, seemed to him to represent the dialectical inversion of the Enlightenment's vision of a world mastered by Reason" (Wrong, 1970, p. 27).

It is precisely the negation of this vision which defines the ideological contours of the concept of rationalization. Within the *Weltanschauung* of German idealism. Weber's master conception, that bourgeois reason is the historical fate of the modern world—albeit a paradox of unintended consequences—was strikingly similar to the dialectical and immanentist postulates of the Hegelian Absolute. To be correct, it was an inverted immanence. For Hegel, the material and historical world was predicated on the Idea and only subsequently is there a mutual relationship between them. But for Weber, the world *begins* with amorphous, multi-causal social interests and develops with their increasing infusion by Reason. Let us now see how Weber's acceptance of the appearance of a rationalized and static world extends to his notion of the legal order.

III. WEBER'S SOCIOLOGY OF LAW

A. LAW AND OTHER IMPERATIVES

Weber's sociology of law is constructed on a convoluted set of ideal types, and comprises both a typology of the characteristics of legal thought and of the relations between law and other elements of the social structure. His central concern in both cases is to elucidate the binary relation between law and the rise of capitalism, and he situates this problem within the methodological context of a highly abstract model of historical change which is replete with detailed empirical illustrations (see Trubek, 1972). His premise is that only a particular type of legal system is conducive to the growth of capitalism. The crux of his comparative study is the search for factors which would verify this hypothesis. His sociology of law thus has a mission aligned to his sociology of religion.

The key to Weber's sociology of law is to be found in his notion of *rules in general* as they occur in and produce typified social interaction. In his *R Stammler's Surmounting of the Materialist Conception of History,* written in 1907, Weber understands "rules" in two main senses. Firstly, they are general statements about causal links. Second, they are norms by which past, present, or future processes may be measured in the sense of a value judgment. The first notion is an empirical "is," which leads directly to the question "which *actual* regularity would correspond to it?" The second notion is a general statement of an "ought," which leads to the question "what degree of *actual* regularity is causally occasioned by aspiring to it?" (Weber, 1976, p. 21). The latter question is therefore inextricably linked with the notion of the "paradox of unintended consequences."

Weber distinguishes these two notions from a maxim of conduct, by which he refers to an actor's own subjective conception of the relevant norm. Relevance from the standpoint of the norms delimits the object of investigation, and using the rules of a game of cards by way of illustration, Weber shows that the meaning in which such rules are a necessary condition for empirical knowledge of the game is to be differentiated from the meaning which the player accords them during the empirical course of the game.

In principle, for Weber, *legal* rules are no different from other maxims. On the one hand, a rule is conceptually derivative norm, and on the other, it is a maxim of behavior for concrete individuals. For example, the legal concept of "United States of America" is in a logically different category to the empirical-historical structure of the "United States of America." In short, the rules of a game of cards define the scope of that game, but *legal* rules are only one condition of an object which is also delimited by culture, history, interest associations, etc.

Elsewhere, Weber is careful to distinguish between legal rules, usage, fashion, and convention. Although *all* involve some degree of socially-conformative action, only convention and law are coextensive with sanctions. The difference between law and convention is that the former exists with a specific institution of coercion. This is as yet to say nothing of the motives which prompt obedience to legal rules, or the consequences for deviation from them. Weber argues in *Economy and Society* that the *legitimacy* of an order may be guaranteed either subjectively or externally, and that whilst the violation of a convention will only be met with disapproval, an order will be designated as law "if its validity is externally guaranteed by the probabil-

ity that coercion (physical or psychological), to bring about conformity or average violation, will be applied by a *staff* of people holding themselves specially ready for that purpose" (1965, p. 5). It should be noted that this definition, and Weber's insistence that "sociologically speaking, the modern state is an enterprise just like a factory" (1968, p. 1934), is a formal, static notion which resembles Engels' (1970, p. 327) dictum that state power "consists not merely of armed men but also material adjuncts, prisons and institutions of coercion of all kinds." The great difference between these two notions is that Weber consistently defines the state and the legal system by reference to their formal-technical qualities, whereas Marx and Engels always refer to the state's dynamic function in the historical context of the class struggle. Weber's definition insists that law is to be distinguished from other imperatives in two ways. First, other imperatives are non- or pre-legitimate. But this is tautological, and his *a priori* separation of the various elements in the social structure does not, at this point, permit him to enquire why some imperatives are inscribed with legitimate status and others are not. Second, law is the sole imperative endowed with a coercive apparatus. But, as Trubek (1972, p. 726) has added, if rules without an organized coercive machinery are not law, then this notion can be attacked by those "who wish to find law without organized political force, *and* by those who do not want law to refer to every coercively backed action, whether of political authority or not." Anticipating this ambiguity, Weber (1954, p. 6) hints that "in other connections different definitions may be appropriate."

One such "connection" is the distinction drawn between the sociological and the juristic notions of legal order, which in turn hinges on the separation of fact and value. Weber (1954, p. 7) indicates that "whether or not a normative idea which is actually held by human beings belongs to the realm of ethics, or, in other words, whether or not a given norm is one of 'mere' law or convention must be decided by the *sociologist* exclusively in accordance with that notion of the 'ethical' which is actually held by the people in question." The jurist, however, assumes the empirical validity of legal propositions *prius,* and he endeavors to arrange each of them into an internally consistent, gapless system.

This is a valid and useful insight if Weber's intention is to demonstrate that the subjective orientation of different individuals (lawyers, judges, laymen, sociologists, etc.) to law may be as diverse as the interaction among individuals in a social grouping. But his methodology implies far more than this. It implies, crucially, the objective adequacy of the sociologist's own interpretation of the diverse values which confront him. And this involves a double-bind. If actors are oriented by the significance which they attach to their actions in pursuit of an intended value, and if the sociologist constructs an ideal type of what the principle of that significance is, then the sociologist "in making this construct is also guided by what he himself finds significant in data, according to *his* value system" (Harvey, 1972, p. 96). Thus, we are precluded from understanding the *social production* of those norms and values which are actually held as desirable by social actors and social classes. Further, in presenting the sociological notion as scientific, and the juristic as dogmatic and value-laden, Weber slides into another error: the jurist's conception of law is *already* sociologicial and "as a general concept it already involves an abstraction from a multiplicity of concrete circumstances and in its universal applicability across the boundaries of different cultures expresses a highly abstract notion" (Albrow, 1975, p. 27). In other words, Weber agrees that the juristic notion of legal order is an ideological artifact, but refuses to accept that this involves a definite social production. This failure stems from the sociologist's own belief in the value of the formal rationality of abstract logic, which itself involves a social production.

B. THE CATEGORIZATION OF LEGAL THOUGHT

Weber's categorization of legal thought is a subgroup of his concept of rationalization, and the various ideal type systems are differentiated along two axes according to the manner in which they handle lawmaking and lawfinding activities. One axis (substantive/formal) measures the degree to which the system is differentiated or autonomous. The other (irrational/rational) measures the degree to which the system deduces legal propositions in a universal manner. *Substantively-irrational* decisions are those influenced by concrete factors of the particular case as evaluated on an ethical, emotional, or political basis. *Formally-irrational* decisions are those deduced by a logic which is both internal to the system yet unpredictable, and are based on oracles and other revelations. *Substantively-rational* lawmaking exists where decisions involve reference to external norms such as ethical imperatives and other forms of expediential rules. *Formally-rational* lawmaking refers to decisions which are based on universally-applied rules which form a highly logical system, and is epitomized by the Pandectist Civil Code. There is, therefore, a logical coherence between Weber's notion of rational action and formally-rational lawmaking.

Formally-rational lawmaking involves the "highest measure of methodological and logical rationality" and proceeds from the following five postulates: "first, that every concrete legal decision be the 'application' of an abstract legal proposition to a concrete 'fact situation'; second, that it must be possible in every concrete case to derive the decision from abstract legal propositions by means of legal logic; third, that the law must actually or virtually constitute a 'gapless' system of legal propositions, or must, at least, be treated as if it were such a gapless system; fourth, that whatever cannot be 'construed' legally in rational terms is also legally irrelevant; and fifth, that every social action of human beings must always be visualized as either an 'application' or 'execution' of legal propositions, or as an 'infringement' thereof" (Weber, 1954, p. 64).

This concern with the types of legal thought rather than the substantive content of legal propositions reflected the highly formal and abstract nature of the Pandectist Civil Code. But Weber was aware that various intra- and extra-legal factors could undermine such a "gapless system." He therefore saw that legal formalism was occasionally challenged by "new demands for a 'social law' to be based upon such emotionally colored postulates as 'justice' or 'human dignity' and . . . (these) have arisen with the emergence of the 'modern class problem'" (Weber, 1968, p. 886). The disadvantaged groups associated with the "modern class problem" claim as their legitimation "substantive justice rather than formal legality," and are products of a "self-defeating scientific rationalization of legal thought as well of its relentless self-criticism. To the extent that they themselves do not have a rationalistic character, *they are a flight into the irrational*" (Weber, 1968, p. 889). Weber does not, it appears, consider these trends as irrational because they happen to contravene *his* personal system of values, but because parties will always be disappointed when the facts of life are "construed" in order to make them fit the abstract propositions of law. The expectations of these parties "are oriented towards the economic or the almost utilitarian *meaning* of a legal proposition. However, from the point of view of legal logic, this meaning is an 'irrational' one" (Weber, 1968, p. 885). It therefore seems that Weber, the most notable proponent of a value-free sociology, can condemn demands for substantive justice not by reference to his own political preferences but by recourse to an "independent" construct of rational action. This is a clever strategy, and quite in keeping with his actual political carrer. He advocated a brand of national power politics tantamount to imperialism; a passionate supporter of the German war effort up to 1917, he aided Neumann in forming the conservative National Social Party and vigorously participated in drafting the post-1918 Weimar constitution.

C. LAW AND DOMINATION

What, however, is unique and valuable about Weber's sociology of law is the marriage which he sought to precipitate between the ideal types of legal thought and the ideal types of political structure which corresponded to them. Two distinct typologies are interlaced in this project to explain why it is that "the State in the sense of the rational State has existed only in the western world" (Weber, 1966, p. 249). The area of communion in this ideal type combination lies in the collusion of action with power. Weber (1968, p. 53) defines power as "the probability that one actor within a social relationship will be in a position to carry out his will despite resistance." It is a mark of his Hegelian heritage that Weber is anxious to anchor the Prussian state in a condition of value consensus, and accordingly he is compelled to find a mediating principle between naked power and the definition of the state as "a human community that successfully claims the monopoly of the legitimate use of *violence* within a given territory" (Weber, 1946, p. 78). He thus distinguishes between two ideal types of power, namely, domination and legitimacy. All social action is profoundly influenced by structures of dominance, and "in a great number of cases the emergence of rational consociation from amorphous communal action has been due to domination and the way in which it has been exercised" (Weber, 1954, p. 322). Domination is defined as "the probability that a command with a given specific context will be obeyed by a given group of persons" (Weber, 1968, p. 53). To be more precise,

> *domination* will thus mean the situation in which: the manifested will (*command*) of the *ruler* or rulers is meant to influence the conduct of one or more others (the *ruled*). . . . Looked upon from the other end, this situation will be called *obedience*" (Weber, 1954, p. 328).

How, then, is obedience induced? Since *legitimate* domination can only survive with some minimum level of consent on the part of the dominated, the very concept of domination for Weber implies "a minimum of voluntary obedience" (Weber, 1968, p. 212). The use of naked power is an insufficient basis for stable domination and, therefore, "every domination always has the strongest need of self-justification through appealing to the principle of its legitimation" (Weber, 1968, p. 954). It should be stressed, again, that although Weber's definition of the state includes reference both to coercion and to voluntary obedience, his search for the formal aspects of political legitimation leads him to defuse the structural conditions from which legitimation arises and instead to emphasize the consensual conditions of its survival. Weber offers us a theoretical model, at the most general level, of the empirical processes in which non-statutory norms arise as valid customary law. Action which is subjectively experienced as habitual eventually comes to be recognized as binding. Subsequently, "with the awareness of the diffusion of such conduct among a plurality of individuals, it comes to be incorporated as 'consensus' into people's semi- or wholly conscious 'expectations' as to the meaningfully corresponding conduct of others" (Weber, 1954, p. 67). Finally, these consensual understandings are guaranteed by a coercive apparatus which thus distinguishes them from customary norms. Such rule emergence Weber labels as "unconscious." New legal norms may be created in innumerable ways: the standardization of the consensual understandings: by legal prophets; by charismatic revelation; from "above" (Weber, 1954, pp. 75–82).

Weber's next step is to explore the ways in which different types of domination and "consensual understandings" seek to legitimate their authority within the political apparatus, and in this schema there are three types of action. *Traditional authority* depends on an established belief in the sanctity of immemorial social practices. *Charismatic authority* rests on devotion to the specific and exceptional heroism, sanctity, or exemplary character of an individual actor. *Rational authority* rests on a belief in the validity of legality of patterns of normative rules and the right of those elevated to authority under such rules to issue commands. Each type finds itself expressed concretely in pure form: respectively, in a patriarchy, in an individual, and in a rational legal bureaucracy: Methodological protocol requires the careful reader not to situate these types within a framework of actual historical development. But if rational legal authority is the fate of

the modern West, then it is difficult not to see its triumph as the result of an evolutionary determinism. Charismatic authority is a disruptive force which tends to be routinized with the progress of rationality, and traditional authority is undermined by a scientific *Weltanschauung*. In common with Nietzsche, who saw history as a process of birth and decay in which great men stamp their imprint on social change, Weber presents charisma as a dialectical mediation between different authority types. And in common with de Tocqueville, who saw bureaucracy as a giant power wielded by pygmies, Weber's profound pessimism at the prospects for individual freedom in the modern world derives from his observation that Bismarck's bureaucratic polity actively stifled the emergence of a charismatic political leadership.

The marriage between the types of legal thought and the types of domination is a matrix which implies that a professional bureaucracy and formal logical rationality constitute the unique features of Western legal systems. The first condition for the existence of formal rationality is intra-juristic. Only in the West was "conscious" lawmaking made possible, and this through the separation of lawmaking and lawfinding activities, which had been a characteristic of precapitalist Germany. The West developed both a distinctive group of legal professionals, a group which had a high degree of autonomy from economic, political, and religious pressures, and also a unique method of legal education. Emphasis was placed not on legal training *per se*, but on the inculcation of legal theory and legal science. But Weber is also concerned to outline the extra-juristic or "objective" factors operative in this process. This is a vision of a world in which economic factors provide "the possibility for the spread of a legal technique if it is invented" (Weber, 1954, p. 131), but which can never be directly causative of the social production of new legal rules. Nowhere can material elements play a decisive role. It is a world in which an immense number of factors contributed to the growth of legalism: the alliance of objective interest between patrimonial monarchic powers and the rising bourgeoisie, and the bureaucratization of all areas of social life from the Roman Catholic church to its canon law. In its turn, this rational legalism performed unique and indispensable functions for the promotion of capital accumulation. Its precision led to calculability in the chaos of the uncoordinated market of *laissez faire* capitalism; its impersonality reduced the instability of authority types associated with charisma and tradition—"the domination of capital is the only one which cannot be ethically regulated, because of its impersonal character" (Weber, 1968, p. 1186); and its apparent intransigence masked a flexibility which permitted the expansion of substantive principles into such important notions as freedom of contract and corporate personality.

IV. THE POLITICS OF DISENCHANTMENT: SUBJECT AND OBJECT

It was argued at the beginning of this paper that the intellectual history of sociological approaches to order and domination has been marked by the attitudes of two competing versions of neo-Kantian epistemology. Both versions derive from conflicting conceptions of the relation of man to society, of man to his environment, and of the appropriate method of elucidating the nature of these relations.

One version incorporates a vision of man in society which asserts that social structures are historically and causally prior to man. Social facts are seen as external objects which constrain social action. This separation of man from his reified environment establishes a particular methodology for understanding social relationships in which the disassociation of subject (observer) and object (society) requires that the observer define an object solely by reference to the intrinsic properties of that object. It therefore involves a theoretical empiricism whereby a social object is to be understood by the extrapolation of the methods of natural science to the objects of social theory. The scientific method(s) is used as

an heuristic device to unlock the doors which guard an Alladin's cave of pre-given treasures. But this venture is caught within an insoluble paradox: the search for objectivity both affirms the constraining power of social facts yet also embodies the contradictory notion that the observer has autonomy in his intellectual practice.

The alternative version is based on an epistemology which asserts that social structures derive from the complex of individual action, from the complex of subjective meanings which actors designate to reciprocated patterns of action. Here, the essence of an object can never be grasped because the conceptual categories employed by the observer are an integral part of the complex of values and meanings deemed problematic. In order to understand the rationale of other meanings and values, the observer must temporarily discard his or her own value system. Declining to assess different values, the observer must instead understand them in terms of the significance which they hold for the observed actor. But this involves the paradox that the values of the observed actor must be selected by the observer's own perception of them. And in so doing, the observer succeeds in condensing the appearance and the essence of the objectified subject. The unintended result is a personal description of other value systems rather than knowledge of their social production.

We have argued that Weber's epistemology overtly avoided evolutionary or historical determinism, and involved a rejection of both horns of the neo-Kantian dichotomy. The particular combination of elements which he selected confined itself to the manner in which social structures emerged from the meaning attached to social action by objectified subjects. He therefore accepted the primacy of subjective values in a disenchanted and irrational world in which German Social Democracy emphasized the objective importance of the class struggle as the *leitmotiv* of development from one mode of production to another.

Weber's solution to the subject/object antinomy posed by neo-Kantianism was the use of a logically precise fiction—the ideal type—whereby an observer seemed best able to maximize the distance between himself and the society of which he was a part. Weber's view of sociology was that it should perform "the very modest preparatory work of formulating type concepts and general uniformities" (Roth, 1976, p. 307). But this incurs the mind-twisting problem of whether "the product of such a selection . . . is a subjective artifact or corresponds to empirical reality" (Harvey, 1972, p. 980). In this contemplative schema of value neutrality, there can be no correspondence between the sociologist and the social conditions responsible for his intellectual production. The effect, ironically for one so bemused with the paradox of unintended consequences, resembles the iron cages of positivism. On the one hand, Weber decried the bureaucratization and routinization of Western capitalism but, on the other, he exempted himself from such constraint simply by admitting the preference of his own value system.

Weber's sociology, then, was undoubtedly an ideological artifact.[4] It was ideological for the trivial reason that all social theory embodies ideological presuppositions. Declaratory statements on what society ought to be are inextricably related to statements on what society is. But there are two notions in Weber's sociology of law which are peculiarly ideological: his notion of the relation between obedience and legitimized domination, and his pessimism concerning the potential of the modern world to escape from the irrational consequences which the belief systems of the Reformation had effected.

Contemporary accounts of Weber's theory of order and domination tend to focus either on his failure to outline the dysfunctional results of formal rationality, or on his reluctance to examine the structural conditions from which different

types that Weber unduly emphasized the formal, technical qualities of logical rationality but that, for example, "his definitions are formulated so carefully and his grasp of concrete reality was so firm, that he does not in fact eliminate, even at an abstract, theoretical level, economic domination and violence from his purview" (Wrong, 1970, p. 58). As we have seen, Weber grounded legitimacy in the most diverse of motives. If, as he explicitly stressed, obedience to authority implies a minimum of voluntary obedience, then a comprehensive account of persistent obedience must include consideration of the legitimating ideology which is bestowed on and perpetuated by legal rules. Importantly, it would have to include consideration of the political functions of law and the relation of these to what Weber a priori ignored—class rule. Weber showed how formal, rational law was a necessary but not a sufficient condition for the reproduction of the capitalist economy. What he failed to show was that in history, all economically dominant classes have also in the long run been politically dominant classes.

Weber's subjectivist epistemology, itself reflecting an atomized and disenchanted world, logically precluded him from examining the historical mediations between the possibilities of obedience, consciousness, and the political facts of class domination. Weber portrayed obedience to the imperatives of capitalist economic organization as a subjective process in which each worker evaluates the gains to be had by partaking in commodity production with the losses to be had by abstaining. This was, he (Weber, 1968, p. 110) said, "the fate of the entire working class." But this ignores the question of whether legal rules induce obedience because they are presented as rational and as a reflection of widely-shared social values. If so, is such a presentation distributed in the interests of the stability of a social formation by particular classes within it? If not, how does Weber explain the historical fact that the legal order of capitalist formations is often flagrantly violated by workers' mass movements, and occasionally overthrown? Even

---

[4]The term ideology is not used here in the sense of the Althusserian distinction between science (objective truth) and ideology (subjective fiction), which this author does not accept. Rather, it refers to the far looser meaning of the discourse used to promote any sectarian interests (including those of science) within a social formation.

more, Weber distracts our attention from examining the social conditions which would allow human autonomy. The meaning of formal rationality therefore changes as the Weberian project unfolds, and as Marcuse (1972, p. 214) has observed, in one of his more lucid moments, ". . . in becoming a question of domination, of control, this rationality subordinates itself, by virtue of its own inner dynamic, to another, namely, the rationality of domination."

In a profound sense, Weber's vision of what Western society *was* flowed from his sincere convictions of what it should *not* be. His abhorrence of socialism was based on the belief that it created servile souls, that it embodied the necessary extension of bureaucratic and legal domination to all areas of life. Marianne Weber (1975, p. 118) informs us that his "sense of justice reacted against exceptional laws that impeded the fight of the proletarians," but that Weber wanted "a fatherland organized along the lines of a power state with a growing, hard-working population whose complete political maturity would enable it both to protect its own rights and to share in the responsibility for the fate of the nation" (Weber, 1975, p. 135). Weber thus identified the socialist expropriation of the expropriator as inevitably resulting in the dictatorship of the official. But this characterization is based on the interesting image of a socialism dependent on rational bureaucracy, which according to Weber is optimally efficient under capitalist modes of production, and which requires the domination of labor by economic organizations.

Nevertheless, and to a limited extent, the choice which Weber presented has historically proved correct: whether to have increased material production, or reduced bureaucratic domination? Alternatively, Weber (1947, p. 338) thought that "only by reversion in every field—political, religious, economic, etc.,—to small-scale organization would it be possible to escape its influence." Salvation from this "masterless slavery" could be affected by a charismatic leader, but this was an unlikely event in a world which suppressed charismatic (i.e., non-rational) authority.

And on one of the few occasions when Weber referred to the anarchist solution, he (1968, p. 515) argued that "the only remaining variant of socialism in western Europe equivalent to a religious faith, namely, syndicalism, can easily turn into a romantic game played by circles without direct economic interests." Weber's politics of disenchantment left him with nothing other than a plea for individual responsibility. Whereas Marx's optimism at least invoked the possibility of a collective subject transforming its conditions of existence, Weber condemned the *irrationalities* of the capitalist order whilst fundamentally resigning himself to the permanence of its historical rationality . . .

* * * *

REFERENCES

Abel, T., *Systematic Sociology,* New York: Octagon Books, 1965.

Albrow, M., "Legal Positivism and Bourgeois Materialism," *British Journal of Law and Society,* vol. 2, no. 1 (1975): 14-31.

Droz, J., and Ayçoberry, P., "Structures Sociales et Courants Idéologiques en Allemagnes Préréyolutionnaire," *Annali,* 6. Feltrinelli, Milan, 1964.

Engels, F., "The Origin of the Family, Private Property and the State," in *Marx-Engels Selected Works,* vol. 3, London: Lawrence and Wishart, 1970.

Harvey, M., "Sociological Theory: The Production of Bourgeois Ideology," in T. Pateman (ed.), *Counter Course,* London: Penguin, 1972.

Hawthorn, G., *Enlightenment and Despair.* Cambridge: Cambridge University Press, 1976.

Hegel, G., *The Philosophy of History,* New York: Dover Publications, 1956.

Hegel, G., *The Philosophy of Right,* New York: Oxford University Press, 1973.

Horkheimer, M., *Eclipse of Reason,* New York: Oxford University Press, 1947.

Ilting, K. H., "The Structure of Hegel's Philosophy of Right," in Z. Pelczynski (ed.), *Hegel's Political Philosophy,* Cambridge: Cambridge University Press, 1971.

Kant, I., in P. Gardiner (ed.), *Theories of History.* Glencoe, Ill.: The Free Press, 1959.

―――――, in Z. Pelczynski (ed.). *Hegel's Political Philosophy,* Cambridge: Cambridge University Press, 1971 .

Kelly, R. F., "Historical and Political Interpretations of Jurisprudence and the Social Action Perspective in Sociology," A paper presented in the History of Sociology Section at the 72nd Annual Meeting of the *American Sociological Association,* Chicago, Illinois, 1977.

Marcuse, H., "Industrialization and Capitalism in the work of Max Weber," in H. Marcuse, *Negations,* London: Penguin University Books, 1972.

Marx, K., "Letter to J. B. Schweitzer," in *Marx-Engels Selected Works,* vol. 2, London: Lawrence and Wishart, 1969.

―――――, *The Grundrisse,* London: Penguin, 1974.

―――――, "Difference between the Democritean and Epicurean Philosophy of Nature," in *Marx-Engels Collected Works,* vol. 1. London: Lawrence and Wishart, 1975.

―――――― and Frederick Engels. "The Communist Manifesto," in D. Fernbach (ed.), *Karl Marx,* New York: Random House, 1973.

―――――, *The German Ideology,* London: Lawrence and Wishart, 1974.

Papineau, D., "Ideal Types and Empirical Theories," *British Journal for the Philosophy of Science* 27 (1976): 137-46.

Parsons, T., *The Structure of Social Action,* New York: The Free Press, 1969.

Poulantzas, N., *Political Power and Social Classes,* London: New Left Books and Sheed and Ward, 1973.

Razzel, P., "The Protestant Ethic and the Spirit of Capitalism: a natural science critique." *British Journal of Sociology,* vol. 28, no. 1 (1977): 17-37.

Rheinstein, M. (ed.), *Max Weber on Law In Economy and Society,* Cambridge: Harvard University Press, 1954.

Roth, G., "History and sociology in the work of Max Weber," *British Journal of Sociology,* vol. 27, no. 3 (1976): 306-18.

Trubek, D. M., "Max Weber on Law and the Rise of Capitalism," *Wisconsin Law Review,* no. 3 (1972): 720-53.

Weber, Marianne, *Max Weber: A Biography,* (Harry Zohn, tr. and ed.), New York: Wiley, 1975.

Weber, Max, *From Max Weber: Essays in Sociology* (H. H. Gerth and C. Wright Mills, tr. and ed.). New York: Oxford University Press, 1946.

―――――, *The Theory of Social and Economic Organization* (T. Parsons, ed.), New York: The Free Press, 1947.

―――――, *The Protestant Ethic and the Spirit of Capitalism,* London: Allen and Unwin, 1948.

―――――, "Objectivity in Social Science and Social Policy," in H. Finch and E. Shils (tr. and ed.), *The Methodology of the Social Sciences,* pp. 50-112. Glencoe, Ill.: The Free Press, 1949.

―――――, *Law in Economy and Society* (M. Rheinstein, ed.), Cambridge: Harvard University Press, 1954.

―――――, *The Sociology of Religion,* London: Methuen, 1966.

―――――, "Socialism," (H. F. Dickie-Clark, ed.). *Institute for Social Research,* no. 11. University of Natal, 1967.

―――――, in G. Roth and C. Wittich (eds.), *Economy and Society,* 3 volumes, New York: Bedminster Press, 1968.

―――――, "R. Stammler's Surmounting of the Materialistic Conception of History," (M. Albrow, tr.), *British Journal of Law and Society,* (1), vol. 2, no. 2 (1975): 129-52:(2); vol. 3, no. 1 (1976): 17-43.

Wright, E. O., "To Control or to Smash Bureaucracy: Weber and Lenin on Politics, the State and Bureaucracy," *Berkeley Journal of Sociology,* vol. xix, (1974/75): 69-108.

Wrong, D., *Max Weber,* New Jersey: Prentice-Hall, 1970.

THE MAIN THEMES OF MARX' AND ENGELS' SOCIOLOGY OF LAW

MAUREEN CAIN

Little has been written about Marx' and Engels' approach to law. This is largely because Marx never fully developed his theory of the State although, as Sweezy points out,[1] his original intention as stated in the Preface to the *Critique of Political Economy* was to discuss "state, foreign trade, world market" at some length.[2] He died before he could do this. Thus in piecing together "Marx on law" one is forced to treat sections from different works as additive, as if their central concerns were the same. Sometimes, as in chapter X of *Capital*[3] or Engels' *Anti-Dühring*,[4] the extracts are sufficiently long to stand alone as statements about law. At other times there is merely an allusion to law in a text dealing with other matters. These snippets are more open to the abuse of being interpreted out of context. Because my aim has been to let Marx' and Engels' writings speak for themselves I hope I have avoided this. I began the research for this paper with no pre-conceived categories in terms of which to order the extracts. My method was to copy onto cards all the relevant passages (with notes on their contexts) and then to classify them in terms of what seemed to be important or recurring themes.

Although I do not have any particular Marxist or academic axe to grind, two approaches to "Marx on Law" worried and still worry me. These are the "worker bashing" interpretation and the criminological interpretation. The former view has been held by lawyers, the latter by sociologists. Neither does justice to the complexity and *potential* of Marxist thought. Although I cannot claim to know what Marx and Engels really meant, I hope to show at least that their theory of law was highly sophisticated and that it is still useful not only in analysing and comprehending present day society but also in sparking off ideas dialectically with contemporary theory and in guiding one to fruitful areas of research.

PREVIOUS DISCUSSIONS OF 'MARX ON LAW'

The "putting down the workers" model of Marx' thought is epitomised in the work of Denis Lloyd,[5] who nonetheless recognized that Marx "made a major contribution to the foundation of legal as well as other forms of sociology." Lloyd stated that for Marx "Law was nothing but a coercive system devised to maintain the privileges of the property owning class." Alternatively, law

[1] P. M. Sweezy, *The Theory of Capitalist Development* (1942 Monthly Review Press, New York).

[2] K. Marx, "Preface to A Contribution to the Critique of Political Economy" in K. Marx and F. Engels, *Selected Works* (1969 Progress Publishers, Moscow).

[3] K. Marx, *Capital* (1970 Lawrence and Wishart, London) Vol. 1.

[4] F. Engels, *Anti-Dühring* (1935 Chas. H. Kerr and Co., Chicago).

[5] D. Lloyd, *The Idea of Law* (1964 Penguin, Harmondsworth) 22, 205-7.

SOURCE: *British Journal of Law and Society*, 1, no. 2 (1974), 136-148. Reprinted by permission.

was distilled out of the economic order which gave rise to it, and was an institutionalized form of the prevailing ideology whereby the dominant section of society coerced the masses into obedience.

This is close enough to be recognizably Marx, yet by its dangerous over-simplification it makes it possible to dismiss Marx as incapable of explaining those many laws which have neither this coercive intent nor this effect. Yet in one of his major writings on law Marx, with Engels, comes close to arguing that the law has little to do *directly* with inter-class relationships, the main purpose of laws being to iron out differences *within* the dominant class, and so, *indirectly,* to consolidate their class position.[6] I discuss this more fully below: to mention it here is sufficient to indicate that there is oversimplification in the "worker bashing" view.

Three recent texts have examined Marx' work either to discover in it a radical criminology[7] or to take issue with the radical criminologists' interpretation.[8] These three papers develop from the first, which is more literal in its interpretation, through that of Hirst, which points out the force of Marx' irony and offers a political (and convincing) explanation of Marx' well-known distaste for the "vagabond" and "parasitical" ways of the lumpen-proletarians, to the third[9] which takes the point about irony and seeks to give it a contemporary relevance with the claim that Marx was ridiculing the functionalists (unborn).

My own view is that Marx as a writer is very funny, very bitter, and very passionate. The first two are expected elements of irony; the third, Marx' rage and passionate concern for the sufferings of people, gives way regularly to irony just before it reaches a peak. Having described the processes of dispossession he remarks "In the year 1835, 15,000 Gaels were already replaced by 131,000 sheep."[10] Later "flung on the sea shore, . . . they became amphibious . . . ."

Marx is at his funniest when castigating his philosophical rivals[11] and his powerful blend of anger and irony is most apparent when concrete cases of human suffering,—mangled mineworkers,[12] bemused rustics driven from the land,[13] those bearing heavy sentences for trumped up political offences[14]—are presented. His intellectual grasp is best shown as he moves from weaving and demonstrating patterns of relationships at the highest levels of abstraction to the specific concrete case which illuminates the whole. None of these literary or intellectual skills is demonstrated in his comments on crime.

The problem with Marx, and his interpreters, in his discussions of crime is that he lapses into absolutism. Even in the oft quoted section from *Theories of Surplus Value* Vol. 1,[15] Marx speaks of "the criminal" as a *type of person* and implies that crime is a way of life. These positive definitions lie behind and are intrinsic to the ironic web he weaves in statements such as:

> Crime, through its constantly new methods of attack on property, constantly calls into being new methods of defence, and so is as productive as strikes for the invention of machines.

At his worst in discussing crime Marx is a narrow moralist with a veneer of liberal tolerance. Thus, people may have been driven to villainies of various kinds, for example by being rendered homeless and destitute; penalties for these villainies (as well as for being homeless and destitute *per se*)

---

[6]K. Marx and F. Engels, *The German Ideology* (1965 Lawrence and Wishart, London) 349–83.

[7]P. Walton, paper presented to B.S.A. annual conference, 1971; I. Taylor, P. Walton, and J. Young, *The New Criminology* (1973 Routledge and Kegan Paul, London).

[8]Hirst, "Marx and Engels on Law, Crime, and Morality" (1972) 1 *Economy and Society* 28–56.

[9]Taylor, Walton and Young, *op. cit.*

[10]*Capital,* (1974 Lawrence and Wishart, London) Chap. XXVII, p. 683.

[11]Two good examples are *The Holy Family* (1957 Lawrence and Wishart, London) and *The German Ideology, op. cit.,* both written with Engels.

[12]*Capital, op. cit.,* Chap. XV, Section 9.

[13]*Ibid.,* Chap. X and XXVII.

[14]F. Engels, "The Late Trial at Cologne" in *Selected Works op cit.*

[15]Quoted at length by both Hirst, *op. cit.* and Taylor, Walton and Young, *op. cit.*

were undoubtedly brutally harsh, this being the best known way of encouraging the landless to value the opportunity to become wage labourers. But both the understanding of the cause and the disgust at the savage punishments carry the implication that the villainy simply exists in itself.[16] Similarly, Engels, when arguing that the bourgeois family causes prostitution by creating a demand for it, treats the prostitute and the prostitution as absolute and given in themselves— even in the course of a polemic to the effect that sexual and familial relationships should and will be re-formed.[17]

What Marx and Engels have to say about crime, therefore, may produce a wry smile, but the quality of potential, of being complete but not finished, is lacking. Unlike their remarks on law, these comments do not set the mind a-scampering, tantalised, identifying relationships with other theories, seeking contemporary applications, formulating research problems. And if they do not they should perhaps be spared resuscitation by donnish critics.

LAW, THE STATE AND IDEOLOGY

Criminological interpretations of Marx, as Hirst has pointed out,[18] have crime as their focal concern. This in itself distorts what Marx had to say,[19] for his focus of interest was always the forces and relations of production, the social organisation of the means of life. Marx' and Engels' discussion of law, on the other hand, *arises out of* their more general work. Allusions to law form part of their theory of the State and their sociology of knowledge.[20]

[16]For a full discussion of these phenomena see *Capital, op. cit.,* Chaps. XXVII and XXVIII.

[17]See Engels, "Origin of the Family, Private Property, and the State" in *Marx' and Engels' Selected Works, op. cit.,* Vol. 3.

[18]Hirst, *op. cit.*

[19]This would not matter if the distortion were in order to develop new theories: it matters when what is intended is a commentary.

[20]I deal with this second aspect at greater length in a forthcoming article.

Nowhere is law defined. The authors deal only with legislation in their discussions of how law is created. They comment on enacted law whether or not it is enforced; one can assume that rules actually enforced by the courts are subsumed under their general discussion. Thus by and large they build their argument on the common sense view that we all know what law means. In so far as in their discussions of ideology they are accounting for other people's constructions and understandings, this is legitimate: law *is* what we all know it means. Law as it exists in "massy" reality is an objectified ideological form. Marx and Engels are interested in *ideology,* a concept integral to their theory of the social order. Law, religion, philosophy, doubtless even social science, are *theoretically equivalent* as manifestations of this. The distinctions between these forms, as their comments on education show,[21] are not given in the world but are created by it. The allocation of ideological areas for examination is itself an ideological form.

In order to understand ideology (and therfore law) either in general or, what interested Marx and Engels much more, in either a particular historical or an idealised epochal manifestation, it is necessary to look at the bases of power in society, at the formation of classes, and at the structure of the State. In a paper about law these remarks must be scant and oversimplified, creating merely the context for the later exposition.

The basic fact of man's past has been the thrust for survival, individually and as a species.[22] The "means of life" at a time are a function of geography, history, and current knowledge.[23] Thus they are social as well as physical creations. The organization of people in relation to them (relations of production) is the social phenomenon which gives rise to classes, groups of people who stand in a particular relation to the means of

[21]K. Marx, *Pre-Capitalist Economic Formations* (ed. E. J. Hobsbawm, 1964 (Lawrence and Wishart, London).

[22]This does not involve Marx in a denial that men can choose, for example, to die for a cause.

[23]Again, for Marx, this is not an absolute concept.

production, such as slaves, capitalists, peasants, proletarians, and housewives.

> To claim that pre-bourgeois history, and each phase of it, has its own economy and an economic base of its movement, is at bottom merely to state the tautology that human life has always rested on some kind of production—*social* production—whose relations are precisely what we call economic relations.[24]

Capitalist society, which is most relevant for the present analysis, is characterised by *private property*. This is a unique way of conceptualising the relationship between people and things, although it has its conceptual origins in the personal and private use of tools.[25] This mode of thought is embodied in a peculiarly comprehensive set of legal rights in relation to the use and disposition of real, or fictitious but legally and socially existing, things. Capital is private property which enables the owner to buy the labour power of another individual, and use it to create surplus value. Workers, to the extent that they do not receive the full value of the labour power they expend, are exploited.

So brief a description leaves out all the dynamics and most of the theory. My hope is that it will give the student new to Marx a grip on some basic terms to help him through the ensuing discussion, but he should bear in mind Marx' warning:

> The proletariat and wealth are opposites; as such they form a single whole. They are both forms of the world of private property. The question is what place each occupies in the antithesis. It is not sufficient to declare them two sides of a single whole.[26]

In order to maintain their position of dominance, capitalists *as a class* gradually create a set of linked organisations (the State) with the dual purpose of protecting their common internal class interests, such as the establishment of clearly understood rules for commercial transactions, and of protecting them against external threats from other classes or States. Engels clarifies the theory as follows

> The modern state . . . is only the organisation which bourgeois society provides for itself in order to support the general external conditions of the capitalist mode of production against encroachments of the workers as well as of individual capitalists . . .[27]

The State, for Marx and Engels, is always peopled, never a metaphysical entity—peopled with officials, gaolers, and, late on in its development, with policemen. And these officials are directed, one way or another, by members of the bourgeois class.

> If power is taken on the basis of right . . .then right, law, etc., are merely the symptom of other relations upon which state power rests. The material life of individuals . . . their mode of production and form of interest which *mutually*[28] determine each other . . . this is the real basis of the state. . . . The individuals, who rule in these conditions, besides having to constitute their power in the form of the state, have to give their will . . . a universal expression as the will of the state, as law. . . .[29]

The argument then moves on two important steps. First, the State develops a seeming independence of material conditions "Having public power . . . the officials now stand, as organs of society, *above* society."[30] Or sometimes

> . . . periods occur in which the warring classes balance each other so nearly that state power, as osten-

---

[24]Marx, *Pre-Capitalist Economic Formations, op. cit.,* p. 86.

[25]*Ibid.,* and also Engels, "Origin of the Family, Private Property, and the State" in *Selected Works, op. cit.*

[26]K. Marx and F. Engels, *The Holy Family* (1957 Lawrence and Wishart, London).

[27]Engels, *Anti-Dürhing, op. cit.,* Vol. 2, p. 290.

[28]My italics.

[29]Marx and Engels, *The German Ideology, op. cit.*

[30]Engels, "Origin of the Family, Private Property, and the State" *op. cit.,* p. 577. Engels goes on in the passage to note the special rules necessary for the protection of policemen as State officials because they are "forced to represent something outside and above" society. This point is taken up by Durkheim, *The Division of Labour in Society* (1964 Free Press, New York).

sible mediator, acquires for the moment a certain degree of independence of both . . . . In (a democratic republic) . . . wealth exercises its power indirectly but all the more surely . . . .[31]

Secondly and similarly, politics and law, religion and philosophy develop a seeming independence both of material conditions and of the State.[32] The important point is that these seemingly autonomous ideological areas develop according to their own inner logic: their links with "massy" reality (in Marx' phrase) may indeed become tenuous.

> The state presents itself to us as the first ideological power over man. . . . Hardly come into being, this organ makes itself independent *vis-à-vis* society; and indeed, the more so the more it becomes the organ of a particular class . . . the consciousness of the interconnection between this political struggle (ruling v oppressed class) and its economic basis *becomes* dulled and can be lost altogether. . . . But once the state has become an independent power *vis-à-vis* society it produces forthwith an ideology. It is indeed among professional politicians, theorists of public law and jurists of private law that the connection with economic facts gets lost for fair. . . .[33]

Engels, in particular, struggles with the apparent contradiction between the notion of ideas as *really* determined, and ideas developing in accordance with the rules of logic which members of the particular discipline regard as proper. In the Old Preface to *Anti-Dürhing*[34] he castigates those who regard logic or the laws of thought as "eternal truth, established once and for all." However, he also argues

> Every ideology, however, once it has arisen develops in connection with the given concept mate-

rial, and develops this material further, otherwise it would not be an independent ideology . . . that the material life conditions of the persons inside whose heads this thought process goes on in the last resort determine the course of this process remains of necessity unknown to these persons.[35]

In *Origin of the Family* Engels indicates how the dilemma might be resolved. Changes in material conditions of existence are necessary before certain concepts, legal or otherwise, can be developed. There is bounded choice about how the material conditions of existence are understood—bounded in that the group which controls the means of production in the new conditions will be constrained to conceptualise and "explain" the situation in a manner supportive of its position. Material conditions can be affected by the way they are conceived but material conditions must be capable of existing in order to be thought about. Thus, appropriation of instruments of production for private use (by the male) necessarily preceded the elaboration of property "rights."

Marx had earlier made a similar point[36] in the well-known section[37] in which he argues that "the mode of production of material life *conditions*[38] . . . intellectual life process in general" and that "consciousness must be explained . . . from the contradictions of material life". The *dialectical* nature of this inter-relationship between thought and things comes out more clearly in the discussion of property.

Engels too indicates one way in which the legal ideology influences behaviour which otherwise would have been directly determined by the economic base. The law can set the ground on which struggles must be fought and by so doing may, in particular cases, influence the outcome.

---

[31] *Ibid.*, p. 578.

[32] The advantages of this process for the ruling group are discussed in the next section.

[33] F. Engels, "Ludwig Feuerbach and the End of Classical German Philosophy" in Marx and Engels, *Selected Works, op. cit.*, p. 616.

[34] In the three volume 1970 edition of *Selected Works, op. cit.*, Vol. 3, p. 60.

[35] "Ludwig Feuerbach and the End of Classical German Philosophy", *op. cit.*, p. 618.

[36] See "Preface to a Contribution to the Critique of Political Economy", *op. cit.*

[37] Discussed by Hirst, *op. cit.*

[38] My italics.

Since in each particular case the economic facts must assume the form of juristic motives in order to receive legal sanction, and since in so doing, consideration of course has to be given to the whole legal system already in operation, the juristic form is, in consequence, made everything and the economic context nothing. . . . (*Feuerbach, op. cit.*, p. 619.)

It is important to remember that it may be necessary to lose a battle to win a war; that it may be more important to uphold values fundamental to the capitalist order than to gain a particular legal victory, e.g., equality before the law is linked with freedom of the individual, the break up of feudal society and ascriptive rights, without which capitalism could not have developed. The ideology now has a second, symbolic consequence in legitimating the entire social structure. But this is pre-empting the discussion in the next section.

As far as the law is concerned, Engels argues that the particular legal form within which and in terms of which conceptual development takes place is not relevant. Renner, of course, has elaborated these developments, though he fundamentally confuses legal words and concepts with what he calls legal norms.[39] Max Weber made a similar point that in a two tiered legal system such as our own, full rationality, yielding above all predictability of outcome, is necessary only in the upper tier in order for capitalism to be able to develop.[40] Engels' remarks deserve full quotation.

If the state and public law are determined by economic relations, so, too, of course, is private law, which indeed in essence only sanctions the existing economic relations between individuals which are normal in the given circumstances. The form in which this happens can, however, vary considerably. It is possible . . . to retain in the main the forms of the old feudal laws while giving them bourgeois

content: in fact, directly reading the bourgeois meaning into a feudal name. But also . . . Roman Law, the first world law of a commodity producing society with its unsurpassably fine elaboration of all the essential legal relations of simple commodity owners (of buyers and sellers, debtors and creditors, contracts, obligations, etc.) can be taken as the foundation.[41]

THE FUNCTIONS OF LAW

If the law as ideology is the first of Marx' and Engels' themes, the second theme in their sociology of law concerns the three functions of law. The State develops after irreconcilable class antagonisms have arisen, when it becomes

necessary to have a power seemingly above society, that would alleviate the conflict and keep it within bounds of "order", and this power, arisen out of society but placing itself above it and alienating itself more and more from it, is the state. . . .[42]

The State is the creation of the class wielding real power, i.e., control over the means of production. By creating a seemingly autonomous State (1) real power relationships are obscured; (2) the exercise of real power is legitimated. The second consequence requires the development of an ideology "explaining" the State together with the development of a further ideology based on this earlier explanation. This second, higher order, ideology explains the use of "State" power in certain situations. This second higher order ideology is jurisprudence, which, among other things, tells lawyers what the law is for.

Real power relationships are obscured because legal forms of power (the right to vote, the right to enter freely into contracts) are equally available to all. Engels inveighs against legal forms which "put both parties on an equal footing *on paper.*" He continues:

---

[39]K. Renner, *The Institutions of Private Law and their Social Functions* (1949 Routledge and Kegan Paul, London).

[40]M. Rheinstein (ed.) *Max Weber on Law in Economy and Society* (1954 Harvard U.P., Cambridge) Chap. VII.

[41]Engels, "Ludwig Feuerbach and the End of Classical German Philosophy", *op. cit.*, p. 616.

[42]Engels, "Origin of the Family, Private Property, and the State", *op. cit.*, p. 58.

The power given to one party by its different class position, the pressure it exercises on the other—the real economic position of both—all this is no concern of the law. . . . That the concrete economic situation compels the worker to forego even the slightest semblance of equal rights—this again is something the law cannot help.[43]

Marx puts the point even more succinctly

The recognition of the rights of man by the modern state means nothing more than did the recognition of slavery by the state of old.[44]

This is probably familiar territory which needs little elaboration. One further example is relevant, given the improvements in the legal position of women. Men have, as Engels noted "a dominating position which requires no special legal privileges."[45] Thus, women can be liberated to fulfil a useful economic role and the dominant values such as equality can be reinforced while real power relationships remain unchanged except in so far as their greater obscurity may strengthen them.

Before leaving the parallel mystifying and legitimating functions of law it is important to note that both Marx and Engels were aware that by emphasizing the autonomy of the State and law it was possible to create the mythology of a "total society" in whose interests these institutions operated, coupled with the belief that the State and law by reason of their apparent autonomy are value neutral. This last point does not even follow in logic. However, that the State should operate in the interests of the mythical whole community is in fact written into is as a guiding principle.

What is good for the ruling class should be good for the whole of society with which the ruling class identifies itself. Therefore the more civilisation advances the more it is compelled to cover the ills it

necessarily creates with the cloak of love, to embellish them, or to deny their existence.[46]

The third function of law is of a rather different order. In *The German Ideology* Marx and Engels for the first time discuss law as representing the "average interests" of the ruling class—the interests of the class conceived as a whole rather than of particular sections or individuals.

Their (the capitalists) personal rule must at the same time be constituted as an average rule. Their personal power is based on conditions of life which as they develop are common to many individuals, and the continuance of which they, as ruling individuals, have to maintain against others and, at the same time, maintain that they hold good for all. The expression of this will, which is determined by their common interests, is law.[47]

Within the ruling class the law, it seems, operates as systems theorists would have us believe. It irons out conflict in the best interests of the whole, and maintains the unity and integrity of the class. But to see law only this way is to fall prey to the mythology of a "total society" outlined above. Because of this characteristic of law, many studies, such as Joel Barnett's examination of Rent Act legislation,[48] will yield considerable information about the effectiveness of different pressure groups, about means of access to ruling élites and about the importance of early contact to define the ground, but little evidence of *inter-class* struggle. In the *German Ideology* Marx and Engels at times come close to seeing law making as a middle class game, wholly irrelevant to proletarians. But they do not maintain this position elsewhere.

Finally it scarcely need be said that law can be used for instrumental short-term purposes. But its utility as a legitimator limits the extent to which this is possible, as has been demonstrated by the fate of the Industrial Relations Act which

---

[43]*Ibid.*, p. 500.

[44]Marx, *The Holy Family, op. cit.*

[45]Engels, "Origin of the Family, Private Property, and the State", *op. cit.*, p. 501.

[46]*Ibid.*, p. 582.

[47]Marx and Engels, *The German Ideology, op. cit.*

[48]M. J. Barnett, *The Politics of Legislation* (1969 Weidenfeld, London).

exposed the fact that law and legislation serve *particular* masters.

LAW AND SOCIAL CHANGE

This third theme is most easily presented as four sub-themes: the development of private property, the relationship between social and legal change, the usefulness of law in the class struggle, and law as a means of social reform. Here, however, the danger of distortion arising from the extraction of quotable sections is greatest, since *all* Marx' and Engels' analyses were concerned with change, society was *conceived* in terms of motion.

I have indicated already Marx' and Engels' view of private property as a legal phenomenon, a "general juristic conception" which, true to the second function of law, presents property relations as relations of volition rather than "in their real form as relations of production."[49]

The discussion of property is difficult because the authors use the term to mean *both* the general appropriation of land and things by labour *and* the developing bourgeois forms arising from their historically particular conceptions of relationships between people and things. The law elaborates the distinction between ownership (private property) and possession, and by so doing may well create a gulf between common sense or working class understandings of what it means to say something is mine, and for example the conceptions of lawyers or upper class persons involved in holding companies. Horning has produced evidence of these varying conceptions.[50] Property, however conceived, has always been a social phenomenon. "An isolated individual could no more possess property in land than he could speak";[51] and "Only in so far as the individual is a member—in the literal and figurative sense—does he regard himself as an owner or possessor."[52]

The notion of *private* property is to be found in the appropriation of tools for personal use (which still exists in Horning's factory). This is perhaps the seminal notion, pre-existing, which is elaborated when material conditions change and personal appropriation on a wider scale takes place. As Marx points out, the original meaning of "capital" was "cattle"; taking by *vi et armis,* in feudal Britain the only form of theft, embodies the same idea.[53] In order for something to be *stolen* it has to be *owned.* (Differing conceptions of ownership may also in part account for differential rates of "stealing" between social classes). Thus criminal law developed alongside civil law and, through the eighteenth century in particular, buttressed with its own elaborations the conceptual developments of the notion of private property in the civil law. In civil law, especially, such developments continue. We too ". . . might well reflect on the extent to which civil *law* is linked with private *property* and to what extent civil law determines the existence of a multitude of other relations . . . "[54] Property, of course, is not just in the mind "Actual appropriation takes place not through the relation to these conditions (material) expressed in thought, but through the actual, real relationship to them."[55]

It is, however, a dialectical relationship. This is what is so vital for sociologists of law about Marx' discussion of the development of property. The legal conception *shapes* the external reality, develops with it, and is *developed by* change within the new external world thus created. The hoary old question, which comes first, the law or social change, push or pull, chicken or egg, cannot exist for Marx. The conception *becomes* the material

---

[49]K. Marx, "On Proudhon" (Letter to J. B. Schweitzer) 1865 in *Selected Works, op. cit.,* vol. 1, p. 355.

[50]D. Horning, "Blue collar theft" in E. Smigal and H. Ross (eds.) *Crimes Against Bureaucracy* 46–64.

[51]Marx, *Pre-Capitalist Economic Formations, op. cit.,* p. 81.

[52]*Ibid.,* p. 69.

[53]See Jerome Hall's discussion of this in *Theft, Law and Society* (1952 Bobbs-Merrill, Indianapolis).

[54]Marx and Engels, *The German Ideology, op. cit.,* p. 350.

[55]Marx, *Pre-Capitalist Economic Formations, op. cit.,* p. 92.

world as the material world gives rise to the conception.

My second question, that of the relationship between social and legal change, is already in part answered. In spelling it out the dialectic discussed above must not be forgotten. But the point I specifically wish to make is that for Marx and Engels a legal form cannot hold back developments if a change in the real economic conditions has taken or is taking place. Engels points out that, as feudal society was breaking up

> Where economic conditions demanded freedom and equality of rights, the political order opposed them at every step with guild restrictions. Local prerogatives, differential tariffs, exceptional laws of all kinds in commerce, not only affected foreigners or inhabitants of colonies, but also often whole categories of the State's own subjects.[56]

The demand for legal equality, for free labour, grew. This is the basis of Enlightenment philosophy. But this bourgeois ideology gave and gives the workers a handle, they can extend the same arguments to demand *equality* in other spheres. Material conditions give rise to an idea or an ideal: who can say where it will lead?

The other case of the legislators standing out against change, real economic power having already shifted to the bourgeoisie, occurs in one of Marx' many discussions of the creation of the proletariat.[57] He describes how a century and a half of legislation designed to prevent enclosures—such as the Act of 1533 which restricted the number of sheep for one owner to 2,000—proved fruitless. When the bourgeoisie gained control of the *political* institutions, however, the policy was reversed, the forms of feudal land tenure were abolished. The aims were now to extend large scale agriculture, to increase the supply of masterless "free," proletarians, to increase the dependence of the new proletarians on the market for goods also, and to increase "efficiency" on

the farm and so provide a surplus for the manufacturers. Thus Marx demonstrates, obliquely for it was not his central purpose, that legal noises when not backed by real power achieve nothing beyond irritation, but that legal institutions in the control of the economically powerful can undoubtedly facilitate and expedite real economic change.

In the light of this, what can proletarians hope to achieve by using legal institutions? Marx and Engels suggest that much is possible through such usage. In the first place, an alliance may be formed with some of those within the bourgeoisie who need their help to achieve a particular sectional aim. Marx suggests that this happened at times during the struggle for the shorter working day.

> However much the individual manufacturer might give the rein to his old lust for gain, the spokesmen and political leaders of the manufacturing class ordered a change of front and of speech towards the work people. They had entered the contest for the repeal of the Corn Laws, and needed the workers to help them to victory.[58]

The notion of the "average interests" of the bourgeoisie is apparent again here. Marx emphasises also the point that the death rate of wage earners was alarming, that it was in the "average interests" of the manufacturers, therefore, to take action to improve conditions. "It would seem, therefore, that the interest of capital itself points in the direction of the normal working day."[59]

Two other factors were at work:

> After the factory magnates had resigned themselves and become reconciled to the inevitable, the power of resistance of capital gradually weakened, whilst at the same time the power of attack on the working class grew with the number of its allies in the classes of society not immediately interested in the question.[60]

---

[56]Engels, *Anti Dürhing, op. cit.,* Vol. 1, p. 105.

[57]The present example occurs in *Capital* Vol. 2, Chap. XXIV, *Primary Accumulation* (1930 Everyman, London).

[58]Marx, *Capital* Vol. 1, Chap. X, p. 281 (1970 Lawrence and Wishart, London).

[59]*Ibid.,* p. 266.

[60]*Ibid.,* p. 296.

Moreover, the working class itself became more organized and more determined, so that "the Factory Inspectors warned the government that the antagonism of the classes had arrived at an incredible tension."[61]

The lessons of this for a politically conscious working class are first, that changes can be achieved if differences *within* the bourgeoisie are exploited. A united bourgeoise, as in the case of the mines where landed and manufacturing interests were coincident,[62] is more difficult to persuade. However, (lesson two) if workers present a sufficient threat (as in the last extract) concessions can be achieved. The final lesson is that class aliances, must be formed where possible. Let Engels have the last word:

> But if the laws were in the hands of a government dominated by or under pressure from the workers, it would be a powerful weapon for making a breach in the existing state of things.[63]

Marx leaves one major effect of this, the impetus given to technological development dangling as an unintended consequence. This is unsatisfactory. Why should unintended consequences so fortuitously and so frequently have effects favourable to the dominant economic class? Unintended consequence is little more than a residual sociological category meaning "we don't know." Carson has attempted to go beyond this in the case of factory legislation, pointing out *inter alia,* that those bourgeois operating with steam, the more advanced technology, initially favoured such legislation as a weapon against their less technologically advanced competitors, whose costs were lower.[64]

The final question to be raised is, can the law bring about social reform? Marx and Engels discuss this point not because it is raised by their

theory (which largely precludes it) but because they are constrained to do so by those with whom they are arguing, especially Proudhon and his followers. Marx in 1865 inveighs against Proudhon for mistaking the "legal expression" of property relations (as relations of volition) for their "real form" as relations of production.[65] In the *German Ideology* he had remarked "such concepts (as right) if they are divorced from the empirical reality underlying them can be turned inside out like a glove."[66]

In 1872 Engels developed this critique further, arguing strongly against attempts to bring about piecemeal reform by legal changes (separate solutions for so called political questions) and in particular emphasizing the point that the *criterion* of reform which would be used (human rights, etc.) is itself contingent upon existing relations of production.[67] He recognized that such attempts do take place and argued that if they really operated against the interests of the ruling groups then the law would not be applied or would be only partially applied. (There is a great risk of circularity in actually working with this idea). More probably, such attempts lead to the improvement of the position of one section of the ruling class *vis-à-vis* another rather than to any improvement in the relative position of the workers. For example, in response to Proudhon's argument in favour of a legal limit on the rate of interest he says "the only difference will be that renters will be very careful to advance money only to persons with whom no litigation is to be expected."[68]

Because forms of law are ultimately dependent on relations of production, because the effects of law, in diverse and subtle ways are usually to maintain an existing set of such relations, because, therefore, legal "reforms" cannot really change the pattern of interclass relationships, improving the access of the poor to law is a doubtful

---

[61] *Ibid.,* p. 292.
[62] *Ibid.,* p. 464.
[63] Engels, *The Holy Family, op. cit.,* p. 472.
[64] W. G. Carson and B. Martin, *The Factory Acts* (Forthcoming, Martin Robertson, London).

[65] "On Proudhon", *op. cit.,* p. 357.
[66] *Op. cit.*
[67] Engels, *op. cit.,* pp. 495–574.
[68] *Ibid.*

advantage. In attacking Sue, a young Hegelian, Marx writes

> (According to Sue) the only failing of French legislation is that it does not provide for payment of the lawyers, does not foresee exclusive service of the poor, and makes the legal limits of poverty too narrow. As if righteousness did not begin in the very lawsuit itself and as if it had not been known for a long time in France that the law gives us nothing but only sanctions what we have.[69]

CONCLUSIONS

If the foregoing is to be more than another exercise in literary criticism, the question "where does that get us?" has to be asked. It takes us, I think, a very long way. Theoretically we now see that Marx' and Engels' work not only influenced Durkheim and Weber, as has long been known, but also that it has links through Durkheim with modern functionalism, and, through whom I do not know, with phenomenology. Marx' comments point up criticisms of each of these two contemporary approaches. By showing that a *schema* very like that of Parsons works within a class but not between classes they emphasize again that the systems approach's main weakness is its empirical lack of fit rather than its logical flaws. In their discussions of the role of the subjective in world creation they remind us that in the last resort there is a human body which needs water, however either is conceptualised, if it is going to go on being a creative subjectivity.

The stimulation to current research is as great

as the intellectual delights. Briefly, their remarks about law, the State, and ideology give guidelines for research about State personnel, about their relationships with capital and capitalists, about their beliefs, the occupational pressures to which they are subjected, and their professional socialisation. We are encouraged to regard jurisprudence as a higher order ideology, explaining lawyers to themselves. Which lawyers are exposed to this, and which take it on board? What are the limits to the autonomous development of legal thought in terms of its own concepts and thought-rules? The ramifications are endless.

We move on to the functions of law. Here emergence studies come into their own, and are given direction. We can explore the dimensions of intentionality and unintended consequence. And what of those on the receiving end? Do laws really legitimate and mystify? How are they understood by their various enforcers?

Law and change should speak for itself. We have four ready made research topics I would argue that the first, the role of legal concepts in world creation and its converse, is the most important. I would want to investigate how everyone's world comes to be shaped by the lawyer's world and that of his capitalist clients of the past, how commonly understood statements like "I bought a second-hand car" *came* to be commonly understood. And as I indicated in the text, we must also question the *extent* to which such understandings, for example of what it means to own something, *are* shared.

For the rest, the fact that a reading of Marx and Engels will incite to laughter and to anger should not put them beneath the dignity of the sociologist of law.

---

[69]Marx and Engels, *The German Ideology, op. cit.*

DICHOTOMY AND CONTRADICTION IN THE SOCIOLOGY OF LAW

ALAN HUNT

I. INTRODUCTION

This paper sets out to review developments over the last decade that have had an impact on the sociology of law.[1] In particular I focus upon two lines of development. First the reemergence of theoretical explorations in the sociology of law after the barren years stretching into the 1970s, during which time the sociology of law was almost exclusively characterized by empirical investigation of "the legal process." I will concentrate my attention on the work of Unger, Black, and Trubek, who will represent the awakening of theoretical consciousness within the sociology of law. The second major development to which attention will be given is the emergence of an extensive and varied body of work from a Marxist perspective directed toward advancing a theorization of law. The most recent stage of development involves the tentative beginnings of a meaningful debate between very different theoretical traditions, in particular Marxist and non-Marxist, directed toward the project of the theorization of law.

It is important to stress at the outset that my intention is not to engage in a bibliographical exercise of simply cataloguing recent developments. Rather, it is my intention to make use of this overview to identify current problems confronting the sociological examination of law. In particular, I will advance one general thesis that it is best to introduce at the outset. The thesis is that there exists a fundamental unity between the concerns of contemporary Marxist and non-Marxist theories of law that manifests itself in the extent to which both traditions are impaled upon a dichotomy that inhibits their further advance. This dichotomy finds a variety of expressions within differing theoretical and conceptual traditions. Its varieties will be discussed later, but its general form is the dichotomy between *coercion* and *consent*.

In contending that there exists a manifest unity between the otherwise opposing theoretical traditions, I do not hold to a convergence theory. On the contrary, I want to argue that the different positions enshrine radically different attempts to grapple with the theoretical and practical implications of the general dichotomy that they embody. Thus the issue under discussion is not a theoretical convergence but is a parallelism in which alternative or divergent theories grapple with a common set of problems, albeit these problems being differentially identified and conceptualized within the specific theoretical trajectories. Additionally I want to draw attention to the political and practical implications of the positions advanced. But I would wish to comment that the possibility exists, and is to some limited

---

[1]This paper is an attempt to revise and extend my "Perspectives in the Sociology of Law" (Hunt 1976), which stressed the basic unity in the sociology of law of the 1960s and early 1970s.

Source: Versions of this paper were presented to the Socio-Legal Conference, Sheffield, April 1980 and to the Law and Society Association, University of Wisconsin, Madison, June 1980. Copyright © Alan Hunt.

extent being realized, of a fruitful exchange and debate between Marxist and non-Marxist perspectives in the sociology of law. This possibility exists because of developments within both traditions that has allowed them both to go beyond the ritual encounter between Marxist instrumentalism and .normative integration positions.[2]

The themes introduced above will be explored through a consciously selective discussion of some of the more important texts; it is therefore necessary to reiterate that this essay does not engage in an extensive bibliographical survey of recent developments. The range of substantive work, both theoretical and empirical, that falls under the very general label of "non-Marxist" is very diverse. The discussion will focus on the work of Roberto Unger, Donald Black, and David Trubek. The selection of these authors must be taken to imply an assertion of the importance of their work not only in itself but more specifically because it highlights the parallelism referred to above. With regard to work within the Marxist tradition, I am anxious to emphasize the recent development of a number of divergent theoretical and political tendencies; but, again, I consciously eschew a comprehensive bibliographical survey.

II. TRAJECTORIES IN THE SOCIOLOGY OF LAW

This paper has the objective of assessing the current condition of the sociology of law; it is not intended to offer a bibliographical survey of the field. Rather, attention will be focused primarily on the trends in the theoretical resources and developments deployed. This focus on "theory" is not intended to minimize the importance of empirical studies but rather to argue against the common misapplication of the distinction between empirical and theoretical studies that posits theme as two distinct and separate fields.

On the contrary, there is a basic continuity in that all empirical studies are "theoretical" irrespective of the intentions of their authors in that they necessarily deploy, whether consciously or not, concepts, classifications, hypotheses, and the like that have their origins in the arena of theory, and have necessary and unavoidable consequence when they are deployed within any specific piece of empirical enquiry. The most significant criticism that can be leveled against empirical studies is that they are, all too often, inadvertent to the theory that they deploy and consequently are unable to take account of its problems and limitations.

There is another justication that may be claimed for focusing upon *theoretical* work within the sociology of law, which is that it reveals much more directly the major changes of emphasis and the associated implications and problems that are brought into play.

There is a further reason for concentrating on theoretical developments. It was a characteristic criticism during the early 1970s that one of the major weaknesses of the dominant tradition of American sociology of law was the weakness of its theoretical development.[3] It is, therefore, of considerable significance that there has more recently been a revival of serious theoretical contributions; this development marks both a response to criticism from radical commentators but, more significantly, to a growing sense of dissatisfaction within the dominant tradition. This was in turn sparked off by a deeply felt "crisis" that enveloped law and legal institutions from the end of the 1960s, with which the untroubled perspective of normative integration theories of law was incapable of grappling.[4] As Unger argues,

> the crisis of social order becomes a conscious subject of human concern whenever consensus breaks

---

[2]Referred to by Trubek as "the stifling debates between instrumental Marxism and liberal legalism" (Trubek 1977, p. 553).

[3]See, for example, Currie (1971) and Hunt (1976).

[4]For the present purpose "normative integration" is an equivalent designation to that more commonly referred to as "liberal legalism"; the former is preferred in so far as it designates a theoretical core rather than provides a politico-theoretical description, see Hunt (1979).

down or loses its ability to command allegiance (Unger 1976, p. 264).

It has become a commonplace for writers of widely divergent theoretical and political positions to deploy the contention that there exists a "crisis" in contemporary society or, more specifically, that there exists a "crisis of law and order." Although writers, otherwise widely opposed, agree that there is a "crisis," they differ significantly in the nature of the crisis posited. We need at this stage only to enter the caution that the existence and nature of this invoked crisis should not be accepted uncritically but must be examined at two levels: first, as to whether an identifiable "real" crisis does, in fact, exist and, second, as to the role that the posited crisis plays in the different theoretical positions.[5]

The character of the period in which the re-emergence of a wide-ranging theoretical debate has occurred is one in which law has become increasingly politicized. There exists a tendency within bourgeois democratic systems for law to become more centrally and directly implicated in governmental and political processes.[6] This process poses very sharply the inherent limitations of any analysis founded on an uncritical acceptance of the doctrine of the separation of powers or of legalism in general. Where law is impelled by the logic of events to play an even more central role, the hallowed ideological tenets of such positions become undermined. One major feature of the greatest importance is that the question of the relationship between law and the state has become a central concern in non-Marxist sociology

of law. This is apparent, for example, in Donald Black's more recent text, in sharp contrast with its absence from his earlier writing, which in other respects provides a significant continuity.[7] His concern about the return to anarchy that he posits and the decrease in law is not premised upon any diminution of the role and scope of the state; quite the contrary it is the very growth of the interventionist state that creates the conditions for this new anarchy.

The concern with the law–state relation is even more directly apparent in Unger (1976). At the very center of his concern is the tension between bureaucratic law and legal order. It is also apparent in his emphasis upon the disintegration of the rule of law.

> . . . in seeking to discipline and to justify the exercise of power, men are condemned to pursue an objective they are forbidden to reach (Unger 1976, p. 18).

Conflated with his religious anxiety about modern society with its "consensus without authority" and "stability without belief" is a central focus upon the impact and implications of the welfare or interventionist state, or to pass to the terminology of a different tradition, with the phenomenon of statism.

A similar set of concerns is found in the work of Tay and Kamenka, in which their concern is focused around the rise of "bureaucratic-administrative" regulation, which poses a challenge to individualistic or *Gesellschaft* law. They are not so much concerned with its impact upon modern capitalist societies but rather problematize the extent to which modern socialism, in advancing a critique of individualism, has not inescapably committed itself to bureaucratic-administrative regulation with some admixture of *Gemeinschaft* attributes with its appeal to spontaneous community regulation (Kamenka and Tay 1975). Extending beyond the concerns of Tay and Kamenka, it should be noted that one central feature of contemporary socialist and Marxist de-

---

[5]It would be a fruitful area of enquiry to examine the range of different postulations of a crisis of law and order in order to establish the characterization given to this crisis. Whatever the specific inadequacies of particular alternative accounts of the crisis is, however, not in itself any ground for concluding that no crisis exists; rather, we should be warned against the naive assumptions of many radical positions, which pose "the crisis" as an ever-present and self-evident reality.

[6]In the case of Britain, the process whereby law becomes invoked in the resolution of "hegemonic crisis" is extensively invoked in Hall et al. (1978). With reference to the United States, the same process is central to the thesis of Balbus (1973).

[7]Note the contrast between Black (1976) and (1972).

bates about law revolves around the problem of the place of law in socialist society. The two most important poles of recent debates have, on the one hand, been those that have revived the work of Pashukanis, with his insistence upon the withering away of law and the development of a non-legal social order.[8] On the other hand, E. P. Thompson in his commitment to the rule of law is committing himself to a perspective in which socialist legality completes the mission of bourgeois legality by overcoming the formalism of its concepts of individual rights and justice (Thompson 1975).

The extreme form of the concern with the law–state relation is to be found in Hayek's jurisprudence, which is explicitly directed to the project of delegitimizing the whole positivist, and (in Hayek's strange identification of positivism and socialism) socialist tradition by refusing the title "law" to state legislation, which is presented as the major contributor to the undermining of the rule of law and of the Great Society in general.[9]

Yet this concern is not the property of liberal sociologists of law or conservative economists; it has its ramifications in recent Marxist writings. The question of the law–state relation figures strongly in Poulantzas' characterization of a new stage of "state authoritarianism," which he explicitly sought to distinguish from a simply instrumentalist theory of a reversion of liberal democracy toward fascism (Poulantzas 1978). A similar set of concerns is also present in the much more politically and theoretically heterogeneous writings of those concerned with the question of corporatism.[10]

III. THE GENERAL DICHOTOMY: COERCION AND CONSENT

The most significant trend within contemporary theoretical studies is the parallelism exhibited between different and competing theoretical orientations. These apparently divergent theoretical positions make use of a conceptualization of "law" that is developed around a shared dualism. The general form of this dualism is that between "coercion" and "consent"; but it should be noted that this conceptualization takes a variety of verbal forms. To take an example in which the dualism is very explicit and is posed in its most simple form, we may look briefly at Timasheff, one of the earlier pioneers of theoretical sociology of law. In developing his definition of law as "ethico-imperative co-ordination," we note the particular terminological form within which he develops his dualistic conception of law, which rests on two variables—"ethics" (consent) and "power" (coercion). Law for Timasheff is essentially "ethics + power" which

> may be thought of as two circles which cross one another. Their overlapping section is law (1940, p. 248).

In the development of law, his crudely evolutionist treatment of "the triumph of law," the upward march of civilisation is marked by law with a larger ethical content and conversely lesser reliance on power. Law, then, is conceived as a simple paradigm lying between the polarities of ethics and power, and its advance and progress is marked by an increase in its ethical basis and a decline in its reliance on power.

This evolutionary dualism, presented with estimable sharpness in Timasheff, is but a clearer statement of a much wider and pervasive dualism that characterizes and greatly marks the history of both sociological and jurisprudential debates. Its presence is to be found in such diverse locations as Durkheim's distinction between repressive and restitutive law, on the one hand, and, on the other, in the trajectory of the controversy over the role of sanctions that is the keystone of the debates surrounding jurisprudential positivism.

Nor, it must be stressed, are dichotomy and dualism restricted to theories of law. The whole history of sociology is characterized by the successive engagement between rival dichotomous

---

[8]See Beirne and Sharlet (1980); Pashukanis (1978).

[9]See, in particular, Vols. I and III of Hayek (1972) and (1979).

[10]See, for example: Winkler (1975), Jessop (1977), and Schmitter and Lembrach (1980).

conceptions. I have enjoyed, and repeat for others who have not come across it, Philip Corrigan's observation that of all the different ways in which social theory has attempted to depict the social world, they all come like the animals to the Ark, two-by-two.[11] It is not the object of this paper to engage in an excursion into the sociology of sociology, but one last general comment on the wider location of dichotomous conceptions of law may be in order. The consent/coercion dualism with reference to law has a particular direct relationship with that unproductive and schematic divide in the sociology of the late 1960s and early 1970s between conflict and consensus models in sociology. The two terms stand as direct embodiments of the apparent polarity of concerns of that largely negative and unproductive phase; and to some degree, elements of that opposition necessarily live on despite the timely death of that wider confrontation. Its echoes will recur in the subsequent discussion. The baldly stated negative assessment of conflict sociology must not detract from its positive historical contribution of disrupting the dominant complacency engendered by the long reign of structural functionalism. Conflict theory played a particular important role in the development of radical criminology and radical sociology. In fostering these trends, its positive contribution was to create the conditions for the emergence of more adequate and sophisticated debates of the present period. It is to be welcomed that some of the prime movers of radical criminology and sociology such as Chambliss, Quinney, Taylor, Walton, and Young have come a long way to correct the excesses of the conflict theory period.

The persistence in the theorization of law of the coercion–consent dichotomy leads one to ask: what is the harm? Why should its persistence be seen as a stumbling block over which divergent theoretical positions continue to stumble? The specific negative consequences of particular manifestations will be examined in the more detailed discussion that follows.

The general deficiency inherent in dichotomous conceptions of law is that they have, as a

necessary effect, a tendency to result in an unstable analysis that lurches between the polarities set up. They produce an "either-or" effect in which each theorization is reduced unavoidably to emphasizing "either" the element of consent "or" the element of coercion. The commitment is made, and in the views to be examined it is found in every one of them, to conceptualizing law as not being reducible to either one of the two elements and consequently to searching for a theorization that stands upon the *combination* of the elements as a reality not reducible to either element. Yet in all cases the analysis that emerges fails to escape from a view in which law is presented as constituted of particular proportions of consent and coercion along a unilinear dimension between the two polarities. In its most simple form individual theorist A, B, or C can be differentiated as proposing a location of law within a linear paradigm:

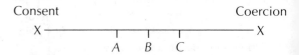

The result is that the elements themselves remain discrete and, despite the commitment thereto, are not seen in the combinatory effect.

This deficiency is but a specific manifestation of the ubiquitous dilemma of social philosophy that revolves around the oppositions of freedom–unfree, consciousness–being, determinism–voluntarism, and so on. The dichotomy between consent and coercion is but a specific embodiment of these wider oppositions. In particular, it has its root in the individualistic problematic that underlies the theorization of law, namely, that of the basis of individual adherence to law. Coercion and consent are but the most general form of the variety of solutions that philosophy, jurisprudence, and sociology have provided at one time or another. Although it is not either the claim or the intention of this essay to offer a general solution that supersedes the deficiencies inherent in dichotomous conceptions of law, it is my purpose to show the way in which that problem must be seen as deriv-

---

[11]Corrigan (1975), p. 216.

ing from some of the most important and perennial intellectual problems.

There is a further level of difficulty that stems from the linear consent–coercion model of law. Its impact is greatest on the non-Marxist or liberal positions to be discussed, but it is not absent from Marxist texts. It arises from the inherent tendency of liberal theory to place a positive valuation on consent; in simple terms for law to be based on consent or for consent to constitute the preponderant element is "good." It is most frequently associated with a metatheoretical or ideological evolutionary view of a historical process toward consent and freedom and away from unfreedom and coercion. The effects of such evolutionary positions often have these most serious effects where they remain implicit. They are frequently expressed in terms of some variant of "social contract" theory that is premised on the positive evaluation and thus elevation of positive or active consent as a condition of human freedom.

The general dichotomy has been introduced and some of its wider implications considered. The next two sections of the paper examine its role in two broadly drawn and contrasting theoretical traditions through the discussion of the work of some of their more important contemporary exponents.

IV. CONTEMPORARY SOCIOLOGY OF LAW: OLD PROBLEMS AND NEW VARIANTS

There have been some significant theoretical developments in the sociology of law in the last few years. During the formative period of the sociology of law in the United States in the 1950s and early 1960s, there existed a widespread consensus as to the nature of the project of the sociology of law. This consensus was formed around the interweaving of two apparently different traditions. Most pronounced and visible was the continuing dominance of the perspectives of American Realism[12] organized around the problematic of examining the operational failures of

the legal process to meet legal ideals operating with the presumption of the perfectability of the legal process to meet these ideals. Indeed, it is important to place due emphasis upon the continuing impact of the Realist perspective. This is nowhere more apparent than in Trubek's proposed "new realism" (Trubek 1977). Harnessing yet again the realist aphorism of the contract between "law in books" and "law in action," that is, between the ideal and reality, he seeks to harness this as an articulated methodology for checking reality against the ideal. Yet the original Realist unproblematic presumption was of the perfectability of law; they presumed some operational deficiency revealed through empirical study followed by scientifically informed reform, "social engineering" could be overcome such that "the gap" between reality and ideal could be narrowed or closed. The manner in which the relation between legal ideals and legal reality has been theorized, particularly by Trubek and Unger, is more sophisticated than the version offered by the early Realists. Yet, nevertheless, both the theoretical terms and their practical points of reference remain central to modern sociology, and, as I shall argue in a later section, are not by any means distant from the concerns of contemporary Marxist writers.

* * *

Our discussion of contemporary liberal legal theory should properly start with Roberto Unger since he has rapidly come to exercise a powerful influence within recent legal theory. His earlier and most generalized excursion into social theory in *Knowledge and Politics* (Unger 1975) is itself impressive if only for the breadth of its concerns and for its sweeping claims to provide an alternative to the classical tradition of social theory, which is taken as embracing almost every major form of social theory developed over the last three centuries. It is important to note that Unger himself locates the problems of legal theory as "the immediate subject of my interest" (1975, p. 3). It is, however, in *Law in Modern Society* that he addressed problems of legal theory (Unger 1976). In this text, despite the continued presence

---

[12] I have traced more fully this fidelity to the Realist tradition in Hunt (1976) and (1978).

of an overarching concern with the development of "total criticism," he nevertheless takes his stand more firmly within the terrain of positions that are part of the partial criticism that in *Knowledge and Politics* he had argued were irremediably scarred by the antimonies inherent in liberal theory (1975, p. 7). He now proposes to resolve the predicament of social and legal theory through an attempted integration of the two major contemporary competing paradigms, the instrumentalist or conflict perspective and the consensus perspective.[13] Yet, despite his commitment to a synthesis that overcomes the systematic deficiencies of both, his method of combination is inherently additive and nonsynthetic; his general hypothesis is

> that some social settings might best be understood in light of the doctrine of consensus and others from the perspective of the theory of instrumentalism (1976, p. 127).

He proceeds to posit the existence of two types of law that embody the general characteristics of the two alternative theoretical perspectives. "Interactional law" is allied to consensus theory and "bureaucratic law' to instrumental theory. The strength of Unger's analysis, although I shall argue it is severely limited, resides in the break he effects with the normative integration theories of contemporary sociology of law within which law operates as a general and pervasive mechanism of societal integration through the linked processes of social control and socialization buttressed by the legitimizing properties of law. He effects this breach with normative integration theories through his emphasis on the conflict or tension between the two different "modes of order" that coexist within the contemporary legal order.

It should, however, be noted that this position is not particularly original. It is firmly and powerfully present in Weber's classic discussion of the tension between formal and substantive justice.[14] It is only the more crude appropriations of Weber that emphasized a simpler and, therefore, more evolutionary thesis of the triumph of formal rationality in the legal order of capitalist society. But even though Weber's analysis rests on the problematic tension between formal and substantive rationality, he nevertheless places unqualified priority upon formal rationality, which he saw as the only alternative when confronted with the rising demand for substantive justice articulated in its most powerful form by the labor and socialist movement. Just so does Unger throw in his lot with legal rationality/formalism. He identifies three functionally significant components of legal systems—formal, procedural, and substantive; but of these three it is formalism that lies at the core of the development of modern Western rule of law. His emphasis is such that formalism in his analysis wholly subordinates the other components. The result is that he presents, as did Weber before him and as does Hayek today, the demand for substantive justice as the source of the dangerous erosion of formalism. As I will argue more generally, despite his apparent commitment to liberal political values, he is led inexorably toward conservatism and pessimism, which even his sociological version of Christian theology cannot disguise.

We find then in Unger a specific variant of the general dichotomy that lies at the heart of the tension inherent in the liberal doctrine of the rule of law. It is expressed as the tension between "collective values" and "bureaucratic welfare tyranny." Despite his apparent commitment to achieve synthesis, he evades the challenges and thereby reinforces the fundamental conservatism of his position by the evasive observation that it is beyond the remit of his present enquiry (Unger 1976, p. 129). However, the general outline of the synthesis that he desires is clearly indicated. Yet his "solution" cannot be treated as one that marks a development in social theory that over-

---

[13]His orientation to these competing paradigms is not dissimilar to that earlier advanced by Dahrendorf, in which both are recognized as grasping different aspects of reality (Dahrendorf 1959).

[14]See for fuller discussion of this central feature of Weber's sociology of law (Hunt 1978), Chapter 5.

comes or supersedes the dualism. Rather, his transcendental theology posits an immanent process of social transformation the resultant of which abolishes both the theoretical problem and the dichotomy within law. He relies upon the assertion of an immanent essentialism reconciling "individual freedom" and "community cohesion":

> The more perfect this reconciliation becomes, the more does the society's emergent interactional law reveal the requirements of human nature and social existence (1976, p. 264).

Far from advancing a theoretical synthesis we return to the old "search for this latent or living law" which seeks to "discover a universal given order in social life" (1976, p. 242). This quest for an immanent or spontaneous normative order in large measure marks a return to an older and more conservative tradition epitomized in general by Durkheim's search for the "ideological community" (Therborn 1976) and more particularly within the sociology of law by Ehrlich's espousal of "living law" (Ehrlich 1962). Yet the temptation should be avoided to immediately apply a conservative label to Unger's position. His claim, most explicit in *Knowledge and Politics,* to discern evidence of the realization of his synthesis in the contemporary developments within the "Welfare-corporate state" and within actual socialist societies should caution us against too hurried political labeling. It is sufficient to note that Unger's attempt to resolve the general dichotomy in the social and legal order takes the form of a synthesis whose starting point is an essentially metaphysical concept of "community."

The pursuance of community is grounded in a general pessimism about the trajectory of modern legal development. Talcott Parsons's late and perceptive review of *Law in Modern Society* (Parsons 1977) provides a very striking illustration of the contrast between two generations of sociological theorists. Parsons notes important areas of agreement and convergence between his own

position and that advanced by Unger. I am disposed to place considerable weight on what Parsons identifies as his fundamental disagreement which leads him to brand Unger's theoretical position as unacceptable:

> Perhaps the main reason I am critical of Unger is that I do not share his—perhaps fashionable—pessimism about the drastic erosion of the rule of law (1977, p. 148).

Parsons has been the embodiment of the most systematized commitment to a positive evaluation of the modern trajectory of the capitalist democracies. Unger can be read as representative of the more recent self-doubt and anxiety that finds its reverberations at all levels of political and social theory and that cuts across traditional political and theoretical boundaries. The pessimism to which Parsons refers finds its expression within both neoconservative jurisprudence (Hayek 1973, 1976, and 1979; Jenkins 1980) and contemporary Marxist debates about law (Thompson 1978, 1978a, 1978b, and 1978c).

* * *

Donald Black presents an apparently sharp contrast to Unger's social philosophical theorization. I confess at the outset to a deep-seated dislike for the rigid positivism and formalism that characterizes his most general theoretical intervention, *The Behavior of Law* (Black 1976). Such a response is sufficient to discourage me from engaging in a general review of his work. Yet, despite the profound difference in methodology and theoretical orientation between Black and Unger, I will seek to demonstrate that there are two important continuities. Black presents his own specific formulation of the general dichotomy, and, second, his position is marked by a pervasive pessimism about the role of law in modern capitalist democracies in spite of his apparent commitment to universalistic sociology purged of all concern with current policy objectives (Black 1972).

Black has noted the continuing impact of the legal realist tradition; he rejects its prostitution of scientific method to the pursuit of policy objectives subsumed under the dichotomy between "law in books" and "law in action." But in seeking to impose a strict divide between "pure sociology of law" and "applied sociology of law" (1972, p. 1087) and thereby to break with the tradition imposed by legal realism, he actually bears witness to its influence by adopting its underlying positivism and behaviorism. His injunction that

> law consists in observable acts, not in rules (1972, p. 1091)

replicated Oliver Wendell Holmes's aphoristic characterization of law as

> the prophecies of what the courts will do in fact, and nothing more pretentious, are what I mean by the law (Holmes 1897, p. 461).

The step that Black effects is to transform the pragmatic positivism of the early realists into a formalistic behavioralist variant.

In order to locate the presence of the general dichotomy it is necessary to trace briefly Black's methodology. His starting point, as the title of his book indicates, is to treat law as a behavioral phenomenon, purged of all value judgments and ideals. Law "behaves" or varies in relation to other observable social phenomena or "dimensions." He posits two dimensions to the variation of law; the first is quantitative, reducible to "more law/less law." The second dimension is provided by "the style of law," which in turn corresponds to styles of social control. The styles of law are merely listed, no indication is given of where the classification is derived from, but it may be noted in passing that like many other typologies that have been advanced within the sociology of law, they have a scarcely concealed evolutionary implication in the transition from the "penal" style (i.e., primitive), through "compensatory" and "therapeutic," to (the more advanced) "conciliatory" style (1976, p. 4). "Style of law" as the second dimension in the variation of law plays little part in the subsequent elaboration. The variations in styles of law are introduced in an arbitrary manner and are not systematically integrated within the body of the theory. The difficulty in quantifying "style" and the ever present danger that the identification of "style" may carry evaluative connotations probably explains the limited attention it receives.

The book thereafter is predominantly concerned to advance quantitatively expressed hypotheses concerning the behavior of law. In the main, they are couched in terms of variations of "more" or "less" law. He nowhere indicates how this quantification of law is to be undertaken. It is assumed without specification of any method of measurement that quantitative variations are self-evidently identifiable. Thus, to take just one example, in dealing with the relationship between law and stratification he advances the hypothesis that "law varies directly with stratification," that is, the more stratification a society has, the more law it has (1976, p. 13). The startling evidence for this hypothesis is to repeat the well-trodden anthropological data about the limited role and extent of law in "simple" society, this taken with the assumption that in some self-evident sense "modern" society has more law. The spurious scientificity of his appeal to quantification does not, however, appear to permit any exploration of the relation between law and the variety of forms and degrees of stratification in "modern" society. Stripped of their scientism, his hypotheses are sociological commonplaces distorted to fit universalistic pretensions. Black's purportedly sophisticated theoretical enterprise is nothing more and nothing less than systematic common sense; and no systematization of common sense can turn it into good sense.[15]

Yet behind the appeal to the quantification of legal phenomena we find lurking the general dichotomy between coercion and consent. The general couplets that run through his hypotheses of less/more law, undifferentiated/differentiated

---

[15]On "common sense," its ideological and conservative character, and "good sense," see Gramsci (1971), p. 419ff.

society, and simple/modern society are completed by noting their congruence with the dichotomy between consensual and coercive characteristics of law. This emerges most explicitly in his rejection of the Durkheimian equation between simple/undifferentiated society and repressive law (1976, p. 40).

It is further manifest in his predilection for curvilinear hypotheses; for example, in positing the quantitative growth of law with social differentiation, he posits a subsequent diminution of law:

> As social life evolves beyond interdependence to symbiosis . . . law declines (1976, p. 40).

The complex symbiotic differentiation of modern society manifests itself not only, according to Black, in a decrease in law but a growing emphasis upon "conciliatory," in contrast to "penal," styles of law.

The variety of curvilinear hypotheses that are advanced provided evidence not only of the presence of the coercion/consent dichotomy but also of the deep social and political pessimism that underlies his apparently neutral and apolitical stance. His evolutionary perspective posits first an increase in the quantity of law and then its decrease; it is this decrease that he decrees as the "return to anarchy" (p. 132). Black's prediliction for quantitative behavioralism commits him, since it constrains him to see the variance of law in terms of increases and decreases, to a cyclical vision of legal and social development. Such a cyclical element is, as Eder argues, the reintroduction of an archaic philosophy of history (Eder 1977, p. 138). Far from the value freedom whose shrine he prays before, Black's sociology of law is transparently ideological. It is but an ideological anxiety that besets liberal intellectuals and paves the way for neoconservatism.

> Encounters replace the social structures of the past, and people increasingly have closeness without permanence, depth without commitment (Black 1976, p. 135).

The breakdown of community and the advance of social equality combine to produce conditions in which law tends to decrease; the result is the situational society in which there is no place for the rule of law and the values of liberal legalism. It is remarkable how, despite the sharp theoretical differences between them, the conclusions arrived at by both Black and Unger replicate the deep pessimism of the liberal intelligensia in the United States.

*   *   *

David Trubek's project of developing a "new realism," referred to at the beginning of this section, marks the clearest and most explicit continuity that has stamped American sociology of law with much of the intellectual imprint of the prewar realism. It needs to be stressed that his "new realism" marks a significant attempt to go beyond the unproblematic treatment of "the gap between legal ideals and legal reality." His position is further significant in that it is marked by an explicit commitment to engage in a meaningful dialogue with the more recently emerging Marxist trend within American sociology of law. It is for this reason that my attention will be primarily focused upon his lengthy review article of Isaac Balbus's *Dialectics of Legal Repression* (Balbus 1973). I will not at this stage be concerned to comment on his critique of Balbus but, rather, to concentrate on the second half of his essay, in which he advances his "new realism" (Trubek 1977). With respect to Trubek's earlier writing, I only want to draw attention to the extent to which he more than any other contemporary writer in the field of the sociology of law is concerned with the theoretical lineage of the field; this concern has manifested itself in the extent to which he goes beyond the conventional deferential bow to the legacy of Max Weber (Trubek 1972a, 1972b). He has sought to reexamine the Weberian legacy, and this concern has its reverberations in the more recent essay.

The element that is "new" in Trubek's realism is the way in which he problematizes "the gap" between legal ideals and reality by abandoning the assumption of the perfectability of law; "the gap" is presented as itself being a necessary consequence of the structural characteristics of liberal democracy.

> The gap between the ideals of law and its performance is a central and pervasive feature of legal existence (1977, p. 544).

Yet it is significant that, despite the abandonment of the simple-minded social engineering of the early Realists, its effects remain contagious such that despite the apparently greater sophistication of his "mediative perspective" (1977, p. 543ff) his concern is still with "the cure" for the realist dichotomy, in that

> law represents an effort to mediate fundamental conflicts (p. 542),

but one that is doomed to remain imperfect.

Within this reworking of the problematic of legal realism and of mainstream sociology of law, we find lurking the general dichotomy. Law in books/law in action is the manifestation of the opposition between ideal/reality; the central content of this opposition within liberal democracy is seen as that between the ideal of social equality and the persistence of structures of hierarchy and dominance. The polarity between equality and hierarchy is, of course, but another form of the opposition between consent and coercion.

There are two significant features to be found in the development of Trubek's attempt to overcome the simple opposition of ideal and reality, consent and coercion. The first concerns the methodology he proposes; it is this that ties him closest to the realist tradition but to which he gives a significantly idealistic inflection. This arises because he insists on giving methodological priority to ideals as the starting point against which legal reality is to be examined.

> Such a system *must begin* [my emphasis] with ideals basic to our society.... I propose that we examine law in terms of its contribution to these values (p. 546).

And again:

> A legal order is not an end in itself. The system must be justified by its contribution to more fundamental social ideals (p. 547).

It should be noted that a very similar idealism is present in Unger's work and constitutes an important continuity, which is made explicit by Trubek's frequent citation of Unger. For Unger,

> the deepest root of all historical change is manifest or latent conflict between the view of the ideal and the experience of actuality (Unger 1976, p. 157).

Two negative consequences follow from such idealist positions. The first is that in giving priority to ideals, the ideals themselves are regarded as unproblematic, they form the taken-for-granted and uncontested presumption of society as a purposive and organic enterprise of Hegelian character bent on the realization of ideals that march through the pages of history. No space is left for a critical examination of, for example, the ideological role of the ideal of equality in capitalist democracies. The second consequence of the idealist methodology is that it necessarily involves the positing of a conception of a universal human nature that is realized in the historical process. This is most explicit in Unger and is not disputed by Trubek:

> the universal is human nature . . . the particulars are the forms of social life and the individual personalities by which that humanity is represented (Unger 1976, p. 261).

Trubek seeks to combine this methodology with theoretical elements appropriated from the Marxist tradition or, more particularly, from the historical analysis of law developed by E. P. Thompson in *Whigs and Hunters* (1975) and his colleagues in parallel work (Hay 1975). Thompson's emphasis upon the complex and contradictory character of law clearly, from his explicit acknowledgments, made a considerable impact upon Trubek.

We reach, then, not a simple conclusion (law = class power) but a complex and contradictory one. On the one hand it is true that law did mediate class relations to the advantage of the rulers... On the other hand, the law mediated these relations through legal forms, which imposed, again and again, inhibitions upon the actions of the rulers (Thompson 1975, p. 242).

Thompson makes a more specific contribution to Trubek's position because it was *Whigs and Hunters* that "first suggested to me the perspective outlined in this essay" (Trubek 1977, p. 543), which he identifies as "the mediative perspective" that asserts that:

a significant feature of legal life in liberal capitalist societies is the simultaneous assertion and negation of basic ideals of equality, individuality, and community. The legal order neither guarantees these ideals, nor does it simply deny them: it does both (p. 544).

Trubek does not adopt the specifically Marxist connotations of "mediation," which, for reasons he does not explain, he sees as closely related to the theory of alienation. Rather, he proposes to adopt "the ordinary English language sense," which he identifies as:

a communicative intervention aimed at reconciling or compromising conflicting ideas or interests (p. 543).

What Trubek has failed to notice that there is in "the ordinary English language sense" a second meaning to the word, and it is this one that both Marx and Thompson employ of mediation as the process of the forming of a link or connection between different objects or processes.

This is not a semantic disputation; important consequences follow from the initial identification of the concept. My reservation about Trubek's mediation = conciliation is threefold: first, that it imports a consensual character to the process of mediation, second, that it implies ends and objectives of human agencies as constitutive of the process, and, third, that it carries un-avoidably functionalist implications. What Trubek misses about the alternative definition of mediation, which is developed in Marxist literature, is that all social activity involves processes in which "things" (whether they be artifacts, language, institutions, etc.) mediate between people and the social and natural environment in which they live *and* have differential effects in transforming the nature of that relation. Applying this directly to problems of the sociology of law, one of the most important questions that Marx asked (but, it should be noted, did not provide a direct answer) was:

the really difficult point to be discussed is how the relations of production as legal relations take part in the uneven development (of material production) (Marx 1969, p. 109; Cain and Hunt 1979, p. 122).

Marx here poses the role of law as a process of "mediation" of legal relations as the form in which relations of production are operative and that have definite effects and consequences. It is this set of central issues that Marx and Thompson pose without importing the "solution" that is introduced by Trubek's identification of mediation as conciliation.

The above exploration of the concept "mediation" is not intended to teach lessons to Trubek about "ordinary English language" or to claim a privileged interpretation of Marx, but it does serve to emphasize two points. First, the joining of a meaningful exchange between Marxists and non-Marxists involves certain problems that make it unwise to attempt simply borrowing or lifting from one theoretical tradition into another. It should be emphasized that this caution should be seen as applying not only to the adoption of elements of Marxism but likewise to the incorporation within Marxism from other traditions. An interesting example of the latter problem can be seen in the problems that arise when Marxists seek to make use of the Weberian concepts of legitimacy and domination; the difficulty arises from the way in which Weber's concepts are produced and thus linked to the analysis of the interpersonal relation between rulers and ruled, which is not directly compatible with the theoretical framework of class analysis. To avoid misunderstanding, let me stress that I do not seek to place any barrier in the way of cross-fertilization between disparate theoretical traditions but, rather, to enter a caution against the simple borrowing or transplanting of individual concepts.

The manner in which Trubek employs the concept of mediation as the equivalent of conciliation has one further interesting consequence. His general position does, as I have argued, provide evidence of the presence of the general dichotomy between coercion and consent as the underlying mode of theorization of his sociology of law. Beyond this general presence, Trubek gives a particular inflection through his equation of mediation and conciliation, which emphasizes the proximity of Trubek's position to the sociology of law of the 1950s and 1960s with its central assumption of the normative integration or consensual character and function of law.

One significant point of differentiation between Trubek, on the one hand, and Unger and Black, on the other, is that there is no note or sign of the pessimism regarding the trajectory of law in contemporary capitalist democracies that has been pointed to in the case of both Unger and Black. Rather, Trubek exhibits a much closer lineage with the liberal confidence in the effectivity of law. He holds out a continuing and renewed faith in the role of law in the contemporary period.

* * *

III. THE GENERAL DICHOTOMY OF MARXISM

The most significant trend within contemporary theoretical discussions of law is the general parallelism between Marxist and non-Marxist orientations. The major manifestation of this congruance is the extent to which both positions operate with the shared dichotomy between "coercion" and "consent." The general dualism of the concept "law" within the history of jurisprudential and sociological thought has been discussed earlier, but the presence of this same dualism within Marxist approaches requires more comment.

The more Marxism has succeeded in overcoming its greatest general weakness, namely, its tendency toward an instrumental reduction of law to the state and the state, in its turn, to organized violence,[16] the more it has, paradoxically, manifested the dualism coercion/consent that characterizes "bourgeois" legal thought. Those Marxists who still cling to a simple faith in the necessary abyss between Marxist (= "science") and non-Marxist thought (= "bourgeois ideology") may see in this shift within Marxist studies of law evidence of revisionism, of the ever-present vice of contamination with bourgeois sociology. The import I draw is very different: it is that the fundamental difficulty and problem confronting all legal theory lies in the exploration and resolution of the dualism of coercion and consent.

The coercion–consent dualism finds its most general expression in Marxist theory through the very widespread recent influence of Gramscian theory. The somewhat belated "discovery" of Gramsci, in particular by British and American Marxists, has focused primarily upon the issues posed by the concept hegemony through which Gramsci struggles to come to an understanding of the social processes through which particular forms of class relations are sustained and reproduced in such a way that relations of exploitation and domination persist without general or frequent recourse to state coercion. Thus law cannot adequately be understood as a dependent instrument of state coercion but must be under

---

[16]I refer to a "tendency" within Marxism toward instrumentalism because Marxism has a certain openness in its formulation by Marx, which allows a range of emphases in interpretation and elaboration. This range of positions within the Marxism of Marx and Engels was demonstrated with respect to their treatment of law in Cain and Hunt (1979). The reduction of Marxism to an instrumentalist theory of law and state can claim some very real textual authority, and it has continued to exercise a persistent influence that has important correlates with the wider politico-strategic debates that have occurred with Marxism since the death of Marx and Engels but which are beyond our present concerns.

stood in its educative and moral dimension securing the conditions of class relations. Central to Gramscian thought is a reworking of the theory of ideology such that there is no invokation of an instrumentalist view of ideology as a mechanism of deception, "brain-washing," or mystification.

Within such a perspective the central focus has been upon the noncoercive face of law seen as contributing to the securing and reproducing of

the "spontaneous" consent given by the great masses of the population to the general direction imposed on social life by the dominant fundamental group [ruling class] (Gramsci 1971, p. 12).

Yet there coexists in Gramsci an emphasis upon the repressive role of law and state. Perry Anderson, in seeking to defend the Leninist continuity in Gramsci and to salvage a "revolutionary" Gramsci from the hands of modern revisionism, documents a continuing recognition in Gramsci of the repressive dimension of law and state (Anderson 1976–1977). But this presence only demonstrates the significance and problematic character of coercion and consent, since Gramsci nowhere attempts to grapple with the implications of holding both the "traditional" thesis on the role of coercion and his own primary focus on hegemony as "permanently organised consent" (Gramsci 1971, p. 80). The solution offered by Anderson, while exhibiting both Leninist and Trotskyist respectability, merely asserts the primacy of coercion over consent.[17] The controversy within Marxism epitomized by Anderson's discussion of Gramsci has advanced little beyond the rival assertion of the primacy of coercion or consent.

Despite this perhaps pessimistic overview of the impact of Gramsci, it should be stressed that in a more general sense the espousal of a Gramscian perspective has had profoundly positive results. Gramsci has been the main vehicle that has facilitated the emergence of Marxist analyses of law precisely because it no longer requires an invocation of the primacy of coercion in state and class relations. In this sense the very existence of Marxist analyses of law owe much to the wider dissemination of Gramsci's writings.

The important place attributed to Gramsci in the genesis of Marxist approaches to law needs one important qualification. It is Gramsci's general concerns and problems that have been influential and have both encouraged and facilitated the examination of law. Yet there is an element within his writings that presents something of a barrier to the development of a systematic Marxist theory of law. It is well-known that he relies heavily on the distinction between "state" and "civil society"; it enables him to direct attention to the hegemonic processes operative in civil society. Yet precisely this distinction creates an initial obstruction in the theorization of law since its location within the state–civil society distinction is problematic. The immediate and self-evident proximity of law and state suggests that law should be located within the state. It is precisely the concern with hegemonic processes that is most suggestive for the theorization of law. Yet this is obstructed by the state–civil society distinction itself.

It should perhaps be stressed that this problem of the initial location of law is not only present in Gramsci. Exactly the same problem presents itself in Althusser's work. His key paper "Ideology and the Ideological State Apparatuses" (Althusser 1971) introduces the distinction between the ideological and the repressive state apparatuses (ISA and RSA). He engages in no substantive discussion of law; it is simply "placed" as part of the RSA. The result of both Gramsci's and Althusser's conceptualizations of the relation between the state and the remainder of the social totality, in so far as it has consequences for the theorization of law, is to introduce an undesirable bifurcation in our approach to law. On the one hand, it is approached as an apparatus of the state, but, on the other, it is studied precisely because of the extent

---

[17]Anderson (1976–1977), pp. 42–44; the "fundamental," "ultimate," "inevitable" reality of bourgeois class power is force, or "the determination of the capitalist state in the final instance by coercion."

to which law is implicated in every facet of social life.

The practical consequence of this bifurcation or rupture within the conceptual framework within which law is located is the presence of two rather different bodies of theory; the first focuses on the regulation of the social relations of production (in particular, property and contract relations) and the second on the role of law in the preservation of class domination (in particular, embodied in criminal and constitutional law). The two differential emphases, it should be noted, correspond to the general dualism between consent and coercion, and at the same time to the commonplace legal distinction between private and public law.[18]

The general theoretical problem that presents itself in the development of Marxist theory of law is the manner in which the common sense reality of the opposition between "consent" and "coercion" is to be theorized in such a way as to produce a *unitary* theory. It is this difficulty upon which work written under the influence of Gramsci has suffered in its failure to integrate its conceptual framework. This theoretical flaw is present in what is the most sustained attempt to develop and apply a Gramscian analysis of law that has so far been published: I refer to the important text by Stuart Hall and his collaborators, *Policing the Crisis* (Hall 1978).

Policing the Crisis takes as its central concern precisely the period in contemporary political history that it is argued marks a shift from:

> a consensual to a more coercive management of the class struggle by the capitalist state (Hall 1978, p. 218).

The text documents in great detail the political and ideological conditions under which the "shift" from consensual to coercive management is prepared and orchestrated. What is omitted, despite two extensive theoretical discussions (Chapters 6 and 7), is an analysis of the part played by law and legal apparatuses in the shift toward coercion and political authoritarianism. In keeping with the explicitly Gramscian approach, stress is laid on the manner in which the autonomization of law in bourgeois democracies contributes to the creation and reproduction of consent. Yet in the transition to authoritarianism, law reappears dressed in different clothing of coercive legislation and punitive judges as the bearer of an unavoidably instrumentalist relationship to the capitalist class and capitalist state (and this despite the conscious attempts of the authors to root out all traces of instrumentalism in their Marxism). The new coercive face of law is for the time being enshrined by the protection of its universal above-the-struggle legitimacy, which is the legacy of its consensual role. It should be noted in passing, although not made explicit in the text, that this facility of law to act as the bearer of repression is limited temporally: repressive law cannot hide behind the consensual mask indefinitely. The imagery that reoccurs in much Marxist and radical writing on law is of "the iron fist in the velvet glove."[19] The fundamental weakness of this imagery is that it necessarily rests upon a theorization that ascribes axiomatic priority to the repressive character of law. Yet it is precisely this necessary primacy that the authors seek to avoid. Their attempt to overcome this apparent contradiction in their theorization deserves some comment.

They seek to provide a theoretical unification by introducing a single fundamental process identified as *domination,* which is articulated as having two faces, the repressive and the consensual/hegemonic forms of domination. I should make clear that my criticism of *Policing the Crisis* carries major elements of self-criticism. I have attempted to resolve a growing awareness of the problem posed by the coercion–consent

---

[18]Paul Hirst (1979), p. 96 makes a similar point in commenting on the two types of Marxist theory of law although he locates the differentiation with respect to an emphasis on two different functions of law (regulation of relations of possession and the regulation of the struggle between classes).

[19]See the most explicit use of "the iron fist and velvet glove" imagery in the study of the American police by the Center for Research on Criminal Justice (1975).

dichotomy by advancing a distinction between "repressive domination" and "ideological domination" (Hunt 1976, 1978). The proposed synthesis, in its basic formulation very similar to that found in *Policing the Crisis,* lay in the extent to which both are forms of a single general process, namely, domination.

In these formulations I was at pains to insist that the distinction between ideological and repressive domination was an analytical distinction made:

> in order that in their re-combination the full complexity of the processes of domination may be explored (Hunt 1976, p. 36).

In very similar terms *Policing the Crisis* proposes the theoretical unification by means of *power* as the central concept taking two distinct forms coercion/domination and consent/direction.

It now seems to me that positions of this type are semantic solutions that contribute little to the difficulties posed by the persistence of the general dichotomy between coercion and consent. The necessary effect of the presence of the dichotomy is that law comes to be seen as being constituted of two different characteristics and in its existence to oscillate like a pendulum between them. Paul Hirst makes the interesting observation that there are two distinct schools of Marxist analysis of law; one trend focuses upon law as a mechanism through which the regulation of property relations is achieved, and the other gives priority to the role of law in the maintenance of class rule, that is, whereby the subordinate classes are repressed. These two variants identified by Hirst embody at the most general level the dualism between coercion and consent (Hirst 1979).

Hence it follows that, although considerable attention has been focused upon Gramscian trends in the theorization of law, the same problems and difficulties manifest themselves in other trends within Marxist theory of law. It is not intended to embark on a comprehensive survey of the different trends that can be identified; rather to focus attention upon two other influential tendencies: Pashukanis' theory of the "legal form" and Edward Thompson's historical antistructuralist analysis.

At first sight it appears most strange that early legal debates and controversies in the young Soviet Republic should have attracted so much attention in the 1970s. The writings of Evgeny Pashukanis have received special attention, and new translations have become available.[20] Their contemporary relevance manifests the general tendency within recent Marxist theory theory to construct its theory in such a manner as to avoid the accusations of simple economic and/or class reductions so frequently directed against Marxism by its critics. More specifically in relationship to the theory of law is that Pashukanis set out deliberately to advance a theoretical alternative to the prevailing orthodoxy of instrumentalism in which law is presented as an instrument to be wielded in the self-conscious pursuit of the interests of a dominant economic class. It is further not without significance that Pashukanis' attempt to found his theorization of law upon a sophisticated understanding and application of the methodology elaborated by Marx in the opening chapters of *Capital* coincides with the tendency of contemporary Marxism to reimmerse itself in detailed reading of and exegetical controversies around Marx's major theoretical texts. The reverberations and adaptions of Pashukanis in recent Marxist debates are exemplified in Balbus (1977), Picciotto (1979), Fine (1979), and Hirst (1979, 1980).

Pashukanis sought to go beyond the mere attribution of a class content to substantive law. In place of such limited analyses he proposed to derive the irreducibly bourgeois character of the legal from the indissoluble internal connection between the commodity exchange relationship and the legal form characterized by exchange relations between formally equal legal subjects. It is not my intention to examine the problems as-

[20]For many years the only available translation, and that a very defective one, was in Hazard (1951). More recently two very useful and much improved translations have become available: Pashukanis (1978) and Beirne and Sharlet (1980).

sociated with Pashukanis' derivation of the legal form from commodity relations,[21] but, rather, to examine its relation to the dualism of coercion and consent.

Pashukanis directed his critique explicitly against two trends in Marxist and sociological thought: the one places primary emphasis on the ideological dimension of law, the other upon the instrumental or coercive dimension. Although he did not express it in the terminology used here, it is clear that Pashukanis' object of attack is both wings of coercion-consent dualism. For him no mere combination of the contradictory elements of coercion and consent adequately provides a basis for the theorization of bourgeois law. To what extent did Pashukanis succeed in providing a theory that overcame the limitations of the dichotomous conceptions of law? With due recognition for the wider heuristic significance of Pashukanis' analysis of the legal form, it can only be concluded that, not only did he fail, but that, albeit in amended form, he reproduces the same dualism. Indeed, there is some evidence that he was himself aware of the problematic implications of his early commodity form analysis; the basis for this contention is to be found in subsequent modification and self-criticisms. Care should be taken about how much reliance should be placed upon these works because it is difficult to determine the extent to which these were self-criticisms or accommodations to Stalinist pressure.[22]

Pashukanis reproduces the dualistic analysis of law in the radical separation between private law and state law, particularly criminal law, upon which he insists. In combating legal positivism he insists upon the primacy of private law as an organic social form that has its origin in the juridic relation of separation and exchange between legal subjects within commodity relations. Thus all law is necessarily private law in that it is the embodiment of the relations of commodity exchange. This organic conception of law bears marked similarities to Eugene Ehrlich's sociological conception of the origin of law in spontaneous customary norms, although he does not, of course, lapse into the latter's metaphysical conception of essence of law residing in the social or popular will of a people (Ehrlich 1962).

In sharp contrast he retains a theory of the state as a coercive apparatus,

> bourgeois society supports its class state by its system of criminal law and thereby holds the exploited class in obedience. . . . The criminal jurisdiction of the bourgeois state is organised class terror (Beirne and Sharlet 1980, p. 115).

Thus he introduces a sharp polarity between two modes of law, the criminal law as a means of securing class domination and the civil law as the mechanism governing the exchange relations between atomized legal subjects.

He was not entirely unaware of the conflict between his express theoretical objective and his reproduction of that which he sought to replace. To provide a bridge that overcame the dualism between private law and state law, he introduces what is undoubtedly the weakest feature of his general theory. He subsumes his attempt to theorize state and criminal law into a theory of punishment.[23] His focus upon punishment allows

---

[21]See the following for important aspects of "the Pashukanis debate": Balbus (1977), Arthur (1977), Redhead (1978), Hirst (1979) and (1980), Picciotto (1979), and Fine (1979).

[22]See the discussion in Beirne and Sharlet (1980) and Redhead (1977) on the "interpretation" of the self-criticisms. Although the criticism of his positions became more vociferous after 1927, he remained a very powerful figure well into the 1930s. I am inclined to accord status to his writings up to about 1932; although after that his writings degenerate and are completely incompatible with his general theory.

[23]There is in this regard an illustrative parallel between Pashukanis and Durkheim. It is the most distinctive feature of Durkheim's sociology of law that his treatment of criminal law is reduced to a theory of punishment; this is most clearly evident in his "Two Laws of Penal Evolution" (Durkheim 1973), in which he sought to modify the earlier counterposition between mechanical and organic solidarity. It is precisely the absence of a theory of the state that led Durkheim to slide from criminal law to punishment in his analysis. In Pashukanis's case it is the contradiction between his commodity theory of private law and his Marxist-Leninist theory of the state that results in his slippage from criminal law to punishment.

him to erect a correspondence between the equivalence inherent in the commodity exchange, enshrined in the labor theory of value, and the "equivalence" established in punishment through the absolute divisibility of both imprisonment and monetary fines that characterizes punitive sanctions in bourgeois societies.[24] The weakness of his treatment lies precisely in the fact that the identity he seeks to establish lies in nothing more than the verbal equation achieved by the dual usage of equivalence and the assertion that the verbal correspondence evidences a real correspondence.

The identification of Pashukanis' failure to overcome the dualism between private law and state law, between coercion and consent, should not detract from the importance of his analysis of the legal form of exchange relations and its consequential role in modern legal systems. His failure is testimony to the intractable nature of the problem posed.

*   *   *

The other major trend within Marxist studies of law is epitomized by the interventions of Edward Thompson. It should be noted that there are important parallels between Thompson's work and the earlier discussion of the Gramscian theory of law. Thompson's work has a dual significance. It insists, first, upon the essential contribution of historical analysis as a primary characteristic of Marxist methodology and with it seeks to deny the possibility of general theoretical solutions that are divorced from concrete historical analysis. It will, however, argue that the very prominent critique of structuralist Marxism, in which Thompson requires Louis Althusser to stand in the dock on behalf of widely divergent positions, involves a theoretical position that no more satisfactorily resolves the problems that have formed the focus for this essay than the position that he seeks, through the most vivid polemic, to demolish. The second dimension of Thompson's intervention raises more directly than any of the positions that have been discussed throughout this essay the explicitly political implications of the theorization of law. It is a mark of the contemporaneous character of Thompson's historical work that whatever the historical period he studies, it is always linked to what he sees as currently important political questions. The politics of legal theory is highlighted in the current controversy over the "rule of law."

Thompson's impact on the field of Marxist legal theory is a result of the shift of his own concerns from the nineteenth to the eighteenth century. In *Whigs and Hunters* (Thompson 1975) and in the parallel volume *Albion's Fatal Tree*, the focus is upon the manner in which law and legal developments are implicated into the construction and constitution of the modern English society. The most general form of his conclusion is developed most fully by his collaborator Douglas Hay: law assumes preeminence in the course of the eighteenth century in so far as it became the most pervasive expression of the legitimizing ideology, replacing the role of religion in the preceding epoch and in constituting the new form of hegemony of the modern bourgeoisie (Hay 1975, pp. 55–56).[25] Thompson's individual study of "the Black Act" of 1723 starts quite deliberately with a period that marks the darkest, most repressive period in the history of English criminal law, expressed in the dramatic rise in the number of capital offences added to the statute books. Yet it is this repressive law, manifest in the Black Act, that Thompson chooses to employ against those he accuses of reducing law to a direct expression of class rule.[26] The contemporary political impli-

---

[24]An interesting line of comparison is suggested by the striking similarity in emphasis upon the divisibility of punishment and its association with conceptions of "responsibility" that are to be found, respectively, in Durkheim, Pashukanis, and more recently in Foucault (1977).

[25]Exactly the same thesis was advanced by Poulantzas: "The centre of legitimacy shifts away from the sacred towards legality" (1979, p. 87).

[26]Thompson's method of criticism of his opponents is fraught with problems; the "some Marxists," "structural Marxists," and "theoretical illiterates" that haunt his waking hours, and from the intensity of his polemic, probably his sleeping hours as well, are disembodied creatures whose actual positions are never addressed. Rather, these figures do service as leaden caricatures to be ridiculed through his

cation should not be missed: as the 1980s open with conservatism in the ascendant and with the banner of "law and order" at the head of their advance, the temptation to see law as a direct expression of "their interests must be resisted."

The reality of law reveals a deep paradox:

> It is true that the law did mediate existent class relations to the advantage of the rulers. . . . On the other hand, the law mediated these class relations through legal forms, which imposed again and again, inhibitions upon the actions of the rulers (Thompson 1975, p. 264).

It is the task of historiography and of theory to explore and expound this paradox and to draw out its implications for current political practice. My objective in discussing Thompson is to examine two aspects of his writing: first, to examine the theoretical treatment of the paradox of law and, second, to consider the politics of law that he advances.

The question that must be addressed to Thompson's theoretical position is the extent to which he succeeds in breathing substance into the paradoxical historical reality of law. The investigation of the paradox may, on the other hand, reduce itself to yet another version of the ubiquitous dichotomy that has been traced in this essay through such an array of disparate authors.

Thompson's onslaught against "schematic Marxism" revolves around their application of the base–superstructure metaphor. If law is pigeon-holed as part of the superstructure, it can only be a dependent entity adjusting itself to the requirements of the economic infrastructure. On the contrary, he insists that far from being separated off within a dependent superstructure:

law as deeply imbricated within the very basis of productive relations, which would have been inoperable without this law (1975, p. 261).

Yet in *Whigs and Hunters* Thompson offers no alternative to the discredited reductionism of base and superstructure.

These theoretical issues are taken up again in the iconoclastic text of *The Poverty of Theory* (1978). Here he announces a more ambitious project: to restore Marxism to its original inspiration as historical materialism by saving it from the distortion introduced by Marx's obsessive concern with the critique of bourgeois political economy. The sins of Althusser can be traced to this vice in the old man. But in belaboring Althusser with every argument that can be pressed into service, Thompson, to avoid the risk of contamination, also dispenses with the need for close examination of the concepts he deploys. One senses that he experiences some discomfort at realizing that much of Althusser's project amounts to an attempt to provide some conceptual and theoretical clothes on the frame of Marx's and Engels' tentative formulations of "relative autonomy," for Thompson has long insisted upon "relative autonomy" to rebut economistic interpretations, "a helpful talisman against reductionism" (1978a, p. 289). To establish his distance Thompson, in his overtly theoretical text, finds the means of differentiation in the term "human experience" as the:

> necessary middle term between social being and social consciousness. . . . It is by means of experience that the mode of production exerts a determining pressure upon other activities (ibid., p. 290).

Human experience does service as "the missing link" whose mission it is to overcome the aridity of Althusser's determinism. Yet the extraordinary feature of Thompson's solution, which without a trace of even false modesty, he likens to Mendel's genetic solution to Darwin's unspecified process of transmutation of species, is that having been unveiled before his expectant audience, it undergoes no examination and no elaboration.

---

splendid polemic. For example, I am very fond of his dig at Althusser: "when I close my eyes and think of what an 'ideological state apparatus' might look like I can only think of Robin Day" [T.V. current affairs journalist] (Thompson, p. 9). Dashing though the polemic is, it intrudes to such an extent that it violates the principle of taking one's adversaries seriously. I do not see it as my task to defend Thompson's adversaries, but to note its limiting effects on his arguments.

The actual role fulfilled by Thompson's "human experience" is twofold. At the most general it necessitates the reaffirmation of historiography as the primary root to social knowledge and understanding; it is historical study rather than theoretical discourse that generates new knowledge. It is important to emphasize the contradictory dimension of this celebration of historical study. The positive dimension is to be found in the very encouraging trend in recent sociology of law to engage in detailed historical studies of the development and effectivity of law for which Thompson's own study, *Whigs and Hunters*, will long remain a major beacon and measure of achievement. But on the other hand, Thompson's procedure is far less acceptable insofar as he advances historical study as a proof of his solution of the great intellectual problem of social causation. In theoretical terms it is no solution and is certainly far less thought out than that offered by Althusser or, for that matter, by his own ally Raymond Williams (1977, pp. 83–89), or by G. A. Cohen (1978), or even by that advanced within the Althusserian tradition by Erik Olin Wright (1978). In the absence of any theoretical solution, what remains is Thompson's vivid imagery of the contradictory reality of law:

> I found that law did not keep politely to a "level" but was at *every* bloody level; it was imbricated within the mode of production and productive relations themselves (as property rights, definitions of agrarian practice) and it was simultaneously present in the philosophy of Locke; it intruded brusquely within alien categories, reappearing bewigged and gowned in the guise of ideology; it danced a cotillion with religion, moralising over the theatre of Tyburn; it was an arm of politics and politics was one of its arms; it was an academic discipline, subjected to the rigour of its own autonomous logic; it contributed to the definition of the self-identity both of rulers and ruled; above all, it afforded an arena for class struggle, within which alternative notions of law were fought out (1978a, p. 288).

Behind this dazzling inventory lies our old friend the dichotomy between coercion and consent.

We must at the end of a long journey relish and value the historical insights of his work, but adjudge him to have committed a grave theoretical misrepresentation in that he fails to resolve the paradox of law but breathes fresh life into the dichotomous conception of law.

* * *

I have argued that the different trends in recent discussions about law exhibit a range of responses concerning the contemporary politics of law. One of the major elements that accounts for the impact of Thompson's recent writings is the explicitly political implications that he draws out and has subsequently elaborated. The concluding chapter of *Whigs and Hunters* seeks to derive contemporary lessons concerning the rule of law. His argument is mounted against "orthodox Marxism," which he accuses, in the main I believe with justification, of adopting the position that:

> the rule of law is only another mask for the rule of class. The revolutionary can have no interest in law, unless as a phenomenon of ruling-class power and hypocrisy; it should simply be his aim to overthrow it (1975, p. 259).

This critique of the Left's response to law is made more explicit in subsequent writings and is applied to current controversies within the politics of law: the defence of the jury as a profoundly democratic institution, opposition to jury vetting, state trials and state secrets, and police powers (Thompson 1978b, 1979, and 1980). These contemporary interventionist essays raise two separable but related sets of questions. The first concerns the orientation of radicals and socialists to the role of law in modern capitalist democracies, and the second concerns the role of law and legality in socialist societies.

I have argued that modern sociology of law exhibits, more or less directly, concerns with the politics of law. It is not surprising that those writing in the context of the Marxist tradition are more explicit and directly concerned with the political implications of their positions. The position of liberal and non-Marxist writers reveals a marked pessimism concerning the trajectory of law in contemporary society. This concern is mirrored in Thompson's writings but is given a very distinctive and much more optimistic inflection.

Thompson broadly accepts that current of recent discussion that points toward the emergence of more authoritarian forms of state power within the capitalist democracies. His dispute with "orthodox Marxism" is that he accuses it of sitting back and complacently interpreting these trends as conformation of the necessarily repressive character of the bourgeois state. This position further results in a cynical lack of concern with the politics of law encouraging a denunciatory response to the erosion of civil liberties; its emphasis is to greet such developments as the shedding of the consensual mask of capitalist law and state to reveal, ever more starkly, its repressive essence.

The root of the disagreement with orthodox Marxism lies in radically different conceptions of the lineage and historical role of class societies. Orthodox Marxism presents each phase of class society (slavery, feudalism, capitalism) as replacing one form of class domination by another; each system of class dominance exhibits state forms that are overturned by the succeeding class to be replaced by a form appropriate to its class interests. The capitalist state and capitalist law are the form appropriate to the maintenance of its class domination. Hence the task of socialist action is to remove capitalist law and state and to replace it with socialist law and state. There is no continuity between the different orders, and any defence of elements within capitalism, except for purely tactical reasons, can only breed illusions and obscure the necessity of the ultimate goal of smashing the bourgeois state. The result:

> the ambivalence *within the "Left"* towards civil liberties is the most alarming evidence of all that the libertarian nerve has become dulled (1978b, p. 10).

Thompson's scenario is radically different: the achievement of class power by the bourgeoisie, and the advent of the rule of law that was one of its major achievements, was an aspect of "revolutionary inheritance" (1979, p. 8). The kernel of the radical and democratic content of civil liberties and the rule of law remains even though it is also at risk in the current stage from the hands of the bourgeoisie and their state and political institutions. The bourgeois epoch heralded an advance on the long haul toward freedom; bourgeois freedom has always been limited in its development by social and economic inequality, on the one hand, and the narrow integument of the formalism that marks bourgeois legalism. The more the limited gains of the bourgeois inheritance are threatened, the more is it politically essential for socialism, as the inheritor of the radical democratic transition. His writings are peppered with reference to the "free-born Englishman"; a major part of Thompson's socialist humanism rests on his insistence that this radical democratic legacy persists and in it resides "the peculiarities of the English" (Thompson 1965), and that it can be reignited in the name of a political perspective that is at one and the same time democratic, humanist, and socialist.

Within Thompson's general perspective the politics of law take on its specific significance. His position is encapsulated in two formulations that take on something of the quality of slogans: "law matters" and "the rule of law seems to me to be an unqualified human good" (1975, p. 266). The first slogan points toward the need for socialists to intervene in the politics of law: to defend the jury, to protect civil liberties, to advance affirmative legislation, and so on. The more controversial and important position that he advances concerns "the rule of law." The controversial character of his position derives from its rejection of the almost instinctive response of the Left to regard the rule of law as a prime example of an ideological fiction, to be denounced and exposed along with the separation of powers and judicial neutrality as the most transparent guises of bourgeois constitutionalism. What Thompson defends in the name of the rule of law is not entirely clear or consistent. Certainly he tends to conflate the rule of law and civil liberty; thereby he hangs the defence of the former on the more self-evident defence of the latter. But he also emphasizes the importance of the rule of law as constituting a mechanism of restraint upon rulers. He adds a further dimension by proposing a conception of the rule of law as constituting a framework within which the class struggle can be fought out. The implications of Thompson's thesis in defence of the rule of law have not received systematic attention, but the need is revealed as soon as importance of its implications become clear; the great importance of his intervention lies precisely in the fact that it is now placed firmly on the contemporary political and intellectual agenda of the Left.

The second dimension of Thompson's excursions into the politics of law, and most directly through his treatment of the rule of law, is the question of the relationship between law and socialism. Thompson's position is a manifestation of his response to "actual socialism," and his anti-Stalinism takes the form of a declaration of faith in the inseparable connection between legality and democracy and the centrality of socialist legality and socialist democracy in a future socialist society. Thompson refuses the apparently libertarian perspective offered, for example, by Pashukanis, of identifying the emergence of an explicitly nonlegal social order as the basis for founding advanced participatory democracy. These issues play a limited role in Thompson's argument, yet their presence adds a wider perspective. My intention in drawing attention to them is to stress that the debate about the trajectory of law has for socialists this added dimension in which law constitutes a "problem" raising difficult issues concerning the nature of the socialist project. It is in this context that his perspective on the politics of law is, on the one hand, activist stressing law as an arena of struggle, and indeed has led him to direct involvement therein; but, on the other hand, there is an absence concerning the theorization of the rule of legality under socialism. Thus, despite his insistence that his perspective is not restricted to a defensive strug-

gle to retain bourgeois legality and civil liberties, the strategic direction remains cloudy and ill-defined. This problem of identifying a strategic direction for the politics of law poses an important challenge to those who stand by Thompson's insistence on the contemporary significance of legal politics but have reservations concerning his failure to explore more fully the different dimensions of "the rule of law" and its wider implications for socialist strategy.

CONCLUSION

The examination of the major trends within recent sociological theories of law has revealed the enduring presence within the different theoretical perspectives of a dichotomous conception of law organized around the polar opposition between coercion and consent. It has been argued that at one level to conceptualize law in terms of the dimensions of coercion and consent succeeds in embracing important characteristics of law. Yet none of the positions examined succeeds in advancing a coherent presentation of a mode of combination of the apparently opposed characteristics of law so as to produce a unitary conception not reducible to a choice between opposites or a fluctuation between them. On the contrary, each of the positions examined is forced to make a choice, conscious or otherwise, between the polarities. Liberal theorists have understandably opted for attaching primacy to the consensual dimension or potential of law. For very different reasons recent Marxist theories, in reaction to positions that had previously held sway within Marxism, have also been anxious to give emphasis to the consensual facet of law.

Thus by different roots and within the logic of their respective theoretical frameworks, both trends exhibit major elements of continuity. One important consequence of this marked parallelism between liberal and Marxist theories of law is that it creates the conditions that make possible a meaningful and potentially fruitful dialogue. The greater the recognition that can be achieved of the proximity of their theoretical concerns, the greater will be the motivation toward the engagement in this dialogue. The emergence and clarification of theoretical problems is not unconnected with the more explicit concern with and attention to the politics of law. Sociology of law is emerging from a period in which its primary concerns were limited to the internal examination of the "legal process" within a largely taken-for-granted social engineering set of assumptions, while the realist tradition has been shown to have continuing effects that reinforce and bolster this narrow conception of the role of sociological study of law. The persistence in widely different positions of some conception of a crisis of law or legal order has given rise, despite the lack of clarity or agreement as to the nature of "the crisis," to a more conscious concern with the wider problem of the part played by law within the social order and thus with the politics of law.

BIBLIOGRAPHY

Althusser, Louis (1971). "Ideology and Ideological State Apparatuses," in *Lenin and Philosophy*, New Left Books, London.

Anderson, Perry (1976–1977). "The Antinomies of Antonio Gramsci," in 100 *New Left Review* 5–94.

Arthur, Chris (1977). "Towards a Materialist Theory of Law," in 7 *Critique* 31.

Balbus, Isaac (1973). *The Dialectics of Legal Repression: Black Rebels Before the American Criminal Courts*, Russell Sage, New York.

Balbus, Isaac (1977). "Commodity Form and Legal Form," in 11(3) *Law and Society Review* 871–888.

Beirne, P., and Sharlet, R. (1980). *Pashukanis: Selected Writings on Marxism and Law*, Academic Press, London, tr. P. Maggs.

Black, Donald (1972). "The Boundaries of Legal Sociology," 81 *Yale Law Journal* 1086.

Black, Donald (1976). *The Behavior of Law*, Academic Press, New York.

Cain, Maureen, and Hunt, Alan (1979). *Marx and Engels on Law*, Academic Press, London.

Center for Research on Criminal Justice (1975). *The Iron Fist and the Velvet Glove*, Center for Research on Criminal Justice, Berkeley.

Cohen, G. A. (1978). *Karl Marx's Theory of History: A Defence*, Oxford University Press, London.

Corrigan, Philip (1975). "Dichotomy Is Contradiction" 23 *Sociological Review* 211–243.

Currie, Elliot (1971). "Sociology of Law: The Unasked Questions," 81 *Yale Law Journal* 134–147.

Dahrendorf, Ralf (1959). *Class and Class Conflict in an Industrial Society*, Routledge and Kegan Paul, London.

Durkheim, Emile (1973). "Two Laws of Penal Evolution" 2 *Economy and Society* 285–308.

Eder, Klaus (1977). "Rationalist and Normative Approaches to the Sociological Study of Law," in 12, *Law and Society*, 133–144.

Ehrlich, Eugen (1967). *Fundamental Principles of the Sociology of Law*, Russell and Russell, New York.

Fine, Bob et al. (1979). *Capitalism and the Rule of Law*, Hutchinson, London.

Fine, Bob (1979). "Law and Class," in Fine et al. (1979).

Foucault, Michel (1977). *Discipline and Punish*, Allen Lane, London.

Gramsci, Antonio (1971). *Selections from the Prison Notebooks*, Lawrence and Wishart, London.

Hall, S. et al (1978) *Policing the Crisis: Mugging, the State, and Law and Order*, Macmillan, London.

Hay, D. et al. (1975). *Albion's Fatal Tree: Crime and Society in Eighteenth Century England*, Penguin, Harmondsworth.

Hay, Douglas (1975). "Property, Authority and the Criminal Law," in Hay et al. (1975).

Hayek, F. A. (1973). *Law, Legislation and Liberty: Vol. I: Rules and Order*, Routledge and Kegan Paul, London.

Hayek, F. A. (1976). *Law, Legislation and Libety: Vol. II: The Mirage of Social Justice*, Routledge and Kegan Paul, London.

Hayek, F. A. (1979). *Law, Legislation and Liberty: Vol. III: The Political Order of a Free People*, Routledge and Kegan Paul, London.

Hazard, John (1951). *Soviet Legal Philosophy*, Harvard University Press, Cambridge, Mass.

Hirst, Paul (1979). "The Law of Property and Marxism," in Hirst, Paul, *On Law and Ideology*, Macmillan, London.

Hirst, Paul (1980). "Law, Socialism and Rights," in Carlen & Collison (Eds.), *Radical Issues in Criminology*, Martin Robertson, Oxford.

Holmes, O. W. (1897). "The Path of Law," 10 *Harvard Law Review* 457–478.

Hunt, Alan (1976). "Perspectives in the Sociology of Law," in Carlen, P. (Ed.), *Sociology of Law*, Sociological Review Monographs, No. 23, Keele.

Hunt, Alan (1978). *The Sociological Movement in Law*, Macmillan, London; Temple University Press, Philadelphia.

Hunt, Alan (1979). "The Sociology of Law of Gurvitch and Timasheff: A Critique of Theories of Normative Integration," in Spitzer, S. (Ed.), *Research in Law and Sociology*.

Jenkins, Iredell (1980). *Social Order and the Limits of Law*, Princeton University Press, Princeton, N.J.

Jessop, Bob (1977). "Recent Theories of the Capitalist State," 1 *Cambridge Journal of Economics*, 353–373.

Kamenka, Eugene, and Tay, Alice (1975). "Beyond Bourgeois Individualism: the Contemporary Crisis in Law and Legal Ideology," in Kamenka, E., and Neale, R. S. (Eds.), *Feudalism, Capitalism & Beyond*, Edward Arnold, London.

Marx, Karl (1969). *Grundrisse*, Penguin, Harmondsworth.

Mitzman, K. (1970). *The Iron Cage: An Historical Interpretation of Max Weber*, Knopf, New York.

Parsons, Talcott (1977). "Review of Unger's *Law in Modern Society*," 12(1) *Law and Society Review* 133–149.

Pashukanis, Evgeny B. *Law and Marxism: A General Theory*, Ink Links, London.

Picciotto, Sol (1979). "The Theory of the State, Class Struggle and the Rule of Law," in Fine, B. et al., *Capitalism and the Rule of Law*, Hutchinson, London.

Poulantzas, N. (1978). *State, Power, Socialism*, New Left Books, London.

Redhead, Steve (1978). "The Discrete Charm of Bourgeois Law," in 9 *Critique* 113–120.

Schmitter and Lembruch (1980). *Trends Towards Corporatist Intermediation*, Sage, London.

Therborn, Goran (1976). *Science, Class and Society*, New Left Books, London.

Thompson, E. P. (1965). "The Peculiarities of the English," *The Socialist Register*.

Thompson, E. P. (1975). *Whigs and Hunters: The Origin of the Black Act*, Penguin and Pantheon, New York.

Thompson, E. P. (1978a). *The Poverty of Theory*, Merlin, London.

Thompson, E. P. (1978b). "Introduction" to Friedman, J. *Review of Security and the State*, State Research, London.

Thompson, E. P. (1979). "Rule of Law in English History," in 10 *Haldane Society Bulletin* 7–10 (Spring).

Thompson, E. P. (1980). *Writing by Candlelight*, Merlin, London.

Timasheff, N. S. (1940). *An Introduction to the Sociology of Law*, Harvard University Press, Cambridge, Mass.

Trubek, David (1972a). "Max Weber on Law and the Rise of Capitalism," 3 *Wisconsin Law Review* 720–753.

Trubek, David (1972b). "Toward a Social Theory of Law," 82(1) *Yale Law Journal* 1–50.

Trubek, David (1977). "Complexity and Contradiction in Legal Order," 11 *Law and Society Review* 529–569.

Unger, Roberto (1975). *Knowledge and Politics*, Free Press, New York.

Unger, Roberto (1976). *Law in Modern Society*, Free Press, New York.

Williams, Raymond (1977). *Marxism and Literature*, Oxford University Press, London.

Winkler, John (1975). "Corporatism," 2 *British Journal of Law and Society*.

Wright, Erik Olin (1978). *Class, Crisis and the State*, New Left Books, London.

CHAPTER TWO

LAW AND CLASS

The selections in this chapter address the problem of the historical specificity of law as a form of social regulation. Why does law appear so conducive to the rule of capital? Readers should be aware that this basic question leads quickly to a region that until recently was theorized as "reform *or* revolution?" Some writers have suggested that by its very nature law is an inherently bourgeois form of social regulation. If this is true, then the attempt to provide legislation with a socialist content is a self-defeating strategy for the socialist movement. On the other hand, if law is an arena of active class struggle in which gains and losses can potentially be made by any of the contending classes, then legal struggles under capitalism are of immense importance.

In "Property, Authority and the Criminal Law," the historian Douglas Hay offers us a brilliant interpretation of the subtle interplay between property, forms of personal dependence, and criminal law in eighteenth-century England. Hay shows us how law assumed such unusual dominance in England as the main legitimizing ideology that displaced the religious authority of previous centuries. Why was it, he asks, that the number of capital offences for crimes against property increased nearly fourfold between 1688 and 1820, and, simultaneously, an increasing number of convictions for theft was not accompanied by an increase in the number of executions? His answer reveals that this paradox has less to do with the regulation of crime than with the maintenance of property relations. Hay vividly documents that the criminal statutes were part of a practice surrounded by the elements of terror, majesty, justice, and mercy. The rhetoric of the death sentence, the ever-present sanction of the gallows, the localized and personal system by which the rural poor (and occasionally the gentry) were convicted, often released on technicalities, or pardoned—all these produced a chaotic system by which respect for property and property owners was effected through the rule of law. So successful was the particular system of criminal law—a system that ensured political domination of the poor without the need for a police force or a large standing army—that its ultimate intention cannot be seen in terms of its physical control of rural populations. It must, much more, be understood as a mechanism for enforcing the moral and psychic domination of the gentry, and, therefore, of property.

The second reading is E. P. Thompson's now famous conclusion to *Whigs and Hunters*. This offers a timely rejoinder to those who consider law to be simply an outgrowth of class power and therefore to be ignored. In the 25 years since the Hungarian uprising of 1956—in such books as *The Making of the English Working Class* and *The Poverty of Theory,* and in the pages of *The New Reasoner, New Left Review,* and *The New Statesman*—there has not been a more fervent and gifted opponent of Stalinism (and champion of radical populism) in the socialist movement than the pen of E. P. Thompson. As Steve Redhead documents in the last chapter of *Marxism and Law,* the focus of the controversy that now surrounds Thompson's work is the thorny status of civil rights and liberties in class societies.

Thompson provides us with a compelling and provocative thesis in "The Rule of Law." He argues that it is true that law mediates class relations to the advantage of the rulers. But it is also true, in countless cases, that law has imposed inhibitions on the rulers. Law mystifies class rule, but its rhetoric and rules are a great deal more than mere sham. There are, he therefore continues, profound differences between extralegal power and the rule of law. The rule of law itself—its imposition of effective inhibitions upon power and the defence of the citizen from power's all-intrusive claims—Thompson asserts to be an unqualified human good. To deny or to belittle this good is a desparate error of intellectual abstraction, a self-fulfilling error that disarms us before power and that discards a whole inheritance of struggle *about* law.

The next essay is a detailed historical analysis of a piece of legislation and the rise of organized labor, and the profound effects that these wrought on the political economy of the United States. In "Judicial Deradicalization of the Wagner Act and the Origins of Modern Legal Consciousness, 1937-1941," Karl Klare examines the deradicalization and incorporation of the American working class through, and as revealed in, the Supreme Court's early Wagner Act decisions. Klare stresses that the initial history of the Wagner Act must be understood as a radical and democratic device. Klare shows that the Act represented real gains for the working class in that it guaranteed certain aspects of labor activity and collective bargaining. The Act was enacted only after arduous working class struggles against the interests of capital and despite its bitter opposition. But Klare also reveals how the subsequent judicial interpretation of the Act by the Supreme Court was adapted to the needs of capital. The question of which readers ought now to be aware, as Klare warns, is whether collective bargaining established in law can ever be anything other than an institutionalized structure, not for the expression of working class interests, but for controlling and disciplining the labor force and for rationalizing the labor market.

Because legal reform culminated in the consolidation of the oppression of workers, Klare leaves us with the conclusion that capitalist law is an expression of the same alienation that characterizes capitalist social relations in general: "one cannot expect that work will be emancipated from its alienated character without the abolition of the social relations, including legal relations, that produce that character."

Sol Picciotto's "The Theory of the State, Class Struggle and the Rule of Law" inveighs against Thompson that debate over the rule of law seldom travels beyond the ambiguous dichotomy of coercion and legitimacy. The demand for the rule of law—in such periods as the social and economic crisis of the 1970s—expresses either a demand for the application of coercion in social relations, or for the control of such coercion through the due process of law. Picciotto asserts that we must begin elsewhere in our analysis if we are to understand the specific ways in which law mediates class relations. In so doing Picciotto returns us to the analysis of the historical development of legal forms. Picciotto reminds us that class struggle is the basic source for the "liberalization" of state and legal forms. But the development of more adequate forms of regulation "can only contain the underlying contradictions of capital, at a higher and more acutely contradictory level of development." Against Thompson he warns that although trial by jury, for example, is better than trial by ordeal, this improvement must not prevent us from seeing its bourgeois characteristics and hence its limitations. The working class movement, he concludes, must strive not to uphold the unattainable ideals of the rule of law, but to transcend them in ways that challenge the dominance of capitalist social relations themselves.

PROPERTY, AUTHORITY AND THE CRIMINAL LAW

DOUGLAS HAY

I

The rulers of eighteenth-century England cherished the death sentence. The oratory we remember now is the parliamentary speech, the Roman periods of Fox or Burke, that stirred the gentry and the merchants. But outside Parliament were the labouring poor, and twice a year, in most counties in England, the scarlet-robed judge of assize put the black cap of death on top of his full-bottomed wig to expound the law of the propertied, and to execute their will. . . .

This was the climactic moment in a system of criminal law based on *terror:* "if we diminish the terror of house-breakers," wrote Justice Christian of Ely in 1819, "the terror of the innocent inhabitants must be increased, and the comforts of domestic life must be greatly destroyed." He himself had dogs, firearms, lights and bells at his own country home, and took a brace of double-barrelled pistols to bed with him every night. But his peace of mind mostly rested on the knowledge that the death sentence hung over anyone who broke in to steal his silver plate. A regular police force did not exist, and the gentry would not tolerate even the idea of one. They remembered the pretensions of the Stuarts and the days of the Commonwealth, and they saw close at hand how the French monarchy controlled its subjects with spies and informers. In place of police, however, propertied Englishmen had a fat and swelling sheaf of laws which threatened thieves with death. The most recent account suggests that the number of capital statutes grew from about 50 to over 200 between the years 1688 and 1820.[1] Almost all of them concerned offences against property.

This flood of legislation is one of the great facts of the eighteenth century, and it occurred in the period when peers and gentry held power with least hindrance from Crown or people. The Glorious Revolution of 1688 established the freedom not of men, but of men of property. Its apologist, John Locke, distorted the oldest arguments of natural law to justify the liberation of wealth from all political or moral controls; he concluded that the unfettered accumulation of money, goods and land was sanctioned by Nature and, implicitly, by God. Henceforth among triumphant Whigs, and indeed all men on the right side of the great gulf between rich and poor, there was little pretence that civil society was concerned primarily with peace or justice or charity. Even interests of state and the Divine Will had disappeared. Property had swallowed them all: "Government," declared Locke, "has no other end but the preservation of property."[2] Most later writers accepted the claim uncritically.

Source: From Douglas Hay, Peter Linebaugh, John G. Rule, E. P. Thompson, and Cal Winslow, *Albion's Fatal Tree* (New York: Pantheon Books, 1975), pp. 17-63. Reprinted by permission.

[1] Sir Leon Radzinowicz, *A History of English Criminal Law and its Administration from 1750,* 4 vols., 1948-68, vol. I, p. 4.

[2] *The Second Treatise of Government,* 1690, sections 85 and 94.

William Blackstone, the most famous eighteenth-century writer on the law and constitution, declared it self-evident that "there is nothing which so generally strikes the imagination, and engages the affections of mankind, as the right of property; or that sole and despotic dominion which one man claims and exercises over the external things of the world, in total exclusion of the right of any other individual in the universe."[3] The common and statute law, it seems, extended throughout not only England but the cosmos. When Christian edited the twelfth edition of Blackstone's *Commentaries on the Laws of England* in 1793, he reduced the claim only a little, to "that law of property, which nature herself has written upon the hearts of all mankind."

Once property had been officially deified, it became the measure of all things. Even human life was weighed in the scales of wealth and status: "the execution of a needy decrepit assassin," wrote Blackstone, "is a poor satisfaction for the murder of a nobleman in the bloom of his youth, and full enjoyment of his friends, his honours, and his fortune." Again and again the voices of money and power declared the sacredness of property in terms hitherto reserved for human life. Banks were credited with souls, and the circulation of gold likened to that of blood. Forgers, for example were almost invariably hanged, and gentlemen knew why: "Forgery is a stab to commerce, and only to be tolerated in a commercial nation when the foul crime of murder is pardoned."[4] In a mood of unrivalled assurance and complacency, Parliament over the century created one of the bloodiest criminal codes in Europe. Few of the new penalties were the product of hysteria, or ferocious reaction; they were part of the conventional wisdom of England's governors. Locke himself defined political power as the right to create the penalty of death, and hence all lesser ones. And Shaftesbury, the enlightened rationalist who attacked both Hobbes and the Church for making fear the cement of the social order, at the same time accepted that the "mere Vulgar of Mankind" might perhaps "often stand in need of such a rectifying Object as *the Gallows* before their Eyes."

Eighteenth-century lawyers were well aware that never before had the legislature passed such a mass of new capital statutes so quickly. They floundered, however, when seeking for explanations. Many men, including learned ones, blamed the ever-increasing depravity of the people. In the 1730s Lord Chancellor Hardwicke blamed "the degeneracy of human nature"; almost a century later, Justice Christian indicted "the wicked inventions, and the licentious practices of modern times." He drew a picture of a besieged government gradually making harsh new penalties as outrages demonstrated the uselessness of the old. But other observers were aware that the larger changes of trade, commerce and manufacturing might have something to do with the increasing weight of the statute book. Justice Daines Barrington cited "the increase of trade": the great circulation of new and valuable commodities made any comparison of England's laws with those of other states unsound, for "till a country can be found, which contains equal property and riches, the conclusion cannot be a just one." In similar vein, the editor of the sixth edition of Hawkins's *Pleas of the Crown* wrote in 1788 that "the increase of commerce, opulence, and luxury" since the first edition of 1715 "has introduced a variety of temptations to fraud and rapine, which the legislature has been forced to repel, by a multiplicity of occasional statutes, creating new offences and afflicting additional punishments."

Undoubtedly this is a more persuasive explanation than "degeneracy." The constant extension of inland and foreign trade from the late seventeenth century, the exploitation of new mines, the wealth of London and the spas and the growth of population all increased the opportunities for theft. The relationship of each of these factors to the level of crime is still uncertain; indeed, whether there was any increase in the amount of theft *per capita* is the subject of current

---

[3]William Blackstone, *Commentaries on the Laws of England* (12th ed. by Edward Christian), 1793–5, vol. II, p. 2.

[4]John Holliday, *The Life of Lord Mansfield*, 1797, p. 149.

research. What is certain is that Parliament did not often enact the new capital statutes as a matter of conscious public policy. Usually there was no debate, and most of the changes were related to specific, limited property interests, hitherto unprotected for one reason or another. Often they were the personal interest of a few members, and the Lords and Commons enacted them for the mere asking.

Three bills from mid-century illustrate the process. An act of 1753 prescribing hanging for stealing shipwrecked goods was brought in on behalf of the "Merchants, Traders and Insurers of the City of London" whose profits were being diminished by the activities of wreckers; the existing laws were declared to be too gentle. In 1764 Parliament decreed that the death penalty would apply to those who broke into buildings to steal or destroy linen, or the tools to make it, or to cut it in bleaching-grounds. But the penalties were contained in an incidental clause in an act passed to incorporate the English Linen Company, whose proprietors included Lord Verney and the Right Honourable Charles Townshend, the death penalty was routinely added to protect their investments. Finally, a law of 1769 suggests how the class that controlled Parliament was using the criminal sanction to enforce two of the radical redefinitions of property which gentlemen were making in their own interests during the eighteenth century. The food riot was an organized and often highly disciplined popular protest against the growing national and international market in foodstuffs, a market which alarmed the poor by moving grain from their parishes when it could compel a higher price elsewhere, and which depended on a growing corps of middlemen whom the rioters knew were breaking Tudor and Stuart legislation by wholesale trading in food. Country gentlemen often tolerated such a "riot," or at least handled it sensibly, but Parliament was not prepared to let property suffer.[5] Some mills had been torn down

in the nation-wide riots of 1766 and 1767, and the 1769 act plugged a gap in the law by making such destruction a capital offence. If death for food rioters was an excellent idea, so was transportation for enclosure rioters. Within three days the bill was enlarged so that gentlemen busy on the expropriation of common lands by Act of Parliament were as well protected as the millers. By the time the bill became law two weeks later, it had also become a transportable offence to meddle with the bridges and steam-engines used in the mines which were bringing ever-increasing revenues to the gentry and aristocracy. As the decades passed, the maturing trade, commerce and industry of England spawned more laws to protect particular kinds of property. Perhaps the most dramatic change in the organizational structure of British capital was the growth of promissory notes on banks as a medium of exchange, and the increase in negotiable paper of all kinds. This new creation was exposed to fraud in many ways never foreseen by the ancient criminal law. The result was a rash of capital statutes against forgeries and frauds of all kinds, laws which multiplied towards the end of the century.

These, then, were the legal instruments which enforced the division of property by terror. They were not the largest parts of the law—much more dealt with land, "with its long and voluminous train of descents and conveyances, settlements, entails, and incumbrances," and commerce, for which the eighteenth-century judges at last created a coherent framework.[6] The financial details of the marriage settlement, so often the sacrament by which land allied itself with trade, provided the best lawyers with a good part of their fees. But if most of the law and the lawyers were concerned with the civil dealings which propertied men had with one another, most men, the unpropertied labouring poor, met the law as criminal sanction: the threat or the reality of whipping, transportation and hanging. Death had long been a punishment for theft in England, and several of the most important statutes were passed in Tudor times. But the gentry and mer-

[5]E. P. Thompson, "The Moral Economy of the English Crowd in the Eighteenth Century," *Past and Present*, no. 50, February 1971, pp. 76–136.

[6]Blackstone, *Commentaries*, vol. I, p. 6.

chants and peers who sat in Parliament in the eighteenth century set new standards of legislative industry, as they passed act after act to keep the capital sanction up to date, to protect every conceivable kind of property from theft or malicious damage.[7]

Yet two great questions hang over this remarkable code. The first concerns the actual number of executions. The available evidence suggests that, compared to some earlier periods, the eighteenth-century criminal law claimed few lives. At the beginning of the seventeenth century, for example, it appears that London and Middlesex saw four times as many executions as 150 years later. Equally interesting is the fact that in spite of the growth in trade and population, the increasing number of convictions for theft, and the continual creation of new capital statutes throughout the eighteenth century, the number of executions for offences against property remained relatively stable, especially after 1750. The numbers of executions did not increase to match the number of convictions because of the increasing use of the royal pardon, by which transportation could be substituted for hanging, on the recommendation of the judges. Sir Leon Radzinowicz, in the most complete study of the subject, has shown that in London and Middlesex the proportion of death sentences commuted increased as the century progressed. He has argued that Parliament intended their legislation to be strictly enforced, and that the judges increasingly vitiated that intention by extending pardons freely.[8] But this is an unsatisfactory conclusion. A conflict of such magnitude between Parliament and the judiciary would have disrupted eighteenth-century politics, and nothing of the sort happened. With few exceptions, gentlemen

congratulated themselves on living in a century when the bench was wise and incorruptible, one of the glories of the constitution. Secondly, we shall see that the men who controlled Parliament were precisely those who usually brought their influence to bear in requesting pardons for condemned convicts from the judges and the king. We have yet to explain the coexistence of bloodier laws and increased convictions with a declining proportion of death sentences that were actually carried out.

This first problem is related to a second one. Most historians and many contemporaries argued that the policy of terror was not working. More of those sentenced to death were pardoned than were hanged; thieves often escaped punishment through the absence of a police force, the leniency of prosecutors and juries, and the technicalities of the law; transported convicts were so little afraid that they often returned to England to pick pockets on hanging days; riot was endemic. The critics of the law argued that the gibbets and corpses paradoxically weakened the enforcement of the law; rather than terrifying criminals, the death penalty terrified prosecutors and juries, who feared committing judicial murder on the capital statutes. Sir Samuel Romilly and other reformers led a long and intelligent campaign for the repeal of some laws, arguing from statistics that convictions would become more numerous once that fear was removed. The reformers also used the arguments of Beccaria, who suggested in 1764 that gross and capricious terror should be replaced by a fixed and graduated scale of more lenient but more certain punishments. His ideas were widely canvassed in England, as well as on the continent. Even Blackstone, the high priest of the English legal system, looked forward to changes on these lines. Yet Parliament resisted all reform. Not one capital statute was repealed until 1808, and real progress had to wait until the 1820s and 1830s.

Why the contradiction? If property was so important, and reform of the criminal law would help to protect it, why did gentlemen not embrace reform? Given the apparently fierce inten-

[7]The extension of benefit of clergy (the right to a lesser sentence of transportation on first conviction for the capital crime of grand larceny) made it increasingly impossible to avoid the gallows. The development of clergy since the sixteenth century was countered in the eighteenth by many statutes removing it from particular kinds of larceny. Other capital statues at the same time extended the death penalty to offences never punished so severely before.

[8]Radzinowicz, vol. I, pp. 151–9, 163–4.

tions of the legislature, why was the law not changed to make enforcement more certain? Historians searching for the roots of the modern criminal law and the modern police usually devote most of their attention to the triumph of reform in the nineteenth century. But the victors in the eighteenth century were the conservatives, the hangers and gibbeters, and they resolutely ignored over fifty years of cogent criticism. Two immediate explanations are commonly given. The gentry undoubtedly refused to create a regular police force, a necessary part of the Beccarian plan. Moreover, the lack of secondary punishments, and the unsatisfactory nature of those in use, such as transportation, made it seem desirable to keep the death penalty for the incorrigible rogue. Neither fact, however, explains why there was such unbending opposition to the repeal of even those capital statutes that were seldom used. This determination of Parliament to retain all the capital statutes, even when obsolete, and to continue to create new ones, even when they were stillborn, suggests that the explanation for the failure of reform lies deeper in the mental and social structure of eighteenth-century England. A few historians have attempted explanations, but they are usually vague or tautological: that the industrial revolution, as a time of social change, induced conservatism; that the French Revolution did the same; that legal reform in England is always, and inevitably, slow. These explanations ignore the underlying assumptions of the governors of England, and do not show how the old criminal law matched that mental world. For it is difficult to believe that Parliament would have been so complacently conservative about the unreformed law unless they were convinced that it was serving their interests. And here the testimony of conservatives is more helpful than the claims of reformers.[9]

Timothy Nourse antedated Beccaria and Romilly by a good half-century, but he expressed an enduring belief of the gentry when he declared that many of the common people were "very rough and savage in their Dispositions, being of levelling Principles, and refractory to Government, insolent and tumultuous." Civility only made them saucy:

> The best way therefore will be to bridle them, and to make them feel the spur too, when they begin to play their Tricks, and kick. The Saying of an *English* gentleman was much to the purpose, That three things ought always to be kept under, our Mastiff-Dog, a Stone-Horse, and a Clown: And really I think a snarling, cross-grained Clown to be the most unlucky Beast of the three. Such Men then are to be look'd upon as trashy Weeds or Nettles, growing usually upon Dunghills, which if touch'd gently will sting, but being squeez'd hard will never hurt us.

The instruments to deal with such "stubborn, cross-grain'd rogues" were at hand: "*Beadles, Catchpoles, Gaolers, Hangmen, . . .* such like Engines of Humanity are the fittest Tools in the World for a Magistrate to work with in the Reformation of an obdurate Rogue, all which, I say, may be so used and managed by him as not to endanger his own Fingers, or discompose his thoughts."[10] This is language far removed from Romilly's cool calculation of rates of conviction, or even Justice Christian's hysterical talk of alarms, watch-dogs and double-barrelled pistols. Nourse knew instinctively that the criminal law is as much concerned with authority as it is with property. For wealth does not exist outside a social context, theft is given definition only within a set of social relations, and the connections between property, power and authority are close and crucial. The criminal law was critically important in maintaining bonds of obedience and deference, in legitimizing the status quo, in con-

[9]Historians have accepted the assumptions of the reformers, which are also those of modern criminology: that the criminal law and the police are no more and no less than a set of instruments to manage something called crime. Effective detection, certain prosecution and enlightened rehabilitation will accomplish this practical task. (Radzinowicz, *Ideology*

and Crime, 1966). Criminology has been disinfested of grand theory and class purpose. Much of it has thereby become ideology.

[10]Timothy Nourse, *Campania Foelix* (2nd Edn, 1706), pp. 15-16, 273-4.

stantly recreating the structure of authority which arose from property and in turn protected its interests.

But terror alone could never have accomplished those ends. It was the raw material of authority, but class interest and the structure of the law itself shaped it into a much more effective instrument of power. Almost a century after Nourse, another defender of the unreformed system described the other side of authority: "Could we view our own species from a distance, or regard mankind with the same sort of observation with which we read the natural history, or remark the *manners,* of any other animal," he wrote in 1785,

> there is nothing in the human character which would more surprise us, than the almost universal subjugation of strength to weakness—than to see many millions of robust men, in the complete use and exercise of their faculties, and without any defect of courage, waiting upon the will of a child, a woman, a driveller, or a lunatic. And although . . . we suppose perhaps an extreme case; yet in all cases, even in the most popular forms of civil government, *the physical strength lies in the governed.* In what manner opinion thus prevails over strength, or how power, which naturally belongs to superior force, is maintained in opposition to it; in other words, by what motives the many are induced to submit to the few, becomes an inquiry which lies at the root of almost every political speculation. . . . Let civil governors learn hence to respect their subjects; let them be admonished, that the physical strength resides in the governed; that this strength wants only to be felt and roused, to lay prostrate the most ancient and confirmed dominion; that civil authority is founded in opinion; that general opinion therefore ought always to be treated with deference, and managed with delicacy and circumspection.[11]

These are the words of Archdeacon Paley, and they were published a few years after the Gordon Riots. Paley is not usually quoted as an exponent of "delicacy and circumspection," but as the most eloquent defender of the old criminal law as

a system of selective terror. He was cited by almost every subsequent opponent of reform, and has often been considered by later writers as little more than an ingenious apologist or uncritical conservative. But he was in fact an acute observer of the bases of power in eighteenth-century England, and although he did not make the connection explicit, the criminal law was extremely important in ensuring, in his words, that "opinion" prevailed over "physical strength." The opinion was that of the ruling class; the law was one of their chief ideological instruments. It combined the terror worshipped by Nourse with the discretion stressed by Paley, and used both to mould the consciousness by which the many submitted to the few. Moreover, its effectiveness in doing so depended in large part on the very weaknesses and inconsistencies condemned by reformers and liberal historians. In considering the criminal law as an ideological system, we must look at how it combined imagery and force, ideals and practice, and try to see how it manifested itself to the mass of unpropertied Englishmen. We can distinguish three aspects of the law as ideology: majesty, justice and mercy. Understanding them will help us to explain the divergence between bloody legislation and declining executions, and the resistance to reform of any kind.

II

MAJESTY

If we are to believe an undated couplet from Staffordshire, at first sight the majesty of the law did not always impress:[12]

COUNTRYMAN: What mummery is this,
'tis fit only for guisers!
TOWNSMAN: No mummery Sir,
'tis the Stafford Assizes,

for coupled with wealth, a considered use of imagery, eloquent speech, and the power of death, the antics surrounding the twice-yearly visits of the high-court judges had considerable psychic force. They were accorded far greater importance

---

[11]William Paley, *Principles of Moral and Political Philosophy,* 1785, Book VI, ch. 2.

[12]Dudley Wilks, *Fragments of Stafford's Past,* Stafford, 1932, p. 32.

by contemporaries than by most historians, who have been concerned more with county government, particularly at Quarter Sessions, than with the majesty of the law. The assizes were a formidable spectacle in a country town, the most visible and elaborate manifestation of state power to be seen in the countryside, apart from the presence of a regiment. The town was crowded, not only with barristers and jurors, but with the cream of county society, attending the assize ball and county meetings, which were often held in the same week. Tradesmen and labourers journeyed in to enjoy the spectacle, meet friends, attend the court and watch the executions. . . .

In the court room the judges' every action was governed by the importance of spectacle. Blackstone asserted that "the novelty and very parade of . . . [their] appearance have no small influence upon the multitude": scarlet robes lined with ermine and full-bottomed wigs in the seventeenth-century style, which evoked scorn from Hogarth but awe from ordinary men. The powers of light and darkness were summoned into the court with the black cap which was donned to pronounce sentence of death, and the spotless white gloves worn at the end of a "maiden assize" when no prisoners were to be left for execution.

Within this elaborate ritual of the irrational, judge and counsel displayed their learning with an eloquence that often rivalled that of leading statesmen. There was an acute consciousness that the courts were platforms for addressing "the multitude." Two stages in the proceedings especially were tests of the rhetorical power of the bench. The first, the charge to the grand jury, was ostensibly directed to the country gentry. Judges gave close attention to content and to delivery. Frequently charges were a statement of central policy, as well as a summary of the state of the law and the duties of gentlemen. Earlier in the century they castigated Jacobitism; and in the 1720s the judges used them to denounce "unfounded and seditious" criticisms of government policy on the South Sea Bubble. Tone was important: before he went on circuit in 1754, Sir Dudley Ryder reminded himself, "When I would

speak to [the] Grand Jury I should mean to persuade them to do their duty, I should therefore speak to them as I would to a number of my tenants whom I would instruct and persuade, and therefore make them fully acquainted with everything necessary to that end, or as I would to my son." The flavour of paternalism was important, for usually the charge was also directed at the wider audience in the court room. It was often a secular sermon on the goodness of whichever Hanoverian chanced to be on the throne, the virtues of authority and obedience, the fitness of the social order. . . .

The second rhetorical test for the judge demanded not the accents of paternalism, but the power and passion of righteous vengeance. The death sentence, we have suggested, was the climactic emotional point of the criminal law—the moment of terror around which the system revolved. As the cases came before judge and jury at assizes, the convicted were remanded for sentencing on the last day; and on that day the judgements were given in ascending order of severity, reserving the most awful for the last. Before passing sentence of death, the judge spoke about the crimes and the criminals. "A wise and conscientious judge," wrote Thomas Gisborne,

will never neglect so favourable an occasion of inculcating the enormity of vice, and the fatal consequences to which it leads. He will point out to his hearers the several causes, when they are sufficiently marked to admit of description and application, which have conducted step by step the wretched object before them through the several shades and degrees of guilt to a transgression unpardonable on earth. He will dwell with peculiar force on such of those causes as appear to him the most likely, either from the general principles of human nature, or from local circumstances, to exert their contagious influence on the persons whom he addresses.[13]

Most published sentences come up to Gisborne's standard. The aim was to move the court, to im-

[13]Thomas Gisborne, *An Enquiry into the Duties of Men in the Higher and Middle Classes of Society in Great Britain,* 1794, p. 270.

press the onlookers by word and gesture, to fuse terror and argument into the amalgam of legitimate power in their minds. For execution was a fate decreed not by men, but by God and Justice. The judge might deepen the effect when visibly moved himself. In 1754 at Chelmsford the Chief Justice condemned a girl to hanging and dissection for murdering her baby. He had pressured the jury to bring in a simple verdict of guilty (at first they found her insane); but having exacted justice, he then expressed the helplessness of men before it: "Before I pronounced the sentence," he confided to his diary, "I made a very proper speech extempore and pronounced it with dignity, in which I was so affected that the tears were gushing out several times against my will. It was discerned by all the company—which was large—and a lady gave me her handkerchief dipped in lavender water to help me."

In its ritual, its judgements and its channelling of emotion the criminal law echoed many of the most powerful psychic components of religion. The judge might, as at Chelmsford, emulate the priest in his role of human agent, helpless but submissive before the demands of his deity. But the judge could play the role of deity as well, both the god of wrath and the merciful arbiter of men's fates. For the righteous accents of the death sentence were made even more impressive by the contrast with the treatment of the accused up to the moment of conviction. The judges' paternal concern for their prisoners was remarked upon by foreign visitors, and deepened the analogy with the Christian God of justice and mercy. Moreover, there is some reason to believe that the secular sermons of the criminal law had become more important than those of the Church by the eighteenth century. Too many Englishmen had forgotten the smell of brimstone, and the clergy—lazy, absentee and dominated by material ambition—were not the men to remind them. The diminished effectiveness of damnation to compel obedience was accentuated by the decline of the ecclesiastical courts since early Stuart times to mere arbiters of wills and marriages and occasional cases of slander. In sharp contrast, the sanctions of the criminal law had not lost their bite: "The government has wisely provided corporal and pecuniary punishments, and Ministers of Justice for the execution of them," Sir James Astry told his juries; "for the punishment of the Pocket, or a sound Whipping to some, is more effectual Rhetorick, than the preaching of Divine vengeance from the Pulpit; for such lewd Wretches has a sordid notion, that Preaching is only a Trade, and to the ministers of gospel, Godliness is great gain. . . ." Timothy Nourse was more succinct: "a good strong pair of Stocks, and a Whipping-post, will work a greater Reformation than Forty Doctrines and Uses." Religion still had a place within the ritual of the law: a clergyman gave the assize sermon, and others attended the condemned men on the scaffold. But we suspect that the men of God derived more prestige from the occasion than they conferred upon it. A suggestion of this can be seen in an evangelical pamphlet published in 1795. In the metaphors of power, judges usually had been likened to God, deriving their authority from divine authority, mediated through the Crown. But the author reversed the metaphor in his attempt to resurrect religion: he likened the deity to an English high court justice, and called the Day of Judgement the "Grand Assizes, or General Gaol Delivery." The secular mysteries of the courts had burned deep into the popular consciousness, and perhaps the labouring poor knew more of the terrors of the law than those of religion. When they did hear of hell, it was often from a judge. Sentencing a murderer at Gloucester in 1772, Justice Nares reminded him that his gibbeted bones would never enjoy Christian burial, but would hang "as a dreadful spectacle of horror and detestation, to caution and deter the rest of mankind." But he reminded him that he also had an immortal soul, and exhorted him to seek salvation: "Then, although your sins are as scarlet, they may be white as snow,—'tho they be as crimson, they shall be as wool."

The assizes were staged twice a year in most counties. Quarter Sessions, held twice as often, could not match them as spectacles, but as courts of law they derived some of their impressiveness by association. The magistrates on the county bench had visited and dined with the circuit judges a few months before; the wealthier JPs had entertained their lordships at their homes, spoken familiarly with them in court. Indeed, their wives and daughters sometimes turned the assizes to their own purposes, giving a competitive display of charm before the assize ball: "By a condescension sufficiently extraordinary," wrote a bemused Frenchman, "the judge permits his Bench to be invaded by a throng of spectators, and thus finds himself surrounded by the prettiest women of the county—the sisters, wives or daughters of grand jurors. . . . They are attired in the most elegant négligé; and it is a spectacle not a little curious to see the judge's venerable head, loaded with a large wig, peering among the youthful female heads." To most of those in the court-room, the spectacle was less amusing and more serious than the foreign barrister found it: it was a reminder of the close relationship between law, property and power.

For certain offences, the full majesty of the criminal law could be summoned outside assize times, and when Quarter Sessions were not sitting. The court of King's Bench would allow prosecution by information for serious misdemeanours, including riot, aggravated assaults and some game offences. The offender was usually tried at the next assizes, but he could be compelled to appear at Westminster, tried in the most awesome surroundings, and pilloried or whipped among the crowds of the metropolis. It was said to be a popular belief that one could be "put into the Crown Office" for any offence, at any time. It happened just often enough to give colour to the story. Finally, on a great many occasions throughout the century the full panoply of the law was sent into the counties in the form of a Special Commission to try a particular, dangerous offence. The Special Commission was used when exemplary hangings or at least exemplary trials were deemed necessary for the public peace. Gentlemen often petitioned for them when riot in their counties was becoming too serious, or

when the violence associated with popular crimes (such as smuggling) verged on insurrection against their authority. The assize judges descended from London, the sermon was preached in the nearest cathedral, and the breach in the social and moral order was healed with the rituals of justice: speeches, fear and the sacrifice of lives on the gallows. As at the regular assizes, at least in the provinces, those executed at Special Commissions were mostly local men, with neighbours, parents, brothers and sisters in the watching crowd.

JUSTICE

"Justice" was an evocative word in the eighteenth century, and with good reason. The constitutional struggles of the seventeenth had helped to establish the principles of the rule of law: that offences should be fixed, not indeterminate; that rules of evidence should be carefully observed; that the law should be administered by a bench that was both learned and honest. These achievements were essential for the protection of the gentry from royal greed and royal tyranny, and for the regulation, in the civil side of the courts, of the details of conveyancing, entailing, contracting, devising, suing and releasing. Since the same judges administered the criminal law at its highest levels, on the same principles, even the poorest man was guaranteed justice in the high courts. Visitors remarked on the extreme solicitude of judges for the rights of the accused, a sharp distinction from the usual practice of continental benches. It was considered to be good grounds for requesting a royal pardon if the judge "did (contrary to the usual custom) lean against the prisoner." The assize judge's attention to the rights of the prisoner did much to mitigate the prohibition against legal counsel in felonies. It was a tradition which permeated the courts, and it was sustained too by the public nature of trials. . . .

Equally important were the strict procedural rules which were enforced in the high courts and at assizes, especially in capital cases. Moreover, most penal statutes were interpreted by the judges in an extremely narrow and formalistic fashion. In part this was based on seventeenth-century practice, but as more capital statutes were passed in the eighteenth century the bench reacted with an increasingly narrow interpretation. Many prosecutions founded on excellent evidence and conducted at considerable expense failed on minor errors of form in the indictment, the written charge. If a name or date was incorrect, or if the accused was described as a "farmer" rather than the approved term "yeoman," the prosecution could fail. The courts held that such defects were conclusive, and gentlemen attending trials as spectators sometimes stood up in court and brought errors to the attention of the judge. These formalisms in the criminal law seemed ridiculous to contemporary critics, and to many later historians. Their argument was (and is) that the criminal law, to be effective, must be known and determinate, instead of capricious and obscure. Prosecutors resented the waste of their time and money lost on a technicality; thieves were said to mock courts which allowed them to escape through so many verbal loopholes. But it seems likely that the mass of Englishmen drew other conclusions from the practice. The punctilious attention to forms, the dispassionate and legalistic exchanges between counsel and the judge, argued that those administering and using the laws submitted to its rules. The law thereby became something more than the creature of a ruling class—it became a power with its own claims, higher than those of prosecutor, lawyers, and even the great scarlet-robed assize judge himself. To them, too, of course, the law was The Law. The fact that they reified it, that they shut their eyes to its daily enactment in Parliament by men of their own class, heightened the illusion. When the ruling class acquitted men on technicalities they helped instil a belief in the disembodied justice of the law in the minds of all who watched. In short, its very inefficiency, its absurd formalism, was part of its strength as ideology.

"Equality before the law" also implied that no man was exempt from it. It was part of the lore of politics that in England social class did not preserve a man even from the extreme sanction of death. This was not, of course, true. But the impression made by the execution of a man of property or position was very deep. As executions for forgery became increasingly common throughout the century, more such respectable villains went to the gallows. The crime was punished with unremitting severity even though it was often committed by impecunious lawyers of good family. This rigour was distressing to many middling men: the agitation led by Johnson against the execution of the Reverend Dr. Dodd, a former Royal Chaplain and Lord Chesterfield's old tutor, was enormous. Dodd died at Tyburn in 1777 but he lived in popular culture for a long time, his case persuasive evidence that the law treated rich and poor alike. The occasional sentence of transportation or death passed on gentlemen with unusual sexual tastes or guilty of homicide, cases widely reported in the *Newgate Calendar* and other versions, similarly served to justify the law. Undoubtedly the most useful victim in this respect was Lawrence Shirley, Lord Ferrers, who killed his steward, was captured by his tenantry, tried in the House of Lords, sentenced to death, executed at Tyburn, and dissected "like a common criminal" as the publicists never tired of repeating. He was hanged in his silver brocade wedding-suit, on a scaffold equipped with black silk cushions for the mourners. But hanging is hanging, the defenders of the law repeated enthusiastically. An enormous literature surrounded his execution in 1760, much of it devoted to celebrating the law. Later in the century the event was often recalled as an irrefutable proof of the justice of English society. An anti-Jacobin in the 1790s advised his "brother artificers":

> We have long enjoyed that Liberty and Equality which the French have been struggling for: in England, ALL MEN ARE EQUAL.; all who commit the same offences are liable to the same punishment. If the *very poorest and meanest man* commits murder, he is hanged with a hempen halter, and his body dissected. If the *Richest Nobleman* commits a

murder, *he* is hanged with a hempen halter, and his body dissected—*all are equal here.*[14]

Hannah More used the same argument in her anti-Jacobin pamphlets for the poor; Ferrers became one of the best-known villains of the century. In some counties the story of the wicked aristocrat who met a just end on the scaffold was told at popular festivities until well into the 1800s.

In the parlour of the Justice of the Peace, *stare decisis* and due process were not always so much in evidence as in the high courts. Many justices convicted on flimsy evidence, particularly when they were subservient to a local magnate, and when they were enforcing the game laws. It was perfectly possible to combine arbitrary powers with an obeisance to the rules, however, and it appears that most JPs made an effort to appear, at least, to be acting legally. Moreover, even at the level of the justice the rules of law could be used effectively on behalf of a labouring man. It was not unknown for labourers caught deer-stealing to make an ingenious use of the contradictory statutes protecting informers to escape punishment. The occasional success of such ruses, and the attempts to use them, probably helped sustain the belief that the integrity of the law was a reality and not merely the rhetoric of judges and gentlemen. Perhaps even more important in this respect were the frequent prosecutions brought by common informers, where the poor could go before a JP and use the law in their own interests. Prosecutions under the excise, game and turnpike acts—often against farmers and tradesmen who on most other occasions were those who used the courts—occasionally allowed the powerless to make the law their servant, whether for personal revenge or the sake of the reward. Moreover, Justices of the Peace sometimes intervened in the administration of the poor laws, prosecuting callous overseers who forced paupers to marry to remove them from the rates, or who dumped them over parish boundaries to die at the expense of their neighbours. Every county saw trials for such cruelties every few years, and the gentlemen who brought them clothed the issue in the language of constitutionalism. An extremely pervasive rhetorical tradition, with deep historical roots, was invoked and strengthened on all such occasions. The law was held to be the guardian of Englishmen, of all Englishmen. Gentlemen held this as an unquestionable belief: that belief, too, gave the ideology of justice an integrity which no self-conscious manipulation could alone sustain. The real guarantees of the law were, moreover, confirmed in several celebrated political trials: Lord Mansfield's finding against general warrants in 1765, the Middlesex jury's acquittals of the leaders of the London Corresponding Society in 1794. In the latter case the striking contrast with the Scottish trials under Braxfield the year before was treated as an object lesson in the superiority of the English courts and bench.

Yet the idea of justice was always dangerous, straining the narrow definitions of the lawyers and the judges. It was easy to claim equal justice for murderers of all classes, where a universal moral sanction was more likely to be found, or in political cases, the necessary price of a constitution ruled by law. The trick was to extend that communal sanction to a criminal law that was nine-tenths concerned with upholding a radical division of property. Though Justice seemed impartial in crimes against the person, wrote Mandeville,

> Yet, it was thought, the sword she bore
> Check'd but the Desp'rate and the Poor;
> That, urged by mere Necessity,
> Were tied up to the wretched Tree
> For Crimes, which not deserv'd that Fate
> But to secure the Rich, and Great.[15]

In times of dearth, when the rulers of England were faced with food riots by men desperate with hunger and convinced of the rights of their case, the contradiction could become acute. At such times two conceptions of justice stood in sharp opposition: an older, Christian version of natural

---

[14] *Job Nott's Advice,* Staffs. RO, D1778, bdl. 57.

[15] *The Fable of the Bees,* 1705.

rights, which guaranteed even the poorest man at least life, and the justice of the law of property, sanctioned by the settlements of the seventeenth century. Keith Thomas has suggested that the erosion of the moral sanctions surrounding charity, and the ambiguity accompanying the birth of a more rationalized and less indulgent attitude to poverty, produced strong conflicts of guilt and blame, with seventeenth-century witch trials as their partial expression.[16]. A century later, the ambiguities had still not been altogether resolved in the law, which in its ideological role had to reconcile popular ideas of justice with the absolute claims of property. From time to time writers in jurisprudence took up with distaste the ancient civil doctrine that a starving man had the right to steal enough food to keep himself for a week. Hale had written in the seventeenth century that the rule had long been disused in England. Blackstone argued that in this, as in all things, English law was founded on the highest reason, "for men's properties would be under a strange insecurity, if liable to be invaded according to the wants of others; of which wants no man can possibly be an adequate judge, but the party himself who pleads them."[17] The judges agreed, for it was impossible to admit poverty as a legal defence without wholly eroding the property statute. Rather than acknowledge an archaic, alien and dangerous legal doctrine, the bench stressed their deep concern for the little personal property that the ordinary Englishman did have. From time to time they passed harsh sentences for certain crimes, such as the theft of clothes, which they proclaimed in court to be particular misfortunes of the poor. A great many words were lavished also on particular statutes for the same reason. An

act of 1713 punished with death any house-breaker who stole goods worth forty shillings or more. Opposing repeal in a major debate in 1811, Lord Eldon declared "that the property of the industrious cottager should be protected, who is often obliged to leave his cottage, and his little hoard of perhaps not more than 40s deposited in a tin-box in a corner of a room."

It is difficult to assess the weight such arguments had with the mass of Englishmen. Eldon's was jejune: few cottagers had savings of £2, the wages of a month or more, in the harsh year 1811. Equally few cottagers could afford to go to law to recover stolen goods. Ideologies do not rest on realities, however, but on appearances, and there were enough prosecutions on behalf of poor men to give colour to the Lord Chancellor's claims. Usually such cases were begun or paid for by employers, landlords or local associations for the prosecution of felons. The motives for men of property to assist the poor to prosecute were a tangle of self-interest and paternalism. Some gentlemen simply believed that the law was the birthright of every Englishman, and most were anxious to convict a thief who might prey on them as well. The consequence was that more poor men were able to use the law than the system of legal fees would otherwise have allowed. The poor suffer from theft as well as the rich, and in eighteenth-century England probably far more poor men lost goods to thieves, if only because the rich were few and their property more secure. In recognizing that fact, and extending its protection, however imperfectly, to ordinary men, the criminal law did much to justify itself and the gentlemen who administered it. . . .

The justice of English law was thus a powerful ideological weapon in the arsenal of conservatives during the French Revolution. Wicked Lord Ferrers, juries and *habeas corpus* were leading themes in anti-Jacobin popular literature. They were usually contrasted with tyrannical French aristocrats, the inquisitorial system of law and *lettres de cachet*. In countering the influence of Tom Paine, the conservatives repeatedly emphasized the central place of law in the English

---

[16]Keith Thomas, *Religion and the Decline of Magic*, 1971, p. 561.

[17]Blackstone, *Commentaries*, vol. IV, pp. 31-2. Perhaps Blackstone sensed that the claims of poverty were not extinquished, for he resorted to chauvinist humbug. Theft might be justified on the continent, "where the parsimonious industry of the natures orders every one to work or starve," but it had no place in England, "where charity is reduced to a system, and interwoven in our very constitution." Many other writers also wrestled with the problem.

constitution. Gillray caught the spirit of the argument perfectly in a print of 1801. He drew two trees. One, the blasted and rotten stump of Opposition, was surmounted by a French cap of Liberty, and on its few remaining branches hung the withered fruits of Blasphemy, Sedition, Anarchy, Democracy. The other tree, flourishing and green, he gave roots of Kings, Lords and Commons, sweet apples of Peace, Happiness and Prosperity, and he labelled its massive trunk JUSTICE. It is important, however, to distinguish the argument against Paine from the wider ideological use of justice throughout the century. The author of *The Rights of Man* was in a peculiar position with respect to the law. As one of "the middling sort" he was a man of moderate property, and he thought like one. He was not a critic of the institutions of the law. Indeed, Paine claimed that Quarter Sessions and assizes, as bodies of local administration, were two of the few organs of proper self-government. Nor did he criticize the law's tenderness for property. The only effective answer to the Tory position would have been a thoroughly egalitarian critique and this Paine was unwilling to begin. An egalitarian on the subject of hereditary monarchy and corrupt aristocracy and landed wealth, he was no leveller of all property distinctions. Hence he had to suffer the conservatives' encomiums of justice in silence.[18]

Although Paine never lent his pen to the task, the institutions of the law were in fact exceedingly open to radical criticism. The conservatives based their defence on comparisons with French tyranny, the occasional punishment of a great man, the limited protection the law gave to the poor. They did not dare to attempt a reasoned examination of the whole legal system for the

edification of the mob. All men of property knew that judges, justices and juries had to be chosen from their own ranks. The jury, the supposed guarantee that an Englishman would be tried by his equals, had a sharp property qualification. The reason, simply put, was that the common Englishman could not be trusted to share in the operation of the law. A panel of the poor would not convict a labourer who stole wood from a lord's park, a sheep from a farmer's fold, or corn from a merchant's yard. As Gisborne pointed out, even as witnesses "many of the common people ... are found to make use of a very blameable latitude in their interpretation of the ninth commandment; and think that they are guilty of no breach of it in deviating, though upon oath, from strict truth, *in favour* of the party accused."[19] The cottager who appeared in court charged with the theft had no illusions about being tried by "his equals and neighbours," whatever the writers of law books claimed. The twelve men sitting opposite him were employers, overseers of the poor, propertied men. In most cases they were the equals and neighbours of the prosecutor, not the accused, and this was especially true in cases of theft. The point is not that such juries convicted against the evidence, but rather that a more democratic jury might not have convicted at all. In the constitutional struggles of the seventeenth century, "middling men" of moderate property had wanted the widest possible extension of trial by jury; the Crown had tried to restrict it because juries shielded sedition. There was another small group, however, who had also wanted to control juries. Winstanley and the Diggers repudiated them as protectors of property against the rights of the poor. There were no Diggers in the eighteenth century, but cottagers and labourers were undoubtedly aware that English justice was still the creature of judges and juries.

Eighteenth-century "justice" was not, however, a nonsense. It remained a powerful and evocative word, even if it bore a much more lim-

---

[18]The one exception is his trenchant criticism of special juries. By an act of 1729, civil suits and misdemeanours could be tried by a jury with a special property qualification; it ensured that gentry and aristocracy would always pack a jury with friends and neighbours if the occasion required. Paine reflected acidly, in print, on the advantages of special juries to the Government when it prosecuted *The Rights of Man* as seditious libel. But this is virtually his only criticism of criminal procedure; he accepts the property qualification for ordinary juries as a matter of course.

[19]Gisborne, op cit., p. 284, note b.

ited meaning than a twentieth-century (or seventeenth-century) egalitarian would give it. In a society radically divided between rich and poor, the powerful and the powerless, the occasional victory of a cottager in the courts or the rare spectacle of a titled villain on the gallows made a sharp impression. Moreover, it would be wrong to suggest that the law had to be wholly consistent to persuade men of its legitimacy. "Justice," in the sense of rational, bureaucratic decisions made in the common interest, is a peculiarly modern conception. It was gaining ground in the eighteenth century. Most reformers worked to bring about such law, and of all such schemes Jeremy Bentham's was the logical conclusion. Yet his plan for a criminal code that was precise, consistent and wholly enforced was alien to the thought of most eighteenth-century Englishmen. They tended to think of justice in personal terms, and were more struck by understanding of individual cases than by the delights of abstract schemes. Where authority is embodied in direct personal relationships, men will often accept power, even enormous, despotic power, when it comes from the "good King," the father of his people, who tempers justice with mercy. A form of this powerful psychic configuration was one of the most distinctive aspects of the unreformed criminal law. Bentham could not understand it, but it was the law's greatest strength as an ideological system, especially among the poor, and in the countryside.

MERCY

The prerogative of mercy ran throughout the administration of the criminal law, from the lowest to the highest level. At the top sat the high court judges, and their free use of the royal pardon became a crucial argument in the arsenal of conservatives opposing reform. At the lowest jurisdiction, that of the Justice of the Peace, the same discretion allowed the magistrate to make decisions that sometimes escaped legal categories altogether. Although he frequently made obeisance to the rules when convicting, as we have seen, he could dispense with them when pardoning, and

the absence of a jury made it even easier for him to do so. Latitude in the direction of mercy caused some critics to complain that many justices, partly from laziness or carelessness "but frequently from benevolent views improperly indulged," judged cases "partly or entirely by their own unauthorized ideas of equity."[20] This element of discretion impressed Weber when he examined the office of JP. He compared it to Arabic "khadi justice"—a formalistic administration of law that was nevertheless based on ethical or practical judgements rather than on a fixed, "rational" set of rules. It could combine rigid tradition with "a sphere of free discretion and grace of the ruler."[21] Thus it allowed the paternalist JP to compose quarrels, intervene with prosecutors on behalf of culprits, and in the final instance to dismiss a case entirely. The right of the pardon was not limited, however, to high court judges and Justices of the Peace. The mode of prosecution, the manner of trial and the treatment of condemned convicts gave some of the same power to all men of property. "Irrationality," in the sense used by Weber, and the "grace of the ruler" which grew from it pervaded the entire administration of the law.

Almost all prosecutions were initiated by private persons, at their discretion, and conducted in accordance with their wishes. Accustomed to organized state police and rigorous state prosecution, French visitors were inclined to marvel at this peculiar English institution. Charles Cottu, a French judge who toured the Northern Circuit in the early nineteenth century, exclaimed,

> The English [that is, state officials] appear to attach no importance to a discovery of the causes which may have induced the prisoner to commit the crime: they scarcely even affix any to the establishment of his guilt. I am ignorant whether this temper of mind arises from their fear of augmenting the already excessive number of public offenders, or whether it proceeds from their natural humanity;

[20]Gisborne, op cit., p. 28.
[21]*From Max Weber*, ed. H. H. Gerth and C. Wright Mills, 1970, pp. 216-21.

it is however an undoubted fact, that they make no effort to obtain proofs of the crime, confiding its punishment entirely to the hatred or resentment of the injured party; careless too, about the conviction of the accused, whether his victim shall yield to feelings of compassion, or give way to indolence.[22]

Cottu did not appear to have heard, or understood, the traditional arguments of English gentlemen against a constabulary and state prosecution: that it could lead to despotism, a political police serving the Crown. He did understand, however, the consequences of private prosecution. The victim of the crime could decide himself upon the severity of the prosecution, either enforcing the letter of the law, or reducing the charge. He could even pardon the offence completely by not going to court. The reformers' objections to this system are well known. Private prosecution was capricious and uncertain, and too often rogues escaped due to the distaste, compassion or fear of their victims. But reformers failed to acknowledge the great power this conferred on the prosecutor to make the law serve his own purposes. In Cottu's words, the accuser became "the arbitrator of the culprit's fate," and the law became an expression of his will. In short, it was in the hands of the gentleman who went to law to evoke gratitude as well as fear in the maintenance of deference.

In a rural parish with a relatively settled population there were many alternatives to a rigorous prosecution. The accused man could be made to post a bond not to offend again, or be given the choice of leaving the neighbourhood. The threat of prosecution could be held over his head to ensure his future good behaviour. He might also be allowed to escape the law by making compensation for his crime, and the negotiations between Richard Ainsworth and his master Nicholas Blundell in 1709 were repeated in all parts of England, throughout the century. Ainsworth was caught stealing, begged Blundell repeatedly not to prosecute, and entered into negotiations to

work on one of his master's houses in return for forgiveness. Other accused men simply appealed to the merciful feelings of the man who held them in his power. The wretched thief begging on his knees for forgiveness is not a literary conceit, but a reality described in many legal depositions. Critics of the law objected, however, that many prosecutions were dropped through fear as well as compassion. Certainly it is true that feeling against some prosecutors ran so high that they went in fear of their lives from popular opinion, or felt obliged to defend their actions in the press. Yet where certainty of enforcement had to be sacrificed to public opinion, even then graciously granted mercy could produce gratifying deference. Especially where the prosecutor was a landed gentleman, acts of mercy helped create the mental structure of paternalism. The papers of any large landed proprietor are peppered with appeals for pardons, and earnest thanks for them—pardons for poachers, for stealers of holly, for embezzlers of coal. "I hope his Lordship will not insist upon your acquainting my Master of it," wrote one poacher to a steward, "as it would be productive of very great injury to me . . . we are afraid the crime is so great that it will not admit of any excuse and therefore all we can say is that our future good behaviour shall be such that his Lordship will not repent of his Lenity and goodness in forgiving us." The phrases of benevolence constantly recur on the other side: "it may so happen that my Good Lord Stafford may be inclined (as he generally is) to pardon the offenders. . ." Such acts were personal ties, not the distant decisions of bureaucracies. They also bridged great vertical distances in the social order: in this case, between some day labourers caught pilfering, and the Lord Lieutenant of the county. We cannot, of course, infer gratitude from begging letters, but there is enough evidence to suggest that much of it was genuine. Many prosecutors, peers included, made the most of their mercy by requiring the pardoned man to sign a letter of apology and gratitude, which was printed in the county newspaper.

The nature of the criminal trial gave enormous

[22]Charles Cottu, *The Administration of Justice in England*, 1822, p. 37.

discretion to men of property other than the prosecutor. Because the law did not allow those accused of felony to employ an attorney to address the jury, a poor man's defence was often a halting, confused statement. If he had a clear alibi he was lucky: to establish innocence in more complicated cases might be very difficult, even when the judge was sympathetic. Character witnesses were thus extremely important, and very frequently used. It was not uncommon for a man accused of sheep-stealing, a capital offence, to bring a dozen acquaintances to court to testify to his honesty. If the jury did convict, such favourable testimony might still induce the judge to pass a lesser sentence, or recommend a pardon. Yet in character testimony too, the word of a man of property had the greatest weight. Judges respected the evidence of employers, respectable farmers and neighbouring gentlemen, not mere neighbours and friends. A labourer accused of a serious crime learned again his enormous dependence on the power of property to help him, or abandon him, as it chose: "I am now going to take a dredful tryal and god nose but my poor Life may Lay at Stake," William Sheffield wrote to his masters a month before the assizes,

> therefore I hope Both of you will stand my friend this time jest to Come and give me a Careckter for the time that I lived with you and I hope you will do that for me the judg I am told will Look upon that as a great thing in my Behaff.... So pray my dear mastters Consider my Unhappy state this time for gods sake and stand my frend and if plees god it should Ever Laye in my power I will neaver think nothing two much to make you amends Eaver to Lay my selfe at your feet if I can be of haney serviss to you for your passt goodness to me in so doing...[23]

If respectable character witnesses did not succeed in convincing the jury to acquit, their support was the first step in influencing the judge to consider a pardon. A free or conditional pardon from the king was the hope of almost every capital convict in the eighteenth century, and many men under lighter sentences also struggled to obtain it. For the historian it epitomizes the discretionary element of the law, and the use of mercy in justifying the social order.

Pardons were very common. Roughly half of those condemned to death during the eighteenth century did not go to the gallows, but were transported to the colonies or imprisoned. In many cases the judge made the decision before he left the assize town, but if he did not intend to recommend mercy, it was still possible to petition the king, through the Secretary of State, up to the moment of execution. The grounds for mercy were ostensibly that the offence was minor, or that the convict was of good character, or that the crime he had committed was not common enough in that county to require an exemplary hanging. The judges also used the pardon when necessary to meet the requests of local gentry or to propitiate popular feelings of justice. The bench could ultimately decide whom to recommend for mercy and whom to leave to hang, but they were not usually willing to antagonize a body of respectable feeling. Justice Ashurst, asked to endorse a pardon for a horse-stealer from Cambridge, reported to the king, "I had whilst on Circuit received such favourable Accounts of him as induced me to reprieve him & had those accounts remain'd uncontradicted I should have thought there could be no objection . . . for a free Pardon . . . But I have this day received a letter from some Gentlemen of the University desiring to retract their former applications for mercy...."[24] The judges were well aware that the gentry of the county were charged with government and criminal justice between assize times, and hence usually gave their opinions a serious hearing. The pardon could be used, however, to show mercy when the death penalty seemed too severe, and this discretion became

---

[23]William Sheffield to Evans, Hinds and Best, re his trial at Aylesbury, Lent 1787; PRO, HO 47/6. Sheffield's employers found it inconvenient to attend; he was condemned, although Best wrote on his behalf.

[24]Report of Justice Ashurst, 10 April 1787, re John Higgins; PRO, HO 47/6.

part of the explicit justification of the law to the poor. In passing sentence of death on a prosperous sheep-stealer in 1787, Sir Beaumont Hotham argued that the law understood the trials of the poor and properly held the rich rogue to stricter account. "He noted the difference between a poor wretch in distress committing such a crime, and a man of seeming reputation;—that the latter, under the mask of a fair and upright character, was enabled to make depredations on his neighbours and the public, without being suspected, therefore was not to be guarded against, and consequently, in his eye, was much more culpable than the poor man, who commits such acts from real want."[25] Since most death sentences were pronounced for theft, the most recent historian of the pardon concludes that it moderated the barbarity of the criminal law in the interests of humanity. It was erratic and capricious, but a useful palliative until Parliament reformed the law in the nineteenth century.

Such an analysis stresses the narrowly legal use of the pardon, but ignores its social significance, the crucial point that interests us here. As in so many other areas of the law, custom and procedure allowed wholly extra-judicial considerations great influence. The pardon allowed the bench to recognize poverty, when necessary, as an excuse, even though the law itself did not. But the manner in which a pardon was obtained made it an important element in eighteenth-century social relations in three other ways. In the first place, the claims of class saved far more men who had been left to hang by the assize judge than did the claims of humanity. Again and again in petitions the magic words recur: "his parents are respectable persons in Denbighshire"; his father is "a respectable farmer"; his brother is "a builder of character and eminence in London." There are very few petitions that plead what one in 1787 called "the common excuse for larceny, poverty and distress." It may have been the common excuse, but those requesting pardons

knew it held little weight—only two of the hundreds of petitions that year bothered to mention it. In contrast, the excuse of respectability was pleaded *in extenso*. Even need, rarely admitted as a legitimate excuse for a poor man, could become a compelling reason to forgive a richer one. When an officer returned from India was caught stealing silver from inns as he travelled by sedan chair through Oxfordshire, Lord McCartney testified to his valour in imperial wars, and urged that he must have been distressed. This evidence and the support of a "very reputable" family procured a full pardon. Similar considerations that would never have saved a labourer from the gallows worked in favour of the respectable. When the son of a secretary of the London Foundling Hospital was condemned for a serious burglary, he was saved from execution out of consideration for his mother, and "Seven unmarried Sisters and a Brother" who would "unavoidably Share the Ignominy due only to his Crimes." John Say's case was similar: he came from "an exceedingly Worthy & respectable family who will feel the disgrace of a Public Execution beyond expression, his Young Sister also now at Boarding School will be irreparably Injured by a disgrace which no time can Obliterate & which will greatly affect her future Interests thro' Life." The future interests of the sisters of condemned labourers were never mentioned in petitions, because they had no prospects. When the families of poor convicts were taken into consideration, it was usually through fear that execution would create too many orphans to be supported on the parish rates.

The pardon thus served to save a good many respectable villains. It was all very well to hang Dr. Dodd and Lord Ferrers, but to hang every errant son of the rich who tried his hand at highway robbery to pay gambling debts would have made too great a carnage in the better circles. Pardons also favoured those with connections for another reason: mercy was part of the currency of patronage. Petitions were most effective from great men, and the common course was for a plea to be passed up through increasingly higher

---

[25] *An Account of the Life, Trial, and Behaviour of William Bagnall* (WSL, Broadsheets 2).

levels of the social scale, between men bound together by the links of patronage and obligation. The bald language of place-seekers recurs here too; trading in life and death became part of the game of interest. "If anything can be done in consequence of the inclosed letter," wrote Lord Viscount Hinchingbrooke, "I shall be very thankful for it—as the writer of it is a particular friend of mine in the county of Huntingdon. . .

Petitions for pardons were occasionally opposed, but usually by determined prosecutors. Where a prosecutor had second thoughts or wished to indulge his humanity after exacting terror and recovering his property, he sometimes was the first to add his name to a plea for mercy—and thereby gave it greater weight. Most successful petitions, however, were begun by other men of respectable position, with good connections, and their activity on behalf of the condemned could only enhance their reputations as men of compassion and magnanimity. To the poor, the intercession of a local gentleman was proof of his power to approach the throne. He took no blame if the petition failed, for an unanswered plea was attributed to the determination of the king, who was popularly believed to sign all death warrants. A successful outcome was attributed to mercy at the same exalted height— and Blackstone argued that "these repeated acts of goodness coming immediately from his own hand, endear the sovereign to his subjects, and contribute more than anything to root in their hearts that filial affection, and personal loyalty, which are the sure establishment of a prince." And all the chaplains, country gentlemen and peers who had helped to obtain a pardon shared somewhat in the reflected glory of the merciful ruler.

The pardon is important because it often put the principal instrument of legal terror—the gallows—directly in the hands of those who held power. In this it was simply the clearest example of the prevailing custom at all levels of criminal justice. Here was the peculiar genius of the law. It allowed the rulers of England to make the courts a selective instrument of class justice, yet simul-taneously to proclaim the law's incorruptible impartiality, and absolute determinacy. Their political and social power was reinforced daily by bonds of obligation on one side and condescension on the other, as prosecutors, gentlemen and peers decided to invoke the law or agreed to show mercy. Discretion allowed a prosecutor to terrorize the petty thief and then command his gratitude, or at least the approval of his neighbourhood as a man of compassion. It allowed the class that passed one of the bloodiest penal codes in Europe to congratulate itself on its humanity. It encouraged loyalty to the king and the state:

> And Earthly Power doth then show likest God's
> When mercy seasons justice.

And in the countryside the power of gentlemen and peers to punish or forgive worked in the same way to maintain the fabric of obedience, gratitude and deference. The law was important as gross coercion; it was equally important as ideology. Its majesty, justice and mercy helped to create the spirit of consent and submission, the "mind-forged manacles," which Blake saw binding the English poor. But consent, in Archdeacon Paley's phrase, must be managed "with delicacy and circumspection." To understand fully the social functions of the eighteenth-century criminal law, we must understand how it embodied those virtues too.

DELICACY AND CIRCUMSPECTION

Deference in eighteenth-century England, although pervasive, was not complete. The gentry managed to maintain order without anything resembling the political police used by the French, but it was order that often seemed to rest on precarious foundations. The common Englishman was renowned for his riots, and also for his dislike of standing armies. Although the ideology of justice could be used by gentlemen to quiet a mob, and with success, words sometimes lost their magic. Then the discretion embodied in the law allowed the authorities to use terror with great flexibility. Examples of this delicate adjustment of state power are legion, especially in decisions about executions, the most emotive act in civil government. In 1756 Justice Willes was holding the Warwick Assizes when food riots broke out in the county. He announced his intention of trying and executing immediately all rioters brought before him, adjourning the court from week to week until order had been restored. Within days he convicted four,

> And, when I passed Sentence upon Them, I said a good deal to show the heinous nature of their crime, and the great folly of the attempt . . . and I ordered the captain and another notorious offender to be executed on Wednesday next; and told . . . the others. . . that I would adjourn 'till Monday s'en night, and that then, if the insurrection was quite at end, I would apply to his Majesty to pardon them; but if not, I would immediately execute the two other persons that were convicted.

No one thought it strange to hang some men for crimes committed by others. The Secretary of State wrote to Willes to congratulate him, and expressed the hope that other judges would follow his example in similar cases. "The King, the Duke, the whole court, are full of Commendation, & the general voice is, that these Insolent Rioters could not have fallen into better Hands."

Gentlemen were very sensitive to opinion in their neighbourhoods, for there might be serious consequences if the show of force was either not quite impressive enough, or so brutal that it outraged men and destroyed the mystique of justice. Lord Hardwicke, when Chief Justice, ordered a Cornish rioter's body to hang in chains, a refinement of capital punishment that added infamy to death. He agreed to respite that part of the sentence, however, when the local gentry informed him that

> in the present circumstances of affairs it would be more advisable not to do it, for tho' his crimes, as your Lordship says, demand the most terrifying Example yet there must be the greatest regard had for the Peace of our Country, which we were apprehensive might be again disturbed if that measure was pursued. It is undoubtedly in theory right and

would be extremely necessary in most parts of the Kingdom, but in this there has been such an unaccountable run in his favour, that if any of his particular Friends should cut Him down, which would be a fresh insult upon Authority, The Rabble would call it the last blow, and the spirit might revive . . . . We are in hopes that the examples are carried far enough to work upon the Fears of his friends, without giving them the opportunity of any new Triumph.[26]

Edmund Burke used the same argument a half-century later in the case of the Gordon rioters. A week of looting, arson and unchecked defiance of authority severely shook the foundations of order. Burke therefore advised the government to limit the number of executions in spite of the gravity of the offence: "If I understand the temper of the publick at this moment, a very great part of the lower, and some of the middling people of this city, are in a very critical disposition, and such as ought to be managed with *firmness and delicacy*." He continued, "In general they rather approve than blame the principles of the rioters . . . This keeps their minds in a suspended and anxious state, which may very easily be exasperated, by an injudicious severity, into desperate resolutions; or by weak measures, on the part of the Government, it may be encouraged to the pursuit of courses, which may be of the most dangerous consequences to the public. . ." His recommendation was for six executions with maximum publicity, a calculated blend of terror and mercy under the strict rule of law.[27]

The rulers of eighteenth-century England spent much time gauging opinion in this way. The facade of power had to be kept undamaged. The gentry were acutely aware that their security depended on *belief*—belief in the justice of their rule, and in its adamantine strength. Hence, punishment at times had to be waived or mitigated to meet popular ideas of justice, and to prevent popular outrage from going too far and

---

[26]Brit. Mus. Add. MSS, 35,585 fos. 299–303.
[27]"Some Thoughts on the Approaching Executions," *Works*, 1812, vol. IX, pp. 268–71. My emphasis.

thereby realizing its own strength. The aim above all was to avoid exposing the law and authority either to ridicule or to too close scrutiny. Contempt of court was therefore punished severely: the convict who heard the death sentence with no sign of repentence, and who instead damned the judge, could hope for no pardon. It was also important for those administering and using the law to be circumspect, discreet—to leave unsaid anything that might mar the illusion of power. Hence a gentleman who trifled with the mob or called into question the ultimate justice of the law was execrated by his fellows as a knave and a fool. Lord George Gordon did both. The impotence of England's governors in the face of disorder, and the measure of their contempt for class traitors, was epitomized by a curious scene in the House of Commons in June 1780. As Gordon's supporters raged outside and threatened to break in upon the Honourable Members, several MPs followed him about the House with their hands on their swords, vowing to run him through if the mob broke in. When Gordon continued his wayward career a few years later by publishing a protest of the convicts of Newgate against capital punishment for theft, he was committed to prison as a libeller of justice. Most gentlemen thought him mad.

Discretion was necessary in thousands of small things, too. It permeated the operations of the law. The decisions that moved the levers of fear and mercy were decisions of propertied men, and they made them privately, among themselves. At the most informal level, before Justices of the Peace—country gentlemen—the operation of the law was often the result of an agreement on tactics between the JP and the prosecutor, especially when the latter was a friend or powerful neighbour. At the level of prosecution, the gentry particularly were likely to allow the offender to escape if they were not completely sure of a conviction: it was better to feign mercy rather than reveal impotence. Since the legal process was largely a secret between landowner and magistrate, nothing was easier to arrange. . .

. . . The opacity of the law also made it possible for the rulers of England to act in concert in managing hangings, arranging backstage the precise moment of the emotional climax. This was crucial not only at times of disorder; it was part of the routine administration of the law. The Hanoverians themselves sometimes took seriously their legal prerogatives in this respect. Shortly after he came to the throne, George III agreed to the routine mitigation of the death sentence to one of transportation in the case of a highway robber. He gave instructions, however, that

> as his Majesty hopes so to terrify this unhappy Man, on the present occasion that he may not hereafter be guilty of the like offense; it is the King's intention that *he should not be acquainted of his Majesty's having extended his royal mercy towards him, 'till he comes to the place of execution.* It will be proper therefore, that you give orders to the sheriffs, for this purpose, so that he be carried with the others, who are to suffer; to the place of execution, and that he be informed, then, and not before then, of the reprieve. . . .[28]

''Circumspection'' is a euphemism in such circumstances. The private manipulation of the law by the wealthy and powerful was in truth a ruling-class conspiracy, in the most exact meaning of the word. The king, judges, magistrates and gentry used private, extra-legal dealings among themselves to bend the statute and common law to their own purposes. The legal definition of conspiracy does not require explicit agreement; those party to it need not even all know one another, provided they are working together for the same ends. In this case, the common assumptions of the conspirators lay so deep that they were never questioned, and rarely made explicit.

It is important to recognize this fact, for it raises some important methodological questions for the student of authority and the law. There is a danger, which perhaps this essay has not avoided, of giving the impression that a system of authority is *something*, rather than the actions of

[28]C. Jenkinson to Recorder of London, 22 May 1761; PRO, SP 44/87, fos. 19 and 20 (my emphasis).

living men. The invisible hand of Adam Smith's political economy was metaphor, shorthand for an effect rather than a cause; it was a description of recurrent patterns of useful behaviour forged out of the energy, conflicts and greed of thousands of individuals in a capitalist market. In a somewhat similar way, much of the ideological structure surrounding the criminal law was the product of countless short-term decisions. It was often a question of intuition, and of trial and error. In handling a mob it was useful to appeal to ideals of English justice: but that was a lesson that was slowly learned over many generations, and rarely raised to the level of theory. The necessity of gauging reactions to executions was an immediate problem of public order, not a plot worked out by eighteenth-century experts in public relations for a fee. The difficulty for the historian of the law is twofold. He must make explicit convictions that were often unspoken, for if left unspoken we cannot understand the actions of the men who held them. Yet in describing how convictions and actions moulded the administration of justice, he must never forget that history is made by men, not by the Cunning of Reason or the Cunning of System. The course of history is the result of a complex of human actions—purposive, accidental, sometimes determined—and it cannot be reduced to one transcendent purpose. The cunning of a ruling class is a more substantial concept, however, for such a group of men is agreed on ultimate ends. However much they believed in justice (and they did); however sacred they held property (and they worshipped it); however merciful they were to the poor (and many were); the gentlemen of England knew that their duty was, above all, to rule. On that depended everything. They acted accordingly.

Seen in this light, much of the historical literature on the eighteenth-century ruling class seems misconceived. Their attitudes to the law are often made a test of their moral worth. Romilly and the other reformers usually have received alphas, as the forerunners of the armies of liberal enlightenment and humanitarianism, and as the "winners." But in praising the reformers we caricature the conservatives. Descriptions of a ruling class in terms of abstract moral judgement have contradictory results because they are profoundly unhistorical. The substantial literature on the county magistrate is another case in point. Historians have reached divergent conclusions, although the present consensus seems to be that their rule was "in general upright and humane." Still, pessimists (to borrow the terms of another moral debate) can find evidence that many JPs were "pretty great tyrants," and at least one optimistic historian has hailed them as the finest governors the world has ever known. These peculiarly idealist explanations, which count or weigh the number of good acts against the number of bad, then judge whether or not to admit the eighteenth-century ruling class into the heavenly kingdom of twentieth-century respectability, hinder rather than aid understanding. Nor does it help to take a relativist moral tack, and assert that the rulers of England were about as humane as the society that they lived in, some a bit better, some a bit worse. Humanity and inhumanity are real dispositions, rooted in individuals, and more or less general, perhaps, in groups of men with similar experiences. But conscious dispositions can be shaped by much deeper social imperatives, justifications are not always the same as motives, and even the sincerest convictions and most authentic emotional responses may be called forth, or subdued, or even at times reversed, by the patterns of power within a culture or a class. Men were merciful and merciless in the eighteenth century: the historian's task is to answer the questions when, and why. It is not something we can judge in the light of eternity. Rather, we should be content to know why Lord Montagu was able to please his ladies by saving a man's life, and why a Midlands cleric was prepared to use the gallows to help his parishioner find God.

The second question raised by a discussion of the law as ideology is evidential: how can we prove that it worked? Much of the evidence cited here comes from the avowed intentions and observations of the rulers, not the ruled. Perhaps much of what the gentry interpreted as the deference and gratitude of the poor was in fact conscious deception. Perhaps the ordinary Englishman played the role assigned to him, but was never convinced by the play. The eighteenth century produced much genteel cant about justice, but it also produced a large popular literature marked by cynicism and disrespect for the law. And there were many more forceful demonstrations of incredulity, including riots at executions, and rogues who mocked their judges.

Much research remains to be done before we can give confident answers to some of these questions. But two general points may be made. In the first place, most of the evidence that we have of loud popular disrespect for the law comes from London, and London differed in important ways from the rest of eighteenth-century English society. It had a highly transient population, and a large body of disorderly and parasitic poor, living on the gathered wealth of commerce, the port and the disorderly and parasitic rich. In sharp contrast to the provinces, the men hanged at Tyburn were mostly born in distant places. They had come to London from the country, and in doing so left behind the close and persisting personal relationships that still characterized much of English society. And it was in such intimate dealings of fear and gratitude that much of the ideology of justice was realized. Some historians have suggested that "urban alienation" accounts for London disorder and crime in the eighteenth century. It may be more correct to say that the instruments of control there were weaker, in part because the class relationships that fostered deference were. Resistance to the law, disrespect for its majesty, scorn for its justice were greater. Equally, judicial mercy in London was more often a bureaucratic lottery than a convincing expression of paternalism.

The provinces too erupted in disorder: food riots, militia riots, excise riots, turnpike riots, gang poaching, endemic and often violent smuggling. The hegemony of the law was never complete and unbroken, even in the most deeply rural, most traditional counties. The fabric of authority was torn and reknit constantly. The important fact remains, however, that it was reknit readily. The closer mesh of economic and social ties in rural society, the public nature of those relationships compared to the complexity and obscurity of much of metropolitan life, allowed the creation of an ideology that was much more pervasive than in London. When it was momentarily challenged in a county riot or by a defiant labourer, no serious harm resulted; the prevailing code was, in fact, usually strengthened. An ideology endures not by being wholly enforced and rigidly defined. Its effectiveness lies first in its very elasticity, the fact that men are not required to make it a credo, that it seems to them the product of their own minds and their own experience. And the law did not enforce uniform obedience, did not seek total control; indeed, it sacrificed punishment when necessary to preserve the belief in justice. The courts dealt in terror, pain and death, but also in moral ideals, control of arbitrary power, mercy for the weak. In doing so they made it possible to disguise much of the class interest of the law. The second strength of an ideology is its generality. Provided that its depths are not explored too often or by too many, it remains a reservoir of belief throughout the society and flows into the gaps made by individual acts of protest. Therefore, those using it are concerned above all with surface appearances. Undoubtedly the gentleman accepting an apology from the man in his power, the thief or the rioter, would have been gratified to know that the contrition was public and convincing, that it served to sustain general belief in the justice of the social order, it sufficed. It became part of the untested general idea, the ideology which made it possible to stigmatize dissent as acts of individuals, of rogues and criminals and madmen.

The hypothesis presented here is that the criminal law, more than any other social institution, made it possible to govern eighteenth-century England without a police force and without a large army. The ideology of the law was crucial in sustaining the hegemony of the English ruling class. This argument, if sound, helps us to explain their resistance to suggestions for drastic legal reform. It also casts some light on the membership of that ruling class, and the character of their society.

III

The long resistance to reform of the criminal law has perplexed later writers. The conservatives who opposed reform have been generally criticized, but historians have failed adequately to explain the growth in numbers of capital statutes and the simultaneous extension of the pardon. When the criminal law is seen not simply as a coercive instrument to punish crime, however, both problems seem largely resolved.

The post-revolution Parliaments passed more and more capital statutes in order to make *every* kind of theft, malicious damage or rebellion an act punishable by death. Although most executions took place under Tudor statutes rather than these fresh-minted ones, the new legislation gave the power to make terrible examples when necessary. Sometimes the new laws merely recreated the death penalty for offences which had been affected by the development of benefit of clergy; more often they added it to newly defined offences, including some not foreseen by the lawmakers of Elizabeth's time, such as the forging of banknotes. But if gentlemen in Parliament were willing to hang a proportion of offenders every year in order to stage the moral drama of the gallows, it is extremely doubtful that they ever believed that the capital statutes should be strictly enforced.[29] The impact of sentencing and hanging could only be diminished if it became too common: "It is certain," wrote Burke, "that a great havock among criminals hardens, rather than subdues, the minds of people inclined to the same crimes; and therefore fails of answering its purpose as an example."[30] Equally important, a return to the severities of the Tudors and early Stuarts probably would not have been tolerated by the people. At that period and earlier the gentry and the great houses usually had small armies of their own with which local disaffection could be crushed when necessary. But from the later seventeenth century the importance of managing opinion had made nuance, discretion and less obvious coercion a necessary part of the art of ruling. If London rioted at Tyburn, how much worse would disorder be if the executions were four times as numerous? In the counties, three or six hangings in each, twice a year, afforded splendid occasion for lessons in justice and power; but scores of victims would have revolted the people. Although some gentlemen in Parliament did pen bloody new laws in the heat of anger and an uncompromising spirit of revenge, they saw the wisdom of pardons when confronted with long gaol calendars and the spectre of county towns festooned with corpses.

Considerations such as these probably influenced the judges most in determining their general policy over the century. For although it is asserted that after 1750 a constantly declining proportion of death sentences was actually carried out, this is only true in London. In the home counties the proportion of condemned who were executed remained fairly steady over the same period. But the common element in both jurisdictions was the effect of the differing policies on the absolute numbers hanged. In both cases, the number of the condemned who actually died on the gallows was relatively constant over much of the century. The law made enough examples to inculcate fear, but not so many as to harden or repel a populace that had to assent, in some measure at least, to the rule of property.

The second great paradox about the old criminal law, the delay in reform long after a good case had been made that capital statutes allowed theft

---

[29]This is Paley's doctrine, embraced by every subsequent conservative apologist. Radzinowicz explicitly rejects it on the grounds that the divergence between the law and its administration was increasing (Radzinowicz, vol. 1, p. 164, no. 59). His argument ignores the probability that Parliament passed many laws in part *because* they knew they would not be rigorously enforced; that is, that they legislated on the basis of their experience.

[30]"Some thoughts on the Approaching Executions," *Works*, vol. IX, p. 270.

to increase by making prosecutions uncertain, may also be resolved. Romilly and Eden and the other reformers proposed to replace capital punishment with lesser penalties, and the model which they followed implicitly and sometimes used publicly was that of Beccaria: "a fixed code of laws, which must be observed to the letter."[31] But Beccaria's plan made no provision for the needs of government. The conservative gentlemen of England balked not only at the "unconstitutional" police that such plans required: they instinctively rejected rational plans as pernicious. A complete rationalization of the criminal law would remove those very elements of discretion, such as the pardon, which contributed so much to the maintenance of order and deference. Beccaria's thought, as Venturi has pointed out, was no mere *mélange* of humanitarianism and reason. His machine-like system of judgement and punishment would work only where differences of power between men did not exist, where the "perhaps unnecessary right of property" had disappeared. His principal European opponents seized on this fact: his ideas, they claimed, spelt the end of all authority.[32]

In England the opposition was muffled, since the rhetoric of Whiggism denied that arbitrary measures existed and claimed that the criminal law was *already* fixed and determinate. Most of the opponents of reform therefore argued only that it was impossible to create a schedule of crimes and punishments complete enough to do "justice" to the subtle differences between cases. But there were hints even in England of the deeper fears for authority. In 1817 Christian, always a frank defender of the unreformed law, recalled Livy's description of the fixed laws enacted after the expulsion of the Roman kings:

> The King was a man from whom you might obtain by petition, what was right, and even what was

wrong: with him there was room for favour and for kindness: he had the power of showing his displeasure, and of granting a pardon; he knew how to discriminate between a friend and an enemy. The laws were a thing deaf and inexorable, more favourable and advantageous to the weak than to the powerful: they admitted of no relaxation or indulgence, if you exceeded their limits.

"He knew how to discriminate between a friend and an enemy"—no criminal code could do that, in Christian's opinion. And had not the French Revolution shown that rigid laws could favour the poor rather than the propertied? With such reforms, the judge concluded, "we should all be involved in republican gloom, melancholy, and sadness."[33]

Throughout the period we have been considering, the importance of the law as an instrument of authority and a breeder of values remained paramount. The English ruling class entered the eighteenth century with some of its strongest ideological weapons greatly weakened. The Divine Right of Kings had been jettisoned in the interests of gentry power, but the monarchy lost as a consequence much of its potency as a source of authority, and so too did religion. At the same time control had flowed away from the executive in the extreme decentralization of government which characterized the century. With Stuarts plotting in Europe, Jacobitism suspected everywhere at home, and a lumpily unattractive German prince on the throne, English jsutice became a more important focus of beliefs about the nation and the social order. Perhaps some of the tension abated after the last Jacobite attempt in 1745, which may help to aocunt for Blackstone's relatively favourable attitude to reform in mid-century. But within a few decades renewed assaults on the structure of authority—the riots of 1766 and 1780, Wilkes and the French Revolution—determined the English ruling class to repel any attacks on the mystery and majesty of the law.

In doing so they apparently sacrificed some security of property. Romilly and the rest of the

[31]Cesare Beccaria, *On Crimes and Punishments,* trans. Henry Paolucci, New York 1963, ch. 4, p. 16.

[32]Franco Venturi, *Utopia and Reform in the Enlightenment,* Cambridge, 1971, p. 101, quoting Beccaria, ch. 30. On this statement compare Paolucci on Beccaria, op. cit., p. 74, no. 39.

[33]Christian, *Charges,* pp. 278–9.

reformers were undoubtedly right that convictions in the courts were uncertain, and that the occasional terror of the gallows would always be less effective than sure detection of crime and moderate punishments. Yet the argument had little weight with the gentry and aristocracy. In the first place they had large numbers of personal servants to guard their plate and their wives. Their problem was not attack from without but disloyalty within their houses. No code of laws or police force would protect them there. Their own judgement of character and the fair treatment of servants within the family were the only real guarantees they could have. Nor did the technicalities of the law bother country gentlemen when they did come to try pilferers of their woods and gardens. For as MPs they passed a mass of legislation that allowed them, as JPs, to convict offenders without the trouble of legalistic indictments or tender-minded juries. In cases involving grain, wood, trees, garden produce, fruit, turnips, dogs, cattle, horses, the hedges of parks and game, summary proceedings usually yielded a speedy and simple conviction. The other crime from which the gentry commonly suffered was sabotage: arson, cattle-maiming, the destruction of trees. Although all these offences were punished by death, few offenders were ever caught. Here too gentlemen knew that a reform of the capital statutes would not increase the certainty of a conviction. Moreover, sabotage was primarily an attack on their authority rather than their property. Their greatest protection against such assaults was acquiescence in their right to rule: the belief in their neighbourhoods that they were kind and just landlords and magistrates. In one area alone were they exposed to the danger of great financial loss from theft. Their largest possession was land. The only way it could be taken from them illegally was by forgery—and it is significant that forgery was punished with unmitigated severity throughout the century, by death.

Lower down the social scale, the property of men in trade and manufacturing and farming was much less secure. In the eighteenth century very few of the offences from which such men suffered were punishable on summary conviction. Instead, to recover embezzled banknotes or shoplifted calico or stolen sheep, it was necessary to go to the expense and trouble of a full criminal trial. Its outcome was always uncertain: the technicalities of indictment or the misplaced sympathies of juries allowed many thieves to escape. After the trial came the misplaced sympathies of petitioners for pardons. Martin Madan, anxious to see property secured by a more rigorous execution of the laws, argued that "the outside influences of great supporters" had too great effect on the prerogative of mercy. The result was that the great indulged their humanity at the expense of lesser men's property.

There was, therefore, a division of interest among propertied Englishmen about the purpose of the criminal law. The reformers' campaign spoke to humanitarians of all classes, men revolted by the public agonies of the condemned at the gallows. But their argument that capital punishment should be replaced by a more certain protection of property appealed mostly to that great body of "middling men," almost half the nation, who earned from £25 to £150 a year at mid-century, and created more than half England's wealth. Although they could use the discretionary elements of the law to a limited degree, their property was the prey of thieves undeterred by terror. Their complaints did not impress a tiny but powerful ruling class, whose immense personal property in land was secure, who could afford to protect their other goods without public support, and who in any case were most concerned with the law as an instrument of authority.

It is in such terms that we must work toward a definition of the ruling class of eighteenth-century England. Far from being the property of Marxist or *marxisant* historians, the term is a leitmotiv in studies of the period. Partly this is due to the testimony of the sources: gentry and aristocracy claimed the title with complete assurance. Its historical usage, however, remains imprecise. Usually it has been defined in terms of income or status: the rents of the great landed estate, or the exact meaning contemporaries gave to the word "gentleman." Class, however, is a social relationship, not simply an aggregare of individuals. As a relationship based upon differences of power and wealth, it must be sought in the life of the institutions that men create and within which they meet. The law defined and maintained the bounds of power and wealth, and when we ask who controlled the criminal law, we see a familiar constellation: monarchy, aristocracy, gentry and, to a lesser extent, the great merchants. In numbers they were no more than 3 per cent of the population. But their discretionary use of the law maintained their rule and moulded social consciousness. An operational definition of the ruling class—asking who controlled a critical institution like the law, and how they manipulated it—is a more useful approach than drawing horizontal lines in Blackstone's list of forty status levels. For it is necessary to define in detail what it means to rule.

Many historians, confronted with the hegemony of the eighteenth-century ruling class, have described it in terms of absolute control and paternal benevolence. Max Beloff argued that after the Restoration they enjoyed an unparalleled sense of security which explained "the leniency with which isolated disturbances were on the whole treated, when compared with the ferocity shown by the same class towards their social inferiors in the times of the Tudors and early Stuarts."[34] It seems more likely that the relative insecurity of England's governors, their crucial dependence on the deference of the governed, compelled them to moderate that ferocity. More recent writing has stressed the importance of patronage; Harold Perkin has argued that this was the central bond of eighteenth-century society. Patronage created vertical chains of loyalty; it was, in fact, "the module of which the social structure was built." Powerful men bound less powerful ones to them through paternalism, controlling the income, even the "life-chances" of the dependent client on tenant or labourer. Such ties, repeated endlessly, formed a "mesh of verti-

cal loyalties." Social control in the eighteenth century seems a gentle yoke from this perspective: a spontaneous, uncalculated and peaceful relationship of gratitude and gifts. The system is ultimately a self-adjusting one of shared moral values, values which are not contrived but autonomous. At one point the author concedes that insubordination was "ruthlessly suppressed." But mostly social solidarity grew quietly: "those who lived within its embrace . . . [called it] friendship."[35] Coercion was an exceptional act, to handle exceptional deviance.

Yet it is difficult to understand how those loyalties endured when patronage was uneven, interrupted, often capricious. Many contemporaries testified to the fickleness of wealth: disappointed office-seekers, unemployed labourers or weavers, paupers dumped over parish boundaries. Riot was a commonplace; so too were hangings. Benevolence, in short, was not a simple positive act: it contained within it the ever-present threat of malice. In economic relations a landlord keeping his rents low was benevolent because he could, with impunity, raise them. A justice giving charity to a wandering beggar was benevolent because he could whip him instead. Benevolence, all patronage, was given meaning by its contingency. It was the obverse of coercion, terror's conspiracy of silence. When patronage failed, force could be invoked; but when coercion inflamed men's minds, at the crucial moment mercy could calm them.

A ruling class organizes its power in the state. The sanction of the state is force, but it is force that is legitimized, however imperfectly, and therefore the state deals also in ideologies. Loyalties do not grow simply in complex societies:

---

[34]Max Beloff, *Public Order and Popular Disturbances 1660-1714*, 1938, p. 154.

[35]Herold Perkin, *The Origin of Modern English Society*, 1969, pp. 32-49, a sustained historical use of the idea of "social control" currently orthodox in the sociological literature. The origins of the concept lie at least as far back as Durkheim's "social conscience," and it has a marked ideological history of its own. Its increasingly common usage in historical writing, often with little critical exmination, therefore bears watching. Its assumption of the relative autonomy of normative sanctions seems dubious, particularly in descriptions of the power of the state.

they are twisted, invoked and often consciously created. Eighteenth-century England was not a free market of patronage relations. It was a society with a bloody penal code, an astute ruling class who manipulated it to their advantage, and a people schooled in the lessons of Justice, Terror and Mercy. The benevolence of rich men to poor, and all the ramifications of patronage, were upheld by the sanction of the gallows and the rhetoric of the death sentence.

THE RULE OF LAW

E. P. THOMPSON

... We might be wise to end here. But since readers of this study may be provoked to some general reflections upon the law and upon British traditions, perhaps we may allow ourselves the same indulgence.

From a certain traditional middle ground of national historiography the interest of this theme (the Black Act and its evolution) may be evident. But this middle ground is now being eroded, from at least two directions. On one hand the perspective within which British political and social historians have been accustomed to view their own history is, quite properly, coming under challenge. As the last imperial illusions of the twentieth century fade, so preoccupation with the history and culture of a small island off the coast of Europe becomes open to the charge of narcissism. The culture of constitutionalism which flowered here, under favoured conditions, is an episode too exceptional to carry any universal significance. If we judge it in terms of its own self-sufficient values we are imprisoned within its own parochialism.

Alternative perspectives must diminish the complacency of national historical preoccupation. If we see Britain within the perspective of the expansion of European capitalism, then the contest over interior rights and laws will be dwarfed when set beside the exterior record of slavetrading, of the East India Company, of commercial and military imperialism. Or, to take up a bright new conservative perspective, the story of a few lost common rights and of a few deer-stealers strung from the gallows is a paltry affair when set beside the accounts of mass repression of almost any day in the day-book of the twentieth century. Did a few foresters get a rough handling from partisan laws? What is that beside the norms of the Third Reich? Did the villagers of Winkfield lose access to the peat within Swinley Rails? What is that beside the liquidation of the *kulaks*? What is remarkable (we are reminded) is not that the laws were bent but the fact that there was, anywhere in the eighteenth century, a rule of law at all. To ask for greater justice than that is to display mere sentimentalism. In any event, we should adjust our sense of proportion; against the handfuls carried off on the cart to Tyburn (and smaller handfuls than have been carried off in Tudor times) we must see whole legions carried off by plague or dearth.

From these perspectives concern with the rights and wrongs at law of a few men in 1723 is concern with trivia. And the same conclusion may be reached through a different adjustment of perspective, which may coexist with some of the same arguments. This flourishes in the form of a sophisticated, but (ultimately) highly schematic Marxism which, to our surprise, seems to spring up in the footsteps of those of us in an older Marxist tradition. From this standpoint the law is, perhaps more clearly than any other cultural or institutional artifact, by definition a part of a 'superstructure' adapting itself to the necessities of an infrastructure of productive forces and productive relations. As such, it is clearly an instrument of the *de facto* ruling class: it both defines and defends these rulers' claims upon resources

Source: From E. P. Thompson, *Whigs and Hunters: The Origin of the Black Act* (New York: Pantheon Books, 1975), pp. 258-269. Reprinted by permission.

and labour-power—it says what shall be property and what shall be crime—and it mediates class relations with a set of appropriate rules and sanctions, all of which, ultimately, confirm and consolidate existing class power. Hence the rule of law is only another mask for the rule of a class. The revolutionary can have no interest in law, unless as a phenomenon of ruling-class power and hypocrisy; it should be his aim simply to overthrow it. And so, once again, to express surprise at the Black Act or at partial judges is unless as confirmation and illustration of theories which might easily be demonstrated without all this labour—simply to expose one's own naivety.

So the old middle ground of historiography is crumbling on both sides. I stand on a very narrow ledge, watching the tides come up. Or, to be more explicit, I sit here in my study, at the age of fifty, the desk and the floor piled high with five years of notes, xeroxes, rejected drafts, the clock once again moving into the small hours, and see myself, in a lucid instant, as an anachronism. Why have I spent these years trying to find out what could, in its essential structures, have been known without any investigation at all? And does it matter a damn who gave Parson Power his instructions; which forms brought "Vulcan" Gates to the gallows; or how an obscure Richmond publican managed to evade a death sentence already determined upon by the Law Officers, the First Minister and the King?

I am disposed to think that it does matter; I have a vested interest (in five years of labour) to think it may. But to show this must involve evacuating received assumptions—that narrowing ledge of traditional middle ground—and moving out onto an even narrower theoretical ledge. This would accept, as it must, some part of the Marxist-structural critique; indeed, some parts of this study have confirmed the class-bound and mystifying functions of the law. But it would reject its ulterior reductionism and would modify its typology of superior and inferior (but determining) structures.

First, analysis of the eighteenth century (and perhaps of other centuries) calls in question the validity of separating off the law as a whole and placing it in some typological superstructure. The law when considered as institution (the courts, with their class theatre and class procedures) or as personnel (the judges, the lawyers, the Justices of the Peace) may very easily be assimilated to those of the ruling class. But all that is entailed in "the law" is not subsumed in these institutions. The law may also be seen as ideology, or as particular rules and sanctions which stand in a definite and active relationship (often a field of conflict) to social norms; and, finally, it may be seen simply in terms of its own logic, rules and procedures—that is, simply *as law*. And it is not possible to conceive of any complex society without law.

We must labour this point, since some theorists today are unable to see the law except in terms of "the fuzz" setting about inoffensive demonstrators or cannabis-smokers. I am no authority on the twentieth century, but in the eighteenth century matters were more complex than that. To be sure I have tried to show, in the evolution of the Black Act, an expression of the ascendancy of a Whig oligarchy, which created new laws and bent old legal forms in order to legitimize its own property and status; this oligarchy employed the law, both instrumentally and ideologically, very much as a modern structural Marxist should expect it to do. But this is not the same thing as to say that the rulers had need of law, in order to oppress the ruled, while those who were ruled had need of none. What was often at issue was not property, supported by law, against no-property; it was alternative definitions of property-rights: for the landowner, enclosure—for the cottager, common rights: for the forest officialdom, "preserved grounds" for the deer; for the foresters, the right to take turfs. For as long as it remained possible, the ruled—if they could find a purse and a lawyer—would actually fight for their rights by means of law; occasionally the copyholders, resting upon the precedents of sixteenth-century law, could actually win a case. When it ceased to be possible to continue the fight at law, men still felt a sense of legal wrong: the propertied had obtained their power by illegitimate means.

Moreover, if we look closely into such an agrarian context, the distinction between law, on the one hand, conceived of as an element of "superstructure," and the actualities of productive forces and relations on the other hand, becomes more and more untenable. For law was often a definition of actual agrarian *practice*, as it had been pursued "time out of mind." How can we distinguish between the activity of farming or of quarrying and the rights to this strip of land or to that quarry? The farmer or forester in his daily occupation was moving within visible or invisible structures of law: this merestone which marked the division between strips; that ancient oak— visited by processional on each Rogation Day— which marked the limits of the parish grazing; those other invisible (but potent and sometimes legally enforceable) memories as to which parishes had the right to take turfs in this waste and which parishes had not; this written or unwritten customal which decided how many stints on the common land and for whom—for copyholders and freeholders only, or for all inhabitants?

Hence "law" was deeply imbricated within the very basis of productive relations, which would have been inoperable without this law. And, in the second place, this law, as definition or as rules (imperfectly enforceable through institutional legal forms), was endorsed by norms, tenaciously transmitted through the community. There were alternative norms; that is a matter of course; this was a place, not of consensus, but of conflict. But we cannot, then, simply separate off all law as ideology, and assimilate this also to the state apparatus of a ruling class. On the contrary, the norms of foresters might reveal themselves as passionately supported values, impelling them upon a course of action which would lead them into bitter conflict—with "the law."

So we are back, once again, with *that* law: the institutionalized procedures of the ruling class. This, no doubt, is worth no more of our theoretical attention; we can see it as an instrument of class power *tout court*. But we must take even

this formulation, and see whether its crystalline clarity will survive immersion in scepticism. To be sure, we can stand no longer on that traditional ground of liberal academicism, which offers the eighteenth century as a society of consensus, ruled within the parameters of paternalism and deference, and governed by a "rule of law" which attained (however imperfectly) towards impartiality. That is not the society which we have been examining; we have not observed a society of consensus; and we have seen the law being devised and employed, directly and instrumentally, in the imposition of class power. Nor can we accept a sociological refinement of the old view, which stresses the imperfections and partiality of the law, and its subordination to the functional requirements of socio-economic interest groups. For what we have observed is something more than the law as a pliant medium to be twisted this way and that by whichever interests already possess effective power. Eighteenth-century law was more substantial than that. Over and above its pliant, instrumental functions it existed in its own right, as ideology; as an ideology which not only served, in most respects, but which also legitimized class power. The hegemony of the eighteenth-century gentry and aristocracy was expressed, above all, not in military force, not in the mystifications of a priesthood or of the press, not even in economic coercion, but in the rituals of the study of the Justices of the Peace, in the quarter-sessions, in the pomp of Assizes and in the theatre of Tyburn.

Thus the law (we agree) may be seen instrumentally as mediating and reinforcing existent class relations and, ideologically, as offering to these a legitimation. But we must press our definitions a little further. For if we say that existent class relations were mediated by the law, this is not the same thing as saying that the law was no more than those relations translated into other terms, which masked or mystified the reality. This may, quite often, be true but it is not the whole truth. For class relations were expressed, not in any way one likes, but *through the forms of law*; and the law, like other institutions which from time to time can be seen as mediating (and masking) existent class relations (such as the Church or the media of communication), has its own characteristics, its own independent history and logic of evolution.

Moreover, people are not as stupid as some structuralist philosophers suppose them to be. They will not be mystified by the first man who puts on a wig. It is inherent in the especial character of law, as a body of rules and procedures, that it shall apply logical criteria with reference to standards of universality and equity. It is true that certain categories of person may be excluded from this logic (as children or slaves), that other categories may be debarred from access to parts of the logic (as women or, for many forms of eighteenth-century law, those without certain kinds of property), and that the poor may often be excluded, through penury, from the law's costly procedures. All this, and more, is true. But if too much of this is true, then the consequences are plainly counterproductive. Most men have a strong sense of justice, at least with regard to their own interests. If the law is evidently partial and unjust, then it will mask nothing, legitimize nothing, contribute nothing to any class's hegemony. The essential precondition for the effectiveness of law, in its function as ideology, is that it shall display an independence from gross manipulation and shall seem to be just. It cannot seem to be so without upholding its own logic and criteria of equity; indeed, on occasion, by actually *being* just. And furthermore it is not often the case that a ruling ideology can be dismissed as a mere hypocrisy; even rulers find a need to legitimize their power, to moralize their functions, to feel themselves to be useful and just. In the case of an ancient historical formation like the law, a discipline which requires years of exacting study to master, there will always be some men who actively believe in their own procedures and in the logic of justice. The law may be rhetoric, but it need not be empty rhetoric. Blackstone's *Commentaries* represent an intellectual exercise far more rigorous than could have come from an apologist's pen.

I do not know what transcultural validity these reflections may have. But they are certainly ap-

plicable to England in the eighteenth century. Douglas Hay, in a significant essay in *Albion's Fatal Tree,* has argued that the law assumed unusual pre-eminence in that century, as the central legitimizing ideology, displacing the religious authority and sanctions of previous centuries. It gave way, in its turn, to economic sanctions and to the ideology of the free market and of political liberalism in the nineteenth. Turn where you will, the rhetoric of eighteenth-century England is saturated with the notion of law. Royal absolutism was placed behind a high hedge of law; landed estates were tied together with entails and marriage settlements made up of elaborate tissues of law; authority and property punctuated their power by regular "examples" made upon the public gallows. More than this, immense efforts were made (and Hay has explored the forms of these) to project the image of a ruling class which was itself subject to the rule of law, and whose legitimacy rested upon the equity and universality of those legal forms. And the rulers were, in serious senses, whether willingly or unwillingly, the prisoners of their own rhetoric; they played the games of power according to rules which suited them, but they could not break those rules or the whole game would be thrown away. And, finally, so far from the ruled shrugging off this rhetoric as a hypocrisy, some part of it at least was taken over as part of the rhetoric of the plebeian crowd, of the "free-born Englishman" with his inviolable privacy, his *habeas corpus,* his equality before the law. If this rhetoric was a mask, it was a mask which John Wilkes was to borrow, at the head of ten thousand masked supporters.

So that in this island and in that century above all one must resist any slide into structural reductionism. What this overlooks, among other things, is the immense capital of human struggle over the previous two centuries against royal absolutism, inherited, in the forms and traditions of the law, by the eighteenth-century gentry. For in the sixteenth and seventeenth centuries the law had been less an instrument of class power than a central arena of conflict. In the course of conflict the law itself had been changed; inherited by the eighteenth-century gentry, this changed law was, literally, central to their whole purchase upon power and upon the means of life. Take law away, and the royal prerogative, or the presumption of the aristocracy, might flood back upon their properties and lives; take law away and the string which tied together their lands and marriages would fall apart. But it was inherent in the very nature of the medium which they had selected for their own self-defence that it could not be reserved for the exclusive use only of their own class. The law, in its forms and traditions, entailed principles of equity and universality which, perforce, had to be extended to all sorts and degrees of men. And since this was of necessity so, ideology could turn necessity to advantage. What had been devised by men of property as a defence against arbitrary power could be turned into service as an apologia for property in the face of the propertyless. And the apologia was serviceable up to a point: for these "propertyless," as we have seen, comprised multitudes of men and women who themselves enjoyed, in fact, petty property rights or agrarian use-rights whose definition was inconceivable without the forms of law. Hence the ideology of the great struck root in a soil, however shallow, of actuality. And the courts gave substance to the ideology by the scrupulous care with which, on occasion, they adjudged petty rights, and, on all occasions, preserved proprieties and forms.

We reach, then, not a simple conclusion (law = class power) but a complex and contradictory one. On the one hand, it is true that the law did mediate existent class relations to the advantage of the rulers; not only is this so, but as the century advanced the law became a superb instrument by which these rulers were able to impose new definitions of property to their even greater advantage, as in the extinction by law of indefinite agrarian use-rights and in the furtherance of enclosure. On the other hand, the law mediated these class relations through legal forms, which imposed, again and again, inhibitions upon the actions of the rulers. For there is a very large difference, which twentieth-century experience

ought to have made clear even to the most exalted thinker, between arbitrary extra-legal power and the rule of law. And not only were the rulers (indeed, the ruling class as a whole) inhibited by their own rules of law against the exercise of direct unmediated force (arbitrary imprisonment, the employment of troops against the crowd, torture, and those other conveniences of power with which we are all conversant), but they also believed enough in these rules, and in their accompanying ideological rhetoric, to allow, in certain limited areas, the law itself to be a genuine forum within which certain kinds of class conflict were fought out. There were even occasions (one recalls John Wilkes and several of the trials of the 1790s) when the Government itself retired from the courts defeated. Such occasions served, paradoxically, to consolidate power, to enhance its legitimacy, and to inhibit revolutionary movements. But, to turn the paradox around, these same occasions served to bring power even further within constitutional controls.

The rhetoric and the rules of a society are something a great deal more than sham. In the same moment they may modify, in profound ways, the behaviour of the powerful, and mystify the powerless. They may disguise the true realities of power, but, at the same time, they may curb that power and check its intrusions. And it is often from within that very rhetoric that a radical critique of the practice of the society is developed: the reformers of the 1790s appeared, first of all, clothed in the rhetoric of Locke and of Blackstone.

These reflections lead me on to conclusions which may be different from those which some readers expect. I have shown in this study a political oligarchy inventing callous and oppressive laws to serve its own interests. I have shown judges who, no less than bishops, were subject to political influence, whose sense of justice was humbug, and whose interpretation of the laws served only to enlarge their inherent class bias. Indeed, I think that this study has shown that for many of England's governing elite the rules of law were a nuisance, to be manipulated and bent in what ways they could; and that the allegiance of such men as Walpole, Hardwicke or Paxton to the rhetoric of law was largely humbug. But I do not conclude from this that the rule of law itself was humbug. On the contrary, the inhibitions upon power imposed by law seem to me a legacy as substantial as any handed down from the struggles of the seventeenth century to the eighteenth, and a true and important cultural achievement of the agrarian and mercantile bourgeoisie, and of their supporting yeomen and artisans.

More than this, the notion of the regulation and reconciliation of conflicts through the rule of law—and the elaboration of rules and procedures which, on occasion, made some approximate approach towards the ideal—seems to me a cultural achievement of universal significance. I do not lay any claim as to the abstract, extra-historical impartiality of these rules. In a context of gross class inequalities, the equity of the law must always be in some part sham. Transplanted as it was to even more inequitable contexts, this law could become an instrument of imperialism. For this law has found its way to a good many parts of the globe. But even here the rules and the rhetoric have imposed some inhibitions upon the imperial power. If the rhetoric was a mask, it was a mask which Gandhi and Nehru were to borrow, at the head of a million masked supporters.

I am not starry-eyed about this at all. This has not been a star-struck book. I am insisting only upon the obvious point, which some modern Marxists have overlooked, that there is a difference between arbitrary power and the rule of law. We ought to expose the shams and inequities which may be concealed beneath this law. But the rule of law itself, the imposing of effective inhibitions upon power and the defence of the citizen from power's all-intrusive claims, seems to me to be an unqualified human good. To deny or belittle this good is, in this dangerous century when the resources and pretentions of power continue to enlarge, a desperate error of intellectual abstraction. More than this, it is a self-fulfilling error, which encourages us to give up the struggle against bad laws and class-bound procedures, and to disarm ourselves before power. It is to throw away a whole inheritance of struggle *about* law, and within the forms of law, whose continuity can never be fractured without bringing men and women into immediate danger.

In all of this I may be wrong. I am told that, just beyond the horizon, new forms of working-class power are about to arise which, being founded upon egalitarian productive relations, will require no inhibition and can dispense with the negative restrictions of bourgeois legalism. A historian is unqualified to pronounce on such utopian projections. All that he knows is that he can bring in support of them no historical evidence whatsoever. His advice might be: watch this new power for a century or two before you cut your hedges down.

I therefore crawl out onto my own precarious ledge. It is true that in history the law can be seen to mediate and to legitimize existent class relations. Its forms and procedures may crystallize those relations and mask ulterior injustice. But this mediation, through the forms of law, is something quite distinct from the exercise of unmediated force. The forms and rhetoric of law acquire a distinct identity which may, on occasion, inhibit power and afford some protection to the powerless. Only to the degree that this is seen to be so can law be of service in its other aspect, as ideology. Moreover, the law in both its aspects, as formal rules and procedures and as ideology, cannot usefully be analysed in the metaphorical terms of a superstructure distinct from an infrastructure. While this comprises a large and self-evident part of the truth, the rules and categories of law penetrate every level of society, effect vertical as well as horizontal definitions of men's rights and status, and contribute to men's self-definition or sense of identity. As such law has not only been imposed *upon* men from above: it has also been a medium within which other social conflicts have been fought out. Productive relations themselves are, in part, only meaningful in terms of their definitions at law: the serf, the free labourer; the cottager with common rights, the inhabitant without; the unfree proletarian, the picket conscious of his rights; the landless labourer who may still sue his employer for assault. And if the actuality of the law's operation in class-divided societies has, again and again, fallen short of its own rhetoric of equity, yet the notion of the rule of law is itself an unqualified good.

This cultural achievement—the attainment towards a universal value—found one origin in Roman jurisprudence. The uncodified English common law offered an alternative notation of law, in some ways more flexible and unprincipled—and therefore more pliant to the "common sense" of the ruling class—in other ways more available as a medium through which social conflict could find expression, especially where the sense of "natural justice" of the jury could make itself felt. Since this tradition came to its maturity in eighteenth-century England, its claims should command the historian's interest. And since some part of the inheritance from this cultural moment may still be found, within greatly changed contexts, within the United States or India or certain African countries, it is important to re-examine the pretensions of the imperialist donor.

This is to argue the need for a general revaluation of eighteenth-century law, of which this study offers only a fragment. This study has been centred upon a bad law, drawn by bad legislators, and enlarged by the interpretations of bad judges. No defence, in terms of natural justice, can be offered for anything in the history of the Black Act. But even this study does not prove that all law as such is bad. Even this law bound the rulers to act only in the ways which its forms permitted; they had difficulties with these forms; they could not always override the sense of natural justice of the jurors; and we may imagine how Walpole would have acted, against Jacobites or against disturbers of Richmond Park, if he had been subject to no forms of law at all.

If we suppose that law is no more than a mystifying and pompous way in which class power is registered and executed, then we need not waste our labour in studying its history and forms. One Act would be much the same as another, and all, from the standpoint of the ruled, would be Black. It is because law *matters* that we have bothered with this story at all. And this is also an answer to those universal thinkers, impatient of all except the *longue durée,* who cannot be bothered with cartloads of victims at Tyburn when they set these beside the indices of infant mortality. The victims of smallpox testify only to their own poverty and to the infancy of medical science; the victims of the gallows are exemplars of a conscious and elaborated code, justified in the name of a universal human value. Since we hold this value to be a human good, and one whose usefulness the world has not yet outgrown, the operation of this code deserves our most scrupulous attention. It is only when we follow through the intricacies of its operation that we can show what it was worth, how it was bent, how its proclaimed values were falsified in practice. When we note Walpole harrying John Huntridge, Judge Page handing down his death sentences, Lord Hardwicke wrenching the clauses of his Act from their context and Lord Mansfield compounding his manipulations, we feel contempt for men whose practice belied the resounding rhetoric of the age. But we feel contempt not because we are contemptuous of the notion of a just and equitable law but because this notion has been betrayed by its own professors. The modern sensibility which views this only within the perspectives of our own archipelagos of *gulags* and of *stalags,* for whose architects the very notion of the rule of law would be a criminal heresy, will find my responses overfussy. The plebs of eighteenth-century England were provided with a rule of law of some sort, and they ought to have considered themselves lucky. What more could they expect?

In fact, some of them had the impertinence, and the imperfect sense of historical perspective, to expect justice. On the gallows men would actually complain, in their "last dying words," if they felt that in some particular the due forms of law had not been undergone. (We remember Vulcan Gates complaining that since he was illiterate he could not read his own notice of proclamation; and performing his allotted role at Tyburn only when he had seen the Sheriff's dangling chain.) For the trouble about law and justice, as ideal aspirations, is that they must pretend to absolute validity or they do not exist at all. If I judge the Black Act to be atrocious, this is not only from some standpoint in natural justice, and not only from the standpoint of those whom the Act oppressed, but also according to some ideal notion of the standards to which "the law," as regulator of human conflicts of interest, ought to attain. For "the law," as a logic of equity, must always seek to transcend the inequalities of class power which, instrumentally, it is harnessed to serve. And "the law" as ideology, which pretends to reconcile the interests of all degrees of men, must always come into conflict with the ideological partisanship of class.

We face, then, a paradox. The work of sixteenth- and seventeenth-century jurists, supported by the practical struggles of such men as Hampden and Lilburne, was passed down as a legacy to the eighteenth century, where it gave rise to a vision, in the minds of some men, of an ideal aspiration towards universal values of law. One thinks of Swift or of Goldsmith, or, with more qualifications, of Sir William Blackstone or Sir Michael Foster. If we today have ideal notions of what law might be, we derive them in some part from that cultural moment. It is, in part, in terms of that age's own aspiration that we judge the Black Act and find it deficient. But at the same time this same century, governed as it was by the forms of law, provides a text-book illustration of the employment of law, as instrument and as ideology, in serving the interests of the ruling class. The oligarchs and the great gentry were content to be subject to the rule of law only because this law was serviceable and afforded to their hegemony the rhetoric of legitimacy. This paradox has been at the heart of this study. It was also at the heart of eighteenth-century society. But it was also a paradox which that society could not in the end transcend, for the paradox was held in equipoise upon an ulterior equilibrium of class forces. When the struggles of 1790–1832 signalled that this equilibrium had changed, the rulers of England were faced with alarming alternatives. They could either dispense with the rule of law, dismantle their elaborate constitutional structures, countermand their own rhetoric and exercise power by force; or they could submit to their own rules and surrender their hegemony. In the campaign against Paine and the printers, in the Two Acts (1795), the Combination Acts (1799–1800), the repression of Peterloo (1819) and the Six Acts (1820) they took halting steps in the first direction. But in the end, rather than shatter their own self-image and repudiate 150 years of constitutional legality, they surrendered to the law. In this surrender they threw retrospective light back on the history of their class, and retrieved for it something of its honour; despite Walpole, despite Paxton, despite Page and Hardwicke, that rhetoric had not been altogether sham.

JUDICIAL DERADICALIZATION OF THE WAGNER ACT AND THE ORIGINS OF MODERN LEGAL CONSCIOUSNESS, 1937-1941*

KARL E. KLARE

I. THE PROBLEM

When passed, the National Labor Relations (Wagner) Act was perhaps the most radical piece of legislation ever enacted by the United States Congress. Enacted in the wake of the great strikes of 1934, at an unusually tense and fluid historical moment, it represented, in the words of one historian, "an almost unbelievable capitulation by the government".[1] It appears that a small number of the most sophisticated representatives of business favored passage of the Act on the theory that some such measure was essential to preserve the social order and to forestall developments toward even more radical change. Nonetheless, most employers, large and small, bitterly opposed passage of the Act, and its enactment touched off several years of fierce and concerted resistance to labor and law throughout the ranks of American business. This massive employer resistance was met by one of the most dramatic strike waves in the annals of labor, culminating in the "sit-down" movement and the rise of the Congress of Industrial Organizations (CIO).

It is of transcendent importance in understanding what follows to appreciate that the Wagner Act did not fully become "the law" when Congress passed it in 1935, or even when the Supreme Court ruled it constitutional in 1937, although obviously these legal events enhanced the legitimacy of the labor movement. The Act "became law" only when employers were forced to obey its command by the imaginative, courageous, and concerted efforts of countless unheralded workers.[2] This was one of the rare in-

---

*This Article is part of a work-in-progress that will explore the entire trajectory of American labor law from 1935 to the present. Footnotes and legal citations have largely been deleted from this reprinted version.

This Article is dedicated to Hallie R. Carmen.

[1] P. CONKIN, FDR AND THE ORIGINS OF THE WELFARE STATE 63 (1967).

Source: From *Minnesota Law Review*, vol. 62, no. 3 (1978), pp. 265-339. Copyright © 1978 by Karl E. Klare. Reprinted by permission.

[2] The two most crucial early breakthroughs in collective bargaining, which laid a political foundation for more widespread employer acceptance of and obedience to the Wagner Act, were probably General Motors' agreement with the United Auto Workers and United States Steel's about-face decision to deal with the Steel Workers Organizing Committee. Both events occurred before the April 12, 1937, decision of the Supreme Court upholding the Act, NLRB v. Jones & Laughlin Steel Corp., 301 U.S. 1 (1937), but after the sit-down strike wave had begun; in particular, both occurred against the backdrop of the momentous Flint sit-down strike against General Motors in the winter of 1936-1937 and are directly traceable to that strike and its surrounding events and circumstances. *See* I. BERNSTEIN, TURBULENT YEARS 457-73, 519-51 (1970).

stances in which the common people, often heedless of the advice of their own leaders, seized control of their destinies and genuinely altered the course of American history.

The Wagner Act and the rise of organized labor unquestionably effected profound changes in the American political economy. Collective bargaining became fairly widespread, unions attained a significant role in the partisan political system, the labor market was rationalized in certain important ways, many people improved their standard of living and job security, and millions of workers experienced a new sense of participation and dignity.

Nevertheless, at the beginning of labor's New Deal, many employers feared that the Act would lead to state control of business and compulsory arbitration of the terms and conditions of employment, if not a usurpation of the prerogatives of private property ownership itself. These fears proved to be exaggerated, however, for whatever its achievements, the Act did not produce a fundamental transformation of the premises and institutions of capitalist society. True, private ownership was burdened by state regulation that allowed most workers the right to organize and bargain collectively. But state regulation is characteristic of advanced capitalism; rather than radically revising property relations or the social distribution of power, it protects them. Likewise, although workers in unionized industries generally enjoy a higher standard of living and more security now than did most workers a generation ago, the Act did little to enhance their decision-making role regarding the use of society's means of production, the organization of the work-process, and other decisions that affect their industrial lives. Moreover, New Deal reform appears to have fostered the co-optation of the workers' movement and, with the exception of certain periods such as the post-World War II strike wave, a diminution of labor's combativeness. Indeed, it has been argued that collective bargaining has become an institutional structure not for expressing workers' needs and aspirations but for controlling and disciplining the labor

force and rationalizing the labor market. One need not accept these claims fully to recognize that, since World War II, organized labor has become more integrated into the economic system of advanced capitalism, progressively more dependent on its erstwhile corporate adversaries, and largely conventional in the political arena.

How this transformation of the labor movement took place is the broad underlying question motivating this Article. Obviously many processes were at work—political, social, economic, and cultural. I will make no attempt to canvass them here. I will focus only on what was contributed to the deradicalization and incorporation of the working class by developments within the relatively autonomous dimension of legal consciousness, legal institutions, and legal practice, as revealed in the Supreme Court's early Wagner Act decisions.[3] I do not argue that there is a direct causal relationship between the Supreme Court's decisions and the integration of the working class into the postwar social order. But those decisions did have two more indirect consequences worth noting. First, they provided the beginnings of the conceptual integration of the working class by laying the intellectual groundwork upon which were later erected the prevailing political theories of the postwar period, which in turn have in significant measure been internalized by and become the self-conception of the leadership of the labor movement.[4] Second, in the process of

---

[3] By focusing on the Supreme Court, I do not mean to imply that other legal institutions, notably the National Labor Relations Board, did not also contribute to the integrative process here described. I have emphasized the Court because some of the most significant issues in this process are highlighted by the Court's several attempts to define its relationship to the Board and to other courts.

[4] The argument relies on the theory of hegemony articulated in the work of the Italian Marxist philosopher Antonio Gramsci. *See* A. GRAMSCI, SELECTIONS FROM THE PRISON NOTEBOOKS (Q. Hoare & G. Nowell Smith eds. and trans. 1971). *See generally* C. BOGGS, GRAMSCI'S MARXISM (1976); J. CAMMETT, ANTONIO GRAMSCI AND THE ORIGINS OF ITALIAN COMMUNISM (1967); Anderson, *The Antinomies of Antonio Gramsci,* NEW LEFT REV., November 1976–January 1977, at 5; Williams, *The Concept of "Egemonia" in the Thought of Antonio Gramsci: Some Notes on Interpretation,* 21 J. HIST. IDEAS 586 (1960). By "hegemony" Gramsci meant "the permeation

adopting some and foreclosing other paths of doctrinal development under the relatively general terms of the Act, the Court began to elaborate the boundaries of "legitimate" labor activity. This process not only had some immediate political consequences in the 1930's but its ultimate, more enduring, significance was the creation of the rudiments of what later became an increasingly formalized and regulated institutional structure for the state administration of the class struggle.

It is not suggested that the Supreme Court engaged in a plot or conspiracy to defeat or co-opt the labor movement, nor do I think that the Court can adequately be understood as an instrument of particular economic interests.[5] I emphatically re-

ject any such reductionism or determinism. That the Court did so much to guide the long-run development of the labor movement into domesticated channels and, indeed, to impede workers' interests is, in fact, ironic precisely because it was so often attacked by contemporaries as overly friendly to labor. Many decisions of the prewar period were intended to be, and were then understood as, tremendous victories for organized labor. But these prolabor victories contained the seeds of long-term defeats, because through them the Court, including its most liberal members, set in motion a distinctive style of legal analysis characteristic of modern American legal consciousness that came to stand, whatever the intentions of its authors, as an ineluctable barrier to worker self-activity.

II. THE SETTING

At the outset, it is appropriate to situate the focus of this Article within its historical and political context.[6] What follows is a provisional and sche-

---

throughout civil society . . . of an entire system of values, attitudes, beliefs, morality, etc., that is in one way or another supportive of the established order and the class interests that dominate it." C. BOGGS, *supra* at 39.

[5] I adopt the concept of the "relative autonomy" of legal consciousness, institutions, and practice, notwithstanding my obvious commitment to the view that the legal process is deeply imbedded in the political process and not only reflects the political and class structure of American capitalism but serves to maintain and reproduce it. The view that law reflects the political and class structure does not require or imply the reductionist argument that the legal process is directly responsive to the needs and preferences of dominant social and political actors. *See* Balbus, *Commodity Form and Legal Form: An Essay on the "Relative Autonomy" of the Law*, 11 LAW & SOC'Y REV. 571, 572-73 (1977). Indeed, though determinism regrettably remains the popular conception of Marxist method, the most creative work on law within the Marxist tradition begins with the rejection of economic determinism as an explanatory mode. This intellectual tradition has sought to develop a theory adequate to explain the way in which law ultimately reflects and sustains the social order, yet has its own internal logic and unique modes of discourse and institutional patterns that are to some extent independent of the will of powerful, nonlegal, social and political actors and that represent an important constitutive element of the social totality in their own right.

Different approaches have been attempted toward such a theory, including Balbus' thesis of "structural homologies" and the thesis developed in the following pages of lawmaking as a form of social and political practice. It must be conceded, however, that at present no comprehensive theory of the relative autonomy of law exists. The effort here is simply to acquaint the reader with this intellectual project and to indicate some paths of ongoing research. *See generally* D. HAY, P. LINEBAUGH, J. RULE, E. P. THOMPSON, & C. WINSLOW, ALBION'S FATAL TREE (1975); E. P. THOMPSON, WHIGS AND HUNTERS: THE ORIGIN OF THE BLACK ACT (1975); Gabel, *Intention and Struc-*

ture in Contractual Conditions: Outline of a Method for Critical Legal Theory, 61 MINN. L. REV. 601 (1977); Pashukanis, *The General Theory of Law and Marxism*, in SOVIET LEGAL PHILOSOPHY 111 (H. Babb trans. 1951); Tushnet, *A Marxist Analysis of American Law*, 1 MARXIST PERSPECTIVES (forthcoming); Tushnet, *Perspectives on the Development of American Law: A Critical Review of Friedman's "A History of American Law,"* 1977 WIS. L. REV. 81; Gabel, Book Review, 91 HARV. L. REV. 302 (1977) (R. DWORKIN, TAKING RIGHTS SERIOUSLY); A. Fraser, *Legal Theory and Legal Practice*, in Arena, A. Marxist Journal of Criticism & Discussion, Nos. 44-45 (1976) (published in Greensboro, Victoria, Australia; copy in Harvard University Library).

Analogous lines of development also appear in recent debates between the instrumentalist, structuralist, and neo-Hegelian positions within the neo-Marxist theory of the state. *See* Gold, Lo, & Wright, *Recent Developments in Marxist Theories of the Capitalist State* (pts. 1-2), MONTHLY REV., October 1975, at 29 & November 1975, at 36; Wolfe, *New Directions in the Marxist Theory of Politics*, 4 POL. & SOC'Y 131 (1974).

[6] This Article will consider the work of the Court from the 1937 decision upholding the Act, NLRB v. Jones & Laughlin Steel Corp., 301 U.S. 1 (1937), to Pearl Harbor. After Pearl Harbor, the creation of the National War Labor Board and such other wartime enactments as the War Labor Disputes Act, so radically altered the legal status of labor that the conceptual scheme of the NLRA was temporarily abandoned. The

matic outline of the relationship of the Article to the revisionist controversy in American historiography, followed by a location of the issues herein discussed within the crosscurrents of modern American jurisprudence. Considerations of space prevent me from fully developing or defending the positions advanced; they are offered simply to provide a sense of the background and to alert the reader to my political assumptions.

A. THE THEORY OF CORPORATE LIBERALISM

The assumptions of Progressive historiography dominated writing about the Constitution and the Supreme Court, particularly regarding the problem of social reform, in the period from the beginning of the century through the Court-packing crisis of 1937.[7] Progressive historiography viewed

the American past as a slow but steady march toward the democratization of society. The animating force behind this progress was the conflict between privileged and nonprivileged groups identified either on a sectoral or regional basis or more typically on the basis of economic interest. Characteristically, propertied interests were viewed as being in perennial conflict with groups who possessed relatively little or no property—the farmer, the consumer, the small businessperson, the worker—in short, the "people." Progressive historiography regarded liberalism as a movement of the underprivileged, assisted by the enlightened middle class, to curb the power and interests of the propertied and business classes.

The rise of the historiographical tradition was connected to the ferment generated by the Progressive political movement of the early twentieth century. This movement was the political articulation of the liberalism of that era and took as an article of faith that the American democratic destiny would evolve through governmental regulation of business in the interests of the public. The Interstate Commerce Act (1887), the Sherman Antitrust Act (1890), and the Federal Trade Commission Act (1914), for example, were seen as so many milestones of liberal achievement in the defense of the common people. In fact, the entire branch of modern legal thought known as administrative law, whatever its origins in the ancient common law writs, is symbiotically connected to the Progressive vision.

The Progressive tradition viewed the Supreme Court as hopelessly out of touch with modern reality and beyond the reach of the democratic process. The institution of judicial review was particularly attacked as a key mechanism by which the representatives of Big Business were able to place a brake on needed social reform. In Max Lerner's formulation,

---

system of labor relations that emerged during World War II involved routine state intervention into the substantive terms of collective bargaining; settlement of labor disputes by compulsory mediation or arbitration without resort to economic action; the prohibition of concerted activity, enforced both by the law and by the politics of the "no-strike pledge"; the development of governmentally sanctioned union security devices that served as a basis for stabilizing (and bureaucratizing) the leadership of labor; and delegation to labor's leadership of the role of disciplining rank-and-file employees in the name of productivity and at the expense of the militant defense of workers' interests. Concurrently, top labor leaders were co-opted onto various boards and agencies, thus increasing their distance from the rank-and-file while cementing their new "junior partner" role in national politics.

The War's end was followed by one of the most momentous strike waves in American history, but a dramatic shift in the political climate soon occurred within both labor and the nation at large. The restrictions imposed on labor by the Taft-Hartley Act abruptly foreclosed any radical departures within the legal plane, just as the Cold War foreclosed any opening to the left on the political plane. The nascent working-class radicalism of the 1930's and early 1940's was arrested, and the potentiality for reform of the workplace was forestalled for a generation.

Until recently very little work had been done on the situation of labor in the 1940's, the imagination of far more social historians being captured by the 1930's. This deficiency, which seriously distorts our understanding of the labor movement, is now being remedied by a new generation of historians. *See generally American Labor in the 1940's*, RADICAL AMERICA, July–August 1975 (Special Issue).

[7]*See* Lerner, *The Supreme Court and American Capitalism*, 42 YALE L. J. 668, 672–78 (1933) (tracing the impact of Progressivism as an historiographical school and as a political movement on the acrimonious pre-New Deal de-

bate over the political role of the Supreme Court). Classical works on this tradition include C. BEARD, AN ECONOMIC INTERPRETATION OF THE CONSTITUTION OF THE UNITED STATES (1913); C. BEARD, THE SUPREME COURT AND THE CONSTITUTION (1912); J. SMITH, THE SPIRIT OF AMERICAN GOVERNMENT (1907).

[c]apitalist enterprise in America generated, as capitalism has everywhere generated, forces in government and in the underlying classes hostile to capitalist expansion and bent upon curbing it: it became the function of the Court to check those forces and to lay down the lines of economic orthodoxy. . . . [The Court] . . . may be regarded from other angles. But if we seek a single and consistent body of principles which will furnish the rationale of the judicial power in the last half century, we must find it in the dynamics of American business enterprise.

The heirs of Progressivism therefore viewed the dramatic 1937 turn of the Court toward an attitude of judicial deference to legislative authority (classically but somewhat naively viewed as the repository of the popular will) as a triumph for democracy, a great divide that fundamentally resolved the problem of the role of the courts in a liberal democratic society.

In the 1960's, some historians began to rethink the legacy of Progressivism, both as a political movement and as a description of the American past. There arose a revisionist version of American history, known as the theory of corporate liberalism.[8] The proponents of this theory rejected Progressive historiography as historically

inaccurate and politically misleading. In their view, liberal economic and political reform was not adequately described as an imposition upon Big Business. On the contrary, most significant modern reforms were enacted with the tacit approval, if not ardent support, of major corporate interests, because the more sophisticated sectors of the business community recognized that government intervention in the private sector was essential to rationalize the chaos of a market economy, to enhance the stability, predictability, and security of the competitive capitalist system, and to provide a stable political environment in which the corporations could get on with the business of making reasonable profits. In short, the revisionist historians argued that, notwithstanding the laissez-faire and social-Darwinist rhetoric sometimes circulated for public consumption, Big Business systematically sought and achieved a political capitalism in which the state played a crucial, rationalizing role designed to protect corporate interests and retrieve the business world from recurring market crises. Whatever reforms and concessions were enacted in the process furthered these ends and forestalled even more radical measures that might have been enacted into law or imposed by extra-parliamentary pressures had popular discontent been permitted to crystallize into a coherent oppositional political force.

Corporate liberal research has thus far produced its most significant results with regard to the Progressive Era proper. Although attempts have been made to assimilate New Deal politics into the corporate liberal theory, in my view these have inadequately confronted the central difficulty presented by the Wagner Act. Although over the long run the institutionalization of collective bargaining has served corporate interests in economic stability and predictability, the historical record makes emphatically clear that the business community, with few exceptions, did not initially conceive collective bargaining to be in its long-run interests, resisted passage of the Act, and later attempted to shape it to its own ends only when forced to obey it by working

[8]*See, e.g.,* G. KOLKO, RAILROADS AND REGULATION, 1877–1916 (1965); G. KOLKO, THE TRIUMPH OF CONSERVATISM (1963); R. RADOSH, AMERICAN LABOR AND UNITED STATES FOREIGN POLICY (1969); J. WEINSTEIN, THE CORPORATE IDEAL IN THE LIBERAL STATE: 1900–1918 (1968); W. WILLIAMS, THE CONTOURS OF AMERICAN HISTORY (1961); W. WILLIAMS, THE TRAGEDY OF AMERICAN DIPLOMACY (1959); Radosh, *The Corporate Ideology of American Labor Leaders from Gompers to Hillman,* STUDIES ON THE LEFT, November–December 1966, at 66; Sklar, *On the Proletarian Revolution and the End of Political-Economic Society,* RADICAL AMERICA, May–June 1969, at 1; Sklar, *Woodrow Wilson and the Political Economy of Modern United States Liberalism,* STUDIES ON THE LEFT, Fall 1960, at 17; D. Eakins, The Development of Corporate Liberal Policy Research in the United States, 1885–1965 (1966) (unpublished Ph.D. dissertation in University of Wisconsin Library). *See generally 'New Left Historians' Of the 1960s,* RADICAL AMERICA, November 1970, at 81.

It should be noted that, besides the theory of corporate liberalism, the postwar period produced another major school, led by the so-called "consensus" historians, notably Daniel Boorstin and Louis Hartz, that also defined itself in opposition to Progressive historiography. *See* R. HOFSTADTER, THE PROGRESSIVE HISTORIANS 437–66 (1968).

people and their allies in the federal government. In short, although the corporate liberal thesis is a good starting point from which to describe the general contours of the emergence of post-World War I monopoly capitalism, both it and the conventional interpretation of New Deal labor law reform, influenced by the Progressive tradition, are inadequate to explain fully the events of the period.[9]

A major goal of this Article is to supply the groundwork for a more intricate explanation of this most perplexing problem of New Deal historiography, affirming both the context of class struggle that surrounded the early years of the Wagner Act and the role of the Act in stabilizing and preserving the social order of American capitalism.

B. THE CRISIS OF THE LEGAL ORDER

During the Depression, capitalism entered a period of profound, world-wide crisis, not only economically but also in politics, culture, and law. The particular manifestation of this crisis in law was the incipient disintegration of liberal legalism.

"Legalism" has been defined as "[t]he ethical attitude that holds moral conduct to be a matter of rule following, and moral relationships to consist of duties and rights determined by rules."[10] "Liberal legalism" is a particular historical incarnation of the legalist outlook, which characteristically serves as the philosophical foundation of the legitimacy of the legal order in capitalist societies.[11] Its essential features are the commitment to general, democratically promulgated rules, the equal treatment of all citizens before the law, and the radical separation of morals, politics, and personality from judicial action. Liberal legalism also consists of a complex of social practices and institutions that complement and elaborate upon its underlying political philosophy and jurisprudence. With respect to its modern Anglo-American form, these include adherence to precedent, separation of the legislative (prospective) and the judicial (retrospective) functions, the obligation to formulate legal rules on a general basis (the notion of *ratio decidendi*), adherence to complex procedural formalities, and the search for specialized methods of analysis ("legal reasoning"). All of these institutions are designed to serve the fundamental desideratum of separating morals, politics, and personal bias from adjudication.[12] The rise and elaboration of the ideology, practices, and institutions of liberal legalism have been accompanied by the growth of a specialized, professional caste of experts trained in manipulating legal reasoning and the legal process.

Not surprisingly, the crisis of liberal capitalism revealed itself within law as a breakdown of the separation between law and politics and between

---

[9]Thus, conceding the influence of the revisionist school, this Article nonetheless reflects the more recent development toward a critical perspective on the theory of corporate liberalism, particularly insofar as it exaggerates the self-consciousness and rationality of the dominant business sectors, and the ability of the system to reform itself, and minimizes the significance of popular resistance. See TWENTIETH-CENTURY AMERICA: RECENT INTERPRETATIONS 6-8 (B. Bernstein & A. Matusow eds. 1969); Block, *Beyond Corporate Liberalism*, 24 SOC. PROB. 352 (1977). See also Schatz, *The End of Corporate Liberalism: Class Struggle in the Electrical Manufacturing Industry, 1933-1950*, RADICAL AMERICA, July-August 1975, at 187.

On the other hand, the conventional interpretation of the Wagner Act, as imposed upon the business community in the interests of the American worker by an enlightened government, is also inadequate. This interpretation fails to do justice to the massive, extraparliamentary struggle waged by the working class during the period, without which the legislation probably would have meant very little, nor does it confront the profoundly conservative implications of New Deal labor law reform.

[10]J. SHKLAR, LEGALISM 1 (1964).

[11]See generally L. FULLER, LEGAL FICTIONS (1967); M. HORWITZ, ORIGINS OF JUDICIAL REVIEW (tent. ed. 1973); F. NEUMANN, *The Change in the Function of Law in Modern Society*, in THE DEMOCRATIC AND THE AUTHORITARIAN STATE 22 (H. Marcuse ed. 1957); Horwitz, *The Legacy of 1776 in Legal and Economic Thought*, 19 J. L. & ECON. 621 (1976); Kennedy, *Legal Formality*, 2 J. LEGAL STUD. 351 (1974).

[12]The historical development and interrelationships of these practices and their connection to liberal legalist jurisprudence are traced in M. HORWITZ, *supra* note 11. See generally Horwitz, *supra* note 11.

Horwitz points out that, although the central institution of separation of powers is ordinarily justified as a device to subordinate the judiciary to the popular will as expressed in legis-

law and private interests,[13] as a tendency for law and politics to merge or for law to become politicized. The political character of adjudication was already fairly apparent to labor activists, but the Supreme Court decisions of the early (pre-1937) New Deal striking down reform legislation cast the politics of the Court into stark relief.

Within academic legal circles, the primary manifestation of the crisis of liberalism was the rise of the legal realist reaction to "conceptualist formalism." "Formalism" refers to styles of legal reasoning that assume that the processes of deriving legal rules to govern new situations and of applying ascertained rules to given sets of facts can be relatively determinate, objective, and value-free operations, which proceed according

───────────

lation, it arose historically in the United States in connection with the development of the institution of judicial review as a conservative justification for checking and impeding the redistributive and egalitarian tendencies imagined to be inherent in popularly elected legislatures.

Liberal legalist jurisprudence is closely related to the classical liberal political tradition. The metaphysical underpinnings of the enumerated practices are supplied by the central philosophical themes of that tradition: the notion that values are subjective and derive from personal desire, and that therefore ethical discourse is conducted profitably only in instrumental terms; the view that society is an artificial aggregation of autonomous individuals; the separation in political philosophy between public and private interests (between state and civil society); and a commitment to a formal or procedural rather than a substantive conception of justice.

These themes are sounded in the great writings of the classical liberal political tradition, as exemplified in the work of Thomas Hobbes, John Locke, and David Hume. The interrelationship of the ethical, psychological, social, and political assumptions characteristic of the liberal tradition is developed in R. UNGER, KNOWLEDGE & POLITICS (1975); the connection of these metaphysical assumptions to liberal legalist jurisprudence and the unity of liberal legalist thought are discussed in chapter 2 of that work and in R. UNGER, LAW IN MODERN SOCIETY (1976). The connection of the metaphysical premises of the liberal tradition to liberal legalism is also explored in Kennedy, *Form and Substance in Private Law Adjudication*, 89 HARV. L. REV. 1685, 1766–78 (1976).

[13]There is, of course, no claim implied here that at any time prior to the crisis of the 1930's the legal order was in fact autonomous from politics, but only that it became increasingly difficult in the 1930's to maintain the legalist belief that this was, could, or should be so.

to specialized modes of analytical deduction. Logically and historically, formalism is connected to formal conceptions of justice. "Conceptualism" is a particular version of formalism that was the prevailing mode of thought among the legal elite in the United States in the period roughly from 1885 to 1930. The characteristic conceptualist glosses to formalism are the belief that very abstract and general principles of law can be used to resolve very concrete legal problems and an identification of legal reasoning with natural science.

"Realism" denotes a movement in legal thought that united thinkers of disparate political philosophies in an attack on conceptualism. As a style of legal reasoning, realism denies the objective and autonomous character of rule-formulation and rule-application and assumes the indeterminacy of legal concepts and rules. It sees legal reasoning as a purposive or instrumental, rather than a purely deductive, enterprise, and it asserts that proper judicial action requires and may legitimately involve inquiry into the social policies intended to be served by legal rules and the practical social consequences of a court's decisions.

Plainly, realism threatened to undermine the legitimacy of the legal process by politicizing it. This could not be otherwise when it was proposed that the decision of cases explicitly turn on the judge's assessment of competing notions of social policy. This is by definition the danger that liberal legalism had hitherto sought to avoid. The realists did not call for the demise of the rule of law, but they did urge candor about the ethical and political character of all legal decisions and believed that instrumental decisionmaking was proper and just. In Felix Cohen's words,

> creative legal thought will more and more look behind the traditionally accepted principles of "justice" and "reason" to appraise in ethical terms the social values at stake in any choice between two precedents.

> "Social policy" will be comprehended not as an emergency factor in legal argument but rather as the

gravitational field that gives weight to any rule or precedent, whether it be in constitutional law, in the law of trademarks, or in the most technical details of legal procedure.[14]

Realist jurisprudence released a radically destabilizing force within legalism. This was not widely perceived at first, partly because realism spread initially among academics, not judges, and partly because, other than a generalized inclination of many toward President Roosevelt and the New Deal, the realists shared no explicit political program. In time, when realism ascended to the bench, its subversive content became more apparent. This in turn provoked a conceptualist counterattack, although this reaction was to be obscured by its adoption of the language and style of realist discourse. The cases I will discuss occur against the backdrop of the traumatic encounter between conceptualism and realism.

It is commonly believed that during the New Deal a "revolution" occurred in American legal thought in general, and labor law in particular, that swept away the cobwebs of archaic conceptualism and, for the first time, gave the poor and the downtrodden a fair hearing in the courts of the land. It is imagined that this revolution coincided with, indeed resulted from, the triumph of legal realism, particularly in the Supreme Court, in the persons of Justices Black, Douglas, and Frankfurter, but also more generally in the legal establishment.

This period clearly marked a new era in our legal history. Whether "revolution" is the appropriate word to describe that transformation is another question. Likewise, whereas legal realism undoubtedly came into its own, whether it consigned conceptualism to the dustbin of history is also problematic. In my view the dividing line between the Old Court and the New is much more indistinct than is commonly supposed. The early Labor Board cases were an attempt—at the

height of the so-called labor law revolution—to forestall the disintegration of legalism that is the necessary consequence of the merger of law and politics and to assimilate realism to mainstream legalist jurisprudence by diluting its implicit political content. Put another way, liberal legalism exhibited the same resilience in its moment of crisis as did the American political system as a whole during the Depression. The Labor Board cases marked the emergence of a distinctively modern legal consciousness that eventually superseded realism in the direction of a new "social conceptualism." In effect, each side in the debate tacitly refrained from pushing the internal logic of its position to its ultimate conclusions and was eventually absorbed into its adversary. The resultant, hybrid style of legal reasoning was more attentive to social and political realities and more self-conscious and candid about the political character of adjudication than its conceptualist predecessor. But like the latter, it was premised on the notion that a disjunction between law and politics is necessary to legitimate the judicial role, and it sought in the reasoned elaboration of neutral principles a method for upholding the law/politics distinction. The new social conceptualism reproduced the formal, undemocratic, and uncritical character of the old. The New Deal solution to the crisis of legalism was to update legal consciousness and to make it more responsive to contemporary social exigencies—that is, to give a new life to the liberal legal order—while at the same time preserving its contradictions and mystifications. The Labor Board cases were a significant early episode in this process.

C. THE WAGNER ACT: GOALS AND PERCEPTIONS

It is not easy to discern and articulate the goals of the NLRA. The legislative history is often vague and inconclusive, and on many issues that were subsequently the subject of burning debate, Congress simply expressed no legislative intent. Nonetheless, from the "Findings and Policy" incorporated in section 1 of the Act and from the

---

[14]Cohen, *Transcendental Nonsense and the Functional Approach*, 35 COLUM. L. REV. 809, 833–34 (1935).

labor law cases and literature, it is possible to identify at least six statutory goals:

1. Industrial Peace: By encouraging collective bargaining, the Act aimed to subdue "strikes and other forms of industrial strife or unrest," because industrial warfare interfered with interstate commerce; that is, it was unhealthy in a business economy.[15] Moreover, although this thought was not embodied in the text, industrial warfare clearly promoted other undesirable conditions, such as political turmoil, violence, and general uncertainty.

2. Collective Bargaining: The Act sought to enhance collective bargaining for its own sake because of its presumed "mediating" or "therapeutic" impact on industrial conflict.

3. Bargaining Power: The Act aimed to promote "actual liberty of contract" by redressing the unequal balance of bargaining power between employers and employees.

4. Free Choice: The Act was intended to protect the free choice of workers to associate amongst themselves and to select representatives of their own choosing for collective bargaining.

5. Underconsumption: The Act was designed to promote economic recovery and to prevent future depressions by increasing the earnings and purchasing power of workers.

6. Industrial Democracy: This is the most elusive aspect of the legislative purpose, although most commentators indicate that a concept of industrial democracy is embedded in the statutory scheme, or at the least was one of the articulated goals of the sponsors of the Act. Senator Wagner frequently sounded the industrial democracy theme in ringing notes, and scholars have subsequently seen in collective bargaining "the means of establishing industrial democracy, . . . the means of providing for the workers' lives in industry the sense of worth, of freedom, and of participation that democratic government promises them as citizens."[16] Indeed, one carefully argued study has gone so far as to conclude that

> Congress viewed the objective of the Act as establishing throughout the country as the normal relationship between employer and employees, a system whereby employees would participate through their representatives in governing all matters affecting their conditions of work. . . . When judges and the public become more familiar with the principles of industrial democracy it is to be expected that any autocratic conduct by an employer will come to be viewed as a serious breach of the employees' rights to self-organization and collective bargaining.[17]

Enumerating the statutory premises in this manner makes apparent why the Wagner Act was, at first, perceived by employers as such a radical threat. Although it demands an effort of

---

[15]Ironically, section 13 of the Act emphatically affirms the right to strike, and its sponsors must have known that in the short run the Act would encourage workers to exercise this right on a massive scale, which is exactly what happened. Thus, the industrial peace rationale only makes sense on the assumption that employers would eventually come to their senses and accept collective bargaining as more productive from the long-run standpoint of the business system than intransigent efforts to hold back the clock. In other words, the Act gave workers a powerful weapon in industrial warfare so that industrial warfare would, in the long run, be dissipated. Not only does this show that the sponsors of the Act had a rather awesome confidence in their own foresight, but also that they were fully prepared to wait on the sidelines while revitalized unions clobbered backward employers into submission. *See* Lynd, *The United Front in America: A Note*, RADICAL AMERICA, July–August 1974, at 29. Not surprisingly, once section 13 served its purpose, the Court and Congress began to impose elaborate restrictions on the right to strike and other potentially disruptive activity.

[16]Shulman, *Reason, Contract, and Law in Labor Relations*, 68 HARV. L. REV. 999, 1002 (1955). Cox writes more cautiously that Congress *possibly* intended, in promulgating the section 8(5) duty to bargain, that "the divine right of the king must yield to a constitutional monarchy, in which a large measure of industrial democracy will prevail. Wages, hours, and conditions of employment should be determined by mutual consent." Cox, *The Duty to Bargain in Good Faith*, 71 HARV. L. REV. 1401, at 1408 (1958), (footnote omitted).

[17]Weyand, *Majority Rule in Collective Bargaining*, 45 COLUM. L. REV. 556. 599 (1945). Weyand's formulation suggests a fundamental ambiguity in the concept of industrial democracy that is not resolved by the legislative history: is the contemplated industrial democracy to be "participatory" or "representational"? As will be seen, the subsequent development of the law was directed almost entirely toward the latter model, with only a passive role allowed rank-and-file employees in day-to-day industrial affairs.

historical imagination sufficient to penetrate the narcotic haze of hindsight to understand this perception, the Act by its terms apparently accorded a governmental blessing to powerful workers' organizations that were to acquire equal bargaining power with corporations, accomplish a redistribution of income, and subject the workplace to a regime of participatory democracy. The Act's plain language was susceptible to an overtly anticapitalist interpretation.[18]

To corporate management, the Act was unquestionably the most unpopular piece of New Deal legislation affecting industry. The bill was denounced in vivid terms by representatives of a wide spectrum of business interests, and most employers, large and small, opposed its passage. The *Commercial and Financial Chronicle* had called Senator Wagner's predecessor bill, "one of the most objectionable, as well as one of the most revolutionary, pieces of legislation ever presented to Congress," while the Associated Industries of Oklahoma thought the new bill would "out-SOVIET the Russian Soviets." Nor was opposition to the Act limited to verbal assaults. The business community embarked upon a path of deliberate and concerted disobedience to the Act between 1935 and 1937, a response marked by determination and often by violence. Large and respected corporate employers engaged vast resources in systematic and typically unlawful antiunion campaigns involving such tactics as company unionism, propaganda, espionage, surveillance, weapons stockpiling, lockouts, pooling agreements for the supply of strikebreakers, and terrorism.

What provoked this extraordinary campaign of lawlessness and opposition to the statute? It is difficult to say with certainty whether the dominant motive was simply opposition to the Act's promotion of unionism and redistribution of bar-

gaining power or a more fundamental fear that the Act was a prelude to state regulation of the substantive terms of the wage-bargain and the loss of management's exclusive right to direct the production process. From the available evidence, however, it is at least possible to conclude that, in addition to the purely economic costs of collective bargaining, business opposition to the Act was in significant measure prompted by two fundamental considerations. First, the Act's radical potential justifiably produced a fear that collective bargaining meant the loss of control over the production process, the fatal subversion of the hallowed right of managerial freedom to run the enterprise. In short, business took the Act's rhetoric of industrial democracy seriously. This common denominator of fear of loss of managerial control runs through much of business' perceptions of the Act. Business was particularly outraged because the statute went beyond merely legalizing union activity and providing for representation elections, but in addition created an affirmative *duty* on the part of employers to bargain with the employees' exclusive representative over terms and conditions of employment. This requirement raised the spectre that section 8(5) could lead to administrative scrutiny of the substantive terms of employment contracts, indeed, to compulsory arbitration of the terms of employment, and was viewed as a dramatic departure from the concept of managerial control.

The other motif prominent in expressions of business opposition to the Act was the fear that the Act would encourage and promote labor radicalism and class conflict as a necessary consequence of promoting any kind of unionism. A Cleveland Chamber of Commerce resolution of the era, for example, expressed concern about " 'professional labor agitators whose primary objective is to foment antagonism, with a view to an organized power, socially, politically and economically dangerous to the American Commonwealth.' " In fact, business had good reason to fear that the Act would lead, at least in the short run, to labor conflict and, therefore, in the context of the times, to the possibility of increased

---

[18]Obviously such a radical reading of the Act is not compelled by the legislative history. It does, however, find substantial support in that history and in the text of the Act; and moderate and conventional interpretations of the Act, however more plausible they may seem now, cannot conclusively be said to be *commanded* by the legislative history either.

working-class militancy and political radicalism. As the sponsors of the Act themselves must have foreseen, their rhetoric of industrial peace notwithstanding, the inevitable short-run impact of the Act would be a substantial increase in strikes.

It is even more difficult accurately to specify working people's perceptions of, and attitudes toward, the Wagner Act. Conventional labor historiography has tended to equate the aspirations and goals of working people with those of the leadership of organized labor and, apart from the well-known rivalry between the AFL and the CIO over the craft versus industrial models of unionization, has assumed widespread consensus among working people as to what was desired: legal protection of the right to organize; equalization of bargaining power by—and to the extent of—promoting unions as units of countervailing economic power; use of this power to achieve higher standards of living through wage-bargaining; and an industrial democracy limited to the notion that the bargaining unit is a political constituency to which should be extended the traditional democratic right to vote for or against representation, but that democratic participation is largely exhausted by that choice. From this perspective, it follows that the Wagner Act embodied the highest aspirations of labor and that its passage and success not only marked the irreversible emergence of labor as a political force in American life, but was triumphant testimony to the possibilities of democratic reform within the framework of capitalism.

Recent reexaminations of the American labor history of the 1930's suggest, however, that, whereas the foregoing goals may have reflected the attitudes of union leadership, a vastly more complicated and variegated situation is revealed beneath the plane of articulate historical actors at the level of ordinary, historically anonymous, working people. The conventional view exaggerates the unitary character of what labor sought generally in the 1930s and particularly from the collective bargaining law. It appears that the leadership of labor was in many respects quite distant from the rank and file and often acted at cross-purposes to its desires. There is evidence to support the claim that the collective bargaining model that eventually prevailed in the United States may not accurately reflect the aspirations of at least a significant number of those who were foot-soldiers in the industrial battles of the New Deal era. Rather, these working people may have contemplated a far more radical restructuring of relationships within the workplace in which industrial democracy, as an ongoing, participatory process both in the factory and the union, was at least as important as improved living standards. From this perspective, working people fought with determination to make the Act a reality—many giving their lives—because it imported more to them than the right to engage in endless economic combat for whatever benefits could be wrung from their corporate adversaries; it meant a commitment of government assistance toward the achievement of an objectively decent living standard and some control over the industrial decisions that affected their lives. At the very least, it can be asserted that the Act meant many different things to different people and groups on the labor side and that, for a substantial number, although they may have had only a vague idea of what the statute actually said, it nevertheless symbolized a significant opening in the direction of radical change.

An important conclusion emerges from the foregoing discussion: the indeterminacy of the text and legislative history of the Act, the political circumstances surrounding its passage, the complexity and fluidity of working-class attitudes toward collective bargaining and labor law reform during the period, and the hostility and disobedience of the business community make it clear that there was no coherent or agreed-upon fund of ideas or principles available as a conclusive guide in interpreting the Act. The statute was a texture of openness and divergency, not a crystallization of consensus or a signpost indicating a solitary direction for future development. This situation presented first the Board and the lower courts, but ultimately the United States Supreme Court, with the task of plotting the contours of the nation's new labor law. In doing so, the Court had to select one set of principles from among the Wagner Act's possible meanings and give to it the imprimatur of law. This task was unavoidably a *political* enterprise that thrust the Court into a central role in shaping the ideological and institutional architecture of the modern capitalist workplace.

Of course, the Court was not presented with treatises on political philosophy or industrial sociology in the argument of cases nor was it asked to write such treatises in its decisions. The Court decided issues of law in particular cases. Yet in many cases, the Court easily could have reached one or more alternative results, while employing accepted, competent, and traditional modes of judicial analysis and remaining well within the boundaries of the legislative history of the Act. In a number of cases, the Court overruled decisions of the Board that were fully "responsible" in any traditional sense of appropriate legal discourse and thereby pushed the law in a markedly different political direction. To justify not one result, but the entire set of results, the Court was obliged to articulate a new legal consciousness respecting labor matters, a new intellectual outlook on the nature of the wage-bargain. As this world view matured, it began to set boundaries on the type of questions the Court would ask and the possible scope of results it could reach in the labor field; that is, future decisions were mediated through, and in part determined by, the new legal consciousness. At a certain point, this mediation of legal consciousness may explain particular results in particular cases, where the mere logic of precedent or legislative hisotry, on the one hand, or political result-orientation, on the other, are unable to do so. Though it changed and adapted throughout the postwar period, the outlines of the Court's modern outlook on labor issues were established in the crucible of the late 1930's. To the extent that the vision of the law is a form of legitimating ideology supportive and protective of the institutional structure of the workplace, this vision itself serves as a form of political domination.

The remainder of this Article will attempt to demonstrate that, in shaping the nation's labor law, the Court embraced those aims of the Act most consistent with the assumptions of liberal capitalism and foreclosed those potential paths of development most threatening to the established order. Thus, the Wagner Act's goals of industrial peace, collective bargaining as therapy, a safely cabined worker free choice, and some rearrangement of relative bargaining power survived judicial construction of the Act, whereas the goals of redistribution, equality of bargaining power, and industrial democracy—although abiding in rhetoric—were jettisoned as serious components of national labor policy. This process will be discussed in terms of three central aspects of the Court's deradicalization of the Wagner Act and articulation of a more modern legal consciousness: its emphasis on contractualism; its development of the "public right" doctrine; and its promulgation of certain limitations on the legal protection of employee concerted activity.

III. JUDICIAL TREATMENT OF THE WAGNER ACT: FROM THE SIT-DOWNS TO PEARL HARBOR

A. THE CONTRACTUALIST PHOENIX: THE LABOR LAW REVOLUTION AS THE REVIVAL OF *LOCHNER v. NEW YORK*

In 1931, Walton Hamilton argued that the days of "freedom of contract" were numbered. When the Wagner Act was passed, commentators and courts saw in it the fulfillment of this prophecy with respect to labor contracts. Indeed, it is widely believed today that the Wagner Act effected a detachment of labor relations from the law of contracts that had previously governed it. This notion is seriously misleading. Contract is alive and well in the law of labor relations. To be sure, the collective bargaining agreement is a special kind of contract, with peculiar legal incidents, but despite the strongly anticontractualist overtones of the Act the Supreme Court ensured from the start that contractualism would be the jurisprudential framework of the law of labor relations.

The political ramifications of the Court's revivification of labor contractualism at the moment of its apparent demise can be seen from an analysis of the philosophy or ethos of freedom of contract. Although contrary emphases on social control had never been excluded from the law of contracts, in the nineteenth century, freedom of contract doctrine reshaped and revised that law so as to provide a framework for protecting expectations and facilitating transactions deemed essential or desirable from the standpoint of the emerging capitalist order. In the spirit of laissez faire, the doctrine extolled the social virtue of uncompelled private-ordering of most transactions: the right of private citizens to establish the legal incidents and standards governing most of their relationships. The central moral ideal of contractualism was and is that justice consists in enforcing the agreement of the parties so long as they have capacity and have had a proper opportunity to bargain for terms satisfactory to each. Contractual justice is, therefore, formal and abstract: within the broad scope of legal bargains it is disinterested in the substantive content of the parties' arrangements.

Since its appearance a century or more ago, the moral and social policy of freedom of contract has been assailed by critics who regard as its chief vice the fact that the substantive content of private-ordering reflects the gross disparities of economic power characteristic of capitalist society.[19] In this view, freedom of contract is, in prac-

tice, an institutional framework for the legitimate exercise of coercive power. The amount of freedom created by the system of freedom of contract depends on the structure of economic power, yet differences of economic or class power are ordinarily either ignored or regarded as legitimate in contractualist jurisprudence, particularly in its late nineteenth- and early twentieth-century conceptualist version. The tendency of freedom of contract doctrine has been to treat as naturally preordained an historically contingent system of class relations.

In the context of the labor market, freedom of contract produced oppressive and morally defective results for two reasons. First, the wage-bargain is inherently an unequal exchange, because the value produced by the employee, and appropriated by the capitalist, must ordinarily be greater than the value received back in wages. Second, the wage contract is more than a legal relationship. It establishes an entire system of social relations in the workplace whereby the employer is entitled to control the worker's actions and choices during the major portion of his waking hours. Thus, labor contractualism functions as the institutional basis of domination in the workplace. Private-ordering in the labor market therefore means, for the ordinary American worker, only the freedom to choose one capitalist or another to whom to sell one's labor power. It offers no freedom to opt out of the social relations of capitalism, to participate as a subject in defining the quality of work or of life. It is for this reason that working-class movements have traditionally sought to curtail freedom of contract, through struggles to limit the hours of work, to set minimum wages, or to restrict the employer's discretion in hiring and firing.

The foremost task of the Supreme Court, in the wake of the Wagner Act, was to resolve whether the wage-bargain would remain fundamentally within the contractualist, private ordering

[19]Contractualism has also been criticized by questioning the validity of its underlying metaphysical assumptions. Thus, in contrast to the liberal political tradition, it has been argued that the good is not arbitrary and wholly subjective; that needs and values can arise from shared social experience apart from mere coincidence or situations of domination; that there is a natural, spontaneous component of human sociality; that public and private life are indissolubly linked; that the ideal of community is a meaningful and worthy starting point for political philosophy; and that justice properly has a substantive meaning. Each of these themes has been advanced by major dissenting intellectual traditions in liberal society, located at a variety of positions on the political spectrum; they are reflected in the Marxist tradition from which

this paper draws its inspiration. *See generally* R. UNGER, KNOWLEDGE & POLITICS (1975).

framework. This task was accomplished in the very first cases decided under the Act. *NLRB v. Jones & Laughlin Steel Corp.* and its companion cases are chiefly remembered for their far-reaching innovations in the areas of federalism, the commerce power, and the scope of judicial review, but this fact must not obscure their crucial historical role in updating and preserving the freedom of contract ideal.

Jones & Laughlin began by establishing that employees would be allowed to pool their bargaining power to offset the superior economic position of the employer and that the employer would not be permitted to interfere with its employees' decision whether to adopt a collective posture for wage-bargaining or their choice of a representative for that purpose. Chief Justice Hughes' conception appeared to be that employees had a privilege to create a quasi-fiduciary or protected economic relationship between each of them individually and the others by constituting a collective bargaining unit and designating an "agent" or "agency" (a word commonly used to refer to unions in the early opinions) to represent them. The designation of the bargaining agency constituted the creation of the "protected" relationship, and the unfair labor practices proscribed in section 8 were conceived essentially as torts of injurious interference with the privileged relationship. That is, employer interference with employee choice of a bargaining representative was treated conceptually as similar to employee interference with the employer's protected relationship with its representative, such as would occur, for example, if an employee intercepted the employer's communications with counsel:

> [Legitimate] collective action would be a mockery if representation were made futile by interference with freedom of choice. Hence the prohibition by Congress of interference with the selection of representatives for the purpose of negotiation and conference between employers and employees, "instead of being an invasion of the constitutional right of either, was based on the recognition of the rights of both."

But the Court emphatically rejected any suggestion that the Act abolished private-ordering as the framework of relationships in the workplace:

> The Act does not compel agreements between employers and employees. It does not compel any agreement whatever. It does not prevent the employer "from refusing to make a collective contract and hiring individuals on whatever terms" the employer "may by unilateral action determine." . . . The Act does not interfere with the normal exercise of the right of the employer to select its employees or to discharge them. The employer may not, under cover of that right, intimidate or coerce its employees with respect to their self-organization and representation, and, on the other hand, the Board is not entitled to make its authority a pretext for interference with the right of discharge when that right is exercised for other reasons than such intimidation and coercion.

In the Court's view, the Act did not infringe on normal managerial prerogatives except insofar as the employer was prohibited from invading the employees' privilege to pool their bargaining power and to choose and act through a bargaining agent. The Act was no warrant for a regime of governmental supervision of normal managerial decisions. The Court rejected any inference that the law would inquire into the substantive justice of labor-management relations or the fairness of the wage-bargain. In short, the opinion of Chief Justice Hughes really went no further than the dissenting opinions in the classical freedom of contract cases of *Adair v. United States* and *Coppage v. Kansas;* his conceptual universe was akin to that which inspired those opinions.

Subsequent cases of the period preserved this framework, with a bloc composed of Chief Justice Hughes and Justices Roberts and Stone continuing to adhere to contractualism and a conceptualist style of analysis. In *NLRB v. Mackay Radio & Telegraph Co.,* for example, the Court established the crucial strategic right of struck employers to offer permanent positions to workers hired to replace strikers (so long as the strike was not provoked or prolonged by unfair labor practices). The manner in which the Court reached its conclusion is instructive. The issue before the Court was whether, as a matter of labor policy, the employer should have the weapon of permanent replacement at its disposal. The Court, however, never candidly addressed this question, saying only that it did not follow from section 13 "that an employer, guilty of no act denounced by the statute, [had] lost the right to protect and continue his business by supplying places left vacant by strikers." This statement is a paradigmatic representation of the vices of conceptualist legal reasoning because the question whether the employer was "guilty of [an] act denounced by the statute" was precisely the matter to be decided, and the question whether the employer had a right to protect his business, if to do so would invade the right of his employees to engage in concerted activity, likewise required explicit analysis from the standpoint of the society's labor policy. In each case, the Court merely assumed its conclusion, presenting as compelled by the words of the Act, or by Reason, or simply as a priori true, judgments involving debatable choices from among competing economic and political values. Thus, the conceptualist tradition was upheld and continued as the Court masked the unavoidably ideological content of judicial action.[20]

The *Mackay* rule remains the prevailing law. It is historically important because it was one of the earliest manifestations of the developing premise that once an employer lawfully bargains to impasse, it is free unilaterally to impose terms and conditions of employment, if it has the economic staying power to defeat a strike. Thus, the decision furthered the principle that the Act is disin-

---

[20]The point is not that a realist analysis would have guaranteed a different or better result in *Mackay*. An explicit sociopolitical analysis might have more candidly addressed the real issues involved, but ultimately a realist balancing of competing interests in light of Congress' labor policy might have led to the same result. Neither conceptualism nor realism succeeds in immunizing adjudication from politics, nor is either a method that provides a determinate answer to every legal problem. The effort here is simply to delineate the texture and vision of the legal consciousness developing in the cases under discussion.

terested in the substantive justice of the labor contract since it taught that not only would the wage-bargain not ordinarily be subject to substantive scrutiny, but also that the economic combat of the parties had replaced a "meeting of the minds" as the moral basis of labor contractualism.

NLRB v. Sands Manufacturing Co. was another example of this trend. In *Sands,* a dispute arose between the union and the employer during the term of a collective bargaining agreement. The Court held that the statutory duty to bargain attached in such situations. The dispute in question remained unresolved after discussion, however, and a work-stoppage was threatened. The company thereupon discharged the entire work force and reopened the plant with a wholly new complement of employees. It was contested whether the initial dispute went to a question of contract application or to a proposed modification; in any event, the union refused to compromise its position. Interpreting the contract sua sponte, the Court announced that its terms favored the employer's version and that, therefore, the union was unilaterally insisting upon a midterm modification. The Court held that employees may not use economic power to impose their demands in such a situation, despite the fact that the contract did not contain a "no-strike" clause and, in fact, reserved full liberty of action to the employees in case of impasse in attempts to resolve "misunderstandings" between the company and the work force. The employees' insistence that they would not work except under their interpretation of the contract was held to be a "breach" or "repudiation" of an implied contractual obligation, sufficient to divest the workers of their statutory right to engage in concerted activity. The Court stated,

> The Act does not prohibit an effective discharge for repudiation by the employee of his agreement. . . .
>
> . . . .
>
> . . . If, as we have held, the respondent was confronted with a concerted refusal on the part of [the union] to permit its members to perform their con-

tract there was nothing unlawful in the company's attempting to procure others to fill their places.

The Court's opinion in *Sands* relied on a highly formalistic and contractualist reading of the statute to legitimize the inequalities of bargaining power arising from the unequal social distribution of property ownership. The ban on the use of economic power by the union was, given the record presented, presumably meant to apply equally to attempts to impose a union interpretation of an agreement as well as to achieve a midterm modification of the agreement. That is, if an impasse is reached, the employer could use its economic power, namely its ownership and control of the business, to get its way, but the workers could not use their primary economic weapon, the work-stoppage.

The Court's initial period of contractualist formalism under the Wagner Act was followed by a series of realist victories, written chiefly by Justices Black and Douglas. One series of these cases concerned the definition of "free choice," an essential ingredient of traditional contract doctrine, in the context of alleged employer domination of labor organizations.

The old-fashioned company union was one of the preeminent weapons employers used to defeat the labor movement. Therefore, section 8(2) of the Act was a crucial battleground in the 1930's. If the Act were to fulfill its functions, the company union had to be eliminated. To this end, the Board and the courts developed the remedy of "disestablishing" organizations found to be employer-dominated. The realists pushed this remedy to its limits. In *NLRB v. Falk Corp.*, for example, one issue was whether the remedy of "disestablishment" meant that the company union was to be denied a place on the ballot in an election to choose a new bargaining representative. Justice Black, writing for the Court, upheld the Board's conclusion that the "company-created union could not emancipate itself from habitual subservience to its creator, and that in order to insure employees that complete freedom of choice guaranteed by §7, [the dominated

union] must be . . . kept off the ballot." In other words, if the workers voted for the company union in a fair election, that would not be "free choice." This free choice had a *substantive* content, determined by the history of the workplace, not merely a formal content determined by the mechanics of secret balloting.

The realist tide swept away other formalistic doctrines. In *NLRB v. Waterman Steamship Co.*, Justice Black held that the formalities of the typical seaman's contract, under which each voyage constitutes a separate and distinct contractual relationship, were not controlling under the Act. The words of the Act were

> not limited so as to outlaw discrimination only where there is in existence a formal contract or relation of employment between employer and employee. They embrace, as well, all elements of the employment relationship which in fact customarily attend employment and with respect to which an employer's discrimination may as readily be the means of interfering with employees' right of self-organization as if these elements were precise terms of a written contract of employment. . . . For the purpose of the Act, it is immaterial that employment is at will and terminable at any time by either party.

The Court held that, although the employer had a clear contractual right to discharge his employees after a voyage for any reason whatsoever or no reason at all, it could not exercise that right in such a way as to chill union activity.

Similarly, in *International Association of Machinists v. NLRB*, the Court developed a broad doctrine of "imputed liability" in order to safeguard worker free choice. The Court stated that the technicalities of *respondeat superior* were not applicable to proceedings under the Act:

> The employer, however, may be held to have assisted the formation of a union even though the acts of the so-called agents were not expressly authorized or might not be attributable to him on strict application of the rules of *respondeat superior*. . . . Thus, where the employees would have just cause to believe that solicitors professedly

for a labor organization were acting for and on behalf of the management, the Board would be justified in concluding that they did not have the complete and unhampered freedom of choice which the Act contemplates.

Undoubtedly, the free choice decisions overrode certain traditional doctrines governing the employment contract, but they did not attack contractualism as such. They sought to achieve what the Court saw as the preconditions of "true" or "actual" private-ordering; they were designed to make contractualism work, not to abolish it. There is no intimation in these decisions that, once the preconditions of "actual liberty of contract" were realized, the law would inquire into the substantive results of bargaining. Thus, the new realism preserved the formal and abstentionist posture of traditional contract doctrine, and the political function of labor contractualism—the creation of an institutional framework in which social relations of domination appear in the guise of free exchange—was reaffirmed.

Only the uncertain shadow of the section 8(5) duty to bargain clouded this contractualist horizon. The legislative history of section 8(5) contains repeated indications that the Act was not intended to require the parties to agree to anything, but just to meet and bargain. Nevertheless, it was clear from the pre-NLRA experience of the National Labor Board and the "old" National Labor Relations Board under section 7(a) of the National Industrial Recovery Act, that the duty to bargain would have to mean more, if it were to mean anything, than just a minimal duty physically to meet with employee representatives. The Board and the courts, however, largely avoided setting the parameters of the duty during the period under discussion, because the primary battleground of the 1930's was the field of union organization and recognition, not collective bargaining as such.

In the period before Pearl Harbor, the only major Supreme Court decision under section 8(5) was *H. J. Heinz Co. v. NLRB,* which held that, although an employer was not compelled to agree to a union's demands, if the parties did reach an agreement, the section 8(5) duty required the employer, on request, to incorporate the agreed terms into a written, signed document. It was logically possible to imply from *Heinz* a power in the Board to scrutinize employers' bargaining conduct against a standard of objectively reasonable bargaining practice, but the Court's actual reasoning supplied no basis for anticipating that the Board would be empowered to judge bargaining conduct, much less the content of proposals, under a broad reasonableness standard. Rather, the *Heinz* rule was understood at the time as a minimal imposition designed to stabilize and regularize the collective bargaining relationship, as part of the program to make contractualism work. Thus, although the Court's pronouncements in this area were minimal, it is nevertheless apparent, given that substantive scrutiny was at least a plausible outcome in light of the legislative history, that the Court's preference for purely procedural review represented a matter of conscious choice.[21]

---

[21]The foregoing discussion is not a legal argument that the Board should have been granted the power of substantive scrutiny over wage-bargaining. Nor is it contended that substantive review of the wage-bargain would have been the answer to labor's problems or a guarantee of justice for the American worker. From a theoretical standpoint, the idea of a democratic process establishing what the community regards as fair and just terms of employment is attractive compared to leaving such decisions to the outcome of the raw conflict of class power. I do not share the premise of liberal political theory that there is an inherent contradiction between community intervention and individual or group self-actualization and freedom. Nevertheless, in society as presently constituted, there is no reason to assume that a grant of substantive review powers to an administrative agency would, with any likelihood, result in a democratic process or just terms of employment. The Board is a priori no more likely to serve the needs of employees (or employers) than the courts or the private collective bargaining process.

My political claim, therefore, does not rest on a preference for the assumption by the Board of substantive review powers. Rather my claim is that, had the Court permitted and encouraged the Board to assume such powers, a potentially radicalizing force would have been introduced into the law

The rudimentary foundations of a new juris-prudential synthesis, "social conceptualism," began to appear on two levels in the process of development of the new labor contractualism. On a substantive level, the Court recognized that state regulation of the wage-bargain could coexist with private-ordering. This outlook at once affirmed two seemingly contradictory social values: that it is appropriate and just for the state to rearrange the relative bargaining strengths of capital and labor because the pre-existing disparity of power produced substantively unacceptable results and that the state ought not to intervene in private wage-bargaining to encourage or assure any particular substantive outcome. In logic, these competing social values may be mutually exclusive, but not so in the new judicial consciousness, which accommodated both regulation and private-ordering by refusing to push either principle to its limits.

On a second, methodological level, the emerging legal consciousness became sensitized to the social and political ramifications of legal rules and decisions, but the Supreme Court was not prepared simply to assimilate legal reasoning to social policy analysis. The political realism that indicated the necessity of state intervention in labor bargaining did not inexorably lead to legal realism as an adjudicatory method. On the contrary, the process at work was the reification of ad hoc social policies into "values" or "first principles" that were then conceived to provide determinate—and therefore legitimate—solutions to legal problems, as, for example, with Justice Roberts' concept of the employer's right to pro-tect the business and Justices Douglas' and Black's notion of free choice.

B. THE PUBLIC RIGHT DOCTRINE: NEW DEAL ADMINISTRATIVE LAW AS A CONTRIBUTION TO PLURALIST POLITICAL THEORY

A classical problem of liberal political theory has been to preserve the neutrality of the state in a world understood to be dominated and motivated by the conflict of private interests. Liberal political theory has always conceived of the state as being radically divorced from, or rising above, civil society, the realm of private and group interest. During the early years of the Great Depression, however, the purported neutrality of the state, particularly the federal judiciary was, as had happened before, called into widespread doubt. The New Dealers eventually appointed to the Court confronted a massive crisis of legitimacy. Their difficult task, therefore, was to make the law more responsive to pressing social priorities and the constituencies that the reform programs of the New Deal were designed to aid, while restoring the purported neutrality of the state. That is, although the law was to be mobilized to carry out new regulatory and welfare functions representing the triumph of a particular political coalition, the rhetoric of liberal legalism had to be repaired and enhanced, proving that Americans did, indeed, live under the rule of law, not men.

The articulation of a comprehensive modern administrative law was one of the New Deal jurists' most creative responses to this dilemma. In this jurisprudence, the actions of administrative agencies and tribunals were considered subject to the rule of law and not mere reflections of the shifting interests of partisan power, yet administrative bodies were also conceived to be relatively emancipated from rule-formalism insofar as their responsiveness to changing crystallizations of public interest and policy was deemed legitimate. This uneasy merger of formalism and result-orientation required careful and articulate justification. New doctrinal formulas were

---

by the making of a *public political issue* of the substantive terms of the wage-bargain. Public discussion and criticism of Board decisions respecting the fairness of terms of employment would have had a politicizing and destabilizing impact on the labor movement by creating greater public understanding of the contingent nature of social relationships and the way in which the purportedly neutral decisions of government reflect the preponderant influence of class power on the state. In this sense, the Court's preference for a formal, proceduralist model represented a deradicalization of the potential of the Wagner Act.

needed to enable progressive courts to brush aside some of the finer concerns and details of traditional private adjudication in reviewing the work of the agencies, while at the same time avoiding any appearance of capitulation to partisan interest.

A second challenging aspect of rehabilitating the state's image as neutral arbiter above group conflict was to provide a theoretical justification for the delegation of the lawmaking function (i.e., the setting of enforceable standards of conduct) to socially significant groups. If the Wagner Act and the other New Deal reform measures were to succeed, the law had to allow for some notion of legitimate private lawmaking. The radical disjunction between public and private that characterized classical liberal political theory was no longer tenable in the late capitalist or welfare state in which the government systematically and pervasively intervened in the private sector and, conversely, in which institutions, such as corporations and unions, hitherto deemed to be purely private in nature, increasingly assumed the functions, attributes, or powers of quasi-governmental agencies. On the other hand, the public/private distinction could not be abandoned altogether without subverting the basic philosophical premises of the liberal democratic state. The preservation of the public/private distinction in a world in which it was becoming increasingly incoherent, at least in the classical liberal formulation, became one of the central projects of the new jurisprudence of social conceptualism. One minor but significant early episode in the process was the strategy developed in the NLRA cases of maintaining the forms of private conflict-resolution in the administrative and legal process while superimposing on them a new version of the higher law through the public right doctrine.

In *Jones & Laughlin,* Chief Justice Hughes made a remarkable claim:

> Thus, in its present application, the statute goes no further than to safeguard the right of employees to self-organization and to select representatives of their own choosing for collective bargaining or other mutual protection without restraint or coercion by their employer.
>
> *That is a fundamental right.* Employees have as clear a right to organize and select their representatives for lawful purposes as the [company] has to organize its business and select its own officers and agents. Discrimination and coercion to prevent the free exercise of the right of employees to self-organization and representation is a proper subject for condemnation by competent legislative authority [emphasis added].

Hughes' choice of language implied that the rights guaranteed by the Act were not created by it. Rather, they were basic or inherent rights deriving from a source of law much more fundamental than mere statute. Hughes conceived of the Act as providing for the protection, as a matter of public policy, of a *right inhering in private law* and as striking a general balance between the respective private rights of adverse parties, with the Board assigned the detailed task of weighing and resolving clashes of *private* interests in particular factual settings.

Of course, the historical record flatly contradicted the view that the right to organize was recognized by law prior to 1935 as a fundamental, extrastatutory right, or, indeed, as a right at all. Perhaps Chief Justice Hughes was motivated to use this schema by a desire to depreciate the momentousness of what the Court was actually doing in *Jones & Laughlin.* In any case, the opinion reflects the inertia of legal concepts, the difficulty of conceptualizing radical change even at the moment it is experienced or brought about. Though everyone knew the Act was a marked political departure, the radical innovations it implied in legal theory were at first only dimly understood. The idea of a right had theretofore been associated with a private law conception of adjudication, and it is no surprise, therefore, that Hughes interpreted the Act within this conceptual framework. Moreover, his account of the Act had, in retrospect, a great virtue: it focused attention on the raw fact of class (group) conflict, rather than on the nebulous, and ideological, conception of a public interest rising above such conflict.

The Hughes formulation, however, was short-lived. The outline of an alternative scheme first appeared, implicitly, in *American Federation of Labor v. NLRB*. The case was a political bombshell, because the Court, in effect, allowed Harry Bridges' International Longshoremen's & Warehousemen's Union (CIO) to have a Pacific Coast-wide bargaining unit over the outraged opposition of the rival International Longshoremen's Association (AFL), which stood to lose its small base on the Pacific coast. The Court's holding was that judicial review of Board decisions in representation proceedings was not available unless and until the employer was charged with an unfair labor practice and raised a section 9 issue as a defense. This decision implicitly rested on the idea that the statutory scheme does not protect private entitlements but protects certain public interests. A private litigant was entitled to the orderly completion of the Board's processes, but it had no individual right, entitlement, or claim to the section 9 unit determination preferred by it. Thus, no deprivation of any right was involved in forbidding the courts to hear the claims of aggrieved private parties except under the circumstances provided by the statutory scheme. Under other circumstances, there was literally no claim to be heard.

The case was widely viewed as a prolabor victory, notwithstanding the wrath of the AFL, because the ruling put an end to one of the employers' favorite antiunion delaying tactics. But it had an unfortunate consequence, which CIO as well as AFL leaders were quick to see. If the party aggrieved in the section 9 proceeding was the union, for example, a union that later lost an election because of an improper definition of the bargaining unit, it would have *no* remedy under the Act because it would never be in a position to defend a refusal-to-bargain charge.

The new public right schema was explicitly articulated less than two months later in *Amalgamated Utility Workers v. Consolidated Edison Co.* Alleged employer disobedience to a Court of Appeals enforcement order prompted the union to move that the employer be cited for contempt.

Although the *Board* had standing to make such a motion, it had declined to do so. The issue, therefore, was whether a *private party* could vindicate its rights under the Act by this means. A unanimous Supreme Court said no. Chief Justice Hughes wrote,

> The Board as a public agency acting in the public interest, not any private person or group, not any employee or group of employees, is chosen as the instrument to assure protection from the described unfair conduct in order to remove obstructions to interstate commerce.
>
> When the Board has made its order, the Board alone is authorized to take proceedings to enforce it.
>
> . . . .
>
> It is the Board's order on behalf of the public that the court enforces. It is the Board's right to make that order that the court sustains. The Board seeks enforcement as a public agent, not to give effect to a "private administrative remedy."

As a result, if a successful charging party was aggrieved but the Board refused fully to enforce its order through contempt proceedings, that party was without remedy to protect its rights or even to obtain a hearing. The fundamental rights spoken of in *Jones & Laughlin* were transmuted in the space of three years into privileges created by the statute and therefore measured by the Board's discretion and largesse in administering the statutory scheme. The rights of employees were now conceived to be held and defined at the pleasure of an agency of the federal government.

Once launched, the public right doctrine exhibited a potent power to override private interests. The Court allowed the Board to adjudicate certain contract rights without requiring the Board to join or afford a hearing to one of the contractual parties, employed the public right doctrine to justify its previously mentioned rulings that the technicalities of *respondeat superior* do not apply to section 8 proceedings, and invoked the doctrine to justify the breakdown of traditional concepts of remedies.

The culmination of the public right conception

occurred in *Pittsburgh Plate Glass Co. v. NLRB*. In that case, a CIO affiliate had an overall majority and a majority in each of five of PPG's six flat glass plants. An independent union, with a history of employer domination, claimed a majority in the sixth plant. The Board found appropriate a single bargaining unit encompassing all six plants, thus writing off the independent union for practical purposes. The Court affirmed the Board's action, relying in part on the view that it was permissible for the Board to consider in deciding the case that, if the sixth plant were placed in a separate bargaining unit, the employer could use it to maintain operations in the event of a strike in the larger unit and thereby tip the balance of economic power in its favor.

The Court's holding itself was of modest significance, especially since the Board had receded from its policy of certifying such massive units prior to the *Plate Glass* decision. But the Court's conception of the Board's role under the Act was of preeminent importance. Read broadly, *Plate Glass* implied that determinations as to the appropriateness of bargaining units were strictly reserved to the Board's discretion and that in making such determinations, the Board was authorized to include in its calculations a balancing of the relative economic power of the opposed class forces. Presumably, the balancing of relative economic forces was deemed a matter of neutral, expert judgment, although the Court never explained how one might define or identify a public interest in one or another balance of power between capital and labor. In practice, *Plate Glass* placed enormous political power in the hands of the Board to delimit the contours of legitimate class struggle. Not only was the Board granted wide discretion in enforcing the Act, but it also had the power to define the balance of opposing economic forces on which the substantive outcome of collective bargaining depends.

Of course, it is not suggested that the Court granted the Board carte blanche to restructure American class relations; the historical impact of the case should not be exaggerated. Rather the effort here is to recover the Court's conceptuali-

zation of the statutory scheme, in which the Court recognized that as a practical matter the Board had the power dramatically to shape the terrain on which private-ordering will take place and thereby crucially to influence its outcome. In *Plate Glass* the Court endowed this de facto power with the imprimatur of law. Although institutional and political considerations have led the Board generally to utilize this power discreetly over the years, in the context of the late 1930's, *Plate Glass* brought to fruition an intellectual movement to conceptualize employees' rights as public rights, measured by the discretion of the Board. Unavoidably, the decision in *Plate Glass* created an intellectual justification for the dependency of labor on the state, thereby reinforcing the cultural hegemony of liberal political theory. This dependence hindered labor from conceiving of itself, or acting, as an autonomous movement capable of fundamentally transforming the established social relations of production. The public right doctrine created a justification in political theory for labor's dependence on government, thereby tending to transform a contingent historical relationship into a moral destiny.[22]

C. THE INHIBITION OF WORKER SELF-ACTIVITY

Labor was the beneficiary of an exciting series of legal victories in the early years of Wagner Act interpretation. In procedural matters, the scope of judicial review of Board findings under section 10 was narrowly confined, and the courts were forbidden to review or interdict Board proceedings until they had run their proper course. Thus, the Court made clear that it would protect the Board's processes from judicial invasion and em-

[22]As a postscript to this discussion and a prelude to the next section, it should be noted that the public right doctrine was applied selectively. That is, when the Court disapproved of the Board's action in a particular case, it suddenly reverted to the more exacting standards of traditional private adjudication. Most often, this latter approach was used to defend the property rights of employers from encroachment by the public rights supposedly protected under the Act. The result was severe limitations on the protection of employee concerted activity.

ployer stalling tactics. In substantive matters, the Court liberalized the law of picketing and endowed ordinary union activities with immunity under the antitrust laws. The latter action brought an end to what for generations had been one of the primary legal weapons used by employers against the labor movement.

Intermixed with these cases, however, were several decisions narrowing and limiting legally protected union activity and hampering the effective enforcement of the Act. Chief among these decisions were *NLRB v. Fansteel Metallurgical Corp.*, condemning the sit-down strike; *NLRB v. Mackay Radio & Telegraph Co.*, allowing permanent replacement of economic strikers; *NLRB v. Sands Manufacturing Co.*, withdrawing section 7 protection from certain strike activity in the context of an existing collective bargaining relationship; and *Phelps Dodge Corp. v. NLRB*, establishing the mitigation rule.

The early Wagner Act cases had a much more momentous consequence than can be captured in this simple tally of labor's immediate gains and losses. The unprecedented privileges granted to labor created discord in conventional legal thought. In generating doctrines to justify this new legal status, the Court was called upon to develop a conception of the proper role of unions in the reformed social order.

Two motifs are paramount in the Court's portrait of "legitimate" union activity. First was the fiduciary theme, the Court's view that unions have an institutional role setting them apart from their members. Initially this idea was but a conceptual corollary of the "quasi-tort" schema Hughes articulated in *Jones & Laughlin*, namely, the view that the union was something separate and apart from the employees and the purpose of the Act was to prevent unwarranted employer invasion of the privileged relationship between the employees and their "agent." But the theme soon developed a life of its own. The delineation of legitimate forms of concerted activity contained the unstated proviso that unions wishing the protection of the Board had to keep their members in line. *Sands Manufacturing* and *Fansteel* were ab-

rupt warnings that what, from a management perspective, were the more spontaneous or undisciplined forms of concerted activity, the midterm strike and the sit-down strike, would not be protected by the Act. The public right doctrine implied that union conduct would not be judged solely against the backdrop of competing employer and employee interests, but against the public interest in industrial peace as well. The ideological premise that there is such a general societal interest in the smooth operation of the industrial system was always taken for granted. The union was seen not just as a private fiduciary vis-à-vis the membership of the bargaining unit, but also as a "trustee" of this public interest, and "responsible behavior" by unions became a quid pro quo for the legal privileges extended by the Act.

Second, the Court's wage-bargain theme represented, as the term implies, a conception that the function of a union was to make a wage-bargain; that is, its role was limited to the sphere of exchange. The very power that unions had in arranging the sale of labor power signaled their inevitable participation in reproducing the alienation that characterized the work-process itself and negated the alternative historical and moral claims they might have advanced with respect to the sphere of production.

The negative implications of these two themes provided the underpinnings of a narrow conception of the social relations of the work-place in three fundamental and interrelated ways. First, the treatment of workers as sellers of labor power and as consumers of commodities, but not as producers, hindered them from achieving an alternative perspective in which worker self-activity, the process by which workers produce value by embodying their labor power in things, services, and relationships, would be recognized as the basis of all production in, and reproduction of, society. The Court's vision countered the corollary of this alternative premise, that workers' organizations ought to affirm and advance the proposition that those whose collective efforts make social production possible should have a decisive say in the decisions that affect the process, that they pose themselves morally and institutionally as the authors of their own destinies in the workplace.

Second, since it was imagined that there was an overall societal interest in maintaining the prevailing industrial system, the Court's fiduciary theme encouraged responsible unions to accept the social order as given and to seek to defend and better the lot of their members only within its ground rules. Here again, the fact that the social fabric is itself produced and reproduced through the activity of society's members was obscured and denied.

Finally, since union activity was denominated as something separate from members' self-activity in the workplace, unions could not function as participatory institutions in which workers continuously articulated and redefined their aspirations for the governance and transformation of the work-process. The union was not expected to foreshadow the organizational form of a democratic workplace, nor to provide the workers with an "experiment . . . in self-organization, in initiative and collective decision-making, in short, an experiment in the possibility of their own emancipation."[23] In sum, the Court's narrowly restricted vision of legitimate union activity stood in every sense as a barrier to the possibility that labor would participate in bringing about fundamental social change.

These themes are vividly illustrated by the extraordinary case of *NLRB v. Fansteel Metallurgical Corp.,* which condemned the sit-down strike. In *Fansteel,* massive and undisputed employer unfair labor practices designed to defeat unionization of the plant provoked the employees to stage a sit-down strike in their factory. They were evicted by the police, and many strikers were fined or jailed under state law. The employer then encouraged the formation of a company union, continuing its course of illegal conduct. The Board attempted to undo the effects of

[23]Gorz, *Reform and Revolution,* in THE SOCIALIST REGISTER 125 (1968).

the employer illegality by ordering the company to bargain on request with the bona fide union and to reinstate the strikers. The Court agreed that the employer had committed unfair labor practices, but overruled the reinstatement of the sit-down strikers, holding that under the Act the company could legally discharge the strikers for occupying the plant and that the Board lacked authority under section 10(c) to order reinstatement. In the language of Chief Justice Hughes,

> reprehensible as was that conduct of [the company], there is no ground for saying that it made [the company] an outlaw or deprived it of its legal rights to the possession and protection of its property. The employees had the right to strike but they had no license to commit acts of violence or to seize their employer's plant. . . . But in its legal aspect the ousting of the owner from lawful possession is not essentially different from an assault upon the officers of an employing company, or the seizure and conversion of its goods, or the despoiling of its property or other unlawful acts in order to force compliance with demands. To justify such conduct because of the existence of a labor dispute or of an unfair labor practice would be to put a premium on resort to force instead of legal remedies and to subvert the principles of law and order which lie at the foundations of society.

The extreme formalism underlying the *Fansteel* opinion is evident in Hughes' focus on the legal aspects of the discharge, rather than on the scope of the Board's remedial powers. Hughes reasoned that the strikers' tortious conduct was independent from the employer's unfair labor practices and an adequate basis for divesting them of their status as employees, notwithstanding the language of section 2(3), which provides for the continuation of employee status in contemplation of law notwithstanding its cessation in fact in connection with current labor disputes or unfair labor practices. Accordingly, it followed that the strikers could not avail themselves of the protection and remedies of the statute. Hughes, however, belatedly recognized that the remedial powers of the Board were not limited to the assistance of employees; the ultimate test under section 10(c) was whether reinstatement would serve, under the circumstances, to effectuate the policies of the Act. Responding briskly in the negative, Hughes argued that reinstatement would only give license to tortfeasors and discourage the peaceful settlement of industrial disputes. Concluding this formalist tour de force, Hughes castigated the workers for their sit-down tactic:

> It was a highhanded proceeding without shadow of legal right . . . .
>
> . . . .
>
> . . . This was not the exercise of "the right to strike" to which the Act referred. . . . It was an illegal seizure of the buildings in order to prevent their use by the employer in a lawful manner and thus by acts of force and violence to compel the employer to submit.

The realists bitterly counterattacked, contending that the real question was the Board's expert assessment, arguably proper under section 10(c), that the purposes of the Act would best be served by reinstating the strikers. Since any unlawful acts committed by the strikers had already been punished quite severely under state law, to impose the further penalty of allowing the company permanently to sever the employment relationship would permit employers to subvert the Act by provoking sit-down strikes or other tortious conduct and then reaping the benefits of their unfair labor practices by immunizing themselves from the Board's remedial powers. This, at any rate, was the Board's considered judgment. The real issue of the case, brusquely avoided by the Court, was the soundness and legitimacy of this judgment of social policy.

The best that can be said for Hughes' view is that it blatantly ignored historical and social reality. The Court ignored the fact that the sit-down strikes were essentially a reaction to the widespread and often violent refusal by employers to obey the law between 1935 and 1940. The historical record is clear that the sit-down strikes were an indispensable weapon with which workers stemmed the tide of employer resistance to

unions and to the law; inferentially, they thereby helped create the political conditions for the Court's leftward shift in *West Coast Hotel Co. v. Parrish* and *NLRB v. Jones & Laughlin Steel Corp.* That is, the sit-down strikes contributed to, rather than detracted from, whatever law and order existed in industrial life in 1939 when Hughes delivered *Fansteel*. Moreover, in sharp contrast to contemporary but traditionally conducted strikes, the sit-downs in 1936–1938 caused no deaths and little property damage.

The sit-down strike was important not only because it was so effective tactically, but also because it minimized the risks of picket-line violence. The traditional strike separates the employees from the workplace and from each other. Typically striking workers come together only serially, on the picket line. In the sit-down, however, workers posed themselves as collectively capable of organizing the workplace. The logistics of the sit-down required the constant participation of all in decisionmaking and fostered a spirit of community, cooperation, and initiative. The sit-downs nurtured a new psychological and emotional experience: "The fact that the sit-down gives the worker in mass-production industries a vital sense of importance cannot be over-emphasized."[24] The sit-downs were a utopian breach in the endless regularity and pessimism of everyday life, a "dereifying" explosion of repressed human spirit.

By ignoring these social realities and condemning the sit-down strike, the Court interpreted the Act as standing against the possibility of emancipatory workplace experiments. *Fansteel* condemned a tactic designed to transcend the disjunction between the union and its members; it bolstered the forces of union bureaucracy in their efforts to quell the spontaneity of the rank and file. As such, it marked the end of the radical potential of the 1930's by demarcating the outer limits of disruption of the es-

[24]Brecher, *The Sitdown Strikes of the 1930's: From Baseball to Bureaucracy*, 4 ROOT & BRANCH PAMPHLET 23 (n.d.) (quoting L. ADAMIC, MY AMERICA 408 (1938)).

tablished industrial order that the law would tolerate. The utopian aspirations for a radical restructuring of the workplace, engendered by enactment of the Wagner Act and the intoxicating experience of the rise of the CIO, were symbolically thwarted by *Fansteel*, which erected labor law reform as a roadblock in their path.

D THE ROOTS OF MODERN LEGAL CONSCIOUSNESS

The contours of a more modern legal consciousness, hinted at in the earliest Wagner Act cases, were clearly visible by the beginning of the 1940's as the legal crisis of the previous decade drew to a close. The Court could be divided, somewhat schematically, into three groups. Chief Justice Hughes and Justices Stone and Roberts continued the conceptualist tradition. They were reluctant to abide by the Board's expert judgment and fearful, to some extent, of the new power of labor. Justices Black, Douglas, and Murphy, sometimes joined by Reed, formed the realist contingent. Their opinions evinced a purposive style of legal analysis and a willingness to defer to the discretion of the Board. There is a curious correlation between legal styles and these Justices' understanding of the fundamental purposes of the Act. The conceptualist group persistently emphasized what is probably the most instrumental goal of the Act, industrial peace, whereas the realists stressed the more ethereal goal of employee free choice. Since bringing social policy explicitly into legal analysis was already disturbing to the more traditional judicial mind, the conceptualists probably felt most comfortable coming to grips with urgent and undiscriminating priorities rather than trying to elaborate on more philosophical themes requiring a more thorough-going transformation of their personal assumptions. On the other hand, in Douglas' and Black's emphasis on free choice, an abstract, highly conceptual term, can be seen an intimation of future movement away from their early realism. In the postwar period Black's labor opinions evinced a rigid contractualist formalism, whereas Douglas' disillusionment with Big Labor led him to adopt a stance of tenacious individualism or "anti-institutionalism."

It is appropriate to put Justice Frankfurter in a separate category. Though his opinions sounded the themes of legal realism, he was a legalist through-and-through, and the roots of his later attempt to mediate between realism and conceptualism were already apparent. Much sooner than Black's or Douglas', Frankfurter's work showed glimpses of the emerging "social conceptualism."

Phelps Dodge Corp. v. NLRB, the last Wagner Act case before Pearl Harbor, provides an excellent vehicle for delineating these disparate judicial styles and for sketching the emerging legal consciousness that came to dominate the postwar period. The case tendered four major questions: (1) Does an employer violate section 8(3) by refusing to hire job applicants because of their participation in union activity or affiliation with a union? (2) If so, is the Board authorized under section 10(c) to order the employer to offer jobs to such aggrieved workers? (3) Is the Board authorized to order reinstatement of aggrieved employees who have obtained "substantially equivalent employment" during the course of the litigation? (4) Must aggrieved employees mitigate their damages by seeking alternative work while awaiting redress before the Board? The Court, with some qualifications, answered each question affirmatively, although the respective majorities were formed by different justices.

The separate opinions in *Phelps Dodge* reveal the stages of development in modern legal thought. Justice Stone's opinion, joined by Chief Justice Hughes, was largely a dissent. It reveals both the woodenness of traditional formalism and Stone's tentative gropings toward the social conceptualist style most apparent in Justice Frankfurter's opinion. Stone and Hughes agreed that discrimination in hiring was a section 8(3) violation, but denied that the Board could order an offending employer to offer jobs or pay compensation to the victims. In their view, the employer could be punished by the stigma of a cease-and-desist order, but the aggrieved employee could get no personal redress. This was an odd result in light of the oft-repeated insistence that the Act was "remedial, not punitive," and Stone reached it by a tortured path. He defined the issue to be whether section 10(c) allowed the Board to force a particular employee on an unwilling employer, "a remedial power which few courts had ever assumed to exercise or had been thought to possess." He then proposed to answer this question by determining whether the words in section 10(c) granting the Board's remedial powers, "including" the power of reinstatement, implied that remedies not specifically mentioned were forbidden. The meaning of the word "including," he wrote, "must be determined by [reference to] the purpose of the Act." Though this sounds like realism, Stone immediately eschewed a purposive analysis by concluding that Congress probably did not intend to allow the remedy (a) because of "the traditional reluctance of courts to compel the performance of personal service contracts" and (b) because "an authority to order reinstatement is not an authority to compel the employer to instate as his employees those whom he has never employed." Point (a), with its attempted overlay of traditional contract doctrine onto the statute, is refuted by the fact that Congress overrode this precise reluctance in allowing the reinstatement remedy in the first place. Point (b) merely states the undisputed point that reinstatement is something different from an offer of new employment; the mere fact that they are different is not by itself a reason for a different conclusion of law.

Justice Stone was no more persuasive in his argument that the Board could not order reinstatement of aggrieved employees who obtained substantially equivalent employment because section 10(c) only authorized reinstatement of employees and because the definition of "employee" in section 2(3) excluded unfair labor practice victims who obtained substantially equivalent employment. Both statements represented mechanically restrictive readings of the statutory language. Section 10(c) provides that the Board's powers shall include the reinstatement of employees; section 2(3) provides that employees shall include those who are illegally discharged but who have not found other equivalent employment. The words of the statute did not

by themselves settle the question before the Court, and a construction—that is, a judicial act—was required. In keeping with the formalist style, Stone obscured the volitional elements of judicial action, thereby obscuring the political content of his decision.

Justice Murphy's opinion, joined by Justices Black and Douglas, was at the other end of the spectrum of legal analysis. The motif was starkly realist: judicial deference to the Labor Board's decisions based on the latter's informed view of social policy; in other words, the abandonment of the rule of law as traditionally understood. Though more candid than Stone's, Murphy's opinion also obscured the political nature of judicial action by referring issues to the Board's expertise. Murphy stated that the Board should be allowed to order reinstatement of employees who found new jobs because the Board might conclude that this was a good idea and the Act did not forbid it. On the mitigation question, he argued that (a) the Act does not require mitigation "in so many words," (b) the Board has discretion not to require mitigation deductions, and (c) it is not the Court's business to displace the Board's judgment if it is, when "tested in the light of statutory standards... within the permissible range of the Board's discretion." This "standard," of course, tells us nothing. The phrases "statutory standards" and "permissible range" are without content apart from a judicial elaboration of the meaning of the Act. Thus, this ardent realist slid directly into the formalist trap of imagining that abstract principles decide cases. Murphy did tell us that the Board "might properly conclude" that mitigation should not be required, since such a position might well effectuate the purposes of the Act. But his analysis was not really about the Act's purposes; it boiled down to the view that the Board's rule would make things a little bit tougher for offending employers than Justice Frankfurter's rule. Murphy's approach was radically unstable as a model for judicial reasoning, and it helps to explain the birth of social conceptualism. To remain within the legalist institutional framework, which none of the realists had any manifest purpose to go beyond, the realist judge must eventually legitimate instrumental reasoning by reifying his or her core political and social values, by turning them into doctrines. That is, realism must evolve toward a species of formalism.

I have saved Justice Frankfurter's opinion, written for the Court, until last. It is a remarkable document, symbolizing the transition to a new phase in legal history. Rarely does one opinion traverse the entire spectrum of judicial styles with so little hesitation. At the outset, Justice Frankfurter sounded the realist theme of social policy analysis. His initial discussion of the purposes of the Act strongly resembled a memorandum that he had written for President Roosevelt in 1935.[25] In each, Frankfurter portrayed the Wagner Act as the inevitable codification of settled principles of federal labor policy, citing the experience of the War Labor Board, the Railway Labor Act, and so on. This was interesting as intellectual history, but politically disingenuous, given the extraordinary opposition that greeted the Wagner Act.

Frankfurter's *Phelps Dodge* discussion of the Act's policies was somewhat jumbled. He earnestly argued that the Act did not take away the employer's freedom so long as the employer freely recognized the adverse claims of labor. The Act "leaves the adjustment of industrial relations to the free play of economic forces but seeks to assure that the play of those forces be truly free." The Act does not interfere with the employer's rights so long as the employer does not abuse those rights by doing something the Act condemns. Protection of employees' right to organize "does not curtail the *appropriate* sphere of managerial freedom; it furthers the *wholesome* conduct of business enterprise." In sum, Frankfurter told employers that the first principle was always the "free market," but that the law would take away their freedom so as to make their freedom truly free. No doubt employers found scant reassurance in these contradictory and purportless phrases.

But reading the opinion in the light of the memorandum, one gets a glimpse of what Frankfurter really believed. In the opinion he implied that eventually all reasonable employers would accommodate themselves to collective bargaining. This was an echo of a sentiment in the earlier piece:

> The day of industrial absolutism is done. All our experience since the industrial revolution demonstrates that employers as a class cannot be relied upon, voluntarily and out of the goodness of their hearts, to give a square deal to unorganized labor; this has been precluded by the pressure of immediate self-interest and the inexorable workings of the competitive system. . . .
>
> . . . Once the employer has ungrudgingly accepted the process of collective bargaining with the freely chosen representatives of his employees, differences as to wages and hours are more readily reconciled by negotiation or arbitration. Reasonableness begets reasonableness. On the other hand, stubborn refusal to deal with the representatives chosen by the employees, the irresponsible use of force or economic power, the maintenance of elaborate systems of espionage, black lists, and other familiar devices, to thwart efforts of employees to organize in their own way, only result in an accumulation of bitterness that sooner or later will break out in the most serious manifestations of industrial disturbance. The employers, and especially the leaders in the big association of employers, have a grave responsibility at this juncture. Mock heroics about preferring to go to jail rather than submit to this iniquitous statute, incitements to mass disobedience of its provisions, will tend to produce dangerous frustrations of labor's reasonable human aspirations and play into the hands of extremists who insist that nothing is to be gained by peaceful processes.

As indicated, Frankfurter feared that initially some employers might not have had the good sense to arrange a *modus vivendi* with labor. Such recalcitrant employers were a threat and had to be dealt with for the good of the social

[25]ROOSEVELT AND FRANKFURTER: THEIR CORRESPONDENCE, 1928–1945, at 603 (M. Freedman ed. 1967) [hereinafter cited as ROOSEVELT AND FRANKFURTER] (memorandum from Justice Frankfurter to President Roosevelt, dated 1941; its actual composition, however, is placed by the editor in early 1935, with revisions in 1936).

order. He never quite said this in so many words, although he self-confidently asserted that a driving motive behind enactment of the NLRA was to remove obstacles to the prosperity of labor organizations, a goal that he saw as imperative to the survival of liberal capitalism. Frankfurter's position was almost a parody of the reason/fiat antinomy: if the employers of America were not persuaded by reason to work out an accommodation with collective bargaining, then they would be forced to be reasonable by the raw power of the law and the legions of organized labor. The breadth and self-confidence of this political vision are staggering.

Frankfurter's opinion proceeded to sing paeans to purposive legal reasoning, telling us that statutes cannot be interpreted like mathematical symbols, that "verbal logic from which the meaning of things has evaporated" is anathema, and that industrial experience, history, and the social policy of the Act are the keys to interpretation, not judicial maxims. He praised the Board's expert judgment and discretion, to which Congress had wisely entrusted frontline interpretation of the Act. Based on his purposive analysis, in the light of the historical background, he concluded that discrimination in hiring was a section 8(3) violation remediable by an order to offer employment and that reinstatement of equivalently employed complainants was authorized by section 10(c).

Frankfurter then performed an about-face so subtle that its implications are not visible until a second or third reading:

> [T]he mere fact that the victim of discrimination has obtained equivalent employment does not itself preclude the Board from undoing the discrimination and requiring employment. But neither does this remedy automatically flow from the Act itself when discrimination has been found. A statute expressive of such large public policy as that on which the National Labor Relations Board is based must be broadly phrased and necessarily carries with it the task of administrative application. There is an area plainly covered by the language of the Act and an area no less plainly without it. . . . Because the rela-

tion of remedy to policy is peculiarly a matter for administrative competence, courts must not enter the allowable area of the Board's discretion and must guard against the danger of sliding unconsciously from the narrow confines of law into the more spacious domain of policy. On the other hand, the power with which Congress invested the Board implies responsibility—the responsibility of exercising its judgment in employing the statutory powers.

As far as it goes, this was an orthodox realist argument, but it produced a strange result. The Court remanded the case so that the Board could exercise its statutory responsibility by determining whether the Act's purposes would be effectuated by reinstatement of the particular complainants involved. While assuring the reader that he had no intention of invading the area of remedial policy assigned to the Board, Frankfurter nevertheless provided a list of factors for the Board to consider in reaching its policy decision.

The only problem with all of this is that, on the record presented, the Board had already carefully and explicitly made a finding that the Act's purposes would be effectuated by reinstatement. Frankfurter's motive was not simply to reprimand the Board for supposedly having failed to make a considered policy judgment, but implicitly to pronounce that henceforth the Board would in all cases be required to consider a victim's obtainment of substantially equivalent employment before ordering an employer to make work available. Frankfurter thus read a major restriction into the broad remedial powers granted to the Board under section 10(c) and flatly overruled his own call for deference to the Board's expertise.

Justice Frankfurter took a similar approach on the mitigation issue, although here his faith in the inherent superiority of judicial reasoning was even more explicit. He stated,

> Making the workers whole for losses suffered on account of an unfair labor practice is part of the vindication of the public policy which the Board enforces. Since only actual losses should be made good, it seems fair that deductions should be made

not only for actual earnings by the worker but also for losses which he willfully incurred.

This unvarnished fiat flatly overruled a considered policy judgment of the Board and profoundly undercut effective enforcement of the Act. Having intoned the by now monotonous "public right" slogan, he introduced into federal labor law an absolutely classical private adjudication doctrine. His sole authority for the rule was the ancient maxim that mitigation doctrines serve the beneficent purpose of "promoting production and employment." By placing this strange construction on a statute passed in the midst of the worst depression in American history, Frankfurter made a mockery of his earlier injunction to interpret statutes in the context of the historical and social exigencies that led to their enactment, to avoid "verbal logic from which the meaning of things has evaporated."

A microcosm of modern legal consciousness, *Phelps Dodge* contained a chaotic amalgam of conceptualism and realism, ruleboundedness and ad hoc balancing, deference to nonjudicial sources of law and unhesitating faith in the superiority of the judicial mind. This jurisprudential mélange transcended political lines and attitudes as to whether the proper judicial role is one of activism or restraint. I believe that all of modern legal consciousness partakes of this hodgepodge character. It is a consciousness in which contrasting styles of legal reasoning are simultaneously and unreflectively employed by the same court or even the same judge; in which the public/private distinction is invoked as the basis of judicial decisions, as though it were a concept of scientific precision and with no apparent recognition that the distinction has assumed formidable ideological and mystificatory functions in the welfare state; in which state regulation of private economic activity is assumed to be a legitimate and even compelling mode of achieving progressive reform, while the ideal of the free market is simultaneously upheld as the proper basis of social organization; and in which the antinomy of reason and fiat is understood to

pervade the legal process while at the same time it appears to be a veritable public responsibility of the judge to obscure or veil this fact. The formalist and realist traditions are continued sub silentio in judicial decisions, but in a manner consistent with neither legal vision. The rule of law is preserved, though in an updated, more socially responsive form.

The full rehabilitation of legalism awaited the relative social stability of the Cold War era, when it again became possible to attempt a totalizing jurisprudence, a merger of realism and the social policies it imported into the law with the traditions of formalist jurisprudence.[26] No doubt such attempts to revitalize legalism have dominated postwar American legal thought, to some extent quelling the residual disquiet left over from the legal crisis of the 1930's. For this reason, it is appropriate to conceive of modern legal consciousness as a relatively unified whole, although this is a unity that consists chiefly in a willingness to merge approaches and methods that, if pushed only slightly, appear to be antagonistic. The preeminent characteristic of modern legal consciousness, transcending all political battlelines, is its unreflective and uncritical quality, its at-

[26]Central to the process of the mutual assimilation is the inevitable tendency of realism to evolve into a species of formalism. This tendency arises for several reasons. First, because liberal political theory and social science are unable candidly to confront the reality of class power and class domination in capitalist society, they necessarily serve an ideological and mystificatory role; in particular, the tendency of liberal social thought (which is harnessed by, but ultimately contributes to the transformation of, legal realism) is to present, as scientifically necessary, answers to questions involving choices between competing political values and interests. Second, and more generally, all legal decisions are necessarily made within a context of assumptions (*i.e.*, a "conceptless" jurisprudence is an epistemological impossibility), and the historical tendency is for these underlying assumptions periodically to become reified. Finally, the aforementioned tendencies are exacerbated by the formal character of law itself in the liberal tradition, that is, its requirement that the grounds of decision in particular cases be capable of presentation in a general, suprahistorical rule-form. *See* Blackburn, *A Brief Guide to Bourgeois Ideology*, in STUDENT POWER 163 (A. Cockburn & R. Blackburn eds. 1969); Horton, *The Dehumanization of Anomie and Alienation: A Problem in the Ideology of Sociology*, 15 BRIT. J. Soc. 283 (1964).

tempt to accommodate yet obscure the contradictions of legal thought, which reflect the contradictions of social life in late capitalist society.

IV. CONCLUSION AND POSTSCRIPT

Although certain concrete legal inhibitions were placed on worker self-activity in the period immediately preceding World War II, the primary role of the Court was to fashion and articulate a legitimating ideology for the emerging institutional system governing the workplace. In the postwar period, while continuing this ideological mission, the Court played an enormous role in elaborating the institutional structure of mature collective bargaining. To a degree unprecedented in the capitalist world, the judiciary directly and creatively intervened in the workplace and was crucially involved in designing the architecture of the modern, administered, and regulated system of class relations. It is again an irony that many of the leading developments in this process were widely perceived as victories for labor and intrusions upon the prerogatives of management. Many of the Court's rulings were, in fact, designed to bolster the institutional interests of labor unions. Often, however, this occurred at undue expense to the rights of individual employees and to the initiative of the rank and file. More and more, unions were treated as guarantors of productivity and enforcers of work-discipline, and the chasm separating union leadership from the rank and file was widened. Cases hailed as prolabor victories may therefore someday be regarded as long-run defeats for working people, particularly in an industrial world in which it is debatable whether the institutional interests of labor unions are entirely congruent with the needs and interests of working people.[27]

In retrospect, it should not be surprising that the attempt to ease the oppression of working people through legal reform ended by reinforcing the institutional bases of that oppression, however much it improved the material circumstances of organized workers.

In one sense, the problem of law is the same as the problem of labor. Producing goods and services in the workplace and making law in legislatures and courtrooms are both forms of objectification—that process "whereby human subjectivity embodies itself in products that are available to oneself and one's fellow men as elements of a common world."[28] Because "[m]an and society exist only as *praxis,* outside themselves in the fluctuating interworld their actions compose together,"[29] objectification is the ontological foundation of human freedom and self-actualization. But in the capitalist work-process, objectification takes on the character of alienation: the product, commanded and owned by another, is an estranged, alien power, over and against the producers, who have no way to recall that the world in which they live has been created by themselves. The capitalist work-process, far from being an expression of human freedom, is a realm of unfreedom, of separation between the self and others, between consciousness and actuality, a

---

[27]Central themes of postwar labor doctrine that will be explored in future essays include the following:

(a) the Court's chimerical attempt to keep the law out of the substance of collective bargaining, to separate substance and form in labor law, both as to the substantive terms of contracts and as to scrutiny of the legitimate economic weapons to be available to the parties;

(b) the exclusion of labor unions from bargaining over managerial decisions "which lie at the core of entrepreneurial control";

(c) the enhanced institutional role and responsibilities of labor unions;

(d) the steady erosion of the section 7 right to engage in protected, concerted activity;

(e) the gradual metamorphosis of grievance arbitration from a voluntary and private mode of dispute resolution into a semicompulsory, institutional system for the management of complex enterprises, resulting in the dilution of statutory rights;

(f) the altered conception of labor unions whereby they are increasingly seen not as private associations within civil society, but as semigovernmental agencies whose acts border on "state action," and that therefore may properly be subjected to the closest regulation.

[28]Berger and Pullberg, *Reification and the Sociological Critique of Consciousness,* NEW LEFT REV., January–February 1966, at 60.

[29]Anderson, *Problems of Socialist Strategy,* in TOWARDS SOCIALISM 288–89 (P. Anderson and R. Blackburn eds. 1966).

realm in which no person can recognize him- or herself.

Lawmaking is governed by the same process of alienation. Its structure and function in liberal capitalism make it, too, a form of activity in which the "product," moral and allocational rules and decisions, cannot be recognized as having been created by its purported authors, the people. Law in our society is made by experts socialized in elite institutions and distant from the lived reality of everyday life in capitalist society. Its connection to official violence and coercion, its impersonal, antiparticipatory character, its insistence on the presentation of all moral judgments in the form of general, suprahistorical rules, and its exaltation of property over human dignity, all make it inevitable that the *form* of lawmaking must be a negation of the human spirit, even when the impulse to do justice and to accommodate to changing social priorities forces its way into the *content* of legal decisions.

One cannot expect that work will be emancipated from its alienated character without the abolition of the social relations, including legal relations, that produce that character. Alienation can only be transcended through a comprehen-sive historical metamorphosis of social and political relationships, a process that would profoundly transform the quality of legal arrangements, indeed, the very nature and form of law. Conversely, while legal practice remains a form of alienation, there can be no fundamental change in the character of work or any other aspect of social life. Until lawmaking becomes a quest for justice in each concrete historical setting, until the "rule of law" ideal (the separation of law and ethics) is abolished and ethics brought directly into daily life as a continuous, participatory practice of mediation and redefinition of relations among people who see in each other the possibility of their own fulfillment, that is, until lawmaking becomes a self-conscious, critical form of social practice, there can be no hope of the emancipation of labor. The struggle to transform lawmaking in this manner is intimately linked to the struggle to make the workplace a realm of free self-activity and expression. Labor law reform in the 1930's served as a vehicle for the preservation of liberal capitalism and the alienated social relationships that constitute it. Henceforth, the struggle to emancipate labor must also be a struggle to emancipate law itself.

THE THEORY OF THE STATE, CLASS STRUGGLE AND THE RULE OF LAW

SOL PICCIOTTO

The problem of the rule of law has a powerful political and intellectual fascination. It provides a focus for a range of crucial questions about the nature and relationship of power and order in society. Behind the day-to-day political sloganizing on law and order we find elaborated philosophical and social scientific positions of diverse kinds. In Britain, the recent radical Toryism of Thatcher and Joseph rests, it seems, on the rather less new intellectual positions of F. A. Hayek, the equivalent in legal and constitutional theory of monetarism in economics (Centre for Policy Studies, 1976). Hayek can certainly take the credit for having captured the slogan of the "rule of law" for the libertarian right. More recently we have seen E. P. Thompson urging forward the forces of the libertarian, perhaps even Marxist, left to regain the banner.

What is more, it seems to be agreed on most sides that this resurgence of debate about law has deep social and economic roots. It clearly takes place within a more general crisis of the state, in the context of a period of economic crisis which became apparent in the 1970s. This has brought into question not only the adequacy of the state's performance of its functions in relation to the economy, but more fundamental questions as to the very form of the state and its limits. To take two major examples: there has been considerable

public discussion, in many countries, of the question of terrorism, and of whether the state can continue to act legally and democratically in the face of it; and the trend towards "corporatism" has also received world-wide debate, also in relation to the question of the survival of the rule of law.

However, it would be mistaken to see such issues in terms of the impact of an external economic crisis upon a formerly stable social order. Rather, the crisis involves a deepening and generalization of underlying tensions which made themselves felt in the various social conflicts that gathered momentum during the years of post-war economic expansion, and which can be seen to be part of a general class movement. While there was still an adequate basis for continued capitalist expansion these conflicts could be swallowed up in one way or another in the process of capital accumulation. The crisis is seen to break out when the contradictions of that process of accumulation become so acute that a new basis for accumulation can only be established after a general social restructuring. The crisis must therefore be seen as being that very social restructuring process (see generally, Holloway and Picciotto 1977).

The call for the rule of law in such a social crisis expresses either a demand for the application of coercion in social relations, or for the control of such coercion through the "due process" of law. The coercion is legitimized by being wielded through the state and in the form of law. It is surprising how seldom the debate about law gets beyond this initial ambiguous dichotomy of

Source: From Bob Fine, Richard Kinsey, John Lea, Sol Picciotto, and Jock Young, Eds. (National Deviancy Conference and Conference of Socialist Economists), *Capitalism and the Rule of Law* (London: Hutchinson, 1979), pp. 164–177. Reprinted by permission.

coercion/legitimacy. It is this ambiguity that enables the rule of law to be used as a slogan which is effectively a call for repression, and also to be attacked as such. Stuart Hall and others have recently contributed an exhaustive account of the ways in which the call for law and order has been used in the recent period in Britain in orchestrating an increasingly repressive response to the crisis (Hall *et al.* 1978). At the same time, the rule of law can be used as an appeal for "the imposing of effective inhibitions upon power and the defence of the citizen from power's all-intrusive claims" (Thompson 1975, p. 266). Thompson makes the argument that in order to obtain the consent of the ruled, the ruling class is obliged to resort to legitimizing forms such as law, and thereby is obliged either to act justly or be exposed as having fallen short of the standards of justice thus established (see, for example, ibid., p. 263). Perry Anderson has pointed to the Gramscian elements in this argument (1977, p. 7). Stuart Hall and his collaborators work within a theoretical framework explicitly derived from Gramsci. Anderson's own detailed study of Gramsci clearly shows the limitations of the approach to the theory of the state based on the notion of a "balance between coercion and consent." Anderson himself concedes that "the analytic issues with which Gramsci was most concerned in fact need to be reconceptualised within a new order of categories, beyond his binary landmarks" (ibid., p. 26), and that "the relationship between the two terms [consent and coercion] cannot be grasped by their mere conjunction or addition" (ibid., p. 41). Anderson's own argument, however, scarcely escapes this binary conjunction: he sees bourgeois-democratic power as "simultaneously and indivisibly *dominated by culture* and *determined by coercion*" (ibid., p. 42). This relegates the confrontation with the coercion of the state to the final insurrectionary situation and puts on the immediate agenda a compromise with bourgeois democracy, which seems to leave out of account any view of the coercive nature of bourgeois-democratic legality. In the case of Thompson, his

neo-Gramscian lapses may perhaps be attributed to his overpowering urge to find any stick with which to assault the abstractions of the neo-Marxist structuralists: unfortunately the nearest weapon looks very like a structuralist concept. The main bulk of his own historical work on the other hand makes a great contribution to the theorization of the specific way in which the development of law mediated and contributed to the development of capitalist relations of production (see, for example, Thompson 1976).

A moment's reflection should indeed be enough to convince us that the analysis of law and state power by the mere combination of the contradictory ideas of consent and coercion does not help to explain *what form* of coercion is involved, nor *how* the consent is obtained. We need a different starting-point if we are to try to understand the specific way in which law mediates class relations.

LEGAL RELATIONS AND SOCIAL RELATIONS

It is characteristic above all of law and the legal system, probably more than of any other social institution or part of the state apparatus, that it appears to be essentially neutral, an empty vessel that can be filled with whatever content society chooses. So any attempt to understand law as a social relation of class, or power in any sense, must first explain this appearance of neutrality.

Quite clearly it cannot be satisfactorily explained as nothing more than a "mere mask," an ideological hypocrisy which conceals the reality of class power (although there is a considerable amount of ideological pretence and hypocrisy about the law). It is equally inadequate to see the law simply as an instrument or apparatus manipulated by the ruling.class. While obviously factors such as the cultural and ideological background of judges are very relevant, it is inadequate to attribute the class character of a social institution simply to the social origins of those who control it. Most Marxists would agree that revolutionary change entails the transformation of the very character of social institutions such as the state and the legal system, and not simply the replacement of the personnel which operates them. The main limitation of both these approaches (the "instrumental" and the "mere mask" or ideological) is that they do not provide a perspective of the class relations embodied in the law itself, but tend to accept the *externality* of class to law. This therefore reinforces the picture of law as a neutral and historically unchanging state apparatus.

The characteristic neutrality of law is generally attributed to its autonomy within capitalist society. In capitalism, social relations are not directly relations of power or force: they appear as the relations of free and equal individuals. In precapitalist societies social relations took the form of some sort of social hierarchy, and the government of such a society could consist of commands passed through the hierarchy. Alternatively, in some societies solidaristic groups were able to take decisions regarding social order according to some kind of basic collective process, which however would take account of the different status of groups such as elders, women, etc. In either of these models, the legal and political order of the society is not separate from its social and economic structure. It is under capitalism that a legal order emerges which appears as autonomous. It should be emphasized that this kind of analysis, so far, is by no means confined to the explicitly Marxist approaches, but is fairly common to many social scientific analyses of law. The real issue which divides different approaches is the nature and conditions of the autonomization of law.

We may first of all distinguish what I will call the "sociological" conceptualization of the autonomy of law. Such an approach is based essentially on the analysis of a sphere of social relations separate from what is designated the "economic" sphere of production. This results in the abstract analysis of social relations isolated from their roots in production, from the relationship of human society to nature through production. We may take as an example one of the more sophisticated of recent sociological theorists of law, R. M. Unger. In his formulation, legal autonomy is specified as having four different aspects: substantive, institutional, methodological and occupational autonomy. This "legal order" Unger sees as having "emerged with modern European liberal society" (1976, pp. 52–4). He states the historical conditions of emergence of such a legal order as being (1) a pluralistic social order, and (2) a dominant natural law ideology (ibid., p. 66ff.). He categorizes liberal society, and distinguishes it from the tribal and the aristocratic, in terms of the nature and relationships of the social groupings in each. It can be seen quite clearly that he is concerned to analyse social relations in a way that has no explicit relation whatever to production, in the broad sense, to the "material conditions of life." Unger does relate his abstract schema to analyses of specific historical examples, as a means of illustrating, testing or refining the initial model. For him, theoretical models are "ideals as well as descriptions" (ibid., p. 267); but his combination of abstract ideal types and historical descriptions fails to grasp history as an actual process of social change through struggle.

For Marxist approaches, the essential question is to trace the nature of the relationship between law and the "material conditions of life." In order to grasp the specific characteristics of order and domination embodied in the form of legal relations in any particular society and epoch, it must be related to the nature and historical development of the relations of production. Very much hangs upon the conceptualization of the "relations of production." Lukács has recently reemphasized that Marx's starting-point is the "sum total of relations of production."

> His conclusion, that "It is not the consciousness of men that determines their being but on the contrary their social being that determines their consciousness," does not reduce the world of consciousness with its forms and contents directly to the economic structure, but rather relates it to the totality of social existence. The determination of consciousness by social being is thus meant in a quite general sense. It is only vulgar materialism (from the period of the Second International through to the Stalin period and its consequences) that made this into a unilateral and

direct causal relationship between the economy, or even particular aspects of it, and ideology (Lukács 1978, p. 32).

Lukács goes on to explain in detail how Marx's dialectical method enables him to mount a sustained critique of bourgeois political economy, which cuts itself off from reality since it has no way of relating the working of the abstract laws of the autonomous sphere of economics to the totality of social existence.

Many of the theories of the Marxist renaissance have sought to escape the vulgar materialist heritage pointed to by Lukács. This has not been a movement simply in ideas. The attempts to recapture a living Marxist theory also stem from the experience of many of the social struggles of the 1960s and 1970s, in which it became clear that class struggle was not confined to the narrow sphere of work. Racial and sexual oppression, struggles over issues broad and narrow, from housing to imperialist exploitation, all called for an analysis which could relate them to the dynamics of capitalism as a total system, yet did not reduce them to mere epiphenomena incidental to the "real" struggle at the "point of production."

It is in this context that we must see the popularity of theories which emphasize the "relative autonomy" of legal relations, as well as the state, ideology and much else, from capitalist accumulation.

> Hence, even in a social formation over-determined by the laws of motion of capitalist production, the conditions for that production—or what has come to be called *social reproduction*—are often sustained in the apparently "unproductive" spheres of civil society and the state; and in so far as the classes, fundamentally constituted in the productive relation, also contend over this process of "social reproduction," the class struggle is present in all the domains of civil society and the state (Hall *et al.* 1978, p. 202).

In this kind of view the notion of relations of production is limited to the narrow sphere of the direct production of commodities, which Marx

called the *immediate process of production*. Yet it runs quite counter to Marx's strong emphasis on the analysis of "the capitalist process of production . . . seen as a total, connected process, i.e. a process of reproduction" (1976, p. 724). In fact, the explicit distinction made in formulations such as the one quoted above between "social reproduction" and the "productive relation" reveals quite clearly the limitations of the neo-Marxist structuralist approaches, whose foremost exponent in the field of the theory of the state has been Poulantzas.

In these theories, in fact, relations of production are seen not as social but as technical or economic. They are "determinant in the last instance"; class relations are seen as "rooted" in them, but as actually *constituted* as distributional relations, in a sphere of "civil society" which is inserted *between* the essentially "economic" sphere of production and the state (see Clarke 1977). This enables Poulantzas to develop a "regional" theory of the state which is essentially "politicist," without however avoiding the ultimate reductionism of economism (see Holloway and Picciotto 1977, 1978). He points the way to the development of an equally abstract theory of law. Since, for him, legal relations are seen as *external* to the relations of production, there is no way in which their contradictory development can be grasped as part of the actual historical development of the capitalist mode of production. Some basic characteristics of bourgeois law can be derived *a priori*: "The roots of its [capitalist law's] specific features (abstraction, universality, formalism) . . . have to be sought in the social division of labour and the relations of production" (Poulantzas 1978, p. 86). But since this cannot be traced as an actual historical process, it remains a bare abstraction.

An understanding of how law and a legal system which are economically neutral and seem to operate with an independent rationality can nevertheless have a class character cannot therefore start from the notion of "relative autonomy." In *Capital* Marx speaks of the need for a scientific analysis of the "forms of human life" (1976, ch.

1, section 4). This scientific analysis is vital in order to grasp the class nature of social forms in any society, but expecially so in capitalist society, since under capitalism the main characteristic of class domination is that it is mediated through commodity exchange. Hence the social character of particular social institutions or forms is concealed by the fetishism of the commodity. Thus the form of appearance of social relations (the forms in which they actually appear) conceals their social character and therefore their content. For example, profit conceals the social nature of the surplus product under capitalism and its source in labour, which under capitalism has the specific class character of surplus-value.

However, Marx emphasizes that while the elucidation of the social content of these forms is necessary in order to understand them, a revolutionary perspective requires a method that can grasp the historical and therefore transitory character of both form and content. Thus he points out that classical political economy had already understood the content of profit as value with its source in labour, but having "never once asked the question why this content has assumed that particular form" it failed to grasp its historic character (1976, p. 174). The question why is therefore important for Marx because the scientific analysis of social forms is not a merely logical exercise, but a matter of "reflection *post festum*" on an actual process of history. It is not the case that people bring the products of their labour into relation with each other as values because they see these objects as embodying human labour, but the reverse. There was an actual historical process by which commodity production became dominant (which is still a continuing though ever more contradictory process). It is the actual equation of products in exchange that produces values and thus the equation of human labour. This is the essential materialist basis of the Marxist concept of form, as opposed to the idealism of Hegel, in which "the genesis and mutation of form is only within the power of the mind" (Sohn-Rethel 1978, p. 17). Hence a Marxist analysis of a particular social form cannot be

a purely logical derivation. John Holloway and I have pointed out in relation to the theory of the state the inadequacy of any theory which attempts a simple logical "derivation" of the state from the capital relation, in whatever way the latter is conceived or understood (Holloway and Picciotto 1977, p. 85; 1978, p. 27).

This point may be illustrated by reference to Balbus's essay (1977). Balbus begins explicitly from the 'logic of capital' and states that he derives the "logic of the legal form" as a "homology between the commodity form and the legal form." Thus the legal form tends to be presented as merely a mystifying fetishism, which mystifies simply because it appears as autonomous, yet one that is internally coherent and without internal contradictions or tendency to crisis. Change is only introduced from outside, by reference to the "transformation from competitive, laissez-faire capitalism to monopoly, state-regulated capitalism," which "has resulted in a partial transformation of the content of the homology between economic and political exchange" (1977, p. 586). However, in his closing paragraph he emphasizes that this method of demonstrating structural homologies is only a starting-point, since "the demonstration of structural or synchronic homologies is not intended as a substitute for an analysis of *praxis* which would serve to reunite structure and history, synchrony and diachrony." This indicates at least an awareness of the dangers of Hegelian idealism in his method.

A major contribution to the theorization of law as a social form in the development of capitalist production relations was made by the Bolshevik jurist Pashukanis, whose work has recently been revived in discussions in the West (Pashukanis 1978; Arthur 1976). No one is clearer than he that "Marxist theory considers every social form historically. Consequently it sets itself the task of elucidating those historically given material conditions which brought this or that category into being" (1978, p. 111). However, the limitations of Pashukanis's analysis, in my view, stem from the fact that he confines himself to the analysis of the historical unfolding of the capitalist mode of production at the most general level, namely the full development of commodity production. But commodity production does not become fully developed until labour-power itself also becomes a commodity—that is, when capitalism dominates the social reproduction forces. Although Marx begins with the commodity, the money-form and the general formula for capital, M—C—M, he very soon introduces the unique commodity, labour-power, and goes on to develop his analysis of the expanded reproduction of capital on that basis. This Pashukanis does not do. This does not negate his whole enterprise, since the juridical process which is his main concern does, in its bourgeois form, serve to mediate and confine social relations merely as relations of circulation. So the analysis at the general level of commodity production tells us quite a lot about the forms developed by bourgeois law.

ANALYSING THE DEVELOPMENT OF LEGAL FORMS

At this point it may be helpful to summarize the argument so far. Since there has been much abstract talk of structure and form, it may help to clarify the argument about the relationship between legal and economic relations to think of it in the context of the key example of the wage-labour relation and the employment contract. (The choice of this example also has disadvantages, notably that it has an obvious economic side whereas other legal relations may not.) The individual, subjective relationship of a particular worker and employer is a microcosm of a social relationship. Legal autonomy means that the law establishes a framework for the regulation of that relationship according to established procedures and an independent set of legal rules. A simple "instrumentalist" class view would emphasize the class origins of the judges, lawyers and legislators who create and apply the law, and would conclude that they would consequently tend to favour employers, implying that the same system could produce a more fair or just result if con-

trolled by people with a different class background. While clearly there are "good" and "bad" judges, this can only be a small part of an explanation of the class nature of law. A neo-Marxist structuralist theory would presumably emphasize that although the economic nature of the wage-labour relation is determinant in the last instance, it is constituted or reproduced as a legal relation in the sphere of civil society. The dynamics of this legal relation must be analysed in their "relative autonomy," but the roots of its specific features can be traced to the relations of production. The problem is to explain how the "relatively autonomous" legal logic and procedure can succeed in reinforcing and maintaining the wage-labour relation in a way that is functional for capital.

Form analysis emphasizes that legal relations must be grasped as *part* of social relations as a totality, and their historical development theorized as part of the changes in the social relations of production resulting from the unfolding contradictions and underlying tendencies of the dominant mode of production. However, people's actual relationships in capitalist society are not immediately social: due to the domination of commodity production, social relations are mediated by the exchange of commodities. They therefore appear as fetishized forms: that is, they actually take place in forms which conceal their class nature. People are brought together as "employees," "consumers," "neighbours" because they buy and sell objects (including their own labour-power, which is a rather unique commodity). These are partial and fragmentary relationships, which are reproduced by the underlying process of capitalist accumulation, seen as a contradictory and crisis-ridden process of expanded social reproduction through class struggle. At its most general level, class struggle is the struggle to penetrate and transcend those forms, to restore the humanity to a fetishized society.

The most basic aspect of the fetishization of social relations under capitalism is the separation of the economic and the political and the autonomization of the state (see generally Holloway and Picciotto 1977). Historically this took place on the basis of primary or primitive accumulation of capital by merchants' capital, at a time when the direct relation of exploitation was not yet capitalist wage labour. Thus the first moment of the capitalist state is to *establish and guarantee exchange* as the mediation of production and consumption. This involves the creation and maintenance of individuals as *economic and legal subjects*, the bearers of reified property rights. Thus, as Pashukanis rightly emphasizes, the basic legal category is the legal subject as the bearer of rights and duties (1978, sec. 4). This individual legal subjectivity is enshrined and maintained by legal procedures. A "right" in bourgeois legal form does not create but fragments class solidarity.

This has been the repeated lesson of many struggles, not least over the last few years in Britain. While the left campaigned successfully against the repressive Tory Industrial Relations Act, it has been largely disarmed by the extensive juridification of the employment relationship by measures enacted by a Labour government on TUC advice. These, by extending legal rights on a large scale ("rights" to compensation on redundancy, against "unfair" dismissal, to "equal pay for equal work," etc.) have done much to defuse the collective struggles and strength that brought them about. Substantive gains are achieved through collective struggles building up class solidarity: the channelling of such struggles into the form of claims of bourgeois legal right breaks up that movement towards solidarity, through the operation of legal procedures which recognize only the individual subject of rights and duties. Of course we have learned and must go on struggling to overcome this: in criminal prosecutions through collective defence strategies and solidarity groups; through solidarity tactics in the courtroom or tribunal to try to build a human warmth against the dead hand of legal etiquette and courtroom discipline; in mass campaigns for the assertion or take-up of rights. But these merely enable us to probe the limits of bourgeois law as a

social form. To transcend those limits, even to the smallest extent, requires the political perspective of a movement aiming at the total transformation of social relations. This involves a determination to struggle within but also through and beyond those legal forms, or around and in spite of them. It requires, for instance, a determination such as that of the Trico women strikers to organize collectively and continue a campaign of which individual "cases" are only a part, and in which court judgments, win or lose, affect but do not deflect the strategy. It is particularly difficult to build this kind of campaign around claims of legal rights, even where mass claims are made, because an aggregation of individual claims does not amount to a movement. Thus, for example, campaigns on housing can be undermined by the different legal status of squatters, private tenants, council tenants and owner-occupiers; struggles over factory closures or dismissals can be undermined by the differential rights of individuals to redundancy pay.

Correlative to the legal subject as the individual subject of rights is the principle of individual personal responsibility, which is established as the cornerstone of criminal law. Now, it should be emphasized that the historical struggles for the establishment of the individual as subject of rights, and also as personally responsible for his or her own actions (and nobody else's) were progressive struggles. A right encapsulated in bourgeois legal form is certainly better than no right at all, and individual personal responsibility is certainly better than arbitrary punishment. The point is that under capitalism social "rights" take this form when enshrined in law, and a struggle for social justice must aim to transcend the limitations of this form if it is to succeed. Nor does it mean that the legal form of "rights" should be ignored as totally illusory, since that is the form into which social relations are actually reproduced: the task is to surpass it.

As we have indicated, the individual legal subject is essentially the bearer of commodities, the owner of economic assets producing a revenue. Hence the bulk of law is concerned with property. Even aside from substantive law, this characteristic is embedded in the nature of legal procedures. Civil procedure takes the basic form of a private claim by an individual (or aggregation of individuals) which is basically a claim for damages quantified in money. This means that as a procedural requirement, any interest to be thought of in legal terms must be expressed as a commodity. Legally protected interests boil down to the individual's person or property. But even rights in respect of the person are reified: the physical person is considered as an income-producing asset (so it is cheaper to injure a poor person than a rich one); the only non-physical personal interest recognized by English law is "reputation." Hence all kinds of needs or demands are forced into the commodity form when put forward as legal rights—for example, proposals to control the extent of corporate and state surveillance tend to be discussed in terms of the right of the individual to "privacy." The anomalies it causes may be papered over to some extent by legal devices, but the contradiction runs deep.

Enforcement of legal rules comes to take the form of referral to a process of adjudication, the "trial" of a "case". Again, it is important to emphasize that it was a historical process that produced the form of trial that today seems in its basics to be the essence of rationality. For instance, in English law it was only during the seventeenth century that the accused gained the right to call witnesses, and not until late in the nineteenth century to give evidence in his or her own defence. This of course was part of the process of abstraction of the trial, from being an inquiry by persons involved with an issue by the use of magical or religious ordeal or ritual, to the adversarial contest between competing subjects of right based on formal conventions as to proof of fact and judgment of law. It is in the context of this kind of analysis that we should consider, for instance, the development of the jury, from a pre-capitalist institution of local justice to an abstract mechanism for "finding the facts" as presented before them and allowed by the rules of

evidence and on the basis of the law as ruled by the judge. To try to make of this an instrument for anything that could move towards popular justice would need much more than to ensure that the jury is "randomly selected" (whatever that may mean; see NCCL 1979): for a start it needs an effort to turn that randomly selected group of stony-faced individuals into an actual collection of human beings, whose job is to look at a human problem. However great an improvement this form of trial is on trial by ordeal, this should not prevent us from trying to grasp its bourgeois characteristics and its limitations.

As has already been mentioned, the development of these basic characteristics of the legal form was part of the historical process of autonomization of the state, which predated the establishment of the capitalist mode of production on the fully adequate basis of "free" wage labour. This also involved the centralization within society of the power to apply legitimate physical force and its vesting in the state as the abstract representative of social power, that is, class power. The consequent creation of absolutist sovereignties was only slowly, and through struggle, tempered by the whole process of depersonalizing that centralized power: this was the importance of the constitutionalist struggles waged by the bourgeoisie for the "rule of law." At the same time, since this was the period of primitive capitalist accumulation, this "rule of law" exhibited startling contradictions, and this continues to be the case in any society where the moment of primitive accumulation still figures significantly (though overlain by the subsequent development of the movement of capital). Social relations are not yet dominated by the "equal exchange" characteristic of the "dull compulsion of economic relations," but by the extensive use of direct compulsion, systematic privilege or bribery, coercive creation of property rights and labour forces, etc. To counter this, the establishment of the legal subject as bearer of rights and duties, the establishment of reified property rights and abstract judicial processes, involves the spectacular demonstration of the supremacy of abstract Law, through the insistence on stern formalism, theatricality, the combination of strict justice with benign mercy, etc. (see generally Hay, in Hay *et al.* 1975).

The establishment of the capitalist mode of production on the basis of "free" wage labour lays the basis for the liberal moment of the capitalist state. Once the formal subordination of labour to capital is established—that is, the objective and subjective conditions of labour (means of production and means of subsistence) confront labour as capital monopolized by the buyer of labour-power—the worker enters into wage labour on the basis of the "dull compulsion of economic relations" alone, and not on the basis of any political or social coercion. Production now dominates exchange, which then becomes the sphere of realization in which commodity-capital becomes money-capital and must be returned to the sphere of production in the shortest possible time. The state must now establish the conditions for circulation by guaranteeing and maintaining the *equivalence* of exchange and the reproduction of social relations on the basis of free and equal exchange in the sphere of circulation. But when social relations are viewed from the point of view of *production,* this equality of exchange is seen to be illusory:

> The constant sale and purchase of labour-power is the form; the content is the constant appropriation by the capitalist, without equivalence, of a portion of the labour of others which has already been objectified, and his repeated exchange of this labour for a greater quantity of the living labour of others (Marx 1976, p. 730).

Hence liberal state forms, which develop to facilitate the free play of "market" forces on the basis of the equal treatment of free citizens, have at their heart the relation of production that constantly creates inequality and ultimately crisis, in the state form as well as in economic relations.

In the sphere of legal relations, the moment of liberalization involves the movement to *generality of application* of law. As Neumann points out (1957, p. 28), this involves three elements: "the law must be general in its formulation, its generality must be specific, and it must not be retroactive." Specificity and non-retroactivity are necessary in order to provide certainty so that individuals may plan their private transactions within the framework of the law. Law therefore provides a predictability which enables individual exchanges to take place. However, this analysis, which is close to a Weberian one, fails to catch the dynamics of the process and its contradictions. There is a constant *tension* between the need for generality of application and the need for precision in formulation, which can be traced back to the contradiction between the *formal* equality of exchanges and their actual content. Liberal legal procedures are continually riven by this contradiction. This contradiction continually emerges *within* legal forms themselves, and not simply as an *external* contradiction between the abstract and formal equality of law and the inequalities of economic relations.

Liberal state forms try to rely on the self-reproduction of social relations. The availability of recourse to law aims to facilitate circulation by preventing breakdown in individual transactions: the parties themselves must carry through or reconstitute the terms of disputed transactions in anticipation of the probable outcome of recourse to the available procedure. The reference of such transactions for judicial adjudication very gradually leads to the elaboration of principles of obligation and liability based on generality of application: "reasonableness," "foreseeability," "consideration," etc. But simultaneously with the development and propagation of this liberal "rule of law" we see its progressive breakdown and recuperation. The reference of social conflict situations to courts cannot be left to individuals, but is supplemented with the growth of bodies of state officials who can selectively initiate state intervention to impose exchange equivalence. It is significant that this occurs first in the field of "social welfare," that is in relation to the terms of sale of labour-power, since it is here that, once free of all fetters, the rapaciousness of capital is felt. As we have already pointed out, it is above all the commodity labour-power that cannot be adequately produced on the basis of "equal" exchange alone (see Aumeruddy et al. 1978). It is class struggle that forces on capital even the most basic conditions for social reproduction; and while this simultaneously forces the development of more adequate legal and state forms, at the same time they can only contain the underlying contradictions of capital, at a higher and more acutely contradictory level of development.

Once the bourgeoisie has established its decisive control of parliament, the liberal conflict between generality of application and specificity is increasingly contained by the enactment of specific codes of legislation (Neumann 1957, p. 39). As Neumann points out, this does not develop until after the bourgeoisie has decisively gained control of parliment. [That this control was not established without an important struggle is shown, for example, in Foster's account (1974, ch. 3) of the fight by the radicals of Oldham to control elections, even based on a limited franchise.] To the extent that this control enables the substantive content of law to be legitimized by its origin in a political institution, the role of judges can be reduced to what Neumann calls the "phonograph" approach, "applying the law as it is." This denial to even judges of any part in making law is part of a general denial of any lawmaking or legitimizing capacity to any force outside parliament. Any deliberate challenge to this exclusive legitimizing authority is met with denunciations of extreme fervour—"kangaroo courts," "who is running the country?" etc. But it is also noticeable that where such a challenge manages to develop a significant momentum, there can be pressure to back down so that "the law should not be brought into disrepute" (for example, of course, the dockers' strike in Britain which finally killed the Tory Industrial Relations Act).

The contradiction between generality of application and specificity is a feature of the liberal rule of law that creates the most mystification. The belief that the law is or should be precise is one that runs very deep; yet so is the equally strong contrary pressure for "freedom under the law"—the power of the individual to arrange his or her own affairs without "interference" from specific orders or directions. This contradiction creates a kind of "porosity" in the juridical law enforcement process, a latitude or leeway of indeterminacy which essentially gives scope for the exercise of social or economic power. Anyone who has tried to define a policeman's legal power of arrest, or experienced the ways in which the legal "porosity" is exploited in practice will understand this point. It creates the framework for the exercise of the specific form of state power which at the beginning of this essay I pointed out was so badly grasped by the dichotomy of coercion/consent.

The activities of "law enforcement" officials are structured by this form of generally applicable laws retroactively applied to individual conduct. This mediation of the "application" of laws is also carried out of course above all by the "professionals," the lawyers. This raises all the familiar problems of "access" to the law—the cost, social and cultural barriers, etc. Seen in this light, the pressure to make the law equally accessible to all is simply a desperate attempt to maintain the credibility of the liberal myths. However, this is not to say that it is not important to *demystify* law, especially to *deprofessionalize* it. Here again we can note the lessons of the past few years of militancy around the law in Britain, and the sharp dichotomy between the line of "law for the poor" or "you too have rights" (see, for example, Hodge 1974) and the struggles to work towards a demystification (for example, Release 1978).

It is usual to "periodize" classical liberalism as corresponding to the heyday of competitive capitalism, usually thought of in terms of Britain in the period roughly 1840 to 1875. Yet in English law liberalization had hardly begun by 1875. This is partly explained by the particular relation in Britain between the juridical process and other parts of the state. It is more important however to try to grasp the periodization in terms of the dynamic movement of the development of the capitalist relations of production, rather than in terms of static "ideal types." The formal subjection of labour to capital, as we have seen, lays the basis for the liberal moment, which continues to be a significant element in the social reproduction process dominated by the valorization of capital. But as the capitalist mode of production develops further, new contradictions and new social forms come to the fore, which involve a reformulation of the social structure. From the last decade of the nineteenth century, the increasing domination of monopoly capitalism brings to the fore the complex of contradictions analysed by Marx as the tendency for the rate of profit to fall and its counter-tendencies. These contradictions can no longer be overcome simply by maintaining exchange equivalence in the sphere of circulation, but require increasingly direct intervention to redress imbalances, to create the possibilities of an equivalent exchange, to create the conditions for valorization. This is the response of capital to the increased growth of production on a social scale, the socialization of production.

These underlying tendencies lead through crisis and struggle to the restructuring of the state apparatus, which has meant in the twentieth century the modification of the legal apparatus and its supplementation by new forms. The general codes of the liberal form of law have become the overblown regulatory systems which increasingly require an elaborate bureaucratic apparatus. The old contradiction between generality of application and specificity becomes the conflict between legal certainty and administrative discretion. Compare for instance the general commercial law codes of the nineteenth century, for instance on Sale of Goods, with the modern detailed specification by regulation of what must go into a sausage, etc., etc. The undermining of generality leads to the establishment of specific bureaucratic apparatuses to regulate different areas of social conflict where "market" principles of allocation break down. The general jurisdiction of courts of law is supplemented by the establishment of specific tribunals, which can work more closely with the bureaucratic apparatus. Formal "judicial review" of these tribunals serves to maintain the fiction that the universality of law and observance of procedural "natural justice" are not affected, but this is an increasingly hollow myth.

Even the central areas of private law are increasingly undermined by the need to contain the increasing socialization of the means of production. Thus the principle of individual responsibility and liability, which we have seen is a key concept procedurally as well as ideologically, becomes increasingly undermined, for example by the growth of private and state insurance. Even the institutions of private property are undermined and often reformulated as in shareholder ownership of companies: mortgage, hire-purchase, even leasehold are adapted to give the institutions of finance capital effective control over property legally "owned" by the purchaser or tenant. The struggle to maintain a role for traditional juridical processes is rent by the contradiction of either on the one hand upholding the increasingly hollow myths of the liberal "rule of law," or on the other attempting to reform them. For instance the pressure to revitalize the judiciary must attempt to legitimize judicial activism by some kind of view of the judge as "policymaker" (on the US pattern); but this undermines the established credibility of the delicate balance between parliament and judiciary and opens up the terrible prospect of extraparliamentary lawmaking.

Thus we see that the restructuring of the state apparatus which is part of the general crisis of capitalism creates pressures to break through the limits of the existing forms; yet at the same time, since it is through the state that increasingly the restructuring must take place, state forms themselves become the focus of struggle. The strategy for a working-class movement must be, not to uphold the impossible ideals of the liberal forms of state and the "rule of law," but to insist on the necessity that it be transcended, in forms which challenge the dominance of capitalist social relations.

REFERENCES

Anderson, P. (1977), "The Antinomies of Gramsci," *New Left Review*, no. 100.

Aumeruddy, A., Lautier, B., and Tortajada, R. J. (1978),

"Labour-Power and the State," *Capital and Class,* no. 6, pp. 42–66.

Balbus, I. (1977), "Commodity Form and Legal Form: An Essay on the 'Relative Autonomy' of law," *Law and Society Review,* vol. II, no. 3, pp. 571–88.

Centre for Policy Studies (1968), *Bibliography of Freedom.*

Clarke, S. (1977), "Marxism, Sociology and Poulantzas's Theory of the State," *Capital and Class,* no. 2, pp. 1–31.

Foster, J. (1974), *Class Struggle and the Industrial Revolution,* Weidenfeld & Nicolson.

Hall, S., Critchley, C., Jefferson, A., Clarke, S., and Roberts, B. (1978), *Policing the Crisis: Mugging, the State, Law and Order,* Macmillan.

Hay, D., Linebaugh, P., and Thompson, E. P. (1975), *Albion's Fatal Tree,* Allen Lane.

Hodge, H. (1974), *Legal Rights,* Arrow.

Holloway, J., and Picciotto, S. (1977), "Capital, Crisis and the State," *Capital and Class,* no. 3, pp. 76–101.

Holloway, J., and Picciotto, S. (1978), *State and Capital: A Marxist Debate,* Edward Arnold.

Lukács, G. (1978), "Marx's Basic Ontological Principles," pt. I, ch. 4, in his *Towards the Ontology of Social Being,* Merlin Press.

Marx, K. (1976), *Capital,* vol. I, Penguin.

National Council for Civil Liberties (NCCL) (1979), *Justice Deserted: the Subversion of the Jury,* ed. H. Harman and J. Griffith.

Neumann, F. (1957), *The Democratic and the Authoritarian State,* Collier-Macmillan.

Pashukanis, E. B. (1978), *Law and Marxism: A General Theory,* Ink Links.

Poulantzas, N. (1978), *State, Power and Socialism,* New Left Books.

Release (1978), *Trouble with the Law: The Release Bust Book,* Pluto Press.

Sohn-Rethel, A. (1978), *Intellectual and Manual Labour: A Critique of Epistemology,* Macmillan.

Thompson, E. P. (1975), *Whigs and Hunters,* Allen Lane.

Thompson, E. P. (1976), "The Grind of Inheritance: A Comment," in J. Thirsk and E. P. Thompson (Eds.), *Family and Inheritance: Rural Society in Western Europe 1200–1800,* Cambridge University Press.

Unger, R. M. (1976), *Law in Modern Society,* Free Press, Collier-Macmillan.

CHAPTER THREE

LAW AND STATE

One of the most significant issues so far to surface in *Marxism and Law* concerns the relative merits, and political consequences of, the instrumentalist and structuralist conceptions of law. This was one of the organizing themes of many of the arguments presented in the last chapter. The conceptual dichotomy between instrumentalism and structuralism was originally initiated in the debates between Ralph Miliband and Nicos Poulantzas, waged in the pages of *New Left Review* a decade ago, in the context of the development of Marxist accounts of the capitalist state. In recognizing the historical importance of this dichotomy for the development of Marxist accounts of law, this chapter suggests that the dichotomy is misconceived and must be transcended. In so doing, two new questions are raised. What is the historical specificity of the capitalist state? What is the relation between law and state?

In "Law," a section from his last book, *State, Power, Socialism*, Nicos Poulantzas implicitly takes issue with those such as E. P. Thompson who have counterposed law to terror, and the rule of law to arbitrariness.[1] For Poulantzas this counterposition merely reproduces the political philosophy of the bourgeois state. It becomes clear, as his object unfolds, that Poulantzas is less concerned to refute this counterposition than he is to insert it at another level. Poulantzas argues that law is an integral part of the repressive order and organization of violence in every state. Every state commands a monopoly of violence and ultimate terror, a monopoly of war, and state-monopolized physical violence permanently underlies the techniques of power and the mechansim by which dominated classes consent to the legitimacy of the social order. But Poulantzas continues that law cannot simply be equated with violence. The positive function of law is to interpellate social agents into the politicosocial system, and to provide them with a place endowed with rights and obligations. The specificity of capitalist law must be sought in the social division of labor and in the relations of production. Its specificity, therefore, refers to the class struggle, not to the realm of circulation exchange, to the manner in which agents dispossessed of the means of production are given formal cohesion as abstract individuals and citizens of the nation state. Faced with working class political struggle, law organizes the structure of the compromise equilibrium permanently imposed on the dominated. Only in

[1] The best summary of the relation between law, state and juridico-politico ideology in the work of Poulantzas is found in Bob Jessop, "On Recent Marxist Theories of Law, the State, and Juridico-political Ideology," *International Journal of the Sociology of Law*, 8, no. 6 (1980), 339–368.

this sense, Poulantzas stresses, does law limit the exercise of state power by dominant classes. Whether or not this is sufficient ground to establish a dialogue between Poulantzas and E. P. Thompson, however, remains to be seen.

The second essay, "Whatever Happened to Politics? A Critique of Structuralist Marxist Accounts of State and Law" by Charles W. Grau, reconsiders some of the instrumentalist notions that have been rejected or ignored by structuralism. Grau correctly points out that one does not have to be overly familiar with the development of labor law in the United States, for example, to see that the corporatist form of the wage contract does not derive from the inexorable logic of capitalist development. Largely, it derives from the bitter struggles of the American working class to organize collectively for greater bargaining power in the marketplace. Structuralism bases much of its analysis on a form of ("in the last instance") economic determinism that excludes the role of political struggles in the historical development of the content of legal forms. If law springs not from relations of production or exchange but from class struggle, as Grau avers, then law is autonomous relative to the state itself. Law is mediated by the state, yet within the structural limits imposed by state policy there is considerable room for variation in the content of law. In other words, Grau is suggesting that the transcendance of instrumentalism and structuralism can occur only through their integration.

The major emphasis of Alan Freeman's argument, in his essay "Legitimizing Racial Discrimination through Antidiscrimination Law," is how the process of legitimation operates through the manipulation of the legal doctrine contained in U.S. Supreme Court decisions from 1954 up to the present. Freeman suggests that the concept of racial discrimination may be approached from the perspective of either its victim or its perpetrator. The victim perspective indicates that discrimination cannot be ended until the conditions generating it have been dissolved; from the perpetrator perspective, discrimination results from the actions of blameworthy individuals. Examining Supreme Court decisions in the areas of education and employment, Freeman detects three major periods: the era of uncertainty, 1954 to 1965; the era of contradiction, 1965 to 1974; and the era of rationalization after 1974. In each period, despite the contradictory principles often invoked in particular cases, Freeman shows that the perpetrator perspective has been the only formal conception of a violation admitted in antidiscrimination law. Yet this form would have made even illusory progress in the quest for racial justice impossible. The Supreme Court met this challenge by separating violation from remedy. The implication of Freeman's essay is a powerful corrective to those who believe that the social conditions that produce structured social inequality can be eliminated through law.

The final essay in this chapter puts forward the thesis that the rising costs of crime control are among the most refractory of the problems facing modern capitalist states. In "Social Control in Historical Perspective," Steven Spitzer and Andrew Scull demonstrate that only with the decay of medieval institutions of collective responsibility did the control of crime become a profitable undertaking. With the development in England of a differentiated and loosely articulated society, the informal and voluntary system of social control became increasingly suspect. Prisons and police gradually emerged as institutions of private profit in the middle of the eighteenth century. The authors then argue that the institutions of crime control became increasingly public as part of a much larger movement toward rational management in public administration, finance, and economic policy. This rationalization process clearly corresponded to the needs and aspirations of the commercial and manufacturing bourgeoisie, and the impersonal system of social control that resulted masked the class character of the legal order.

LAW

NICOS POULANTZAS

I. LAW AND TERROR

In fact, it was only at a very late historical stage, when the capitalist State was already being constituted, that law first appeared as a limitation upon state arbitrariness, and as a barrier to a certain form of violence. This "State based on law," conceived as the contrary of unlimited power, gave birth to the illusory opposition Law/Terror. I say illusory, because law and certain rules have always been present in the constitution of power: the Asiatic or despotic State was, for example, based on Babylonian or Assyrian law, the slave State on Greek or Roman law, and the feudal State on the juridical forms of the Middle Ages. Even the most bloody state form has set itself up as a juridical organization, giving itself an expression in law and functioning in accordance with a juridical form: as we know only too well, this was the case with Stalin and the 1936 Constitution, reputedly "the most democratic in the world." Nothing could be more mistaken than to counterpose the rule of law to arbitrariness, abuse of power, and the prince's act of will. Such a vision corresponds to the juridical-legalist conception of the State—to that political philosophy of the established bourgeois State which was opposed by both Marx and Max Weber, and which never made any impression on the theorists of bloody state management, Machiavelli and Hobbes. The split between law and violence is false even, or above all, with regard to the modern State. For

Source: From Nicos Poulantzas, *State, Power, Socialism* (London: New Left Books, 1978), pp. 76-92. Reprinted by permission.

unlike its pre-capitalist counterparts, this supremely juridical State holds a monopoly of violence and ultimate terror, a *monopoly of war*.

Thus, in every State, law is an integral part of the repressive order and of the organization of violence. By issuing rules and passing laws, the State establishes an initial field of injunctions, prohibitions and censorship, and thus institutes the practical terrain and object of violence. Furthermore, law organizes the conditions for physical repression, designating its modalities and structuring the devices by means of which it is exercised. In this sense, law is *the code of organized public violence*. Those who neglect the role of law in organizing power are always the ones who neglect the role of physical repression in the functioning of the State. A clear example of this is provided by Foucault, whost latest work *La volonté de savoir* is a logical sequel to the aberrations of his earlier *Surveiller et punir*.

The chain of Foucault's reasoning may be somewhat schematically represented as follows: (a) the opposition legality-terror is false, because law has always gone together with the exercise of violence and physical repression; (b) in modern societies, the exercise of power is based much less on overt violence and repression than on subtler mechanisms that are supposedly "incongruous" with violence: namely, the mechanisms employed by various "disciplines." "And although the juridical could serve to represent, in a no doubt incomplete manner, a power that was essentially based on blood-letting and death, it is utterly incongruous with the new methods of power, which rest not on right but on technique,

185

not on law but on normalization, not on punishment but on control—and which are exercised at specific levels and in particular forms that go beyond the State and its apparatuses."[1] As Castel puts it, following Foucault, the exercise of power involves a passage from authority-coercion to manipulation-persuasion:[2] in other words, the famous 'internalization' of repression by the dominated masses. Inevitably, Foucault is led to underestimate at the very least the role of law in the exercise of power within modern societies; but he also underestimates the role of the State itself, and fails to understand the function of the repressive apparatuses (army, police, judicial system, etc.) as means of exercising physical violence that are located at the heart of the modern State. They are treated instead as mere parts of the disciplinary machine which patterns the internalization of repression by means of normalization.

Now, while the first point concerning the constitutive relationship between law and the exercise of violence is indeed correct, the second one is by and large false. Adopted by a current of thought that is much broader than, and often very distinct from, Foucault, this second line of reasoning has taken root in the couplet violence/consent or repression-ideology that has long been a characteristic of analyses of power. The central theme is quite straightforward: modern power is grounded not on organized physical violence, but on ideological-symbolic *manipulation,* the organization of consent, and the internalization of repression ("the inner cop"). This conception originated in the early analyses of bourgeois politicojuridicial philosophy—that philosophy which, by counterposing violence and law, saw in the law-based State and the rule of law realities that impose an inherent limitation on violence. In its various modern continuations—ranging from the celebrated Frankfurt School analyses of the replacement of the police by the family as the authoritarian

instance, through those of Marcuse to Bourdieu's analysis of so-called symbolic violence—the theme of internalized expression or, more generally, what we might call the "softening" of physical violence in the exercise of power has become an almost commonplace idea.

For our present purposes, then, this current may be said to have two essential features: on the one hand, underestimation of the role of physical repression, in the strong sense of deadly, armed constraint of the body, and on the other, a conception of power in which the terms of the couplet repression-ideology constitute zero-sum components or quantities. According to this perspective, any diminution or contraction of physical violence in the functioning and maintenance of power cannot but correspond to an accentuation or increase of ideological inculcation (seen as symbolic violence or internalized repression).

There is little fundamental difference between the above conception and the one dominant in a number of currently fashionable analyses that ground consent on the wish of the masses (for fascism or whatever) or on love of the Master.[3] For these also neglect the role of organized physical violence, at the same time reducing power to repression-prohibition. The resulting subjectivization of the exercise of power takes the form of seeking 'the reasons for obedience' in the desire or love of power—factors which here replace the role imputed to ideology in the internalization of repression. If law enters into the picture, it does so not as the coding of physical repression, but as a form of the Master, who induces the desire and love of his subjects simply through his presence, self-expression and discourse. The couplet repression-ideology gives way to the couplet law-love or prohibition-desire. But the role of violence in grounding power is still underestimated, and *all that is ever mentioned are the reasons for consent.*

Of course, the fact that these analyses raise the

---

[1] *La volonté de savoir,* op. cit., pp. 117–18.
[2] R. Castel, *Le psychanalysme,* Paris 1976, pp. 288ff.

[3] There is a long list of such works: from Fr. Lyotard (*L'économie libidinale*) through R. Scherer to P. Legendre (*L'amour du censeur*).

question of consent to power is not at all objectionable—quite the contrary. What is disturbing is both their neglect of the role of organized physical violence in exercising repression, and their reduction of power to prohibition and symbolic or internalized repression. By grounding consent on love-desire of repression, they become unable to grasp the positive *material reasons* for this phenomenon—reasons such as the concessions made to the masses by the existing power, which play a decisive role over and above that of the dominant ideology. At the same time, insistence on the positivity of power should not be allowed to obscure either the question of repression or the role of ideology itself in relation to consent. Yet this is precisely what happens in Foucault's writings. Unlike the above currents, he does have the merit of bringing out one aspect of the power techniques that materially organize the submission of dominated layers—namely, the aspect of the normalization disciplines. But his analyses, too, constantly play down the role of overt physical violence. (A mere symptom of this is his underestimation of the role of law in giving coded form to such violence.)

In the omnifunctional position assigned to them by Foucault, the techniques of power absorb not only the question of physical violence but also that of consent. The latter thereby becomes a non-problem which is either given no theoretical elucidation at all or else is collapsed into the "internalized repression" type of analysis. But over and above the disciplines of normalization, there must be other "reasons" that explain consent. For if those disciplines were enough to account for submission, *how could they admit the existence of struggles?* Here we come to the central impasse of Foucault's analyses: his failure to provide a basis for that celebrated "resistance" to power of which he is so enamoured. In point of fact, there has to be organized physical violence for the very reason that there has to be consent—that is to say, because of the universality and primacy of struggles based on exploitation. It is this primary, inescapable reality which accounts for the fact that *struggles are always at the foundation of power.* If power (the Law, the Master) is instead made the basis of struggle, or if "power" and "resistance" are considered as entirely equivalent terms of a relation, then one is led to derive consent from love or the wish for power, or else to obscure the problematic character of consent itself. In either case, the role of violence is completely passed over.

What then is the truth of the matter? Unlike its pre-capitalist counterparts, the capitalist State holds *a monopoly of legitimate physical violence.* Max Weber must be given the credit for establishing this point and for demonstrating that the legitimacy of its concentration of organized force is a "rational-legal" legitimacy based on law. Indeed, the capitalist State's prodigious accumulation of the means of bodily constraint goes hand in hand with the development of its character as a State based on law. Now, this circumstance gives rise to some quite remarkable effects. The degree of overt physical violence exercised in the various contexts of "private," extra-state power—from the factory to the famous micropower situations—declines as an exact function of the State's monopoly of legitimate physical force. The European capitalist States, in particular, were constituted through pacification of territories torn by feudal wars. And once political power was institutionalized, these States had less recourse to such violence in normal contexts of domination—even though they now enjoyed a monopoly of its legitimate use—than did the various pre-capitalist States. Of course we should not forget: (a) the exceptional forms of capitalist State (fascism, military dictatorship, etc.) which infest to-day's world but which are lost from sight in the short memories and Eurocentric light-mindedness of so many theorists (although when they come to the regimes in the East, they suddenly become aware of violence); (b) the supreme terror of *war* (the First and Second World Wars, others . . . and now the threat of nuclear war: whoever had the idea that modern power is no longer exercised "up to the point of death"?); and (c) the conjunctures of accentuated class struggle. But despite all this, overt violence is employed less frequently than in the past: it is exactly as if the State had to apply less force *to the very degree that* it holds a monopoly of its legitimate use.

However, contrary to a now wisespread illusion, it does not follow that modern power and domination are no longer grounded on physical violence. Even if violence is not concretized in the daily exercise of power as it used to be, it still, and indeed more than ever, occupies a *determining* position. For its very monopolization by the State induces forms of domination in which the numerous methods of establishing consent play the key role. In order to grasp this point, we must go beyond the notion of a simple complementarity of violence and consent, modelled on Machiavelli's image of a Centaur that is half-human, half-beast. Physical violence and consent do not exist side by side like two calculable homogeneous magnitudes, related in such a way that more consent corresponds to less violence. Violence-terror always occupies a determining place—and not merely because it remains in reserve, coming into the open only in critical situations. *State-monopolized physical violence permanently underlies the techniques of power and mechanisms of consent: it is inscribed in the web of disciplinary and ideological devices; and even when not directly exercised, it shapes the materiality of the social body upon which domination is brought to bear.*

There can be no question, then, of replacing the couplet law-terror by a trinomial repression-disciplinary normalization-ideology, in which, despite the presence of a third term, the component parts stand in an unchanged relationship to one another as heterogeneous and distinct magnitudes of a quantifiable power, or as modalities of the exercise of a power-essence. We need rather to grasp the material organization of labour as a class relation whose condition of existence and guarantee of reproduction is organized physical violence. The establishment of techniques of capitalist power, the constitution of disciplinary devices (the great "enclosure"), the emergence of

ideological-cultural institutions from parliament through universal suffrage to the school—all these presupposed state monopolization of violence concealed by the displacement of legitimacy towards legality and by the rule of law. They presuppose this not only in the sense of historical genealogy, but in their very existence and reproduction. To take just one example, the national army is consubstantial with parliament and the capitalist school. But this consubstantiality does not rest only on a common institutional materiality stemming from the social division of labour embodied by these apparatuses; it also rests on the fact that the national army, as an explicit part of the state monopoly of legitimate physical violence, gives rise to the forms of existence and operation of institutions—parliament, school—in which violence does not have to be materialized as such. The regular existence and even the constitution of a law-enacting parliament is unthinkable without the modern national army.

Finally, I should like to say something more about *death itself*. For how is it possible not to see that the changing modes of prosaically dying in one's bed, the veritable taboo on death in modern societies, and the loss of control by "private" citizens over their own death[4] actually converge with the state monopoly of legitimate public terror? Does the State no longer have any function with regard to death? Even when it does not execute people, kill them or threaten to do so, and even when it prevents them from dying, the modern State manages death in a number of different ways; and medical power is inscribed in present-day law.

State monopolization of legitimate violence therefore remains the determining element of power even when such violence is not exercised in a direct and open manner. This monopoly is not the origin of the new forms of struggle under capitalism; and so true is it that power and struggle summon and condition each other that the

---

[4]Ph. Aries, *Histoire de la mort en Occident,* and the works of L. V. Thomas.

role of the mechanisms of organization and consent now correspond to these forms. State concentration of armed force and the disarming-demilitarization of private sectors (which is a precondition of established capitalist exploitation) contribute to shifting the class struggle away from permanent civil war (periodic and regular armed conflicts) towards those new forms of political and trade-union organization of the popular masses against which overt physical violence is, as we know, only conditionally effective. Confronted with a "public" power, a "private" people no longer lives political domination as a natural and sacrosanct fatality: it considers the state monopoly of violence to be legitimate only to the extent that legality and judicial regulation give it the hope, and in principle even the formal possibility, of gaining access to power. In short, at the very time that violence is concentrated in specialized state bodies, it becomes less than ever capable of ensuring the reproduction of domination. As I said earlier, the state concentration of force established peace instead of the private armed conflicts and constantly updated holy wars that used to constitute the *catharsis* of the fatality of power. Under the impact of the same state monopoly, these have given way to permanent disputing of political power; and the rule of capitalist law has installed in the very outposts of power the various mechanisms of organizing consent—including, insofar as it masks the state monopolization of physical force, the mechanisms of ideological inculcation.

Although law, as the organizer of repression and physical violence, thus turns out to play an essential role in the exercise of power, it does not for all that exhibit the purely negative logic of rejection, obstruction, compulsory silence, and the ban on public demonstration. Moreover, it is not only because law is also something other than law that it is never exclusively negative. Even in its repressive role, law involves an eminently positive aspect: *for repression is never identical with pure negativity.* More than a conglomeration of prohibitions and censorship, law has since Greek and Roman times also issued positive in-

junctions: it does not just forbid or leave be, according to the maxim that all is permitted which is not expressly forbidden by law; it lays down things to be done, dictates positive obligations, and prescribes certain forms of discourse that may be addressed to the existing power. Law does not merely impose silence or allow people to speak, it often *compels* them to speak (to bear witness, denounce others, and so on). More generally, institutionalized law has never been so completely identified with prohibition and censorship that state organization has been divided between law-censorship-negativity and "something else"-action-positivity. The opposition itself is partially false, since law organizes the repressive field not only as repression of acts forbidden by law, but also as repression of a failure to do what the law prescribes. Law is always present from the beginning in the social order: it does not arrive *post festum* to put order into a pre-existing state of nature. For as the codification of both prohibitions and positive injunctions, law is a constitutive element of the politico-social field.

Repression then is never pure negativity, and it is not exhausted either in the actual exercise of physical violence or in its internalization. There is something else to repression, something about which people seldom talk: namely, *the mechanisms of fear.* I have referred to these material, and by no means subjective, mechanisms as the *theatricals* of that truly Kafkaesque Castle, the modern State. They are inscribed in the labyrinths where modern law becomes a practical reality; and while such concretization is based on the monopoly of legitimate violence, we must still go into Kafka's Penal Colony in order to understand it.

Finally, although law plays an important (positive and negative) role in organizing repression, its efficacy is just as great in the devices of creating consent. It materializes the dominant ideology that enters into these devices, even though it does not exhaust the reasons for consent. Through its discursiveness and characteristic texture, law-regulation obscures the politico-economic realities, tolerating structural lacunae and transposing these realities to the political arena by means of a peculiar mechanism of concealment-inversion. It thus gives expression to the imaginary ruling-class representation of social reality and power. In this manifestation, which runs parallel to the place it occupies in the repressive machinery, law is an important factor in organizing the consent of the dominated classes—even though *legitimacy* (consent) is neither identical with nor restricted to *legality*. The dominated classes encounter law not only as an occlusive barrier, but also as the reality which assigns the place they must occupy. This place, which is the point of their insertion into the politico-social system, carries with it certain rights as well as duties-obligations, and its investment by the imagination has a real impact on social agents.

Furthermore, a number of the State's activities that go beyond its repressive and ideological role come to be inscribed in the text of the law and even form part of its internal structure. This is true of state economic intervention, but above all of those material concessions which are one of the decisive reasons for consent. Law does not only deceive and conceal, and nor does it merely repress people by compelling or forbidding them to act. It also organizes and sanctions certain *real rights* of the dominated classes (even though, of course, these rights are invested in the dominant ideology and are far from corresponding in practice to their juridical form); and it has inscribed within it the material concessions imposed on the dominant classes by popular struggle.

Nevertheless, it is evident that *the activity, role and place of the State stretch a very long way beyond law and judicial regulation*—a fact which cannot be grasped by a juridical-legalistic conception or by current psychoanalytic theories such as those expressed in Legendre's interesting works.[5]

(a) The activity and concrete functioning of the State by no means invariably take the form of

law-rules: there is always a set of state practices and techniques that escape juridical systematization and order. This is not to say that they are "anomic" or arbitrary in the strong sense of the term. But the logic they obey—that of the relationship of forces between classes in struggle—is somewhat distinct from the logic of the juridical order, and law invests it only at a certain distance and within a specific range.

(b) The State often transgresses law-rules of its own making by acting without reference to the law, but also by acting directly against it. In its very discursiveness, each juridical system allows the Power-State to disregard its own laws and even enters an appropriate variable in the rules of the game that it organizes. This is called *the higher interests of the State (raison d'Etat)*—which, strictly speaking, entails both that legality is always compensated by illegalities "on the side," and that state illegality is always inscribed in the legality which it institutes. Thus, Stalinism and the totalitarian aspects of power in the East are not principally due to "violations of socialist legality." Every juridical system includes illegality in the additional sense that gaps, blanks or "loopholes" form an integral part of its discourse. It is a question here not merely of oversights or blind-spots arising out of the ideological operation of concealment underlying the legal order, but of express devices that allow the law to be breached. Lastly, of course, there are cases where the State engages in straightforward violations of its own law—violations which, while appearing as crude transgressions not covered by the law, are no less part of the structural functioning of the State. The state-institutional structure is always organized in such a way that both the State and the dominant classes operate at once in accordance with the law and against the law. Many laws would never have existed in their present form if a certain rate of ruling-class violation had not been anticipated by, and written into, the workings of the state machinery. Thus, even when illegality is distinct from legality, it is not identified with a kind of parallel organization or

[5] *Jouir du pouvoir*, Paris 1976.

State separated from the *de jure* State of legality, and still less does it form a chaotic non-State counterposed to the real State of legality. Not only does illegality often enter into the law, but illegality and legality are themselves part of one and the same institutional structure.

This is essentially how we should understand Marx's argument that every State is a class "dictatorship." All too often it is taken to mean that the State is a power above the law—where the term law is opposed to violence and force. As we have seen, however, even the most dictatorial of States is never devoid of law; and the existence of law or legality has never forestalled any kind of barbarism or despotism. In Marx's statement, the term "dictatorship" refers to the precise fact that every State is organized as a single functional order of legality and illegality, of legality shot through with illegality.

(c) The activity of the State always overflows the banks of law, since it can, within certain limits, modify its own law. The State is not the simple representation of some eternal law, be it universal prohibition or a law of nature. If such were the case—and this needs to be made clear—law would have *de jure* primacy over the State. (This is indeed the cornerstone of the juridical conception of the State, whose present-day convergence with the analytical, or psychoanalytical, conception of institutions is not difficult to explain.) Now, it is true that every State is consubstantial with a system of law, and that law is not strictly speaking the utilitarian creation of a pre-existing State of naked might. But in a class-divided society, it is always the State, as the practitioner of legitimate violence and physical repression, which takes precedence over law. Although law organizes this violence, there can be no law or right in such a society without an apparatus that compels its observance and ensures its efficacy or social existence: *the efficacy of law is never that of pure discourse, the spoken word, and the issuing of rules.* Just as there is no violence without law, so law always presupposes an organized force at the service of the legislator (the secular arm). Or, more prosaically: strength remains on the side of the law.

II. MODERN LAW

Despite the fact that all legal systems have certain characteristics in common, capitalist law is specific in that it forms an *axiomatic system*, comprising a set of *abstract, general, formal and strictly regulated norms.*

A certain variant of Marxism has sought to base this specificity of the capitalist juridical system in the sphere of circulation of capital and commodity-exchange: "abstract" juridical subjects are thus held to correspond to free commodity-traders, and "formally" free and equal individuals to equivalent exchange and "abstract" exchange-value, and so on.[6] However, we can hardly grasp the reality of capitalist law by remaining within this sphere. The roots of its specific features (abstraction, universality, formalism)—which also embrace the state monopoly of legitimate violence as opposed to the diffusion of such violence among several bearers that characterizes juridical particularism—have to be sought in the social division of labour and the relations of production. It is these which assign to violence its position and role under capitalism. For by virtue of the expropriation of the means of labour from the direct producers, violence is not present directly and as such (as an "extra-economic factor") in the production process. The axiomatic system of capitalist law constitutes the framework wherein agents who are totally dispossessed of their means of production are given *formal cohesion;* it thus also sketches out the contours of a state space relatively separate from the relations of production. The formal and abstract character of law is inextricably bound up with the real fracturing of the social body in the social division of labour—

[6]In my first and long since out-of-print work *Nature des choses et droit* (1966), I also took this position. However, the reader can rest assured that I have no intention of republishing this text.

that is to say, with the individualization of agents that takes place in the capitalist labour process.

Modern law therefore embodies space-time as the material frame of reference of the labour process: a serial, cumulative, continuous and homogeneous space-time. This law institutes individuals as juridico-political subjects-persons by representing their unity in the people-nation. It consecrates, and thus helps to establish, the differential fragmentation of agents (individualization) by elaborating the code in which these differentiations are inscribed and on the basis of which they exist without calling into question the political unity of the social formation. All subjects are free and equal before the law: that is, the discourse of law does not merely hide, but actually expresses the fact that they are different (as subjects-individuals) to the very extent that this difference may be inscribed in a framework of homogeneity. All too often it is said that capitalist law just obscures real differences behind a screen of universal formalism. But in fact, it also helps to establish and consecrate individual and class differences within its very structure, while at the same time setting itself up as a cohesive and organizing system of their *unity-homogenization*. Therein lies the source of the universal, formal and abstract character of the juridical axiomatic. For it presupposes agents who have been "freed" from the territorial-personal bonds of pre-capitalist, and even serf, societies—bonds resting upon a law which was essentially composed of the statuses, privileges and customs of castes or Estates, and in which the political and the economic were closely intertwined. Of course, *law* does not itself *free* these agents: it rather intervenes in the process whereby they are disentangled and separated from the bonds that differentiated them according to class or Estate (those closed classes which served as the fount of signs, symbols and meanings). Law participates in this process by helping to establish and consecrate the new great Difference: *individualization*. The modern legal system works for this individualization either in a parallel, and more or less contradictory, relationship with other state techniques and practices (the normalization disciplines) or else by covering and moulding itself to them.

Now, insofar as they materialize the dominant ideology, capitalist law and the capitalist juridical system present certain further peculiarities. The centre of legitimacy shifts away from the sacred towards legality. Law itself, which is now the embodiment of the people-nation, becomes the fundamental category of state sovereignty; and juridical-political ideology supplants religious ideology as the predominant form. Although these changes coincide with the emergence of a state monopoly of legitimate force, they have much deeper roots than that. The function of legitimacy shifts towards the impersonal and abstract instance of law, at the very time that the agents "loosen" and "free" themselves from their territorial-personal bonds. It is exactly as if the abstract, formal and general character of law had rendered it the mechanism most suitable for fulfilling the key function of every dominant ideology: namely, that of cementing together the social formation under the aegis of the dominant class.

Apart from the fact that it imposes a framework of cohesion on social agents, capitalist law is pre-eminently able to represent their unity by writing it into the social imagination and to *cement* the various processes of individualization. Organized in the mode of the *pure sign* (abstraction, universality, formalism) law takes up a privileged position in the ideological mechanism of imaginative representation "as soon as" the social agents become atomized and severed from their natural means of labour. In the pre-capitalist formations, by contrast, it was the mode of symbolization peculiar to religion ("religion binds people together") which allowed the consecration of links already embedded in the land, the family, and the caste or Estate. These links gave rise to a graduated series of primary symbolizations in the mode of the sacred—a series which the State registered by drawing its legitimacy from its position, at the top of the pyramid of meaning, as the incarnation of the sovereign's word and body. As Marx pointed out, it was in these modes of production that ideology played a dominant role; while in the capitalist mode of production, the specific relations of production assign to the economic a role that is at once determining and dominant. Juridical ideology written into law becomes the dominant area of ideology in a mode of production in which ideology no longer plays the dominant role. We must understand by this that the capitalist form of law comes to constitute the fundamental ideological mechanism from the moment that the extraction of surplus-labour (surplus-value) is activated by the very cycle of reproduction of capital (and not by "extra-economic factors")—from the moment that the sub-symbolizations cementing the various territorial-personal links among social agents are uprooted and destroyed. The rule of capitalist law is grounded on the absence of other signifiers around it.

This specificity of law and the juridical system is inscribed in the peculiar institutional structure of the capitalist State. Indeed, its centralizing-bureaucratic-hierarchic framework is itself possible only through being moulded in a system of general, abstract, formal and axiomatic norms that organize and regulate the impersonal echelons and apparatuses of the exercise of power. What is termed 'administrative law' exactly corresponds to capitalist law's structuring effect on the State. Law and regulation underlie the recruitment of state personnel (through competition and impersonal examination) as well as the functioning of the written text and of the State's *internal* dogma of speech. Its discourse does not embody, reveal or interpret the divine (royal or noble) Word; and nor is it the medium of a more or less direct and personal mystical relationship that each servant entertains with God (the King or Lord). It is rather supposed to give progressively concrete application to abstract and formal law through a logical-deductive chain ("juridical logic") which is nothing other than the trajectory of an order of domination-subordination and decision-execution internal to the State.

If we remember that the state framework is related to the capitalist division of intellectual and manual labour, and that it specifically reproduces intellectual labour, then we shall be able to grasp the relationship between this division and capitalist law. In the legitimacy of the sacred, every subject of power is supposed to bear within himself a share of (divine) *truth,* an inner limit to earthly power (a soul). The mark that is inscribed within him by the body of the (divine) King can never be entirely removed, for status and privilege belong to the realm of natural law. For its part, modern law expresses the capitalist relationship between power and knowledge, as it is condensed in capitalist intellectual labour: outside the law, individuals-subjects contain no knowledge or truth. As law becomes an incarnation of Reason, the struggle against Religion is pursued in the forms of law and juridical ideology, and Enlightenment physical science is conceptualized in juridical categories. Abstract, formal, universal law is the truth of subjects: it is knowledge (in the service of capital) which constitutes juridical-political subjects and which establishes the difference between private and public. Capitalist law thus gives expression to the process whereby the agents of production are entirely dispossessed of their "intellectual powers" to the benefit of the dominant classes and of their State.

That things are so may also be seen in the relationship of law and juridical systematization to the specialization of the state apparatuses—a relationship which is manifested in the emergence of a corps of specialized jurists. Provided that this corps is understood in the broad sense, we can see that, as a network "separated" from society, it probably constitutes the best representative of intellectual labour incorporated in the State. In this broad sense, every state agent—every parliamentarian, politician, policeman, officer, judge, barrister, lawyer, civil servant, social worker, and so on—is an intellectual to the extent that he is a *man of law,* who legislates, knows the laws and regulations, and applies them in concrete ways. *No-one should be ignorant of the law*—that is the fundamental maxim of the modern juridical system, in which no-one but state representatives are able to know the law. This knowledge required of every citizen is not even a special subject of study at school, as if everything were done to keep him in ignorance of what he is supposedly obliged to know. The maxim therefore expresses a relationship whereby the popular masses, whose ignorance of the law's secrets is built into this law and juridical language itself, remain dependent upon, and subordinated to, state functionaries as the makers, protectors and appliers of the law. Modern law is a *state secret* which grounds a form of knowledge monopolized for reasons of State.

This specificity of capitalist law and the capitalist juridical system is therefore based on the existing relations of production and social division of labour; and so it refers us to social classes and the class struggle such as they exist under capitalism. The fact that these are open classes rather than closed castes is of the highest importance with regard to the reproduction both of their positions (extension, contraction, disappearance) and of their agents (specific training-subjection of agents so that they may occupy certain class positions). Evidently, the abstract, formal and general character of the capitalist juridical system allows it to regulate the relationship between the positions of social classes (capital, wage-labour) and those of agents who are not formally "tied" to them. It is this system which can regulate *both* the permanent allocation of agents of the dominated classes among the relevant class positions (peasantry, working class, petty bourgeoisie)—which is nothing other than the role of law in expanding the *real submission* of Labour to Capital—*and* the greater or lesser partitioning of these positions and agents in the relationship between the dominant and dominated classes. For in that bourgeois juridical axiom, which expresses a real national-popular class law, everyone is free and equal before the law on condition that he is or becomes bourgeois. And that, of course, the law at once allows and forbids.

However, this juridical system also corre-

sponds to the peculiar coordinates of political struggle under capitalism.

(a) The axiomatic systematization of law as the framework of formal cohesion assumes a strategic function with regard to the expanded reproduction introduced by capitalism. Whereas precapitalist societies exhibited only simple, repetitive and, so to speak, blind reproduction, this expanded form entails that, at the very level of the reproduction process, a strategic calculation is made by the various fractions of capital and their bearers. In its turn, such calculation requires that the rules of the game should possess a modicum of stability sufficient to allow some degree of *forecasting*. This is made possible by axiomatic law, whose systematic character, based on abstract, general, formal and strictly regulated norms, consists in, among other things, the fact that it carries its own rules of transformation. Thus, any changes in law become regulated transformations within its own system—thanks, in particular, to the role of the Constitution.

(b) It is precisely through a system of general, abstract and formal rules that law *regulates* the exercise of power by the state apparatuses, as well as access to these apparatuses themselves. Within a specific form of domination, this legal system controls the process whereby power is apportioned to the various classes and, above all, the distinct fractions of the bourgeoisie that make up a power-bloc. By thus giving order to their mutual relations within the State, it allows a changed balance of forces in the ruling alliance to find expression at state level without provoking upheavals. Capitalist law, as it were, *damps down* and *channels* political crises, in such a way that they do not lead to crises of the State itself. More generally, capitalist law appears as the necessary form of a State that has to maintain relative autonomy of the fractions of a power-bloc in order to organize their unity under the hegemony of a given class or fraction. This compulsion is further bound up with the State's relative separation from the relations of production—that is to say, with the fact that agents of the economically dominant class (the bourgeoisie) do not directly coincide with the occupiers and agents of the State.

This is moreover the way in which modern law was historically constituted. Its roots go back to the Absolutist State and the seventeenth-century European monarchies. The predominantly capitalist State of Absolutism, which was truly a State of transition to capitalism, already had to confront specific problems of organization concerning relations between the landed nobility and the bourgeoisie. The state's monopolization of war here corresponds to the pacification of social forces ("private wars") which it had been accomplishing since the sixteenth century, and which prepared it for success in that first great war which bore it to the baptismal font: the bloody process of primitive accumulation of capital in favour of the bourgeoisie.

However, the capitalist legal system also takes the dominated classes into account in regulating the exercise of power. Faced with working-class struggle on the political plane, law organizes the structure of the compromise equilibrium permanently imposed on the dominant classes by the dominated. It also regulates the forms in which physical repression is exercised: indeed, we need to stress the fact that this juridical system, these

"formal" and "abstract" liberties are also conquests of the popular masses. In this sense and this alone does modern law *set the limits* of the exercise of power and of intervention by the state apparatuses. It is very clear from its abolition in the exceptional forms of capitalist State (fascism, military dictatorship), that this role of law depends on the class relationship of forces and provides the outline of the barrier to ruling-class power imposed by the dominated classes. Modern law, then, has not intervened against state violence ("law versus terror"); on the contrary, the very letter of the law has played a role in organizing the exercise of violence, always taking into account the resistance of the popular masses. The juridical axiomatic, as I have already indicated, allows political forecasting on the part of the dominant classes: while it expresses a class relationship of forces, it also serves as a prop for strategic calculation by including among the variables of its system the resistance and struggle of the dominated classes.

Finally, with regard to the dominant classes and fractions, the role of law in setting limits expresses the relationship of forces within the power bloc. It becomes concrete above all by delimiting the fields of competence and intervention of the various apparatuses, in which different classes and fractions of this bloc have dominance.

WHATEVER HAPPENED TO POLITICS? A CRITIQUE OF STRUCTURALIST MARXIST ACCOUNTS OF STATE AND LAW

CHARLES W. GRAU

Much Marxist analysis of state and law since 1974 has been structured by the typologies introduced by Gold et al. (1975), who summarized existing Marxist writings on the capitalist state. In their summary, they identified three "categories" of Marxist theories of the state—instrumental, structural, and Hegelian–Marxist. "Instrumental" theories were defined as those that view the capitalist state as a mechanism used by the ruling class either directly through the manipulation of state policies or indirectly through the exercise of pressure on the state (p. 34). "Structuralist theory" categorically rejected instrumental theories, contending instead that the capitalist state performed functions necessary for the reproduction of capitalist society. The need to perform these functions arose outside the state, either in the economy or in class struggle, which posed continuous contradictions requiring resolution. "These functions," the authors contended, "determine the specific policies and organization of the state," although the "concrete ways" in which the state meets the functions varied with the level of capitalist development and forms of class struggle. (pp. 35–36).

Although Gold et al. intended to present these different "traditions" in order to reconcile, synthesize, and extend them (p. 30), an unintended

consequence of their work was to add fuel to the polemical fire. Identifying various writers and works as "instrumentalist"—in order to demonstrate the inadequacies of "instrumental" theory—became an apparent favorite pastime of American Marxists. It was not long before the "debate" spread from the analysis of the capitalist state to the analysis of law. Fraser, for example, attacks "radical lawyers" for "viewing the law . . . merely as the passive reflection of the class interests of socially dominant groups" (1976, p. 131). Overcome by "the rush of emotion that often accompanies personal demystification," radical lawyers supposedly came to believe that "understanding . . . the legal process requires nothing more than the ripping away of the veil of illusion [to reveal] a repressive and exploitative legal system" (p. 127). Even Poulantzas, himself some years earlier embroiled in polemical dialogue with archinstrumentalist Ralph Miliband, is not spared. By missing the "crucial insight" that the experience of individual autonomy and freedom is both real and central to capitalist relations of production, Poulantzas too quickly dismisses freedom and autonomy as a "juridical illusion." By failing to recognize that law "operates on the level of productive relations between classes as well as the level of circulation and exchange," Poulantzas should be regarded as one of the "ultra-sophisticated contemporary radical lawyers" Fraser defiles (Fraser 1976, pp. 141–142). Rather than demystifying the law,

Fraser argues that radical lawyers should strive "to recognize the unique logic embodied in the bourgeois legal system" (p. 131). This supposedly will help them to search out "effective means of enforcing official recognition of claims" rooted in "private needs" (p. 156).

Similarly, Beirne (1979) traces the theoretical development of instrumental Marxist accounts of law, sharply criticizing them for occupying one end of a theoretical continuum with voluntaristic pluralism at the opposite pole. He charges that instrumental Marxists have unwittingly adopted the problematic and methods of conflict theory, defining as their object the ways in which "those with power" manipulate the state and the law to serve their own purposes. In doing so, they have overlooked the importance of the law's autonomy relative to other state institutions and of "the exigencies of particular classes" to the reproduction of the social order. If the ruling classes have a general interest in reproducing the social order as a whole, Beirne reasons, then they have at least some interest in ensuring that the legal system's operation *not* correlate with social class (pp. 377–379). Indeed, he argues, the state must "routinely pursue policies which are at a variance with the interests or wishes of certain fractions of capital" (p. 379). This imperative does not derive from that class's need to mystify its rule, but from a variety of internal and external constraints ranging from the benevolence of the rich to the competing legitimation and accumulation functions posed by O'Connor (1973).

LEGAL CONTENT AND LEGAL FORM

If the *content* of law cannot explain why the overall interests of the capitalist class are embodied in the law, Beirne argues, its *form* can (1979, p. 380). We are told that "the legal form itself has an innate quality which represents and perpetuates the dominant mode of production within any social formation." This innate quality stems in capitalist society from the interaction between commodity owners—"the logic of legal concepts corresponds with the logic of the social relationships of exchange" (p. 381). "Freedom" and "Equality" take on definite meaning as commodity owners freely meet in the market to exchange equivalent abstracted values. The abstraction from the concrete labor embodied in the commodities and the uses for which they were produced fetishizes them, allowing them to dominate human subjects. But the process of commodity exchange also gives birth to the "juridic subject"—as the product of labor becomes a commodity bearing exchange value, so does the human subject become the bearer of an alienable right over the commodity. As subjects exchange commodities, they exchange rights, thus appearing to become "immobile bearers" of rights:

> The concrete rights and obligations established between economic subjects are eventually dissolved into the abstract attributes of the juridic subjects. Concrete political subjects are relegated to abstract political citizens who incorporated egoism, freedom and the supreme value of the personality. The capacity to be a subject of rights is finally disassociated from the specific living personality and becomes a social attribute.

Thus, Beirne concludes, law is "the political form for establishing abstract equivalence between isolated economic subjects" (pp. 381–382).

Like Beirne, Fraser argues that the legal form is rooted in capitalist social relations; unlike Beirne, Fraser maintains that the relations that give rise to law are the relations of *production*, not *exchange*. The relations of exchange mask the deepest contradiction between labor and capital—the appropriation of labor—the mere semblance of exchange (Fraser 1976, p. 140). Thus, law ultimately is rooted in the relations between classes, not individuals:

> Pashukanis fails to incorporate within his theory of law the insight that capitalist society is not primarily characterized by relationships between individuals but is instead fundamentally a relationship between classes. . . . If as Marx claimed in the *Grundrisse*, the autonomous individual is an illusion (albeit a necessary illusion) a concept of law tied to

that concept cannot be of any significance in grasping the legal character of the relationship between classes in capitalist society (1976, p. 441).

Consequently, as the relations of production change, so does the legal form. Increasing concentration of capital gives rise to a "neocapitalist corporate state" characterized by the "symbiotic relationship" between giant corporations and the state (p. 143). In this state, analysis of legal relationships in terms of concepts drawn from contract, property, and tort law becomes irrelevant—the small-scale commodity productions upon which they are based have disappeared (pp. 142–143). The advent of overt economic planning in the neocapitalist economy, Fraser claims, requires increased cooperation and coordination, giving rise to legal forms defined by status rather than contract. The nature of the labor contract, he tells us, is most revealing: no longer is it fixed in *individual* contracts, but in *collective* ones where individual workers' rights and obligations are defined by their *status* as workers. Furthermore, rights are increasingly conceptualized as sociohistorical rather than ontological phenomena, reflecting the need of the corporate state both to organize the reproduction of the neocapitalist social order and to justify it as serving shared needs. Moreover, instead of providing a framework for the interplay of juridic individuals with varied goals, neocapitalist law defines shared goals, and seeks to provide increased access and participation in their pursuit. To promote this consensus, and thus the "free flow of the rational forces of technology, capital and labor upon which social progress and harmony depend," neocapitalist law "dissolves" "parochial particularities" and "unreasonable categories," thereby reaffirming its "impersonal," "rational," and "objective" qualities (p. 148). Furthermore, planned neocapitalism absorbs legal ideals into the political order and penetrates the realm of private law with public purpose. Thus, the new primary role of law in neocapitalism is to maintain unity within the corporate state.

The structuralists have made a substantial contribution to the current Marxist understanding of law by exploring the link between relations of production and exchange, on the one hand, and the legal form, on the other. But their accounts raise several problems. They do not define what the "legal form" is. The absence of definition is reflected in a failure to clearly distinguish between the state and the law; indeed, more often than not they mistakenly equate the two. The failure to distinguish the two hinders attempts to explain the process by which the state and legal form evolve, thereby obscuring the significance of class struggle to the evolution and interpretation of both state and law. These problems combine to dissociate law from politics, a dissociation with implications inadequately explored. Indeed, in their fervor to demonstrate the inadequacies of instrumental Marxism, the structuralists have denied potentially valuable political insights made by "instrumentalists."

Beirne and Fraser emphasize the theoretical importance of the legal form. But just what is the "legal form"? Both Beirne and Fraser contend that the legal form reflects and perpetuates the dominant mode of production. In other words, different modes of production give rise to different legal forms. What, then, are the percapitalist legal forms that correspond to precapitalist modes of production? This transhistorical notion of law is inconsistent with the locus of the legal form in commodity exchange, itself the product of the capitalist mode of production. If bourgeois law stems from commodity exchange, from what does prebourgeois, precommodity-exchange law spring? One solution to this genetic dilemma is that adopted by Pashukanis, who contended that *all* law is bourgeois law, that the legal form itself is the product of commodity exchange relationships, rather than the form that law takes in the capitalist mode of production. But this position fails to explain pre- and postbourgeois phenomena that many would intuitively label as "law." It is difficult to agree with Fraser, for the bourgeois legal form—formally equal juridic subjects possessing and exchanging alienable rights—does not reflect the inequality and exploitation characteristic of productive relations. To the contrary, the legal form *obscures* the fundamental inequality of the relations of production. It does not follow that the relations of production directly *cause* the legal form merely because the legal form protects them. There can be little question that the legal form more closely resembles the relations of commodity exchange than those of production. Indeed, Balbus (1977) has described commodity exchange and the legal form as "homologous," remarkably similar in structure and function. Although such "homology" is insufficient to attribute causality, as Young has argued (1979, pp. 146–147), it strongly suggests a relationship. Nevertheless, this relationship requires logical and historical clarification. The lack of definition of the legal form is reflected in the simple equation of law with state.

LAW AND THE CAPITALIST STATE

"Structuralists" sidestep the issue of the relationship between law and the capitalist state, freely moving from discussion of one to discussion of the other. This is unfortunate, for they point the way to possible statements of the relation. In his critique of "instrumental marxist accounts of law and crime," Beirne (1979) cites three works as examples of instrumental Marxism—Kolko (1962), Domhoff (1970), and Miliband (1969). None of these works focuses on *law*; rather, each examines the capitalist *state*. Nevertheless, they are cited as examples of how "the state *and the legal system* are seen as instruments which can be manipulated" by the ruling classes (emphasis added). In his account of structural Marxism, he again focuses on the state—"*the state*, must therefore routinely pursue policies which are at a variance with the interests of certain fractions of capital" (p. 379, emphasis added). Without resolving the relationship, he proceeds to a discussion of the relationship between commodity exchange and the legal form. The closest he comes to a statement of the relationship is that state policies are "implemented through the medium of the legal form" (p. 380), and that this somehow circumscribes the content of legal norms (p. 382).

Fraser (1976), too, equates law and state. As the role of the state changes as capitalism moves from competitive capitalism to "neocapitalism," law moves from the embodiment of individual rights to the embodiment of corporatist status. Just as Fraser poses direct complementarity between capitalist development and state function, he poses a direct correspondence between state function and legal form. In doing so he commits the very crime of which he accuses radical lawyers, Poulantzas, and Pashukanis—abstraction from relationships between classes. Nowhere is this more evident than in his analysis of the labor contract:

> [The individual] wage contract today is but a distant memory for most workers in the advanced capitalist world. The wages of organized workers are no longer set by the confrontation between individual workers and employers in the labor market. Wages now represent the outcome of a complex interplay of forces in the contest of the bureaucratic process of collective bargaining or arbitration which seeks to exclude workers from all but the most passive forms of participation. Individual workers typically have no standing to negotiate a wage contract on their own behalf; instead they are represented collectively or by a legally certified bargaining agent. Increasingly, the individual worker only gains access to a whole range of rights and powers through voluntary contractual relationships with other private persons through his membership in an officially recognized corporate group. Status, the set of rights and duties attendant upon membership in a particular group, rather than contract has become the paradigmatic legal relationship of the corporate state (Fraser 1976, p. 145).

Fraser is correct in attributing importance to the role played by the evolution of capitalist production and the capitalist state in this development in the legal form. He may even be right that there is an evolution in the legal form. But he is dead wrong in denying the primary importance of political and economic struggle in the demise of the individual wage contract. One does not have to be overly familiar with the development of labor law in the United States to see that the corporatist form of the relationship does not owe to the inexorable logic of capitalist development, but to the bitter struggles of the American working class to collectively organize for greater bargaining power in the marketplace. If the evolution of capitalist development has had a role in ushering in corporatist form of law, it is not through the inexorability of its developmental logic, but through the profits and power it brought monopoly capitalists, rendering collective bargaining more politically acceptable and economically affordable.

Beyond this, the mere labeling of "neocapitalist" law as "corporatist" without reference to the class struggle and to legal content is dangerously misleading, as it mystifies both the process by which the legal form evolves and the relationship between legal consent and legal form. The "law" of Nazi Germany in many ways reached the pinnacle of corporatist development. The Nazis, Neumann tells us, provided "a chorus chanting that labor is no commodity; labor is honor; the relationship between employer and employee is a community relation" (1944, p. 420). In criminal law, culpability for one's acts was replaced for culpability for one's will, only to be placed ultimately in one's personality—one need only be a thief "in essence" to be convicted of theft. One either *was* a thief or one *wasn't* (Neumann 1944, p. 453). Yet this corporatism is a far cry from that Fraser claims to have evolved in the West, where respect for due process remains part of the legal landscape. The critical difference is the process of class struggle that culminated in the supposed development of legal corporatism. In the United States, the demise of the individual labor contract was a concrete victory for the working class, and its endurance owes at least in part to the economic and political strength of that class; in Nazi Germany, the rise of corporatist legal forms signaled the defeat and impotence of the German working class. Rather than representing the political and economic strength of the German working class, "the community and leadership theories in labor relations use[d] a medieval terminology to conceal the complete surrender of the rights of workers by the destruction of the rationality of the individual labor contract" (Neuman, 1944, p. 422). In other words, although the legal form of Nazi Germany and the "neo-capitalist" West might be described as "corporatist," the differing paths by which corporatism evolved are reflected in wide divergences in legal content and legal practice, divergences important not only theoretically, but practically to those aiming to transform society. By failing to examine the evolution of law within the context of class struggle, one object of which was the nature of the labor contract, Fraser has produced an ahistorical and distorted image—distorted in its explanation of corporatism and in its simple equation of law with state and economy. Moreover, the comparison of corporate legal forms in different social formations demonstrates the folly of divorcing the analysis of legal form from that of legal content.

Rather than this simple equation, I want to suggest that the bourgeois legal form and the evolution of the capitalist state are in contradiction, even though legal *content,* modes of judicial reasoning, and the structure of the judicial apparatus have evolved in the directions Fraser suggests. This contradiction is obscured by the simple equation of state and law. The courts are a state apparatus, and as such are faced with the structural and political demands and constraints placed upon the state—they must repress and legitimate, they must facilitate accumulation. Yet, at the same time, courts are charged with the application of the bourgeois legal form, a function not necessarily consistent with other state functions. This charge arises from three sources: a broad ideological commitment to "the rule of law," the professional socialization of a particular strata, lawyers, as the bearers of this ideology, and the historical role of law in regulating the exercise of state power over private individuals (and capitals), thereby organizing the "power game" among both dominant and dominated classes (Poulantzas 1974, Tushnet 1978, Grau 1976).

For the state, this contradiction poses the problem that the judicial apparatus will limit it in the performance of its functions, a problem faced by the U.S. Congress in its initial attempts to promote accumulation through the "regulation" of interstate commerce, and again by Roosevelt in his attempts to deal with the economic stagnation of the 1930s. For the judges who staff the judicial apparatus, the divergence between legal form and state function poses a dilemma, too. To what extent will they consider "policy" in the determination of cases when to do so would fly in the face of formal legalism? To what extent will they adopt systemically dysfunctional policies in the name of formalism? And what are they to do when political forces demand different results than the legal form will allow?

At the most general level, this contradiction is one between the transformation of state role and class struggle on one hand—both of which require the state to be flexible in the formulation of policy and exercise of power—and the rigidity of the bourgeois legal form on the other. The contradiction between state function and legal form is perhaps best illustrated with a familiar example from the criminal law. If one function of the capitalist state is to repress the surplus population's individualized responses to deprivation, that is, crime (Jancovic 1978, Quinney 1979), then the application of the bourgeois legal form to free otherwise legally guilty parties from prosecution directly contradicts that function. It is insufficient to dismiss this phenomenon as a necessary legitimation of the legal system, though, empirically, it may be this to some people. It is just as true that this contradiction delegitimizes the system in the eyes of others. In either event, the legal form, embodied in the legal protections afforded defendants, contradicts a specific and significant state function—repression. And the periodic "resolutions" of this contradiction vary: not only are guilty parties released because their legal rights have been violated, but guilty and innocent parties alike have been repressed regardless of their rights. These particular resolutions depend far less on the inexorable logic of capitalist development than on particular conjunctures of political and ideological forces. Some prosecutors and judges are more committed to defendants' assertions of rights than others; some administrations appoint "lenient" judges more than others. Minority movements have pushed the state to greater respect for these rights through the development and pursuit of strategies to enforce them (Handler 1978, Scheingold 1974).

This is not to say that predominantly legalistic strategies successfully attained the substantive goals sought by these movements, or to downplay the role legal strategies contributed to downfall or disorganization of movement that relied on them. Nor is it to say that these rights are respected in all or even most cases, or that even when they are that their exercise is always "tangible" rather than "symbolic." But regardless of the effect of legalistic strategies on social movements that utilize them, one historical consequence of legalistic strategies in the United States has been the greater respect demonstrated for legal rights than might have been the case. In turn, even though the disorganization of social movements and dominated classes serves important state functions, the legal rights the movements forged have in numerous circumstances impeded the state's operation, particularly when political resources were mobilized to assert them.

Many efforts to expand the state's economic role in the early twentieth century were frustrated by the legal assertions of adversely affected groups. In *U.S. v. E. C. Knight Co.*, 156 U.S. 1 (1895), for example, the American Sugar Refining Company, which had acquired stock that enabled it to control all but one of the sugar refineries in the country, defeated the attempt of the United States to prohibit the acquisition under the newly adopted Sherman Antitrust Act. The court reasoned that production and distribution were two distinct operations, the latter subject to national regulation under the Commerce Clause and the former not, so long as it was conducted in one state. "[I]t does not follow that an attempt to monopolize ... manufacture was an attempt ... to monopolize commerce, even though ... the instrumentality of commerce was necessarily invoked." At one level, the Court was making a definite political allocation, giving to particular interests what Congress, reflecting the political accommodations of a wider set of interests, had taken away. But beyond the directly political consequences of the decision were the dire implications it held for the state in its efforts to "rationalize" the economy in the general interest of the capitalist class (Kolko, 1962).

Amidst the severe economic crisis of the 1930s, courts struck down major state programs designed to address sharp drops in income, production, and employment. The Petroleum Code of National Industrial Recovery Act was invalidated as an unconstitutional delegation of legislative authority to the executive [*Panama Refining Co. v. Ryan*, 293 U.S. 388 (1935)]. Presidential codes defining unfair trade practices, minimum wages and prices, maximum working hours, and collective bargaining rights were struck down as unconstitutional delegations, and because they were said to affect intra- rather than interstate commerce [*Schechter Poultry v. U.S.*, 295 U.S. 495 (1935)]. The Bituminous Coal Conservation Act of 1935 called for producers to pay a 15 percent tax on the disposal of coal at the mine, or to accept a code fixing minimum price and establishing the rights to organize and collectively bargain in exchange for 90 percent reduction of the tax. This act, too, was held unconstitutional because it sought to regulate production, not commerce, and production was a "local" activity [*Carter v. Carter Coal Co.*, 298 U.S. 238 (1936)].

The legal explosion of the postwar years further illustrates the growing magnitude of the contradiction between state and law. Since 1940, the capitalist state's accumulation and legitimation functions have expanded dramatically, encompassing a dramatic growth in state allocations and production (Offe 1974, O'Connor 1973). The expansion of state role required the expansion of

the state apparatus as well as the development of allocative and productive criteria to replace those previously set by the market (Offe 1973). State expenditures grew in two areas corresponding to its legitimation and accumulation functions: the monopoly sector was directly and indirectly subsidized; and the surplus population was provided a certain level of subsistence (O'Connor 1973). Lacking a priori criteria for these allocations, the state required maximum discretion so as to perform its accumulation and legitimation functions (Offe 1974). To paraphrase Davis, the lifeblood of the administrative process is informal discretionary action (Davis 1972, 1969). This discretion implied substantive, rather than procedural ends, and particularistic rather than general applications (see, Neumann 1957, pp. 22–68).

The state's need for discretion contradicts formal legalism, with its values of generality, doctrinal consistency, and procedural due process. Affected groups challenged the spread of administrative discretion by demanding the extension of due process protections. Both the recipients of the state's subsistence payments and the subjects of state economic regulation pressed legal claims that property had been taken from them without the due process of law [Reich 1965, pp. 742–796; *Goldberg v. Kelly*, 397 U.S. 254 (1970)]; that delegations of authority to administrative agencies were unlawful [*Schechter v. U.S. supra; Panama Refining Co. v. Ryan, supra; U.S. v. Southwestern Cable Co.* 392 U.S. 157 (1968)]; and that they had a right to participate in administrative agencies' rulemaking processes [*Environmental Defense Fund v. Ruckelshaus*, 439 F. 2d 584 (D.C. Cir. 1971)]. In response to these demands, due process protections were incorporated into the administrative process. The Administrative Procedure Act, first adopted in 1946, required agencies to: publish procedural and substantive rules [§552 (a)(1)]; provide notice of pending rulemaking [§553 (b)]; allow interested parties to participate in rulemaking [§553 (c)]; adjudicate decisions on the basis of a record after an opportunity for hearing [§554 (e)]; and allow persons compelled to appear before an agency the right to counsel [§555 (b)]. Even more significant is the right to judicial review afforded persons suffering legal wrong because of (final) agency action (§§701 et seq.). Agency decisions found to be arbitrary or capricious, contrary to constitutional or statutory rights, in excess of authority delegated to the agency, attained without observance of procedure required by law, unsupported by substantial evidence in the record, or unwarranted by the facts are to be set aside by the courts (§706). Furthermore, standing to challenge agencies' actions, while not yet extended to trees [*Sierra Club v. Morton* 405 U.S. 727 (1972), Justice Douglas dissenting], has significantly expanded [*Flast v. Cohen,* 392 U.S. 83 (1968); *Association of Data Processing Services Organizations v. Camp,* 397 U.S. 150 (1920); *Barlow v. Collins,* 397 U.S. 159 (1970)]. Nevertheless, in matters of national security, standing to challenge agency actions has remained severely limited [*U.S. v. Richardson,* 418 U.S. 166 (1974); *Schlesinger v. Reservists Committee to Stop the War,* 418 U.S. (1974)]. In summary, the "legalization" of administration fetters the state by allowing particular interests an opportunity to check state action. Far from "dissolving" the "parochial particularities" of neocapitalism as Fraser maintains, the bourgeois legal form permits them to hamper the capitalist state.

If courts have applied law so as to hamper repression, legitimation, or accumulation, they also have promoted and facilitated the performance of state functions *despite* legal rights. There is, for example, ample evidence that the surplus population is selectively repressed by the legal apparatus. "Crime" is defined in terms reflecting the distribution of social power (Taylor, Walton, and Young 1975; Young 1975, pp. 66–69; Reiman 1979, pp. 44–87; cf. Becker 1963). Even among the acts and omissions that are labeled "crimes," the criminal justice system systematically discriminates against lower classes. Poorer people are more likely to get arrested, and if arrested, charged (Reiman 1979, pp. 100–110; Erickson 1973, pp. 41–52). Once arrested and charged, they are more likely to be convicted (Chiricos, Jackson, and Waldo 1972; Blumberg 1967, p. 33; Reiman 1979, pp. 110–114). Finally, if convicted, they are more likely to receive harsher sentences (Chambliss and Seidman 1971, p. 475; Jancovic 1978; Thornberry 1973; Grau 1980; Nagel 1967; cf. Hagan 1974; Pope 1979).

Indeed, the "legalization" of administration has been far from complete. Although the legal form impeded the state's transformation in particular circumstances, the legal apparatus has at the same time grown more integrated within the state apparatus, and legal content has been molded to facilitate state transformation.

Throughout the twentieth century, court reformers and legal elites have attempted to rationalize the judicial apparatus. By promoting "scientific management," more "businesslike" procedures, centralized budgeting and management, judicial control of judicial administration, and merit-selection of judges, legal elites sought to establish hegemony over the judicial apparatus vis-à-vis legislature, ethnic political machines, and nonelite lawyers (Wheeler and Whitcomb 1977; Halliday 1979; see also Auerbach 1976). By the 1960s and 1970s, new technologies and professional managers were diffused throughout the apparatus, thrust there by a massive infusion of state resources through the Law Enforcement Assistance Administration (Heydebrand 1979). The major goals of this movement were to expedite the *processing* of cases, and to *systematize* a hitherto decentralized judicial system (Harrington 1980). From the viewpoint of the state, the systemization of the judicial apparatus promised a more "efficient" performance of courts' functions, primarily their disposition of criminal cases—or in Quinney's terms, repression of the dominated classes (Quinney 1977, pp. 6–13, 43–52).

American courts have also consistently promoted accumulation. In the nineteenth century, the law protected and promoted the "release of creative energy" and "mobilized the resources of the community," thereby encouraging "a steeply rising curve of material productivity" (Hurst

1956, pp. 6, 7). The twentieth century saw the proliferation of substantive law effecting, defining, and regulating the geometrically progressing interpenetration of state and economy. And although significant due process protections have been extended to administration, most administration proceeds along informal channels (Davis 1972, pp. 88–91; Davis 1969, pp. 1–26). At the same time, legal thought has grown more purposive and instrumental, becoming less concerned with the uniform application of general rules and more concerned with the interpretation of rules in light of policies they supposedly embody (Unger 1976, pp. 193–202; Klare 1977). The infusion of "realistic" considerations in judicial decisions has enabled the appellate courts to address the evolving socioeconomic conditions and relationships that correspond to neocapitalism.

Nevertheless, these legal developments have been ambiguous ones. Despite repeated efforts to "reform" the courts, the rationalization of American courts is far from complete (Berkson et al. 1978). Despite greater judicial sensitivity to the policy goals embodied in legal standards and to the social consequences of judicial decisions, formalism has not given way to a coherent realism, but to a hybrid "social conceptualism." This hybrid jurisprudence is only relatively more responsive to the requirements of contemporary social arrangements, because it has attempted to retail all of the contradictions and mystifications of formalism (Klare 1977). In this respect, the law's utility as an overtly political instrument is limited by the ideological functions formalism plays. Despite the expansion of law's authoritative economic role, market-oriented goals remain important in the state's allocation of resources (Hurst 1977, pp. 267–268). In other words, even though the halcyon days of perfect competition and the dominance of the market are irretrievably lost, law continues to embody values central to the market, and does so in the allocation of resources from the state to private parties.

This is of little surprise because the legal form itself is homologous to market relations. Not only does the substance of law embody bygone mar-

ket values, but the legal form itself embodies them. Indeed, it is precisely this contradiction that enables particular interests to frustrate the state from achieving necessary transformations and from performing necessary functions. This contradiction poses a crisis for bourgeois legality. In the long run, capitalist society could not be reproduced if particular interests could permanently prohibit the state from performing its functions or making necessary transformations. In the short run, the state's legitimacy to the various factions and fractions of the dominant class depends on the availability of legal recourse when they feel their particular interests threatened. Internal cohesion among the dominant groups is to an important extent predicated upon the existence of a relatively neutral forum in which each can protect itself from the others. The legal protection of the courts is the final protection when other, more overtly political forums have failed. Yet the presence of this forum becomes increasingly risky—not only can dominant groups utilize it to frustrate the collective interests of the dominant classes, but dominated groups can attempt to use it this way, too. Confronted with such use by dominated groups, a perplexing dilemma is posed. In the interests of legitimacy, the use can be tolerated, and, it is hoped, subverted or diffused (the case Klare describes regarding the Wagner Act). The risk in this case is the cost of concession. Or, if such use cannot be tolerated, the mask of neutrality must be lowered, as it was in Salvadore Allende's case. The risk in this case is that the confrontation will be lost, or that, even if it is won, the loss of legitimacy in the eyes of dominated classes is too costly to sustain.

LAW AND POLITICS

In a state without law, the particular interests in the cases cited above probably would have failed. None of them controlled the state apparatus. None of them had sufficient political resources to prevail in legislatures. None of the substantive results in these cases, or in those where the state prevailed, was predetermined by legal doctrine, state function, or intra- or inter-class politics. Any of the cases could have been decided differently with roughly equal legal justification, or even a change in the distribution of political forces. Yet in each case, the legal form was invoked to check specific manifestations of state power. In each case a particular aggrieved interest sought through law what it could not get directly through politics. In each case the court made a definite political allocation, though most often in the guise of adherence to a priori legal standard. But, for the purposes of this argument, the critical point is that the courts blocked the state from actions that would have expanded its direct participation in the economy. The New Deal era cases blocked the state at a particularly critical conjuncture—the deepest and most serious depression ever faced by capitalism. Although none of the invalidated legislation was in itself necessary to maintain or promote accumulation, together they reflect a transformation in the state's role in modern capitalism.

On the basis of this evidence, it is clear that bourgeois law is a form of political expression, though a political expression articulated in neutral, nonpolitical terms that mask the intrinsic inequalities of capitalist social relations. As a form of political expression within capitalist society, dominated classes also have pursued their political objectives through law. What, then, are the limits of bourgeois law as a form of political expression? Beirne and Fraser both have suggested that the legal form limits the utility of law as an object of class struggle. According to Beirne:

> . . . the range in variation in the context of particular legal norms is circumscribed by the *form* of law and the form of law is contingent on the dominant mode of production in any social formation. The *content* of legal norms may vary only within these determinate limits. Under the capitalist mode of production, for example, there can be no law which abolishes rent, interest, or industrial profit, for that would be to abolish capital itself. But the level of surplus value—or already produced surplus value in the case of rent—extracted by capital will vary according to state policies which are themselves

partly conditioned by the relative strengths and weaknesses in the class struggle (1979, p. 382).

In a similar vein, Fraser argues that radical lawyers should help express "the internal needs of the real individual" partly within the legal process; nevertheless, he admits that "only certain needs can receive expression within the legal process" (1976, p. 154).

Although it is intuitively compelling that the legal form circumscribes the content of legal norms, it is *not* so clear that law cannot be a means of abolishing rent, interest, or industrial profit. Logically, the abolition of these categories and relationships necessarily implies the demise of the capitalist mode of production. Hence, wherever law (or anything else) abolished them, there would be no capitalist mode of production; this formulation of the limits that form places on substance is thereby tautological. But we are dealing with *social*, not logical relationships. Why cannot laws to abolish profit be part of a larger process of social transformation, a transformation where the application of anticapitalist law is backed up by the social power of dominated classes? The critical question is not the logical limitation imposed by the legal form, but the relative strength of the classes directing their power through legal and extralegal means.

Two aspects of the bourgeois legal form effectively limit its political utility to dominated classes. First, the bourgeois legal form is inherently individualized. Individual persons are the bearers and asserters of rights. This individualism disorganizes dominated classes by denying the expression of collective interests. Individualized treatment of each "case" hampers the development of a consciousness that reorganizes the systematic causes of deprivation and domination. Courts recognize narrowly defined legal issues that may bear little resemblence to underlying social issues. Cases are tried only between legal parties with defined legal interests that conflict over narrowly drawn legal issues. Collective needs are denied. The specificity of the rights and the narrowness of the legal issues combine to preclude the introduction of broader, though relevant, social questions. This restriction effectively depoliticizes the case. For example, an unemployed black accused of theft is tried on whether or not he took the property of another; he cannot defend himself by demonstrating the structural relationships between his act, racism, and class, nor by arguing that property is theft.

This individualism continues even in the areas Fraser has identified as expressing a new, corporatist legal form, such as welfare. Although certain groups have been attributed a particular status, the allocations and refusals to allocate are made on an individual basis (Lamb 1975; see also Balbus 1973). In fact, such arrangements have increased the amount of individual surveillance as well as the power exercised by the state over individual welfare recipients (Reich 1964).

The legal form further disorganizes dominated classes by operationally defining concepts such as "freedom" and "equality," hampering critical reflection and the development of oppositional consciousness. Nouns such as "freedom," "right," "equality," "democracy," and "justice" are identified with attributes specific to the capitalist social formation: free enterprise, property, due process, elections. To quote Marcuse (1964, p. 88), "the ritualized concept is made immune against contradiction." "Justice" is equated with the formality of a legal proceeding. And with this functional definition of justice, the legal system continually verifies itself as just by adhering to its formal processes. Moreover, by periodically disallowing state actions, the law verifies itself as a protector against arbitrary state power. Thus by its action, as well as by its pretension, the bourgeois legal form appears to be neutral, even benevolent in its protection of individual from the arbitrary power of the state. Yet even as it protects individuals it sets them up to be preyed upon.

This apparent neutrality, reinforced by legal practice, in turn encourages the law to be viewed and pursued as a reified political object—social movements equate changing the law with transforming society. Collective needs asserted by these movements get articulated in terms of individual rights; political decisions become delegated to a caste of legal professionals. Laws perhaps are changed, and if changed, challenged. Interpreted by the courts, the changed laws acquire meanings other than those held by those who sought the changes. Turned solely to legal ends, the social movement is diffused (Klare 1977).

Do the politically disorganizing effects of the bourgeois legal form preclude its use by social movements seeking to transform society, or are they merely significant impediments to its use? Certainly several of the impediments it imposes amount to political choices or ideological mystifications whose effects could be mitigated by different political choices and an alternate ideology. The law does not have to be seen as neutral to be used to secure political ends. Nor does law have to be held as the ultimate object of struggle. Suppose, for example, that the American workers viewed the Wagner Act not as the end product of their struggles, but as an intermediate product, a further stepping stone to further struggle and increased demands. Suppose further that they insisted on its enforcement on their terms, rather than on the terms the courts ultimately imposed, and that they insisted extralegally as well as legally. It is conceivable the Wagner Act would not have been deradicalized as Klare has so persuasively argued it has.

Even if the bourgeois legal form imposes limits on the variation in the content of legal norms, the variation within those limits may be considered a worthy political object. Accepting for the moment Beirne's assertion that bourgeois law cannot abolish profit, it certainly can limit the rate of profit. Limiting the rate of surplus value and of absolute surplus value certainly are two goals of vital importance to the working class. Nor is it clear that the legal form is a fixed constraint with political use of law, even though it exhibits less malleability than legal content. The structuralists suggest the nature of the legal form is contingent upon the dominant mode of production. What they have failed to address in this context is precisely how transformation in legal form came to pass, and instead have relied on a reductionist argument—as the mode of production goes, so goes the legal form. But the nature of the legal form is contingent upon the level and relative strengths of class struggle as well. The corporatist nature of the labor contract attained by American workers was, as Fraser argues, a transformation in legal form, though it was not as far ranging as he indicates, nor did it occur for the reasons he suggests. Similarly, the transformation of the legal form in Nazi Germany also was a product of class struggle, but one with an entirely different outcome because of the vastly different distribution of power among classes.

CONCLUSION

Structuralist accounts of law have stressed that the bourgeois legal form circumscribes variation in legal content, thereby limiting the role law might play in effecting social change. They argue that law serves the interests of the ruling class, not because its substance embodies their interests, but because its form does. Indeed, it does. But in making this important point, they reduce the legal form to a direct reflection of ruling class interests, a reduction embodied in the direct correspondence they draw between legal form and productive relations or between law and state.

This reductionist theory obscures the contradictory nature of bourgeois law. It embodies ruling class interests, yet can frustrate them. This is most clear when the legal form has been involved to check the state from acting in the general interests of capital. If law was synonymous with state, this would not happen. Yet legal institutions are part of the state, and are faced with the necessities of repressing, legitimating, and promoting accumulation. Legal outcomes reflect the contradictions between state function and legal form. Law serves state functions; yet it frustrates them. The rampant rise of administration has eroded the rule of law, yet administration has become legalized. The former process reflects the structural needs of capitalist reproduction, the lat-

ter, a safeguard to protect particular capitalists' interests from their general interests, a protection against politics, yet a protection itself political.

As production is politicized, the overtly political role of law is thrown into crisis. As actions in the general interest (administration) become more frequent and vital, the perceived need for protection (bourgeois legalism) grows. The politicization of production and, consequently, of law calls for a reexamination of the much defiled "instrumentalists." Although their accounts perhaps are inadequate as a theory of law or the state, they deserve an accounting within such theories. What needs to be recognized is that the object of the instrumentalists' inquiry is the politics of the capitalist state, and that this inquiry is aimed at a different level of abstraction than that of the structuralists. Moreover, it must be realized that capitalist states do not perform functions in the same way heavenly bodies circle the stars. Their performance is the result of political activity carried out by human beings within certain political and ideological forms. If it is true that the capitalist state and the law are structurally limited, it is just as true that within those limits, the content of policies and actions can vary, and that the variation can be theoretically and politically significant. Even the structural limits, such as the legal form, are not as rigidly fixed as "structuralists" suppose. The work of the "instrumentalists" can be singularly important in understanding the ways in which content, and even form, are likely to vary. So long as Marxist practice holds a place for the political use of legality, Marxist theory of the state should encompass the political analysis undertaken by the "instrumentalists," as well as an understanding of its limitations.

REFERENCES

Auerbach, Gerald (1976). *Unequal Justice*. New York: Oxford.

Balbus, Isaac (1973). *The Dialectics of Legal Repression*. New York: Russell Sage.

Balbus, Isaac (1977). "Commodity Form and Legal

Form: An Essay on the 'Relative Autonomy' of the Law," 11 *Law and Soc. Rev.* 571.

Becker, Howard (1963). *Outsiders: Studies in the Sociology of Deviance*. New York: Free Press.

Beirne, Piers (1979). "Empiricism and the Critique of Marxism on Law and Crime," 26 *Social Problems* 374.

Berkson, Larry et al. (1976). *Court Unification: History, Politics, and Implementation*. Washington, D.C.: NILECJ.

Blumberg, Abraham (1967). *Criminal Justice*. New York: New Viewpoints.

Chambliss, William, and Robert Seidman (1971). *Law, Order, and Power*. Reading, Mass.: Addison-Wesley.

Chiricos, Jackson, and Waldo (1972). "Inequality and the Imposition of a Criminal Label," 19 *Social Problems* 553.

Davis, Kenneth Culp (1969). *Discretionary Justice*. Baton Rouge: LSU Press.

Davis, K. C. (1972). *Administrative Law Text*. Minneapolis: West.

Domhoff, G. William (1970). *The Higher Cricles*. New York: Random House.

Erickson, Maynard (1973). "Group Violation, Socioeconomic States and Official Delinquency," 52 *Social Forces* 41.

Fraser, Andrew (1976). "Legal Theory and Legal Practice," 44 *Arena* 123.

Genovese, Eugene (1976). *Roll Jordan Roll*. New York: Vintage.

Gold, David, Clarence Lo, and Erik Wright (1975). "Recent Developments in Marxist Theories of the Capitalist State," 11 *Monthly Review* 29.

Grau, Charles W. (1976). "A Multifunctional Marxist Analysis of Law," unpublished manuscript.

Grau, Charles W. (1980). "Working the Damned, the Dumb, and the Destitute: The Politics of Community Service Restitution," paper presented to the Law and Society Association, Madison, June 1980.

Handler, Joel (1978). *Social Movements and the Legal System*. New York: Academic Press.

Hagan, John (1974). "Extra-legal Attributes and Criminal Sentencing: An Assessment of Sociological Viewpoint," 8 *Law and Society Review* 357.

Halliday, Terrence (1979). "Parameters of Professional Influence: Policies and Politics of the Chicago Bar Association, 1945–79," Ph.D. Dissertation.

Harrington, Christine (1980). "Historical Analysis of Delegalization Reform Movements," unpublished manuscript.

Heydebrand, Wolf (1979). "The Technocratic Administration of Justice," in S. Spitzer (Ed.), *Research in Law and Sociology*, Vol. 2 Greenwich, Conn.: JAI Press.

Holloway, John, and Sol Picciotto (1977). "Capital, Crisis and the State," 2 *Capital and Class* 76.

Hurst, Willard (1956). *Law and the Condition of Freedom in Nineteenth Century America*. Madison: University of Wisconsin Press.

Hurst, J. Willard (1977). *Law and Social Order in the United States*. Ithaca: Cornell University Press.

Klare, Karl (1978). "Judicial Deradicalization of the Wagner Act and the Origins of Modern Legal Consciousness 1937–41," 62 *Minnesota L. Rev.* 265.

Kolko, Gabriel (1962). *Wealth and Power in America*. New York: Praeger.

Lamb, Geoffrey (1975). "Marxism, Access and the State," 6 *Development and Change* 119.

Marcuse, Herbert (1964). *One Dimensional Man*. Boston: Beacon.

Miliband, Ralph (1969). *The State in Capitalist Society*. New York: Basic Books.

Nagel, Stuart (1967). "Disparities in Criminal Procedure," 14 *U.C.L.A. L. Rev.* 1272.

Neumann, Franz (1944). *Behemoth*. New York: Harper and Row.

Neumann, Franz (1957). *The Democratic and the Authoritarian State*. New York: Free Press.

O'Connor, James (1973). *The Fiscal Crisis of the State*. New York: St. Martin's Press.

Offe, Claus (1975). "The Theory of the Capitalist State and the Problem of Policy Formation, in Leon Lindberg (Ed.), *Stress and Contradiction in Modern Capitalism*. Lexington: D.C. Heath.

Offe, Claus (1973). "The Abolition of Market Control and the Problem of Legitimacy," 1 and 2 *Kapitalistate*.

Pashukanis, E. B. (1924). *The General Theory of Law and Marxism*.

Pope, Carl (1979). "Race and Crime Revisited," 25 *Crime and Delinquency* 347.

Poulantzas, Nicos (1974). *Fascism and Dictatorship*. London: New Left Books.

Quinney, Richard (1977). *Class, State and Crime*. New York: Longman.

Reich, Charles (1964). "The New Property," 73 *Yale Law Journal* 733.

Reich, Charles (1965). "Individual Rights and Social Welfare: The Emerging Legal Issues," 75 *Yale Law Journal* 1245.

Reiman, Jeffrey (1979). *The Rich Get Richer and the Poor Get Prison*. New York: Wiley.

Scheingold, Stuart (1974). *The Politics of Rights: Lawyers, Public Policy, and Political Change*. New Haven: Yale University Press.

Taylor, Ian, Paul Walton, and Jock Young (1975). "Critical Criminology in Britain: Review and Propects," in Young et al. infra.

Thornberry, Terrence (1973). "Race, Socioeconomic Status and Sentencing in the Juvenile Justice System," 64 *J. Cr. L. and Crim.* 80.

Tushnet, Mark (1978). "A Marxist Analysis of American Law," 1 *Marxist Perspectives* 96.

Unger, Roberto (1976). *Law in Modern Society*. New York: Free Press.

Wheeler and Whitcomb (1977). *Judicial Administration: Readings and Text*. Englewood Cliffs, N.J.: Prentice-Hall.

Young, Gary (1979). "Marx on Bourgeois Law," in S. Spitzer (Ed.), 2 *Research in Law and Sociology* 133. Greenwich: JAI Press.

Young, Jock et al. (1975). *Critical Criminology*. Boston: Routledge and Kegan Paul.

Young, Jock (1975). "Working Class Criminology," in Young et al. *supra*.

LEGITIMIZING RACIAL DISCRIMINATION THROUGH ANTIDISCRIMINATION LAW: A CRITICAL REVIEW OF SUPREME COURT DOCTRINE

ALAN DAVID FREEMAN

As surely as the law has outlawed racial discrimination, it has affirmed that Black Americans can be without jobs, have their children in all-black, poorly funded schools, have no opportunities for decent housing, and have very little political power, without any violation of antidiscrimination law.[1] The purpose of the discussion is descriptive and explanatory, *not* prescriptive or normative. The Article is not a doctrinal brief; no attempt will be made to reconcile new arguments with existing case law or find instances for optimism in the interstices of depressing Supreme Court opinions. Nor will there be any discussion of issues internal to the legal system, such as the apportionment of tasks between courts and legislatures, federal and state courts, or higher and lower courts.[2] Those issues are simply irrelevant to an author seeking to observe and report on evolution of legal doctrine rather than to participate in its manipulation.

While all of the Supreme Court opinions to be discussed are, of course, technical assertions of legal doctrine, and can be analyzed as such, they are also an evolving statement of acceptable public morality. In their latter role, the opinions not only reflect dominant societal moral positions, but also serve as part of the process of forming or crystallizing such positions. Given a view that law serves largely to legitimize the existing social structure and, especially, class relationships within that structure, the ultimate constraints are outside the legal system. But if law is to serve its

---

[1] For the purpose of this Article, antidiscrimination law is federal constitutional and statutory law, as expounded or interpreted by the United States Supreme Court, defining the conduct to be treated as racial discrimination. I regard this body of law as the best evidence of the current prevailing or official national moral consensus on the subject of racial discrimination. With respect to the inclusion of both constitutional and statutory law, one would have supposed, until recently, that federal statutes shared with the Constitution the same substantive notion of racial discrimination, with the role of the statutes being to add those violators otherwise immune from constitutional coverage because of the state-action doctrine. That there has been a substantive divergence is part of the story to be told in this Article.

I should also add that the almost exclusive emphasis of this Article is on racial discrimination, with the principal model that of black-white relations in the United States. To the extent that other forms of discrimination overlap with the model, this Article speaks to them.

Source: From *Minnesota Law Review,* Vol. 62, No. 6, pp. 1049–1119, copyright by Alan David Freeman. Reprinted by permission.

[2] Such nonsubstantive issues as federalism or institutional competence are, for me, never neutral and never severed from a particular substantive position or at least from a world view with heavy substantive implications. For a characterization, with respect to these issues, of the internal workings of judicial decisionmaking that roughly corresponds to my own view, see Kennedy, *"Form and Substance in Private Law Adjudication,"* 89 *Harv. L. Rev.* 1685 1760–66 (1976).

legitimation function, those ultimate constraints must yield up just enough autonomy to the legal system to make its operations credible for those whose allegiance it seeks as well as those whose self-interest it rationalizes. . . . The discussion is premised upon the lack, even within that sphere, of any objective criteria to which one might appeal to justify particular substantive decisions. Neither formal criteria nor more substantive "shared values" emerge to resolve the underlying value-conflicts in these cases. The supposedly shared values that are asserted always turn out, even when presented sincerely, to be attempts to rationalize self-interest through appeal to universal criteria. The lengthy discussion of Supreme Court opinions that follows is intended to be, among other things, a testament to the manipulability of legal doctrine.

The major emphasis, however, is on how the process of legitimation works through that manipulation of doctrine. The doctrine cannot legitimize unless it is convincing, but it cannot be convincing in the context of antidiscrimination law unless it holds out a promise of liberation. Simultaneously, the doctrine must refrain from delivering on the promise if it is to serve its function of *merely* legitimizing. And finally, the doctrine must occasionally offer at least illusions of reconciliation and resolution, lest it collapse in obvious self-contradiction.[3]

I. THE PERPETRATOR PERSPECTIVE

The concept of "racial discrimination" may be approached from the perspective of either its victim or its perpetrator. From the victim's perspective, racial discrimination describes those conditions of actual social existence as a member of a perpetual underclass. This perspective includes both the objective conditions of life—lack of jobs, lack of money, lack of housing—and the consciousness associated with those objective conditions—lack of choice and lack of human individuality in being forever perceived as a member of a group rather than as an individual. The perpetrator perspective sees racial discrimination not as conditions, but as actions, or series of actions, inflicted on the victim by the perpetrator. The focus is more on what particular perpetrators have done or are doing to some victims than it is on the overall life situation of the victim class.

The victim, or "condition,"[4] conception of racial discrimination suggests that the problem will not be solved until the conditions associated with it have been eliminated. To remedy the condition of racial discrimination would demand affirmative efforts to change the condition. The remedial dimension of the perpetrator perspective, however, is negative. The task is merely to neutralize the inappropriate conduct of the perpetrator.

In its core concept of the "violation," antidiscrimination law is hopelessly embedded in the perpetrator perspective. Its central tenet, the "antidiscrimination principle," is the prohibition of race-dependent decisions that disadvantage

---

[3]While limiting the presentation to antidiscrimination law, I am willing to speculate that the principal techniques described, especially the victim–perpetrator dichotomy and the remedy-violation relationship, are not peculiar to antidiscrimination law, but, rather, typical of other ostensible law reform efforts.

[4]I concede an irony in, but nevertheless will adhere to, my use of "victim perspective." If the real point of the victim perspective is to talk about conditions rather than practices, why talk about victims? Both are true. In the context of race, "victim" means a current member of the group that was historically victimized by actual perpetrators or a class of perpetrators. Victims are people who continue to experience life as a member of that group and continue to experience conditions that are actually or ostensibly tied to the historical experience of actual oppression or victimization, whether or not individual perpetrators, or their specific successors in interest, can be identified now. The victim perspective is intended to describe the expectations of an actual human being who is a current member of the historical victim class—expectations created by an official change of moral stance toward members of the victim group. Those expectations, I suggest, include changes in conditions.

The perpetrator perspective, on the other hand, is the stance of the legal system, or legal ideology, as a third entity subjecting all of contemporary society to its gaze. To the extent the ideology is received, that view also becomes the view of members of the victim group, nonperpetrator members of the nonvictim group, and perpetrator members of the nonvictim group.

members of minority groups, and its principal task has been to select from the maze of human behaviors those particular practices that violate the principle, outlaw the identified practices, and neutralize their specific effects. Antidiscrimination law has thus been ultimately indifferent to the condition of the victim; its demands are satisfied if it can be said that the "violation" has been remedied.

The perpetrator perspective presupposes a world composed of atomistic individuals whose actions are outside of and apart from the social fabric and without historical continuity. From this perspective, the law views racial discrimination not as a social phenomenon, but merely as the misguided conduct of particular actors. It is a world where, but for the conduct of these misguided ones, the system of equality of opportunity would work to provide a distribution of the good things in life without racial disparities and where deprivations that did correlate with race would be "deserved" by those deprived on grounds of insufficient "merit." It is a world where such things as "vested rights," "objective selection systems," and "adventitious decisions" (all of which serve to prevent victims from experiencing any change in conditions) are matters of fate, having nothing to do with the problem of racial discrimination.

Central to the perpetrator perspective are the twin notions of "fault" and "causation." Under the fault idea, the task of antidiscrimination law is to separate from the masses of society those blameworthy individuals who are violating the otherwise shared norm. The fault idea is reflected in the assertion that only "intentional" discrimination violates the antidiscrimination principle. In its pure form, intentional discrimination is conduct accompanied by a purposeful desire to produce discriminatory results. One can thus evade responsibility for ostensibly discriminatory conduct by showing that the action was taken for a good reason, or for no reason at all.

The fault concept gives rise to a complacency about one's own moral status; it creates a class of "innocents," who need not feel any personal re-

sponsibility for the conditions associated with discrimination, and who therefore feel great resentment when called upon to bear any burdens in connection with remedying violations. This resentment accounts for much of the ferocity surrounding the debate about so-called "reverse" discrimination, for being called on to bear burdens ordinarily imposed only upon the guilty involves an apparently unjustified stigmatization of those led by the fault notion to believe in their own innocence.

Operating along with fault, the causation requirement serves to distinguish from the totality of conditions that a victim perceives to be associated with discrimination those that the law will address. These dual requirements place on the victim the nearly impossible burden of isolating the particular conditions of discrimination produced by and mechanically linked to the behavior of an identified blameworthy perpetrator, regardless of whether other conditions of discrimination, caused by other perpetrators, would have to be remedied for the outcome of the case to make any difference at all. The causation principle makes it clear that some objective instances of discrimination are to be regarded as mere accidents, or "caused," if at all, by the behavior of ancestral demons whose responsibility cannot follow their successors in interest over time. The causation principle also operates to place beyond the law discriminatory conduct (action taken with a purpose to discriminate under the fault principle) that is not linked to any discernible "discriminatory effect."

The perpetrator perspective has been and still is the only formal conception of a violation in antidiscrimination law. Strict adherence to that form, however, would have made even illusory progress in the quest for racial justice impossible. The challenge for the law, therefore, was to develop, through the usual legal techniques of verbal manipulation, ways of breaking out of the formal constraints of the perpetrator perspective while maintaining ostensible adherence to the form itself. This was done by separating violation from remedy, and doing through remedy what was inappropriate in cases involving only identification of violations. But since one of the principal tenets of the perpetrator perspective is that remedy and violation must be coextensive, it was necessary to state that tenet and violate it at the same time, no mean task even for masters of verbal gamesmanship. For a while, the remedial doctrines seemingly undermined the hegemony of the perpetrator form, threatening to replace it with a victim perspective. In the end, however, form triumphed, and the perpetrator perspective, always dominant in identifying violations, was firmly reasserted in the context of remedies as well.

II. 1954–1965: THE ERA OF UNCERTAINTY, OR THE JURISPRUDENCE OF VIOLATIONS

In the first era of modern antidiscrimination law, commencing with the Supreme Court's decision in *Brown* v. *Board of Education (Brown I)*, there was little occasion to consider the limits of the perpetrator perspective. For the most part, the Court concerned itself with identifying violations rather than remedying them and was therefore able to remain within the perpetrator perspective tradition of merely declaring the illegality of specific practices. Although it was obvious that school desegregation was going to require something more than a statement of illegality, the Court in its subsequent opinion in *Brown v. Board of Education (Brown II)* chose to relegate the problem to lower courts, leaving ambiguous the scope of the remedial obligation.

The *Brown I* opinion offers no clear statement of the perpetrator perspective, however, containing within its inscrutable text a number of possible antidiscrimination principles that "explain" the result in the case. These in turn are linked to various "meanings" of the equal protection clause and to conceptions of reality even more abstract and ahistorical than the modern perpetrator perspective—meanings and conceptions that still occasionally insinuate themselves into arguments such as the debate about so-called "reverse" discrimination.

A. THE EQUAL PROTECTION CLAUSE

There are at least three different "meanings" that one can ascribe to the equal protection clause, each of which appears to explain a particular kind of controversy under that clause. The first, the "means-oriented" approach, regards the clause as nothing more than a judicial check on legislative mistakes. Under this view, the judicial role is to articulate permissible levels of overinclusion or underinclusion in legislative classifications and send back to the legislature those statutes that have exceeded the allowable tolerances. In its pure form, the principle is perfectly abstract, concerned only with questions of neatness, inasmuch as it serves to check technique rather than goal, it is utterly value-neutral. It is, therefore, a principle suited to the demands of a formalistic, positivist jurisprudence that purports to separate rule application from questions of value.

There is some question, however, whether the principle ever has been, or ever could be, applied in its pure form. On the one hand, the degree of overinclusion or underinclusion that will be tolerated necessarily varies with the subject matter of the legislation. This problem gives rise to the necessity of separating the occasions for "strict" scrutiny from those demanding only "minimal" scrutiny. Since any legislative generalization is likely to fall if subjected to strict scrutiny, the choice between these alternatives takes on a highly substantive content with the judgment involved in that choice becoming the key decision. Alternatively, the technique of means scrutiny may be employed as a cover for condemnation of an inappropriate purpose or for the creation or extension of a new substantive right.

In either event, the means-oriented technique by itself is a procedural abstraction having nothing in particular to do with racial discrimination. Its application to racial discrimination cases depends on value choices external to questions of means alone. And even where means-oriented review is employed to confirm an implicit value choice about racial discrimination, the employment of this ostensibly value-neutral technique will have the effect of representing the problem of racial discrimination, as an ahistorical abstraction removed from the actual setting that gave rise to the implicit value choice for intervention. Moreover, given its preoccupation with the validity of previously chosen means, this version of equal protection is wholly negative in outlook and therefore does not easily lend itself to remedying conditions associated with racial discrimination.

A second meaning of equal protection, which has on occasion produced affirmative remedies for conditions rather than just negative invalidation of practices, is the "fundamental right" rationale. This approach has arisen largely as a way for the Supreme Court to evade self-created limitations on judicial review while seeming to adhere to ground rules such as those offered by the famous footnote in *United States v. Carolene Products Co.*

There is no necessary relation between the fundamental right concept and racial discrimination, since the doctrine is principally concerned with the fundamentality of the abstract right involved—a concern that is ostensibly neutral with respect to the race of the claimants. In fact, however, since racial minorities bear so disproportionately the burdens of economic class in the United States, any claim for substantive distributive justice is in essence a claim on behalf of those minorities. For practical reasons alone, the rejection of those claims forms part of the history of antidiscrimination law.

The fundamental right litigation also forms part of, or at least helps one to understand, the doctrinal, as well as the practical, history of antidiscrimination law. For one thing, many of the same decisions that denied fundamental right claims also refused to characterize the problems involved as ones of actual racial discrimination. The Court accomplished that rejection by employing the narrow conception of violation associated with the perpetrator perspective. In addition, even apart from whether the cases should have been treated as racial discrimination cases, to have recognized substantive fundamental rights would have been tantamount to recogniz-

ing affirmative claims, a practice associated with the victim perspective. By rejecting such claims, the law, when directly confronted with the victim perspective, explicitly rejected it. Thus, what starts out as a victim perspective claim about the results of racial discrimination is transformed into a complaint about not racial but economic injustice, and then denied in those recast terms. The net effect is that the victim of racial discrimination must persevere until the utopian day when everyone is entitled to distributive justice.

The third meaning of equal protection is the oldest one, and the one that speaks directly to discrimination against black people in the setting of American history. This meaning may be found in the tradition that regards the overwhelming goal of the Civil War amendments to be "the freedom of the slave race, the security and firm establishment of that freedom, and the protection of the newly-made freeman and citizen from the oppressions of those who had formerly exercised unlimited dominion over him. Under this conception, the particular target of the equal protection clause is "discrimination against the negroes as a class, or on account of their race" . . .

B. BROWN V. BOARD OF EDUCATION

There are a number of different ways of looking at the *Brown* case, all of which permeate the subsequent evolution of antidiscrimination law. I shall discuss five such: the color-blind constitution theory; the equality of educational opportunity theory; the white oppression of blacks theory; the freedom of association theory; and the integrated society theory.

1. Color-Blind Constitution To explain *Brown* by invoking the slogan that the "Constitution is color-blind"[5] reflects the means-oriented view of

---

[5]The color-blind theory was first given explicit voice in 1896: "Our Constitution is color-blind, and neither knows nor tolerates classes among citizens." *Plessy* v. *Ferguson*, 163 U.S. 537, 559 (1896) (Harlan, J., dissenting); see Posner, "The DeFunis Case and The Constitutionality of Preferential Treatment of Racial Minorities," 1974 *Sup. Cr. Rev.* 1, 21–26; "Developments in the Law—Equal Protection," 82 *Harv. L. Rev.* 1065, 1088–89 (1969).

the equal protection clause. On this view, what was wrong with school segregation was that government was employing an irrational classification—race. This approach, however, does not explain why it was irrational to classify people by race if the purpose was to prevent blacks and whites from going to school together. How else could one rationally achieve segregation by race in public schools? One answer is that the purpose itself is illegitimate, that it is no business of government to seek to segregate by race in public schools. If that is the answer, however, the color-blind constitution theory is not a means-oriented approach at all, but rather one that collapses into substantive equal protection. If that is the case, however, one must consider not legislative rationality, but, as I suggested above, particular relationships between blacks and whites in the context of American history.

A ploy that avoids the quick collapse into substantive equal protection is to bootstrap the means-oriented principle into its own substantive principle. This is done by starting with the means-oriented assumption that racial classifications are almost always unrelated to any valid governmental purpose (purpose here being the wholly abstract world of possible purposes). Since such classifications are likely to be irrational, they should be treated as "suspect," and subjected to strict scrutiny," which they will survive only if found to satisfy a "compelling governmental interest." If the degree of scrutiny is so strict and the possibility of a sufficiently compelling governmental interest so remote that the rule operates as a virtual per se rule, we then seem to have a means-oriented principle that explains the *Brown* case.

The problem with this second formulation of the color-blind theory is that it still contains a substantive assumption: racial classifications are almost always unrelated to any valid governmental purpose. As an abstract matter, this is hardly intuitively obvious. One could easily envision a society where racial or other ethnic classifications are unrelated to any pattern of oppression or domination of one group by another

and, in fact, promote feelings of group identity. Thus, the initial assumption cannot be made except in the context of a particular historical situation, and the source of the assumption that underlies the color-blind theory can easily be found in American history by taking a brief glance at relationships between whites and blacks. Accordingly, the color-blind theory must originate in a notion of substantive equal protection.

Despite this fact, the color-blind theory has tended to become a reified abstraction, to gain a life of its own, and finally to turn back on its origins. Thus, a pure form of the color-blind theory would outlaw any use of racial classifications, no matter what the context, thereby providing easy answers to questions like whether a black community can refuse to participate in an integration plan or whether black students at a public university can establish their own housing units from which whites are excluded. The answers remain easy only so long as the theory remains divorced from its origins in the actuality of black-white relations. By abstracting racial discrimination into a myth-world where all problems of race or ethnicity are fungible, the color-blind theory turns around and denies concrete demands of blacks with the argument that to yield to such demands would be impossible since every other ethnic group would be entitled to make the same demand.

The color-blind theory has never become the law; the Supreme Court has in fact explicitly upheld the remedial use of racial classifications on a number of occasions. Nevertheless, the theory does share certain features with something that is part of the law—the perpetrator perspective. Among these features is the emphasis on negating specific invalid practices rather than affirmatively remedying conditions, with a consequent inability to deal with ostensibly neutral practices. In addition, the color-blind theory exerts an insistent pressure on antidiscrimination law to produce special justifications for deviations from its norm and to limit their duration to facilitate a quick return to the comfortable, abstract world of colorblindness.

2. Equality of Educational Opportunity. *Brown* can also be viewed as a case concerned with equality of educational opportunity. This approach corresponds with the fundamental right concept of equal protection. Under this view, *Brown* did not merely outlaw segregation in public schools; it also guaranteed that black children would have an affirmative right to a quality of education comparable to that received by white children. The Court in its opinion stressed the importance of education, calling it the "very foundation of good citizenship," and "a principal instrument in awakening the child to cultural values, in preparing him for later professional training, and in helping him to adjust normally to his environment." The Court added that where a state undertakes to provide public education, it "is a right which must be made available to all on equal terms."

By way of hindsight, the case stood for both more and less than a guarantee of equal educational quality. It came to stand for more insofar as its holding was quickly extended to other forms of state-imposed segregation. But it stood for a great deal less insofar as black children today have neither an affirmative right to receive an integrated education nor a right to equality of resources for their schools, which, ironically, was a litigable claim under the regime of de jure segregation. While there is no way to prove "objectively" what the opinion in *Brown* meant with respect to a right to educational equality, both a claim for equal resources and a claim for the choice of an integrated education can be supported from the text of the opinion. The Court assumed for its opinion that the black and white schools in the cases under review "have been equalized, or are being equalized, with respect to buildings, curricula, qualifications and salaries of teachers, and other 'tangible' factors." With respect to the fact of integration, the Court quoted a finding of one of the lower courts: " 'Segregation of white and colored children in public schools has a detrimental effect upon the colored children. The impact is greater when it has the sanction of the law; for the policy of separating the races is usually interpreted as denoting the inferiority of the negro group.' " To the extent the text suggests that the detrimental effect, with its attendant denotation of inferiority, would persist even in the absence of state sanction, the case may be read as addressing not the *practice* but the *fact* of racial separation.

For the Court to have recognized affirmative claims to resources or integrated classrooms would have been to adopt explicitly a victim perspective on racial discrimination. Essential to this perspective is the conferral upon the members of the formerly oppressed group a choice that is real and not merely theoretical with respect to conditions over which they had no control under the regime of oppression. Instead, under the perpetrator perspective, the Court recognizes only the right of the black children to attend schools that are not intentionally segregated by the jursidiction that runs them. This right, it is argued, is all that *Brown* stands for anyway, since all the case did was outlaw de jure segregation. And the famous "social science footnote" of *Brown* is today turned inside-out to make the question of whether integration can be compelled nothing more than a matter of empirical study of educational "outputs."

3. White Oppression of Blacks On this view, the *Brown* case was a straightforward declaration that segregation was unlawful because it was an instance of majoritarian oppression of black people, a mechanism for maintaining blacks as a perpetual underclass. This approach, which begins and ends with historical fact instead of trying to find a neutral abstraction from which one can deduce the invalidity of segregation, was eloquently stated by Charles Black in 1960:

> First, the equal protection clause of the fourteenth amendment should be read as saying that the Negro race, as such, is not to be significantly disadvantaged by the laws of the states. Secondly, segregation is a massive intentional disadvantaging of the Negro race, as such, by state law. No subtlety at all. Yet I cannot disabuse myself of the idea that that is really all there is to the segregation cases.

As a method, the white oppression of blacks approach would ask in each case whether the particular conditions complained of, viewed in their social and historical context, are a manifestation of racial oppression. Such an approach would reflect adoption of the victim perspective. It is not an approach congenial to a system of law that wishes to rationalize continued discrimination just as much as it wants to outlaw it. That goal, if it is to be accomplished through a practice that can be convincingly described as "law," requires a gap between social reality and legal intervention, with that gap mediated by an abstract, objective principle against which particular instances of discrimination can be tested and upheld or struck down depending on the results.

4. Freedom of Association The "freedom of association" view sees *Brown* not as an equal protection case at all, but as a case dealing with the due process right of people to associate with one another free of state interference. While it is clear that this was not the actual rationale of the *Brown* opinion, as the Court specifically eschewed reliance on any due process theory and later cases specifically rejected the freedom of association viewpoint, it nevertheless seems worth discussing. For one thing, the freedom of association theory may be a more accurate explanation of the limits of *Brown* in its historical context. Second, the freedom of association theory exemplifies the rationalization that serves to legitimize discrimination and therefore provides an early model for the contemporary perpetrator perspective. Third, it is still a living principle, although one operating in a narrow context, that does serve to explain some contemporary decisions. Finally, the theory shares some significant features with the color-blind theory and further exposes the abstract world view associated with color-blindness.

The freedom of association theory is as much a statement about the right to discriminate as it is about the right not to be discriminated against. All it outlaws is state action. The autonomous individual remains free to discriminate, or not, according to personal preference. Racial discrimination is thus wrenched from its social fabric and becomes a mere question of private, individual taste. This theory serves to explain the few Supreme Court interventions against racial discrimination during the otherwise racist hegemony of *Plessy v. Ferguson*. But it also sheds light on *Brown*, since the ethical norm reflected in national antidiscrimination law at the time of the *Brown* decision was one that recognized the legitimacy of private discrimination. Because of the constraints of the state-action principle, there was nothing illegal, as a matter of *national* law, about blatant and explicit discrimination in employment, housing, or public accommodations, so long as such practices were "private." The freedom of association theory legitimizes that tolerance of racial discrimination by transforming it into a freedom to discriminate. It thus speaks directly to the needs of an era that had not yet fully developed even the perpetrator perspective, inasmuch as only one perpetrator—the state—could be held accountable for racial discrimination.

Where it does apply, the freedom of association theory implies a notion of racial equivalence similar to the color-blind theory's idea that blacks and whites have equal grounds for complaint about instances of racial discrimination. In this sense, the two theories share a world view— the abstract utopia where racial discrimination has never existed and where, ironically, both theories would probably be irrelevant. The only way that discriminations by whites against blacks can become ethically equivalent to discriminations by blacks against whites is to presuppose that there is no actual problem of racial discrimination. It is just like saying today that the principles of freedom of association and color-blindness govern relationships between long- and short-ear-lobed people.

5. The Integrated Society This view is not so much another way of explaining the *Brown* decision as it is an additional perspective from which to regard all of the other theories and explanations. It begins with the assumption that a decision like *Brown,* which merely outlaws a particular practice, nevertheless implies that the practice is being outlawed to achieve a desired end-state where conditions associated with the outlawed practice will no longer be evident. If particular practices are to be outlawed as deviations from a norm, then the norm must include within it a vision of society where there would not be such deviations. It should then be possible to test current conditions against the desired end-state to decide whether progress is being made. The end-state usually associated with antidiscrimination law is some version of the "integrated society." This ambiguous phrase, however, contains within it a number of possibilities as to the content of the end-state, the extent to which it has already been achieved, and in whose interest it is to achieve it.

The most complete version of the integrated society can be found in the science-fiction story where it is the year 2200 and everybody is a creamy shade of beige. Race has not only become irrelevant, it has disappeared altogether under the guiding hand of genetic entropy. A second and slightly less extreme version of the utopia posits a society where racial identification is still possible, but no longer relevant to anyone's thinking or generalizations about anyone else. In this world of racial irrelevance, the sensory data employed in making a racial identification would still be available, but would have returned to the domain of other similar human identification data in such a way as to obliterate the cultural concept of race. Race would have become functionally equivalent to eye-color in contemporary society. In a third version of the integrated society, racial identification persists as a cultural unifying force for each group, equivalent to an idealized model of religious tolerance. Each group respects the diverse character of every other group, and there are no patterns of domination or oppression between different groups.

Each of these visions of the future reflects the achievement of a casteless, if not classless, society in which there is no hierarchy of status that corresponds with racial identification. The essential defect in the color-blind theory of racial discrimination is that it presupposes the attainment of one of these futures. It is a doctrine that at the same time declares racial characteristics irrelevant and prevents any affirmative steps to achieve the condition of racial irrelevance. The freedom of association theory, to the extent it is antidiscriminational at all, also presupposes an already existing future, but it is the tolerance model that it contemplates.

These theories are not alone in presupposing the goal that one is supposedly working toward. Suppose one were to visit the future society of racial irrelevance and discover conditions that in any other society might be regarded as corresponding with a pattern of racial discrimination. Among such conditions might be that one race seems to have a hugely disproportionate share of the worst houses, the most demeaning jobs, and the least control over societal resources. For such conditions to be fair and accepted as legitimate by the disfavored race in future society, they would have to be perceived as produced by accidental, impartial, or neutral phenomena utterly disassociated from any racist practice. Otherwise the future society would fail to meet its claim of racial irrelevance and would not be a future society at all.

Any theory of antidiscrimination law that legitimizes as nondiscriminatory substantial disproportionate burdens borne by one race is effectively claiming that its distributional rules are already the ones that would exist in future society. From the perspective of a victim in present society, where plenty of explicitly racist practices prevail, the predictable and legitimate demand is that those ostensibly neutral rules demonstrate themselves to be the ones that would in fact exist in future society. The legitimacy of the demand is underscored by the fact that those very rules appealed to by the beneficiaries to legitimize the conditions of the victims were created by and are maintained by the dominant race. From the perpetrator perspective, however, those practices not conceded to be racist are held constant; they are presumed consistent with the ethics of future society, and the victims are asked to prove that such is not the case. This is a core difference between the victim and perpetrator perspectives.

A vision of the future also bears on the question of whom attainment of the integrated society benefits. To introduce this issue more precisely, one might ask whether the integrated society is an end in itself, or just a symbolic measure of the actual liberation of an oppressed racial group from the conditions of oppression. To say that the integrated society is an end in itself, apart from the interest of the oppressed group in its own liberation, is basically to say that the goal is in the interest of society at large, or in the interest of the dominant group as well as the oppressed one. It is hardly controversial to contend that integration is for everyone's benefit, or even that it is in some sense for the benefit of the dominant group. Problems arise when interests diverge and the dominant group's desire for integration supersedes the victim group's demand for relief.

C. POST-*BROWN* DEVELOPMENTS

The remainder of the era of uncertainty offered almost no occasions for resolving any of the ambiguities of *Brown* or exposing the difference between the perpetrator and victim perspectives. Instead, the major task for that era, which put off the question of remedy, was to increase the list of perpetrators against whom antidiscrimination law might be directed. This was accomplished largely through the systematic demolition of the state-action doctrine, a process involving liberal interpretation, partial abolition, judicial and legislative circumvention, and a great deal of human effort.

On one of the few occasions that the Court did have a chance to elaborate on the emerging antidiscrimination principle, it opted for steadfast adherence to the perpetrator perspective. In *Swain v. Alabama,* a black man in Talladega County, Alabama, who had been convicted of rape and sentenced to death, brought to the Su-

preme Court a claim of jury discrimination. He offered three facts in support of this claim: first, that while blacks accounted for 26% of the relevant local population, only ten to fifteen percent of the grand and petit jury panels had been black since 1953; second, that in the immediate prosecution, the prosecutor had used his peremptory challenges to exclude all blacks from the jury that tried the defendant; and, third, that no black had ever served on an actual petit jury in a civil or criminal case in the county.

The Supreme Court denied the claim, rationalizing all three facts into irrelevance and invoking much of the doctrine associated with the perpetrator perspective.

An affirmative claim for representation directed against a *system* that was obviously denying that representation was neatly transformed into a burdensome and elusive hunt for the particular villains within that system who were "causing" the result. Necessarily, the Court ignored the results of the system and presumed, despite the obvious fact that blacks were not represented, that the system was operating impartially. To answer what was the core of the defendant's claim—that regardless of causes, it was the results that were the problem—the Court again appealed to the color-blind theory:

> But a defendant in a criminal case is not constitutionally entitled to demand a proportionate number of his race on the jury which tries him nor on the venire of jury roll from which petit jurors are drawn.... "Obviously the number of races and nationalities appearing in the ancestry of our citizens would make it impossible to meet a requirement of proportional representation."

Swain points up a deep contradiction in antidiscrimination law that sees no absurdity in legitimizing the precise result that would occur under the regime of de jure exclusion struck down in *Strauder*. Strick adherence to the perpetrator form makes results irrelevant; a concern with results violates the form. For a time, in the next era of antidiscrimination law, the Court violated the form, while pretending not to, to produce some results. In the third and present era, the Court returns to strict adherence, pretending never to have deviated from it, while pretending to have produced some results in the interim.

III. 1965–1974: THE ERA OF CONTRADICTION, OR THE JURISPRUDENCE OF REMEDY

A. AN OVERVIEW

A growing tension between the concepts of violation and remedy characterized the second era of modern antidiscrimination law. While the form of the law, with one possible exception, remained squarely within the perpetrator perspective, its content began to create expectations associated with the victim perspective. The perpetrator perspective remained the basic model for a violation, without which there could be no occasion for remedy. Given that finding, however, remedial doctrine took over and, in so doing, subtly changed the concept of violation by addressing itself to substantive conditions beyond the scope of the original violation.

One kind of case that gave rise to this development might be termed the "infinite series" problem. Suppose a jurisdiction that had previously been nearly all white in population experienced a sudden wave of black migration into the area, to the point where its population became sixty percent white and forty percent black. Suppose further that, in response to this population change, the jurisdiction redistricted its legislative body so that each of its ten districts had a population that was sixty percent white and forty percent black. Even under the perpetrator perspective, this action would clearly violate an antidiscrimination principle, whether on the basis of evidence of purposeful racial exclusion or simply on the basis of an effect explicable only in terms of discriminatory purpose. Thus we have a traditional "violation." Because the perpetrator perspective refuses to recognize any claims of racial proportionality or for relief from the plain fact

of political powerlessness, however, all that can be done with a violation of the type described is to call it one and declare the reapportionment invalid.

Now suppose that the same jurisdiction, perhaps because required by local law, again redistricts, this time coming up with a plan that calls for one district that is 100% black and nine districts that are two-thirds white and one-third black. If there is evidence of purposeful discrimination, a court could again declare the practice a violation and send it back again in the hopes that a clean version of the plan will reappear without any evidence of "purpose." If there is no evidence of purpose, however, how do we decide if the plan itself gives rise to an inference of purposeful discrimination? The perpetrator perspective is powerless. To decide whether the second plan is discriminatory requires a comparison of that plan with a hypothetical state of affairs in a community where race is irrelevant. But that comparison is impossible as an abstract matter since, in a community where race was really irrelevant, neither of the plans described would seem odd; there would be no perceived relationship between race and political power.

In a community where race is relevant, however, the second plan must be compared with a scheme that produces racial proportionality, even if this is done only for the limited purpose of deciding whether the second plan is a violation or not. At the moment when the *condition* of racial political power, with its implicit affirmative claim for such power, becomes relevant, the victim perspective enters into the analysis. Without taking the victim perspective into account, there can never be, in this kind of case, either a finding of violation absent explicit evidence of purpose or any remedy for either the initial or any subsequent violation. But once the question of racial political power becomes relevant in a community that once committed a traditional "violation," it is difficult to see why it is not equally relevant in a community where, although no specific violation has been found, race is relevant, and there is extensive racial discrimination in all areas of life. At this point, what arose as remedy in one case threatens to define violation in another, unless the new community can be so severed from the society in which both communities exist as to be hurled by semantic fiat into the future society described earlier.

A second kind of problem case is the "no results" situation. Suppose that for many years a community maintained a blatant de jure system of school segregation by race that was finally declared unconstitutional. Further suppose that despite the ruling of unconstitutionality, no remedial efforts occurred or were required for a number of years, with the result that when those efforts were finally undertaken, the resultant school system looked like one that was still substantially segregated. Why? Because the new basis of school assignment, neighborhood, for example, while itself not a manifestation of discriminatory purpose, nevertheless amplified an existing pattern of pervasive discrimination.

The problem here is embarrassment; it is difficult to call these schools "desegregated" because there has been substantially no change since the era of explicit segregation. To cover the embarrassment requires some integrated schools even though, under the perpetrator perspective, there is no affirmative right to have such schools, nor is it the condition of segregation, as opposed to the practice, that is the violation. By going after the conditions, ostensibly to remedy the original violation, the victim perspective is incorporated, and one wonders whether the very same conditions are equally remediable elsewhere regardless of the remote presence of a no longer existent violation.

A third example is the case of the ostensibly neutral and rational practice. Suppose an employer who for years simply refused to hire any black workers at all suddenly, in response to recently enacted antidiscrimination law, adopts an aptitude test for prospective employees that just happens to exclude all black applicants. There is an inescapable inference that the employer is trying to do implicitly what can no longer be done explicitly, but there is no plausible evidentiary

link between the prior *practice* and the current one. If one wants either to remedy what looks like a continuation of the earlier violation or avoid the no results dilemma, the neutral practice must be the target of inquiry. At that point, however, the analysis again shifts to the victim perspective, demanding that neutral practices producing conditions of discrimination at the very least justify themselves in terms of their own claims to rationality. Here again the plausible contention arises that the very same practices, as well as a lot of similar ones, should be required to justify themselves wherever they appear.

The patterns illustrated by these typical cases, occurring either singly or in combination, are characteristic of the era of contradiction. The following sections will describe the appearance and operation of these patterns in three substantive areas: voting, education, and employment.

B. VOTING

It is not surprising that the contradictions of the perpetrator perspective first began to appear in the area of voting rights. Voting had already passed through the era of merely identifying violations, beginning with the fifteenth amendment itself, which brought racial discrimination in voting explicitly within the perpetrator principle. Although the Court had punctuated its efforts with enormous time-lags, it had occasionally even struck down particular practices as unconstitutional. But none of these efforts had resulted in any significant participation of black voters in twentieth-century Southern political life. While a massive litigation offensive persisted well into the 1960's, it was met by continuing frustrations of the "infinite series" variety, which in turn produced a serious "no results" problem. Thus, for voting, something more than repeated outlawry of particular practices was needed if the fifteenth amendment was ever to make any practical difference.

Voting was a sensible starting place for other reasons as well. Lack of results in voting rights has a particularly noxious symbolic effect, given the key role of political participation in sustaining the form of liberal democracy. To deny a substantial racial minority the right to vote is, whatever the rationalizations offered to support it, a failure to offer even formal, much less substantive, equality. The conferral of voting rights is not only symbolically useful, but it need not impose any serious systemic costs, since voting will only make a difference, if at all, when translated into effective political power.

Confronted with a massive record of systematic deprivations of the right to vote and the apparent inability of the courts to remedy the problem by outlawing specific practices, Congress chose to make the operative provisions of the Voting Rights Act of 1965 depend on the presence of *conditions,* which, though suggestive of actual violations, were not in themselves violations or even causally linked to violations through any process of proof. Thus the basic triggering provisions of the Act depended only on the litigation-proof facts of nonparticipation, or non-registration, in a presidential election, plus the existence of a "test or device," broadly defined. The second-level triggering provisions leading to the employment of federal registrars similarly depended on straightforward conclusive administrative facts. Thus, however much the intent of the Act was just remedial in the sense of finally dealing with those years of actual violations, the effect of the Act was to create an affirmative right to vote, with the functional violation being the conditions associated with the absence of that right.

Once the affirmative right to vote had been conferred on the vast numbers of previously disenfranchised black people, section 5 of the Act became the most important provision. Under section 5, a triggered jurisdiction must demonstrate that any proposed change in voting practice or procedure will not have the purpose or effect of discriminating on the basis of race or color with respect to voting. In the remedial scheme of the Act, this provision made sense as a way of preventing future violations, since jurisdictions so inclined might otherwise creatively manipulate their voting laws to leave black voters formally enfranchised but practically disenfranchised. Without section 5, endless litigation of the "infinite series" variety might have resulted.

A jurisdiction can effectively neutralize the political power of its black voters by altering its geographic boundaries to change the overall racial composition, by switching from ward to at-large systems to decrease minority power, or simply by gerrymandering districts to maximize the political strength of the white population. The Supreme Court itself had deemed an extreme version of the latter to be a constitutional violation in *Gomillion* v. *Lightfoot,* decided prior to the enactment of the Voting Rights Act. To have said that section 5 did not apply to these practices would have been to invite their use to achieve renewed discrimination. Thus the Court, even from within the confines of the perpetrator principle, had no choice but to bring all of these practices under the application of section 5.

By bringing geographic manipulation under substantive scrutiny, the Court was compelled to consider explicit issues of racial proportionality in political power. But since the perpetrator prespective, under the guiding influence of the color-blind theory, is indifferent to affirmative claims for racial political power, it was difficult to ascertain the substantive validity of such practices. These difficulties became evident in *City of Richmond* v. *United States,* the Court's first substantive confrontation with geographic manipulation under section 5. The case dealt with the racial impact of Richmond's annexation of a large, predominantly white, suburban area. On that issue, the Court simultaneously applied section 5 to an annexation and made section 5 inapplicable to annexations. In fact, with respect to the annexation issue, the decision is more typical of the third "era," to be discussed below. The importance of *Richmond* for the present discussion, however, is that while legitimizing annexation as a means of diluting minority voting strength, the Court implied a right to proportional political power within any given geographical unit of government.

The only useful sense in which an annexation

of territory may be evaluated with respect to its discriminatory impact is in terms of the racial population mix before and after annexation, since all the annexation itself does is add people and territory to an existing jurisdiction. To say that section 5 applies to an annexation, then, would seem to imply an inquiry into the percentage population of the minority race in the expanded jurisdiction to see whether its political power has been diluted. *Richmond,* for example, involved the annexation of 23 square miles of territory with a population of 45,705 whites and 1,557 blacks, which changed the racial mix of the entire city from 52% black and 48% white to 42%black and 58% white. If the annexation were tested as to discriminatory *impact,* it would seem to present a clear violation, since a black majority had been transformed into a black minority. The Court avoided that conclusion only by confusing the issue of the annexation's discriminatory impact with the separate issue of the validity of an at-large system of representation. Thus the Court held that the relegation of the black population to minority political status was not a discriminatory "effect" within the meaning of section 5. This is the sense in which the Court nullified the application of section 5 to annexations, since if the change in racial percentage from majority to minority is not discrimination, then the annexation itself becomes immune from scrutiny on that ground.

At the same time, the Court did require Richmond to switch from at-large representation to a ward system, but regarded as sufficient a plan that gave the black population majorities in four of the nine council districts, rejecting a request for control of five districts. Thus, while upholding the basic political effect of the annexation, the reassertion of white political control, the Court guaranteed the black minority a proportional share of political power in the expanded community. That decision would seem to create, despite the perpetrator perspective, an affirmative expectation that the antidiscrimination principle applicable to voting implies a right to proportional political power. That expectation arises

quickly if one makes three plausible assumptions about the *Richmond* decision.

The first assumption is that the issue of at-large versus ward representation is separable from the question of annexation. If, as the Court said, an annexation is valid notwithstanding its reversal of majority power, then unless there is a right to proportional representation, it should make no difference whether the black minority can command control of four seats or none in the expanded community. Since the Court required the four-seat guarantee, it thus becomes difficult to differentiate the case of annexation from a case where geography has remained constant but the black community is underrepresented because of gerrymandering or use of at-large representation with a white majority. In all three situations, the evil is precisely the same—underrepresentation of the black community. The cases can only be distinguished by the rather embarrassing "principle" that a black community has a right to be paid off with proportional power if forced to submit to an annexation that dilutes its power, but has no such right if its power is effectively minimized without a boundary change.

The second assumption is that, apart from the question of burden proof, the standard mandated by section 5—that the particular practice "not have the purpose [or] . . . effect of denying or abridging the right to vote on account of race or color"—is substantively identical to the standard set by the Constitution with respect to the same practice. Under this assumption, the only difference in a jurisdiction not subject to section 5 would be that instead of being able to rely on preclearance review to test the substantive issue, an aggrieved person would have to commence litigation to challenge the practice. And a showing of substantial underrepresentation would presumably be sufficient to make out a prima facie case of discrimination.

The assumption that the standards are the same is rooted in the absence of any rational reason for their being different. Whatever its worth, semantic scrutiny yields no significant difference. Nor does the distinction between remedy and violation suggest a difference if, as common sense would dictate, the notion of remedy refers to the mandatory review part of section 5 rather than its substantive content. The original violation that triggered application of the Voting Rights Act provides little explanatory help, since that violation was merely the occasion for invoking the Act, and there is no pretense of any causal linkage between the practice reviewed under section 5 and the original triggering conditions: To apply different standards would make sense only if it could be said that the kinds of communities subject to section 5 are really ones where race is perceived as more relevant or significant than in those not subject to the statute. The argument would be that even if section 5 creates a right to proportional representation, that right does not pertain in American communities not subject to that law, because in such communities substantial black underrepresentation is hardly indicative of anything. Here again, the argument is essentially that future society already exists, that race is irrelevant. That argument again amounts to no more than a denial of reality.

The third assumption about the *Richmond* opinion, which merely reinforces the other two, is that the Court itself recognized a claim of proportionality not only in what it did, but also in what it said. In rejecting the black community's request for control of five seats in the larger community, the Court said that it could not approve a "requirement that the city allocate to the Negro community in the larger city the voting power or the seats on the city council in excess of its proportion in the new community and thus permanently to underrepresent other elements in the community." The Court's own use of the word "underrepresent" as applied to the white majority implies an expectation of racial proportionality and speaks to a world where race is very relevant to political representation. In the color-blind world, a racial group, black or white, could not be regarded as underrepresented. And as a matter of pure gerrymandering, the enlarged Richmond with its population of 58% white and 42% black, could be districted so as to give as

many as seven seats to the black community or as few as none. The color-blind world would be indifferent to either extreme. But the *Richmond* opinion is concerned about white underrepresentation, a concern that is inconsistent with the color-blind model. If the concept of racial underrepresentation is applicable at all, it should be equally applicable to the black community, which should also be able to claim at least proportional representation. But the Court's comment has today become more than a little ironic, since the solicitous concern expressed for the almost-beleaguered white citizens of "greater" Richmond has hardly given rise to a similar concern for claims of black citizens anywhere.

C. EDUCATION PRIOR TO *SWANN*

For education, the era of contradiction begins with the Supreme Court's decision in *Griffin v. Country School Board*. In *Griffin*, the Court faced a thorough and continuous pattern of resistance to its decision in *Brown I*. To avoid compliance with the Court's desegregation mandate, Prince Edward County had closed its schools and facilitated the operation of private segregated schools through a combination of state and local financial aid. The facts of the case make clear that the county intended to maintain a segregated system of public education, attempting to insulate the program from constitutional scrutiny by disguising it in an ostensibly private form. From within the safe confines of the perpetrator perspective, the Court could have simply told the county and state to stop facilitating or supporting segregated public education. Instead, perhaps motivated by the county's recalcitrance, the Court went a step further and told the district court that it "may, if necessary to prevent further racial discrimination, require the supervisors to exercise the power that is theirs to levy taxes to raise funds adequate to reopen, operate, and maintain without racial discrimination a public school system in Prince Edward County like that operated in other counties in Virginia."

There is a narrow explanation of this curious sentence that is consistent with the perpetrator perspective. The Court might have been saying by way of unstated assumption that so long as public schools remained open throughout the rest of Virginia, any system of private segregated schools in one county would probably be so infected with governmental involvement as to be deemed tantamount to public segregated schools. On this view, to avoid protracted litigation of the infinite series variety with respect to successive forms of "private" segregation, the Court was merely declaring in advance that all such systems would be invlaid. While as a logical matter the county could cleanse itself of any violation by having no education whatsoever, either public or private, the Court somehow knew that this alternative would never be chosen and therefore told the county to reopen its public schools.

The sentence nevertheless subtly offered two promises to the black community of Prince Edward County. These promises may be regarded as more or less disingenuous to the extent one ascribes to the Court a secret reason for the sentence, but the promises are there. One is an affirmative right not only to an education, but to an education comparable to that offered throughout Virginia. This view would regard *Griffin* as partially adopting the "equality of educational opportunity" view of *Brown I,* and recognizing that what is important, from the victim's perspective, is not so much whether the violation has been cured but whether the right results are being obtained. The second promise goes to the specifically racial dimension of that education. The Court had not yet suggested, as of 1965, what it might mean to "maintain without racial discrimination a public school system," but the second promise was that whatever that phrase came to mean, the black students of Prince Edward County had an affirmative claim measured by its content. Later cases began to provide that content.

In 1968, the Court decided two cases that began to set standards for the achievement of desegregation and in so doing further widened the gap between the perpetrator perspective and remedies for violation of its norm. In *Green v.*

County School Board and *Monroe v. Board of Commissioners,* the Court rejected "freedom of choice" as a sufficient remedy for public school segregation. In terms of the perpetrator perspective, *Green* involved the clearer violation of the two since all the school board had done in that case was to superimpose a system of free choice upon its otherwise unchanged system of segregated schools. Thus the board had in no way ceased to operate the same segregated system that it had always operated, and the burden of opting out of that system was placed upon the students and their families. The Court's rejection of this scheme as constituting neither desegregation nor free choice is hardly surprising.

Monroe was more difficult. There the board had established a new system of geographic zoning to replace the old segregated system. But superimposed on the new system was a scheme of free transfers that permitted students to undo the integrated results of the geographic scheme by reestablishing themselves into a racially concentrated pattern. The Court rejected this scheme as well. Among other things, this decision amounted to a repudiation of the freedom of association theory as applied to public education, under which both black and white students would have had a right to choose not to go to school with the students of the other race. In addition, by focusing its attention on the actual racial percentages in the schools operating under the local plan, the Court partially repudiated the color-blind theory, at least within the narrow context of remedies for de jure segregation. Of even more significance, by emphasizing the degree of actual integration, the Court seemed to be shifting toward a victim perspective, concerned with conditions and results rather than merely with the elimination of offensive practices. Moreover, by directing its remedy not only at the behavior of the school board but also at the private behavior of those whites who chose to leave the integrated schools, the Court seemed to be breaking down the dichotomy between state (or other perpetrator-actor) and the rest of society that is so central to the perpetrator perspective.

Narrowly viewed, both *Green* and *Monroe* were nothing more than cases of remedies for traditional violations. But to the extent the cases are concerned with, and promise to the black students, an actual condition of integration, they suggest that the absence of integration might be just as remediable in a jurisdiction that had not previously been guilty of de jure segregation. Even apart from this implicit suggestion, the cases must at least stand for the proposition that an established violation will not be deemed remedied until integrated results are achieved. Thus the more the concept of violation could be expanded, the wider the range in which explicit demands for integrated results could be asserted.

In any neutral practice case, two basic approaches are possible. Given a practice with disproportionate racial impact, one can focus on the practice, asking whether it serves any useful purpose or whether it is itself a manifestation of discrimination. Alternatively one can focus . . . on the victims of the practice, asking whether they are or have become inferior human beings who need to be relieved from the onerous effects of an otherwise valid procedure. The difference between these approaches is crucial to the distinction between the victim and perpetrator perspectives. The latter is just another version of the assumption that future society is already here; its emphasis on compensation for the ill effects of discrete "other violations" can easily be transformed into a case of inaction justified by blaming the victim. The former approach, on the other hand, amounts to a demand that institutions or practices oppressive in their effects justify themselves as legitimate.

D. EMPLOYMENT: THE *GRIGS* CASE

Griggs v. Duke Power Co., the Court's first substantive decision under title VII of the Civil Rights Act of 1964, is as close as the Court has ever come to formally adopting the victim perspective; it is the centerpiece of the era of contradiction. One tribute to its importance is the amount of effort currently being made to repudiate it.

While the actual decision in *Griggs* may be explained in at least two ways that are consistent with the perpetrator principle, the case seems to go beyond that perspective to the extent that it requires neutral practices to justify themselves, radically alters the concept of "intention" in antidiscrimination cases, and implies a demand for results through affirmative action.

The Court posed the issue in *Griggs* as

> whether an employer is prohibited by the Civil Rights Act of 1964, Title VII, from requiring a high school education or passing of a standardized general intelligence test as a condition of employment in or transfer to jobs when (a) neither standard is shown to be significantly related to successful job performance, (b) both requirements operate to disqualify Negroes at a substantially higher rate than white applicants, and (c) the jobs in question formerly had been filled only by white employees as part of a longstanding practice of giving preference to whites.

A unanimous Court, speaking through Chief Justice Burger, answered that question in the affirmative.

That the case was rooted firmly in the perpetrator perspective may be inferred from the behavior of the employer in the case. Prior to July 1965, the employer had blatantly discriminated against black workers, permitting them to work in only one of its five departments, where the highest paying job paid less than the lowest paying job in any of the other four departments. In 1965, the employer abandoned its policy of explicit discrimination. In the same year, however, the employer added a high school diploma requirement for transfer out of the previously "black" department and a requirement that a person had to "register satisfactory scores on two professionally developed aptitude tests, as well as . . . have a high school education" for placement in any department except the previously "black" one. These newly imposed requirements operated to limit severely the opportunities available to black employees and applicants. Thus, the case posed the problem of the "ostensibly neutral practice" introduced as a substitute for blatant racial discrimination and achieving substantially the same results.

By making its rationale dependent on the prior explicit discrimination the Court could have stayed within the perpetrator perspective. But this would have been somewhat disingenuous. For one thing, the prior discriminatory conduct in *Griggs* was legal when it occurred and could not by itself have given rise to a violation. Moreover, to have made the illegality of the test and diploma requirements dependent upon the prior discrimination would have meant that absent such a history the very same practices would be valid however disproportionate their impact. In any event, the Court chose to sever its rationale from any dependence on the prior discrimination, and in so doing left the perpetrator perspective as explaining, at most, why, but not how the Court intervened in *Griggs*.

While the Court was willing to say that all citizens could vote regardless of literacy, they were not equally willing to say that all applicants should be hired, regardless of qualifications. The Court clearly needed a rationale that would describe the instances where tests or other job qualifications could be validly applied even as against black applicants who had suffered inferior educations. To develop such standards, the Court had to take a look at the tests on their merits. Almost inadvertently, then, the opinion switched from blaming the victim to scrutinizing the neutral practices themselves with respect to their claims of rationality. At that point, the background of segregated schools became irrelevant, since standards addressed solely to the merits of the neutral practices limit the issue to whether, under title VII, a particular employee selection procedure that disproportionately excludes black applicants is valid, regardless of the educational experience of the applicants.

Thus, the central rationale of *Griggs* is that selection procedures, even ostensibly neutral ones, that disadvantage minority applicants are not valid unless they can demonstrate themselves to be rational: "The Act proscribes not only overt discrimination but also practices that are fair in form, but discriminatory in operation. The touchstone is business necessity. If an employment practice which operates to exclude Negroes cannot be shown to be related to job performance, the practice is prohibited." The standard of rationality set by the Court seemed to be a tough one, demanding a showing of job-relatedness, the removal of "artificial, arbitrary, and unnecessary barriers," and standards that "measure the person for the job and not the person in the abstract." In short, the opinion amounts to a demand that the myth of a meritocratic scheme of equality of opportunity be transformed into a reality.

Read this way, the case becomes a generalized demand that all objective selection procedures under the coverage of some antidiscrimination law be required to justify themselves as consistent with the notion of equality of opportunity. *Griggs* in no way contradicts the meritocratic model, but assumes that it can be made to work, that those who are deserving can be objectively separated from those who are not.

In addition to legitimizing the assertion of an affirmative claim directed at a systemic practice, *Griggs* changed the notion of "intentional" in antidiscrimination law. This aspect of the opinion derives from the Court's severance of its rationale from the prior discriminatory practices of the defendant employer. The opinion makes it clear that "good intent or absence of discriminatory intent does not redeem employment procedures or testing mechanisms that operate as 'built-in headwinds' for minority groups" and that "Congress directed the thrust of the Act to the *consequences* of employment practices, not simply the motivation." Under the notion of "intention" that emerges from the opinion, then, one is intentionally discriminating if one continues to use a practice or maintains a condition that disadvantages a minority group without being able to justify the rationality of the practice or condition. This idea, too, did not seem easily confined within the employment area to tests alone, nor easily within the employment area at all.

When applied to ostensibly rational practices, the *Griggs* notion of intention merely demands a showing of rationality. When applied to nonrational practices, such as school or voter districting, jurisdictional boundaries, or zoning decisions, all of which are inherently arbitrary, the *Griggs* notion becomes a demand for results and, therefore, an adoption of the victim perspective. If, for example, there are a number of ways to divide a community into districts for school assignment purposes, and the one currently employed produces a great deal of racial concentration in schools, to perpetuate the existing scheme with the knowledge of the racial concentration produced becomes intentional discrimination—unless there is a sufficiently good reason for having chosen that scheme. To follow out the analogy to *Griggs,* such a reason would have to be one that tells the black children, who are confined to schools segregated in fact, why it is *legitimate* that they be so confined. Absent such a reason, the children would have the right to a redistricting that did not produce racial concentration.

E. EDUCATION REVISITED: *SWANN, WRIGHT,* AND *KEYES*

In education, the era of contradiction most thoroughly realized itself in three cases decided during the three years following the *Griggs* decision: *Swann v. Charlotte-Mecklenburg Board of Education, Wright v. Council of Emporia,* and *Keyes v. School District No. 1.* Each of these cases may be explained by and remains formally within the perpetrator perspective, but each, especially when read in light of *Griggs,* creates expectations more consistent with the victim perspective.

All three cases involved explicit findings of de jure segregation. *Swann* and *Wright* involved southern school systems in which the de jure systems were preexisting and remote in time from the actual conditions being litigated. *Keyes* involved a northern city—Denver—where the district court had found de jure segregation in one

part of the city. In addition, all three cases involved challenges to neutral practices that operated to produce racially concentrated schools. In *Swann* and *Keyes,* the practice was the neighborhood school; in *Wright,* it was deconsolidation of a combined city-county school system.

In each case, the Court retained formal adherence to the perpetrator perspective by "linking" the current condition under attack to the actual de jure violation. Thus, in *Swann,* while invoking the magic phrase that the "nature of the violation determines the scope of the remedy," the Court proceeded to show how by inference alone one could conclude either that the prior system of segregation produced segregated neighborhoods, which in turn produced the current condition of segregation, or that the residential segregation led to school siting decisions that continued to produce racial concentration, despite the abolition of de jure segregation. Having linked the current condition to the past violation, the Court was able to conclude that although a prescription of racial balance is not ordinarily within the authority of a federal district court, both an "awareness of the racial composition of the whole school system" and the use of mathematical ratios were appropriate to remedy the current violation.

In *Wright,* the Court could have tied its reasoning to the perpetrator perspective, since the city involved had decided to sever its relationship with the county school system only two weeks after a federal court had ordered pairing of schools. That severance would have changed the racial composition of the system from 66% black and 34% white to 724 black and 284 white (county) and 524 black and 484 white (city). While stressing the factual history and emphasizing that the case involved desegregation rather than lack of racial balance, the Court nevertheless based its decision on the *effect* of deconsolidation: "Thus, we have focused upon the effect—not the purpose or motivation—of a school board's action in determining whether it is a permissible method of dismantling a dual system. The existence of a permissible purpose cannot sustain an action that has an impermissible effect."

In *Keyes*, the Court made a similar effort to tie the condition of segregation to the identified violation. The Court held that proof of a violation with respect to one area of a city, plus racial concentration elsewhere in the system, raised by evidentiary inference (prior similar acts or causal spread) a prima facie case of de jure segregation throughout the system. The school board thereupon became obligated to show that the racial concentration elsewhere was not adventitious, a burden that was not met by a neighborhood school assignment policy.

In all three cases, the Court permitted challenges to neutral practices that produced racial concentration in schools. In none of the cases did the Court demand proof that the original violation caused the challenged racial concentration. In fact, by indulging in causation analysis at least as plausible as that utilized by the Court, one might easily conclude that the real villian in all three cases was discrimination in housing that produced segregated residential patterns. In both *Swann* and *Keyes*, racially concentrated neighborhoods produced the racially concentrated schools; in *Wright*, the relative racial composition of county and city produced the result. Thus regarded, the cases suggest that the de jure segregation merely served as a backdrop for challenges to *conditions* of segregation produced by generalized patterns of discrimination. They further suggest that those same conditions should be equally subject to attack wherever they can be ascribed to patterns of discrimination, which would be anywhere other than the future society.

This conclusion gains much greater force from the fact that the three cases followed the decision in *Griggs*, for two aspects of *Griggs* explain the results in *Swann, Wright,* and *Keyes* much more convincingly than the formal reasoning used in those opinions. One is the notion that ostensibly neutral practices producing racially disproportionate results must justify themselves or be re-

garded as violations. Alternatively, by employing the *Griggs* corollary, one might conclude that the "intentional" violation in the three cases was adherence to a practice (the neighborhood schools) or a decision (the deconsolidation) that produced results associated with segregation. Under this view, retention of the practice in the face of its known resutls becomes a prima facie case of discrimination, again giving rise to a demand for rational justification. Under either appraoch, the rational justification would have to be one that not only explains the action taken, but also makes the condition of discrimination legitimate. Neither the neighborhood school assignments in *Swann* and *Keyes* nor the deconsolidation in *Wright* satisfied those requirements.

Thus by the end of the era of contradiction the Court, while remaining within the perpetrator perspective, had nevertheless managed to offer to black people expectations of proportional racial political power, a working system of equality of opportunity, if not actual jobs, and integrated schools. In the next era, these expectations were systematically defeated and only the perpetrator perspective was preserved.

IV. 1974–?: THE ERA OF RATIONALIZATION, OR THE JURISPRUDENCE OF CURE

A. AN OVERVIEW

The typical approach of the era of rationalization is to "declare that the war is over," to make the problem of racial discrimination go away by announcing that it has been solved. This approach takes many forms. Its simplest and most direct version is the declaration that, despite the discriminatory appearance of current conditions, the actual violation has already been cured, or is being remedied, regardless of whether the remedy prescribed can be expected to alleviate the condition. A more sophisticated approach is to declare that what looks like a violation, based on expectations derived from the era of contradiction, is not a violation at all. This has been accomplished by isolating statutory discrimination from constitutional discrimination to prevent the former from infiltrating the latter and by weakening the previously created statutory standards under the guise of statutory interpretation. The same results have been achieved by renewing insistence on the always manipulable requirement of causation, by emphasizing the form rather than the results of earlier cases, by invoking the purpose-motive distinction to insulate neutral nonrational decisions, or by presuming the rationality of neutral decisions instead of demanding their justification.

Central to the era of rationalization is the pretense—associated with the color-blind theory of racial discrimination—that but for an occasional aberrational practice, future society is already here and functioning. The contradictions implicit in the earlier cases are thus resolved largely by pretending they were never there. This resolution has in turn facilitated a quick and easy return to the comfortable and neat world of the perpetrator perspective. As a result, the actual conditions of racial powerlessness, poverty, and unemployment can be regarded as no more than conditions—not as racial discrimination. Those conditions can then be rationalized by treating them as historical accidents or products of a malevolent fate, or, even worse, by blaming the victims as inadequate to function in the good society. The next few sections will describe, in each of the three substantive areas discussed earlier, the decisions that have brought the era of rationalization into being.

B. VOTING

In *Beer v. United States,* the Court finished the job, which began with its treatment of the annexation issue in *Richmond*, of destroying the expectations of political power that the Court itself had generated by bringing districting procedures under section 5 of the Voting Rights Act of 1965 and by its own treatment of the districting aspect of *Richmond. Beer* was the first case to present a substantive question of section 5's application to legislative redistricting. The city of New Orleans,

a jurisdiction subject to section 5, had a population that was 55 percent white and 45 percent black, with registered voters 65 percent white and 35 percent black. Under the New Orleans districting scheme, there were seven council seats, two of which were elected on an at-large basis. Of the five remaining districts, four had clear white majorities, and black voters comprised 50.2 percent of the voting population in the fifth district. No black had ever been elected to the city council.

New Orleans was obligated by local law to redistrict itself after the 1970 census. After the Attorney General of the United States rejected a plan that provided for no black electoral majorities in any district, a substitute was offered that provided for a black voting majority of 52.6 percent in one district. The validity of this plan was the issue in *Beer,* and the Court had to decide whether the plan had the purpose or effect of discriminating on the basis of race within the meaning of section 5. As suggested above, the determination whether a redistricting plan is racially discriminatory seems to demand a test of that plan against a standard of racial proportionality. Under such a test, a black voting population of 35 percent should control three of seven council seats. A plan that provides a slight majority in one district would seem to fail the test. The Court's response was to rewrite section 5 to change the appropriate inquiry from one about racial discrimination to one about incremental racial discrimination.

The Court's first step was to narrow the scope of its inquiry from the entire new plan to just that portion of the plan involving the five districted seats. Since there had been two at-large seats under the earlier scheme, retaining at-large seats was not a change within the meaning of section 5. Having severed the at-large seats from the case, the Court proceeded to apply the same logic to the five remaining seats, concluding that the concern of section 5 was fulfilled by asking whether the black population was worse off under the new plan than it had been under the old one. Thus rewritten, the concern of section 5 was changed from discrimination to "retrogression." The answer to this narrow question was obvious; the district court, in rejecting the plan, had simply misunderstood the statute.

The opinion did not even allude to the "permanent overrepresentation" of the white community of New Orleans under the approved plan, preferring instead to drag out the color-blind theory to reaffirm that no minority group has any right to proportional representation. The net effect of this decision was to legitimize the status quo by immunizing the preexisting condition of black underrepresentation from statutory or constitutional scrutiny. This implies that the condition of underrepresentation is to be regarded as innocent, fortuitous, unrelated to racial discrimination, and not required to justify itself. It is as if the might Voting Rights Act had been set atop a high-heeled shoe, with its awesome force trained upon a tiny, interstitial moment, surrounded by the remainder of a real problem it could no longer touch.

C. EDUCATION

The era of rationalization began in the same substantive area as modern antidiscrimination law—school desegregation. In *Milliken v. Bradley (Milliken I)*, the Court for the first time applied antidiscrimination law to rationalize a segregated result in a case where a constitutional violation had been found to exist. Despite extensive de jure segregation in the City of Detroit, the Court refused to approve a remedy that would consolidate Detroit schools with those of surrounding suburbs for the purpose of achieving an integrated result. In so holding, the Court rendered irrelevant the district court's conclusion that absent such a remedy, the schools of Detroit would become all-black within a few years. Coupled with the decision a year earlier in *San Antonio Independent School District v. Rodriguez*, which rejected a claim of resource equalization among school districts without regard to ability to pay, the message of *Milliken I* is stark and clear: if whites can find a way to leave the inner city, they may legally insulate their finances and schools

from the demands of blacks for racial equality. The only additional requirement for that sense of security is the availability of easily manipulated restrictive land-use practices, which the Court has graciously provided in other cases.

To achieve this result, the Court had to emphasize the form of *Swann* and *Keyes* over their substance, make results irrelevant, refuse to recognize the implications of *Griggs,* and renew its insistence on proof of causation. Citing *Swann,* the Court pointed out that "[t]he controlling principle consistently expounded in our holdings is that the scope of the remedy is determined by the nature and extent of the constitutional violation." The district court's mistake had been in proceeding on the erroneous assumption that "the Detroit schools could not be truly desegregated . . . unless the racial composition of the student body of each school substantially reflected the racial composition of the population of the metropolitan area as a whole." That the district court so assumed is hardly surprising, however, if one reads *Swann* and *Keyes* in light of *Griggs'* concept of intentional violation or its treatment of neutral practices. Even if one takes a narrower view and simply analogizes the neighborhood school policy, which seemed to be the real cause of the segregation in *Swann* and *Keyes,* to the district boundaries in *Milliken,* the district court's assumption again seems sensible.

It is not clear why the Court thought district boundaries were sacrosanct while neighborhood school assignments were not. The Court offered no comparative judgment, merely announcing that the boundary lines were a manifestation of the sacred principle of local autonomy: "No single tradition in public education is more deeply rooted than local control over the operation of schools; local autonomy has long been thought essential both to the maintenance of community concern and support for public schools and to quality of the educational process." But it was not even the principle of local autonomy that the Court was exalting in *Milliken;* it was the precise fact of the district boundaries existing in the Detroit metropolitan area that served to facilitate the operation of virtually all-white suburban schools. The principle of local autonomy may be a fine one as applied to an area of relative equality. In the usual suburb-city context where it is invoked, however, "local autonomy" is a codeword for rationalizing and protecting the prior appropriation of financial resources, environmental amenity, and, in this case, racial homogeneity. In short, it is a principle of vested rights.

Moreover, the local autonomy discussion, although central to the historical meaning of *Milliken I,* was not even relevant to the rationale of the case. Since the Court refused to advance the implicit thrust of *Griggs-Swann-Keyes,* which would have made the conditions of racial concentration produced by the boundary lines at least a prima facie violation, there was no occasion to demand that the boundary lines be justified as either rational or innocently nonrational. The only practice deemed to be a violation at all was the de jure segregation of the City of Detroit. Here, as in the voting cases, the crucial step toward the result was to narrow the concept of violation. To accomplish that step, the Court had to return to the secure world of the perpetrator perspective:

> Before the boundaries of separate and autonomous school districts may be set aside by consolidating the separate units for remedial purposes or by imposing a cross-district remedy, it must first be shown that there has been a constitutional violation within one district that produces a significant segregative effect in another district. Specifically, it must be shown that racially discriminatory acts of the state or local school districts, or of a single school district have been a substantial cause of inter-district segregation. Thus an interdistrict remedy might be in order where the racially discriminatory acts of one or more school districts caused racial segregation in an adjacent district, or where district lines have been deliberately drawn on the basis of race. In such circumstances an interdistrict remedy would be appropriate to eliminate the interdistrict segregation directly caused by the constitutional violation.

Under the strict causation requirements of *Milliken I,* the law does not offer even a feeble presumption that the extensive ghettoization of the City of Detroit in relation to its surrounding suburbs has anything to do with racial discrimination. Having rejected the implications of *Swann* and *Keyes*—that results mattered and that school desegregation remedies would be used to counter the effects of residential segregation—the Court insured that residential racial concentration will be subject to scrutiny, if at all, only in the difficult to litigate and virtually impossible to remedy domain of housing discrimination. Under the combined force of *Rodriguez* and *Milliken,* black city residents are thus worse off in terms of legal theory than they were under the "separate-but-equal" doctrine of pre-*Brown* southern school litigation, where a claim of equivalent resources for black schools was at least legally cognizable. And even if it makes sense within the narrow world of the perpetrator perspective to say that school desegregation should not be a remedy for housing discrimination, the effect of *Milliken I* is far worse than neutral with respect to housing. By offering the lure of suburban isolation, the decision invites "white flight," thereby stimulating even greater racial concentration in housing.

The remedial counterpoint to *Milliken I* appears in *Milliken II,* where the Court upheld a district court order requiring the State of Michigan to pay one-half the support of various remedial programs that the lower court had made a part of its desegregation plan for Detroit. The case exhibits both of the characteristics typical of remedial counterpoint cases—the illusion of vigorous remedial action, the effect of which has been limited to a narrowly defined violation, and the affirmation of voluntary tokenism. The facts of *Milliken II* are so odd, however, that it is unclear which of these two features predominates. The oddness stems from the lack of adversity in the case: both the Detroit School Board and the State of Michigan favored the remedial programs, and the only issue before the Court was whether the state could be made to contribute.

From the perspective of the school board, the case may be an exercise in voluntary tokenism, with the crucial fact being the school board's willingness to spend more money than would otherwise be required to make up for the effects of past segregation. This view gains further force from the fact that the state defendant also supported some of the special programs on the merits, objecting only to the expense of implementing the order. Thus read, the case stands for nothing more than the proposition that a local government *may* choose to do more than the Constitution requires in remedying school segregation.

The Case may also be read, however, as rejecting a claim, at least on the part of the State of Michigan, concerning the propriety of the remedial order apart from the issue of money. Thus interpreted, *Milliken II* stands for the bold proposition that special remedial programs, even expensive ones, may be required to remedy the effects of past segregation. The most striking aspect of this interpretation is the idea that something more than pupil reassignment may be required to undo a past system of segregation. When read together with the prior cases, however, this proposition loses significance. For one thing, the remedial programs may be the only possible remedy in Detroit, since the one aspect of segregation that will not be remedied after *Milliken I* is racial concentration. Pupil reassignment is unlikely to cure segregation in a school system whose students are nearly all black. Second, the obligation to finance special programs would seem in view of *Pasadena* to last only until a court announces that desegregation has been accomplished in Detroit. In this respect, *Milliken II* remains ambiguous, with the ambiguity analogous to the gap between *Swann* and *Pasadena*. One could either insist that the remedial programs be maintained until the actual effects of segregation on Detroit's students are eliminated or neutralized or be ready to abandon the programs as soon as some barely plausible empirical measure of change is offered.

A third feature of *Milliken II* viewed as an instance of remedial vigor is that the compelled state expenditures upheld in *Milliken II* gain significance from the Court's refusal in the 1973 *Rodriguez* case to adopt any generalized principle of statewide resource equilization for school systems. The combined force of *Rodriguez* and *Milliken I* puts the urban school system in the untenable position of being able to claim neither resources of the state or suburbs on any generalized continuing basis nor student access to the actual suburban school systems. Against that background of "separate-but-unequal," the $5,800,000 in state money disputed in *Milliken II* looks significant. In the larger context, however, the money, just like the ward plan in *Richmond*, looks more like a payoff to the black community to gain its quiet acquiescence in the demise of antidiscrimination law.

D. EMPLOYMENT

If *Griggs* was the most important case of the era of contradiction, the only one offering a genuine threat to the hegemony of the perpetrator perspective, then the major task of the era of rationalization must be the obliteration of *Griggs*. And so it is in the area of employment that one finds the case that will likely become the centerpiece of the era of rationalization: *Washington v. Davis*. While not quite obliterating *Griggs*, the Court has so undermined it that it has ceased to be a credible threat. This overall result has been achieved in three discrete steps: *Griggs'* apparent implications for all of antidiscrimination law have been squelched by limiting its doctrine to title VII; its forceful assault on the system of equality of opportunity from within the structure of title VII has been blunted by softening the scrutiny required; and its apparent application to analogous title VII problems has been denied by refusing to extend it to the other major substantive area where it had been applied by the lower courts for some time—seniority. The first two of these steps appear in *Washington* v. *Davis;* the third required an additional case.

As noted above, *Griggs* was apparently significant for other than title VII cases insofar as it implied that neutral practices producing racially disproportionate results would have to be justified; that, for the purposes of antidiscrimination law, intent would mean no more than voluntary conduct producing racially disproportionate results; and that the best way to avoid or at least defer the impact of the first two was to initiate a voluntary affirmative action program. In *Washington v. Davis,* the Court explicitly rejected the first two implications, thereby removing any suggestion of obligation from the third and relegating it to the easier world of voluntary tokenism.

Washington v. Davis involved a test that purported to measure verbal ability, vocabulary, reading, and comprehension. The test was challenged in its role as a criterion for admission to the training program for District of Columbia police officers. Given a failure rate that was four times as high for blacks as for whites, the plaintiffs asserted, in an action commenced before title VII became applicable to governmental employment, that the test was prima facie unconstitutional. The Court held that absent direct or inferential proof that the test was employed with a design to produce racially disproportionate results, the disproportionate failure rate was not itself significant enough to create a prima facie case and that there was no requirement that the test demonstrate any rationality at all. Using an intriguing kind of inside-out reasoning, the Court quickly rebutted the common sense notion that racial discrimination under the fifth or fourteenth amendments meant the same thing as racial discrimination under title VII. Mr. Justice White's terse offering was that "[w]e have never held that the constitutional standard for adjudicating claims of invidious racial discrimination is identical to the standards applicable under Title VII, and we decline to do so today."

To support its position, the Court offered a "parade of horribles" argument that would be embarrassing in a first-year law class: "A [contrary] rule . . . would raise serious questions about, and perhaps invalidate, a whole range of tax, welfare, public service, regulatory, and licensing statutes that may be more burdensome to the poor and to the average black than to the more affluent white." For precedent, the Court turned to cases like *Wright v. Rockefeller,* which involved electoral districting, but failed to explain why a conclusion that an inherently nonrational decision like districting need not be justified in rational terms compels the conclusion that an ostensibly rational practice like testing is equally secure from scrutiny.

Thus, with quiet efficiency the Court eliminated all extra-title VII implications of *Griggs.* The alternative holding of *Washington v. Davis* went a step further, softening the severe scrutiny thought to be required by *Griggs* to the point where *Griggs* is no longer much of a threat even in title VII cases. *Griggs* itself had never reached the question of degree of rationality demanded from the tests, since the case offered a strong inference of purposeful discrimination and the employer declined to offer any proof concerning the validity of the test. *Griggs* did, however, use strong language in its insistence on job-relatedness, business necessity, and the elimination of "built-in headwinds" to minority employment. In addition, *Griggs* cited with approval the tough stance on job-relatedness taken by the Equal Employment Opportunity Commission (EEOC) and paid homage to the EEOC as deserving of deference in its administrative interpretations of the statute. This strict insistence on proof of job-relatedness seemed doctrinally secure as late as 1975, when the Court in *Albemarle Paper Co. v. Moody* insisted on genuine proof of job-relatedness and again relied on the EEOC guidelines.

In three respects, the Court in *Washington v. Davis* dropped any pretense of strictness with respect to job-relatedness and simultaneously abandoned its posture of deference to the EEOC: the test was ultimately validated by nothing more than intuitive generalization. There may have been evidence that the challenged test correlated with some degree of significance with another test given to trainees at the end of the training program, but there was no evidence that either the entrance test or the final test in any way related to qualities or abilities relevant to being a police officer. In fact, there was no proof that the test given at the end of the training program measured anything taught in that program, even assuming that the program was related to future performance as a police officer. The most that was established was that the test correlated with another test, which in itself is hardly surprising. But that other test may or may not measure something, which something, even if measured, may or may not have anything to do with the job for which the training program is supposed to prepare those who pass the initial test. In this context, the Court's conclusion, shared with the district court, that "some minimum verbal and communicative skill would be very useful, if not essential, to satisfactory progress in the training regimen seems little more than an assumption of the desired conclusion.

Thus, while *Griggs* remains good law with respect to title VII cases involving tests and other objective hiring criteria, it has lost a good deal of its force even in those areas. And . . . the Court rejected the unanimous views of eight courts of appeals by refusing to apply the *Griggs* approach to its other major area of application—seniority. In *International Brotherhood of Teamsters v. United States,* the Court conceded that the *Griggs* approach to neutral practices under title VII would serve to invalidate seniority systems that perpetuated the effects of prior racial discrimination even where such discrimination was not proved or provable as a separate violation of the Act. The Justices nevertheless concluded, by a seven-to-two majority, that the qualified exemption clause of section 703(h) insulated such seniority systems from attack as violations in themselves. To reach its result, the Court chose to construe the qualified exemption for seniority contrary to the way it had construed the very similar qualified exemption for tests in *Griggs*. In addition, the Court distinguished as remedy rather than violation its own willingness to uphold awards of retroactive seniority in hiring dis-

crimination cases. That position had been taken just a year earlier in *Franks v. Bowman Transportation Co.,* which turned out to be a remedial counterpoint decided in advance of the case narrowing the violation. The majority relied on the legislative history of the original 1964 Civil Rights Act, which, although seeming to support its position, is difficult to reconcile with equally persuasive arguments based on the legislative history of the 1972 amendment-reenactment of title VII. The latter argument simply presumes some congressional awareness of the numerous and consistent lower court decisions construing section 703(h).

Ultimately, however, the doctrinal intractability of *Teamsters* is irrelevant. The point here is not that *Teamsters* was wrong or that *Griggs* was right. It may even be conceded that as a purely logical matter *Griggs* could have been decided the other way. The point here is that *Teamsters* is basically inconsistent with *Griggs* and that it amounts to a rigorous reassertion of the perpetrator perspective. To challenge the effects of seniority, which means lay-offs or reduced opportunities for better jobs, it is now necessary, however disproportionate the racial impact, to prove that those suffering the consequences are identifiable victims of post-1965 instances of hiring discrimination. If all you can show is pre-1965 discrimination, however blatant, you have no claim, unlike *Griggs,* where the Court seemed to regard as relevant that the testing scheme was perpetuating the employer's pre-Act discrimination or the effects of years of school segregation. But even for post-1965 hiring discrimination, the effect of *Teamsters* is to place the difficult burdens on the victims, who must identify their perpetrators before being entitled to relief rather than rely on the impact of the seniority system to establish a prima facie case and thereby switch the burden to justifying its results to the defendants. Finally, if the *Griggs* standards continue to be relaxed, it will be that much more difficult to establish the hiring discrimination that is prerequisite to any remedy altering the adverse impact of seniority systems.

SOCIAL CONTROL IN HISTORICAL PERSPECTIVE: FROM PRIVATE TO PUBLIC RESPONSES TO CRIME.

STEVEN SPITZER and ANDREW T. SCULL

The rising costs of crime control are among the most refractory of the problems facing modern capitalist states. In the United Kingdom, for instance, the costs of justice and law more than doubled between 1951 and 1973, increasing from 0.6% to 1.4% of the gross national product (Gough, 1975:60). From 1902 to 1960 expenditures on local police in the United States increased more than 30-fold—from $50,000,000 to $1,612,000,000 (Bordua and Haurek, 1970:57)—and had reached a level of $3,803,000,000 by 1970 (U.S. Bureau of the Census, 1975:416). Moreover, in the United States since 1942, expenditures on corrections by state-run systems have at least doubled every decade, moving from $14,000,000 in 1902 to $1,051,000,000 in 1970 (U.S. Bureau of the Census, 1975:416).

The rapid escalation of these costs, which has been paralleled by a massive expansion of other forms of state activity (Gough, 1975), has contributed to the "fiscal crisis of the state" (O'Connor, 1973). In an effort to alleviate this crisis, the state has struggled to divest itself of at least some of its most expensive control functions. One strategy has been to encourage, on at least a limited scale, the "privatization" of police and cor-

rectional services—thereby both reducing social expenses and stimulating investment in the private sector. (On the police, see Kakalik and Wildhorn, 1971; Klare, 1975. On corrections, see Griggs and McCune, 1972; Rutherford, 1973; Bailey, 1974; Scull, 1977, chapter 8.) This development has been part of a broader process through which the spheres of public and private activity have become progressively less distinct.

The interpenetration of public and private services is, of course, not without historical precedent. In fact, the notion that the state should be considered solely responsible for the control of crime and other "public" services was not really established in England and America until the latter part of the 19th century. Prior to that period, social protection and services were frequently offered as part of an explicit contractual arrangement between two interested parties. Radzinowicz (1956:259), for example, noted that "the enlistment of Police Officers in private service in the form in which it flourished in the eighteenth and early nineteenth centuries transformed the Police Offices into police markets." Well into the 19th century the English policeman was "a member of a liberal profession, whose fortune and standing in life depended on the goodwill of his private clients" (Radzinowicz, 1956:255). Until 1835, the handling of the poor

Source: From David F. Greenberg (Ed.), Corrections and Punishment (*Beverly Hills, Calif.: Sage, 1978*), pp. 265-86. *Reprinted by permission.*

in England also took on many features of a profit-able business. Sidney and Beatrice Webb (1927:412) described the "adoption of the plan of dealing with the nuisance of destitution very much as with the nuisance of town dung, namely by handing it over at a fixed price to the speculator who saw his way to make the largest pecuniary profit from the contract." Among the varieties of "poor farming" were "contracting for the maintenance of all the persons having any claim on the Parish; contracting merely for the management of the workhouse; contracting for infants and children; and, in the latter decades, contracting for lunatics" (Webb and Webb, 1927:412). The last arrangement evolved into a "trade in lunacy" (Parry-Jones, 1972), wherein a system of private profit-making madhouses be-came the dominant form of institutional provision for the mad in England until 1850. This relatively "pure" form of private enterprise may be com-pared with the operation of 18th century English gaols which, although public in name and oper-ated under official auspices, were actually almost universally administered as the private profit-making concerns of the gaolers. According to the Webbs (1922:5), "so completely was it assumed and accepted that the keeping of the gaol was a profitable business that it was exceptional for any salary to be attached to the post; and, down to 1730, this unsalaried office was even made the subject of purchase and sale."

The examples outlined above present us with a fascinating research question: How can we ex-plain *both* the emergence of profit-making con-trol arrangements during the period between the end of the 17th and the beginning of the 19th centuries, and the subsequent movement from private to public forms of "deviance manage-ment" in the modern era? In order to shed some light on these developments we will concentrate on the process through which crime control was "privatized" and then "socialized" in England. The decision to embark upon a historical investi-gation of changes within English rather than American society was dictated by three consider-ations: (1) the privatization and socialization of

crime control occurred first and most com-prehensively in England; (2) the historical mate-rials on England are far superior to those available on America; and (3) the reforms introduced in England not only predated, but in many cases provided the model for, similar innovations in the United States. (On the police, see Reith, 1952, chapter 6; Richardson, 1970; Rubenstein, 1973. On gaols jails and prisons, see McKelvey, 1936; Lewis, 1965.)

Before beginning our discussion, we will try to eliminate any conceptual confusion by identify-ing what we take to be the essential characteris-tics of private and public varieties of crime con-trol. It should be noted, however, that these characteristics are rarely, if ever, found in pure form in the societies we have studied. Instead, they represent end points in a theoretical con-tinuum along which responses to crime have been and continue to be organized and carried out.

By public crime control arrangements we mean those which are characteristically sup-ported by taxation, organized on a bureaucratic basis, and operated directly by full-time em-ployees of the state. Private forms, by contrast, are predicated on a market or contractual rela-tionship and may be distinguished from services and arrangements offered voluntarily or through some sense of community obligation on the one hand and from modes of control that are or-ganized and directly implemented by a single monopolistic entity (i.e., the state) on the other. In their simplest form, private arrangements may in-volve the offer of a monetary reward, fee, or gratuity by a private individual, group (corpora-tion), or the state to *anyone* who will perform specific services (protection, apprehension of of-fenders, recovery of stolen property, etc.). When efforts to achieve crime control take this form, those paying for and those providing services are normally unknown to each other in advance of the transaction, and their relationship tends to be fortuitous and temporary rather than regularized and stable. Postings of rewards by the state or private individuals are examples of this form. At a more developed level these arrangements may involve an independently negotiated contract between a single party (individual or corporation) and a specific individual or organization willing to provide services on an exclusive basis. Personal bodyguards, private investigators, and corporate security forces are examples of this pattern. Finally, in the advanced stages of capitalist society, when private profit making and public services are most intertwined, the state may underwrite or contract out for the private provision of public services on an ongoing basis. The state, in this instance, serves as an intermediary between those offering control services (corporations and agencies) and those consuming them (the "public"), and the provision of services which have come to be defined as the responsibility of the state (including crime control) provide yet another opportunity for private profit.

It should be clear from this discussion that it is not the source of funding in itself that defines crime control as public or private, but the character of the *relationship* between those seeking and those supplying services. If the services are supplied by "public servants" as part of their routine responsibilities as agents of the state, the services are public. On the other hand, if these services are furnished through the workings of a competitive, profit-oriented market, they are private. It is only when the enforcement of the law and the punishment of criminals takes place exclusively within the domain of public bureaucracies at public cost that we can say that socialization of crime control is complete.

THE NATURE AND DEVELOPMENT OF PRIVATE CRIME CONTROL

It was not until medieval institutions of collective responsibility began to decay that the control of crime could become a profitable undertaking in English society. The ancient Saxon and Norman institutions of hue and cry (*hutesium et clamor*), *posse comitatus* (the sheriff's power of calling out every man between 15 and 50 years of age), collective fines, outlawry, and the frankpledge were

predicated upon the feasibility of collective, informal, unitary, and spontaneous reactions to crime. The character of this system is suggested by Pollock and Maitland's (1968:578–579) description of how thieves were expected to be handled prior to the 18th century:

> When a felony is committed, the hue and cry . . . should be raised. . . . The neighbours should turn out with the bows, arrows, knives, that they are bound to keep and besides much shouting, there will be horn-blowing; the "hue" will be "horned" from vill to vill. Now if a man is overtaken by hue and cry while he has still about him the signs of his crime, he will have short shrift. Should he make any resistance, he will be cut down. But even if he submits to capture, his fate is already decided. . . . He will be brought before some court (like enough it is a court hurriedly summoned for the purpose), and without being allowed to say one word in self-defence, he will be promptly hanged, beheaded or precipitated from a cliff, and the owner of the stolen goods will perhaps act as an amateur executioner.

Although "civic responsibility" for the apprehension and punishment of evildoers was not always a sufficient spur to action (fines were frequently invoked for nonperformance),[1] as long as the suppression of crime was a community affair and could be accomplished without specialized agents and facilities there was little opportunity for profiteering from its control. When specialization initially occurred—as in the establishment of the office of constable in the late 13th century (Critchley, 1972)—officials went without pay, their duties to be discharged out of civic rather than pecuniary motives. But as feudalism declined and England was transformed from a series of relatively homogeneous and tightly integrated communities into a differentiated and loosely articulated society, the informal and voluntary system of social control became increasingly suspect. In a society where interests were becoming more distinct, associations more transitory, relationships more fragmentary, and public order

---

[1]For an illustration of how the principle of collective liability was resurrected in the 18th century see Thompson (1975).

more fragile (see Beloff, 1938), it made less and less sense to rely on the alacrity and spirit of the people to secure obedience and tranquility. Rather than appealing to something as unreliable as "public spirit," emphasis was increasingly placed on personal needs. Private interests thus came to replace social obligations as the main-spring of the control system. By the 18th century the system had reached a point where the architects of legal control were beginning to ask "private individuals for no higher motive than self-interest, and were confident that they could, by a system of incentives and deterrents—rewards and punishments, bribes and threats—so exploit human greed and fear that there would be no need to look for anything so nebulous and un-realistic as public spirit" (Pringle, 1958:212).

The twin spurs of fear and greed were thus intended to work hand in hand. Fear was nourished by the extension of capital penalties to a wide range of offenses,[2] while greed was ap-pealed to through a burgeoning network of incen-tives and rewards. Of the two motivating forces, the latter proved to be more determinative, be-cause, in the absence of an effective prosecutorial agency and regular police, some means had to be discovered to inflict punishments (whatever their intensity) on those who violated the law. Because of the long-standing view of police as a "system of tyranny; an organized army of spies and inform-ers, for the destruction of all public liberty, and the disturbance of all private happiness" (J. P. Smith cited in Thompson, 1963:22) and because of the inadequacy of "spontaneous enforce-ment," any concerted attempt to regulate crime had to be undertaken "from a distance."[3] It was

generally assumed, therefore, that the regulation of crime could best be achieved by manipulating the latent conflicts of interest and aspirations for gain within both criminal and "respectable" segments of society. The initiative of the law-abiding and the depravity of the "dangerous classes" were to be harnessed as a single force—a force that could function in lieu of direct official intervention. At least in theory, society would be disciplining itself, and the incentives provided by private citizens and the government were no more than a convenient stimulant to proper action.

It was within this context that a system of pri-vately organized crime control could emerge and begin to flourish by the middle of the 18th cen-tury. The incentives that evolved during this period were explicitly designed to induce collab-oration of the citizenry in the suppression of crime. Private interests were seen as the key to the system, and, if these interests could be skill-fully adjusted to the interests of the criminal jus-tice system, they were expected to act, in the words of one reformer, "with the certainty of gravitation" (Chadwick, 1829:288). In some cases, inducements involved no more than the reduction or elimination of civic obligation. One such measure was the so-called "Tyburn Ticket," which entitled anyone bringing a certain class of felons to justice to a lifelong exemption from the burden of serving "all offices within the parish or ward where the felony was committed" (Colqu-houn, 1806:391). In other instances there were categorical pardons for accomplices, statutory and ad hoc rewards offered by government, as well as special rewards and gratuities announced by private individuals, insurance companies, prosecution societies, property owners associa-tions, and groups of residents. Informing was en-couraged by the promise of pardons and shares of

---

[2]Radzinowicz (1948:4) estimated that the number of capi-tal statutes in England grew from about 50 to over 200 be-tween the years 1688 and 1820. But as Thomson (1950:65) suggested, "the policy of mere terror did not deter; for so long as detection and capture were so uncertain, and juries were reluctant to convict where conviction meant disproportionate penalties, these offences continued in abundance."

[3]The character of objections to the establishment of a pre-ventive police may be gauged from the conclusions of an 1822 commission: "It is difficult to reconcile an effective sys-tem of police with that perfect freedom of action and exemp-

tion from interference which are the great privileges and blessing of society in this country; and Your Committee think that the forfeiture or curtailment of such advantages are too great a sacrifice for improvements in police, or facilities in detection of crime, however desirable in themselves if abstractedly considered" (cited in Thomson, 1950:66).

any goods seized by the authorities, and those who informed soon became known as "voluntary police" who were "always on the alert to discover any infringement of the law which might prove a source of profit to themselves" (Radzinowicz, 1956:146).

The long-range and indirect nature of the incentive arrangements fostered a system of payment by results. In consequence, many crime control services took on the character of *piecework* rather than work for wages. One commentator of the period argued that constables should not be "compelled day after day . . . to go in search of some atrocious ruffian" (Allen, 1821:29), only to be informed that he had merely done what was expected. "Extra remuneration for extra service" was considered far preferable to a general increase in salaries. Similarly, because keepers of gaols were paid through fees rather than wages, they too were more like independent purveyors of services than salaried employees.

The changing character of the private system and the reasons for its transformation can be grasped most clearly if we consider two of its specific features—policing and imprisonment. Policing for profit had its origins in the office of the constable. Although this office traditionally "rested on the principle of unpaid performance of duty by members of the community as their turn came round" (Tobias, 1975:106), it gradually took on pecuniary potential as (1) citizens chose to pay deputies to perform these disagreeable services in their places, (2) constables were able to demand rewards and portions of recovered goods in exchange for their services, and (3) private individuals and organizations began to contract those with experience in law enforcement for specific protective or investigative duties.

The growth of deputization was such that by the first decades of the 19th century "there were few parishes in which the office was not filled by a deputy" (Radzinowicz, 1956:278). Hart (1951:24) reported that, "as the duties of constables increased in volume and perplexity, the office became more and more unpopular. The middle classes in particular regarded it as a waste

of their time, and disliked having to assume for a whole year an unpaid, arduous office which might entail enforcing unpopular laws. They therefore took to paying deputies to do the job for them." Eventually, according to Radzinowicz (1956:278), "by taking bribes, by frauds and extortions, they [the deputies] made such a profitable trade of their offices that many were prepared to serve for nothing." When salaries were attached to the office, they remained quite low (less than £100 a year in 1822). Nevertheless, profits could be gained privately from rewards and forfeitures and publicly from such routine duties as serving warrants and serving as a witness for the prosecution and by claiming a wide range of "operating expenses." In some cases, magistrates even "ordered a fine when otherwise they might have sentenced an offender to imprisonment; for if they sent him to prison, then the officer would get nothing 'for his pains'" (Radzinowicz, 1956:242).

The reluctance of authorities to raise salaries as well as the growing opportunities for enterprising constables did much to promote the appearance of specialists in police services. "An officer who had risen high enough in his profession to become personally known could aspire to more than occasional remuneration for petty services. The next step in his career would be to obtain a number of well paid special employments consisting of permanent or temporary duties, for which he might be hired by any one willing and able to pay" (Radzinowicz, 1956:257). Wealthy individuals, merchants, the Bank of England, theaters, and other places of entertainment were frequent employers of police.[4] But services of this type were not only arranged through private agreement; they could also be secured through the mediation of police offices themselves. At the beginning of the 19th century, it was common practice for the police offices to "send officers

---

[4]Outside incorporated towns, private police were frequently hired by railway companies and industrial concerns to maintain order among "large bodies of unruly workmen" (Mather, 1959:80).

from London at the request and expense of private individuals," and officers who received nominal stipends from the parish were encouraged to accept "additional gratuities from interested persons" (Radzinowicz, 1956:261).

When the provision of private police services received the countenance of official authority, the stage was set for the growth of what became the apotheosis of the incentive system—the Bow Street Police Offices (Pringle, 1958; Fitzgerald, 1888). As a marketplace for the trading in police services, this office became " 'a pecuniary establishment to itself,' the headquarters of a closely knit caste of speculators in the detection of crime, self-seeking and unscrupulous, but also daring and efficient when daring and efficiency coincided with their private interest" (Radzinowicz, 1956:263). At about the same time (the beginning of the 19th century), the first large-scale collective sponsorship of policing was undertaken with the founding of the Thames River Police. This force, consisting of twice as many officers as employed by all the Metropolitan Police Offices, was charged with suppressing threats to maritime commerce. The West India Merchants, a group whose interests this experimental force was directly intended to serve, absorbed 80% of the initial operating costs (see Colquhoun, 1800). In 1800, two years after it began operation, the Marine Police Establishment was established as a publicly authorized and supported force "for the more effectual Prevention of Depredations on the River Thames and Vicinity" (House of Commons, 1799–1800:723).

Paradoxically, this first venture in organized policing, although private in origin, provided the springboard for the development of policing as a publicly administered and financed service.[5] The Thames River Police were to be the model for the subsequent development of the Metropolitan Police in 1829 and the progressive socialization of policing throughout the 19th century.

Prior to the reforms of the 19th century, imprisonment (much like policing) frequently afforded an opportunity for private gain. But to understand the peculiar history of incarceration in England, one must keep in mind that imprisonment was always among the most costly forms of punitive control. This fact provided a strong disincentive to its use as a routine form of punishment in the premodern era and led to efforts "to enforce a line of conduct on a defaulter by pledges of payments rather than by detaining his body" (Pugh, 1968:2). However, with the weakening of collective responsibility, some form of custodial imprisonment became essential, if only to secure a defendant's appearance for trial or a condemned man's presence for infliction of sentence. By the Middle Ages, the primitive lockups which served such functions were also being used to some extent for coercive imprisonment, in the first place "as a means of securing the payment into the Exchequer of debts due to the Crown" (Pugh, 1968:5) and later as a sanction against all types of debtors. While the expenses of the first gaols sometimes came out of the royal purse, the Crown increasingly "relieved itself of such expenses, together with the costs of maintenance, by requiring a subject to keep a goal in return for land, or by selling a right to do so in return for cash" (Pugh, 1968:5). All gaols remained nominally the king's, but in practice they were in a wide variety of hands—the possession of local landed magnates, of ecclesiastical potentates, or of town corporations under royal charter, each of whom "clung to them as income-yielding properties" (Webb and Webb, 1922:3).

As this overview suggests, the distribution and administration of gaols was haphazard and fortuitous. Some attempts were periodically made to ameliorate this situation: for example, the 1532 Gaols Act placed nominal responsibility for gaol management on the justices of the peace and endeavored to rationalize the distribution of gaols; but such efforts met with little success (Pugh,

---

[5]It is significant that the success of the Thames River Police experiment depended on a renunciation of the desultory incentive (piecework) system in favor of established wages. The instructions to the first officers were clear: "you are to receive no fee or gratuity from any person whatsoever, for any duty you perform" (Colquhoun, 1800:642).

1968:343–344). From the late 16th century on, these medieval gaols were supplemented by a number of houses of correction, for the most part modeled on the London Bridewell (1557) and supposedly under the direct administration of the justices of the peace. Originally, these places were intended to serve as a deterrent to the able-bodied idler and vagrant and, under mercantilist principles, to add to the national wealth by setting the poor to work. By the end of the 17th century, however, the distinctive features of the houses of correction had all but disappeared, and they were essentially used interchangeably with gaols as places of pretrial detention, as a punishment for various minor offences, and as a means of keeping debtors in custody. Since neither church dignitaries nor landowners nor local justices were in the least inclined to busy themselves with the sordid day-to-day business of administering gaols or houses of correction, such places were used simply as sources of income, being leased out to those desirous of speculating in this form of human misery. Thus, "both institutions were, in effect, run as private ventures of their masters or keepers" (Webb and Webb, 1922:15).

Such businesses were conducted in a multitude of settings. Of the 518 gaols that John Howard surveyed in 1777, six (all in London) were relatively sizable establishments, each containing 90 or more prisoners; but in the provinces, only seven housed as many as 50 inmates, and well over a hundred confined fewer than 10 (Webb and Webb, 1922:131). Small operations like these could scarcely afford to provide specialized accommodations, and few of the gaols of the period were purpose-built. Many, indeed, consisted of little more than a room or two in a tavern or gatehouse, more or less ill adapted to serve as a place of confinement. At West Wycombe, for example, the "gaol" consisted "of two small rooms in the back court of the keeper's public house, about seven feet by three, and six feet high: apertures in the doors: . . . the windows are almost closed up by strong planks nailed across for security" (Howard, 1792:282). In small, often decaying structures of this sort, pris-

oners were thrown together in a single heterogeneous mass: "Debtors and felons, men and women, the young beginner and the old offender, . . . idiots and lunatics" (Howard, 1792:8)—all subject to the depredations of entrepreneurial gaolers, "low-bred, mercenary and oppressive, barbarous fellows, who think of nothing but enriching themselves" (*Gentleman's Magazine*, 1767).

Like other "deviant farmers" of the period, gaolers extracted their living from those whom they kept confined, a practice which obviated the need to pay them a wage and hence kept demands on local taxpayers to a minimum. "Every incident in prison life, from admission to discharge, was made the occasion for a fee" (Webb and Webb, 1922:5), and tables of legitimate charges were often ratified by the local justices at quarter sessions. For an appropriate additional payment, prisoners could obtain better food and accommodation "on the master-side" with the gaoler's family (Howard, 1792:238). Similarly, "the tap for the sale of beer was a recognized and legitimate source of profit to the keeper. . . . There was a public house in every prison. . . . In the King's Bench [prison in London] there were at one time no less than thirty gin shops, and in 1776, 120 gallons of gin were sold weekly besides other spirits and eight butts of beer a week." So profitable was this trade and so anxious were the keepers to further it that not infrequently "the treatment of the prisoner depended upon his consumption of liquor" (George, 1965:291).

Even the physical decrepitude of many of the gaols was turned to advantage. To guard against escapes, prisoners were chained: but "if they have the money to pay, their irons are knocked off, for fettering is a trade by which some gaolers derive considerable emolument" (W. Smith, 1776:12; see also Pugh, 1968:178–180). So long as the gaol required but minimal subventions from local taxpayers, most magistrates were only too willing to turn a blind eye to the keepers' methods—a willingness accentuated by the physical hazards of the alternative. Howard (1777:379) reported that a standard response among the gaolers whom he questioned about magistrates' tours of inspection was, "Those gentlemen think that if they came into my gaol they should soon be in their graves." And in view of the massive prevalence of typhus or "gaol fever," such an attitude was scarcely unrealistic. There was tacit agreement to leave undisturbed any arrangements from which both parties apparently benefited.

THE TRANSFORMATION OF PRIVATE INTO PUBLIC CONTROL

Although the system of profit-oriented crime control seemed to address the needs and mirror the priorities of 18th century English society, its dominance and appeal were relatively short-lived. Like most social arrangements, it was transformed by pressures operating from both within and without.

When we examine the internal structure of 18th century private controls it is clear that the very principles upon which these controls were founded contributed to their demise. While unbridled self-interest may serve as a powerful stimulus to action under certain conditions, it must always be articulated within a collectively oriented system if that action is to serve social rather than personal ends. The problem with the arrangements that evolved during this period was that they failed to integrate opportunities for gain within a coherent administrative framework. Without this integration, an effective link could not be forged between individual and collective interest. As long as the market in crime control services remained diffuse and decentralized, the activities of independent profit-seekers could only be imperfectly coordinated at best. Moreover, since the spurs to action tended to be ad hoc and provisional (rather than part of a centrally conceived and directed plan), a net of incentives was woven which, instead of trapping the "criminal classes," grew ever more tangled and porous. Finally, it may be argued that the method of payment-by-results upon which the system was so firmly established actually encour-

aged the very behavior it was designed to eliminate.

The irrationality and inefficiency of the "trading in justice" may be illustrated by a few brief examples. As its very foundations the administration of justice was corrupted by structurally generated pressures to turn "offices of burden" into "offices of profit" (see George, 1965:23ff.). The justice of the peace or magistrate "was the product of the system which aimed at making the administration of justice self-supporting by exacting a fee for every act that was performed. These fees were individually small in amount, and they could only be made to yield an income to magistrate and clerk by a perpetual flow of business which it thus became the interest of both of them to promote" (Webb and Webb, 1906:326). Consequently, "the transition from 'encouraging business' to a corrupt or oppressive use of magisterial authority in order to extort fees or levy blackmail was, to a Trading Justice, seldom perceptible" (Webb and Webb, 1906:326). Pringle (1958:57) even noted that "to keep up the flow of business some magistrates employed barkers and runners to tout for customers and when business was slack the magistrates even allowed credit, issuing warrants and summonses on easy terms."

In a similar fashion, because of their position in the structure of rewards, constables were encouraged to instigate crime. Thief-takers were turned into thief-makers by the opportunities for lucrative bargaining and piecework.[6] This pattern took two major forms: (1) consorting with organized thieves in the commission of an offense and then acting as a go-between (for a fee) to effect the return of the stolen property and (2) trapping innocent victims into crimes to obtain rewards. The first practice was "encouraged by the great banking-houses, who were eager to recover their property, or a portion of it, on any terms" (Fitzgerald, 1888:141). Thief-takers were more likely to compound the felony than bring

[6]For a similar account of how police in New York were more "private entrepreneurs than public servants" and the abuses of the fee system, see Richardson (1970:23-50).

the felon to justice because "when a sum like £20,000 had been stolen, and perhaps half of it might be recovered by negotiation, the statutory reward of £40 per robber became too trivial to be "considered" (Pringle, 1958:161). The second practice was perpetuated by constables and others who were willing to stage offenses and then falsely accuse novices or young offenders. "Thief-makers were ruthless ... not shrinking ever from 'swearing away' the life of an innocent, and their trade prospered in proportion to the progressive multiplication of rewards" (Radzinowicz, 1956:327).

The system of rewards as a whole led to a "horrible trade in blood demands" and was linked to an increase in crime "fostered and cultivated by the very persons set to watch over and prevent it (London *Times,* 1817, cited in Radzinowicz, 1956:338). Informers were part of this trade and were taken to task by reformers of the day because they did not take, "nor wish to take measures to prevent parties infringing the law, but merely to entrap them in order to get the penalty" (*Parliamentary Papers,* 1834:1). The practice of pardoning felons was likewise scored by critics like Edward Sayer (1784:25), who argued that it created "an asylum opening itself for the reception of offenders into the bosom of Justice herself."

The organization of incarceration for profit reflected, in yet another way, the internal contradictions of privatized control. For example, in 1701 the House of Lords refused to pass a bill "regulating" the overcrowded King's Bench and Fleet Prisons on the ground that, if the number of prisoners fell, "the profits thereby accruing will not be proportional recompense to the officers to attend the Courts, so that the king's four Courts at Westminster will be without prisons and without officers to assist them" (House of Commons, 1701). Moreover, since "mere parsimony could not ... make the gaol yield a profit ... many eighteenth century gaolers ... varied the squalid misery of prison life by deliberate torture for the purpose of extortion, and ... a whole system of skillful extortion under the pressure of wanton

discomfort and physical pain, and the sale of licentious indulgence to those who consented to pay, prevailed in the majority of contemporary prisons" (Webb and Webb, 1922:21). Whether the purpose of incarceration was deterrence through proportional punishment or rehabilitation, these arrangements were palpably counterproductive. But even more inconsistent with effective control were the habits of prison wardens who were willing to sell the "right to escape to such [debtors] as could afford their terms" (Webb and Webb, 1922:28).

The *external* changes promoting the abandonment of private and the adoption of public means of crime control form part of and are predicated upon a much larger movement toward rational management in public administration, finance, and economic policy—indeed, of social life as a whole. On the most fundamental level, such rationalization was compelled by competition: in the private sector, between firms for markets; at the level of state administration, between states for political power (Weber, 1961). And the process was a progressive and self-perpetuating one: that is, increased rationalization in one sector reacted back on and reinforced pressures toward rationalization in the other, fueling a sustained and cumulative advance in the direction of the increased systematization of human activity.

We might trace briefly just a few of the connections. Beyond a certain point, further developments of markets and long-distance trade were hindered by a locally based, arbitrary system of law enforcement, which was effective as a means of sustaining and reinforcing the authority and social position of a rural landed class[7] but which was highly inefficient as a means of guaranteeing the kind of stable, predictable, orderly environment that alone permits sophisticated forms of markets to flourish. Private, localized, and personal forms of control entailed the sacrifice of efficiency and certainty in the enforcement of the law and thereby also of a mea-

---

[7]See the superb analysis in Hay (1975), to which we are indebted here.

sure of public order and tranquillity. Indeed, "the English propertied classes in the eighteenth century were prepared to put up with a level of casual violence from their inferiors which would lead to martial law and the suspension of civil rights were it to occur today" (Stone, 1976:26). Moreover, such a system necessarily weakened the safeguards of *some* forms of property—"the property of men in trade, and manufacture and farming" (Hay, 1975:60). But the landed elite, who had "large numbers of personal servants to guard their plate and their wives" and who "as M.P.s . . . passed a mass of legislation which allowed them, as J.P.s, to convict . . . pilferers of their woods and gardens . . . without the trouble of legalistic indictments or tender-minded juries" (Hay, 1975:59), suffered no equivalent disabilities. On the contrary, *their* interests were threatened by a rationalization of the criminal law, which promised to substitute central for local authority and to remove perhaps the strongest single support of the social order over which they presided—all for the sake of benefits which would largely accrue to another class.

For the bourgeoisie, on the other hand, a rationalized crime control apparatus had a quite different significance. Although the factory system had allowed them to achieve greater control over such internal sources of disorder and loss as employee pilferage, dishonesty, and so forth (indeed, in the early stages of the Industrial Revolution this was perhaps its most significant advantage over the putting-out system), it did nothing to solve the pressing problem of external disorder—the ill-regulated, at times almost anarchistic, social context within which business was perforce conducted. Yet such an uncertain and unpredictable environment was at least as severe a limitation on the growth of a sophisticated exchange economy as the more obvious problem of effective control over the conduct of one's employees.

Riot was tolerated by the English ruling class in the 18th century; in fact, it formed an important channel of communication between the masses and their masters, a quasi-legitimate means of securing redress of grievances (Hobsbawm,

1959; Thompson, 1971). But "in the nineteenth century breaches of the peace, if committed by armed crowds, were deemed an incipient rebellion and an acute danger to the state; stocks collapsed and there was no bottom in prices. A shooting affray in the streets of the metropolis might destroy a substantial part of the national capital" (Polanyi, 1944; 186-187).

"The market system was more allergic to rioting than any other economic system we know" (Polanyi, 1944: 186). A stable public order was a precondition of rational calculation on the part of industrial capitalists, and in the absence of such calculability the development of all sectors of the market system—investment, production, trade—was held within strict limits. This problem of the establishment and maintenance of external order was, moreover, save in unusual circumstances,[8] something not amenable to private solutions. In the first place, with the growth of national and international markets, the geographical area which required pacification was simply too extensive, and the number and diversity of the actors whose interests and activities had to be combined and coordinated were simply too great. Even more serious, while capitalists as a class required a hitherto unprecedented degree of social order, it was in the interests of no one of them, *as an individual,* to provide or to contribute to its provision; for those who "irresponsibly" refused to do so would continue to enjoy the benefits of a more stable operating environment while giving themselves a competitive cost advantage. As a "collective good," order had to be collectively provided.

Even as the growing political power of the commercial classes brought with it a decreasing tolerance for disorder, the type of society that

[8]One such exception was the entrepôt trade centering on the Thames River, in which a limited number of actors dominated a form of economic activity essentially taking place within a geographically circumscribed area. This unusual situation permitted the development of a collaborative private solution to the problem of pilferage and thievery at the docks; and, not surprisingly, we find here one of the earliest (and privately supported) moves toward professionalized policing—the Thames River Police (see Colquhoun, 1800).

those same classes were busily creating was systematically undermining traditional sources of restraint and threatening the stability of the social system itself. Vertical linkages in the stratification order were first weakened, then in many cases destroyed, as the market undercut the significance of purely local ties and allegiances and as traditional bonds of obedience and deference to one's "natural superiors" gave way before the calculating impersonality of the wage labor system. This breakdown of the paternalistic foundations of society and the traditional institutions of control coincided with the sharpening of class antagonisms, heightening the dangers associated with perpetuating the 18th century reliance on the army as the ultimate protection against disorder. For the use of the military entailed "an alternation between no intervention and the most drastic procedures—the latter representing a declaration of internal war with lingering consequences of hate and resentment" (Silver, 1967:12).[9] Then, too, industrial capitalism promoted "what was taken at the time to be the virtually universal deterioration of family life. The stupendous social dislocation had affected this most fundamental of social institutions, and if anything was calculated to alarm the middle classes into a consciousness of possible social disaster, it was the notion that the most stabilizing of social maintenance systems was imperilled" (Marcus, 1974:211).

At the same time, however, the development of industry and markets had already proceeded sufficiently far to force the development of more efficient managerial techniques and a trained managerial class (Pollard, 1965), as well as the development of a much higher level of economic activity and a greater monetarization of the economy. These latter developments had massive effects on the possibilities for effective state action. The changing structure and trend of the economy

offered the state "ever-increasing possibilities of action, not only because greater production affords more extensive levying of taxes, but also because a more highly developed exchange economy allows one to establish taxes with greater accuracy" and to raise them with greater ease (Ardant, 1975:166). And the new administrative techniques and the emerging class of administrators and managers permitted the state to make effective use of its new fiscal muscle. Thus, those controlling the state apparatus found themselves pressed toward and capable of a far more effective and thoroughgoing intervention and control of social life than had hitherto been feasible; and, as these possibilities became realities, the resulting increase in the orderliness and predictability of social existence prompted further rationalization of economic life.

As a whole, then, the rationalization process clearly corresponded to the needs and aspirations of the commercial and manufacturing bourgeoisie, while it undermined the basis of the authority of the old rural aristocracy. The very entrenchment of the peers and gentry in the local political apparatus and their consequent ability to resist efforts to bring into being a more "rational" criminal justice system through permissive legislation placed further pressure on the bourgeoisie to opt for a national approach. Practically speaking, the administrative "reforms" of the English political system—the shift from a system based on (local) judicial and legislative power to one increasingly dominated by executive power and staffed by salaried professional workers (see Webb and Webb, 1963)—had their structural roots in the growing political power of the middle class, an increased power not so much produced as recognized and ratified in the 1832 reform of Parliament.

The rationalization of crime control consisted of a number of separate but closely interrelated changes. The control system increasingly came to be predicated on *instrumental* rather than *symbolic* methods: gross and capricious terror attended by the ceremonial trappings of authority (as in the public hangings at Tyburn) were replaced by a system which (at least in theory) was designed to work uniformly, evenhandedly, and with machinelike precision. The rise of imprisonment as the dominant response to crime brought to the fore a form of punishment precisely suited to uniform administration, allowing the infliction of a· standardized penalty of graduated intensity which could be adapted to match the gravity of the crime. In a caricature of marketplace rationality, it made possible the exaction of an infinitely variable "price" which the offender had to "pay" for his crime. Control was increasingly tied to certainty rather than severity of punishment, for Sir Samuel Romilly and other English penal reformers were convinced that "the occasional terror of the gallows would always be less effective than sure detection of crime and moderate punishments" (Hay, 1975:59). Hence the necessity of a professionalized police, for without adequate police, there could be no certainty of punishment and, therefore, at best an imperfect deterrent. With an organized police force there accrued still another advantage: instead of merely reacting to crime after the fact, crime might even be prevented. In parallel fashion, once the criminal had been caught, imprisonment in its newly emerging forms promised—vainly as it turned out—not simply to punish but also to rehabilitate him.

The rationalization of the system incorporated a wholly new emphasis on impersonal forms of control, with an associated decrease in the arbitrariness with which laws were enforced. Traditional responses to crime had been permeated by personal considerations. In a social order premised upon the fusion of political, economic, and social domination, squires, parsons, and wealthy landowners directly and personally supervised the apparatus of politico-legal coercion. At all levels, the law was used to reinforce the structure of personal ties and dependencies. The very discretion which the reformers condemned so vehemently played a crucial role in this process. The system of private prosecution, for example, allowed the gentry to become the arbitrators of the criminal's fate, for they could prosecute or not, as they chose. Likewise, the free and frequent use of the pardon, while undermining the certainty of the law, "helped create the mental structure of paternalism" (Hay, 1975:42). For pardons more often than not depended upon the intercession of propertied men in behalf of the condemned, and such acts were both the product of and a powerful reinforcement of personal ties running vertically through the stratification order. A similar reliance on deference and personal dependency was evident in the standard use of the yeomanry—a cavalry force largely composed of small landowners—for police purposes in times of civil disturbance and riot. Such tactics reflected the conviction that "the people would in many instances be debarred from violence by seeing those arrayed against them to whom they were accustomed to look up to as their masters" (an English MP of 1817, cited in Silver, 1967:9). And, of course, the actions of gaolers, thieftakers, and private police were usually fairly directly motivated by their personal (rather than impersonal) interests.

But the underlying structural supports of this "irrational," personalistic response to crime were slipping away beneath those who sought to defend it. At an ever-increasing pace, the market dissolved away local and communal ties, replacing the master-servant relationship with the cash nexus—the conviction that the employer "owed his employees wages, and once these were paid, the men had no further claim on him" (Mantoux, 1928:428). A social system whose notion of reciprocity did not extend beyond the wage contract could not long sustain paternalism as its reigning ideal. Moreover, the laborer was becoming, as Adam Smith, David Ricardo, Thomas Malthus, and other political economists recognized, no longer a human being but a thing—a "factor of production" along with land and capital, responding to market imperatives, not personal ties.[10] And on yet another level, the rise of a single national market to a position of overriding importance in English society was steadily un-

[10]Compare, for example, Adam Smith's comment (1776:183) that "the demand for men, like that for any other commodity, necessarily regulates the production of men; quickens when it goes slowly, and stops when it advances too fast."

dermining the rationale of a fragmentary, locally based response to crime.

One of the central achievements of capitalism as a system of domination was that "into the center of the historical stage it has brought a form of compulsion to labour for another that is purely economic and 'objective'" (Dobb, 1963:17). Just as the invisible hand of the marketplace provided an unequaled means of mystifying control over the work force, so the class character of the legal order could be masked by appearing to place that order firmly beyond the influence of human agency. The rise of the bourgeoisie to a position of cultural and political hegemony thus corresponded to a growing emphasis on impersonal forms of social control. For, through impersonal control, the newly dominant class could ideologically separate the enforcement of "constitutional" authority from its own social and economic ascendance; that is, it could present the surface appearance that society was now subject to "the rule of law and not of men." Here, then, was yet another support for a system of crime control with quasi-automatic regularity, uniformity, and efficiency and with as little evidence of human activity as possible. The public execution—that elaborate morality play with its individual performers—was replaced by the gray passionless prison—a mechanical "mill for grinding [anonymous] rogues honest and idle men industrious" (Jeremy Bentham to Jacques Brissot in Bentham, 1843:226). Without the necessary sentiments of deference among those to be controlled, "the use of social and economic superiors as police exacerbated rather than mollified class violence" (Silver, 1967:10), and manufacturers who noted this effect sought to depersonalize police operations by placing them in the hands of trained professionals. As with the transformation of the self-interested, profit-oriented gaoler into the salaried employee of a publicly financed prison system, the bureaucratization of police work placed day-to-day operations of the control system in the hands of faceless agents of the state, men who no longer operated in their own self-interest, but (presumably) in the general interest, and who discharged their responsibilities "ac-

cording to *calculable rules* and 'without regard for persons'" (Weber, 1946:215, emphasis in the original).

It was through this process, therefore, that the management of crime was rationalized and transformed into a responsibility of the state. But because these changes occurred within the context of class struggle and required the dissolution of long-standing social arrangements, they were not effected at the same rate throughout English society. There were many pockets of resistance to the standardization of the criminal law, the establishment of a preventive police, and the assimilation of prisons under state control. Resistance was strongest in areas where the grip of the landed gentry and their paternalistic institutions were most secure. Although the consolidation of crime control under a single national system was heralded by a series of legislative and administrative reforms between 1828 and 1835, "an extensive social reform is not effected overnight by the mere passage of a bill through Parliament. The administrative process by which it is implemented commonly stretches over a number of years, and resistance is encountered at every turn from those who have a vested interest in frustrating the measure" (Mather, 1959:112).

The metropolitan experiment in preventive police was undertaken swiftly and on a massive scale, but "police reform outside London was gradual, patchy and unspectacular compared to what happened in the Metropolis" (Hart, 1951:31). Despite the establishment of the London police in 1829, at least 53 boroughs (29% of the whole) possessed no police force in 1839, and as late as 1848 at least 22 corporate towns (12%) remained in this position (Mather, 1959:112). While efforts to establish a nationwide police force were given impetus by the industrial violence of the 1830s and 1840s, "the organization of the new police on a county basis meant that the rural districts of a county, remote from industrial unrest but heavily rated on account of the large amount of landed estate situated within them, would be footing the bill for the maintenance of public order in the relatively distant manufacturing towns and villages, where property of highly rateable value was more scarce" (Mather, 1959:131). Thus, although the introduction of salaried police into rural areas could not be completely halted, it could at least be delayed by magistrates who, "as the principal landowners of the county, had a vested interest in keeping down the rates" (Mather, 1959:131).

By the same token, uniform, centrally directed, and bureaucratically organized prison practices could be completely implemented only when the last vestiges of parochial power had withered away. The compromised character of legislative activity at the end of the 18th and first half of the 19th century offers one indication of how the struggle between bourgeois and landed interests evolved. The Prison Act of 1791 was drafted to apply the principles of projected national penitentiary to all places of confinement in England and Wales. Nevertheless, the act "could not decide to make the gaoler simply the salaried servant of the Justices, and, because it shrank from explicitly commanding the levy of a rate, it failed to abolish his fees, or the profit-making character of his post" (Webb and Webb, 1922:41). In 1823 an act was passed "for consolidating and amending the laws relating to the building and regulating of certain gaols and houses of correction in England and Wales" (Webb and Webb, 1922:74). But the act did "not contemplate . . . the appointment of Government inspectors to insist on the law being obeyed, nor did the Act provide any machinery for compelling negligent or recalcitrant local authorities to comply with its requirements" (Webb and Webb, 1922:75). Moreover, the act applied to only 130 prisons and did nothing to reform the debtors' prisons or the gaols and bridewells in local districts. The system of inspection was intended to standardize and regulate the conditions of confinement, but "it was not until the passing of the Prisons Act of 1865 that the inspectors . . . could rely on anything more than 'the uncertain weapons of persuasion and publicity, backed by the imponderable authority of a Secretary of State'" (Moir, 1969:139). With the passage of that act, central control was strengthened significantly, and "all 193 local prisons were forced

into the uniform regimen prescribed by the Home Office, and the local variations in diet, treatment and discipline which had resisted with such vigour the attempts of the inspectors were at last ironed out" (Moir, 1969:139).

While the commitment to personally administered, privately organized, and locally based crime control was not overturned without opposition, by the last quarter of the 19th century its fate was sealed. As the 20th century unfolded, social control was increasingly organized and carried out as a public effort—coordinated, financed, and implemented by the state.

CONCLUSION

The historical transformation of social control arrangements has seldom received systematic attention. Most of the accounts that we do possess are largely descriptive. To the extent that "explanations" *are* offered, they appeal to a number of factors, singly or in combination: some accounts emphasize the spread of humanitarian ideas and the activities of charismatic reformers; others postulate a crudely deterministic relationship between what is alleged to be a dramatic upsurge in crime rates and the adoption of more effective methods of control; while still others claim that reactions to crime are shaped by the conditions attending the emergence of an industrial and urbanized society.

In contrast to these accounts, we have argued that the privatization and subsequent socialization of crime control was conditioned by historically specific changes in the political and economic structure of English society. Taken together, these changes were to prove decisive for the development of what we know today as the "crime control establishment"—an establishment which both reinforces the priorities and reflects the problems of the modern capitalist state.

REFERENCES

Allen, L. B. (1821). Brief considerations on the present state of the police of the metropolis, London.

Ardant, G. (1975). "Financial policy and economic infrastructure of modern states and nations." Pp. 164–242 in C. Tilly (ed.), *The formation of national states in Western Europe*. Princeton, N.J.: Princeton University Press.

Bailey, R. H. (1974). "Can delinquents be saved by the sea?" *Corrections Magazine*, 1 (September):77–88.

Beloff, M. (1938). *Public order and popular disturbances, 1660–1714*. London: Oxford University Press.

Bentham, J. (1843). *Works* (vol. 10; J. Bowring, ed.). Edinburgh.

Bordua, D. J., and Haurek, E. W. (1970). "The police budgets's lot: Components of the increase in local police expenditures, 1902–1960." Pp. 57–70 in H. Hahn (ed.), *Police in urban society*. Beverly Hills, Calif.: Sage.

Chadwick, E. (1829). "Preventive police." *London Review*, 1:252–308.

Colquhoun, P. (1800). *A treatise on the commerce and police of the River Thames*. Montclair, N.J.: Patterson Smith.

——— (1806). *A treatise on the police of the metropolis*. Montclair, N.J.: Patterson Smith.

Critchley, T. A. (1972). *A history of police in England and Wales*. Montclair, N.J.: Patterson Smith.

Dobb, M. (1963). *Studies in the development of capitalism*. New York: International Publishers.

Fitzgerald, P. (1888). *Chronicles of Bow Street Police-Office*. Montclair, N.J.: Patterson Smith.

Gentleman's Magazine (1767), July.

George, D. M. (1965). *London life in the eighteenth century*. Middlesex, Eng.: Penguin.

Gough, I. (1975). "State expenditures in advanced capitalism." *New Left Review*, 92 (July–August):53–92.

Griggs, B. S. and McCune, G. R. (1972). "Community-based correctional programs: A survey and analysis." *Federal Probation*, 36 (June):7–13.

Hart, J. M. (1951). *The British police*. London: George Allen and Unwin.

Hay, D. (1975). "Property, authority and the criminal law." Pp. 17–63 in D. Hay, P. Linebaugh, J. G. Rule, E. P. Thompson, and C. Winslow (eds.). *Albion's fatal tree: Crime and society in eighteenth century England*. New York: Pantheon.

Hobsbawm, E. J. (1959). *Primitive rebels*. New York: W. W. Norton.

House of Commons (1701). *Journals* (May 15).

——— (1799–1800). *Journals, 55*:723–784.

Howard, J. (1777). *The state of prisons in England and Wales*. Warrington.

——— (1792). *The state of prisons in England and Wales* (4th ed.). Warrington.

Kakalik, J. S. and Wildhorn, S. (1971). *The private police industry: Its nature and extent* (vol. 2). Santa Monica, Calif.: Rand Corporation.

Klare, M. T. (1975). "Rent-a-cop: The boom in private police." *Nation*, 221 (November): 486–491.

Lewis, W. D. (1965). *From Newgate to Dannemora: The rise of the penitentiary in New York, 1796–1848*. Ithaca, N.Y.: Cornell University Press.

Mantoux, P. (1928). *The Industrial Revolution in the eighteenth century*. London: Cape.

Marcus, S. (1974). *Engels, Manchester and the working class*. New York: Vintage.

Mather, F. C. (1959). *Public order in the age of the Chartists*. Manchester: Manchester University Press.

McKelvey, B. (1936). *American prisons: A study in American social history prior to 1915*. Chicago: University of Chicago Press.

Moir, E. (1969). *The justice of the peace*. Middlesex, Eng.: Penguin.

O'Connor, J. (1973). *The fiscal crisis of the state*. New York: St. Martin's Press.

Parliamentary Papers (1834). "Report from the select committee on police of the metropolis." 16:407–421.

Parry-Jones, W. (1972). *The trade in lunacy*. London: Routledge and Kegan Paul.

Polanyi, K. (1944). *The great transformation*. Boston: Beacon.

Pollard, S. (1965). *The genesis of modern management*. Middlesex, Eng.: Penguin.

Pollock, F., and Maitland, F. W. (1968). *The history of English law* (vol. 2). Cambridge: Cambridge University Press.

Pringle, P. (1958). *The thief-takers*. London: Museum Press.

Pugh, R. B. (1968). *Imprisonment in medieval England*. Cambridge: Cambridge University Press.

Radzinowicz, L. (1948). *A history of English criminal law and its administration from 1750* (vol. 1). London: Stevens.

_____ (1956). *A history of English criminal law and its administration from 1750* (vol. 2). London: Stevens.

Reith, C. (1952). *The blind eye of history.* London: Faber and Faber.

Richardson, J. F. (1970). *The New York police: Colonial times to 1901.* New York: Oxford University Press.

Rubinstein, J. (1973). *City police.* New York: Ballantine.

Rutherford, A. (1973). "Youth corrections in Massachusetts." Pp. 283–297 in S. L. Messinger, S. Halleck, P. Lerman, N. Morris, P. V. Murphy, and M. E. Wolfgang (eds.), *Crime and justice annual.* Chicago: Aldine.

Sayer, E. (1784). *Observations on the police or civil government of Westminster with a proposal for a reform.* London.

Scull, A. T. (1977). *Decarceration: Community treatment and the deviant: A radical view.* Englewood Cliffs, N.J.: Prentice-Hall.

Silver, A. (1967). "The demand for order in civil society: A review of some themes in the history of urban crime, police and riot." Pp. 1–24 in D. Bordua (ed.), *The police.* New York: Wiley.

Smith, A. (1776). *The wealth of nations.* (A. Skinner, ed.). Middlesex, Eng.: Penguin.

Smith, W. (1776). *State of the gaols in London, Westminster, and Borough of Southwark.* London.

Stone, L. (1976). "Whigs, marxists, and poachers." *New York Review of Books,* 23 (February):25–27.

Thompson, E. P. (1963). *The making of the English working class.* New York: Vintage.

_____ (1971). "The moral economy of the English crowd in the eighteenth century." *Past and Present,* 50 (spring):73–136.

_____ (1975). *Whigs and hunters: The origin of the Black Act.* New York: Pantheon.

Thomson, D. (1950). *England in the nineteenth century.* Middlesex, Eng.: Penguin.

Tobias, J. J. (1975). "Police and public in the United Kingdom." Pp. 95–113 in G. L. Mosse (ed.), *Police forces in history.* Beverly Hills, Calif.: Sage.

U.S. Bureau of the Census (1975). *Historical statistics of the United States: Colonial times to 1970.* Washington, D.C.: U.S. Government Printing Office.

Webb, S., and Webb, B. (1906). *English local government: The parish and the county* (vol. 1). London: Archon.

_____ (1922). *English local government: English prisons under local government* (vol. 6). London: Archon.

_____ (1927). *English local government: English Poor Law history: Part I, The old Poor Law.* London: Longman's Green.

_____ (1963). *The development of English local government.* London: Oxford University Press.

Weber, M. (1946). *From Max Weber: Essays in sociology.* New York: Oxford University press.

_____ (1961). *General economic history.* New York: Collier.

CHAPTER FOUR

LAW AND IDEOLOGY

Some of the most exciting developments in the recent history of Marxist theory have taken place in the concept of ideology. Until the last decade ideology tended to be understood either as thought that mechanically served the interests of ruling classes, or else as false or socially determined consciousness. The first essay in this chapter, Colin Sumner's "The Ideological Nature of Law," observes that law is many things at the same time. Legal ideology contains much more than bourgeois economic ideology. Law reflects the ideologies of different fractions within the bourgeoisie and the ideologies of other classes. But it also reflects the ideologies of occupational groups, minority groups, and the ideologies related to family structure, morality, the environment, political representation, and so forth. Yet, while law is an ideological form of the fullest complexity, it is not equally pluralistic. It is also and basically a reflection of class inequality and expresses the ideologies of the dominant class.

Law is therefore a major weapon of class domination. Sumner argues that legal discourse operates within the terms of the general ideologies reflected by dominant social relations, rather than in terms of the specific versions of the ideologies held by the dominant classes and their representatives. Law in capitalist society designates power relations according to general ideologies reflecting a social structure that divides people economically, politically, and ideologically. And Sumner concludes:

> The legal system is first and foremost a means of exercising political control available to the propertied, the powerful and the highly educated. It is the weapon and toy of the hegemonic bloc of classes and class fractions whose rough consensus it sustains. As such, it lies hidden beneath a heavy shroud of discourse, ritual and magic which proclaim the Wisdom and Justice of The Law.

In "Reification in Legal Reasoning," Peter Gabel begins by examining the nature of legal reasoning, as the foundation of the legal form. His study also furnishes us with a phenomenological psychology of law. Gabel argues that legal reasoning is an inherently repressive form of interpretive thought, that it arises within consciousness at moments of collective uncertainty about the legitimacy of the world around us. Although this form of thought originates within the consciousness of the dominant class, it is interiorized by everyone because of the lack of a humanizing environment. Gabel characterizes legal reasoning as a "reification," a distortion of meaning, mistaking a constructed abstraction for reality. In the case of legal reasoning, reification is not simply distortion, but is also a form of coercion, an acceptance of the world as constructed within the framework of capitalism.

In his historical study of slavery in the United States, Eugene Genovese investigates how the law constituted a principal vehicle for the hegemony of the Southern ruling class. In "The Hegemonic Function of Law," Genovese argues that "since the slaveholders, like other ruling classes, arose and grew in dialectical response to the other classes of society—since they were molded by white yeomen and black slaves as much as they molded them—the law cannot be viewed as something passive and reflective, but must be viewed as an active, partially autonomous force, which mediated among the several classes and compelled the rulers to bend to the demands of the ruled." How a worldview appropriate to a slaveholding regime was constructed—and resisted by slaves—in the course of legal formulation and practice is the focus of Genovese's rich argument. The legal form was ideally appropriate for the promotion of a slave economy, in that law based on the fetishism of commodities attempted to regulate beings as objects in a commodity relationship, cloaking the domination of one human group by another.

Our final selection in this chapter is included explicitly to confront those in the socialist movement who continue to understand class struggles apart from the claims of Marxist feminism. In "Toward a Theory of Law and Patriarchy," Janet Rifkin offers us the thesis that the struggle for sexual equality can only be successful if it challenges, rather than reifies, the male paradigm of law. She conceives of patriarchy as any system by which males hold dominant power and in which capabilities assigned to women are relegated to the mystical and aesthetic and excluded from the practical and political realms, these realms being regarded as separate and mutually exclusive. In her essay Rifkin argues that legal ideology under capitalism preserved, transformed, and updated preexisting patriarchal forms to serve the interests of the emerging bourgeoisie. Legal rules enabled the creation of a social order where women are excluded from the public world of production and exchange.

THE IDEOLOGICAL NATURE OF LAW

COLIN SUMNER

The law in its majesty impartiality forbids rich and poor alike to sleep under bridges, to beg in the streets, and steal bread.
Anatole France, quoted in Hunt, 1976, p. 184

Law has rarely been explicitly defined as a concept in Marxist theory and one is often left with the impression that empiricism has prevailed. That is, law has usually been dealt with as "the law in the books." This is understandable but seems unsatisfactory since it is a definition which takes the state's word for what counts as law. However, perhaps the implicit definition is the correct one—after all, is not the point about law that it is what the state says it is? Subjectively, the law may be what you think it is, but surely objectively it is a collection of ideologies, sanctioned in the correct manner by the institutionalized executors of social power, which define the socially permissible modes of social intercourse? It is distinguished from ordinary ideology by its political backing. It is distinguished from politicians' speeches and policies by the fact that it has received political backing in the manner laid down by custom or constitution. It is distinguished from administrative decisions not by due process or rights of appeal but by the fact that it expresses approved rules of conduct in a general form and by the fact that these rules have been agreed upon in the proper manner by the proper persons in power. What counts as the "proper" mode of law-creation is, of course, itself a matter

Source: From Colin Sumner, *Reading Ideologies: An Investigation into the Marxist Theory of Ideology and Law* (1979) (London: Academic Press, 1979), pp. 266–277. Reprinted by permission.

in the control of the powerful.

This definition will cover stateless societies which are often excluded by Marxist definitions which usually suppose a state. It will allow for minority legal systems which operate within a nation-state: these systems only ever operate by permission of the social power-holders. Judge-made law is included, since the judiciary are institutionalized as executive agents of social power. Inoperative or unenforced rules are also included: as properly sanctioned ideologies they are laws, even though their existence may discredit the legal system.

Definitions of law which point to the necessity of collective consensus, which see it as an expression of some transcendental force, which depoliticize it, which reduce it to mere decisions of the powerful, or which limit it to those ideas which serve ruling class interests—all such definitions miss the precise sense of law as a conjoint expression of power and ideology. The crucial questions about the origins of law always relate to the power bloc behind the legislation, the nature of the problem this bloc wants to solve, the ideologies in which this problem is perceived and understood, and the political opposition to the proposed legislation. Law is a hybrid phenomenon of politics and ideology; a politico-ideological artefact.

It may be argued that some ideologies are sanctioned by the power-holders in a different manner to that laid down as necessary for legal enactment and that these ideologies are often more effective than a statute or judge's decision. An example of this is a government incomes policy which is sanctioned by a political pact between the party in power, the trade unions, the employer's representatives and media-influenced "public opinion." My definition may thus seem to collude with the state in playing down the fact that modes of social practice are often controlled without legal enactment or procedure. I do not think it does. That is the whole point about law, as it is now and as it always has been. Law is a public, ideological front which can often conceal the true workings of a social formation. It is very much an ideological means of controlling social practice; sometimes more practical means of social control are necessary. Law depends on some kind of ideological consensus amongst a number of classes and class fractions; that consensus cannot always be produced on important issues or problems. In such situations, social control has to go on behind the law's ideological curtain. In short, the use of law is not always culturally possible and therefore not politically expedient and, in political practice, politics is always in command. Law lies in the cradle of political practice and is, therefore, subject to the pressures and imperatives of politics. This is the answer to Balibar's question: as an instance in a social formation, law is a politico-ideological phenomenon produced in a form of political practice, that practice geared to the creation, definition and maintenance of power relations. As such it is only one weapon within a whole armoury.

It is important not to overstate the political sources of law. Thus, I use the phrase "sanctioned by the instituted social powers" rather than "created by." Legislation and judicial decisions are always political since their immediate causes are the legislators and the judges, agents of political practice, and their immediate purpose is the resolution of conflict but, less immediately, the balance of class forces, economic necessity, ideological pressures and political pressure groups are always other important causal considerations. Moreover, something Gramsci said should not be forgotten:

> ... once the conditions are created in which a certain way of life is "possible", then "criminal action

or omission" must have a punitive sanction, with moral implications, and not merely be judged generically as "dangerous" (Gramsci, 1971, p. 247).

It does not concern us here which problems are treated punitively and which are dealt with by restitutive law, but what is important is to realize, with Gramsci, that once a mode of production is established, along with corresponding modes of political and cultural intercourse, the law of the land must develop in order to regulate that social formation. In other words, legal enactments mostly respond to social problems and are not simply unilateral political declarations of ideology. To a certain extent, therefore, the social system dictates to judges and legislators. Only to an extent though: what is vital is the recognition that problems only appear in a certain manner depending on the social structural context in which they exist and are only perceived through the ideological grids of the people observing them. Thus the system may require legislative action, but it does not dictate to legislators how they are to see the problem or how to deal with it. This fact often reduces parliament to a "talking shop" (Lenin's phrase) and judicial decisions to wonders of cultural ignorance: the system often goes on without them.

It is a false argument which mitigates the political and ideological nature of law on the grounds that much law is "technical." In its most sophisticated form, the argument would be that most legal enactments today reflect technical problems within social practice and thus are little to do with class relations. However, this is not only a politician's viewpoint (whether bourgeois or Marxist); it is also a false one. Technical relations of practice are always bound up with the class relations of practice. Thus, in economic life, the reorganization of production is not simply a technical adjustment but one which affects the classes and class relations articulated conjointly with the technical relations (see Bettelheim, 1974, for a good analysis of this issue). The distinction between law which reflects political ideology and law which is a mere technical instrument is made in both modern Western and Russian legal systems. It is a spurious distinction which often works to conceal the political and ideological nature of so-called technical instruments.

If it is possible to sum up these brief remarks on the nature of law in one argument, I would say that law is only an instrument of class rule through the mediating arenas of politics and ideology and that, therefore, it is not just an instrument of class rule. It is also, at the very same time, an instrument of party politics, a protector of revered ideas and an agency for the prevention of social chaos. Moreover, it can only successfully operate on the basis of a politico-ideological consensus (whether spontaneous or constructed). Law is all of these things at the same time and that is one reason why class rule has continued for as long as it has.

Ideologies arise out of economic, political and cultural practices and thus not only reflect class relations but also the technical divisions encapsulated within class relations. Law does not, therefore, just contain bourgeois economic ideology. It also reflects the ideologies of fractions of the bourgeoisie and the ideologies of other classes—through the political activities of these classes and class fractions. Moreover, it reflects the ideologies of occupational groups, minority groups and pressure groups. And, in terms of the range of ideologies, law expresses ideologies relating to the family morality, the environment, political representation, immigration, communication, public association and so on—as well as ideologies relating to the economy. Law is truly an ideological form of the fullest complexity. Having said all this, it must be reiterated that law does not reflect these ideologies equally. Some classes, some occupational groups, some pressure groups and some individuals have more power than others in the legislative process. It is not as pluralistic as other ideological forms because it is subject to the political process and, hence, the relative ability of different classes and groups to establish their ideas as law. Political success requires money and power as well as po-

tent ideas, even more so than other fields of superstructural practice. Thus law as an ideological form is less pluralistic, than, say, the novel or music. It is a much closer reflection of class inequality than other forms. It tends to express the ideologies of the dominant class and their political and cultural representatives. I want to render a Marxian analysis capable of dealing with all forms of law, law as it exists in a complex society, but I most certainly do not want to deny that law is still a major weapon of class domination. When the chips are down, the essential function of the legal system is revealed as itself: the reproduction of class power.

Now it is necessary to turn to the inner determination of law, for like all things, it is not just an effect of externals. It is also necessary to say something about the peculiarity of law as an ideological form. These two matters are of course connected.

Legal enactments are partly ideological and partly political forms. In their ideological being, they exist as discourses. In their most developed form these discourses are written down and carefully circumscribed. They take on a magical form as sacred texts: the canons of social order. In quantity, the magic of their expression is compounded by their bureaucratic organization in a whole range of statutes and law reports and by its professional production in a language peculiar unto itself. Legal discourse in modern societies is thus bureaucratized magic expressed in legalese. It is therefore not only a discrete phenomenon but downright impenetrable: unless one has been initiated in the ancient skills of finding and reading the law, skills only available, of course, to the legal profession and its initiates. Legal discourse is worthy of study in itself by students of contemporary culture: if they can wrest themselves away from the "high" culture of novels and the "approved" culture of the proletariat. As an impenetrable discourse it ranks second to none: at least sociology does not use Latin.

The privacy of legal discourse (embodied in its impenetrability) stands in stark contrast to its essential peculiarity, which is to delineate power relations within a society in terms of the most general social ideologies available to that social formation. (Perhaps this is the secret of the lawyer's self-imposed "omnicompetence": he is in possession of the code which enables him to tell us in general what we can and cannot do.) In its discourse, law does not designate power relations in terms of the actual class (or group) version of the ideologies at work in the legislative process. Rather, it designates them in the terms of a general discourse abstracted from that sectional version. In this way, the actual definitions and ideas which produced the legal proposal are usually concealed in the final discourse and the proposal, being stated in abstracted terms, takes on a universal, moral character separated from its current economic, political and ideological thrust. Thus, in modern times, the latest attempts to suppress the unionized power of the working class, in order to prise more surplus value out that class, can be seen to take the form of legislative proposals to protect the freedom of the individual from the collective pressure of 'the closed shop.' What is essentially a matter of class power and interest becomes transformed into a legislative proposal which raises the universal moral question of the individual versus the collective. And, of course, as individuals we can all sympathize with the freedom of the individual, especially if the other issues at stake are minimized and distorted by the mass media.

It is insufficient to object that this legal abstraction from specific, historical ideologies is merely a characteristic of bourgeois ideology in general. Certainly, bourgeois ideology focuses superficially upon the appearances of capitalist social relations and thus talks in terms of "the individual," "liberty," "property" and "equality": that is, the liberty of the individual to be exploited equally by those who own the productive property. But all ruling classes express their own interests as abstract, universal interests, as Marx and Engels point out in *The German Ideology* (1976). Moreover, and this is the finer point, one does not need to present one's own interests as universal interests in an abstract way. These interests can

be presented as universal in a quite concrete and practical way. Economic policy is often presented in this manner: thus the interests of capital are openly presented to the populace by bourgeois politicians as the interests of the whole people. No: it is the demands of the legal form itself which require the universalization and moralization of private and seedy self-interest to be presented in an abstract manner. Law must command some kind of consensus. It must thus express itself in a general manner. Therefore, legal discourse signifies within the terms of the general ideologies reflected by the dominant social relations rather than within the terms of the specific versions of those ideologies held by the dominant classes and their representatives. Consequently, law signifies in terms of the freedom of the individual rather than the freedom of the bourgeoisie to expand their capital at the expense of the working class, or the freedom of the workers to work for capital or starve. Similarly, it signifies in terms of the sanctitude of property in general rather than the sanctitude of the productive property of the bourgeoisie or the sanctitude of the labourer's only productive property, his health. Freedom, property and equality are key general ideologies arising from the general nature of capitalist social relations and are expressed as such in various branches of bourgeois law (freedom of the individual, freedom of association, etc.). *The generic social function of law is to express, regulate and maintain the general nature of the dominant social relations of a social formation.* It is therefore only natural that it does this through the discourse of the general ideologies necessitated by these general forms of social relation. It is the peculiarity of legal discourse as a social form that it should signify in this way. Law must always delineate the power relations of social practice (or the permissible modes of social intercourse) through the general ideologies necessitated by the dominant social relations of a society.

This argument clearly cuts across any simplistic reduction of legal discourse to an expression of bourgeois ideology. If the argument is taken a step further, this becomes even more obvious.

What I want to suggest is that some of the key items in the legal lexicon are overdetermined in modern society in that they not only reflect the general ideologies of its social structure but also the imperatives of any moral code. It seems to me that it is an inevitability that a moral code (and law is one such thing, sanctioned by social power) must talk in terms of right and wrong, duty and neglect, obligation and fulfilment, and guilt and innocence. How could a moral discourse talk otherwise, given that it is a discourse which prescribes the acceptability of modes of social intercourse? Thus property rights is not simply a concept which reflects a social structure with private property. It also reflects the notion of right. If I am correct, then, our modern legal dictionary is becoming less of a mysterious puzzle. Some of its concepts relate, through ideology and power, to the social structure, others relate to the imperatives of moral discourse. Of course, what is actually said to be reasonable conduct, or neglect, or criminal behaviour (and so on) is an historically situated matter determined by the social forces at work rather than by any discursive imperatives.

A substantial part of legal discourse is not even particularly legal, of course, but is merely descriptive of the facts to be dealt with. This part of the discourse is difficult to evaluate when it exists in a judicial decision, for what count as "the facts of the case" are the product of the filtering mechanisms of the trial and pre-trial investigations. Facts can be constructed either by accident, by the court procedure or by lies, just as much in the legal system as in any other form of social practice. In any case, whether true, false or somewhere in between, "the facts" are a substantial part, or reference point, of legal discourse.

One further aspect of the form of legal discourse is that it usually contains doctrines and concepts which express the general ideologies of social relations of a prior epoch. That is, some of its key elements may have originated in earlier historical contexts. This does not mean that they are fossilized residues or forms isolated from modern social life, although they could be. Very often such concepts or doctrines correspond with modern needs in a way which their proponents could not have imagined. Thus the concept of trespass (*vi et armis*) derives originally from the feudal ideologies of landowners, reflecting feudal relations of production where territoriality and battles for land were crucial features. A writ of trespass in the twelfth century enabled plaintiffs to recover damages for forcible entry into land, or (at a later time) into goods held in the person's possession. It gave birth to the modern law of torts (civil wrongs such as negligence) and to the modern law of theft which began as a trespass into goods held on bailment). It still remains of course, but in a much more restricted sense of unlawful entry. Thus the legal conception of trespass has had an interesting history where its functions have been largely hived off as property relations expanded and developed but where it retains the essence of its original meaning. Clearly, to understand the modern functions of this type of concept it is necessary to study the development of the meaning of the concept right from its historical roots.

Legal discourse is thus an ideological formation of some complexity and richness containing contemporary general concepts, the language of moral discourse, descriptive accounts and references, and doctrines and terms from the distant past. There is no doubt that it contains sufficient internal complexity for us to imagine that its internal dialectic is purely ideological, purely a matter of continually reconciling concepts and doctrines. It most certainly provides an interesting game for lawyers to play with, and part of its magic must surely lie with the fact that it provides a mass of principles, concepts, statutes and case decisions all relating to specific issues and needing to be sifted and applied to a present situation. However, one must not forget that as a system of discourse which is linked to the social structures of the day, law only works through its successful regulation of that social system in terms of the interests and ideologies of the dominant social classes. Thus the inner dialectic of law rests here. Law designates power relations in terms of general ideologies reflecting a social structure which divides people economically, politically and ideologically. Its internal dialectic is fired by the eternal contradiction between its generalities and the specificities of contemporary social problems. Lawyers, of course, will see it differently and posit legal history as the history of a set of concepts developed solely by lawyers. In my view, law moves within, and is moved by, its relation to the problems posed for it by the social structure. This relation is mediated practically, in the form of the institutions of law creation and enforcement. The central tensions within law enforcement and law creation are thus set by the relation between legal discourse and social practice. The history of law is the history of this relation as it is mediated by the legal profession, the legislature and the law enforcement agencies.

Finally, as an instrument of social change or development, the law's internal character is important. One cannot just talk of the intractability of certain social contradictions or of the manner of enforcement. As a discourse, law takes a general form and, therefore, it is in principle, and sometimes in practice, useful for all-comers. Law can thus be pulled in directions other than those intended by the legislators. It can become an instrument for the mitigation of the harsher effects of the class structure and other inequalities.

We have looked at the social determinations of ideologies embodied in the law and commented upon the nature of legal discourse. It is also necessary to say something briefly about the ideology of Law. The legal form hitherto has always been seen as something supernatural, magical, God-given and sacred. Perhaps today, it is also seen as an expression of objective rationality of True reason. Many people today, and presumably in the past, have seen through this mystical veil and perceived the secular nature of law. The ideology of Law as something above the mundane run of things is still popular however. What is the basis of this ideology? It seems to me that the inner structure of legal practice and its key social function in attempting to maintain order combine to give legal discourse and institutions an external appearance as something special and mysterious. Professional secrecy, esoteric language, grand ceremony, special clothing, carefully structured courtrooms, the rituals of legislation and the occupational status of the judge are all internal factors which work to present the appearance of magic. But I think that the reasons run deeper than these factors which are only superficial conditions. What we have to consider is that, in essence, law is little different from political policy, administrative decision and military strategy. In itself therefore it would be seen for what it is, a form of political control, without much difficulty. Now clearly such transparency is contrary to the interests of ruling classes who always want to give their directions some universal legitimacy. It is also contrary to the interests of lawyers who need special status and esoteric services in order to continue—who would pay so much for mere political administrators? Lawyers' interests are, however, secondary and depend on the main condition which is the structural necessity of all ruling classes to obtain some kind of consent for their direction and supremacy. Consent can be obtained much more easily if the rulers' main policies and principles of administration can be seen as the expression of something transcendental, whether this be a God or Absolute Reason or the Necessity of Order. The production of this mystification of law began a long time ago and we inherit some of the older illusions. However, the mystification of the nature of law (as a form) is still necessary today and will be as long as there is class domination. In short, the ideology of Law is an ideology *necessitated* by political relations of domination: it enables them to continue on a regular basis. Lawyers develop this ideology to a fine point because it is in their interests to do so. But they cannot conceal the fact that law is little different from other means of political control. Despite their insistence that law is distinguished by its "proper" constitution, it is clear that what counts as proper is a political question and not one for God or True Reason. It is also clear that the ideology and rituals of propriety within legal practice serve an important function in concealing the sectional nature of law-making.

The law is a rich combination. Not only does it conceal politics through its magic, its rituals of propriety, its moral universals, its esoteric language and its historical longevity, but it has the added benefit of sharing in all the legitimacy that the state as the executor of social power has managed to acquire for itself. Since the remote state has a magic of its own and since the rulers of a society have the available tools to create the impression that they are worthy, the law basks in the sunshine of the rulers' patronage and charisma. In this way, we have the nice paradox that law avoids the dirty images of politics and shares in its good side. Law's structural position enables it to be presented as an expression of universal truth under the aegis of beneficent and meritorious authority.

Perhaps because law holds out so many fake promises, people feel all the more disillusioned when they are broken. To begin with, the ideology of Law offers us truth, magic, impartiality and merit whilst denying the filthy side of politics. Secondly, the specific ideologies within legal enactments tell us what the world ought to be like on the basis of illusions about what it is like. Both these ideologies, those of the inside and those of the outside, are of course closely interlinked. When they collapse as effective grips on one's mind, then the whole ideological edifice collapses like a pack of cards. It becomes crystal clear that the whole business—the discourse, the procedure, the ceremony, the ritual, the prestige, the magic—is part of a colossal facade. Of course, the legal system coerces, punishes and executes "criminals" and of course it may leave many ordinary people without access to civil remedy and therefore in financial difficulty. The legal system has its instrumental side. But it has this other aspect—as Law—its ideological side. This aspect is a complete and utter façade. If we

take modern capitalist society, for example, it is no exaggeration to say that the legal system is first and foremost a means of exercising political control available to the propertied, the powerful and the highly educated. It is the weapon and toy of the hegemonic bloc of classes and class fractions whose rough consensus it sustains. As such, it lies hidden beneath a heavy shroud of discourse, ritual and magic which proclaim the Wisdom and Justice of The Law. This shroud is of central importance to our social formation. Once it is torn into tatters, that hegemonic bloc of classes and class fractions which sustains the rule of capital is in trouble, because inequality and domination can only be justified mystically and that is precisely the ideological function of the law.

To sum up, legal discourse represents an historically constituted unity of politics and ideology and therefore stands for something much wider than itself. As a representation of social structure in the language of general and moral ideology sanctioned by the institutionalized executors of social power, it is a significant feature of all social formations mapping social history at the same time as it redirects it. It is a form which is central to ruling class hegemony because of its cultivated sacredness. It is an emblem of the universal pretensions of a ruling class and an abstracted expression of the concrete interests of that class and its allies.

REFERENCES

Charles Bettelheim, *Cultural Revolution and Industrial Organization in China* (1974), New York: Monthly Review Press.

Antonio Gramsci, *Prison Notebooks* (1971), London: Lawrence and Wishart.

Alan Hunt, "Law, State and Class Struggle," *Marxism Today*, 1976, vol. 20, no. 6, pp. 178–187.

Karl Marx and Friedrich Engels, *Collected Works* (1976), vol. 5, London: Lawrence and Wishart.

REIFICATION IN LEGAL REASONING

PETER GABEL

Legal reasoning is an inherently repressive form of interpretive thought which limits our comprehension of the social world and its possibilities.[1] This interpretive thought emerges

[1]The main influences on the ideas presented in the essay are the works of Marx (1967), Freud (1962, 1964), Heidegger (1962), Jameson (1971), Laing (1967), and especially Sartre (1976). In my description of the legal thought-process, I have used a number of Sartre's terms, the meaning of which may be unclear to readers unfamiliar with his later work. Those that are not adequately defined through their usage in the text are the following: *Synthetic* is used in the sense of "synthesizing" rather than in the sense of "artificial." Our lived experience of the world is always synthetic because we experience the world in every moment toward the realization of a coherent and understandable end. Thus a carpenter goes about fixing a door by experiencing the materials and tools available to her not as inert "things," but as synthetically unified and directed toward the realization of her objective. The *comprehension* of this objective is experientially prior to the analytical thinking that she will use to reach her goal. Thus, we can say that she *apprehends* her tools synthetically toward the comprehended project of fixing the door, and she "thinks about" how to use those tools analytically on the basis of this prior comprehension. This is also true of the judge who "intends" to legitimate (comprehension) and who uses legal reasoning analytically for this purpose. The word *dialectical* describes the movement of consciousness in action. Human experience is always meaningful action that unifies and conserves what is given toward the realization of a novel objective that surpasses what is given. This is what it means to say that action (or practice) is a dialectical movement. *Dialectical reason* is the activity of thought attempting to conform itself to this movement. The term *worked matter* is Sartre's way of expressing the signifying movement of material objects in history, and it represents an attempt to enrich the overly abstract and objectified Marxian concept of "material conditions." Any material object always reveals itself to our experience as already shaped by past labor toward a use that it signifies in its social appearance. *Passivization* describes an act of direct or

Source: From Steven Spitzer (ed.), *Research in Law and Sociology* (1981), Vol. 3 (Greenwich, CT: JAI Press). Reprinted by permission.

within consciousness at moments of uncertainty about the legitimacy of the concrete world within which we find ourselves, and its function is to institutionalize—with the help of such overpowering psychological symbols as robed judges, quasi-ecclesiastical schools, the Profession, and the Tribunal—the boundaries of a legitimate rationality. It is therefore incorrect to say, as does the instrumentalist, that legal rules and principles directly serve the interests of the dominant class by bringing about certain consequences in the socioeconomic order. Legal outcomes have only the most marginal effect on the movement of socioeconomic processes and social actors who have been conditioned to accept the apparent necessity of these processes do not require anything so abstract as "legal rules" to shape and direct their daily conduct. It is closer to the truth to say that it is action which has an "instrumental" effect on legal thought, as social actors of

indirect power through which a person or group is compelled to feel a loss of agency in their social activity (cf. Klein, 1976). This act of power may be performed by no one in particular; in capitalist society as a whole, for example, it is "capital as a social power," to use Marx's phrase, or capital as a social organization of worked matter, to use Sartre's vocabulary, which passivizes the dominant classes as well as the dominated. I use the phrase "passivized within a role" to describe the way that the forms of interpersonal recognition generated in alienated groups prevent people from reciprocally eliciting each other's full and active humanity, a humanity which can be elicited only through the process of realizing an organically generated collective activity. Sartre describes the collective experience of passivity that is produced by the "weight" of worked matter as an *inertia*. I describe a thought which "factualizes" a passivized situation as a passivizing thought because it intends to deny the feeling of "illegitimacy" that is produced in the alienated group.

262

every class seek to legitimate to themselves the experiential world within which they come to know themselves and their relations with others, under definite historical conditions.

This is not to deny the reality of class domination; it only emphasizes that legal domination arises within the consciousness of every person as a sort of legitimating repression, much like what is called a "resistance" in psychoanalysis. Legal thought originates, of course, within the consciousness of the dominant class because it is in this class's interest to bring it into being, but it is accepted and interiorized by everyone because of the traumatic absence of connectedness that would otherwise erupt into awareness. This is why the legal form becomes "fetishized" as Balbus (1977, p. 582) has put it: people "believe in" the legal order because the legal order substitutes an harmonious abstract world for the concrete alienation that characterizes their lived experience. Thus, while legal thought represses, it also reassures: it is, so to speak, the superego of the public self at the level of social interpretation.

The character of this repressive thought is accurately described by the word "reification," which is properly understood as a certain sort of distortion of meaning that occurs within communication. This distortion is sometimes called the "fallacy of misplaced concreteness" because when we "reify," we draw an abstraction from a concrete milieu and then mistake the abstraction for the concrete. (An example is the well-known expression "law is a means of social control," which suggests that "the law" is substantial, like a fence.) The "misplaced-concreteness" characterization is descriptively accurate, but it lays insufficient emphasis on the intersubjective and paradoxical meaning of reified communication. For in reification we do not simply make a kind of private error about the true nature of what we are talking about: we participate in an unconscious conspiracy with others whereby everyone knows of the fallacy, and yet denies that the fallacy exists. More specifically, in a reified communication the speaker: (1) misunderstands by asserting that an abstraction is concrete; (2) understands

that he misunderstands or knows that the communication is "false"; and (3) denies both to himself and to the listener that he knows either of these things by the implied assertion that the communication is "true," or concrete. Thus, reification is not simply a form of distortion, but also a form of unconscious coercion which, on the one hand, separates the *communicated* or *socially apparent* reality from the reality of experience and, on the other hand, denies that this separation is taking place. The knowledge of the truth is both repressed and "contained in" the distorted communication simultaneously.

An example relevant to the development of "legal reification" can be found in any first-grade classroom. It is 8:29 and the children are playing, throwing food, and generally engaging in relatively undistorted communication. At 8:30, the teacher (who is replacing the father and who, in later years, will be replaced by the judge) calls the class to attention: it is time for the "pledge of allegiance." All face front, all suffer the same social rupture and privation, all fix their eyes on a striped piece of cloth. As they drone on, having not the slightest comprehension of the content of what they are saying, they are nonetheless learning the sort of distorted or reified communication that is expressed in the legal form. They are learning, in other words, that they are all abstract "citizens" of an abstract "United States of America," that there exists "liberty and justice for all," and so forth—not from the content of the words, but from the ritual which forbids any rebellion. Gradually, they will come to accept these abstractions as descriptive of a concrete truth because of the repressive and conspiratorial way that these ideas have been communicated (each senses that all the others "believe in" the words and therefore they must be true), and once this acceptance occurs, any access to the paradoxically forgotten memory that these are mere abstractions will be sealed off. And once the abstractions are reified, they can no longer be criticized because they signify a false concrete.

And yet this false concrete that emerges within reified communication is not merely a *concep-*

tion of reality, not merely an "ideological representation"; the pledge of allegiance is itself a living sequence during which a ritual of the Other is enacted through everyone. Each child enacts a humility, as does the teacher, who is merely playing the role of sovereign; each draws the act down upon himself; each institutes in every gesture (even in the modulation of the vocal chords) an obedience to "a presence that is everywhere elsewhere" (Laing, 1967, p. 84), such that the represented world is also realized in the body, such that the social body of a collectivity becomes the expression of a *gap* that gives reality the feel of pseudo-reality, in which each movement is lived in the as-if. The terrible truth of reification is that it is alive within each of us as the haunted embodiment of an alienated desire, such that representational "communication" is itself the expression of an alienated communion in which everyone is other to himself, knows this, and can do nothing, or almost nothing, about it. And because appearance floods reality in this way, intimating a "reality" that is already an absence of itself, it becomes impossible to divorce the false consciousness that signifies a false concrete from the false concrete itself. There is a dim and intuitive comprehension that something is very wrong, but this comprehension is the only trace of itself, like the "other side" of a mobius strip.

In this paper, I want to investigate the way that the alienated communion of a group "legalizes" itself in representational thought. My discussion of alienation will be limited to a brief introductory description of the organization of groups within capitalism, and of the way in which living within these groups feels in many ways like the way children feel when they are "passivized" by the pledge of allegiance. The better part of the essay describes the way that "the law" emerges within our alienated culture as a kind of quasi-religious belief-system which simultaneously compensates for our feelings of loss within these alienated groups and conceals these feelings from us.

I. LAW AS A DENIAL OF A COLLECTIVE FEELING OF ILLEGITIMACY, AND AN AFFIRMATION OF THE LAW-LIKE NATURE OF THE NORMAL

I take it as given at the outset of this essay that human relationships within contemporary capitalism are characterized by a traumatic absence of connectedness that does not wish to become conscious of itself. The source of this absence of connectedness is the passivity, impotence, and isolation generated by the structure of groups, as those groups are themselves organized by the movement of capital. Within these groups, no one is normally aware of his or her sense of unconnectedness, passivity, impotence, and isolation, because this felt reality is *denied* by the socially communicated reality. Each person denies to the other that he or she is suffering, because this collective denial has been made a condition of what social connection there is. One cannot assert that the pledge of allegiance is insane and still remain "with" one's friends and family—so we forget that this pledging is insane and reinforce the collective coercion.

Within these alien collectivities, each person experiences himself as a thing-like function of "the system," understood as the semi-autonomous structure which constitutes the group's inertia. Each person experiences himself this way because each person is recognized in this way by everyone else, and human beings are such that they experience themselves as they are recognized (Hegel, 1967). Thus, a "small businessman" experiences himself as a "small businessman," a "secretary" as a "secretary," a "child" as a "child." These role-experiences are thing-like in that each is subject to rigid determinations within the group's socially defined and socially communicated structure. Thus, within an American family, a child must experience himself as a child because he is treated as a child within the family system which constitutes each of its subjects. Yet to say that each person experiences himself as thing-*like* is to express the meaning of alienation: each actor is passivized within a role that denies him recognition as a connected, active, potentiated, and intersubjective *person*. One is never, or almost never, a person; instead, one is successively a "husband," "bus passenger," "small businessman," "consumer," and so on (cf., Laing, 1967).

The experiential starting point for understanding the function of "the law" in this milieu is to recognize, to sense, that this thing-like quality that pervades each of these groups is felt as *illegitimate*. Even as we are passivized into imprisoning roles, and even as this reification is denied by each of us to the other, there is a collective tendency to explode the whole thing. This is true within the smallest sub-group (two people talking in a room), and it is true within the totality within which each sub-group is situated. Although each sub-group does have a semi-autonomy from the entire group (from "capitalism"), it is nonetheless situated within the living totality that is capitalism, and in fact each sub-group is given its fundamental determination from the totalizing effect of the movement of capital. Thus, one cannot discover the final intelligibility of the way clerical workers chat in the halls, or the way businessmen expound over lunch, without situating each tone and gesture within the organization of the entire human group. The clerical workers *secret themselves* from their bosses, and this is what it means to move into the hall and "gossip." The bosses *talk too loud* at lunch in order to reinstitute their nervous privilege to do so. Each "alienation" is expressive of the totalizing movement of an internal class-struggle, and this class-struggle as a whole is felt as illegitimate, because each person is able to experience himself only as thing-like, as passivized within a role. And because this sense of illegitimacy is always threatening to erupt into awareness, there is a need for "the law."

The function of "the law" is to give each of us the impression that the system operates according to a normative law. The law is a denial; at the level of social interpretation, of our collective experience of illegitimacy. Through the law we tell ourselves, through the collective terror and coercion that I have described, that what is, ought to be—that the system follows a law. This profound tautology expresses what I mean when I say that the function of law is legitimation.

II. THE PHENOMENOLOGY OF THE LEGAL OPINION

When I say that the law represents the system as if the system followed a normative law, I mean that the law is an instance of the *system* thinking itself, the word "thinking" being used in an active, transitive sense (cf., Sartre, 1976). When a judge engages in legal reasoning, he is, of course, a person who is thinking. But he is a person passivized within a role, fulfilling what is often called "the judicial function," and his thought corresponds itself to the movement of the system as a whole. Precisely to that extent that the "small businessman" has become a "small businessman," the "secretary" a "secretary," and so on—precisely, that is, to the extent that intersubjectivity has been reduced to a series of interlocking roles and functions—to that extent the judge's legitimating thought becomes a sort of carapace which fits itself over those roles in order to *think* them legitimatively. In other words, we might say that it is capital that engages in legal reasoning through the judge, precisely because it is capital which totalizes the objectified interpersonal relations which legal reasoning interprets.[2] One could say that the judge is dissociated or "decentered" from his own subjectivity by virtue of his own alienation, and so he is reduced to performing a certain "thinking function" whereby he represents what is as if it were "legal."

---

[2] Although this essay describes legal reasoning as form of alienated thought within capitaism, the description is equally applicable to the legitimating thought of any alienated group, whether the group thinks of itself as "capitalist," "communist," or a divinely ordered cult. I mean to describe not capitalist law in particular, but a self-justificatory mode of thought. The description of legitimation at a social level is also applicable to what is ordinarily called rationalization at a personal level.

The development of legal thought within the judge can be described in terms of three movements of his consciousness. These movements are: (1) the apprehension of the concrete as the synthetic and thing-like process that it in fact is; (2) the taking-for-granted of the apprehended concrete as what I will call a "presupposed norm"; and (3) the generation of a conceptual analysis that covertly (or "unconsciously") embodies this norm as its synthetic underpinning. I will describe this process in some phenomenological detail, using examples wherever possible to make the description more understandable.

A. THE APPREHENSION OF THE SYSTEM AS A WHOLE AS A SYNTHETIC AND THING-LIKE PROCESS

Legal reasoning is an application of what is ordinarily called the scientific method to the realm of human interaction. Through a process of induction that is called "reasoning by analogy," certain perceived similarities in a series of "fact-situations" provide the basis for an abstract law which is given the form of an abstract rule or principle. This abstract law is then applied to other "fact-situations" through a deductive thought-process known as applying the law to the facts. When a fact-situation does not clearly come within a particular rule or principle, the legal thinker must again reason by analogy in order to decide whether the rule or principle should be applied to it. He or she may conclude that the law does not apply, or that it does apply, or that the law should apply, in which case the rule may be modified so as to "cover" the fact-situation in question. This is obviously a highly formalized description of legal reasoning, but it is accurate enough for my purpose here.[3]

There are two epistemological features of this

[3]I would emphasize that this description of legal reasoning is not limited in its application to the late 19th-century conception of law as "science." It is rather a description of the way that analytical reasoning generally reveals itself in all legitimating thought, of which classical "legal science," with its separation of law and morals, its formalistic style, and its treatment of the parties as atomized units, is but one example.

thought-process which must be emphasized at the outset. First of all, legal reasoning requires an a priori "passivization" of human situations, such that a law may be drawn from them and applied to them interchangeably. Each situation appears as a "set of facts" which can be compared with analogical interchangeability to any other set of facts in order to determine whether the two situations reveal the same abstract legal features (contract, tort, crime, etc.). Second, each situation is imbued, a priori, with a certain cultural meaning, such that it is possible to know a priori whether one situation is "like" another. The process of recognizing similarity or difference between two fact-situations is not a matter of empirically investigating two collections of data, but rather of "recognizing" whether the two situations reveal the same cultural meaning. One could say that the judge "has a feeling" about each situation and their immanent relationship to one another (a feeling we ordinarily call "common sense"), and he applies this feeling to them both, deciding whether the same law applies to them. It is only on the basis of this feeling or "sense of the facts" that the judge is able to reason by analogy, and it is only because this feeling is shared by the entire culture that the judge's sense of analogy is accepted as legitimate by the culture within which he is allowed to judge.

On the basis of these two a priori epistemological features of legal reasoning, we can say that the first movement of the judge's consciousness is the apprehension of the entire social field as a synthetic activity that moves like a thing; or, in other words, he has a sense of the whole culture all at once that he passivizes into the movement of a quasi-object, such that each discrete situation of facts reveals itself to his mind against the background of the total "factual" context from which the law has emerged. To take a modern example showing this, suppose that John's car and Mary's car are involved in an accident. John sues Mary for violation of tort law. In order to decide the case, the judge must re-experience the event as a passivized situation of "facts" (John and Mary become abstract "parties," their jal-lopies become abstract "instrumentalities"), and he must decide by a process of immanent recog-nition whether this fact-situation is like others from which the law of torts has emerged and to which it applies. He can do this only through his immanent grasp of the total factual context within which each accident has a cultural significance (a context partially revealed in such concepts as ownership, speeding, insurance, braking, etc., all of which the judge must comprehend pre-conceptually in order to recognize "likeness" among facts). And when I say that the judge grasps this total factual context as a "quasi-object," I mean that he grasps the totality in terms of its normal functioning as a system, or in other words as a kind of *passive activity* (Sartre, 1976) conforming to our shared common sense of the world as it is. This "common sense of the world as it is" is quite simply the socially communi-cated reality of advanced capitalism as a syn-thetic system of external relations, or to put this more precisely, as a synthetic system of intersub-jective relations that have been mutated, through alienation, into relations of interlocking roles and functions.

This sense of the normal movement of the total "factual" context, without which it would be im-possible to apply the law to any discrete situation, has been interiorized by the judge during the course of his conditioning. It is a dialectical common-knowledge or common-sense that each of us possesses by virtue of having been raised within the same culture, as that culture is mediated through concretely experienced social collectives, such as the family, the school, and the workplace, and through social collectives that are experienced more abstractly, such as one's social class and the media. And this common-knowledge or common-sense is itself alienated to the extent that these collectives which communi-cate the "real" through terror and coercion are themselves alienated reciprocities, reciprocities passivized within roles that bear a functional rela-tionship to the system's total functioning. Thus,

the judge as a child "identifies with the father," to use the familiar Freudian vocabulary, meaning that he grasps himself as other-for-father through the father's recognition of him as "my child." But the father is himself a member of a social class that bears a functional relationship to the inter-subjective totality, and the father embodies this class within his own self as what Sartre calls his "class being" (1976, p. 228) (he is "like" other fathers within the class and share their point of view to the extent they share the same practical and functional relationship to the whole). And so in "identifying with the father," the judge in-teriorizes his class which is itself defined and constituted as the collective interior negation of the class against which it struggles, within an in-tersubjective totality that is given its organization by certain determinate economic pressures. Thus, it is accurate to say that the judge knows himself and is "self-conscious" by virtue of his knowl-edge of the whole. He has what one might call an historical sense of the normal that must be a common-sense among all those to whom the same law applies.

The pernicious consequence of this first movement of the judge's consciousness is that it reifies the world as it is. Each discrete "fact-situation" is apprehended in relation to a total context that is experienced as factual a priori. The sense of illegitimacy that everyone feels in re-sponse to the system's normal functioning, and in response to the passivizing violence that this normal functioning imposes on our subjectivity, is denied at the outset by the epistemological as-sertion that what is, is inevitable, universal, time-less: the facts of life. And this is not all. The act of factifying or reifying the "real world" also has the consequence of denying that this world is contin-gent, that it has been created by human beings, and that it can be changed by human beings. In precisely the same way that the natural scientist "reifies nature" by treating the physical world as an object, so the judge as a "legitimation scien-tist" reifies the social world as if it too were an object, immutably moving according to its own internal dynamic. In his very way of knowing the social world, the judge represents it as natural, and it is precisely his intention to show, in the manner of the natural scientist, that the social world follows certain laws.

B. THE APPREHENSION OF THE SOCIAL FIELD AS A 'PRESUPPOSED NORM'

When the judge apprehends a "fact-situation" in order to apply the law to it, he does so because a "disequilibration" has arisen within the system.[4] The normal way of describing this disequilibration is to say that a dispute has arisen between two people, but from the point of view of the judge's consciousness, this dispute appears to him as an objective problem—as a sort of "breakdown" in the normal movement of the social field. The real situation giving rise to the dispute has occurred in time, and the judge re-experiences this real and temporal situation as the movement of animated facts which must be "put right" through the mediation of his legal reasoning. This is what it means to say that the subjectively-experienced dispute appears to him as an objective disequilibration between objectified "parties" within the system as a whole. To return to my example of the auto accident, John and Mary are engaged in an argument over money, hurt pride, and so forth: the judge, on the other hand, is engaged in an analysis of facts to which the law of torts must be applied. When the judge apprehends the social field as a synthetic and thing-like process, therefore, he does so according to an equilibrative tendency immanent to the organization of the facts. He recognizes and evaluates the disequilibration by its relation to what might be called a normal equilibration. For example, an automobile accident gives rise to a justiciable controversy only within a total context

of the normal movement of automobiles, as that normal movement embodies a set of cultural meanings internalized by everyone in the culture. If the normal movement of automobiles corresponded to the normal movement of bumper cars in an amusement park, then it would be likely that an "accident" would not give rise to a dispute and would not be experienced objectively as a disequilibration. There would be no cause of action because an accident would be entirely normal.

As I have already emphasized, the normal equilibration expressed in the movement of each discrete fact-situation is necessarily also an expression of the normal equilibration of the system as a whole. Because the social field as a whole is internalized by every social actor within the culture and conditions his sense of possible action from within his role (which we can describe as the limit that common-sense places upon the realization of his alienated self-interest), each discrete movement of the social field occurs in a relation of synthetic heterogeneity with every other movement: each movement is both a complete expression of the system as a whole and a partial constituent of it, like the relation of an arc to the entire circle. Thus, the normal movement of an automobile today expresses the way people drive *within advanced capitalism,* and the entire culture of advanced capitalism is expressed within its movement: each driver knows via the common-sense that she is an "insured owner" who must get to work by a certain time and who has left home at an hour which takes account of all the other expectable drivers, the likelihood of being arrested by the available number of policemen as that has been affected by recent property tax cuts, the degree of bodily coordination among drivers as that has been affected by the decline in athletic participation in the schools, owing to the decline in available open space, and so on and so on. And the judge applies his common-sense comprehension of the relation between the normal equilibration of these facts before him and the normal equilibra-

---

[4]*Equilibration, equilibrative tendency,* and *disequilibration* are terms that I use to describe the conspiratorial and tenuous effort of an alienated group to maintain a sense of false cohesion in the fact of a perpetual tendency toward collapse and panic. The so-called "capitalist system" is such a group, as are each of the groups which constitute it.

tion of the entire culture in his search for a legal resolution of the case.

Since this equilibrative tendency derives from the totalizing influence of the movement of capital upon the movement of intersubjective action, it is evident that the judge is preparing to make himself the legitimating voice of capital. His objective is precisely to capitalize on the tendency toward equilibration that sustains the system and reinstate this equilibration in the face of a "dispute." The necessity for this reinstatement derives from the fact that the system's equilibrative tendency moves in a delicate balance. Since each of us senses the alienation and illegitimacy of our normal functioning, each dispute contains the seeds of an "irrational breakdown." There is a danger that *real feeling,* like irrational anger, may erupt through our passivized and repressed egos, creating a dangerous reflection on our collective-individual impotence ("fuck this bullshit"). In other words, the totality of disputes poses the danger of an oppositional and liberatory consciousness. In order to perform the passivizing judicial function, the judge must seize upon the dispute as a factual disequilibration, re-experience this disequilibration in relation to the equilibrative tendency of the system as it expresses itself through these facts, and then state this equilibration in the form of a law that "controls" the outcome of the case.

If these ideas seem difficult to grasp in the abstract, consider the concrete predicament that a law review editor faces in deciding whether to print "fuck this bullshit" in a law-review article. A law review is a movement of worked matter that exists in time (it is printed, published, distributed, read, and placed on a shelf). Once it is distributed, it obtains its cultural meaning through the shared experience of a dispersed collective—that is, through those who experience this worked matter as a "law review." It places *them* in a relation of reciprocal equilibration, to the extent that each reader experiences himself in a passivized role that expresses the collective's normal functioning (as a "law professor,"

"lawyer," etc.). By "reciprocal equilibration" I mean that each reader, as an "other lawyer" to each of the other lawyers, conforms his response to the response he attributes to the others, according to a "lawyer norm" that has come to them from the outside, from the class relations that have created their collective function (objectively speaking) or role (subjectively speaking). In this context, "fuck this bullshit" is a disequilibration precisely to the extent that each reader, in imagining how all the others are responding to it, experiences mild shock. This is not how law reviews are supposed to sound if "we lawyers" are to sustain our lofty analytical tone. And in a way, the entire system is thrown into question by the de-reification of law-review language, since lawyers, as a "cog" within the system's equilibration, are partially constituted by their language in their law reviews. If law reviews don't have to seem like law reviews, perhaps nothing has to seem like anything.

In discovering a sentence like this in a manuscript from an author, the editor is forced into a position similar to that of the judge. As an "other" to all of the others that are synthetically constituted by the movement of the law review as worked matter, he knows that his function within the dispersed collective is to make sure that the law review follows its law. It must read normally. If he intends to act in accordance with his interest, he must enjoin the publication of "fuck this bullshit" if he finds, through "reasoning by analogy," that the phrase is sufficiently disruptive to the normal movement of its factual context. Considering the expectability, within this equilibration, of an author saying what she pleases and of a student-editor being somewhat deferential, he may or may not decide that an injunctive remedy is appropriate. But his method of deciding requires precisely an apprehension of the system as a synthetic and thing-like process, and an equilibrative evaluation. Were he to publish an opinion, it would legitimate the law review, whatever the outcome.

Since the system's equilibrative tendency is

taken for granted epistemologically in the judge's organization of the facts, I will call it a "presupposed norm." What is presupposed is the inevitability of the system as it is in its normal movement.

C. THE GENERATION OF A CONCEPTUAL ANALYSIS THAT EMBODIES THE PRESUPPOSED NORM

Thus far I have described only the synthetic field from which the law is drawn and to which it applies. This synthetic field is revealed in the judge's reasoning by analogy. It represents a reification of the social world as it is, because it presupposes the social world as an epistemological a priori.

The next movement of the judge's consciousness is the generation of a conceptual analysis that will embody what has been presupposed. This movement is the actual "application of the law." It is of central importance to the activity of legitimation because it creates the appearance that the social order is a consequence of the legal order. The judge, as a member of a ruling elite, disappears from view; he is merely the conduit of certain abstract rules and principles that "govern the affairs of men."

The activity of conceptual analysis requires both the derivation of concepts from the synthetic field and their application through the method of logical deduction. These two operations are in reality unified in the temporal reflection that is called "legal thinking"; the concepts are always in use, like the material world from which they are abstracted. But, for convenience, I will address each operation separately here.

1. The Reification of Concepts in Ordinary Language
The word "concept" means "seize with." That which is "seized" with a concept is a social experience of an object in the world as the object reveals itself within particular sociohistorical conditions. Our social experience of the world is first of all temporal, by which I mean that we experience everything in time toward the realization of practical and meaningful intentions that have been organized or shaped by our condi-

tioning, by our past way of learning the nature of the world through our relations with others. We do not experience the world first of all with concepts, because concepts are atemporal (Sartre, 1977). It is rather the case that our concepts derive from practical experience and permit us to "freeze" this experience in order to signify the experience to ourselves and to others.

For example, near me sits something that I experience first of all as towards-lighting-up-a-darkness. Everyone in my culture also experiences this thing this way. Together we seize this shared experience with the concept "lamp." The concept "lamp" is an abstraction from our shared practical experience of this thing, which signifies the thing's normal function for us. In the case of the concept "lamp," it is perhaps most accurate to say that the concept signifies a thing which functions towards-lighting-up-a-darkness-to-a-moderate-level. If a thing functions toward lighting-up-a-darkness-very-brightly, we might conceptualize the thing as a "beacon" and not as a "lamp."

There is nothing troubling about a concept as long as its abstract nature is remembered by those who use it. But in the ordinary language that has emerged within our culture, concepts are concretized. For example, when we say "the lamp lights up the room," we attribute to the abstraction the power to perform the function from which it was derived. The concept "lamp" *means* towards-lighting-up-moderately; it was abstracted from our shared experience of a thing's function-for-us. If we now say "the lamp lights up" something, we confuse the concept with the concrete usable thing whose function-for-us we seized with the concept. The abstract concept "lamp," which originated as a shorthand for our shared practical experience of a thing, has been "falsely concretized" or reified, such that normal lightness seems to be created by it, rather than the converse. According to the grammar of our language, the concept "lamp" has become the "subject" of the sentence, as if it were doing something meaningful to the room. Perhaps it would be simpler to say that the reification of the concept gives the impression that the thing itself is a subject, instead of being the object of a shared temporal experience that is merely "captured" or signified conceptually.[5]

The significance of this reification of the concept in its ordinary usage is that an historically contingent social norm is transformed into a timeless fact about the world. Through our use of normal sentences, we collectively fail to recognize that the thing before us was fashioned by human labor in order to perform a social function under historically determinate material conditions; instead, through the repression that the reification of the concept forces on our awareness, we give ourselves the impression that this function is simply "what the thing does." And if we remember that the set of cultural meanings seized with the concept "lamp" obtains its meaningfulness only in relation to the total set of meanings expressed in the culture's normal functioning, we can see that through language taken as a whole we generate a disjunction between the socially-communicated reality and the reality of experience, such that reality as a whole is signified as thing-like in its movement. This seems to me to be the phenomenological-linguistic basis of what Marx called "commodity-fetishism" (Marx, 1967, p. 72).

In our concepts, we reify not only things; we also reify persons precisely to the degree that they are passivized within roles expressing their function. Consider the concept "secretary," an abstract term that freezes the cultural meaning of certain functions performed by a number of human beings. When we say, "she is a secretary," we equate a being with her function. If we say, "a good secretary types 60 words a min-

ute," we attribute a normative behavior to the concretized concept. It is like saying "a good function types 60 words per minute," but we fail to recognize this because the function has become a presupposed "fact" about "what secretaries do." Her function has been reified as the factual activity of the concept which envelopes her. And, of course, her functional activity, as it is determined for her by the technology of the typewriter, the available supply of secretarial labor and so forth, bears a synthetic relation to "what manufacturers do," "what welfare recipients do"—in short, to the reified social field in its totality.

If we now return to the judge whose function it is to construct the law of this social field, we can more easily see how he will embody the presupposed norm in a conceptual analysis of the fact-situation. He will abstract *legitimating* concepts from the presupposed norm and then reify them, so that it will appear that the functioning of the system is simply the factual activity of the legitimating concepts, thereby representing the system itself as legitimate a priori.

2. The Reification of Legal Concepts as a Way of Legitimating the Status-Quo In order to grasp the way that the judge derives legal concepts from his apprehension of the social field, we must remember that his intention is to adjudicate a dispute in such a way that the system will be restored to a normal and legitimated equilibration in the realm of thought. He has, in other words, an unconscious *legitimating intention* and it is towards-legitimating-the-system that he has apprehended the events leading up to the dispute as a disequilibrated fact-situation in the first place. In order now to conceptualize the fact-situation "legally," he must abstract legitimating concepts from the normal movement of the facts, concretize the abstractions, and then re-describe the facts with the aid of these abstractions. This is exactly what it means to apply the law to the facts. Simultaneously, the facts become lawful and the law becomes factual.

Since the law as a generality is supposed to

---

[5]I do not mean to imply that there would be no social context within which one could use the concept "lamp" without reifying it. Whether the concept "lamp" becomes reified depends upon whether or not we are able to "remember" the concept's abstract and provisional character. This, in turn, depends upon whether we are able to actually experience the thing itself as a temporal object fashioned by human beings for a human use, or whether we experience the thing in a fixed and factual way as if it simply had an inborn attribute of "emitting light."

apply to everyone in "the society," the primary legal abstractions drawn from any fact-situation must be universal. Within the operational reasoning of the physical world (the laws of physics), an example of such a universal abstraction is the concept "particle" because it signifies the movement of anything whatsoever, to the extent that the movement of the whole of the material world is apprehended as being made up of parts. An atom, a photon, an electron—all of these can be abstracted to higher levels of universality by the concept "particle." Within legal reasoning as it is applied to the social world, the equivalent to this concept is the concept "party." The bailee, the tort-feasor, the executor, the trustee—all of these abstractions share the universal abstract feature of being "parties in dispute." The "party" is the abstract universal "particle" of the social field, and signifies simply that the social field is comprised of "legal parts" that are, at this highest level of generality, identical to one another.

In order to legalize the normal movement of the social field, each party must be conceptualized as possessing certain universal normative "properties" signifying that the way people do function together normally is also the way people should function together normally. These properties are called "rights" and "duties." Within any fact-situation of whatever kind, each party is presumed to have a "right" to the other's normal functioning (e.g., prompt delivery of the goods, driving at normal speed), and each party is also presumed to have a "duty" to function normally toward the other. If we continue to think of the judge as a "legitimation scientist" who observes the "data" that makes up the social field, we can say that he conceptualizes what he sees as a mass of moving "parties," all identical, all linked to one another through the bonding permitted by the rights and duties possessed by each party. And in so doing, he reifies the interaction of the parties as legitimate a priori, since it appears to him that the parties interact because they *ought* to. From within the legitimating gaze, a party delivers goods on time, or a party remains within the speed limit, or a party disposes of net income properly, *because* he has a duty to do so and *because* the other has a right to it. Once the abstractions are concretized, it appears that this is simply how parties interact, or more precisely, it appears that parties do interact the way they should. "Is" and "ought" are fused in the very way that the social field is conceptualized.

Within any particular fact-situation, the legal party is reconceptualized in terms of the particular function that he or she (perhaps "it" would be the correct pronoun) is obliged to perform. Suppose, for example, that party A is in dispute with part B because B delivered some goods five days late (A would not transfer money to B, B is upset, etc.). The system is in disequilibration and the judge is asked to state its law, which, as we can now begin to see, is nothing more than the legitimating conceptual representation of its normal functioning. He asks first: "What was B's duty?" This is derived by abstracting a concept from B's normal function within the system, reifying the concept in such a way that the function becomes "what B is," and then describing what B does in normative terms as identical to what B ought to do. Thus a "party" of the type B is conceptualized as a "seller," a concept which simply freezes this party's function as it is dictated by the movement of the commodity; this function is then factualized as what sellers do (the common-sense may be; in this case, that sellers deliver goods on time); and then this factualized normal function receives a normative articulation ("sellers have a duty to deliver goods on time"). When a "seller" fails to deliver goods on time to a "buyer," then the buyer's "right" has been "violated." In analyzing the facts this way, all that the judge actually does is to restate the facts in terms of their lawful attributes, such that what happened in the facts appears as a violation of a law immanent to them. And through this restatement, normal equilibration of the seller-buyer world is restored in the realm of thought.

It follows from this that a "rule of law" is merely the normative reification of function—it is a way of describing a normal practice that has been generated by pressures within the system in a legitimating conceptual form. The judge needs to construct such a rule because what he wants to do is to describe what this seller "should have done" by evaluating her factual conduct in relation to what all sellers "should be doing" within the system. This can only be accomplished by evaluating what this seller did in relation to what sellers as a generality (as performers of the "seller-function") actually do, and then representing this evaluation in an "ought" form. For example, the actual rule that is to be applied in the case that we are looking at, the prompt-delivery rule, emerged as a rule receiving wide acceptance from the socio-economic relations of classical free-market capitalism. We can infer from the very fact that this rule was "accepted" and "made sense" that these socio-economic relations generated a normal practice in commodity-exchange transfers that favored the simultaneous transfer of goods for money.[6] Faced with a systemic breakdown, the judge abstracts from this normal practice a legitimating rule that "applies" to all sellers: "Prompt delivery by the seller is a condition precedent to the buyer's duty to pay." When this rule is reified as a "law," the appearance is created that the "commodity-exchange transfer-function," as it is supposed to be performed by all sellers within the system, is *caused* by "the rights and duties of the parties." The judge can then deduce whether *this* seller did what she "ought" to have done by comparing her factual conduct to what all sellers "ought" to do.

This process of reifying the rule turns the world as it is on its head, because it signifies that a norm of intersubjective action is "caused" by an ideological appearance that has been drawn from it. The process of deducing outcome from rule then becomes the process of signifying the causality of the law, of signifying that the social order is the consequence of a legal order that is immanent to it.

[6] I am not saying that normal practice ever conforms in an empirical way to *actual* practice because a variety of factors influence actual practice besides the objective pressures of the market.

3. The Temporal Structure of Legal Reasoning: 'Reliving a Time-Sequence' through the Thought Process of Logical Deduction

Whenever I have referred to the normal movements of facts, I have used the word "movement" as an objectified representation of the temporal activity of real human actors, working in intersubjective reciprocity with one another. Each actor, of course, does not at first experience his activity as that of a moving fact. He lives his activity as what might be called "projective possibility"—that is, as towards the realization of some practical intention that has been defined for him by circumstances. These circumstances are actually a network of coercive social relations that have been shaped by material objects, each of which bears, through the inscription imposed upon it by past labor, a social meaning. The social meaning of the commodity, for example, is towards the network of social relations which constitutes the market. Because the seller is constituted as a seller by the social meaning of the commodity, he adopts *its* meaning as his own. He experiences the commodity as towards the possibility of exchanging it for money. To this extent, the person who sells goods has become passivized and thing-like.

Yet the project of carrying goods to the market is a contingent project that is pervaded, as I have suggested, by a sense of illegitimacy. Because every disequilibration threatens to raise this sense of illegitimacy to a kind of inchoate awareness, it is the function of the judge to interpret the contingency of the seller's project as factual necessity. Therefore, his objective is to apprehend and express the seller's contingent behavior as the movement of a fact. The apprehension of the fact-situation as a synthetic and passive activity, which, as I have shown, describes the first movement of the judge's consciousness, is therefore properly called a "temporalization"; it seizes upon the alienated temporal project of each social actor and represents this project as factual movement. I indicated this implicitly earlier when I described this initial process of apprehension as a process of "re-experiencing" the events that gave rise to the breakdown in order to sense whether they reveal a disequilibration from the norm.

If we review the thought-process of applying the law to the facts as I described it in the previous section, we can see that this is also in reality a "temporalization" of this kind. The process of "deducing the outcome from the rule" is in reality a process of re-experiencing the event itself as that event is signified through legitimating concepts. To return to my sale of goods example, what occurred in the real world was an attempted exchange and breakdown. Through the legitimating prism of the law, however, this occurrence is re-experienced as a temporal movement of imaginary figures who apparently actually possess "rights and duties" as aspects of their being. When I say that the process of deducing outcome from rule is a process of signifying the causality of the law, I mean that the judge is literally guiding an imaginary movement of the collective consciousness through the signifying movement of "deducing." He shows that a particular seller who possesses the universal attribute of "having a duty to deliver on time" (as signified through the general rule) has in this instance mis-acted or violated his attribute by delivering late. The rule states the imaginary attributes; the so-called "application of the rule" is simply a re-experiencing and re-describing of what occurred in the real world, as it is seen through the prism of these attributes. In reaching the outcome, therefore, the judge is simply reliving the time-sequence that has given rise to the dispute, but in a wholly imaginary way. His "legal reasoning" is finally nothing more than a movement of the imaginary—an imaginary that takes on the appearance of the real through the process of reification.

This final aspect of the description has important implications for understanding the role of the legal outcome in the social system—it means that the outcome is significant only in its effect on the collective imagination of the culture, because the outcome "is" nothing more than the signification of an image. Of course, the result of the legal proceeding does have a practical consequence— one person tells another to do something and he does it or is compelled to by somebody with a gun. But this practical consequence has to do with the role of force and not with the role of law, and it is but an incidental concrete aspect of the ritual through which law is brought into the world. In the "legal world" that is signified in the judge's opinion, the signification that the buyer "wins" because her "right" has been violated" is to express the necessary imaginary "outcome" of an imaginary interaction between essentially fictional characters. To the extent that people share in the judge's experience as it is signified in the opinion, they come to believe in a "legal order" that directs the concrete truth of daily life.

III. THE "ONTOLOGICAL" BASIS OF LEGITIMATION; LEGAL REASONING AS A WAY OF RESTORING THE UNALIENATED GROUP IN IMAGINARY FORM

A. THE RELATIONSHIP BETWEEN LEGAL REASONING AND NORMATIVE POLITICAL THEORY

No matter how much people experience their social relations as relations between things, they do not forget that in reality these relations are only thing-*like* (cf., Jameson, 1971: 244–246). For this reason, a law which reifies and legitimates these relations must itself be legitimated by concepts which are abstracted from the subjectivity of those to whom the law applies. A person who asks why he has a legal duty to do something is not answered by being told "because it is your function to do it." Such an answer would suggest that he is actually a thing, which he knows is not the case. The only effective answer to such a question is to justify the duty by reference to a "human nature" which brought the duty into being, or, in other words, the law must appear to spring from normative assumptions about *who* "the parties" are as real people.

These normative assumptions are embodied in the abstractions of normative political theory. The activity of thinking up political theory is formally identical to the activity of thinking up legal reasoning. It consists in apprehending the system as a synthetic quasi-object (the presupposed norm), drawing abstractions from the movement of concrete social actors as they move in their normal functioning, reifying these abstractions, and then creating the appearance, through "political reasoning," that these abstractions have brought the world as it is into being. In political reasoning, the thinker's intention is to attribute a *normative subjectivity* to the members of a culture that is then reified as "human nature," in exactly the same way that legal reasoning reifies the duties of the seller as an ingredient or property of what might be called the "seller's nature." In each case, we are dealing with a reifying thought, but political reasoning backs up legal reasoning by articulating the relationship between the seller as functioning unit and the seller as human being, such that the "duty" corresponding to the seller's function seems to be ultimately derived from his own intentions. Of course, these "intentions" are actually those of the abstract and normative "subject" whose identity has been grafted as a reified fact onto the seller's being (thus, it is said that he entered the contract of his own "free will"); yet the seller feels these intentions as his (or, in other words, it "makes sense" to him to call them his intentions) because his identity as normative subject has been abstracted from his actual alienated functioning in the world (engaging in apparently voluntary transactions in a "private" market).

Thus, it makes sense, in the objective context of a freely competitive market, to describe the necessary systemic function of exchange as the consequence of an intentional interaction between two "free and equal" subjects. Seen as quasi-objects, the participants in an exchange *are* in a certain sense "free and equal"—that is, in the sense in which atoms as "mere facts" appear to the physicist as unattached and identical. The subjective concepts are abstracted from the concrete functioning of the participants, and once reified, they represent the functional interaction as the consequence of the participants' human nature as subjects. Similarly, it makes sense, in the objective context of the cooperative market that we now have, to describe the same exchange as the consequence of an intentional interaction between two "free and equal" subjects "acting in good faith." Seen as quasi-objects, the participants in an exchange today *do* "act in good faith" in the same sense that the bonded atoms in a molecule appear to the physicist as attached to one another. The subjective moral sentiment is abstracted from the objective functional reality, and reified, such that it appears that the necessity of objective cooperation in state-regulated monopoly capitalism is the consequence of the participants' subjective intentions. In both cases, the alienated intention which is forced upon the participants by the movement of the commodity and which mirrors their function, is represented normatively in the abstract.

These are examples of the way that political theory is used within judicial opinions. In any historical period there are also full-blown works of political theory which subjectivize and naturalize the entire system of social relations from which they are abstracted. Thus, liberal political theory, as it emerged in the context of a developing competitive market, described the entire structure of market relations as the consequence of atomized and self-interested "free wills" (utilitarianism and social contract theory). Its conceptual structure made the facts of competitive capitalism "legitimately lawful" by allocating the responsibility for its laws to an hypostasized "we" which supposedly brought the world as it was then into being. This "we" was an abstract collection of free wills who created an abstract "state" that created the laws by which social relations were to be governed. Today, liberal political theory has been modified to conform to the cooperative structure of contemporary capitalism. It is imagined that classical liberal theory was wrong in failing to include a moral component in each subject's free will that would limit liberty as license in the interests of a newly conceived notion of the general welfare. And it is through this new conception of a more moral "we" that the laws of corporate liberalism find their political justification. Seen in this way, a work of normative political theory is a kind of fantastic fable or myth describing the world as it is in a common-sense mythical form, and yet hiding its mythic quality beneath the false concretization of reified abstractions.

Now if we put this brief description of political reasoning together with the description of legal reasoning in the previous section, we can see each judicial opinion as a mythical narrative that restores the system's equilibration in the realm of thought by resolving a dispute according to the requirements of "human nature." The equilibrative tendency within the system is apprehended as the movement of a normative political "we," or in other terms, the intersubjective movement of socio-economic relations is abstracted as a political communion of normative subjects. Through the abstract "political process," "we" create the laws which govern "us." These laws define the "rights and duties" of normative subjects to one another, and are "applied" in the resolution of disputes between "parties." And through the collective fantasy of applying the law, the resolution of each dispute restores a disrupted communion to its lawful state. We are reminded that the system itself is the embodiment of our collective nature.

B. THE TRANSPOSITION OF THE REAL INTO THE IMAGINARY

And yet this description of legal reasoning, which we should now call "politico-legal" reasoning, does not explain its efficacy, its psychological power. If the motive force behind this thought-process is the concealment of "a traumatic absence of connectedness that does not wish to become conscious of itself," it remains for us to understand how the experience of thinking this way provides a psychic gratification that temporarily alleviates the trauma when it threatens to erupt, through the dispute or breakdown, into awareness.

The solution to this dilemma is to be found in the ontological meaning for each person of ex-

periencing the intersubjective movement of socioeconomic relations as a political communion of normative subjects. This experience is captured in the psychoanalytic concept of a "wish fulfillment." Under the pressure of what Freud called the "return of the repressed," or of what we can here describe as the possibility of becoming aware of the social alienation that pervades our entire collective experience, we respond by imagining that we are actually disalienated in an harmonious socio-political connection that is also "the law." No matter what the particular content of the politico-legal thought (feudal/religious, capitalist/liberal, etc.), its universal ontological feature is that it generates an imaginary feeling of "with-ness" by restoring the feeling of being-in-a-group in an imaginary way. In other words, there occurs something like what Freud called a "cathexis," whereby dammed up desire is partially and momentarily gratified through images that are signified in thought. These images are potentiated in such a way that they are able to allow us to experience, through an infinite number of historical forms, what life would be like in the absence of alienation. Thus, to imagine a society of "free and equal citizens" is to *experience*, however dimly, a feeling of collective spontaneity free of interpersonal domination; to imagine a world in which people have "moral obligations" to one another is to experience, however dimly, a feeling of reciprocal recognition and commitment. And even God's harshest commands, as they were embodied in the politico-legal ideology of feudalism, allowed people to experience a feeling of genuine love through the image of possible salvation. It is the cathexis of these ideal images that provides what we might call the emotional correlate of reification: "belief" in the law derives not from mere indoctrination, but from a desire to reify, a desire to believe that the abstract is concrete, that the imaginary is real.

The reason that these ideal images can take an infinite number of historical forms is that our ontology, our social being, is indivisible. We do not want freedom and equality and recognition and justice in an additive fashion; it is, rather, that each of these words signifies an indivisible and whole way of being-in-a-group that will achieve concrete expression only with the elimination of alienation. In the ontological sense, freedom implies equality just as equality implies freedom, and both will be realized in the concrete when either is, neither before the other. There is no limit to the way that this sense of wholeness and sociality can be expressed, since the historical development of forms of social expression is nothing other than an infinite evocation of social being in the course of its becoming. Thus, from the ontological point of view, we can say that the judicial or political "ideologist," as a social theorist of the imaginary, has an infinite variety of images available to him in the construction of his legitimating thought.

From the socio-historical point of view, however, his options are strictly limited by what we could call formal and historical constraints. The "formal" constraint is one that I have emphasized consistently in the course of this essay—in order for politico-legal reasoning to "make sense," there must always be a relative correspondence in form between the imaginary social organization of the legitimating images and the social organization of the concrete socio-economic world from which these images are drawn. Thus, from a purely formal standpoint, for example, the legitimation of the feudal hierarchies required an ideology of Divine Right *or any formal equivalent* that could represent these hierarchies in an imaginary ideal way. The "historical" constraint on the development of politico-legal thought is what gives a relatively determinate *content* to the particular evocation of the ideal that is possible at a given historical moment. Because there must be an historical continuity to the development of ideological forms, the ideological tensions that are continually produced by formal disjunctions between a prevailing ideology and the transforming equilibration of the common-sense must be mediated by a thought that simultaneously conserves the existing forms and images while surpassing them toward new imaginary wholes. In this historical sense, the hierarchies of feudal life, for example, required an ideology of Divine Right *or any mediative equivalent* that could have adjusted the prior cosmology to a new social order.[7]

As an historical figure, therefore, the ideologist is perhaps best seen as a kind of sleight-of-hand man or "bricoleur" (Levi-Strauss, 1966) who seeks to fuse these ontological, formal, and historical dimensions of legitimating thought in the fabrication of a perpetual illusion that everyone wants to believe. The group conspires to create him in order to maintain its collective repression in the face of a perpetual terror that there will be a "breakdown of law," which is to say a breakdown of even the imaginary forms of social cohesion. The only antidote to this perpetual movement of unconscious conspiracy is the development of a concrete disalienating social cohesion unnecessary. And one feature of the development of such a movement must be the development of such a movement must be the delegitimation of the law altogether, which is to say the delegitimation of the notion that social life is created and enforced by imaginary ideas.[8]

[7]My use of the terms "formal" and "historical" corresponds roughly to my understanding of the terms "synchronic" and "diachronic" as they are used in structuralist thought as descriptive of the organization and transformation of concepts (cf. Culler, 1978). Please note that when I refer to a "formal correspondence" in the relation of level thought to socioeconomic practice, I am referring to a correspondence that emerges within existential historical time according to what we might describe as a "legitimation correspondence rate" that is felt as necessry by members of the group. It is impossible to line up the so-called "base" and the so-called "superstructure" by comparing the "economic form" and the "legal form" prevailing in a particular decade or number of decades because real life does not proceed in accordance with the presuppositions about "quantities of time" that are characteristic of positivist methods.

[8]This should not be taken to imply that there would be "no law" in a future and more humane society. To the extent that the transformation of socio-economic life allows for the development of less alienated personal relationships, it will become both possible and important to develop provisional forms of moral consensus that are externalized and communicated as part of a "constitutive" politics (See especially, Klare, 1979.)

REFERENCES

Balbus, Isaac, "Commodity Form and Legal Form: An Essay on the 'Relative Autonomy' of the Law," *Law and Soc. Review* 11 (1977): 571–588.

Culler, Jonathan, *Ferdinand de Saussure,* New York: Viking Press, 1978.

Freud, Sigmund, *The Ego and the Id,* New York: Norton, 1962 (originally published in German, 1923).

————, *The Future of an Illusion,* Garden City, New York: Doubleday, 1964 (originally published in German, 1927).

Hegel, G. W. F., *The Phenomenology of Mind,* New York: Harper & Row, 1967 (originally published in German in 1807).

Heidegger, Martin, *Being and Time,* New York: Harper & Row, 1962 (originally published in German, 1927).

Jameson, Frederic, *Marxism and Form,* Princeton, N.J.: Princeton University Press, 1971.

Klare, Karl, "Law-Making as Praxis," *Telos* 40 (1979): 123–135.

Klein, G., *Psychoanalytic Theory,* New York: International Universities Press, 1976.

Laing, R. D., *The Politics of Experience,* New York: Pantheon Books, 1967.

Levi-Strauss, Claude, *The Savage Mind,* Chicago: University of Chicago Press, 1966.

Marx, Karl, *Capital, Volume I,* New York: International Publishers, 1967 (originally published in German, 1873).

Sartre, Jean-Paul, *Critique of Dialectical Reason: Theory of Practical Ensembles,* London: Humanities Press, 1976 (originally published in French, 1960).

————, *Life/Situations,* New York: Random House, 1977 (originally published in French, 1975).

THE HEGEMONIC FUNCTION OF THE LAW

EUGENE D. GENOVESE

When Mao Tse-tung told his revolutionary army, "Political power grows out of the barrel of a gun," he stated the obvious, for as Max Weber long before had observed as a matter of scientific detachment, "The decisive means for politics is violence."[1] This viewpoint does not deny an ethical dimension to state power; it asserts that state power, the conquest of which constitutes the object of all serious political struggle, represents an attempt to monopolize and therefore both discipline and legitimize the weapons of violence.

One of the primary functions of the law concerns the means by which command of the gun becomes ethically sanctioned. But if we left it at that, we could never account for the dignity and élan of a legal profession in, say, England, that has itself become a social force; much less could we account for the undeniable influence of the law in shaping the class relations of which it is an instrument of domination. Thus, the fashionable relegation of law to the rank of a superstructural and derivative phenomenon obscures the degree of autonomy it creates for itself. In modern societies, at least, the theoretical and moral foundations of the legal order and the actual, specific history of its ideas and institutions influence, step

by step, the wider social order and system of class rule, for no class in the modern Western world could rule for long without some ability to present itself as the guardian of the interests and sentiments of those being ruled.

The idea of "hegemony," which since Gramsci has become central to Western Marxism, implies class antagonisms, but it also implies, for a given historical epoch, the ability of a particular class to contain those antagonisms on a terrain in which its legitimacy is not dangerously questioned. As regards the law specifically, note should be taken of the unhappy fate of natural-law doctrines and assorted other excursions into "revolutionary" legal theory. The revolutionary bourgeoisie, during its rise to power in Europe, counterposed natural-law doctrines to feudal theory but once in power rushed to embrace a positive theory of law, even while assimilating natural-law doctrines to a new defense of property. Nor did the experience of the Communist movement in Russia differ after its conquest of power. However much sentimentalists and utopians may rail at the monotonous recurrence of a positive theory of law whenever revolutionaries settle down to rebuild the world they have shattered, any other course would be doomed to failure. Ruling classes differ, and each must rule differently. But all modern ruling classes have much in common in their attitude toward the law, for each must confront the problem of coercion in such a way as to minimize the necessity for its use, and each must disguise the extent to which state power does not so much rest on force as

[1]Max Weber, "Politics as a Vocation," *From Max Weber: Essays in Sociology* (trans. and ed. H. H. Gerth and C. Wright Mills; New York, 1946), p. 121.

Source: From Eugene D. Genovese, *Roll, Jordan, Roll* (New York: Pantheon Books, 1976), pp. 25–49. Reprinted by permission.

279

represent its actuality. Even Marxian theory, therefore, must end with the assertion of a positive theory of law and judge natural-law and "higher-law" doctrines to be tactical devices in the extralegal struggle.

In southern slave society, as in other societies, the law, even narrowly defined as a system of institutionalized jurisprudence, constituted a principal vehicle for the hegemony of the ruling class. Since the slaveholders, like other ruling classes, arose and grew in dialectical response to the other classes of society—since they were molded by white yeomen and black slaves as much as they molded them—the law cannot be viewed as something passive and reflective, but must be viewed as an active, partially autonomous force, which mediated among the several classes and compelled the rulers to bend to the demands of the ruled. The slaveholders faced an unusually complex problem since their regional power was embedded in a national system in which they had to share power with an antagonistic northern bourgeoisie. A full evaluation of the significance of the law of slavery will have to await an adequate history of the southern legal system in relation to the national; until then a preliminary analysis that risks too much abstraction must serve.

The slaveholders as a socio-economic class shaped the legal system to their interests. But within that socio-economic class—the class as a whole—there were elements competing for power. Within it, a political center arose, consolidated itself, and assumed a commanding position during the 1850s. The most advanced fraction of the slaveholders—those who most clearly perceived the interests and needs of the class as a whole—steadily worked to make their class more conscious of its nature, spirit, and destiny. In the process it created a world-view appropriate to a slaveholders' regime.

For any such political center, the class as a whole must be brought to a higher understanding of itself—transformed from a class-in-itself, reacting to pressures on its objective position, into a class-for-itself, consciously striving to shape the

world in its own image. Only possession of public power can discipline a class as a whole, and through it, the other classes of society. The juridical system may become, then, not merely an expression of class interest, nor even merely an expression of the willingness of the rulers to mediate with the ruled; it may become an instrument by which the advanced section of the ruling class imposes its viewpoint upon the class as a whole and the wider society. The law must discipline the ruling class and guide and educate the masses. To accomplish these tasks it must manifest a degree of evenhandedness sufficient to compel social conformity; it must, that is, validate itself ethically in the eyes of the several classes, not just the ruling class. Both criminal and civil law set standards of behavior and sanction norms that extend well beyond strictly legal matters. The death penalty for murder, for example, need not arise from a pragmatic concern with deterrence, and its defenders could justifiably resist psychological arguments. It may arise from the demand for implementation of a certain idea of justice and from the educational requirement to set a firm standard of right and wrong. "The Law," as Gramsci says, "is the repressive and negative aspect of the entire positive civilising activity undertaken by the State."[2]

The law acts hegemonically to assure people that their particular consciences can be subordinated—indeed, morally must be subordinated—to the collective judgment of society. It may compel conformity by granting each individual his right of private judgment, but it must deny him the right to take action based on that judgment when in conflict with the general will. Those who would act on their own judgment as against the collective judgment embodied in the law find themselves pressed from the moral question implicit in any particular law to the moral question of obedience to constituted authority. It appears mere egotism and antisocial

---

[2] *Selections from the Prison Notebooks of Antonio Gramsci* (trans. and ed. Quintin Hoare and Geoffrey N. Smith; New York, 1971), p. 247.

behavior to attempt to go outside the law unless one is prepared to attack the entire legal system and therefore the consensual framework of the body politic.

The white South shaped its attitude toward its slaves in this context. With high, malicious humor, William Styron has his fictional T. R. Gray explain to Nat Turner how he, a mere chattel, can be tried for the very human acts of murder and insurrection:

"... The point is that *you* are *animate* chattel and animate chattel is capable of craft and connivery and wily stealth. You ain't a wagon, Reverend, but chattel that possesses moral choice and spiritual volition. Remember that well. Because that's how come the law provides that animate chattel like you can be tried for a felony, and that's how come you're goin' to be tried next Sattidy."

He paused, then said softly without emotion: "And hung by the neck until dead."[3]

Styron may well have meant to satirize Judge Green of the Tennessee Supreme Court, who declared in 1846, "A slave is not in the condition of a horse." The slave, Judge Green continued, is made in the image of the Creator: "He has mental capacities, and an immortal principle in his nature that constitute him equal to his owner, but for the accidental position in which fortune has placed him. ∴. The laws ... cannot extinguish his high born nature, nor deprive him of many rights which are inherent in man."[4] The idea that chattels, as the states usually defined slaves, could have a highborn nature, complete with rights inherent in man, went down hard with those who thought that even the law should obey the rules of logic.

Four years before Judge Green's humane observations, Judge Turley of the same court unwittingly presented the dilemma. "The right to obedience ..." he declared in *Jacob (a Slave) v. State,* "in all lawful things ... is perfect in the

master, and the power to inflict any punishment, not affecting life or limb ... is secured to him by law."[5] The slave, being neither a wagon nor a horse, had to be dealt with as a man, but the law dared not address itself direct to the point. Had the law declared the slave a person in a specific class relationship to another person, two unpleasant consequences would have followed. First, the demand that such elementary rights as those of the family be respected would have become irresistible in a commercialized society that required the opposite in order to guarantee an adequate mobility of capital and labor. Second, the slaveholders would have had to surrender in principle, much as they often had to do in practice, their insistence that a slave was morally obligated to function as an extension of his master's will. However much the law generally seeks to adjust conflicting principles in society, in this case it risked undermining the one principle the slaveholders viewed as a *sine qua non.*

Yet, as Styron correctly emphasizes in the words he gives to T. R. Gray, the courts had to recognize the humanity—and therefore the free will—of the slave or be unable to hold him accountable for antisocial acts. Judge Bunning of Georgia plainly said, "It is not true that slaves are only chattels ... and therefore, it is not true that it is not possible for them to be prisoners...."[6] He did not tell us how a chattel (a thing) could also be nonchattel in any sense other than an agreed-upon fiction, nor did he wish to explore the question why a fiction should have become necessary. Since much of the law concerns agreed-upon fictions, the judges, as judges, did not have to become nervous about their diverse legal opinions, but as slaveholders, they could not avoid the prospect of disarray being introduced into their social philosophy. Repeatedly, the courts struggled with and tripped over the slave's humanity. Judge Hall of North Carolina, contrary to reason, nature, and the opinion of his fellow judges, could blurt out, *en passant,* "Being

---

[3]William Styron, *The Confessions of Nat Turner* (New York, 1967), pp. 21-22.

[4]*Ford v. Ford,* 1846, in Catterall, ed., *Judicial Cases,* II, 530.

[5]Catterall, ed., *Judicial Cases,* II, 517.

[6]*Ibid.,* III, 35.

slaves, they had no will of their own. . . ."[7] If so, then what of the opinion expressed by the State Supreme Court of Missouri: "The power of the master being limited, his responsibility is proportioned accordingly"?[8]

The high court of South Carolina wrestled with the conflicting principles of slave society and came up with an assortment of mutually exclusive answers. Judge Waites, in *State v. Cynthia Simmons and Lawrence Kitchen* (1794): "Negroes are under the protection of the laws, and have personal rights, and cannot be considered on a footing only with domestic animals. They have wills of their own—capacities to commit crimes; and are responsible for offences against society." The court in *Fairchild v. Bell* (1807): "The slave lives for his master's service. His time, his labor, his comforts, are all at the master's disposal." Judge John Belton O'Neall in *Tennent v. Dendy* (1837): "Slaves are our most valuable property. . . . Too many guards cannot be interposed between it and violent unprincipled men. . . . The slave ought to be fully aware that his master is to him . . . a perfect security from injury. When this is the case, the relation of master and servant becomes little short of that of parent and child."[9] But in Kentucky, the high court had pronounced in 1828: "However deeply it may be regretted, and whether it be politic or impolitic, a slave by our code is not treated as a person, but (*negotium*) a thing, as he stood in the civil code of the Roman Empire." But one year later we hear: "A slave has volition, and has feelings which cannot be entirely disregarded." And again in 1836: "But, although the law of this state considers slaves as property, yet it recognizes their personal existence, and, to a qualified extent, their natural rights."[10]

The South had discovered, as had every previous slave society, that it could not deny the

slave's humanity, however many preposterous legal fictions it invented. That discovery ought to have told the slaveholders much more. Had they reflected on the implications of a wagon's inability to raise an insurrection, they might have understood that the slaves as well as the masters were creating the law. The slaves' action proceeded within narrow limits, but it realized one vital objective: it exposed the deception on which the slave society rested—the notion that in fact, not merely in one's fantasy life, some human beings could become mere extensions of the will of another. The slaves grasped the significance of their victory with deeper insight than they have usually been given credit for. They saw that they had few rights at law and that those could easily be violated by the whites. But even one right, imperfectly defended, was enough to tell them that the pretensions of the master class could be resisted. Before long, law or no law, they were adding a great many "customary rights" of their own and learning how to get them respected.

The slaves understood that the law offered them little or no protection, and in self-defense they turned to two alternatives: to their master, if he was decent, or his neighbors, if he was not; and to their own resources. Their commitment to a paternalistic system deepened accordingly, but in such a way as to allow them to define rights for themselves. For reasons of their own the slaveholders relied heavily on local custom and tradition; so did the slaves, who turned this reliance into a weapon. If the law said they had no right to property, for example, but local custom accorded them private garden plots, then woe to the master or overseer who summarily withdrew the "privilege." To those slaves the privilege had become a right, and the withdrawal an act of aggression not to be borne. The slaveholders, understanding this attitude, rationalized their willingness to compromise. The slaves forced themselves upon the law, for the courts repeatedly sustained such ostensibly extralegal arrangements as having the force of law because sanctioned by time-honored practice. It was a small victory so far as everyday protection was

---

[7] *Ibid.*, II, 41.

[8] *Ibid.*, V, 179.

[9] *Ibid.*, II, 277, 289, 365.

[10] *Ibid.*, I, 311, 312, 334. See also I, 154 (Judge Cabell of Virginia).

concerned, but not so small psychologically; it gave the slaves some sense of having rights of their own, and also made them more aware of those rights withheld. W. W. Hazard of Georgia ran the risk of telling his slaves about their legal rights and of stressing the legal limits of his own power over them. He made it clear that he had an obligation to take care of them in their old age, whereas free white workers had no such protection, and argued deftly that their being whipped for insubordination represented a humane alternative to the practice of shooting soldiers and sailors for insubordination. His was an unusual act, but perhaps not so risky after all. He may have scored a few points while not revealing much they did not already know.[11]

The legal status of the slave during the seventeenth century, particularly in Virginia, still occasions dispute. We cannot be sure that the position of the earliest Africans differed markedly from that of the white indentured servants. The debate has considerable significance for the interpretation of race relations in American history. It remains possible that for a brief period a less oppressive pattern of race relations had had a chance to develop in the Upper South; it is doubtful that any such alternative ever existed in South Carolina, which as a slave society virtually derived from Barbados. In any case, before the turn of the century the issue had been resolved and blacks condemned to the status of slaves for life.

The laws of Virginia and Maryland, as well as those of the colonies to the south, increasingly gave masters the widest possible power over the slaves and also, through prohibition of interracial marriage and the general restriction of slave status to nonwhites, codified and simultaneously preached white supremacy. Kenneth Stampp writes: "Thus the master class, for its own purposes, wrote chattel slavery, the caste system, and color prejudice into American custom and law."[12] These earliest, Draconian slave codes

served as a model for those adopted by new slave states during the nineteenth century. Over time they became harsher with respect to manumission, education, and the status of the free Negro and milder with respect to protection for slave life; but most of the amelioration that occurred came through the courts and the force of public opinion rather than from the codes themselves. At the end of the antebellum period the laws remained Draconian and the enormous power of the masters had received only modest qualification. The best that might be said is that the list of capital crimes had shrunk considerably, in accordance with the movement toward general sensibility, and that the ruthless enforcement of the eighteenth century had given way to greater flexibility during the nineteenth. The laws, at least as amended during the early nineteenth century, tried to protect the lives of the slaves and provided for murder indictments against masters and other whites. They also demanded that masters, under penalty of fine or imprisonment, give adequate food, clothing, shelter, and support to the elderly. But these qualifications added confirmation to the power of the master over the slaves' bodies as well as labor-time. Nowhere did slave marriages win legal sanction, and therefore families could be separated with impunity. Only Louisiana effectively limited this outrage by forbidding the sale away from their mothers of children under the age of ten. Most significantly, blacks could not testify against whites in court, so that enforcement of the laws against cruel or even murderous masters became extremely difficult.

If harsh laws did not mean equally harsh practice, neither did mild laws mean equally mild practice. Kentucky had one of the mildest of slave codes, including the notable absence of an antiliteracy provision, but it probably suffered more personal violence and lynching than most other states, although much more often directed against allegedly negrophile whites than against blacks. The South had become the region of lynching *par excellence* during antebellum times, but of the three hundred or so victims recorded between 1840 and 1860, probably less than 10 percent

---

[11]W. W. Hazard, "On the General Management of a Plantation," *SA*, IV (July, 1831), 350-351.

[12]Stampp, *Peculiar Institution*, p. 23.

were blacks. Occasionally, the lynch fever struck hard, as in the wake of an insurrection scare. In these cases the most respectable planters might find themselves side by side with the poor whites in meting out fearful summary punishments; but for the blacks the danger of lynching remained minimal until after emancipation. The direct power of the masters over their slaves and in society as a whole, where they had little need for extralegal measures against blacks, provided the slaves with extensive protection against mob violence. So strong a hold did this sense of justice take on the master class that even during the war prominent voices could be heard in opposition to panicky summary actions against defecting slaves. Charles C. Jones, Jr., then a lieutenant in the Confederate army, wrote his father: "A trial by jury is accorded to everyone, whether white or black, where life is at stake. . . . Any other procedure, although possibly to a certain extent justified by the aggravated character of the offense and upon the grounds of public good, would in a strictly legal sense certainly be *coram non judice,* and would savor of mob law."[13] As Lieutenant Jones undoubtedly understood, an easy attitude toward indiscriminate mob violence against blacks would do more than threaten slave property; it would also threaten the position of the master class in society and open the way to initiatives by the white lower classes that might not remain within racial bounds. The masters felt that their own direct action, buttressed by a legal system of their own construction, needed little or no support from poor white trash. Order meant order.

The extent to which the law, rather than mobs, dealt with slave criminals appeared nowhere so starkly as in the response to rape cases. Rape meant, by definition, rape of white women, for no such crime as rape of a black woman existed at law. Even when a black man sexually attacked a black woman he could only be punished by his master; no way existed to bring him to trial or to convict him if so brought. In one case an appel-late court reversed the conviction of a black man for attempted rape, probably of a white woman, because the indictment had failed to specify the race of the victim.

Rape and attempted rape of white women by black men did not occur frequently. Ulrich Bonnell Phillips found 105 cases in Virginia for 1780 to 1864, with a few years unaccounted for.[14] Other states kept poor records on slave crime, although enough cases reached the appellate courts to make it clear that every slaveholding area had to face the issue once in a while. But even these infrequent cases provide a body of evidence of contemporary white southern attitudes.

On the whole, the racist fantasy so familiar after emancipation did not grip the South in slavery times. Slaves accused of rape occasionally suffered lynching, but the overwhelming majority, so far as existing evidence may be trusted, received trials as fair and careful as the fundamental injustice of the legal system made possible. Sometimes slaves did run into injustices even at law. A slave accused of raping a widow in Louisiana in 1859 went to the gallows on evidence that a local planter thought woefully insufficient. No positive identification had been made, he charged, and the evidence as a whole was slender. "I consider him," he wrote in his diary, "to be a victim of what is deemed a necessary example."[15]

The astonishing facts—astonishing in view of postemancipation outrages—are that public opinion usually remained calm enough to leave the matter in the hands of the courts and that the courts usually performed their duty scrupulously. The appellate courts in every southern state threw out convictions for rape and attempted rape on every possible ground, including the purely technical. They overturned convictions because the indictments had not been drawn up properly; because the lower courts had based their convic-

---

[13]Lt. Charles C. Jones, Jr., to C. C. Jones, July 25, 1862, in Myers, ed., *Children of Pride,* p. 939.

[14]Phillips, *American Negro Slavery,* pp. 458ff., or his article on slave crime cited in note 20 above.

[15]Breaux Diary, July 25, 26, 1859.

tions on possibly coerced confessions; or because the reputation of the white victim had not been admitted as evidence. The calmness of the public and the judicial system, relative to that of postbellum years, appeared most pointedly in reversals based on the failure to prove that black men who approached white women actually intended to use force. The Supreme Court of Alabama declared in one such instance: "An indecent advance, or importunity, however revolting, would not constitute the offense...." The punishment for rape remained death; punishment by castration receded, although in Missouri it survived into the late antebellum period.

The scrupulousness of the high courts extended to cases of slaves' murdering or attempting to murder whites. In Mississippi during 1834–1861, five of thirteen convictions were reversed or remanded; in Alabama during 1825–1864, nine of fourteen, in Louisiana during 1844–1859, two of five. The same pattern appeared in other states.

A slave could kill a white man in self-defense and escape conviction, provided that his own life stood in clear and imminent danger. In a celebrated case in Virginia in 1971, Moses, a slave, killed his overseer and escaped conviction despite much controversy in the white community. The court accepted testimony that Moses had served honestly and faithfully and that he had killed only when the overseer tried to kill him. During the nineteenth century the southern courts said plainly that a slave had the right to resist an assault that threatened his life, even to the point of killing his attacker. In practice, these rulings meant that a white man who attacked a slave with a deadly weapon risked the consequences; they did not mean that a slave had the right to make a judgment on the potential effects of, say, a prolonged whipping.

A brace of famous cases in North Carolina brought the theoretical questions to the surface and exposed the ultimate absurdity of defining a slave as chattel. In 1829, Judge Thomas Ruffin, one of the South's most respected jurists, handed down a decision he freely admitted to have

ghastly implications. A lower court had held that, as a matter of law, a master could be charged with committing battery upon a slave, much as a parent could be charged with unduly harsh physical punishment of a child. Judge Ruffin explained the Supreme Court's reversal in words that reveal as much about new attitudes toward the rights of children and the limits of parental authority as about anything else:

> There is no likeness between the cases. They are in opposition to each other and there is an impassable gulf between them—the difference is that which exists between freedom and slavery—and a greater cannot be imagined. In the one the end in view is the happiness of the youth born to equal rights with that governor on whom the duty devolves of training the young to usefulness in a status which he is afterwards to assume among free men.
>
> With slavery it is far otherwise. The end is the profit of the master, his security and public safety; the subject, one doomed in his own person, and his posterity, to live without knowledge, and without the capacity to make anything his own, and to toil that another may reap the fruits. What moral considerations, such as a father might give to a son, shall be addressed to such a being, to convince him what, it is impossible but that the most stupid must feel and know can never be true—that he is thus to labour upon a principle of natural duty, or for the sake of his own personal happiness, such services can only be expected from one who has no will of his own; who surrenders his will in implicit obedience to that of another. Such obedience is the consequence only of uncontrolled authority over the body. There is nothing else which can operate to produce the effect. The power of the master must be absolute to render the submission of the slave perfect. I must freely confess my sense of the harshness of this proposition, I feel it as deeply as any man can. And as a principle of moral right, every person in his retirement must repudiate it. But in the actual condition of things, it must be so. There is no remedy. This discipline belongs to the state of slavery.[16]

[16] J. G. deRoulhac Hamilton, ed., *The Papers of Thomas Ruffin* (4 vols.; Raleigh, N.C., 1918–1920), IV, 255–257; Earnest James Clark, Jr., "Slave Cases Argued Before the North Carolina Supreme Court, 1818–1858," unpubl. M.A. thesis, University of North Carolina, 1959, pp. 34–35.

Never has the logic of slavery been followed so faithfully by a humane and responsible man. As Ruffin knew, no civilized community could live with such a view. Perhaps he had hoped that the legislature would find a way to remove the high court's dilemma. It did not. The court had to reconsider its attitude.

In 1834, in *State v. Will,* the liberal Judge Gaston, speaking for the same court, handed down a radically different doctrine at once infinitely more humane and considerably less logical. Judge Gaston considered some things more important than logical consistency. Will, a slave, had tried to run away from an overseer who was attempting to whip him. The overseer thereupon got a gun and tried to shoot him. Will killed the overseer; accordingly, he entered a plea of innocent by reason of self-defense. The Supreme Court, under Judge Gaston's leadership, overturned Will's conviction and sustained the plea. Judge Ruffin must have been relieved; he remained silent and did not dissent from a ruling that so clearly contradicted the philosophy inherent in his own previous judgment. The aftermath of the case also reveals something about the southern legal system. On the assumption that Will's life would be unsafe from extralegal white retaliation, his master sold him and his wife to Mississippi. A few years later she arranged to be sold back to her old place. Her fellow slaves greeted her with surprise, for they had not expected her to leave her husband. She had not. Will had killed another slave in Mississippi and had been convicted of murder and executed. As the poor woman recalled, "Will sho'ly had hard luck. He killed a white man in North Carolina and got off, and then was hung for killing a nigger in Mississippi."[17]

The courts could never have sustained the right of a slave to self-defense if public opinion had been hostile. For the most part, it was not. Especially in cases in which the victim was an overseer or a poor man, the white attitude was that he got what he deserved. Armsted Barrett, an ex-slave of Texas, recalled that when a brutal overseer finally went too far, two slaves picked up their hoes one day and hacked his head off. The master calmly sold them. In so doing, he protected his investment, for compensation never equaled market value; but we can hardly believe that in such cases of violence against whites monetary considerations easily overpowered the others. In South Carolina a master abused his slaves and was believed responsible for the death of one or more. A committee of local citizens waited on the master to suggest, no doubt with grave courtesy and respect, that he leave the area immediately. He did. In Georgia slaves killed a cruel master without evoking the ire of local whites, who considered that he had deserved his fate. In Missouri, an ex-slave recalled that at the age of ten she had blinded her old mistress by hitting her with a rock in retaliation for the wanton and unpunished murder of her baby sister, who had made a nuisance of herself by excessive crying. The slave girl was owned by the mistress's daughter, who refused to have her punished and said, "Well, I guess mamma has larnt her lesson at last."[18]

In seventeenth-century Virginia a master could not murder a slave. He might cause his death, but he could not, legally, murder him. Would a man willingly destroy his own property? Certainly not. Therefore, no such crime as the murder of one's own slave could present itself to a court of reasonable men. In time, Virginia and the other slave states thought better of the matter. In 1821, South Carolina became the last of the slave states to declare itself clearly in protection of slave life. During the nineteenth century, despite state-by-state variations, slaveholders theoretically faced murder charges for wantonly killing a slave or for causing his death by excessive punishment. The Virginia Supreme Court in 1851 upheld the conviction of a master for causing the death of a slave by "cruel and excessive whipping and torture": "But in so inflicting punishment for the sake of punishment, the owner of the slave acts at his peril; and if death ensues in consequence of such punishment, the relation of master and slave af-

---

[17]E. J. Clark, Jr., "Slave Cases Argued Before the North Carolina Supreme Court," p. 38.

[18]Rawick, ed., *Texas Narr.,* IV (I), 25–26.

fords no ground or excuse or palliation." The court unanimously ruled that a murder had been committed.

South Carolina responded more slowly to the demands for liberalization than did other states, although Chancellor Harper may have been right in declaring: "It is a somewhat singular fact that when there existed in our State no law for punishing the murder of a slave other than a pecuniary fine, there were, I will venture to say, at least ten murders of freemen for one murder of a slave." White folks in South Carolina, gentlemen all, always had played rough with each other and everyone else. When whites were convicted of killing slaves, they usually got off lightly, although less so as time went on. By 1791 the prosecution insisted that a white man deserved the death penalty in a clear case of murder, especially since such crimes against slaves were increasing and had to be deterred. The murderer received a fine of £700, which he was unable to pay; accordingly, he went to prison for seven years at hard labor. The same year a white man convicted of manslaughter of a slave paid £50. After a tougher law was passed in 1821 in South Carolina a man killed a slave, not with premeditation but "in heat of passion," and received a fine of $350.

The law of 1821 established three categories: murder, killing in heat of passion, and killing by undue correction—generally, excessive whipping. The change aimed at increasing the penalty for murder. Judge O'Neall commented: "The act of 1821 changed the murder of a slave from a mere misdemeanor, which it was under the act of 1740, to a felony. . . . It, in a criminal point of view, elevated slaves from chattels personal to human beings in the place of the State." The authorities enforced the law as best they could, but its strength may be measured by the sentence meted out to a woman convicted of killing a slave by undue correction in 1840—a fine of $214.28.

The courts moved to eliminate the excuses for killing blacks. In Louisiana, for example, a white man was found guilty of killing a free man of color who had insulted him. The court observed that whites did not have to suffer insults from

Negroes, slave or free, and had adequate recourse at law; therefore, the provocation could not excuse the defendant's extralegal action. In Texas a white man killed another man's slave, who had raised a hand to him. He was found guilty of manslaughter and appealed, but the high court sustained the verdict, citing precedent in Tennessee, and added, "The only matter of surprise is that it should ever have been doubted."

When whites did find themselves before the bar of justice, especially during the late antebellum period, they could expect greater severity than might be imagined. The penalties seldom reached the extreme or the level they would have if the victim had been white; but neither did they usually qualify as a slap on the wrist. If one murderer in North Carolina got off with only eleven months in prison in 1825, most fared a good deal worse. Ten-year sentences were common, and occasionally the death penalty was invoked.

The greatest difficulty in securing enforcement of the laws against murdering or mistreating slaves did not stem from the laxness of the authorities or from the unwillingness of juries to convict, or from any softness in the appellate courts. Public opinion might remain silent in the face of harsh treatment by masters, it did not readily suffer known sadists and killers. But neither did it suffer blacks to testify against whites, and therein lay the fatal weakness of the law. Moreover, the authorities and public opinion more readily came down hard upon overseers or small slaveholders than upon gentlemen of standing.

Despite the efforts of the authorities and the courts, masters and overseers undoubtedly murdered more slaves than we shall ever know. If the number did not reach heights worthy of classification as "statistically significant," it probably did loom large enough to strike terror into the quarters. It could happen. It sometimes did. And the arrests, convictions, and punishment never remotely kept pace with the number of victims.

Despite so weak a legal structure, the slaves in the United States probably suffered the ultimate crime of violence less frequently than did those in other American slave societies, and white killers probably faced justice more often in the Old South than elsewhere. The murder of a slave in Barbados drew little attention or likelihood of punishment. Effective protection was out of the question in Saint-Domingue. The Catholic slaveholding countries of Spanish and Portuguese America abounded in unenforceable and unenforced protective codes. Wherever the blacks heavily outnumbered the whites, as they did in so much of the Caribbean, fear of insurrection and insubordination strangled pleas for humanity. The bleak record of the southern slave states actually glows in comparison. These observations reveal something about the sociology of law and power. But they would not likely have provided much comfort to the slaves of South Carolina or Mississippi.

Frederick Law Olmsted pointed out the consequences of the South's position, especially for those regions in which white testimony could not be expected.

> The precariousness of the much-vaunted happiness of the slaves can need but one further reflection to be appreciated. No white man can be condemned for any cruelty or neglect, no matter how fiendish, on slave testimony. The rice plantations are in a region very sparsely occupied by whites: the plantations are nearly all very larg—often miles across: many a one of them occupying the whole of an island—and rarely is there more than one white man upon a plantation at a time, during the summer. Upon this one man each slave is dependent, even for the necessities of life.[19]

South Carolina tried to protect its slaves in cases of wanton cruelty or murder by providing that the master had responsibility for their condition, so that physical evidence on a body or the condition of a corpse could constitute circumstantial evidence adequate for conviction. What the law gave, the law took away, for it also provided that a master's oath of innocence had to be respected. Apart from the general absurdity of such a provi-

sion, the State Supreme Court's outstanding jurist, John Belton O'Neall, fumed, "This is the greatest temptation ever presented to perjury, and the Legislature ought speedily to remove it."

The tenacious opposition to black testimony against whites proved a disadvantage to the planters themselves. If, for example, a white man robbed a plantation, the testimony of the owner's slaves had to be ignored. If a white man killed another's slave and thereby also robbed him of hundreds or thousands of dollars, the slaveholder had to settle accounts by personal violence or not at all unless some other white man had witnessed the crime. In Louisiana in 1840 the ultimate irony occurred, when a white man who had incited slaves to insurrection had to be acquitted because their confessions could not be used against him. In this as in so many other ways, the racism of the whites worked against them; but they regarded these expensive inconveniences as necessary evils and bore them doggedly.

"It is remarkable at first view," wrote George Fitzhugh, the proslavery ideologue of Virginia, "that in Cuba, where the law attempts to secure mild treatment to the slave, he is inhumanely treated; and in Virginia, where there is scarce any law to protect him, he is very humanely governed and provided for."[20] This self-serving sermon, with its exaggeration and its kernel of truth, became standard fare for the apologists for slavery and has won some support from subsequent historians. The slaveholders did not intend to enforce their severe legislation strictly and considered it a device to be reserved for periods of disquiet and especially for periods of rumored insurrectionary plots. In practice this easy attitude confirmed the direct power of the master. For example, although state or local laws might forbid large meetings of slaves from several plantations, the planters normally permitted religious services or balls and barbecues unless they had some reason to fear trouble. The local authorities, generally subservient to the planters, usually looked

---

[19]Olmsted, *Seaboard*, p. 487.

[20]George Fitzhugh, *Cannibals All! Or, Slaves Without Masters* (Cambridge, Mass., 1960 [1857], p. 79.

the other way. Thus in Ascension Parish, Louisiana, the local ordinance declared: "Every person is prohibited from permitting in his negro quarters any other assemblies but those of his slaves and from allowing his slaves to dance during the night." Enforcement of such an edict would have required that masters constantly punish their slaves, who were not to be denied, and thereby ruin the morale of their labor force. Planters who agreed to such an edict had either let themselves be swept away by some momentary passion or intended it for emergency enforcement. The laws of most states also forbade teaching slaves to read and write. Most slaveholders obeyed these laws because they thought them wise, not because they expected punishment of violators. In many of the great planter families various individuals, especially the white children, taught slaves to read. Some slaveholders violated the laws against giving slaves guns to hunt with, although they no doubt screened the beneficiaries with care. The law existed as a resource to provide means for meeting any emergency and to curb permissive masters. But the heart of the slave law lay with the master's prerogatives and depended upon his discretion. In this sense alone did practice generally veer from statute.

A slaveholding community did not intervene against a brutal master because of moral outrage alone; it intervened to protect its interests. Or rather, its strong sense of interest informed its moral sensibilities. "Harmony among neighbors is very important in the successful management of slaves," wrote a planter in an article directed to his own class. A good manager among bad ones, he explained, faces a hopeless task, for the slaves easily perceive differences and become dissatisfied.[21] It does no good, wrote another, to enforce discipline on your plantation if the next planter does not.[22] These arguments cut in both directions. They called for strict discipline from those who tended to be lax and for restraint from those who tended to be harsh.

What the law could not accomplish, public opinion might. A brutal overseer threatened by arrest could be made to understand that, however his trial might turn out, the community would welcome his departure. J. H. Bills reported from one of his plantations in Mississippi: "A jury of inquest was held yesterday over the body of a negro fellow, the property of the John Fowler estate, whose verdict was, I understand, that he came to his death by a blow given him on the head by Mahlon Hix a few days before. Hix left the country this morning."[23]

A more difficult question concerned atrocities by respected masters. When in Richmond, Virginia, Fredrika Bremer heard some slaveholders talking about a rich neighbor who treated his slaves savagely. They condemned him, but had nevertheless accepted an invitation to his party. When questioned, they explained that they did not wish to offend his wife and daughters. Miss Bremer thought that his money and power had played a part in their decision. She noted a five-year sentence handed down on a master for barbarously killing a favorite house slave. When the entire community expressed outrage at the crime and approved the prison term, she concluded that that was about what it took to provoke a meaningful reaction.

Ex-slaves from various parts of the South recalled community interventions and moral pressure on cruel masters. Hagar Lewis of Texas said that her master filed charges against some neighbors for underfeeding and excessive whipping. A. M. Moore, an educated preacher from Harrison County, Texas, added, "I've known courts in this county to fine slaveowners for not feeding and clothing their slaves right." George Teamoh of Virginia recalled that his mistress gave runaways from cruelty refuge on her place. Lou Smith of South Carolina recalled a slave's slipping off to tell white neighbors that his master had

[21]H. C., "On the Management of Negroes," *SA,* VII (July, 1834), 367–370.

[22]A Minister of the Gospel, "Tatler' on the Management of Negroes," *SC,* IX (June, 1851), 84–85.

[23]Bills Diary, Sept. 24, 1852.

savagely whipped a slave and left him bleeding. The neighbors forced the master to have the slave attended by a doctor. And others testified that brutal masters had constant trouble from irate fellow slaveholders, one of whom, however, seemed willing to take direct action unless something atrocious had occurred.

Cruel and negligent masters did not often face trial. Some did, primarily because of the efforts of other slaveholders. A slaveholder in certain states could be convicted on circumstantial evidence alone, if the decision in *State of Louisiana* v. *Morris* (1849) may be taken as a guide. Even then, no conviction was likely without an aroused public opinion. These convictions, inadequate as they were, reminded the community of what was expected of individual behavior.

Fortunately for the slaves, in many communities one or two souls among the slaveholders ran the risks of personal retaliation to keep an eye on everyone else's plantations. Captain J. G. Richardson of New Iberia, Louisiana, made no few enemies by compelling prosecution of delinquent fellow slaveholders, and others like him cropped up here and there. The private papers of the slaveholders, as well as their public efforts, suggest that they could become enraged at local sadists and would take action in the extreme cases.

Moral suasion and active intervention had limits. Much cruelty occurred because average masters lost their tempers—something any other master had to excuse unless he saw himself as a saint who could never be riled—and little could be done about someone who stopped short of atrocities as defined by other slaveholders and who did not much care about his neighbors' criticism. Yet moral pressure, if it could not prevent savages from acting savagely, did set a standard of behavior to which men who cared about their reputations tried to adhere.

Although we do not have a thorough study of the place of the slave laws in the southern legal system and of the relationship of the southern legal system as a whole to that of the United States and Western Europe, tentative appraisals

must be risked if much sense is to be made out of the broader aspects of the master-slave relationship. Two questions in particular present themselves: the general character of the southern legal system; and the relationship between the legal status of the slave and his position in what appears to many to have been extralegal practice.

The two questions merge. The dichotomy, made current by Ulrich Bonnell Phillips, of a decisive distinction between law and practice or custom, requires critical examination. W. E. B. Du Bois's comment on the proslavery apologetics to which such a distinction has sometimes been applied says enough on the level on which he chose to leave the matter:

> It may be said with truth that the law was often harsher than the practice. Nevertheless, these laws and decisions represent the legally permissible possibilities, and the only curb upon the power of the master was his sense of humanity and decency, on the one hand, and the conserving of his investment on the other. Of the humanity of large numbers of Southern masters there can be no doubt.[24]

The frontier quality of much of the Old South inhibited the growth of strong law enforcement agencies, but this quality itself cannot be separated from the geographic advance of slave society. The plantation system produced an extensive pattern of settlement, relative to that of the Northwest, and resulted in the establishment of a multitude of separate centers of power in the plantations themselves. At the same time, the nonplantation areas found themselves developing as enclaves more or less detached from the mainstream of southern society. Thus, whereas the frontier steadily passed in the free states and even the formative stages of civilization rested on a certain civic consciousness, it not only passed less rapidly in the slave states but actually entrenched itself within the civilization being built. This process imparted a higher degree of appar-

---

[24]W. E. B. Du Bois, *Black Reconstruction in America* (New York, 1962 [1935]), p. 10; see also Dwight Lowell Dumond, *Antislavery Origins of the Civil War in the United States* (Ann Arbor, Mich., 1959), pp. 43–44.

ent lawlessness—of the extralegal settlement of personal disputes—to southern life. Its spirit might be illustrated by the advice given to Andrew Jackson by his mother: "Never tell a lie, nor take what is not your own, nor sue anybody for slander or assault and battery. *Always settle them cases yourself!*"[25]

This "violent tenor of life," to use an expression Johan Huizinga applied to late medieval Europe,[26] provided one side of the story; the intrinsic difficulty of developing a modern legal system in a slave society provided another. Southerners considered themselves law-abiding and considered northerners lawless. After all, southerners did not assert higher-law doctrines and broad interpretations of the Constitution. Rather, as Charles S. Sydnor has argued, they understood the law in a much different way and professed to see no contradiction between their code of honor, with its appeal to extralegal personal force, and a respect for the law itself. Notwithstanding some hypocrisy, their views represented a clumsy but authentic adjustment to the necessity for a dualistic, even self-contradictory, concept of law prefigured in the rise of a rational system of law in European civilization.

At first glance, the legal history of Western Europe represents an anomaly. The law arose in early modern times on rational rather than traditional, patrimonial, or charismatic foundations, however many elements of these remained. As such, it assumed an equality of persons before the law that could only have arisen from the social relationships introduced by the expansion of capitalism and the spread of bourgeois, marketplace values, although to a considerable extent it derived from Roman tradition. Max Weber's distinction between "capitalism in general" and "modern capitalism," however sugges-

tive, cannot resolve the apparent contradiction.

As Weber clearly understood, the ruling class of Roman society, and therefore the society itself, rested on slave-labor foundations. We do not have to follow Rostovtzeff, Salvioli, and others in projecting an ancient capitalism or a cycle of capitalisms in order to establish a firm link between ancient and modern civilization in Western Europe, as manifested in the continuity of legal tradition. Slavery as a mode of production creates a market for labor, much as capitalism creates a market for labor-power. Both encourage commercial development, which is by no means to be equated with capitalist development (understood as a system of social relations within which labor-power has become a commodity). Ancient slave society could not, however, remove the limits to commercial expansion—could not raise the marketplace to the center of the society as well as the economy—for its very capitalization of labor established the firmest of those limits. The modern bourgeoisie, on the other hand, arose and throve on its ability to transform labor-power into a commodity and thereby revolutionize every feature of thought and feeling in accordance with the fundamental change in social relations. It thereby created the appearance of human equality, for the laborer faced the capitalist in a relation of seller and buyer of labor-power—an ostensibly disembodied commodity. The relationship of each to the other took on the fetishistic aspect of a relationship of both to a commodity—a thing—and cloaked the reality of the domination of one man by another. Although ancient slavery did not create a market for labor-power, it did, by creating a market for human beings and their economic products, induce a high level of commercialization that, together with the successful consolidation of a centralized state, combined to bequeath a system of law upon which modern bourgeois society could build. The rise of capitalism out of a seigneurial society in the West owed much to cultural roots that that particular kind of seigneurialism had in a long slaveholding past.

[25]Quoted in Sydnor, "Southerner and the Laws," p. 12. This article is the most important contribution we have to this problem. I have drawn on it freely but also departed from it in some essentials.

[26]Johan Huizinga, *The Waning of the Middle Ages: A Study of The Forms of Life, Thought and Art in France and the Netherlands in the Fourteenth and Fifteenth Centuries* (London, 1924).

The slave South inherited English common law as well as elements and influences from continental Roman and Germanic communal and feudal law. But by the time the slave regime underwent consolidation, the legal system of the Western world had succumbed to a bourgeois idea of private property. The southern slaveholders had been nurtured on the idea but also had to draw upon earlier traditions in order to justify their assimilation of human beings to property. In so doing, they contradicted, however discreetly, that idea of property which had provided the foundation for their class claims.

The slaveholders could not simply tack the idea of property in man onto their inherited ideas of property in general, for those inherited ideas, as manifested in the bourgeois transformation of Roman law and common law, rested precisely upon a doctrine of marketplace equality within which—however various the actual practice for a protracted period of time—slavery contradicted first principles. The southern legal system increasingly came to accept an implicit duality: a recognition of the rights of the state over individuals, slave or free, and a recognition of the rights of the slaveholders over their slaves. Since the slaveholders' property in man had to be respected, the state's rights over the slaveholders as well as the slaves had to be circumscribed. At first glance, this arrangement appears simple enough: considered abstractly, a system in which the state, representing above all the collective will of the slaveholding class, could lay down rules for the individual slaveholders, who would, however, have full power over their chattels. But the slaves, simply by asserting their humanity, quickly demolished this nice arrangement. The moral, not to mention political, needs of the ruling class as a whole required that it interpose itself, by the instrument of state power, between individual masters and their slaves. It is less important that it did so within narrow bounds than that it did so at all. The resultant ambiguity, however functional in quiet times, ill prepared the South to meet the test of modern war.

Even in peacetime the slaveholders had to pay dearly for their compromises. Among other things, as Charles S. Sydnor saw and as Robert Fogel and Stanley Engerman have reflected on further, the reintroduction of precapitalist elements into the legal system weakened the economic organization and business capacity of the planters.[27] These questions await a full exploration at other hands.

The immediate concern is with the effect of the imposed duality created by the reintroduction as well as the continuation of precapitalist ideas of power and property into an inherited system of bourgeois-shaped rational jurisprudence. This momentous reintroduction was effected with some ease because the idea of the state's having a monopoly of the legal means of coercion by violence had had only a brief history—roughly, from the conquest of state power by the bourgeoisies of England and Holland during the seventeenth century and of France at the end of the eighteenth. Nor had traditional ideas simply disappeared. Not only from the Left, but more powerfully from the Right, they continued to do battle within even the most advanced capitalist countries.

The slaveholders fell back on a kind of dual power: that which they collectively exercised as a class, even against their own individual impulses, through their effective control of state power; and that which they reserved to themselves as individuals who commanded other human beings in bondage. In general, this duality appears in all systems of class rule, for the collective judgment of the ruling class, coherently organized in the common interest, cannot be expected to coincide with the sum total of the individual interests and judgments of its members; first, because the law tends to reflect the will of the most politically coherent and determined fraction, and second, because the sum total of the individual interests and judgments of the members of the ruling class generally, rather than occasionally, pulls against the collective needs of a

[27]Sydnor, "Southerner and the Laws," pp. 8-9; Fogel and Engerman, *Time on the Cross*, pp. 128-129.

class that must appeal to other classes for support at critical junctures. But the slaveholders' problem ran much deeper, for the idea of slavery cannot easily be divorced from the idea of total power—of the reduction of one human being to the status of an extension of another's will—which is phenomenologically impossible, and more to the point, as Judge Ruffin had to face, politically impossible as well. Repeatedly, the slaveholders' own legal apparatus had to intervene, not primarily to protect the slaves from their masters, but to mediate certain questions among contending manifestations of human action. In so doing, it discredited the essential philosophical idea on which slavery rested and, simultaneously, bore witness to the slaves' ability to register the claims of their humanity.

Confronted with these painful and contradictory necessities, the slaveholders chose to keep their options open. They erected a legal system the implications of which should have embarrassed them and sometimes did; and then they tried to hold it as a reserve. They repeatedly had to violate their own laws without feeling themselves lawbreakers. The slave laws existed as a moral guide and an instrument for emergency use, although the legal profession and especially the judges struggled to enforce them as a matter of positive law; wherever possible, the authority of the master class, considered as a perfectly proper system of complementary plantation law, remained in effect. But since no reasonable formula could be devised to mediate between counterclaims arising from the two sides of this dual system, much had to be left outside the law altogether.

Several of the many ramifications of this interpretation bear on the position and condition of the slaves. We have already found reason to qualify the oft-repeated charge that the legal system of the South did not offer the slaves the protection offered by the slave codes of the Catholic countries. Further observations are now in order. The ethos informing the Catholic slave codes did play a significant role in shaping the slave societies of Portuguese and Spanish America, but the role of the law itself cannot readily be deduced either from that ethos or from the codes themselves. The system of enforcement in the United States, conditioned by Anglo-American standards of efficiency and civic discipline, generally exceeded that in, say, Brazil, where effective power lay with the *senbores de engenbo*—the great sugar planters. And the Spanish slogan, *¡Obedezco pero no cumplo!* (I obey, but I do not comply) says enough. More to the point, the slave codes of Brazil, the various Caribbean colonies, and Spanish South America had been drafted by nonslaveholders in the several metropolitan capitals and had had to be imposed upon resistant planters with enormous power of their own. The British, for their part, showed great reluctance to impose a slave code on the Caribbean planters. The slave codes of the southern United States came from the slaveholders themselves and represented their collective estimate of right and wrong and of the limits that should hedge in their own individual power. Their positive value lay not in the probability of scrupulous enforcement but in the standards of decency they laid down in a world inhabited, like most worlds, by men who strove to be considered decent. These standards could be violated with impunity and often were, but their educational and moral effect remained to offer the slaves the little protection they had.

For the slaves, two major consequences flowed from the ambiguities of the system. First, they constantly had before them evidence of what they could only see as white hypocrisy. An ex-slave commented on the antimiscegenation laws and their fate at the hands of the white man: "He made that law himself and he is the first to violation." No respect for the law could easily rise on such a foundation. Since the slaves knew that the law protected them little and could not readily be enforced even in that little, the second consequence followed. For protection against every possible assault on their being they had to turn to a human protector—in effect, a lord. They had to look to their masters for protection against patrollers, against lynching, against the strict enforcement of the law itself, as well as against hunger and physical deprivation. And they had to look to some other white man to shield them against a harsh or sadistic master. Thus, the implicit hegemonic function of the dual system of law conquered the quarters. But not wholly and not without encouraging a dangerous misunderstanding.

As the masters saw, the working out of the legal system drove the slaves deeper into an acceptance of paternalism. As the masters did not see, it did not drive them into an acceptance of slavery as such. On the contrary, the contradic-tions in the dual system and in the slave law per se, which had developed in the first place because of the slaves' assertion of their humanity, constantly reminded the slaves of the fundamental injustice to which they were being subjected. Paternalism and slavery merged into a single idea to the masters. But the slaves proved much more astute in separating the two; they acted consciously and unconsciously to transform paternalism into a doctrine of protection of their own rights—a doctrine that represented the negation of the idea of slavery itself.

TOWARD A THEORY OF LAW AND PATRIARCHY

JANET RIFKIN

I. IDEOLOGY, LAW AND POWER

The nature and meaning of patriarchal social order and of patriarchal culture has recently become the subject of intense scholarly questioning. Historians, literary scholars, political theorists, economists, anthropologists, sociologists, psychologists, and law teachers have been attempting through their respective disciplines, to understand the origin of patriarchy and the perpetuation of a patriarchal social order. By patriarchy, I mean any kind of group organization in which males hold dominant power and determine what part females shall and shall not play, and in which capabilities assigned to women are relegated generally to the mystical and aesthetic and excluded from the practical and political realms, these realms being regarded as separate and mutually exclusive.

Law plays a primary and significant role in social order. The relationship between law and patriarchy, however, needs to be clarified and developed. I intend to suggest a theoretical framework in which the fundamental connections between culture, patriarchy and law can begin to become clearer. In this context, I will examine the cultural and anthropological origins of patriarchy: how law is a paradigm of maleness; how law and legal ideology under capitalism preserved, transformed and updated pre-existing pa-

triarchal forms to serve the interests of the emerging bourgeoisie; and finally, why legal change does not lead to social reordering. I want to emphasize that my efforts are directed primarily toward developing a theoretical base from which many of these issues can be more exhaustively reviewed and studied in the future.

Law is powerful as both a symbol and a vehicle of male authority. This power is based both on an ideology of law and an ideology of women which is supported by law. One function of ideology is to mystify social reality and to block social change. Law functions as a form of hegemonic ideology. Thus, a court could rule that

> civil law, as well as nature herself, has always recognized a wide difference in the respective spheres and destinies of man and woman. Man is, or should be, woman's protector and defender. The natural and proper timidity and delicacy which belongs to the female sex evidently unfits it for many of the occupations of civil life.[1]

By the acceptance of this as a statement of reality, law is reinforced as a powerful ideological force of social cohesion and stability.

The ideology of law is also tied to its manifestation as a written set of formulations, principles and regulation. "Freezing ideas and information in words makes it possible to assess more coolly and rigorously the validity of an argu-

Source: From *Harvard Women's Law Journal* (1980), 83–95. Reprinted with permission.

[1] *Bradwell* v. *State,* 83 U.S. (16 Wall.) 130, 141 (Bradley, J., concurring).

ment, ... thus, 'reinforcing a certain kind and measure of [increased] rationality.' "[2] The power of law as ideology is to mask or distort social reality in the name of tradition. Law, in relation to women, is seen as a measured and rational set of beliefs which at the same time asserts a mythological vision which is believed by many to present an accurate statement of the world.

A good example of this phenemonon is found in the suffragist movement of the early twentieth century. "Operating within the male-dominant paradigm, the form, language, and mode of Suffragist protest was set not so much by the objective conditions of female oppression as by their response to the idealizations and mystifications and legalities which rationalized continuance of the *status quo*."[3] Thus, the suffragist, in not challenging the ideology of law which supported an ideology of women, perpetuated mystifications which supported the status quo.

The power of legal ideology is so great that it often becomes hard to differentiate between legal principles and social customs. For example, American women have long worked outside the home in significant numbers. This fact of women's work in the labor market is constantly restricted by specific laws, and is at odds with the basic legal ideology that females should be excluded from the public sphere of work. The legal ideology of these restrictions carries forward the basic message that women *are to be* at home. The legal ideology of women does not bend to accommodate the economic reality of working women.

In 1908, when a substantial number of American women were working, the United States Supreme Court upheld a maximum hours law which applied to women only, reasoning that "her physical structure and a proper discharge of her maternal functions—having in view not merely her own health, but the well being of the race, justify legislation to protect her from the greed as well as the passion of man."[4] The ideological statement that women should be at home was couched in the context of the capitalist framework of competition for jobs. Economic competition between women and men was recognized, and in the name of protecting women, the hierarchical, male-dominated sex/gender system was reinforced. This reinforcement is supported by the ideological assertion that women are in need of greater protection than men.

The power of law as ideology continues into the present and may be examined in light of massive litigative efforts to change the status of women in contemporary society. The reliance on litigation reflects the belief in law as a source of social change, while ignoring the ideological power of law to mask social reality and block social change. Court battles about "women's issues" are waged and sometimes won with the result that a new body of rights is created and deployed in battle, but the basic sexual hierarchy is not changed. Although the hierarchy may be threatened in that each battle subjects the traditional law and legal ideology to examination and reivew, the litigation of "rights" never reaches the question of collective social organization.

In the area of the law of abortion, for instance, one sees that while the decisions relating to contraception and abortion have been thought of in terms of the expansion of a woman's right to privacy and reproductive freedom, a challenge asserting a competing claim surfaces after every expression of an apparently broadened claim. Thus, after the decision in *Roe v. Wade*[5] recognizing a limited constitutional right to abortion, cases were brought alleging that the rights of fathers were violated, arguments were made that the rights of parents would be violated if minors had full rights to choose abortion, and laws and restrictions threatened doctors who performed abortions.

Another significant example of this pattern is

[2]Kellner, "Ideology, Marxism, and Advanced Capitalism," 42 *Socialist Rev.* 38 (1978), at 45, quoting A. Gouldner, *The Dialectic of Ideology and Technology* 41 (1976).

[3]Elshtain, "Moral Woman and Immoral Man: A Consideration of the Public-Private Split and Its Political Ramifications," 4 *Pol. & Soc'y.* 453, 469 (1974).

[4]*Muller v. Oregon*, 208 U.S. 412, 422 (1908).
[5]410 U.S. 113 (1973).

in the legal war over affirmative action, where there have been numerous lawsuits brought by individuals claiming that granting members of minority groups preference discriminates against members of the majority group. Here the struggle is articulated as a battle between individuals competing for jobs and education. This focus ignores and obscures the more fundamental social and political questions of power which generate these lawsuits.

The crucial point is that these legal battles reflect anger and dissatisfaction which, in reality, potentially threaten the patriarchal hierarchy. The power of law is that by framing the issues as questions of law, claims of right, precedents and problems of constitutional interpretation, the effect is to divert potential public consciousness from an awareness of the deeper roots of the expressed dissatisfaction and anger. The ideology of law serves to mask the real social and political questions underlying these problems of law. At the same time, the paradigm of law which historically has been and continues to be the symbol of male authority is not only unchallenged but reinforced as a legitimate mechanism for resolving social conflict. In the end, patriarchy as a form of power and social order will not be eliminated unless the male power paradigm of law is challenged and transformed. In order to challenge the male paradigm of law, the origin of law as a form of male authority and power must be discovered and examined more thoroughly.

Although the relationship between the women and the law has been the subject of a number of recent books, law school courses, undergraduate programs, and law review articles, few of these efforts have helped to elucidate the complexity of the relationship between law and patriarchal power. Similarly, the practice of law now includes "women's" litigation and women litigators. Litigation has resulted in challenges to statutory restrictions and common law practices in areas such as marriage and parenting, abortion, pregnancy disabilities, and equal employment benefits and opportunities. Nonetheless, these litigation efforts have not challenged the fundamental patriarchal social order. Litigation and other forms of formal legal relief, however, cannot lead to social changes, because in upholding and relying on the paradigm of law, the paradigm of patriarchy is upheld and reinforced.

The fact that little exploration of the connection between law and patriarchy has been done can be largely attributed to the fact that the study of law takes place primarily in the context of law school where the focus is exclusively on legal principles and case study. The study of law in law school is confined to a narrow doctrinal analysis of law and largely excludes an approach which examines the connections between law and social theory. For the most part, law school does not provide students with a framework of ideas to aid them in formulating personal values to help them explore the relationship between social values and law. Because traditional legal education ignores the cultural, political and social foundations of law, it is not possible, in the law school context, to illuminate the relationship of patriarchy and law.

II. NATURE, CULTURE AND WOMEN

The efforts to find and explain the origins of patriarchy have led some scholars to examine mythology, fables and kinship bonds. Kate Millett, for example, in *Sexual Politics,* claims that "myth and kinship ties are the most lasting vestiges of that vast historical shift whereby patriarchy replaced whatever order preceded it and instituted that long government of male over female."[6] In this context, she turns to Aeschylus's Oresteia trilogy and its final play *The Eumenides,* in which he presents a confrontation between paternal authority and maternal order. In the first two plays, we have seen Clytemnestra, rebelling against the masculine authority of husband and King, kill Agamemnon upon his return from Troy, and her son Orestes revenge his father's death by killing her. In so doing, Orestes provokes the rage of the Furies, who accuse him of matricide. In the third play they put him on trial, assured that justice will be done. They are not prepared, how-

---

[6]K. Millett, *Sexual Politics* (1970), at 110.

ever, for the emergence of the new form of patriarchal justice articulated by Athena, who says:

No mother gave me birth. Therefore, the father's claim
And male supremacy in all things, save to give
Myself in marriage, wins my whole heart's loyalty.
Therefore a woman's death, who killed her husband,
is,
I judge, outweighed in grievousness by his. . . .[7]

Through Athena's deciding vote, Orestes is acquitted and his patrimony is reinforced. The Furies lament helplessly:

The old is trampled by the new!
Curse on you younger gods who override
The ancient laws. . . ![8]

In this fable, law emerges as the symbol of patriarchal authority. The complex and fundamental connections, however, between law and patriarchy in a more general historical context have not been adequately developed, and these connections are essential to an understanding of political and social power.

In *The Elementary Structure of Kinship,* Levi-Strauss, in analyzing the meaning of the universality of incest taboos, also analyzes the role of women in pre-state societies. He suggests that the concept of women as the property of men that is based in the universal notion of the exchange of women emerges as a fundamental tenet of culture. The origins of social order then are grounded on the conception of women as the property of men; the patriarchal social order is the basis of culture itself.

Levi-Strauss begins by asking where nature ends and culture begins. He suggests that the "absence of rules seems to provide the surest criterion for distinguishing a natural from a cultural process."[9] He finds that the incest taboo is a phenomenon which has the "distinctive characteristics both of nature and of its theoretical contradiction, culture. The prohibition of incest has the universality of bent and instinct and the coercive character of law and institution."[10] The rule against incest gives rise to rules of marriage, which although varying somewhat from group to group, are universally based on the taboo against incest. The rules of marriage also universally are based on the idea of exchange, and in particular, the exchange of women. The exchange of women is a universal mode of culture, although not everywhere equally developed. Levi-Strauss asserts further that the incest taboo "is at once on the threshold of culture, and in one sense, . . . culture itself."[11] Since, as he shows, the exchange of women is integrally connected to the incest taboo, it can also be said that the exchange of women, as objects of male property, is also on the threshold of culture, in culture and is culture itself.

Levi-Strauss states that the role of exchange

in primitive society is essential because it embraces material objects, social values and women. But while in the case of merchandise this role has progressively diminished in importance in favour of other means of acquisition, as far as women are concerned, reciprocity has maintained its fundamental function, . . . because women are the most precious possession . . . [and] a natural stimulant.[12]

He asserts the universality of the exchange of women: "The inclusion of women in the number of reciprocal prestations from group to group and from tribe to tribe is such a general custom that a whole volume would not be sufficient to enumerate the instances of it."[13]

The notion of women as male property is then at the heart of cultural-social order. Matrimonial exchange is only a particular case of those forms of multiple exchanges embracing material goods, rights and persons:

The total relationship of exchange which constitutes marriage is not established between a man and a

---

[7]Quoted in Id. at 114.

[8]Id. at 173.

[9]C. Levi-Strauss, *The Elementary Structures of Kinship,* 2d ed. (J. Bell & J. von Starmer trans., 1969), at p. 8.

[10]Id. at 10.

[11]Id. at 12.

[12]Id. at 62.

[13]Id. at 115.

woman, . . . but between two groups of men, and the woman figures only as one of the objects in the exchange, not as one of the partners between whom the exchange takes place.[14]

Even where matrilineal descent is established, the woman is never more than the symbol of her lineage. And Levi-Strauss disposes of the myth of the "reign of women" which he says is "remembered only in mythology, [as] an age . . . when men had not resolved the antimony which is always likely to appear between their roles as takers of wives and givers of sisters, making them both the authors and victims of their exchanges."[15]

The origin of culture as reflected in kinship systems is universally based on the idea that women are the property of men to be exchanged between individuals or groups of males. Levi-Strauss sees a "masculinity of political authority"[16] when political power takes precedence over other forms of organization. Early political philosophy, as reflected by the writings of Aristotle, did not challenge this universal social fact. Aristotle, who developed a philosophy of politics and power, also saw political authority as masculine and saw women as nonparticipants in the political world.

> Aristotle radically bifurcates public (political) from private (apolitical) realms. . . . Fully realized moral goodness and reason are attainable only through participation in public life, and this involvement is reserved to free, adult males. Women *share* in goodness and rationality in the limited sense appropriate to their confinement in a lesser association, the household. . . . Indeed, it can be said with no exaggeration that women in Aristotle's schema are *idiots* in the Greek sense of the word, that is, persons who do not participate in the *polis*.[17]

The political analysis of Aristotle upholds a male-dominant power paradigm which "serves to perpetuate an arbitrary bifurcation between that which is politics and that which is not. . . . Implicit within the paradigm is a concept of persons which admits into the privileges of full personhood . . . only those individuals who hold dual statuses as both public and private persons"—i.e., men.[18] The male-dominant paradigm of political power is also the paradigm of law. The historical image of maleness—objective, rational and public—is the dominant image of law.

Law, in mythology, in culture and in philosophy, is the ultimate symbol of masculine authority and patriarchal society. The form of law is different in varying social groups, ranging from kinship bonds, custom, and the tribal rules in pre-state societies, to written codes in modern society. The point, however, is that law in state and non-state contexts is based on male authority and patriarchal social order.

III. PATRIARCHY, LAW AND CAPITALISM

In *Law and the Rise of Capitalism,* Michael Tigar and Madeline Levy show that the Thirteenth Century in England and in continental Europe "saw the creation and application of specific rules about contracts, property and procedure which strengthened the power of the rising bourgeoisie."[19] They show that these "rules were fashioned in the context of a legal ideology which identified freedom of action for businessmen with natural law and natural reason."[20]

In their study, however, Tigar and Levy do not examine the emerging law in relation to women. They do not discuss, for example, how the rise of capitalism profoundly changed the nature of work, the family, and the role of women. I maintain that law, which emerged "as a form of rationality appropriate to the social relations generated by the emergence of entrepreneurial

---

[14]Id. at 115.

[15]Id. at 118.

[16]Id. at 116.

[17]Elshtain, *supra* note 3, at 455 (emphasis in original).

[18]Id. at 472.

[19]M. Tigar and M. Levy, *Law and the Rise of Capitalism* 6 (1978).

[20]Id.

capitalism,"[21] retained the pre-existing hierarchy of masculine authority and made more explicit the subordination of women to men by increasingly excluding women from working in trades and relegating them to the private world of the home, which itself also became more and more non-productive.

The feudal world, which was organized for war, was essentially a masculine world. Although laws and custom put wives under the power of their husbands, records indicate, nonetheless, participation by some noble women in social, political and legal activities. Women also demonstrated great productive capacity when society was organized on the basis of family and domestic industry. At the end of the Fourteenth Century, one-fourth of the cloth woven in York was produced by women. Laws, restrictive in some spheres, there encouraged women's economic participation. The Act of 1363, for example, declared that:

> [T]he intent of the king and of his council is that women, that is to say brewers, bakers, carders and spinners, and workers as well of wool as of linen-clothing . . . , and all other that do use and work all handiworks, may freely use and work as they have done before this time.[22]

This attitude began to change, however, during the next century as legal regulations promulgated by various guilds became increasingly restrictive of women's participation. Many of these laws reflected the blatant threat of competition to the male workers. In Bristol in 1461, it was complained that weavers employed their wives, daughters, and maidens "by the which many and divers of the king's liege people, likely men to do the king service in his wars and in the defence of this his land, and sufficiently learned in the said craft, goeth vagrant and unoccupied, and may not have their labour to their living."[23]

Sometimes a guild prohibited employment of women, though generally widows could work in their husband's craft. As late as 1726, the Baker's craft in Aberdeen which was distressed by the competition of women who used their own ovens and sold the produce themselves passed a law which mandated a severe fine to any freeman in the baking trade who allowed a woman to use his oven. Other craft guilds were equally restrictive of women working in trades. Rachel Baxter, for example, was admitted to the tailor's craft provided "that she shall . . . have only the privilege of mantua-making, and no ways make stays, or import the same to sell from any other place . . . and it is hereby declared that thi[sic] presents to be no precedent to any woman in tyme coming."[24]

Thus, with the emergence of capitalism and through the power of legal regulation, women were affected in several fundamental ways: individual wages were substituted for family earnings, enabling men to organize themselves in the competition of the labor market without sharing with the women of their families all the benefits derived through their combination; the withdrawal of wage-earners from home life to work upon the premises of the masters and the prevention of the employment of the wage-earner's wife in her husband's occupation, and the rapid increase of wealth which allowed the upper class women to withdraw altogether from business.

Whereas the system of family industry united labor and capital in one person or family group, capitalism brought them into conflict and competition; men and women struggled with each other to secure work and wages. The keystone of the male journeymen's superior economic position in capitalism lay in their ability to restrict their own numbers by promulgating and enforcing laws which specifically limited numbers, imposed long apprenticeship programs and limited the number of apprentices.

The pre-existing patriarchal culture supported historically by kinship bonds and custom was

[21]Fraser, "The Legal Theory We Need Now," 37 *Socialist Rev.* 147, 154 (1978).

[22]E. Lipson, *The Economic History of England,* 7th ed. (1937), at p. 361.

[23]Id.

[24]E. Bain, *Merchant and Craft Guilds* 257 (1887).

transformed in capitalism through law in the service of new economic interest.

> [C]ustomary and traditional modes of conceptualizing bonds of obligation and duty were of diminishing relevance in bourgeois society, where people experienced a growing and radical separation between public life and private life. . . . [F]amily, and personal dependence begin to dissolve and crumble under the corrosive impact of the single universalist principles of social solidarity underlying capitalist social relations—*exchange*.[25]

The role of law in early capitalism was to help create a climate in which production for exchange could thrive. To accomplish this, law, always a symbol of male authority, fostered competition between women and men and severely limited female participation in the world of market production. Law became a primary and powerful tool of the rising bourgeoisie. Legal regulations were enacted which symbolized a continuation of the male authority of the past and which transformed and updated patriarchal society to serve new capitalistic interests. Laws were used increasingly to restrict women from working in trades, relegating them to the private world of the home. Thus, legal rules helped to create a social order where women were excluded from the public world of production exchange. And these new laws, justified in the name of the natural order, were accepted as an accurate vision of the world.

[25]Fraser, supra note 21, at 154–155 (emphasis in original).

CONCLUSION

This discussion has suggested that there are fundamental connections between culture, patriarchy and law. The origins of culture, according to Levi-Strauss, are grounded in the conception of women as the property of men and that patriarchal social order is the basis of culture itself. Law emerges as the symbol of patriarchal authority in varying ways. With the emergence of capitalist society, law became a crucial, substantial and ideological mechanism which updated a preexisting patriarchal social order to meet the needs of emerging capitalist interests. Through law, women were relegated to the private world of the home and family and excluded from the public world of monetary exchange.

Although the recent litigation efforts to change the role of women in society have resulted in alleviating some oppressive practices, the paradigm of law as a symbol of male authority has not been challenged. Indeed, the reliance on litigative and legislative strategies has reinforced the belief that the law-paradigm is a legitimate mechanism for resolving conflict and that it is a source of social change. As long as the male-dominant power paradigm of law remains unchallenged, the basic social hierarchy will not change. The struggle for sexual equality can be successful only if it challenges, rather than reifies, the male paradigm of law.

CHAPTER FIVE

LAW AND SOCIALIST CONSTRUCTION

One of the themes implicit in the four preceding chapters is that social regulation under capitalism appears to reach its apex in law. But what will the characteristics of social regulation be during the transition from capitalism to socialism, the period that Marx described as the first phase of communism? Indeed, based on an understanding of the experience of a variety of existing socialist societies, how realistic are Marx's and Engels's declarations as to the withering away and ultimate disappearance of law with the progressive consolidation of socialism? The answers to these questions are several and contradictory at the present moment. A Marxist theory of law must, at the very least, elaborate upon and identify the quality of legal forms that have emerged in different national contexts and different levels of the process of socialist construction.

The first essay in this chapter, "Pashukanis and Socialist Legality" by Piers Beirne and Robert Sharlet, is an account of Evgeny Pashukanis's adamant opposition to the notion of a socialist or proletarian law in the USSR after 1917. This opposition must be seen in light both of the continued survival of capitalist economic forms during the New Economic Policy (1922–1927) and the extreme authoritarianism that culminated in the Stalinist Constitution of 1936. Although Pashukanis later recanted his assertions that all law was bourgeois and that there could never be a socialist law, students should be aware that it is now impossible to distinguish between those modifications to his theory of law that he may actually have intended and those that were forced on him by a political climate in which personal survival became increasingly hazardous. Note too the awful irony of Pashukanis's strictures on the bourgeois nature of law. In common with the long, tragic tradition of Russian nihilism and anarchism, the movement that Pashukanis created led to a vacuum that was quickly displaced and then savagely destroyed by a jurisprudence of terror.

The next essay, Steve Redhead's "Marxist Theory, the Rule of Law and Socialism," focuses on this last issue and at the same time integrates it with several of the themes of earlier chapters. Redhead argues that Marxist theory is currently laboring under the dominance of Pashukanis's opposition to any form of socialist legality. If law is a peculiarly capitalist phenomenon then it is incompatible with socialist relationships. Redhead records that the unifying theme of much of E. P. Thompson's work lies in its condemnation of those who fail to distinguish between the rule of law and the exercise of extralegal, arbitrary power. But in so doing Thompson himself ignores the different forms that the rule of law assumes. The forms of legality, as Thompson has several times pleaded, must be examined in their specific historical, national, and cultural contexts. To identify the very real differences between Pashukanis and Thompson we must, therefore, not isolate their arguments from their own specific historical trajectories. These trajectories are, respectively, the USSR from the New Economic Policy to the notion of Stalinist legality, and contemporary struggles over "Law and Order" issues. The great value of Thompson's work, for Redhead, is that it has opened up a political space for theorization of the role of law under socialism that Pashukanis deemed necessary to close.

The subject of James Brady's "A Season of Startling Alliance" is the new social and legal order in China. Brady contrasts the attitudes of the now-vilified Gang of Four with those of the present political leadership in post-Maoist China. Since Mao's death, the new legal order represents a general return to conservatism, elitism, and bureaucratic control. Brady shows that the most important principles and policies of Maoism have been overturned. The elimination of revolutionary committees and the weakening of various mass organizations in China have left the bureaucracy without an effective popular counterweight. This change from revolutionary to revisionist policies, Brady points out, is best illustrated by the tenets of the 1978 Constitution. This depressing history is aggravated by Brady's view that at no time have Chinese domestic policies more closely resembled those of the post-Stalinist USSR than now.

We should add here that Lenin himself always insisted that the first task of any socialist revolution is to smash the machinery of the bourgeois state, but then to build a new state that would displace all bureaucratic forms.[1] This can only be accomplished by the leadership of revolutionary mass democracy. At the end of his essay Brady offers us hope that the preconditions for revolutionary mass democracy are still present in China, and that they will eventually defeat the centrist national leadership.

The final reading in this chapter is Boaventura de Sousa Santos's "Popular Justice, Dual Power and Socialist Strategy." Santos argues that the socialist movement now has an urgent need for a Marxist theory of law rather than a Marxist theory *against* law. This must be based on a supersession of the reform/revolution dichotomy as historically known. Such a theory implies the nonbourgeois use of bourgeois legality by the working class, and the creation and expansion of instances of alternative socialist legality. Santos urges that the theoretical foundation of this task is the elimination of such theses as the base/superstructure metaphor, a reevaluation of the European working class movement between the Second and Third Internationals, and the reanalysis of various revolutionary struggles. Through a discussion of the

[1]Students should refer here especially to Etienne Balibar, *On the Dictatorship of the Proletariat* (London: New Left Books, 1977), 99–123 on the destruction of the state apparatus. A word of warning: Balibar's argument was offered in the context of events that surfaced at the twenty-second Congress of the French Communist Party. Balibar was in part reacting against the removal of the concept of the dictatorship of the proletariat from the P.C.F.'s agenda. More critical considerations may be found in Chapters 1 and 5, and in the postscript to the English edition of this book. Balibar's essay was originally intended as part of a collective work with Louis Althusser that was never completed. Althusser's contribution may be found in *22 Congrès* (Maspero), and Balibar's in *Ouvrons la fenêtre camarades* of 1979.

concept of dual power (the interlocking of two dictatorships: the dictatorship of the bourgeoisie, and that of the proletariat and peasantry combined), Santos underscores the valuable lessons to be gained from revolutionary struggles in Portugal (the conceptualization of dual power as working class versus bourgeois justice) and Brazil.

PASHUKANIS AND SOCIALIST LEGALITY

PIERS BEIRNE AND ROBERT SHARLET

Evgeny Bronislavovich Pashukanis (1891–1937) has been the only Soviet Marxist legal philosopher to have achieved significant scholarly recognition outside of the U.S.S.R.[1] The pre-eminent Soviet jurist of the 1920s and early 1930s, Pashukanis fell victim to the great purges of the late 1930s and was thereafter reviled as an "enemy of the people" until his posthumous legal rehabilitation in 1956.[2]

As a student at the University of St. Petersburg before World War I, Pashukanis had been active in the Russian revolutionary movement and, as a result of his involvement, found it necessary to complete his education abroad at the University of Munich where he specialized in law and political economy. The available details on his early life are sketchy, but it is known that he joined the Bolsheviks in 1918, briefly served as a local and circuit judge in the Moscow region, and then for several years into the early 1920s worked as a legal adviser in the People's Commissariat of Foreign Affairs while, simultaneously, he cultivated a blossoming career in juristic scholarship.[3]

In 1924 Pashukanis emerged from relative obscurity with the publication of his major theoretical work *The General Theory of Law and Marxism*,[4] which quickly placed him in the front ranks of the field of aspiring Soviet Marxist philosophers of law. He regarded this treatise primarily as an introduction to the problems of constructing a Marxist general theory of law and by no means as the definitive statement on the subject. In this spirit, he appropriately subtitled his monograph *An Experiment in the Criticism of Basic Juridical Concepts*, emphasizing that he had written the book primarily for "self-clarification" with the hope that it might serve as a "stimulus and material for further discussion."[5]

Pashukanis' *General Theory* was warmly received by the reviewers and went into a second edition in 1926 followed by a third edition in 1927 which eventually encompassed three printings.[6] The originality of Pashukanis' theory of law—which was largely outlined in the first Russian edition of *The General Theory of Law and*

---

[1]His major treatise was *Obshchaia teoriia prava i marksizm*, first published in Moscow in 1924 and subsequently translated into French, German, Japanese, Serbo-Croat and into English in its third edition of 1927 as *The General Theory of Law and Marxism*. In J. Hazard (ed.), *Soviet Legal Philosophy* (1951), Harvard University Press, Cambridge, translated by H. Babb, pp. 111–225.

[2]According to the official *spravka*, Pashukanis was legally rehabilitated by the Military Division of the RSFSR Supreme Court in March 1956.

[3]The sources for this biographical information are Robert

Source: This is a slightly amended version of pp. 1–36 (Editors' Introduction) in Piers Beirne and Robert Sharlet (Eds.), *Pashukanis: Selected Writings on Marxism and Law*, (London: Academic Press, 1980). References to Pashukanis's texts appear at the end of this essay. Reprinted by permission.

Sharlet's interview with the late L. Ia. Gintsburg in Moscow, 1974; and J. Hazard, *Settling Disputes in Soviet Society: The Formative Years of Legal Institutions* (1960). Columbia University Press, New York, pp. 17–18. The English reader should see generally E. Kamenka and A. Tay, "The Life and Afterlife of a Bolshevik Jurist," *Problems of Communism* (1970), vol. 19, no. 1.

[4]See pp. 37–131 of *Pashukanis: Selected Writings on Marxism and Law* for translation of the first Russian edition.

[5]E. B. Pashukanis, "Predislovie" to *Obshchaia teoriia prava i marksizm* (1926), Moscow, 2nd corrected and supplemented edition, p. 3.

[6]See R. Sharlet, "Pashukanis and the Rise of Soviet Marxist Jurisprudence, 1924–1930", *Soviet Union* **1**, 2 (1974), pp. 103–121, esp. pp. 103–112.

Marxism in 1924, and successively revised in a number of works after 1927—lies in the contraposition of three notions with what Pashukanis took to be the *modus operandi* of Marx's *Capital*. From Hegel Pashukanis borrows the familiar distinction between essence and appearance, and also the notion in *The Philosophy of Right* that the Roman *lex persona* was an insufficient basis for the universality of rights attached to individual agents under capitalist modes of production.[7] And from Pokrovsky, an Old Bolshevik and the leading Russian historian between 1910 and 1932, Pashukanis borrows the assertion that the development of Russian capitalism must be understood in the context of the historical primacy of mercantile capital.[8]

Pashukanis saw that it was not accidental that Marx had begun his analysis of the inner dialectic of the capital-labour relationship (the production of surplus value) with a critique of the categories of bourgeois political economy. It was not simply that the categories of rent, interest, industrial profit etc. mystified the essential qualities of this relationship. Rather, in order to apprehend the historically specific form of the relationship of capitalist exploitation, one had first to pierce the veil of appearances/semblances/forms which the real relationship inherently produced, and on which it routinely depended for its reproduction.

Pashukanis therefore infers that had Marx actually written a coherent theory of state and law, as indeed he had twice promised,[9] then it would necessarily have proceeded along the same lines as his iconoclastic analysis of the categories of

political economy and the social reality which they mysteriously yet inaccurately express and codify.

Pashukanis consistently argues that there is an homology between the logic of the commodity form and the logic of the legal form. Both are universal equivalents which in appearance equalize the manifestly unequal: respectively, different commodities and the labour which produced them, and different political citizens and the subjects of rights and obligations. The salience of this insight has only very recently been recovered by Marxists,[10] and there are now some healthy indications that the sterile dichotomy between instrumentalist and formalist approaches to law is likely to be transcended. If Pashukanis' main argument is correct, then it obliges us to ask two crucial questions. First, the *specific* content of legal imperatives does not explain why the interests of dominant classes are embodied in the legal form. Why, for example, are these interests not embodied in the form on which they episodically depend, namely, naked coercion? Second, if under capitalism the struggle between competing commodity producers assumes legal form through the principle of equivalence, then it follows that the class struggle between proletariat and bourgeoisie must also typically appear in the medium of the legal form.[11] And how, then, are we able to transform legal reformism into a revolutionary political practice?

[7]For Pashukanis' own account of his Hegelian heritage, see E. B. Pashukanis, "Hegel on State and Law," *Sovetskoe gos udarstvo* (1931), pp. 1-32.

[8]See M. N. Pokrovsky, *History of Russia from the Earliest Times to the Rise of Commercial Capitalism* (1910-1912), translated and edited by J. D. Clarkson and M. R. M. Griffiths, Martin Lawrence, London, n.d. See further G. M. Enteen, *The Soviet Scholar-Bureaucrat: M. N. Pokrovskii and the Society of Marxist Historians* (1978), Pennsylvania State University Press, Pennsylvania and London.

[9]See K. Marx, "Letter to Weydemeyer" (February 1st, 1859), in *Marx and Engels Selected Correspondence* (1942), International Publishers. New York, p. 119; and K. Marx, *The Grundrisse* (1857-1858), translated by M. Nicolaus (1973), Random House, New York, p. 108.

[10]For example, see A. Fraser, "Legal Theory and Legal Practice," *Arena*, no. 44-45 (1976), pp. 123-156; C. Arthur, "Towards a Materialist Theory of Law," *Critique*, 7 (1976-1977), pp. 31-46; I. Balbus, "Commodity Form and Legal Form: An Essay on the 'Relative Autonomy' of the Law," *Law and Society* (1977), vol. II, no. 3, pp. 571-588; J. Holloway and S. Picciotto, "Capital, Crisis and the State." *Capital and Class*, summer 1977, no. 2, pp. 76-101; C. Arthur, introduction to Evgeny B. Pashukanis, *Law and Marxism: A General Theory* (1978), Ink Links, London, pp. 9-31, a translation from the German edition of *Allgemeine Rechtslehre and Marxismus: Versuch einer Kritik der juristischen Grundbegriffe*; S. Redhead, "The Discrete Charm of Bourgeois Law: A Note on Pashukanis," *Critique*, 9 (1978), pp. 113-120.

[11]Other than in some of his early writings, such as *On the Jewish Question* (1843), Marx himself had very little to say on the importance of the legal *form*. But see F. Engels and K. Kautsky, "Juridical Socialism," *Politics and Society* (1977), vol. 7, no. 2, pp. 199-200, translated and introduced by P. Beirne.

By the late 1920s, as a result of his scholarly reputation, Pashukanis had become the *doyen* of Soviet Marxist jurisprudence, eclipsing even his juridical mentor Piotr Stuchka. However, after 1928 Pashukanis' theory as a Marxist critique of bourgeois jurisprudence became increasingly incompatible with the new political and economic priorities of the first Five Year Plan, especially the necessity for a strong dictatorship of the proletariat and its ancillary, Soviet law which, after 1937, would become socialist law.

In the ensuing ideological struggle on the "legal front" of the Soviet social formation, Pashukanis made the first of his eventual three self-criticims in late 1930.[12] After that experience his theory underwent substantial revision during the period of the first and second Five Year Plans (1928–1937), as Pashukanis became the principal spokesman for the Stalinist conception of the Soviet state, while simultaneously striving to maintain his political commitment to the Marxist concept of the withering away of law. However, as soon as Stalin's "revolution from above" subsided with the essential completion of collectivization and a new legal policy of stabilization was demanded, the intrinsic ambivalence of Pashukanis' dual commitment to the respective marxisms of Stalin and Marx became apparent. This contributed to his downfall in early 1937. Following Pashukanis' purge, his successor as legal *doyen*, Andrei Vyshinsky, began the almost immediate demolition of the considerable structure of his predecessor's influence and, concomitantly, the systematic reconstruction of the Soviet legal system. Vyshinsky ushered in the era of the "Soviet socialist state and law" which has prevailed to this day in Soviet jurisprudence and legal practice.

Finally, in the process of destalinization after Stalin's death in 1953, Pashukanis' name was

[12]See E. B. Pashukanis, "The Situation on the Legal Theory Front" (1930), translated in J. Hazard (ed.), *Soviet Legal Philosophy* (1951), *op cit.* pp. 237–280. Pashukanis' second self-criticism appeared in 1934, his third—"State and Law under Socialism" (1936)—is fully translated in P. Beirne and R. Sharlet (eds.), *Pashukanis: Selected Writings on Marxism and Law* (London: Academic Press, 1980), pp. 346–361.

"cleared" of the politico-criminal charges which were the cause of his demise, and since then his status as a legal philosopher has been partially rehabilitated in the Soviet Union. Ironically, in the U.S.S.R. today Pashukanis is posthumously honoured as one of the founders of the jurisprudence of Soviet socialist state and law, a formulation the full implications of which he had resisted almost to the eve of his arrest.

MARXISM AND SOVIET JURISPRUDENCE FROM WAR COMMUNISM TO THE NEW ECONOMIC POLICY

The *General Theory of Law and Marxism* is a theory of the historical specificity of the legal form, and Pashukanis ostensibly introduces his argument with a critique of three trends in bourgeois jurisprudence dominant in the U.S.S.R. before 1921: Renner's social functionalism, Petrazhitsky's and Reisner's psychologism, and Kelsen's legal positivism. The reader quickly learns that the gist of this critique contains two observations directed against the consequences of economic reductionism. The first concerns the ontological nature of ideological categories in general, and in particular the nature of legal regulation as a specific form of ideological category. The second concerns those instrumental forms of economism which reduce law to the status of an epiphenomenon within the compass of the base/superstructure metaphor.

Pashukanis notes that within the sphere of political economy concepts such as commodity, value and exchange value are indeed ideological categories, but that this assignation by no means signifies that they indicate *only* ideas and other subjective processes. They are ideological concepts principally because they obscure objective social relationships. Yet the ideological character of a concept does not nullify the material reality of the relationships that the concept expresses. Nor does the fact that they are ideological concepts excuse us from searching for the objective conditions which they express yet somehow wrap in mystery. What needs to be proved is not that juridic concepts can and do become integrated into the structure of ideological processes, but that these concepts have *more* than an ideological existence. Pashukanis therefore asserts that law is also a real form of social being, and in so doing he seems astutely to have avoided the troublesome charge that both social scientists *and* theorists of ideology, in the final reckoning, base their assertions on a positivist epistemology.

Pashukanis is equally concerned to rebut the view that law is capable of voluntaristic manipulation by dominant social classes. Stuchka, for example, one of the early RSFSR Commissars of Justice and the author of *Decree No. 1 on the Soviet Court,* had misconstrued the nature of law in his *The Revolutionary Role of Law and State* as a "system of relationships which answers to the interests of the dominant class and which safeguards that class with organized force." Pashukanis retorts that such a definition[13] is useful both in disclosing the class content of legal forms and in asserting that law is a social relationship, but that it masks the real differences between the legal form and all other social relationships which involve regulative norms. Indeed, if law is seen simply as a form of social relationship, and if one asserts that law regulates social relationships, then one must engage the tautology that social relationships regulate themselves.

Pashukanis correctly avers that the social organization of collectivities as diverse as bees and primitive peoples require rules. But not all rules are legal rules: some rules are customary and traditional and may be based in moral, aesthetic or utilitarian considerations. Further, not all social relationships are legal relationships; under certain conditions the *regulation* of social relationships *assumes a legal character* (1924). Marxist theory must investigate not merely the material content of legal regulation during definite histori-

cal periods, but must also provide a materialist explanation of legal regulation as a definite historical form. The crucial question therefore involves the elucidation of the social conditions in which the domination and regulation of social relationships assumes a legal character.

Pashukanis argues that the fundamental principle of legal regulation is the opposition of private interests. Human conduct can be regulated by the most complex rules, but the legal element in such regulation begins where the isolation and antithesis of interests begin. "A norm of law acquires its *differentia specifica . . . ,*" he says, "because it presupposes a person endowed with a right and actively asserting it." (1924, p. 72.) Accordingly, and following some of Marx's Hegelian-inspired comments in *The Law on the Theft of Woods* (1842) and *On the Jewish Question* (1843), Pashukanis distinguishes between those rules which serve the universal interest and those which serve a particular interest. The former are technical rules and are based on unity of purpose, the latter are legal rules and are characterized by controversy. Thus, the technical rules of railroad movement presuppose a single purpose, for example the attainment of maximum haulage capacity, whereas the legal rules governing the responsibilities of railroads presuppose private claims and isolated interests. Again, the treatment of invalids presupposes a series of rules both for the patient and for the medical personnel; but inasmuch as these rules are established to achieve a single purpose—the restoration of the patient's health—they are of a technical character. But when the patient and the physician are regarded as isolated, antagonistic subjects, each of whom is the bearer of his own private interests, they then become the subjects of rights and obligations, and the rules which unite them become legal rules.

Pashukanis asserts that Marx himself had pointed to the basic conditions of existence of the legal form. Thus, Marx had indicated that the basic and most deeply set stratum of the legal superstructure—property relations—was "so closely contiguous to the foundation that they are

---

[13]This definition was officially adopted by the Commissariat of Justice in 1919, and incorporated into *RSFSR Laws* (1919). See also P. I. Stuchka, "Marksistskoe ponimanie prava," *Kommunisticheskaia revoliutsiia* (1922), no. 13–14, pp. 37–38; and "Zametki o klassovoi teoriia prava," *Sovetskoe pravo* (1922), no. 3.

the very same relationships of production expressed in juridic language." Law is some specific social relationship and can be understood in the same sense as that in which Marx termed capital a social relationship. The search for the unique social relationship, whose inevitable reflection is the form of law, is to be located in the relationships between commodity owners. The logic of legal concepts corresponds with the logic of the social relationships of commodity production, and it is specifically in these relationships—not in the demands of domination, submission or naked power—that the origin of law is to be sought. We might add that Lenin himself had said, in relation to the law of inheritance, ". . . [it] presumes the existence of private property, and the latter arises only with the existence of exchange. Its basis is in the already incipient specialization of social labour and the alienation of products in the market."[14]

Pashukanis recalls that the ascendant bourgeoisie's central antagonism with feudal property resided not in its origin in violent seizure, but instead in its immobility in exchange and circulation. In particular, it was unable to become an object of mutual guarantees as it passed from one possessor to another in acquisition. Feudal property, or the property associated with the feudal order, violated the abstract and cardinal principle of capitalist societies—"the equal possibility of obtaining inequality" (1924, p. 83).

At a certain stage of development (with the appearance of cities and city communes, markets and fairs) the relationships of human beings are manifested in a form which is doubly mysterious: they appear as the relationships of objects which are also commodities, and as the volitional relationships of entities which are independent and equal *inter se:* juridic subjects. Law thus appears side by side with the mystical attributes of value and exchange value. Moreover, it is in the concrete personality of the egoistic, autonomous subject—the property owner and the bearer of private interests—that a juridic subject such as *persona* finds complete and adequate embodiment.[15]

The historically-specific object of a commodity, for Pashukanis, finds its pure form in capitalist economies. The authority which the capitalist enjoys, as the personification of capital in the process of direct production, is essentially different from the authority which accompanies production through slaves or serfs. Only capital stands in stark, unhierarchical contrast to the mass of direct producers. Capitalist societies are first and foremost societies of commodity owners. Commodities have a dual and a contradictory character. On the one hand a commodity is and represents a use-value. But commodities necessarily embody different use-values because the qualitatively distinct social needs which they fulfil, and the quality and quantity of labour expended in their production, are necessarily different and unequal. And, on the other hand, a commodity is and represents an exchange-value. One commodity may be exchanged for another commodity in a definite ratio. The values encountered in this exchange are expressed by and facilitated through the mediation of another commodity, money, as the form of universal economic equivalent.

The potential for commodity exchange assumes that qualitatively distinct commodities enter a formal relationship of equivalence, so that ultimately they appear as equal. The exchange of commodities thus obscures a double abstraction in which concrete labour and concrete commodities are equalized *inter se* and are reduced to abstract labour and abstract commodities. This

---

[14]V. I. Lenin, *What the "Friends of the People" Are and How They Fight the Social Democrats* (1894), *LCW,* vol. I, p. 153.

[15]The concept of *persona* in Roman jurisprudence originally derived from the function of an actor's stage mask. The mask enabled the actor to conceal his real identity and to conform to the role written for him. Transposed into the legal realm, as a permanent condition, man must assume a legal mask in order to engage in the activities regulated by legal rules. See further, O. Gierke, *Associations and Law* (1977), translated and edited by G. Heiman, University of Toronto Press, Toronto.

abstraction in turn perpetuates the fetish that commodities themselves, including money, contain living powers: commodities thus dominate their very producers, human subjects.

Pashukanis illustrates how commodity fetishism complements legal fetishism. Exchange transactions based on the *vi et armis* principles of feudalism create a form of property which is too transient and too unstable for developed commodity exchange. *De facto* possession must be transformed into an absolute and constant right which adheres to a commodity during its circulatory process. Pashukanis notes that Marx had tersely stated in *Capital I,* that "commodities cannot send themselves to a market and exchange themselves with one another. Accordingly we must turn to their custodian, to the commodity owner" (1924, p. 75).

The legal form itself is therefore cast as both an essential part and simultaneously as a consequence of the exchange of commodities under capitalism. At the very same time that the product of labour is assuming the quality of commodities and becoming the bearer of value, man acquires the quality of a juridic subject and becomes the bearer of a right. In the development of legal categories, the capacity to perfect exchange relationships is merely one of the concrete manifestations of the general attribute of legal capacity and the capacity to act. Historically, however, it was specifically the exchange arrangement which furnished the notion of a subject as the abstract bearer of all possible legal claims. Nor does the juridic form of property contradict the factual expropriation of the property of many citizens; the attribute of being a subject of rights is a purely formal attribute, qualifying all persons alike as "deserving" of property but in no sense making them property owners.

It is only under developed commodity exchange that the capacity to have a right in general is distinguished from specific legal claims. Indeed, a characteristic feature of capitalist societies is that general interests are segregated from and opposed to private interests. The constant transfer of rights in the market creates the notion of an immobile bearer of rights, and the possibility therefore occurs of abstracting from the specific differences between subjects and of bringing them within one generic concept. Concrete man is relegated to an abstract man who incorporates egoism, freedom and the supreme value of personality; the capacity to be a subject of rights is finally disassociated from the specific living personality and becomes a purely social attribute. The legal subject is thus the abstract commodity owner elevated into the heavens (1924, p. 81), and acquires his *alter ego* in the form of a representative while he himself becomes insignificant. The specific characteristics of each member of *Homo sapiens* are, therefore, dissolved in the abstract concept of man as a juridic subject.

In order for property to be exchanged and alienated there must be a contract or accord of independent wills. Contract is therefore one of the central concepts in law, and once it has arisen the notion of contract seeks to acquire universal significance. In contradistinction to theorists of public and constitutional law, such as Leon Duguit, Pashukanis holds that all law is necessarily private law in that it emanates from commodity exchange. The distinction between private law and public law is therefore a (false) ideological distinction and it reflects a real contradiction in capitalist societies between the individual and the social interest. This contradiction is embodied in "the real relationships of human subjects who can regard their own private struggles as social struggles only in the incongruous and mystifying form of the value of commodities" (1924, p. 109).

Pashukanis argues that the political authority of the state appears to be disassociated from the economic domination and specific needs of the capitalist class in the market. He thus hypothesizes that the capitalist state is a *dual* state: a political state and a legal state. Thus he says that:

> the state as an organization of class domination, and as an organization for the conduct of external wars, does not require legal interpretation and in

essence does not allow it. This is where . . . the principle of naked expediency rules (1924, p. 92).

Class dominance, i.e. the dominance of the bourgeoisie, is expressed in the state's dependence upon banks and capitalist sectors, and in the dependence of each worker upon his employer. But it should not be forgotten that in the political class struggle—most evidently, as its critical phases—the state is the authority for the organized violence of one class on another. The legal state, on the other hand, reflects the impersonal, abstract and equivalent form of commodity exchange. The legal state is the third party that embodies the mutual guarantees which commodity owners, *qua* owners, give to each other.

The *leitmotif* of early Soviet Marxist thought on law at the time of the October Revolution and immediately thereafter, was the imperative of implementing the Marxist concept of the withering away of law. This initial eliminationist approach to law was best exemplified by Stuchka, a Bolshevik revolutionary and a jurist, who in the days following the seizure of power was assigned the task of taking physical and political possession of the premises and institution of the highest court of imperial Russia. On arriving at the court building in what is now Leningrad, Stuchka found that the judges had fled the scene leaving behind only a number of frightened and bewildered clerks and messengers. To put this group at ease, Stuchka reassured them that although previously the judges had occupied the chambers while they themselves had waited in the antechambers, from that time on the clerks and messengers would sit in the judges' chairs and their former occupants would be relegated to the antechambers.[16]

The first Soviet attempt to implement the process of the withering away of law began less than a month after the October Revolution. The Bolsheviks' first legislation on the judiciary abolished the hierarchy of tsarist courts, which were soon after replaced by a much less complex dual system of local people's courts and revolutionary tribunals.[17] This initiated a process of simplification and popularization that in the immediate post-revolutionary days and months swept away most of the inherited tsarist legal system, including the procuracy, the bar, and all but those laws vital to the transitional period between capitalism and communism (e.g. *Decree* Abolishing Classes and Civil Ranks, Nov. 1917). Even the remaining legal minimum was subject to interpretation by a new type of judge, usually untrained in law. These new judges were encouraged to guide themselves by their "revolutionary consciousness" in applying the law. The Bolsheviks' objective was that even these remnants would ultimately become superfluous and wither away or disappear. Their vision was of a new social formation in which people would be able to settle their disputes "with simplicity, without elaborately organized tribunals, without legal representation, without complicated laws, and without a labyrinth of rules of procedure and evidence."[18] However, harsh reality quickly impinged upon this vision as civil war engulfed the country. Confronted with the exigencies of governance under the most difficult conditions, the Bolsheviks deferred this transformative process and, as early as 1918, as John Hazard has conclusively demonstrated, began the process of re-legalization, which culminated in a fully articulated legal system based largely on foreign bourgeois models and perfected in the first federal constitution (1924) during the early years of the New Economic Policy.

Pashukanis concludes his argument in *The General Theory of Law and Marxism* by opposing those who would wish to construct a proletarian system of law after the 1917 revolution. Marx himself, especially in *The Critique of the Gotha Programme*, had grasped the profound inner connection between the commodity form and the

[16]P. I. Stuchka, "Na ministerstvom kresle," in P. I. Stuchka, *13 let bor'by za revollutsionno-marksistskuiu teoriiu prava* (1931), Moscow.

[17]See *Dekrety sovetskoi vlasti* (1957), Moscow, vol. I, pp. 124-126.

[18]Hazard, *Settling Disputes in Soviet Society* (1960), *op. cit.*, p. vi.

legal form, and had conceived of the transition to the higher level of communism not as a transition to new legal forms, but as the dying out of the legal form in general. If law has its real origin in commodity exchange, and if socialism is seen as the abolition of commodity exchange and the construction of production for use, then proletarian or socialist law was a conceptual, and therefore a practical, absurdity. While the market bond between individual enterprises (either capitalist or petty commodity production) and groups of enterprises (either capitalist or socialist) remained in force, then the legal form must also remain in force.

The purportedly proletarian system of law operative under NEP was, Pashukanis asserts, mere bourgeois law. Even the new system of criminal administration contained in the *RSFSR Criminal Code* (1922) was bourgeois law. Pashukanis notes that although the *Basic Principles of Criminal Legislation of the Soviet Union and Union Republics* had substituted the concept of "measures of social defence" for the concept of guilt, crime and punishment (1924, see p. 124), this was nevertheless a terminological change and not the abolition of the legal form. Law cannot assume the form of commodity exchange and be proletarian or "socialist" in content. Criminal law is a form of equivalence between egoistic and isolated subjects. Indeed, criminal law is the sphere where juridic intercourse attains its maximum intensity. As with the legal form in general, the actions of specific actors are dissolved into the actions of abstract parties—the state, as one party, imposes punishment according to the damage effected by the other party, the criminal.

Pashukanis points out that the Soviet Union of 1924 had two systems of economic regulation. On the one hand there were the administrative-technical rules which governed the general economic plan. On the other were the legal rules (civil and commercial codes, courts, arbitration tribunals etc.) which governed the commodity exchange that was the essential feature of NEP. The victory of the former type of regulation would

signify the demise of the latter, and only then would Marx's description of human emancipation be realized. Five years later, in "Economics and Legal Regulation," Pashukanis still clung precariously yet tenaciously to his dictum that "the problem of the withering away of law is the yardstick by which we measure the degree of proximity of a jurist to Marxism" (1929, p. 268).

It must be stressed that The General Theory of Law and Marxism was written during NEP at a critical juncture in Soviet development. Pashukanis argued that in certain respects NEP had preserved market exchange and the form of value, and that this was a consequence of "proletarian state capitalism" (1924, p. 89).[19] Lenin himself had fully appreciated the contradictory character of the different modes of production encouraged by NEP. The Supreme Economic Council, set up in 1917 with the explicit aim of introducing socialist methods of production into both industry and agriculture, had achieved such limited success that in May 1921 Lenin observed: "there is still hardly any evidence of the operation of an integrated state economic plan."[20] Arguing that there was much that could and must be learned from capitalist techniques (Taylorism), Lenin wrote in December 1921 that NEP marked "a retreat in order to make better preparations for a new offensive against capitalism."[21] The painful experiences of War Communism had indicated that socialism would not be attained overnight, and that unless the political domination of the proletariat was ensured, it would not be attained at all. The temporary solution was to allow the peasantry limited ownership of the agricultural means of production. But this was to be a regulated retreat:

[19]In 1927 Pashukanis asserted that the term "proletarian state capitalism" was an error. See J. Hazard (ed.), *Soviet Legal Philosophy* (1951), *op. cit.*, pp. 179ff.

[20]V. I. Lenin, "To Comrade Krzhizhanovsky: the Praesidium of the State Planning Commission" (May 1921), *LCW*, vol. 42, p. 371.

[21]V. I. Lenin, *Draft Theses on the Role and Function of the Trade Unions Under the New Economic Policy* (1922), *LCW*, vol. 33, p. 184.

The proletarian state may, without changing its own character, permit freedom to trade and the development of capitalism only within certain bounds, and only on the condition that the state regulates (supervises, controls, determines the form and methods of etc.) private trade and capitalism.[22]

The general feeling among the Bolsheviks, then, was that NEP was a temporary, necessary and regulated retreat; one step backward, and two steps forward. Lenin warned that "It will take us at least ten years to organize large-scale industry to produce a reserve and secure control of agriculture. . . . There will be a dictatorship of the proletariat. Then will come the classless society."[23] The seeds of this progression were already at hand, however, and in May 1921 he observed that: "the manufactured goods made by socialist factories and exchanged for the foodstuffs produced by the peasants are not commodities in the politico-economic sense of the word; at any rate, they are not only commodities, they are no longer commodities, they are ceasing to be commodities."[24]

Under NEP Pashukanis' theoretical achievements earned him more than just the praise of his contemporaries. During the years 1924-1930, he assumed a number of important positions in the Soviet academic hierarchy and was named to the editorial boards of the most influential law and social science journals. Through these strategic positions and key editorial posts, Pashukanis extended and strengthened the influence of the commodity exchange school of law on Marxist jurisprudence.[25]

When *The General Theory of Law and Marxism* appeared in 1924, Pashukanis was a member of Stuchka's Section of Law and State,

and of the Institute of Soviet Construction, both of the Communist Academy which he subsequently described as "the centre of Marxist thought."[26] Later, he was to become a member of the bureau or executive committee of the Institute and of the Section, as well as head of the latter's Subsection on the General Theory of Law and State.

During 1925, the Section of Law and State formally launched the "revolution of the law" with the publication of a collection of essays entitled *Revoliutsiia prava*. Pashukanis served as co-editor and contributed a major article on Lenin's understanding of law.

In 1926, the second edition of *General Theory* was published. During that year Pashukanis joined the law faculty of Moscow State University and the Institute of Red Professors, the graduate school of the Communist Academy. *Bol'shaia sovetskaia entsiklopediia* also began publication in 1926, and Pashukanis was named chief editor for law shortly afterwards.

The third edition of *General Theory* was issued in 1927, the year *Revoliutsiia prava* was established as the official journal of the Section of Law and State with Pashukanis as a co-editor. Beginning that year, the Section's periodic reports reflected Pashukanis' increasing predominance. His annual intellectual output in books, articles, essays, *doklady*, reviews and reports was prodigious. Along with Stuchka, Pashukanis dominated the scholarly activity of the Section. As an indication of his growing impact on Soviet legal development, he was assigned the task of preparing a textbook on the general theory of law and state, and was chosen to represent the Communist Academy on the commission for drafting the fundamental principles of civil legislation, created by the U.S.S.R. Council of People's Commissars.

During this period Pashukanis began to assume additional positions and editorships. He became Deputy Chairman of the Presidium of the Communist Academy, and a co-editor of *Vestnik*

[22]*Ibid.*, p. 185.

[23]V. I. Lenin, "Report on Party Unity and the Anarcho-Syndicalist Deviation" (March 16, 1921), *LCW*, vol. 32, p. 251.

[24]V. I. Lenin, "Instructions of the Council of Labour and Defence to Local Soviet Bodies" (May 1921), *LCW*, vol. 32, p. 384.

[25]See R. Sharlet, "Pashukanis and the Rise of Soviet Marxist Jurisprudence," *op. cit.*, pp. 112-115.

[26]Pashukanis' phrase in "Disput k voprosu ob izuchenii prestupnosti," *Revoliutsiia prava* (1929), no. 3, p. 67.

kommunisticheskoi akademii, the major Marxist social science journal. He had previously been named a founding editor of the journal *Revoliut-siia i kul'tura,* a new publication designed to promote the cultural revolution. His co-editors on these publications were the most eminent Marxist social scientists, including Lunacharsky, Pokrovsky and Deborin.

In 1927 in "The Marxist Theory of Law and the Construction of Socialism,"[27] Pashukanis undertook two objectives. First, he once again warns of the political dangers involved in trying to erect proletarian or socialist legal forms, and he asserts that the dialectic of the withering away of law under socialism consists in "the contrast between the principle of socialist planning and the principle of equivalent exchange" (1927, p. 193). Thus, he took issue with those such as Reisner[28] who saw *Decree No. 1 on the Court,* or the *RSFSR Civil Code,* as evidence that NEP utilized private property and commodity exchange to develop the forces of production. But this was to imply that in this context private property and commodity exchange had a "neutral" character. What was important, Pashukanis pointed out, was that one should understand the use of these forms not from the perspective of developing the forces of production, but from "the perspective of the victory of the socialist elements of our economy over the capitalist ones" (1927, p. 192). Provided that remnants of the capitalist mode of production were in practice eliminated and that subsequent social rules in the U.S.S.R. were of a technical–administrative nature, then Pashukanis could argue prescriptively and, possibly, descriptively, that law would disappear *only* with the disappearance of capitalism.

This 1927 article contains some interesting emendations to his *General Theory of Law and Marxism.* The most important of these, in response to Stuchka's "State and Law in the Period of Socialist Construction,"[29] is the admission of "the indisputable fact of the existence of feudal law" (Pashukanis, 1927, p. 195). Pashukanis now indicates that we find "purchase and sale, with products and labour assuming the form of commodities, and with a general equivalent, i.e. money, throughout the entire feudal period" (1927, p. 195). But although feudal and bourgeois law may have a common form, their content and class nature is essentially different. Feudal law is based on the will of the simple commodity owner, while bourgeois law is based on the will of the capitalist commodity owner. This is a most important concession because, although Pashukanis will not yet admit the primacy of *production* relations within historical materialism, it allows him to posit the existence of what he refers to as "Soviet law, corresponding to a lower level of development than that which Marx envisioned in *The Critique of the Gotha Programme* . . . [and which] is fundamentally different from genuine bourgeois law" (1927, p. 194).

In 1929, in "Economics and Legal Regulations," Pashukanis explicitly discusses the reflexive status of the legal form, a question that was only implicit in his analysis of ideological forms in *The General Theory of Law and Marxism.* He uses two arguments to refute the criticism of Preobrazhensky, Rubin, and Böhm-Bawerk that economic regulation under conditions of socialism (in the U.S.S.R.) is similar, in certain respects, to the regulation exercised by capitalist states under conditions of monopoly capitalism and imperialism (chiefly in Germany and England).

Pashukanis argues, first, that these sorts of criticisms tend to be based on the false polarity of base and superstructural forms. "The social," he retorts, ". . . is the *alter ego* of the economic" (1929, p. 241). He continues, significantly, "in

[27]E. B. Pashukanis, "Marksistskaia teoriia prava i stroitel'stvo sotsializma," *Revoliutsiia prava* (1927), no. 3, pp. 3–12, translated in present volume on pp. 186–99.

[28]M. A. Reisner, *Pravo, nashe pravo, chuzhoe pravo, obshchee pravo* (1925), Moscow, translated in J. Hazard (ed.), *Soviet Legal Philosophy* (1951), *op. cit.,* pp. 83–109.

[29]P. I. Stuchka, "Gosudarstvo i pravo v period sotsialisticheskogo stroitel'stva," *Revoliutsiia prava* (1927), no. 2. See also the criticism in S. I. Raevich, book review, *Sovetskoe pravo* (1928), no. 2 (32), p. 98.

every antagonistic society, class relationships find continuation and concretization in the sphere of political struggle, the state structure and the legal order . . . productive forces [are] decisive in the final analysis" (1929, p. 244). Superstructural forms, in other words, are incomprehensible apart from those social relationships to which they initially owe their existence. This marks the crucial transition in Pashukanis' work. Even if he has as yet neither identified the proper place of the political within the complex of the social relationships of production, nor posited that the political has primacy in Marxist political economy, he has at the very least conceded that productive relationships are in some sense "determinant factors in the final analysis." Quite clearly, the *origin* of law could not now be explained by commodity exchange—primitive *or* generalized— and Pashukanis seems to have recognized the inferiority of his radical position in the debates with Stuchka that were contained within the Communist Academy and not made public until 1927.[30]

Pashukanis' second argument is a weak rebuttal of the assertion that, because NEP relationships in part conformed to the law of value, and also to the law of the proportional distribution of labour expenditures, therefore the primitive socialist economy contained *capitalist* contradictions. These notions, he replies, stem from a simplistic understanding of Engels' concern with the leap from the kingdom of necessity to the kingdom of freedom. To hold that the form of

value exists in the U.S.S.R. is to miss, as did Preobrazhensky, the crucial point that the U.S.S.R. is a dynamic formation founded on "the economics of co-operation and collectivization" (Pashukanis, 1929, p. 251), and "the union of the working class and the peasantry" (1929, p. 254). What matters, concretely, is not where the U.S.S.R. *is,* but where it *will be.* The U.S.S.R. is in a necessary phase preparatory to Engels' quantum leap. Further, it is trivial to claim that the law of the proportional distribution of labour expenditures is effective in the U.S.S.R. This law is effecitve in all social formations. What matters here is how it is determined, and in the U.S.S.R. it is determined by "the economic policy of the proletarian state" (1929, p. 257).

The regulation of the national economy by the proletarian state under NEP, Pashukanis continues, is qualitatively distinct from the domestic economic intervention of capitalist states during the 1914–1918 War. In contradistinction to the latter's "57 varieties" of socialism represented by wartime state control, the proletarian state has three unique characteristics by which it will effectively realize the dialectical transformation of quantity into quality: the indissolubility of legislative and executive, extensive nationalization and the firm regulation of production in the universal rather than the particular interest. The more these characteristics are actualized, says Pashukanis,

> the role of the purely legal superstructure, the role of law—declines, and from this can be derived the general rule that as [technical] regulation becomes more effective, the weaker and less significant the role of law and the legal superstructure in its pure form (1929, p. 271).

Pashukanis' responsibilities continued to multiply when he was appointed Prorector of the Institute of Red Professors, which was also known as the "theoretical staff of the Central Committee."[31] In 1929, the Institute started a journal for correspondence students with Pashukanis as

---

[30]Indeed, it is most likely that "Economics and Legal Regulation" was an indirect response to Stuchka's *Vvedenie v teoriiu grazhdanskogo prava* of 1927. Here Stuchka had reiterated that exchange must be subsumed within the concept of production because ". . . the distribution of the agents of production is itself only one of the aspects of production". See P. I. Stuchka, *Izbrannye proizvedeniia* (1964), Riga, p. 565, and R. Sharlet, "Pashukanis and the Commodity Exchange Theory of Law 1924–1930," unpub. Ph.D. diss., Indiana University, 1968, p. 210. The Communist Academy effected a compromise in 1929, in its first syllabus on the general theory of law. The concept of law was now rooted in the process of commodity production *and* exchange. See A. K. Stal'gevich, *Programma po obshchei teoriia prava* (1929), Moscow, p. 11, and see R. Sharlet (1968), *op. cit.*, p. 210.

[31]A. Avtorkhanov, *Stalin and the Soviet Communist Party* (1959), New York, p. 21.

chief editor. By this time, the influence of his commodity exchange theory of law on the syllabi for the Institute's law curriculum and correspondence courses was pronounced.

Finally, in 1929–1930, Pashukanis reached the apex of the Marxist school of jurisprudence and the Soviet legal profession. In a major reorganization, the Institute of Soviet Law was fully absorbed and its publication was abolished. All theoretical and practical work in the field of law was concentrated in the Communist Academy. In turn, the Section of Law and State and the Institute of Soviet Construction of the Communist Academy were merged, and the journal *Revoliutsiia prava* was reoriented and renamed. Pashukanis became director of the new Institute of the State, Law and Soviet Construction (soon renamed the Institute of Soviet Construction and Law); chief editor of its new journal, *Sovetskoe gosudarstvo i revoliutsii, prava*; and a co-editor of *Sovetskoe stroitel'stvo*, the journal of the U.S.S.R. Central Executive Committee.

An indication of Pashukanis' influence on the Soviet legal profession was the gradual emergence of the commodity exchange orientation within the Marxist school of law. Just a few years after the appearance of *The General Theory of Law and Marxism,* the group of Marxist jurists working with Pashukanis in the Communist Academy became known as the commodity exchange school of law. This group, led by Pashukanis, dominated Marxist jurisprudence and was strongest in the general theory of law and in the branches of criminal law and civil–economic law. As the commodity exchange theory of law became identified with *the* Marxist theory of law, Pashukanis gradually assumed the unofficial leadership of the Marxist school of law. By 1930, the Communist Academy was bringing all Soviet legal scholarship and education under its control, and Pashukanis, as the pre-eminent Marxist theorist of law, was soon being acknowledged as the leader of the Soviet legal profession.

As Pashukanis' prestige soared in the late 1920s, a critical accompaniment, at first low-keyed but later swelling in volume, began to be heard. From 1925 to 1930, Pashukanis was criticized for overextending the commodity exchange concept of law, confusing a methodological concept with a general theory of law, ignoring the law's ideological character, and even for being an anti-normativist. Other critics disagreed with Pashukanis' positions on feudal law, public law and the readiness of the masses to participate in public administration. He was denounced by one critic as a "legal nihilist."

Nearly all of Pashukanis' critics were Marxists. Most were members of the Communist Academy. Within the Communist Academy, as the commodity exchange school of law became ascendant, it divided into two wings: the moderates and the radicals. All of Pashukanis' critics within the Communist Academy were associated with the moderate wing of the commodity exchange school. This group was led by Stuchka, and the radical wing was led by Pashukanis. Outside of the Communist Academy, A. A. Piontkovsky, at that time a member of the rival Institute of Soviet Law, was Pashukanis' major critic.[32]

Stuchka's criticism, which began to appear publicly in 1927, was by far the greatest challenge to Pashukanis. Basically, Stuchka, as a leader of the moderate wing of the commodity exchange school, criticized Pashukanis' overextension of the commodity exchange concept of law from civil law to other branches of law. Specifically, he criticized Pashukanis for overextending the notion of equivalence, insufficiently emphasizing the class content of law, reducing public law to private law, and denying the existence of either feudal law or Soviet law.

Stuchka apparently had been criticizing Pashukanis within the Communist Academy before the first publication of his criticism in 1927. In his article "State and Law in the Period of Socialist Construction," Stuchka footnoted his criticism of Pashukanis to the effect that their mutual opponents, presumably those outside the Com-

---

[32]On the two wings of the commodity exchange school see R. Scheslinger, *Soviet Legal Theory* (1945), Kegan Paul, London, pp. 153–156.

munist Academy's legal circles, had been exaggerating the extent of their differences. Stuchka conceded that differences existed between him and Pashukanis and that under the circumstances, it was best to bring them out into the open. In this article, however, he tended to minimize these differences.

Stuchka's contributions to building a Marxist theory of law were undisputed by his contemporaries. During the early 1920s, he had, first, argued for a materialist conception of law and for a class concept of law against prevailing idealist conceptions. Second, he was responsible for the conception of a revolutionary role for Soviet law during the transitional period from capitalism to communism.[33] Perhaps Stuchka's greatest contribution to the development of the Soviet legal system was his insistence, which grew in intensity throughout the 1920s, on the necessity for "Soviet" law during the transition period, although he had no illusions about this body of law becoming a permanent feature of the Soviet system. In an article in early 1919, Stuchka clearly stated that "We can only speak of proletarian law as the *law of the transition period. . . ."* He underscored the temporary nature of proletarian law by characterizing it as "a simplification, a popularization of our new social system."[34] At the end of the decade Stuchka summarized his recognition of the importance of law as an agent of socio-economic development by writing in the Foreword to his collected essays: "Revolution of the law is revolutionary legality in the service of furthering the socialist offensive and socialist construction."[35]

In this context, Stuchka criticized Pashukanis' theory of law for its

> omissions, its one-sidedness insofar as it reduced all law to only the market, to only exchange as the

instrumentalization of the relations of commodity producers—which means law in general is peculiar to bourgeois society.[36]

If Stuchka's criticism was sharp and constructive, then the criticism put forward by Piontkovsky was definitely hostile. Piontkovsky was a specialist in criminal law, an advocate of the development of a specifically Soviet legal system, and a member of the Institute of Soviet Law until its absorption by the Communist Academy. Piontkovsky's main and most effective criticism was that Pashukanis had mistaken an ideal-type concept, the commodity exchange concept, for a theory of law. He developed this in his book, *Marxism and Criminal Law,* which was published in two editions. Possibly because Piontkovsky was outside the legal circles of the Communist Academy, his criticism of Pashukanis' work was more explicit and much more blunt. He effectively incorporated into his own criticism the criticism of Pashukanis' colleagues, but without being subject to the restraints that they apparently imposed upon themselves in the interest of unity within the Communist Academy.

Piontkovsky valued Pashukanis' *General Theory of Law and Marxism,* but with definite reservations. He devoted a large part of his book to what he termed the "dangers" of Pashukanis' theory, while at the same time, in his second edition, he defended himself against countercriticism from Pashukanis' followers. One of these had written that Piontkovsky's study had nothing in common with Marxism and by no means explained reality, to which Piontkovsky replied:

> Of course, our point of view has nothing in common with that Marxism that is limited only to the explanation of reality, but has . . . something in common with that Marxism . . . which is a "guide" to action.[37]

[33]A. Vyshinsky, "Stuchka," *Malaia sovetskaia entsiklopediia* (1930), vol. 8, pp. 514-515.
[34]P. I. Stuchka, "Proletarskoe pravo," in P. I. Stuchka, *13 let . . .* (1931), *op. cit.* pp. 24, 34.
[35]P. I. Stuchka, "Foreword" to *13 let . . .* (1931), *op. cit.,* p. 4.
[36]P. I. Stuchka, *Vvedenie v teoriiu grazhdanskogo prava* (1927), in P. I. Stuchka, *Izbrannye proizvedeniia* (1964), *op. cit.,* pp. 563-564.
[37]A. Piontkovsky, *Marksizm i ugolovnoe pravo: sbornik statei* (1929), 2nd ed., Moscow, pp. 32-33, 39.

By the end of the decade, the volume of criticism of Pashukanis' radical version of the commodity exchange theory of law had grown considerably. The two directions from which the criticism emanated, from both inside and outside the Communist Academy, could no longer be easily distinguished. Stuchka's and Piontkovsky's criticism began to converge as the criticism took on an increasingly political tone in 1930. One critic observed that Pashukanis had repaired to the "enemy's territory" and had lapsed into "bourgeois legal individualism." Another critic, in a similar tone, characterized Pashukanis' commodity exchange theory of law as a "collection of mechanistic and formalistic perversions."[38]

The most salient aspects of these debates involved the fundamental questions concerning the role of state and law in the lower phase of communism. These questions indicated a certain dissatisfaction and uneasiness with the type of thought characteristic of Marxist legal circles during the 1920s. Most fundamental was Stuchka's question of the relationship of dictatorship to law. As he wrote, "We know Lenin's definition of dictatorship as 'a power basing itself on coercion and not connected with any kind of laws.'" But then Stuchka goes on to ask, "What should be the relationship of the dictatorship of the proletariat *to its law* and to law in general as the means of administration?"[39]

The other important question, raised from outside the Communist Academy by Piontkovsky, involved the relationship of Pashukanis' general theory of law to the vital tasks of political and economic development in a social formation dominated by feudal social relationships. Piontkovsky pointed out that Pashukanis' theory of law was "*not revolutionary*" in the sense that it was not designated for a voluntarist approach to social change.[40]

"REVOLUTION FROM ABOVE" AND THE STRUGGLE ON THE LEGAL FRONT

Despite growing criticism of Pashukanis' theory the impact of his commodity exchange school of law on the withering away process began to become apparent in the late 1920s. Pashukanis and his colleagues assiduously devoted themselves to bringing about the realization of his prediction that private law and the legal state would gradually begin to wither away upon the elimination of the institutions of private property and the market. From their point of view, the prevailing political and economic trends were favourable. The doctrine of "socialism in one country," signalling the forthcoming end of the strategic retreat of the New Economic Policy, was first officially expressed in 1925 at the XIVth Party Conference. Later in the same year, the XIVth Party Congress adopted the policy of industrialization, which meant that a substantial growth of the socialist sector of the economy could be anticipated. For the commodity exchange school of law, the imminent end of the New Economic Policy and the subsequent growth of the state sector meant a significant weakening of the juridical superstructure. By 1927 the XVth Party Congress was calling for the construction of socialism, an objective that for Pashukanis and his colleagues required the gradual elimination of law. The growth of the socialist base, argued Estrin, meant "the simplification and contraction" of the "legal form"—in other words, a withering away of law.[41]

The revolutionaries of the law directed their main attacks against the NEP codes as the core of the real legal culture, and against the legal education system as the nexus between the real and ideal legal cultural patterns and the means by which they were transmitted and maintained. They reasoned that if the thicket of bourgeois laws could be gradually thinned out, the ground

---

[38]Quoted in E. B. Pashukanis, "The Situation on the Legal Theory Front" (1930), *op. cit.*, pp. 253, 250.

[39]P. I. Stuchka, "Dvenadtsat' let revoliutsii gosudarstva i prava," in P. I. Stuchka, *13 let . . .* (1931), *op. cit.*, p. 189.

[40]A. Piontkovsky, *Marksizm i ugolovnoe pravo* (1929), *op. cit.*, p. 87.

[41]A. Ia. Estrin, "XVth Congress of the Party and Questions of Law," *Revoliutsiia prava* (1928), no. 2, p. 13. See also R. Sharlet, "Pashukanis and the Withering Away of Law in the USSR," in S. Fitzpatrick (ed.), *Cultural Revolution in Russia, 1928-1931* (1978), Indiana University Press, Bloomington, pp. 169-188.

could eventually be cleared, with the remaining legal structures becoming increasingly superfluous and falling into disuse towards that time when they would be razed. Tactically, this meant the necessity of initially replacing the NEP codes with shorter, simpler models which would compress (and hence eliminate) the finer distinctions of bourgeois justice. The longer-term thrust was towards radically reforming legal education for the purpose of preparing cadres who would be socialized into and trained to preside over the transition from the legal realities of NEP to a future without law.

Their primary target was the notion of equivalence, which they regarded as the unifying theme of bourgeois legal culture and the factor most responsible for its cohesion. Against the symmetry of economic-legal equivalence, they opposed the asymmetrical principle of political expediency in their radical efforts to recodify NEP law and reform legal education during the first and second Five Year Plans.

Expediency as a principle of codification meant that the draft codes of the transitional legal culture were characterized by flexibility and simplicity, in opposition to the stability and formality of the NEP codes based on equivalence. Although only a few of the draft codes of the Pashukanis school were actually adopted (in the emerging Central Asian republics), their recodification efforts nevertheless had a subversive effect on the administration of civil and criminal justice during the first half of the 1930s. The draft codes were widely distributed in the legal profession, while their basic principles were constantly elaborated upon in the legal press and taught in the law schools. The revolution of the law appeared to be winning, creating what was subsequently called an atmosphere of legal nihilism.

In the legal transfer culture, criminal law became "criminal policy" (*ugolovnaia politika*), reflecting its extreme flexibility, while many of the procedural and substantive distinctions characteristic of bourgeois criminal jurisprudence were discarded in the interest of maximum simplicity. Similarly, the civil law of equivalent commodity exchange was supplanted by the new category of economic law, encompassing the economic relationships between production enterprises within the Five Year Plans, which were enforced as technical rules based on the criterion of planning expediency. All of this was taught in the law schools, where the legal cadres were being prepared to preside over the gradual withering away of the law.[42]

Although the second Soviet attempt to carry out the withering away of law progressed well into the 1930s, Pashukanis and the commodity exchange school, as advocates of his theory, collided with the process of Soviet rapid industrialization at the XVIth Party Congress in June 1930. The conflict between industrialization and withering away, which had been implicit since 1925, now clearly emerged. Until 1928, this implied conflict had been largely academic while NEP and the policy of economic recovery were still in effect. However, once large-scale industrialization and forced collectivization were underway, a collision was inevitable as it became apparent that the intervention and active support of strong and stable legal and political systems would be necessary in the U.S.S.R. Consequently, the commodity exchange school of law began its rapid decline in the late 1920s, culminating in 1930 as Marxist jurisprudence was brought into line with the "socialist offensive along the whole front."

Stalin, as General Secretary, in his address before the Central Committee Plenum of April 1929, warned against promoting hostile and antagonistic attitudes towards law and state among the masses. He argued instead that the intensification of the class struggle by the kulaks required the strengthening, rather than the weakening, of the dictatorship of the proletariat.[43] This tendency culminated at the XVIth Party Congress in the rejection of the concept of the gradual withering away of law and state. On that occasion Stalin reconceptualized this process:

[42]See R. Sharlet, "Stalinism and Soviet Legal Culture," in R. C. Tucker (ed.), *Stalinism* (1977), Norton, New York, pp. 161-162.

[43]J. Stalin, *Problems of Leninism* (1947), 11th ed., State Publishing House, Moscow, pp. 344-345.

We are for the withering away of the state, while at the same time we stand for strengthening the dictatorship of the proletariat which represents the most potent and mighty authority of all the state authorities that have existed down to this time. The highest development of state authority to the end of making ready the conditions for the withering away of state authority: there you have the Marxist formula. Is this "contradictory"? Yes, it is "contradictory." But it is a living, vital contradiction and it completely reflects Marxist dialectics.[44]

The Communist Party's rejection of the gradualist notion of withering away made it necessary, therefore, to redefine the transitional role of law and state and seriously undermined the theoretical foundations of the commodity exchange school of law.

In 1932, in his *Doctrine of State and Law,* Pashukanis recognized that he should not have equated law as an historical phenomenon with the equivalent exchange of commodities. In class societies every relationship of production has a specific form in which surplus labour is extracted from the direct producers, and he now argues that "the nature of the bond between the producer and the means of production is the key to understanding the specificity of socio-economic formations" (1932). The factor that determines the typical features of a given legal system is therefore the form of exploitation. We might add that by now Pashukanis himself must seriously have wondered whether the primacy of the individual subject within his theory of law had its origins not in the legacies of Hegel, Marx and Pokrovsky, but rather in that subjectivist epistemology represented in bourgeois jurisprudence by Jhering, Laband, Jellinek and possibly Max Weber—all of whom he would undoubtedly have read during his studies at the University of Munich.

Sensitive to the political dangers which he detects in his own earlier work, in Stuchka, and in the Second International, Pashukanis raises the delicate question of whether social relationships which are not relationships of production or exchange can enter into the content of law. He asserts that law in bourgeois society does not serve only the facilitation of commodity exchange, and bourgeois property is not exhausted by the relationships between commodity owners. To argue that law is reducible simply to economic relationships is in the end to identify it with economic relationships, which in turn both excludes all but property and contract law, and denies the reflexive effect of the legal superstructure on economic relationships. And to hold to this latter argument would clearly be inappropriate in the context of the end of the first Five Year Plan and the beginning of the second. Pashukanis responds that law cannot be understood unless we consider it as the basic form of the policy of the ruling class. "A legal relationship is a *form* of production relationship," he continues, "because the active influence of the class organization of the ruling class transforms the factual relationship into a legal one, gives it a new quality, and thus includes it in the construction of the legal superstructure" (Pashukanis, 1932; p. 297).

Pashukanis accordingly now reformulates his definition of Law provided in *The General Theory of Law and Marxism* as "the form of regulation and consolidation of production relationships and also of other social relationships of class society" (1932, p. 287). He adds that this definition is incomplete without reference to a coercive apparatus (the state) which guarantees the functioning of the legal superstructure. But the dependence of law on the state does not signify that the state creates the legal superstructure. The state is itself "only a more or less complex reflection of the economic needs of the dominant class in production" (1932, p. 291). To emphasize the primacy of the state would be to miss the distinction, so crucial for the working class in its struggle with capitalism, between the various forms of rule (democracy, dictatorship etc.)[45] and the class essence of all states. "Bourgeois theorists

---

[44]J. Stalin, "Political Report of the Central (Party) Committee to the XVIth Congress, 1930," in J. Hazard (ed.), *Soviet Legal Philosophy* (1951), *op. cit.,* p. 234.

[45]Marx himself had first appreciated the salience of this distinction in *The Eighteenth Brumaire of Louis Bonaparte* and *The Civil War in France.*

of the state," says Pashukanis, "conflate characteristics relating to the form of government and characteristics relating to the class nature of the state" (1932, p. 280). Following Lenin, Pashukanis stresses that the techniques of legal domination are less important than the goals to which they are directed. Soviet law, in each of its stages, was naturally different from the law of capitalist states. Further:

> ... law in the conditions of the proletarian dictatorship has always had the goal of protecting the interest of the working majority, the suppression of class elements hostile to the proletariat, and the defence of socialist construction ... As such it is radically different from bourgeois law despite the formal resemblance of individual statutes (1932, p. 293).

In the course of the "revolution from above" of forced collectivization and rapid industrialization, a politically chastened but still theoretically active Pashukanis tried unsuccessfully, as it transpired, to re-define his concept of the state during the transitional period. In effect, Pashukanis superimposed the Stalinist concept of the state in Soviet socio-economic development onto the remnants of his original theory of law. Then by simultaneously presiding over the theoretical articulation of the Stalinist state as well as the practical process of the withering away of criminal law, Pashukanis inevitably contributed to the growth of a jurisprudence of terror. As bourgeois criminal law and procedure were superseded in application by a simplistically vague and highly flexible "Soviet criminal policy"—shaped by Pashukanis and his associate Nikolai Krylenko through several proposed draft codes—legal forms were co-opted for extralegal purposes, judicial process was subordinated to political ends, and law itself was used to legitimate and rationalize terror. The jurisprudence of terror institutionalized and routinized political terror within the context of formal legalism. In effect, terror was legalized and the criminal process overtly politicized. Through the legalization of terror, the concomitant criminalization of a wide range of political (and even social) be-

haviour, and the politicization of the co-opted administration of justice, the jurisprudence of terror became a highly effective instrument of Party policy. Speaking in late 1930, Pashukanis expressed the basic premise of the jurisprudence of terror which he seemed to recognize as an inevitable stage on the road to communism and the ultimate withering away of the law. Rejecting the notion of a stable system of law, he argued for "political elasticity" and the imperative that Soviet "legislation possess maximum elasticity" since "for us revolutionary legality is a problem which is 99 per cent political."[46]

The inherent contradiction between the ideas of a strong state and weak criminal law did not become fully evident until the waning of the revolution from above was embodied in the XVIIth Party Congress's (1934) policy emphasis on the need for greater legal formality and stability in Soviet jurisprudence as a means of consolidating the gains of the previous turbulent years. Paradoxically, it was Vyshinsky, the Procurator-General of the U.S.S.R. and soon to become prosecutor of the major purge victims, who became the spearhead of Stalinist criticism of the adverse effect of Pashukanis' and Krylenko's legal nihilism on the administration of ordinary ("non-political") criminal justice.[47]

Similarly, Pashukanis and another associate Leonid Gintsburg exercised an equally strong influence on civil jurisprudence through their concept of economic law. Hazard, then an American student at Pashukanis' Moscow Institute of Soviet Law, subsequently reported:

> Law, concerning the rights of the individuals was relegated to a few hours at the end of the course in economic–administrative law and given apologetically as an unwelcome necessity for a few years due to the fact that capitalist relationships and bourgeois psychology had not yet been wholly eliminated.[48]

[46]E. B. Pashukanis, "The Situation on the Legal Theory Front" (1930), op. cit., pp. 278-280.

[47]See R. Sharlet, "Stalinism and Soviet Legal Culture," op. cit. f49.

[48]J. Hazard, "Housecleaning in Soviet Law," American Quarterly on the Soviet Union (1938), vol. 1, no. 1, p. 15.

The final two translations in the present volume illuminate how emasculated the brilliant insights of *The General Theory of Law and Marxism* had become after the XVIth Party Congress and the introduction of the second Five Year Plan. It is at this point that we no longer need to speculate on whether the intellectual revisions to the main thrust of Pashukanis' work were induced by strictly political and opportunist pressures. In the *Course on Soviet Economic Law,* written with Gintsburg and published in 1935, Pashukanis offers a lengthy, simplistic and functionalist account of the nature of Soviet economic law under the transitional conditions of socialism. Conceived within the manifest constraints to conform with the Stalinist interpretation of Marx's and Engels' brief and unsatisfactory analyses of the period transitional between capitalism and the higher phase of communism, the *Course* defines Soviet economic law as "*a special (specific) form of the policy of the proletarian state in the area of the organization of socialist production and Soviet commerce*" (Pashukanis and Gintsburg, 1935, p. 306).[49] Bourgeois law serves the interests of the capitalist class in capitalist production; Soviet law serves the interests of the proletariat organized as the ruling class under socialism. The special nature of the production policies (i.e. planning) of the proletarian state are revealed through the concept of socialist (revolutionary) legality. Bourgeois legality, according to Pashukanis and Gintsburg:

> is the will of the ruling class . . . directed at the support of the basic conditions of the capitalist mode of production. Socialist (revolutionary) legality expresses the will of the last of the exploited classes, which has taken power, of the proletariat. (1935, p. 314).

Just as criminal policy came to be regarded as counterproductive after the XVIIth Party Congress, so too economic law during the second

Five Year Plan began to encounter muted criticism from the direction of a countervailing tendency toward the need to return to the concept of contract (albeit a *planned* contract) as a method of stabilizing and more effectively managing the planning process. Pashukanis, as the principal theoretical exponent of both criminal policy and economic law, became increasingly politically vulnerable in the mid-1930s.

In "State and Law under Socialism," published on the eve of the new Constitution of 1936, Pashukanis weakly confronts the most serious criticism that the commodity exchange theory of law had always explicitly invited—that it was a left communist, or perhaps anarchist, theory which, if implemented, would greatly impede the construction and reproduction of socialist relations of production in the U.S.S.R. Pashukanis apologetically quotes Lenin's *State and Revolution* to the effect that:

> . . . we want a socialist revolution with people as they are now—with people who cannot do without subordination, without supervision, without "overseers and auditors" . . . it is inconceivable that people will immediately learn to work *without any legal norms* after the overthrow of capitalism (1936, p. 349)

STALINISM AND SOVIET JURISPRUDENCE

The demand for greater contractual discipline within the planned economy, the revival and strengthening of Soviet family law so long submerged within economic law, and, above all, the publication of the draft of a new constitution in June 1936, all clearly foreshadowed an impending major change in Soviet legal policy. The new constitutional right of ownership of personal property and the provisions for the first all-union civil and criminal codes implied the reinforcement rather than the withering of the law. Stalin's famous remark later that year that "stability of the laws is necessary for us now more than ever" signalled the new legal policy, and the promulgation of the Stalin Constitution a few weeks later,

---

[49]To Pashukanis' credit he still refused to recognize the concept of "proletarian law." But even this incorporated somewhat of a major retreat, however, by his terminological nicety of the "class law of the proletariat" (1935, p. 307).

in December 1936, formally opened the Stalinist era in the development of Soviet legal culture.[50]

As the symbol of the defeated revolution of the law Pashukanis was arrested and disappeared in January 1937. The purging of Pashukanis and his associates cleared the way for the re-articulation of the dormant Romanist legal ideals of stability, formality and professionalism. The process of re-building Soviet legal culture began immediately under the aegis of Vyshinsky, Pashukanis' successor as *doyen* of the legal profession. While Pashukanis had been the theorist of NEP legal culture, explaining its rise and predicting its demise, Vyshinsky, the practitioner, was its consolidator by reinforcing and converting it into the Soviet legal culture.[51]

Vyshinsky's critique of Pashukanis involves an intellectual contortionism replete with invective-laden and often self-contradictory statements.[52] Vyshinsky argues that law is neither a system of social relationships nor a form of production relationships. "Law," he stresses, "is the aggregate of rules of conduct—or norms; yet not of norms alone, but also of customs and rules of community living confirmed by state authority and coercively protected by that authority."[53]

Soviet socialist law, the argument continues, is radically unique in both form and content because:

> it is the will of our people elevated to the rank of a statute. In capitalist society, allusions to the will of the people served as a screen which veiled the ex-

ploiting nature of the bourgeois state. In the conditions of our country, the matter is different in principle: there has been formulated among us, a single and indestructible will of the Soviet people—manifested in the unparalleled unanimity with which the people vote at the elections to the Supreme Soviet of the U.S.S.R. and the Supreme Soviets of the union and autonomous republics . . .[54]

> The specific mark of Soviet law . . . is that it serves, in the true and actual sense of the word, the people—society—. . . In the U.S.S.R. for the first time in history the people—the toiling national masses themselves—are the masters of their fate, themselves ruling their state with no exploiters, no landlords, no capitalists.[55]

Law is now to be viewed as a set of normative prescriptions, enforced by the state (whose own character is unproblematic), in accord with Stalin's conception of the character and duration of the transitional phase. The conditions for the existence of Soviet socialist law are the necessity "to finish off the remnants of the dying classes and to organize defence against capitalist encirclement."[56] Soviet socialist law must incorporate and instill revolutionary legality and stability. "Why is stability of statutes essential? Because it reinforces the stability of the state order and of the state discipline, and multiples tenfold the powers of socialism . . ."[57]

Ignoring the internal class contradictions of the new Soviet state, Vyshinsky applauds Stalin's teaching that "the withering away of the state will come not through a weakening of the state authority but through its maximum intensification."[58] The *process* of withering away is of necessity postponed until:

> all will learn to get along without special rules defining the conduct of people under the threat of punishment and with the aid of constraint; when people are so accustomed to observe the fundamen-

[50]See R. Sharlet, "Stalinism and Soviet Legal Culture," *op. cit.,* pp. 168–169.

[51]See R. Sharlet, "Stalinism and Soviet Legal Culture," *op. cit.,* p. 169.

[52]This critique is largely contained in four sources. See A. Ia. Vyshinsky, "The Fundamental Tasks of the Science of Soviet Socialist Law" (1938), in J. Hazard (ed.), *Soviet Legal Philosophy* (1951), *op. cit.,* pp. 303–341; "The Marxist Theory of State and Law," *Bolshevik* (1938); "The XVIIIth Congress of the CPSU and the Tasks of the Theory of Socialist Law," *Sovetskoe gosudarstvo* (1939), no. 3; J. Hazard (ed.), *The Law of the Soviet State* (1948), Macmillan, New York, translated by H. Babb.

[53]A. Vyshinsky, "Fundamental Tasks of the Science of Soviet Socialist Law" (1938), *op. cit.,* p. 337.

[54]*Ibid.,* p. 339.

[55]A. Vyshinsky, *The Law of the Soviet State* (1948), *op. cit.,* p. 75.

[56]*Ibid.,* p. 62.

[57]*Ibid.,* p. 51.

[58]*Ibid.,* p. 62.

tal rules of community life that they will fulfil them without constraint of any sort.[59]

The legal culture of NEP along with the statutory legislation of the intervening years, so long castigated as bourgeois, was redefined as a socialist legal culture. The need to systematize the legal culture, so long obstructed as inconsistent with its withering away, became the new agenda for the legal profession. Jurists, driven from the law schools, the research institutes, and the legal press by the revolution of the law, reappeared as participants in the reconstruction of legal education and research. Disciplines banished from the law curriculum by the radical jurists were reintroduced beginning in the spring term of 1937. New course syllabi and textbooks for every branch of law, especially those eliminated or suppressed by the legal transfer culture, began to appear with great rapidity. New editions of earlier texts were purged of Pashukanis' influence and quickly re-issued. Carrying out the mandate of Article 14 of the Stalin Constitution, numerous jurists were mobilized to prepare drafts for the all-union civil and criminal codes. Finally, a vulgar neo-positivist jurisprudence, based on "class relations" and largely derived from the Stalin Constitution and even the *Short Course*, replaced the tradition of revolutionary legal theory epitomized by Pashukanis.[60]

By way, not of conclusion, but as preparation for future work, we must briefly outline the importance of a question confronted but unanswered in Pashukanis' project that is also unanswered, and unfortunately unaddressed, in our own time. How, precisely, are we to understand the historical configuration of state and law in social formations where capitalist property has been abolished but where communism has by no

means yet been achieved? How are we to resolve the apparent paradox that the legal practices of most, if not all, social formations dominated by the political rule of the proletariat have included the form, and very often the content, of the legal rules typically associated with capitalist modes of production?

To explain this question, as did Stalinism, in terms of capitalist encirclement and the construction of socialism in one country, is to avoid the issue. This is so for at least two reasons. First, as Marx always and Lenin usually argued, under socialism the proletarian dictatorship has two features which radically demarcate it from all other state *dictatures:* the extent of its powers and the duration of its domination must be limited, and these must ultimately inhere in the consent of its citizens. These features are structural preconditions of socialism, and without wishing to lapse into utopianism or idealism, they seem necessary irrespective of the specific economic, political or ideological histories of a given social formation. This would therefore exclude that common explanation of the intensity and longevity of the Soviet polity which pointed to the essential continuity of pre- and post-revolutionary political practices. Further, these qualities of the proletarian dictatorship—clearly discernible as the early Roman, and not the post-Reformation concept of dictatorship[61]—must dialectically contain the capacity for self-transformation. State and legal forms, even while they are actively utilized by the proletariat or by the party which truly represents it, must simultaneously be in the process of immanent transformation. As Lenin himself put it in 1919, "The communist organization of social labour, the first step towards which is socialism, rests, and will do so more and more as time goes on, on the free and conscious discipline of the working people themselves."[62] As such, we are convinced that only intellectual sophistry could

---

[59]*Ibid.,* p. 52.

[60]Published in November 1938, *The History of the Communist Party of the Soviet Union (Bolshevik): Short Course* almost immediately became the Stalinist forerunner of what, for China later, Mao's *Little Red Book* was the functional equivalent.

[61]See particularly, V. I. Lenin, "A Great Beginning" (1919), *LCW,* vol. 29, p. 420.

[62]*Ibid.,* p. 420.

assert that, at least since the late 1920s, the proletarian dictatorship in the U.S.S.R. is a *dictatorship* (in the classical sense) of the *proletariat*.

The second reason in part involves the absence of the conditions necessary to the truth of the first. If the historical development of the U.S.S.R. cannot be characterized as the development of the dictatorship of the proletariat, then how can it best be understood? If it is the case that capitalist property relationships have been abolished, and that they have been replaced by state property and collective farm property as the 1936 Constitution proclaimed, then one must inquire how it is that the agencies of the proletarian dictatorship have been used not only to prevent the external threats posed by capitalist encirclement, but much more so to repress what are perceived as internal dangers? This, to us, can only be explained by the endemic existence of class contradictions within the U.S.S.R. At the very least, therefore, we must reject the mechanistic identification of transformations in legal forms of capitalist property with the abolition of exploiting classes.[63] What is needed is a

transformation in social relationships themselves. We are left with an ironic twist to Lenin's dictum, when applied to the U.S.S.R. since his death, that the dictatorship of the proletariat is the continuation of the class struggle in new forms. This was the thrust of Pashukanis' own concern.

REFERENCES

These texts have been translated in P. Beirne and R. Sharlet (Eds.), *Pashukanis: Selected Writings on Marxism and Law*, translated by Peter Maggs (London: Academic Press, 1980).

Pashukanis, E. B., 1924. *The General Theory of Law and Marxism* in ibid., pp. 40-131.

_____, 1927. "The Marxist Theory of Law and the Construction of Socialism," pp. 188-199.

_____, 1929. "Economics and Legal Regulation," pp. 237-272.

_____, 1932. "The Marxist Theory of State and Law," pp. 275-301.

_____, 1935. *A Course on Soviet Economic Law*, edited with L. Ia. Gintsburg, pp. 304-345.

_____, 1936. "State and Law under Socialism," pp. 348-361.

---

[63]Any distinction between economic and legal property faces the logical difficulty that economic property is usually conceptualized in legal terms (ownership, use, possession etc.). This problem has recently been posed, unsatisfactorily, by several authors. See E. Balibar, *On the Dictatorship of the Proletariat* (1977), New Left Books, London, pp. 66-77; C. Bettelheim, *Class Struggles in the USSR 1917-1923* (1976), Monthly Review Press, New York, pp. 20-32; A. Glucksman, "The Althusserian Theatre," *New Left Review* (1972), p. 68;

N. Poulantzas, *Political Power and Social Classes* (1973), New Left Books, London, p. 72. But, see the interesting and important reformulations contained in G. A. Cohen, *Karl Marx's Theory of History: A Defence* (1978), Princeton University Press, Princeton; and P. Corrigan, H. Ramsay and D. Sayer, *Socialist Construction and Marxist Theory* (1978), Monthly Review Press, New York and London.

MARXIST THEORY, THE RULE OF LAW AND SOCIALISM

STEVE REDHEAD

If I have argued elsewhere that the rule of law is an "unqualified human good" (Whigs and Hunters, 1975) I have done so as a historian and a materialist. The rule of law, in this sense, must always be historically, culturally and, in general, nationally specific.

E. P. Thompson[1]

Since Pashukanis considered the economic institution of commodity exchange to be peculiar to capitalism, he concluded that private law and its derivative, the legal state, were exclusively capitalist phenomena. He argued that law in Soviet society was "bourgeois law," which was primarily necessary for the regulation of the capitalist elements of the NEP economy. From his point of view, there neither was nor could be in the future any such phenomenon as "proletarian" or "socialist" law.

R. Sharlet[2]

The increasing intellectual and political crisis of Marxist theory, from the 1960s onwards, is perhaps best signified by Marxist debate about the "rule of law." The need for a more adequate Marxist account of "legality" under capitalism and socialism[3] has constantly been emphasized

in this period, reflecting, initially, the "rediscovery" of what Marx and Engels (and, depending on political preference, Lenin, Stalin, Trotsky, etc.) actually said about law, and then, later, a certain dissatisfaction with such enigmatic and often contradictory statements of the major figures of classical Marxism.

It is perhaps not surprising, given the desire to develop as sophisticated a critique of "bourgeois" *legal* philosophy as that already being forged in the spheres of politics and economics, that when the work of the Bolshevik jurist E. B. Pashukanis came to be resurrected in the West[4] it should be seen as a ready-made foundation[5] for a historical materialist theory of

[1]E. P. Thompson, "Trial by Jury," *New Society,* 29 November 1979.

[2]R. Sharlet, "Pashukanis and the Withering Away of Law in the USSR," in S. Fitzpatrick (Ed.), *Cultural Revolution in Russia 1928–1931* (Bloomington: Indiana University Press, 1978).

[3]Both "potential," and "actually existing" or "transitional" socialist societies.

[4]First in the late 1960s and early 1970s in the Federal Republic of Germany and West Berlin as part of the attempt to develop a historical materialist theory of the state. See J. Holloway and S. Picciotto, "Introduction: Towards a Materialist Theory of the State," in J. Holloway and S. Picciotto (Eds.), *State and Capital: A Marxist Debate* (London: Edward Arnold, 1978).

[5]Much as Karl Renner's *The Institutions of Private Law and Their Social Functions* (London: Routledge and Kegan Paul, 1949) had earlier been seen as the "classic" text on Marxist theory of law. However, Renner's claim to be midwife to the embryonic legal theory within Marx's writings (*Capital,* in particular) is more dubious than that of Pashukanis. Nevertheless, just as Pashukanis' work must be seen in the context of Russia in the 1920s and 1930s, no proper understanding of Renner's contribution to Marxist scholarship is possible without situating his legal theory within the movement of Austro-Marxism. T. Bottomore and P. Goode (Eds.), *Austro-Marxism* (Oxford: Clarendon Press, 1978) and R. Loew, "The Politics of Austro-Marxism," *New Left Review,* 118 November/December 1979, enable a start to be made in this task. See also R. Kinsey, "Karl Renner, Austro-Marxism and

law. Much debate has since raged over the precise nature and usefulness of Pashukanis' theory, particularly in *The General Theory of Law and Marxism*. In this essay, I want instead to concentrate on the implications of what is perhaps Pashukanis's most lasting contribution to Marxist thought, namely, the question of the withering away of law.[6] In order to assess the significance of positions on law derived from Pashukanis, which deny the necessity and possibility of any form of "proletarian" or "socialist" legality, it is important to consider the intervention in the debate over the "rule of law" by the English social historian, E. P. Thompson. In my view, Thompson, despite the problems of his own theoretical analysis of law, has paved the way for a significant engagement in a political "space" that has been previously abandoned by the socialist movement to such an extent that phrases like "law and order" and the "rule of law" have become almost exclusively a right-wing province. Such a strategy of conceding a certain terrain to the growing political forces of reaction receives considerable theoretical justification from the commodity exchange school of law, headed in the 1920s and 1930s by Pashukanis.

I. THE RULE OF LAW AND MARXIST LEGAL THEORY: E. P. THOMPSON AND BEYOND

In this section of the text it is necessary to review Thompson's radical intervention in Marxist theory of law, which began with the "infamous last ten pages"[7] of *Whigs and Hunters* and has continued almost unabated since.[8] The focus of

much of this writing is the political necessity of defending "civil liberties"—for example, trial by jury—against the encroachment of increasingly authoritarian states, both in capitalist and other social formations. Thompson, as we shall see, is acutely aware that the question of the rule of law cannot be restricted just to the nature of the relationship between the legal form and the commodity form, as Pashukanis and his followers would have it. The question of "socialist legality" is always implicitly posed by Thompson's tantalizing defence of hard-won legal rights within capitalism.

Let us first consider what it is that Thompson says about the "rule of law" that is so startling and such a radical break from previous Marxist theorizing on law. His position within a Marxist theory of law, against what he sees as the "structuralist"[9] enemy, is neatly summarized in

---

the Law," paper delivered to British Sociological Association "Law and Society" Conference, University of Warwick, England, April 1979, for an exploration of this problem.

[6]I am grateful for the comments of those who attended a reading of an earlier version of part of this essay (particularly Ronnie Warrington, who emphasized this aspect of Pashukanis' writings, though he may not agree with my interpretation of its significance for contemporary politics) at the Communist University of London, July 1979.

[7](Harmondsworth: Penguin, 1977), pp. 258–269, first published by Allen Lane in 1975.

[8]E. P. Thompson, "The Poverty of Theory," in *The Poverty of Theory, and Other Essays* (London: Merlin Press, 1978),

especially pp. 288–289; "The Rule of Law in English History," *Bulletin of the Haldane Society of Socialist Lawyers* no. 10, Spring 1979; "The State and Its Enemies," *New Society*, October 19, 1978; "The Secret State," *Race and Class*, XX, 3 (1979); "Introduction" to J. Griffith and H. Harman, *Justice Deserted: The Subversion of the Jury* (London: National Council for Civil Liberties, 1979); "On the New Issue of Postal Stamps," *New Society*, November 8, 1979; "Law and Order and the Police," *New Society*, November 15, 1979; "The Rule of the Judges," *New Society*, November 22, 1979; "Trial by Jury," *New Society*, November 29, 1979; "Anarchy and Culture," *New Society*, December 6, 1979; "The End of An Episode," *New Society*, December 13, 1979.

[9]Although Thompson is sometimes accurate in his caricature of Althusser's influence on Marxist, and "post-Marxist," legal theorizing, for all his brilliant polemic, Swiftian irony, and spirited defence of his historians' trade, much of his "structuralism" is a straw man, or at least has become such in recent years. For instance, B. Hindess and P. Hirst have made a radical break with Althusser's project in several recent publications: *Mode of Production and Social Formation* (London: Macmillan, 1977); (with A. Cutler and A. Hussain) *Marx's 'Capital' and Capitalism Today*, Vols. 1 and 2 (London: Routledge and Kegan Paul, 1977 and 1978); (Hirst alone) *On Law and Ideology* (London: Macmillan, 1979). See also Hirst's own reply to Thompson's "The Poverty of Theory," "The Necessity of Theory," in *Economy and Society*, 8, no. 4 (November 1979). Although these texts raise new problems of their own, and indeed are subversive of much that is taken for granted as "adequate" Marxist theory, they are not easily answered by Thompson's attack. Ironically, in parts, they do in fact coincide with Thompson's own efforts to take seriously the *specific effectivity* of the rule of law, as I shall indicate later in the text of this essay.

Thompson's own last ten pages. In this conclusion to his "excursion into the murky waters" of the eighteenth century to study an old English statute, the infamous Black Act of 1723,[10] he proceeds to sketch a Marxism—in his view, of Althusserian parentage—that conceptualizes law as:

> perhaps more clearly than any other cultural or institutional artifact, by definition a part of the "superstructure" adapting itself to the necessities of an "infrastructure" of productive forces and productive relations. As such it is clearly an instrument of the *de facto* ruling class.... [T]he rule of law is only another mask for the rule of a class.[11]

He then moves onto his "theoretical ledge," which "would accept, as it must, some part of the 'Marxist–Structuralist' critique." He claims that "indeed" some parts of *Whigs and Hunters* "have confirmed the class-bound and mystifying functions of the law." However, Thompson says that he would reject its "ulterior reductionism" and would modify Althusser's "typology of superior and inferior (but determining) structures." He then points to the problem of analytically "separating off the law as a whole and placing it in some typological structure." This is the crux, as he shows in "The Poverty of Theory," of his quarrel with the legal theory, detected by Thompson, in Althusserian accounts[12]:

For I found that law did not keep politely to a "level" but was at *every* bloody level; it was imbricated within the mode of production and productive relations themselves (as property-rights, as definitions of agrarian practice) and it was simultaneously present in the philosophy of Locke; it intruded brusquely within alien catagories, reappearing bewigged and gowned in the guise of ideology: it danced a cotillion with religion, moralising over the theatre of Tyburn; it was an arm of politics and politics was one of its arms; it was an academic discipline, subjected to the rigour of its own automomous logic; it contributed to the definition of the self-identity both of rulers and of ruled; above all, it afforded an arena for class struggle, within which alternative notions of law were fought out.[13]

This "imbricationist"[14] view of law has come to be associated with Thompson. What is at stake here, as I have indicated,[15] is not so much the accuracy of Thompson's perception of Althusserian Marxist contributions to theories of law but, rather, the exact nature of his own conception of the problem of the rule of law.

In the social history of the emergence of the Black Act, Thompson finds a law that expresses the "ascendancy" of a ruling class. But that is not to say that he found that the rulers needed law to oppress the ruled, while the ruled needed no law. The crucial conflict, which Thompson uncovered, was over the definition of eighteenth-

---

[10]For an attempt to draw out the lessons of the Black Act for American criminal justice of the mid-1970s, see G. Ray, "Book Review of *Albion's Fatal Tree* (D. Hay et al., Eds., Harmondsworth: Penguin, 1977) and *Whigs and Hunters*," in *Crime and Social Justice*, Fall/Winter 1976.

[11]*Whigs and Hunters*, op. cit., p. 259.

[12]There is a need for careful consideration of the subtleties and inconsistencies of Thompson's debate with what he regards as the "Stalinist" tendencies of Althusserian theory. Clearly this task goes much further than conflict over what theoretical progress can be made in the area of legal theories. There is already a vast literature emerging on the "culturalism" versus "structuralism" positions, which is tending to strengthen the impression (which Thompson himself has played no small part in creating) that these are "schools" that have been already accurately characterized by the original protagonists (e.g., Althusser and Thompson) and that must be staunchly adhered to on one side or the other. R. Johnson has pointed out that this is not necessarily the case: "Culture and

the Historians" and "Three Problematics: Elements of a Theory of Working-Class Culture," in J. Clarke et al. (Eds.), *Working Class Culture: Studies in History and Theory* (London: Hutchinson, 1979); "Edward Thompson, Eugene Genovese and Socialist-Humanist History," *History Workshop*, 6 (1978). See also the ensuing debate: K. McClelland: "Some Comments on Richard Johnson," *History Workshop*, 7 (1979); G. Williams, "In Defence of History," *History Workshop*, 7 (1979); Simon Clarke, "Socialist Humanism and the Critique of Economism," *History Workshop*, 8 (1979); G. McLennan, "Richard Johnson and His Critics: Towards a Constructive Debate," *History Workshop*, 8 (1979).

[13]"The Poverty of Theory," op. cit., p. 288.

[14]For a comprehensive review of Thompson, Hay, et al.'s social history of law contrasted with more orthodox "social histories" of law, see D. Sugarman, "Theory and Practice in Law and History," extended version of paper given to British Sociological Association "Law and Society" Conference, University of Warwick, England, April 1979.

[15]See footnote 9.

century property rights. The ruled, he states, would actually fight for their rights by means of law, for "as long as it remained possible." We have then, against the background of the English "people's" struggle in the sixteenth and seventeenth centuries against royal absolutism, Thompson's now well-known "contradictory" conclusion that law cannot simply be equated with class power.

It is this contradictory nature of law in Thompson's theory that needs to be dwelt upon, for it contains the kernel of his approach to the rule of law. How can law be both of a class and yet *not* of a class? How can a Marxist social historian of world renown come to the apparently naive conclusion that, despite its partial class nature, legality is a "human good"? The answer lies in a passage that Thompson himself has fondly quoted[16] from *Whigs and Hunters* in support of his argument that the question of the rule of law be taken seriously by Marxism and not dismissed as merely a "mask for the rule of a class." It is worth quoting at length:

> ... the inhibitions upon power imposed by law seem to me a legacy as substantial as any handed down from the struggles of the seventeenth century to the eighteenth and a true and important cultural achievement of the agrarian and mercantile bourgeoisie, and of their supporting yeoman and artisans.
>
> More than this, the notion of the regulation and reconciliation of conflicts through the rule of law—and the elaboration of rules and procedures which on occasion, made some approximate approach towards the ideal—seems to me a cultural achievement of universal significance. I do not lay any claim as to the abstract, extra-historical impartiality of these rules. In a context of gross class inequalities, the equity of the law must always be in some part sham. Transplanted as it was to even more inequitable contexts, this law could become an instrument of imperialism. For this law has found its way to a good many parts of the globe. But even here the rules and rhetoric have imposed some inhibitions upon the imperial power. ... I am not

starry-eyed about this at all. This has not been a star-struck book. I am insisting only upon the obvious point, which some modern Marxists have overlooked, that there is a difference between arbitrary power and the rule of law. We ought to expose the shams and inequities which may be concealed beneath this law. But the rule of law itself, the imposing of effective inhibitions upon power and the defence of the citizen from power's all-intrusive claims, seems to me to be an unqualified human good. To deny or belittle this good is, in this dangerous century when the resources and pretensions of power continue to enlarge, a desperate error of intellectual abstraction. More than this, it is a self-fulfilling error, which encourages us to give up the struggle against bad laws and classbound procedures, and to disarm ourselves before power. It is to throw away a whole inheritance of struggle *about* law and within the forms of law, whose continuity can never be fractured without bringing men and women into immediate danger.[17]

I make no apology for spending time on Thompson's own words. It is important to pay attention to what he has actually written as he has been misquoted[18] and misunderstood. The argument he puts forward is in many ways an anathema to the left and, as such, has been susceptible to abuse and misuse. But to reproduce his argument is not to plead a defence; at least not entirely. There are significant problems with Thompson's thesis. Before coming to an assessment of its value, and contrasting it with Pashukanis's view of the problem of legality and socialism, it is important to examine them.

First, as reviewers[19] have pointed out, those "last ten pages" of *Whigs and Hunters* rest rather

[16]"The Rule of Law in English History," op. cit.

[17]*Whigs and Hunters,* op. cit., pp. 265–266.

[18]For instance, see the debate in the *Times Literary Supplement* over the use of Thompson's "rule of law" thesis in J. Griffith *The Politics of the Judiciary* (London: Fontana, 1977); especially, K. Minogue, "The Biases of the Bench," *Times Literary Supplement,* January 1978; K. Minogue, "The Politics of the Judiciary," *Times Literary Supplement,* February 3, 1978; E. J. Hobsbawm, "The Politics of the Judiciary," *Times Literary Supplement,* February 10, 1978.

[19]For example, G. Pearson, "Eighteenth Century English Criminal Law," *British Journal of Law and Society,* 3, no. 1 (1976).

uneasily on top of the preceding 250 or so; not only this, but also the companion volume of essays on the social history of law and crime in eighteenth-century England[20] frequently contradicts the "rule of law" thesis. The historical evidence, unearthed by the labors of Thompson and his social history colleagues, and which Thompson is fond of using against Althusserian Marxism—that is, the "facts"—simply do not back up the argument that he advances. As he himself acknowledges:

> This study has been centered upon a bad law, drawn by bad legislators, and enlarged by the interpretations of bad judges. No defence, in terms of natural justice, can be offered for anything in the history of the Black Act. But even this study does not prove that all law as such is bad. Even this law bound the rulers to act only in the ways which its forms permitted; they had difficulties with these forms; they could not always override the sense of natural justice of the jurors; and we may imagine how Walpole would have acted against Jacobites or against disturbers of Richmond Park, if he had been subject to no forms of law at all.[21]

The argument about the rule of law being beneficial, or an unqualified human good, rests, then, as an ill-fitting conclusion to the study of a "bad" law. Nonetheless, we should be grateful to Thompson for raising the issue in such a bold manner; it is too important to be seen as mere afterthought.

A more significant objection to Thompson needs to be made, however. This concerns the whole question of the definition of the "rule of law." In popular discourse the phrase is rarely defined; we *know* what it means. In judicial discourse there is a similar lack of conscious definition. To take one example at random, Donaldson J. in the now-defunct National Industrial Relations Court (the NIRC as it was "affectionately" known) in England:

> All courts exist to uphold the rule of law. . . . The

justification for law, the courts and the rule of law is that they protect us from unfair and oppressive actions. . . . If the rule of law is to have any meaning, the courts must in the last resort take action against these few ("who want to use the laws which suit them and disobey those which do not") and impose some penalty.[22]

The "rule of law" is also widely used in the "law and order" campaigns[23] in capitalist countries in the 1970s by politicians and the media, as well as the judiciary. How, then, does Thompson mean it to be understood? There is also a tendency in his usage to take its meaning for granted. Where he does take the trouble to specifically define it, it is emphasized as meaning "imposing of effective inhibitions upon power and the defence of the citizen from power's all-intrusive claims,"[24] as we have seen. This clearly begs too many of the critical questions, not least the nature of "power." For the most part, however, it is evident that Thompson sees the rule of law as the opposite side of the coin to "arbitrary" power or authority. This is, in my view, the most incisive though flawed, incisive point that he has made, whether in discussing eighteenth- or twentieth-century Britain or twentieth-century Russia or Eastern European satellites. For Thompson, no one can afford to ignore this distinction, though many have done so to their—and others'—cost. Indeed, the great bulk of Thompson's prolific output over the years has contained this direct political message. It is dedicated to reminding Marxists, and others, of the dangers of ignoring that distinction in practice. It is precisely this that is the source of his "political" tirade against Althusserianism, and the basis for understanding his own political

[20] *Albion's Fatal Tree,* op. cit.

[21] *Whigs and Hunters,* op. cit., p. 267.

[22] *Heatons Transport Ltd.* v. *Transport and General Workers Union,* 1972, 2 All E. R. 1222.

[23] In the Federal Republic of Germany, for instance [see S. Cobler, *Law, Order and Politics in West Germany* (Harmondsworth: Penguin, 1978)] and, especially, Britain. The most detailed theoretical account of law and order campaigns in Britain is itself heavily dependent on a reworking of Thompson's contribution to Marxist theory of law: S. Hall, C. Critcher, T. Jefferson, J. Clarke, and B. Roberts, *Policing the Crisis: Mugging, the State and Law and Order* (London: Macmillan, 1978), particularly Ch. 7.

[24] *Whigs and Hunters,* op. cit., p. 266.

trajectory[25]—that is, his "departure" from the Communist Party of Great Britain after the Hungary crisis in 1956 and his continuing attempt to preserve a libertarian socialist tradition. Thus, it is at the heart of a great deal of his writing, but in *Whigs and Hunters* and beyond he has made it crystal clear with regard to the law. The "rule of law" is manifestly, then, for Thompson, about law, legality, equity, and so on, as against the arbitrary use of power.

As has already been seen, Thompson feels he has to give his "adversary"—the caricatured "Structuralist" theory of law—its due; to some extent, at least. The law often is, and certainly was in the case of the Black Act, "ideological" and assimilated to the "state apparatus of a ruling class," Thompson admits, although his own refusal to rigorously, and self-consciously, define concepts[26] and phrases such as these in a clear and unambiguous manner is particularly infuriating. But he also wants to say, whether or not there is much concrete evidence in his study of the Black Act, that law is "good" as well as "bad." It is "good" in that it can be used *against* that ruling class and in that eighteenth-century subordinate classes in England *did* use it as "long as it remained possible." Law is for Thompson caught by its own logic; the ruling classes are trapped in their own modes of domination; not all states, laws, police, and so on are "bad."

But we surely need to go further. What are these "good" elements of law in their historical "specificity"? In at least one piece[27] Thompson has enumerated them as "habeas corpus," the jury system, rights of the press and of speech, and

rights of trade union organization, for instance. It is clear from Thompson's recent outpourings since *Whigs and Hunters* that of these the jury, especially, is regarded as a major battleground. As has been documented,[28] at the very moment of its "democratization," the English jury system, whose history Thompson has so avidly followed, has come under attack. Increasingly in the 1970s, a decade that saw the "property qualification" for jury membership abolished, thereby massively changing the sex and age composition of English juries, Thompson and other defenders of civil liberties have had to painfully record the "subversion" of defendants' rights to challenge jurors, to ask jurors occupations and so on, while simultaneously witnessing the development of overt jury vetting by the prosecution.[29] Thompson has taken great delight in showing that this "precapitalist" legal institution ("the jury system originated when the bourgeoisie was not yet a glint in feudalism's eye")[30] not only prevented the terror of the capital offences created by the Black Act becoming a manifest reality in the eighteenth century by refusing to convict on many of the prosecutions that were brought, but is also a vital means of struggle within the law in the twentieth century. It is particularly vital in overtly "political" trials in Thompson's view; it is also part of the campaign against the growth of the "unaccountable and unrepresentative state," an increasingly common worldwide form of political representation. The libertarian tradition that Thompson seeks to preserve finds the "good" aspects of law, in particular, the jury system, a crucial arena for radical political intervention.[31]

Taking this as an example of the "rule of law" in its "good" hat (for instance, the jury limiting

---

[25]See Thompson, Foreword and Afternote in "The Poverty of Theory," op. cit., and J. Ree, "Socialist Humanism," *Radical Philosophy*, 9 (Winter 1974).

[26]Thompson's peculiar skill is to weave his conceptual framework into the "empirical" detail precisely *without* separating it off as an "abstraction" or distinct entity; this frequently leaves the reader crying out for a glossary of concepts, similar to those often provided with "structuralist" texts, so that his theoretical insights could be employed more widely in relation to issues other than those Thompson has dealt with.

[27]"The Rule of Law in English History," op. cit.

[28]Griffith and Harman, *Justice Deserted*, op. cit.

[29]At the time of writing, this issue is being increasingly confused by English court decisions.

[30]"The Rule of Law in English History," op. cit.

[31]I have argued elsewhere that recent "socio-legal" research on the English jury has ignored or misunderstood the political importance of the jury as an arena of struggle; see S. Redhead, "Book Review of J. Baldwin and M. McConville: *Jury Trials*," *Modern Law Review*, 42 (November 1979).

the arbitrary right of the state to prosecute for "political" offences), the problem of the definition that Thompson has given to the phrase is clearly demonstrated. Thompson's distinction between the rule of law and arbitrary, extralegal power fails to adequately take into account the different *forms* of the "rule of law." Unfortunately for Thompson, it is not necessarily the case that all law applies logical intervention with reference to standards of universality and equality, as he seems to suggest in *Whigs and Hunters;* witness Nazi law, for instance. Particular forms of the rule of law in eighteenth-century England did not appear to achieve this to a very great extent either, though they may have done so more thoroughly in the two centuries following the industrial revolution. The jury in the eighteenth century, and earlier, may well have been an important bulwark against the arbitrary power of the state. Thompson shows this, in certain cases, to be so. It does not follow that the jury in the twentieth century necessarily performs the same function.[32] The same goes for other aspects of the "rule of law" that Thompson has selected. While contributing an emphatic warning, to those who would listen, that it is crucial to remember the distinction between arbitrary authority and the rule of law, Thompson has not always seemed aware of the different forms of "legality" though he has suggested a further distinction between the "rhetoric of law" and the "rule of law." Recently, however, perhaps in recognition of a problem in his work, he has in fact added, rhetorically at least, a missing dimension in his discussion of the rule of law:

> There is no such abstract entity as the Rule of Law, if by this is meant some ideal presence aloof from the ruck of history, which it is the business of judges to "administer" and of policemen to "enforce." That is all ideology. It used to be the ideology of kings and despots. It is now the ideology of the authoritarian state. . . . If I have argued elsewhere that the

rule of law is an "unqualified human good" (*Whigs and Hunters,* 1975) I have done so as a historian and a materialist. The rule of law, in this sense, must always be historically, culturally and, in general, nationally specific. It concerns the conduct of social life, and the regulation of conflicts, according to rules of law which are exactly defined and have palpable and material evidences—which rules attain towards consensual assent and are subject to interrogation and reform.[33]

Here, then, is the high point of Thompson's intervention in the debate over the "rule of law"; that "rule of law," in all its forms, must be distinguished from arbitrary power.

I have suggested that it is necessary to assess the significance of Thompson's work on the "rule of law" within previous attempts to understand law from a Marxist perspective. I have indicated some parts of Thompson's thesis, where he has made advances and where problems are generated, but not so far "situated" his radical intervention within Marxist theories of legality. Previous Marxist attempts to theorize law have been notoriously "reductionist" in general and "economistic" in particular. They have usually taken one of two forms, stressing either the mystifying nature of law, masking the reality of class power with an "ideological" face, or the coercive nature of law, that is, its use as an instrument by ruling classes[34] (or both; there is no reason why such conceptions should be mutually exclusive). One alternative to such economistic conceptions of law, which would see the need to theorize law as a specific discourse and a specific practice,[35] may conceivably lead to a rejection of the conceptual framework of classical Marxism in its entirety.[36] It has claimed that:

[32]See N. Blake, "Juries and Civil Liberties: A Political History," *Bulletin of the Haldane Society of Socialist Lawyers,* no. 11, Autumn 1979.

[33]"Trial by Jury," op. cit.

[34]See M. Cain and A. Hunt, *Marx and Engels on Law* (London: Academic Press, 1979), pp. ix–xi.

[35]B. Edelman, *Ownership of the Image: Elements for a Marxist Theory of Law* (London: Routledge and Kegan Paul, 1979), attempts to use Althusser's notion of "interpellation" of subjects to accomplish this task.

[36]Cutler et al., *Marx's 'Capital' and Capitalism Today,* Vols. 1 and 2, op. cit.

Marxists have classically considered law as being merely the juridical expression of the relations of production and the relations of actual possession involved therein.... Such an analysis is naively apolitical; law becomes an "expression" a recognition of what is, rather than an arena of struggle, a form with potential effects.[37]

In many senses this injunction to take seriously the specific effectivity of national legal systems is curiously close to Thompson's imbricationist view of the "rule of law"; the irony is that the theoretical frameworks within which such statements are made emerge from such different, and antagonistic schools of Marxism.

Thompson's difference from more obvious forms of reductionism in Marxist legal theory is not difficult to recognize. What about the more sophisticated Marxism that has developed in the last decade, taking Pashukanis as a touchstone? The work of the C.S.E.[38] has been in sharp contrast to both the crudely reductionist theories of law previously developed within Marxism, *and* Althusserian and "post-Althusserian"[39] developments. Although Thompson's polemic against "Structuralism" is championed by the C.S.E. "school," his theory of law receives severe criticism. Picciotto,[40] for instance, sees Thompson as defending a "bourgeois" individualism that in his view defuses "legal" struggles into "bourgeois" legal rights. Despite Picciotto's perceptive recognition of the historical specificity of the forms of the "rule of law"—for instance, he, too, stresses the point that the function of the jury in the English legal system changes significantly over time—the castigation of Thompson as simply an antistatist, bourgeois individualist, albeit of a

left-wing variety, needs considerably more argument. Nevertheless, there is a crucial consequence of Thompson's vagueness over the forms of the "rule of law" that emerges here. The "rights" that Thompson conceives to be part of the "rule of law" in English society are not all necessarily of the same kind, nor do they form an aggregate of "freedoms" that have evolved with the progressive advancements of capitalism. As Hall[41] has argued, what are sometimes referred to as:

> ... "natural rights" were generated in the struggle of the rising commercial classes against arbitrary and absolutist power. They constitute one of the great historic achievements of a rising bourgeoisie. But they were, of course, predicated on a particular form of society—market societies, societies of private property, of "contract" and free exchange and rooted in a "possessive individualist" image of human nature. Not only were the poor, the property-less, the unenfranchised and women not thought fit and proper subjects of this naturalistic universe; the very form in which "liberty" was conceived was *intrinsically hostile* to democracy. Professor Macpherson has shown, definitively, that this main liberal tradition was either "undemocratic or anti-democratic." ... These natural rights had to be profoundly transformed and others which were utterly foreign to the universe of natural rights had to be defined and fought for.... We are arguing, then, that the civil rights and freedoms which make our society what it is are rights which were defined and won in struggle against the dominant interests in society, not bestowed on society by them.

Thus it can be emphasized again that the "rule of law" that Thompson talks about in the context of the Black Act is not at all the same, in form, as that which is perceived as a site of struggle today. It has been massively transformed, almost beyond recognition.

The forms of legality must, as Thompson has somewhat belatedly remembered, be analyzed "specifically," that is, historically, culturally, and nationally. Whereas the Marxist theory of law

[37]Ibid., Vol. 2, pp. 247–248.

[38]That is, the Conference of Socialist Economists; see issues of C. S. E. journal, *Capital and Class,* and National Deviancy Conference/Conference of Socialist Economists, *Capitalism and the Rule of Law* (London: Hutchinson, 1979).

[39]Hirst, in Appendix 2 of *On Law and Ideology,* op. cit., emphasizes the theoretical difference between Pashukanis and the enterprise pursued in *Marx's 'Capital' and Capitalism Today,* op. cit.

[40]S. Picciotto, "The Theory of the State, Class Struggle and the Rule of Law," in *Capitalism and the Rule of Law,* op. cit.

[41]S. Hall, *Drifting into a Law and Order Society* (London: Cobden Trust, 1980), pp. 8–10.

derived—at least initially—from the writings of Pashukanis is concerned to analyze these forms of the "rule of law" with the aid of Pashukanis' general theory of law as a specific form of commodity society, it is not committed to a search for a theory of socialist legality. (I want to go on in the next section to consider why it is that Pashukanis', and associated theories, limit their analyses to "bourgeois law.") Despite the theoretical problems of Thompson's writings about law, in considering the "rule of law" as a universal cultural achievement he has advanced the position that law in any modern social formation is essential. For Thompson it is impossible to envisage a (socialist *or* capitalist) society without law.[42]

It is only in the context of the transition to socialism that Edward Thompson's brave stand, against the critics and all the self-generating problems of his particular historical tradition, on the need to distinguish between the "rule of law" and the absence of the rule of law can be appreciated. It is only in that context that the "rule of law" can be seen as the crucial focus for modern-day socialist strategy. It is most clearly identifiable if that other "guru" of New Left legal theorists is considered: Evgeny Pashukanis.

II.   PASHUKANIS, 'THE WITHERING AWAY OF LAW,' AND SOCIALISM

There are two major points of criticism of Pashukanis' work[43] that, in its relatively uncritical

[42]Though Hirst would reject Thompson's "rule of law"/ arbitrary power distinction as being based on a "philosophical essentialisation of law" (*On Law and Ideology*, op. cit., p. 149), he would seemingly agree with Thompson's emphasis on the need to conceive of a socialist legality (though not a communist one). See *On Law and Ideology*, ibid., p. 144, footnote 1.

[43]The most important text is, of course, *The General Theory of Law and Marxism*, first published in the Soviet Union in 1924. It is currently available in three English editions: J. Hazard (Ed.), *Soviet Legal Philosophy* (Cambridge, Mass.: Harvard University Press, 1951), from the 1927 Russian edition; C. Arthur (Ed.), *Law and Marxism*, (London: Ink Links, 1978), from the 1929 German edition; P. Beirne and R. Sharlet (Eds.), *Pashukanis: Selected Writings on Marxism and Law* (London: Academic Press, 1980), tr. P. Maggs, pp. 40–131, from the 1924 Russian edition.

reception in the West in recent years,[44] have frequently been overlooked. One is the question of the conception of legal subject in Pashukanis' theoretical framework, which is heavily based on the theory of fetishism of commodities as outlined by Marx in *Capital* Vol. 1. In essence, Pashukanis' work (and to a much less sophisticated extent, Karl Renner's) is a development of the theory of commodity fetishism into a highly sophisticated theory of legal fetishism. However, the theory of fetishism has come under increasing criticism in Marxist theory.[45] It has at last[46] been recognized that this debate, as yet unresolved, imposes severe limitations on the usefulness of Pashukanis's theory of law, although much writing in the area of Marxist legal theory—even the more stimulating contributions[47]—carries on utilizing Pashukanis regardless.

The second area of criticism relates to the specificity of Pashukanis' texts to the political and social context of the Soviet Union in the 1920s and 1930s. With the aid of recent research in this area,[48] it is now possible to emphasize Pashukanis' position on the question of "socialist legality" and assess its contemporary significance. It is this second area, then, that must be the focus here.

It must be remembered that Pashukanis' tentative articulation of a coherent Bolshevik posi-

[44]C. Arthur, "Towards a Materialist Theory of Law," *Critique*, 7 (Winter 1976/7), has proved to be a seminal article; to a lesser extent I. Balbus, "Commodity Form and Legal Form: An Essay on the 'Relative Autonomy' of the Law," *Law and Society Review*, 11, no. 3 (Winter 1977), has performed a similar function, recognizing Pashukanis' "pioneering effort."

[45]For perhaps the most damaging critique, see N. Rose, "Fetishism and Ideology; A Review of Theoretical Problems" *Ideology and Consciousness*, 2 (Autumn 1977).

[46]R. Cotterell, "Commodity Form and Legal Form" *Ideology and Consciousness*, 6 (Autumn 1979), p. 118 especially.

[47]For instance, A. Fraser, "Legal Theory and Legal Practice," *Arena*, 44/45 (1976); A. Fraser, "The Legal Theory We Need Now," in *Socialist Review* 40/41, July/October (1978).

[48]R. Sharlet, "Pashukanis and the Rise of Soviet Marxist Jurisprudence, 1924–1930," *Soviet Union*, 1, 2 (1974); "Pashukanis and the Withering Away of Law in the USSR," in S. Fitzpatrick (Ed.), *Cultural Revolution in Russia 1928–1931*, op. cit.; Beirne and Sharlet (Eds.), op. cit.

tion on law in 1924 in *The General Theory of Law and Marxism* was, indeed, as the subtitle to the book, "An Experiment in the Criticism of Basic Juridical Concepts," suggests, an exploratory[49] project in Marxist legal theory. However, in spite of its status—often overlooked in its resurrection in the West—as an early formulation of the ideas of one wing of the "commodity exchange school of law," it does still present a relatively coherent[50] theoretical justification, based on the writings of Marx and Engels, for the decay of "bourgeois law." Law for Pashukanis, of course, is fundamentally capitalist, because in its form it reflects the (fetishized) form of the commodity as analyzed by Marx in *Capital* Vol 1. Therefore, there cannot be, from Pashukanis' standpoint, a "socialist legality" or "proletarian law," as by definition socialism (and eventually "communism," toward which, in the classical Marxist schema, socialism is only a stepping stone, a "transitional phase") is the progressive overthrow of commodity exchange "intertwined" with capitalist relations of production.[51] To the extent that "exchange of equivalents" still exists in this transition to the classless, communist society of the "future," where "property forms" and their "legal regulation"[52] are no longer conceivable, law also exists for Pashukanis; but it is capitalist and not "socialist"

law. Thus, Pashukanis must be seen as developing classic Marxist texts—Marx's *Critique of the Gotha Programme*, in particular—on the question of legality and the transition period of socialism.

Pashukanis' work, then, represents a clear statement of the classical Marxist thesis that the political and juridical forms of capitalist relations of production will wither away in the phase of socialism, the transition period to the communist society that will no longer require them. The rigorous theoretical explanation of why, in his view, this must be so is, as I have suggested, in many ways Pashukanis' most lasting contribution to Marxist theory of law. However, its consequences for modern socialist strategy have not been fully debated or realized.

I have made it clear elsewhere[53] that it is to Pashukanis' eternal credit that, despite the pressure "from above" to enter into self-criticism of *The General Theory of Law and Marxism* in the late 1920s and the 1930s, he resisted almost to the end (his "disappearance" in 1937) the temptation to change his thesis on the withering away of "bourgeois law" and submit to the stranglehold of the Stalinist conception of "proletarian law."

However, it is of the utmost importance to be clear on this point. The assertion that Pashukanis' derivation of a particular position on "socialist legality" from such an experimental text was correct, and deserving of admiration and respect for being maintained in increasingly hostile conditions, must be seen in its context. I would maintain that the Stalinist conception, and practical implementation, of "proletarian law"—under which Pashukanis, presumably, himself met his death—was and is reactionary and should be an anathema to any political movement that claims to inherit the tradition of Marx and Engels. The experience of the "rule of law" in Russia in and since the 1930s should serve as a terrible reminder of this fact. But to say that Pashukanis'

---

[49]Beirne and Sharlet, ibid., p. 2.

[50]Of course, this "coherence" is radically challenged by the criticisms of the adequacy of the theory of fetishism of commodities; see footnote 45.

[51]Pashukanis, in fact, "radically reconceptualized" the relationship between law and exchange relations later in his life, according an "ultimate primacy" to "the relations of production"; see Beirne and Sharlet (Eds.), op. cit., pp. 273-274. I have discussed this review of his earlier position in "The Discrete Charm of Bourgeois Law: A Note on Pashukanis," *Critique*, 9, Spring/Summer (1978), and criticized it as an unsatisfactory resolution of problems created by the theoretical framework of *The General Theory of Law and Marxism*. However, I would agree with Beirne and Sharlet (p. 274) that it is difficult to "distinguish between those reconceptualisations which Pashukanis may actually have intended and those which were produced by the external pressures of political opportunism."

[52]See Hirst *On Law and Ideology*, op. cit., p. 144, footnote 1.

[53]Redhead, "The Discrete Charm of Bourgeois Law," op. cit.

position of opposition to that *particular* conception of "socialist legality" was right in the 1930s in the USSR does not mean to say that a position of opposition to *any* conception of such a legality can be supported. This was, ultimately, Pashukanis' position; he was *against* law.[54] It requires some explanation by reference to the social and political context of post-revolutionary Russian society,[55] without which it is impossible to understand why Pashukanis could hold so strongly to his view of legal relations under socialism and consistently deny alternative conceptions of a socialist legality.

It is, perhaps, important to begin towards the end. In 1936 Pashukanis, in a little-read, previously unavailable[56] "U-turn," did, in fact, bow to Stalinist pressure. In "State and Law Under Socialism,"[57] Pashukanis' courage at last gave way, though even this capitulation was insufficient to save his life. He simply gives approval to the Stalinist conception of Soviet legality that Vyshinskii was to impose so ruthlessly after replacing Pashukanis in 1937.[58] For Pashukanis, 1936-style:

> This law is established by the proletarian dictatorship and is the law of the socialist state. It serves the interests of the working people and the interests of the development of socialist production. The condescending attitude that this law is "bourgeois" benefits only the anarchic theories of the "left-wing" and the champions of bourgeois equality."[59]

[54] B. de Sousa Santos, "Popular Justice, Dual Power and Socialist Strategy," in *Capitalism and the Rule of Law*, op. cit., has emphasized this important factor.

[55] Beirne and Sharlet (Eds.), op. cit., provide a much-needed comprehensive analysis of Pashukanis's writings in their context of post-1917 USSR social formations.

[56] There is a partial translation in M. Jaworskyj (Ed.), *Soviet Political Thought: An Anthology* (Baltimore: John Hopkins University Press, 1967), but the first full English translation is included in Beirne and Sharlet (Eds.), op. cit.

[57] Beirne and Sharlet, ibid., pp. 348-361.

[58] Hazard, in Hazard (Ed.), op. cit., notes that with "Pashukanis' ouster, Vyshinsky was placed at the head of the Institute of Law of the Academy of Sciences and was made editor of its journal, *Soviet State and Law*. . . . He became the spokesman for the new jurisprudence."

[59] Beirne and Sharlet, op. cit., p. 355.

A far cry from the Pashukanis of 1924; but, of course, the political atmosphere had radically altered:

> The Stalinist revolution from above had by 1936 accomplished most of its economic and political tasks, and its incipient proclivities for greater legal formality and stability were now becoming increasingly apparent. The Party pendulum was beginning to swing away from legal nihilism and towards legal stability and socialist legality, and Pashukanis must certainly have been aware of the fact that the leftist tendencies which he seemed to represent were a major obstacle to this impending shift. . . .
> Pashukanis, as theorist and symbol of the earlier legal policy, stood in the path of this swinging pendulum. It was, after all, he who had originally characterised all law as "bourgeois" and through the success of his *General Theory* popularised this view not merely among Marxist legal cadres but even more widely among individuals in positions of authority who thought it convenient to think of themselves as being above the law. Moreover, Pashukanis was clearly identified with opposition to the idea of "socialist law" and he remained the leading advocate for the active process of the withering away of law.[60]

This context is indeed crucial. It does not call into question Pashukanis' undoubted personal and political courage; rather, it may be asked how his resolve to maintain an opposition to Stalin's view of legality could have remained with him so long in such an increasingly unfavorable political climate. Just as by 1936 it was clearly difficult to resist the juggernaut of "proletarian law," in the years before this, and particularly since Pashukanis had shot to fame in the wake of the 1924 text, a certain position on the "withering away of law" had gathered substantial social forces around it.

The Pashukanis-led movement for the withering away of "bourgeois law" was, undoubtedly, as Beirne and Sharlet state, an "active" preparation for a world without law. It is this "condition of existence" of Pashukanis' theory of law under

[60] Ibid., pp. 346-347.

socialism that has not been fully acknowledged in the contemporary use of Pashukanis as *the* Marxist theorist of law. The opposition to any form of socialist legality, which is inherent in his theoretical framework, has been torn out of its historical place in the 1920s; it needs urgently to be relocated there. It is now clear that Pashukanis, and many of his jurist colleagues who came under his wing during his phenomenal rise in the years between 1924 and 1930, were preparing, in "an atmosphere of legal nihilism"[61] for the withering away of law in practice, which meant the dissolution of courts, the legal profession, and legal education.[62] Speaking of the mid- and late-1920s in Russia, when the field of criminology was also coming under attack, Solomon notes that:

> Prominent in the Communist Academy's legal sector were E. B. Pashukanis and his close associate N. V. Krylenko, a leading prosecutor for the R.S.F.S.R. Commissariat of Justice, and later (from 1931) its Commissar. As representatives of a "nihilistic orientation," Pashukanis and Krylenko were urging that law and legal institutions start to disappear with the construction of socialism. . . .[63]

As Sharlet notes, this was in the second Soviet experiment dedicated to the withering away of law, which "began during the NEP period with the slogan *'revoliutsiia prava'* ('the revolution of the law'), gained momentum during the years of the 'proletarian cultural revolution' and First Five Year Plan, peaked during the Second Five-Year Plan and came to a definitive halt only with the arrest and purge of the jurist E. B. Pashukanis and his associates beginning in January 1937."[64] The first period of such a movement began almost immediately after the 1917 revolution[65] and was predicated on the expectation of an extremely short transitional period of "dictatorship of the proletariat." This was, of course, not to be, and the demands of the NEP economy, complemented so neatly by Pashukanis's legal theory, altered the proposed time scales for the transition to the "higher phase of communism." Nevertheless, it must be recalled that even in the second period of the reign of "legal nihilism," the transition was seen as very near to its end. Pashukanis' theory of the withering away of law, and hence of opposition to socialist legality, rests on a profound belief in the imminent disappearance of the "bourgeois world view" in general and "bourgeois legal philosophy" (epitomized by the "general theory" of Hans Kelsen) in particular. As Sharlet[66] points out, "the main objective of the 'revolution of the law' still lay ahead" in 1927, the year of the third edition of *The General Theory of Law and Marxism,* and the "'bourgeois' world-view, thought to be the last citadel of prerevolutionary society on the road to communism, had to be overcome and destroyed. . . ." Pashukanis was ready for the final assault, confident that Marxist criticism—armed with the commodity exchange approach—could overcome the dangerous 'recidivism of bourgeois juridical ideology.'"

With the enormous benefit of more than 50 years of hindsight, the tragic optimism of such a view is only too clear. The "final assault" never materialized; through the traumatic decade that followed, the legal theory that had found so much favor in the NEP period was to suffer an awful fate, and though members of the "commodity exchange school of law" were "posthumously rehabilitated"[67] in 1956, modern-day Russian legal

[61]Sharlet, "Pashukanis and the Withering Away of Law in the USSR," op. cit., p. 186.

[62]Ibid., pp. 184–187.

[63]P. Solomon, "Soviet Criminology—Its Demise and Rebirth 1928–1963," in R. Hood (Ed.), *Crime, Criminology and Public Policy: Essays in Honour of Sir Leon Radzinowicz* (London: Heinemann, 1974), p. 574.

[64]Sharlet, "Pashukanis and the Withering Away of Law in the USSR," op. cit., p. 170.

[65]For an analysis of Russian legal debate in these years, see J. Hazard, "Soviet Law: The Bridge Years, 1917–1920," in W. Butler (Ed.), *Russian Law: Historical and Political Perspectives* (Leyden: Sijthoff, 1977).

[66]"Pashukanis and the Rise of Soviet Marxist Jurisprudence, 1924–1930," op. cit., p. 120.

[67]Ibid., p. 121.

thought views Pashukanis' theory of the withering away of law as "erroneous."[68]

The context of Pashukanis' theory of the demise of "bourgeois law" has been seen to be crucial; so important are the political and social conditions that helped to produce and sustain this theory that a major question mark must be set against the use of Pashukanis to build a Marxist theory of legality in advanced capitalist social formations. Even without the more fundamental problems concerning the adequacy of the theory of the fetishism of commodities, the production of Pashukanis' experimental work in the euphoria and tragedy of post-1917 Russia has proved to be a massive limitation. But what of its usefulness in periods of "transition"? How far can Pashukanis's theory of opposition to "proletarian law" be relied on when a view of legality in "socialist" or transitional social formations is required? Or even more significant, what implications does it have for socialist strategy?

It is perhaps understandable, given the optimism of Pashukanis and many of his colleagues, that little thought was given in the 1920s to what would replace the "fetishized" form, "bourgeois law." There was only agreement, among the "nihilists," that law, by definition, could not take a "socialist" form, and the transition period being almost over, there would be no real need for blueprints of the coming communism (or socialism, depending on which term was politically preferred). Apparently, Krylenko did have:

> . . . a fairly explicit conception of the ways in which public order would be maintained after the eventual withering away of the court. Moral or educational measures would be applied to violators of the community rules. These measures would include suspended sentences, public censure, expulsion from the community, denial of the right to participate in social and political organisations, and deprivation of political rights. The elaborate pyramidical judicial system, with its different types of tribunals, would be abandoned, and control by the central authorities would cease. The judge would

be guided by ethical rules that would reflect the society's complete achievement of socialism.[69]

Pashukanis was nowhere, in his work, quite so explicit about the nature of the imminent world without law, but from the occasional reference it can be concluded that his vision was of the disappearance of very specific "juridical" forms and their replacement, at least in certain areas, by medical practices more reminiscent of positivist criminology. Although it is true that "Pashukanis' position that there could be no 'Proletarian' law, whilst marking him out as a left Bolshevik, did not commit him to the view that arbitrariness and authoritarianism were therefore acceptable,"[70] his particular conception of the eventual withering away of law was later to be ruthlessly exploited by Stalin, though of course under the rubric of "Soviet socialist law." Take, for instance, the question of crime under socialism. Pashukanis' embryonic theory of crime control in *The General Theory of Law and Marxism* is somewhat bizarre, basing itself on the theory of exchange of equivalents that is at the heart of his general theory of law. It is clear from Pashukanis' presentation of his theory that he anticipated the swift demise of the "juridical element"—by which he meant the concepts of guilt and punishment associated with the "free will" philosophy of the Classicist school of criminology—in social relations. In the case of crime this meant that "in place of punishment" there would be a concept of "treatment" or "medical-health," with all the attendant "medicalization" of the theory and practice of crime control. Thus "antisocial" behavior of the future would, it was anticipated, be combated not by lawyers and the courts but, perhaps, by psychiatrists and clinics. We should not need reminding of the use to which such medicalization of "social problems" has been put since the 1930s.[71] However, the example

---

[68]Ibid., p. 121.

[69]Sharlet, "Pashukanis and the Withering Away of Law in the USSR", op. cit., p. 178.

[70]Hirst, *On Law and Ideology,* op. cit., p. 150, footnote 12.

[71]C. Ackroyd et al., *The Technology of Political Control* (Harmondsworth: Penguin, 1977), Ch. 18.

serves to illustrate how underdeveloped Pashukanis' theory of the withering away of law remained when it was formulated in the USSR of the 1920s; it was, perhaps of necessity, sketchy, but it was also ultimately disastrous as a guide to political action.

CONCLUSION

I have examined in this essay aspects of two important contributions to the contemporary quest for an "adequate" Marxist theory of law. Both represent, in their fashion, different political traditions within the Marxist movement; both are, in many ways, products of their time, one in post-revolutionary Russia, the other postwar Britain. Neither has produced satisfactory solutions to the problem of conceptualizing legal relations within a Marxist theoretical framework, though both are becoming internationally influential. However, there is one crucial difference between them, namely, the argument about whether there can or should be a struggle for a socialist legality.

Pashukanis' theory of law, which in its increasingly widespread acceptance as, at least, the starting point for constructing a Marxist theory of law relevant to the modern world has fostered a contemporary "legal nihilism," *logically* leads to a denial of the political necessity of a strategy for socialism that is based on *any* conception of socialist legality. The only "rule of law" under socialism must, for this and associated standpoints, of necessity be aspects of capitalist legal forms that will wither away—albeit as a result of concerted political action for their eventual removal—with the progressive development of a "socialism" or "communism" that will have no need of them. I have cited two significant objections to Pashukanis' opposition to alternative forms of legality, based on research that places the development of his legal theory in the political and social context of Russia in the 1920s and 1930s. First, though opposition to Stalin's conception of socialist legality was of immense importance, Pashukanis' and his comrades' refusal to conceive of any other legality is only under-

standable (and, if at all, applicable) in the specific conditions of a society where the profound expectation of the almost immediate end of the transition to classlessness has been widely generated. Second, such expectation led, in the 1920s, to certain scenarios for the future that were to be disastrous in their political effect. Stalin and henchmen like Vyshinskii viciously transformed the old "rule of law" into a totally new and authoritarian legality, which, as Pashukanis had foreseen in a more hopeful period, entailed the erosion of guilt, punishment, and so on as juridic concepts and their replacement by concepts of treatment and antisocial behavior. Pashukanis' modern use in the West as the foundation of a Marxist theory of legality has not always portrayed such a backcloth; once this "context" is recalled, the disarming effect of a strategy for socialism based on the withering away of bourgeois law is more clearly perceived.

Thompson, on the other hand, does *compel* theorization of a specifically socialist legality on the Marxist movement. His attempt to distinguish between arbitrary authority and "the rule of law" (even in all its "forms") as distinct entities, however, seems to me much less successful. Would, for instance, Thompson see in Stalin's "legality" merely an arbitrary authority or a particular *form* of the "rule of law"?

Nevertheless, the direction in which Thompson has travelled in recent writings does enable political intervention over the "rule of law"—for instance, over "accountability" and "democratization" of the police, the jury, and so on—to be a significant part of socialist strategy. For Marxists to have to take seriously the "rule of law" in particular national social formations at particular historical periods—which means *struggling* over it, defending certain laws and procedures, *and* actively proposing reforms—may smack of a "Kautskyism" that has long been discredited. But it would seem that Thompson's libertarian socialist tradition, pitting, as he sees it, the "good" parts of the "rule of law" against the "bad," at least does not lead Marxism into the unhappy position of writing off law as "bourgeois" and insisting on "transforming" and "transcending" it. The avoidance of the question of socialist legality, the precise nature of legality under socialist societies, in such programs is reminiscent of the movement for the withering away of law in Russia in the late 1920s. Thompson's beloved "liberties"—trial by jury, for example—may well have to be yet again transformed and perhaps transcended, but the question "into what?" cannot be allowed to ring out for too long. For it "is time to constitute a force for the expansion, the democratic deepening and extension of the rule of law,"[72] however painful that may be.

[72]Hall, op. cit., p. 17.

A SEASON OF STARTLING ALLIANCE: CHINESE LAW AND JUSTICE IN THE NEW ORDER

JAMES P. BRADY

The surprise announcement was almost routinely accepted amidst the excitement of impending ceremony and deepening alliance. China, long reluctant to create a regular "legal system" and often denounced as an "outlaw state" by first the Americans and then the Soviets, has at last adopted a new and remarkably conventional westernized set of laws and judicial bureaucracies. American officials were reassured by this: yet another sign of "stability" and "maturity" among the Chinese "moderates" now ruling the country. China-bound corporate executives also appreciate these developments, as they note new legal guarantees for foreign investors and calculate the potential profits from the vast Chinese market. As David Rockefeller plans joint ventures with Communist officials in Peking and Teng Hsiao ping bargains for "defensive" weapons at the Pentagon it is a time for rubbing eyes at these most amazing political and legal developments.

The growing alliance with the United States, like the new legal system, is possible at this time only because certain long standing internal conflicts have been at least temporarily resolved. One cannot but notice that every new turn in foreign and domestic policy, each new law code, each newly refurbished and expanded justice bureau is preceded by yet another shovel full of

condemnation heaped upon the political grave of the now vilified "Gang of Four." These four deposed members of the Communist Party Central Committee are much more than a scapegoated clique. They are symbolic of a national political opposition (which they once led) that stands in clear opposition to current policies in almost all aspects of society, law and justice. In order to understand anything of the origins and implications of contemporary justice practice it is necessary to consider the political ideas and social policies which distinguish the new dominant "moderate" leadership from the defeated "radicals," represented by the Gang of Four.

This paper will break with the prevailing mood of celebration to argue that the emerging legal system and the rise of the new "moderate" leadership are defeats for the Revolution and for the Chinese people as a whole. Current policies in Peking have systematically widened social inequalities in wages, power, and prestige and reverse the egalitarian spirit of the Cultural Revolution (1966 to 1968). The new conservatism is reflected and reinforced in the new laws and justice procedures which lend permanence to existing uneven property relations (including limited capitalism), outlaw key forms of political dissent developed in the Cultural Revolution, weaken the power of workers and citizens in government and production centers, and impose a heavy dominance of specialized professionals in law enforcement and adjudication.

This is more than "leaning to one side" in a rightward swing of dialectical process. China has

Source: An earlier version of this paper was submitted for presentation at the International Sociology Association Conference at Ibadan, Nigeria, July 1980. This paper was originally submitted to *Marxism and Law*, and first published by agreement in *International Journal of the Sociology of Law*, 1981, Vol. 9, No. 1, pp. 41–67.

taken the downhill path to modernization led by the new leadership, down steep gradients of inequality and narrow bureaucratic defiles. There is nothing "moderate" about the new elite. The correct description of their ideas and their policies is *revisionist*. It is their defeated opponents who, despite their many mistakes, can be best described as the *"revolutionary"* alternative for Chinese development.

The revisionists are constrained, however, by fifty years of revolutionary Maoist traditions, by the centuries old public mistrust for lawyers and formal legal procedures, by the need to maintain popular enthusiasm for labor intensive production, and by the fiscal weakness of the state itself. China simply cannot afford to pay all or even most of those who handle crimes, conflicts, rehabilitation, and other social services. The justice professionals must rely upon great numbers of volunteer activists, and thus dare not risk alienating the citizenry by overcentralizing and formalizing justice.

The following discussion will move through three main sections. First is an overview of the competing "revolutionary" and "revisionist" lines, of the leadership, philosophy, and policy over the past 30 years, and particularly in the decade since the Cultural Revolution. Secondly is a discussion of the 1978 Constitution, new criminal statutes, justice agencies and legal professionalism; with a contrasting view of revolutionary Maoist traditions which emphasize popular involvement through community organizations, informal procedures, and the central importance of politics and class in defining crime and handling disputes. Finally is a discussion of future prospects, with attention to emerging patterns of crime and conflict and the social contradictions arising from China's startling new revisionist alliance.

CHINESE CONFLICTS AND WESTERN SYMPATHIES

China watchers in the United States have long recognized the central importance of the "two line struggle." Indeed scholars have "taken sides" against one another in their relation to this conflict, just as earlier they were divided by their stand on the American genocidal adventure in South East Asia. Certainly, the sympathies of those who sit in council with corporate executives and State Department officials have always been clear. The following remarks have been offered recently by one of Henry Kissinger's top aides, Allen Whiting, and by Ross Terril of the established Harvard intelligentsia:

> The fall of Chiang Ching and her three Shanghai associates (who comprised the Gang of Four) removes the most poisonous elements in Peking affecting Sino-American relations.
> When the far leftist Gang of Four. . . . were snuffed out in the tense darkness of one October night in 1976, the 10 year nightmare of Mao's Cultural revolution was belatedly snuffed out with them (Whiting, 1976).
> . . . by 1977 a more pragmatic government headed by the modest Hua Kuo feng had begun to put a new stamp in China's affairs . . . Peking has at least defined the good society in refreshing terms (Terrill, 1978, p. 9, 10).

News editors have, with near unanimity, approved Peking's new "moderates" while condemning the radical opposition as "dogmatic purists" and "shrill voiced ideologues." Unfortunately, such colored accounts tell us more about the interests of the dominant American elite than they do about the "two line" conflict in China.

What then are the origins and issues in this conflict which has so occupied the attention of Chinese leaders, people, and overseas observers? When writing about this in the year before Mao's death I stressed (Brady, 1977a, p. 128) the philosophical nature of the dispute and argued:

> This central struggle is fundamentally a conflict of competing ideas for economic development and political leadership, rather than a battle of personalities and clear political factions. The two Idea-Antagonists have been generally constant while the lists of their human supporters have changed.

I am not at all sure that I would say the same today. The social and economic policies adopted by the dominant revisionists have so favored certain sectors of the Chinese population as to build an increasingly solid *class base* for what had before been an ideological conservatism with overtones of economic interest. In considering this conflict anew it is even more important to understand historical and material developments as expressions of the deepening political antagonism. This will be of necessity a brief discussion, but there is a rich abundance of good sources on the subject.

THE TWO LINE STRUGGLE AS HISTORY AND IDEOLOGY

The Revolutionary Line and its adherents developed over three eras of sweeping social reforms and powerful mass movements: the Civil War (1927 to 1949), the Great Leap Forward (1957 to 1961), and the Cultural Revolution (1966 to 1968). The Civil War formed the communists as a shadow government and an instrument of class struggle, arousing the peasants against the landlords (Selden, 1969; Brady, 1974, pp. 63–80). The Great Leap was focused especially on the rural areas, where collectivization was advanced and living standards and opportunities were expanded with the development of decentralized industry, technology, and higher education (Dutt, 1967, pp. 90–97; Hsu, 1964; Salaff, 1975). The Cultural Revolution was set chiefly in urban zones where the administration of schools, factories, and government was challenged and re-organized along more egalitarian and participatory lines (Gray, 1970; Nee, 1973; Riskin, 1973).

The Revolutionary ethic rests on three key principles: the "mass line" in political leadership, the "continuing revolution" in social development, and "red and expert" for the role of educated specialists. The mass line was created over the course of the Civil War. It has continued in the tradition of strong community organizations and popular mobilization as both an aide

and a counterweight to the government bureaucracy (Mao, 1943; Schurmann, 1966; Selden, 1969). The "continuing revolution" calls for ongoing reforms to eliminate the cultural influence of the old society and to close gaps in wages and prestige between city and rural zones, workers and farmers, mental and manual laborers, men and women. Those with higher education are expected to be both "red and expert," developing specialized skills but seeking neither material privileges nor isolation from the laboring people (Mao, 1956; Mao, 1970; Schram, 1971).

The competing Revisionist Line traces back to three historic courses: post-war Reconstruction (1949 to 1956), recovery from the failures of the Great Leap (1961 to 1965), and the Thermidorean Reaction to the Cultural Revolution (1976 to present). During the Reconstruction era Soviet advisors were most influential, educating young Chinese specialists and pointing economic plans in the Soviet direction of sharp social and political stratification. In the mid-1960s, the excessive dislocation of the Great Leap prompted a reassessment and restoration of material incentives and centralized authority (Donnithone, 1966; Dutt, 1970, pp. 9–19; Hoffman, 1963). Since Mao's death the rightists have mounted a third (and by far the most powerful) offensive.

The ideas and policies advocated by the right have been fairly consistent throughout, although advanced with more boldness at each resurgence. Initially conservatives such as Liu Shao chi (1956) justified their policies with selected excerpts from Mao's (generally radical) writings. In more recent years Teng Hsiao ping and others have begun to cite what they call "the objective laws of socialist development" (Teng, 1978). These laws, being "objective," have no place for political contest or class struggle (M. R. Editors, 1979). The new conservatives are pledged to rapid modernization through the most expedient concentration of available capital and technology (J.M.J.P., 2 Feb 1979). They would build industry upon the nation's strongest urban centers, and seek the cooperation of Western capitalist firms; though this means that the rural zones will lag behind and that China must abandon its tradition of "self reliance."

Modernization, say the conservatives, should be led by technological specialists and bureaucratic administrators working in stable hierarchies free of interference from "mass supervision" by community organizations and without the obligation to engage in political study/self criticism or manual labor. Material incentives, bonuses and steep wage scales are required to spur individual effort and to distinguish clearly the contribution of essential specialists, administrators and skilled labor, for the less crucial functions of ordinary workers and farmers (Hua Kuo feng, 1979).

A summary of developments in the last decade will reveal the central importance of the Two Lines in the drawing of class and power relationships. The direction and velocity of change there should help in understanding current judicial practice and in comprehending future trends and events.

THE STAKES OF STRUGGLE IN THE 1970s: CLASS AND POWER

As the Cultural Revolution upheavals ended with compromise and reform, one could detect important advances toward social equality. The "piece rate" system of payment was abolished along with most individual bonuses; and the 18-grade urban wage scale was collapsed somewhat in favor of the lower grades. In the countryside the 8-level wage scale, also based on occupation, was leveled off with pay rises to the poorer farmers and by the awarding of extra points to those judged by their fellow workers to be most cooperative and helpful in group projects. The "private plots" and "free markets" which had grown quite important in the rural economy were restricted, halting the deepening stratification of the rural population as a consequence of this limited capitalism (Diao, 1970, pp. 64-7; Tiewes, 1974, pp. 337-9; Whyte, 1974).

Educational policy is of central importance in a nation long ruled by an arrogant Mandarin scholar elite; and where gaps between the educated and the ordinary peasants are still enormous. The Cultural Revolution, of course, began in the schools with disputes over admission, curriculum, and the relationship of students to teachers and administrators. By 1970 new reform policies specified that almost all middle school graduates should work for 2 or 3 years in the countryside, with their later admission to the University determined not only by grades, but by the recommendations of their fellow workers (Hsia, 1972, pp. 153-8, 177, 185). The "red and expert" ideal was emphasized in courses of political study, criticism/self-criticism sessions, and in the insistence that students and teachers engage in some regular manual labor. The Universities were directed to concentrate recruitment efforts among peasant and working youths, offsetting somewhat the advantages of those from more affluent cadre or intellectual backgrounds (Cheng, 1976; Mao, 1970; Pfeffer, 1975).

The political system was profoundly changed with the formation of "Revolutionary Committees" which held power in urban production centres, municipal bureaucracies, and schools. These committees included representatives of local mass organizations, along with party officials, government officials, military and technical specialists (Pfeffer, 1972; Townsend, 1974, pp. 35-7). Grass roots associations of workers, women, and students were strengthened and new leadership was chosen, often from among those most active as critics in the previous years' struggles. The Communist Party membership shifted with many of the conservatives demoted or transferred and a host of younger radicals added or advanced (Lee, 1978; Salaff, 1976, pp. 3-19).

The "Gang of Four" itself reflected these changes, including three who had risen as rebel leaders of the Shanghai "power seizure." Chiang Ching, much more than "the wife of Mao," was promoter of new revolutionary art forms; and Wang Hung wen was the fiery leader of the Shanghai textile workers. At 39 years old he was by far the youngest person ever to sit on the Central Committee of the communist party. Mao's own sympathies were obvious as he stood in Peking in Tien An Mien Square wearing a Red Guard arm band and repeatedly appearing at the side of Wang Hung wen (Hinton, 1969, pp. 40–4; Lee, 1978, pp. 146–9).

The radicals, understanding the determination of their conservative opponents, fought against revisionism to the very end. In 1976 they denounced efforts to turn back Cultural Revolution reforms, in the party's journal, *Red Flag*, (19 Feb. 1976) as follows:

> The capitalist roaders energetically peddle the economic thinking of the bourgeoisie, saying that science and technology are more important (than the mass Line) . . . they advocate letting experts run factories . . . support material incentives . . . oppose the activation of both central and local initiatives and re-impose the practice of direct central control . . . lay one sided stress on things big and foreign and oppose self-reliance.

Within weeks of Mao's death the Four found themselves under house arrest, stripped of power and isolated from their followers who were themselves the object of a massive purge and a continuing campaign of vitriolic criticism. Within a few months the new leadership had stabilized, now including Teng Hsiao Ping and many others once bitterly attacked by the radicals as "rightists." Reporters in Peking described streets full of rejoicing after the fall of the Gang; and even people numbed by sudden revelations of Watergate were surprised by the sudden turn of events in China (Lieken, 1979; Onate, 1978).

It should be pointed out that not everyone cheered the fall of the Four in China. There were protest riots and strikes in Shanghai, Fukien, and Hopeh provinces, and elsewhere, though these received less coverage by foreign reporters and were hardly admitted in the Chinese press. The official reason given for the fall was that the Four had systematically wrecked the economy and organized a coup against the government. Any serious examination of these charges shows that the first is untrue (MacDougall, 1977) and the second is simply ludicrous (Bettleheim, 1978).

There were, however, serious weaknesses in the leadership and programs put forward by the revolutionaries and these deserve some mention. It may well be that too much dependence upon the support of Mao led to the neglect of organizing work among those who gained the most from radical policies: the less skilled and temporary workers in the cities and the poorer farmers. That the Four as individuals were often bombastic and dogmatic, and identified with rampaging Red Guards whose behavior verged on anarchism may explain why they alienated nearly all the bureaucracy and the intellectuals, some of whom might otherwise have been expected to support the left. Their radical supporters in middle levels of power were probably not sufficiently experienced or attentive to practical and scientific considerations. Finally, the fall of Lin Piao in 1971, who over-stepped his responsibilities as chief of the army, seems to have seriously discredited the left with the PLA and given power to officers of the right and centre (Bridgham, 1968; Hinton, 1972, pp. 82–9).

The rise of Hua Kuo feng and Teng Hsiao ping in the new ruling center-right coalition has resulted in an almost total overturning of Cultural Revolution. They have mobilized the Chinese media not only to slander the Gang of Four with absurd lies and innuendo, but also to attack radical ideology, intimidate the remaining left opposition and fundamentally to rewrite modern China's history.

Material incentives and individual bonuses have once again become the order in China, with wage gaps widening especially between ordinary workers and the favored intellectuals and officials. Piece work payment and use of temporary low-paid rural labor in the cities is once more common, with the new leadership claiming (Sun Yeh fang, 1979) that "efficiency has shot up." In the countryside, private plots and "free markets" are encouraged, leading to considerable inequality especially since smaller families receive proportionately more land. As farmers turn to concentrate on family plots and economic differences among them grow, collective work and unity can only decline. The class implications in all of this are clear and the leadership informs people that,

> The policy of more pay for more work reflects the objective law of socialist development. Any violation brings on retribution.
> Differences in skill and work should be reflected in the pay of the workers and those making outstanding contributions should be given extra material rewards (Li Hong Rin, 1979).

Education and the role of intellectuals has been reversed even more drastically. A new system of standardized nationwide exams is now administered to graduates of middle schools, with places for only 2 to 5% in the handful of universities. Since Chinese schools are financed entirely by local resources, children from poorer communes and industrial centers will be less well prepared for the exams than will those attending better urban schools attached to bureaus, Universities, and industrial plants. Those who fail the exams will be sent off to work in the countryside, with little chance of returning for higher education. Workers and farmers will no longer choose university candidates from among their co-workers (Pincus, 1979).

The intellectuals, both academic and technological, have been granted new prominence and are released from the ethical restraints of the "red and expert" ideal (Hua Kuo feng, 1979). Changes in the class composition of the student body are paralleled by rises in the wages of teachers, who already belonged to one of the best paid occupations in the country (Pepper, 1977). Teng Hsiao Ping (1978) recently declared,

> ... teachers hold the key to a school's success. We must raise the political and social status of the people's teachers. We must seriously study teachers' wage scales. Proper steps should be taken to encourage people to devote their lives to education.

The new leadership has declared China's historic problem of intellectual arrogance suddenly resolved. The obligation of intellectuals to engage in political study/self-criticism and occasional

manual labor has been abolished (Dittmar, 1973). That this change runs counter to historic experience and Maoist traditions is rather openly acknowledged as evident for example in recent editorials excerpted from the Party's national press organ:

> In the wake of the emphasis of our Party's work being shifted to modernization, it has become increasingly important and urgent for a comprehensive and accurate understanding of the Party's policy toward intellectuals and for bringing their role into full play ... some comrades, however, do not have a corresponding understanding ... some ask if the party's policy of uniting, educating, and remoulding the intellectuals still applies, now that the overwhelming majority are part of the working class. The intellectuals are no longer objects to be united with, educated and remoulded ... leading comrades ... must listen earnestly to the opinion of scientists and technicians (J.M.J.P., 2 Feb. 1979).

Political authority has become increasingly bureaucratic and divorced from the methods of the "mass line." Correspondingly the political role of the populace has been restricted and routinized. The Revolutionary Committee have been replaced by professional administrators appointed by the state in almost all production sites and municipalities. The mass organizations in the neighborhoods, schools and workplaces have declined in terms of influence and mass participation (Buttlerfield, 1978). Along with the purge of its younger and more radical leaders, the Party has increasingly emphasized discipline within its ranks (Lee, 1978, pp. 81-7, 142-8; Yan yi, 1979). Young members from the rebellious generation of the Cultural Revolution today face a dramatic rightward shift and are advised that:

> We must consciously uphold party rules and regulations and enforce strict party discipline. Disciplinary measures must be taken against all violators. ...
> ... of 36 million odd members of our party, nearly one half joined the party since the Cultural Revolution. They need to be educated in fundamental knowledge about the party and in party discipline (Hung ch'i, 2 Feb. 1979).

The ideological and class composition of the Party has changed considerably. Thousands of cadres once denounced and demoted as "rightists" have been "rehabilitated" and returned to posts of leadership. New members are increasingly chosen from among the intellectuals and technologists or from among the offspring of party or government cadres. In discussing the recent selection of "representatives" for the National People's Congress, party commentators included both of these privileged elites together with the workers and farmers in calculating the percentage of cadres chosen from "working-class" origins. Save for the remnants of the old landlord and capitalist classes, China today does not acknowledge any social contradictions based on economics. As one of the leading official theoreticians noted: . . . "there is no basic conflict of economic interests among the people, although there are partial contradictions . . . this kind of contradiction can be resolved by self regulation of the socialist system." (Shang Zhe, 1979.)

The new revisionist ideology defines the state and Party in a bureaucratic role as central coordination and efficiency expert, rather than catalyst for mass mobilization and egalitarian reform. The break with revolutionary tradition and the widening inequalities create potentially explosive tensions. To secure their position the new regime must neutralize the Maoist ideals and radical activists who comprise their real and potential opposition. The left must be branded as "anarchists" and contained by laws. This repressive threat is implicit along with promises for increased production in the mass media, official speeches and public rallies. The following recent excerpt from the Party's official daily is typical:

A characteristic of anarchism is that it opposes centralization and authority, rejects leadership and discipline, and is interested in "absolute democracy" and "absolute freedom". To make personal gains some people take the promise of democracy as a pretext to neglect laws and make trouble, even going to the extent of violating normal social order

and upsetting the highly favorable situation of stability and unity.

What is the contradiction in the socialist mode of production? . . . contradictions commonly observed are . . . between social production on the one hand and the growing material and cultural needs of the members of society, along with the need for change and development on the other . . . the main thing is to continually raise labor productivity (J.M.J.P., 12 Aug. 1979).

POLITICAL CONTEST AND JUSTICE POLICY

The two line struggle and the recent triumph of revisionism is nowhere more evident than in the history of law and justice policy. As I have noted elsewhere, (Brady, 1974; 1977a) China has in fact developed two justice systems reflecting the different ideas and social forces which lie behind the larger conflict in the national political economy. These I have described as the "popular" and "bureaucratic" models; and I need not repeat here the details of their philosophy, organization, history and practice, save to summarize the essential elements of difference which have remained since Mao's death.

The "bureaucratic" model is a natural consequence of the conservative notion that the Chinese revolution has been completed. Advocates (Peng Zhen, 1979; Tung Pi Wu, 1956) argue that law is necessary to consolidate past gains, to regulate future changes, to ensure the steady development of production, and to protect state authority. A set of regular justice bureaucracies, including the courts, police, and procurate share legal power in a check and balance arrangement designed to protect due process and maintain social order (Li, 1973; Lubman, 1969). The agencies are staffed by professionals and administered by specialists trained in the "science of law and jurisprudence" (Liu Shao chi, 1956; Peng Zhen, 1979). Freedom for the citizenry is legally defined in terms of individual rights and prescribed justice procedures. Crime is defined in terms of specific acts punishable by fixed penal sanctions (I.P.L.R., 1958).

The "popular" model is tied to the radical ideals of "continuing revolution," the "mass line", and "self-reliance". Its adherents have resisted codification, arguing that China is yet in a transitional state and that current social arrangements should not be formalized in law while serious inequalities continue (Hsiang Shih, 1969; Stankhe, 1966). The mass organizations grouping workers, farmers, women and neighborhood residents play a major role in both routine peace keeping and in the "mass supervision" of government and local authorities through "ongoing rectification" and periodic "mass campaigns" (Brady, 1977 a, b). Justice professionals are expected to work closely with citizen activists and to maintain procedures which are informal and open to popular participation (I.P.L.R., 1958; Lubman, 1967). Freedom is implicitly defined in social terms, as in the leveling of wage and status differences, the broadening of opportunities, and the responsiveness and democratic style of leadership. Crime is considered not so much in terms of a specific act, as in the attitudes and motives of the offender, and political education is a central part of both crime control, investigation, and rehabilitation (Brady, 1977 a; Li, 1973).

The dialectic of cooperation and confrontation between these two justice systems has continued through the decade of the 1970s. On the one hand there is fundamental agreement that certain forms of behavior, such as robbery, assault, corruption, and adultery are criminal and intolerable. The justice professionals and the citizen volunteers cooperate quite effectively in handling such problems as in the combined efforts of volunteer "security defense" teams and the local police or in the continuing role of lay "people's assessors" in the People's Courts. Likewise the mass organizations help with crime prevention through their efforts in the mediation of local disputes and in the process of "criticism/self criticism" within "small groups" which seeks to overcome egoism and aggression (Cohen, 1972; Lubman, 1967).

On the other hand, conflict between the two justice models has been fairly continuous varying from quiet disputes over jurisdiction and procedure to sometimes violent struggles in the course of mass rectification campaigns (Leng, 1967). The Cultural Revolution shattered the justice system perhaps more completely than any other institution of government, leaving the Courts isolated, the lawyers' offices abandoned, the police weakened and insecure, and the Procurate almost moribund. All of these agencies were sharply criticized by radical activists for their elitism, over-emphasis on formality, isolation from the masses, and most pointedly for their repression of Red Guard students and Red Rebel workers in the early months of the upheavals (Brady, 1974, pp. 310–28). More than a few judges were dragged from their offices to be subjected to massed criticism at open "struggle meetings". Procurators, judges, and some police officials were hustled to May 7th Schools for ideological reform and manual labor in substantial numbers (Casella, 1973; Pfeffer, 1972). The national police chief was one of these national officials subjected to the most unrelenting criticism, and high officials in the Ministries of Justice and Public Security were sacked or transferred. Efforts to professionalize the legal system were dealt a serious blow with the closure of law schools and legal institutes (Cohen, 1973; 1974; Lee, 1978, pp. 117–9).

Some sort of compromise justice system seemed to be in the offing at the time of Mao Tse Tung's death in 1976. The Constitution of 1975 emphasized the importance of the mass line in legal procedures. The abolition of the highly specialized and bureaucratic Procurate continued the anti-professionalism of the Cultural Revolution (N.P.C., 1975; Wang Hsiao t'ing, 1978). Though the courts were restored to formal authority, the judiciary had been broadened to include great numbers of citizen activists who rose to prominence in the mass rectification movement. Judicial procedure in the re-opened courts was considerably less formal, especially in the lower courts, with few prosecuting or defense lawyers present and representatives of mass organizations playing a prominent role in both the investigative and trial processes (Edwards, 1977).

In interviews with western scholars, Chinese judges and legal officials described procedures as follows:

> . . . our practice is to integrate the mass line and work specialized organizations. When a case comes up, the judicial working personnel will go deep among the masses and carry out the investigation and research to identify the truth and . . . check out the evidence and ask the masses for their views. The court gives the final judgement when this work is done, when the facts are clear . . . When a case is influential or bears important educational significance, the materials of the case will be distributed to the public. . . . The masses can then hold a discussion on the case and put forward suggestions (Ruge, 1976).

The police were likewise enjoined to leave their offices and work more closely with representatives of the mass organizations in peace-keeping work. Police ranks were thinned by demotions or temporary removal of publicly criticized cadres to the May 7th Schools. The military was continuing its withdrawal from active peace-keeping; but the military still served important functions (Lambe, 1974). Indeed, it appears that many of the radicals intended that the militia (as a volunteer force drawn directly from the local community) might replace or at least complement the professional public security forces. In perhaps the most dramatic event to precede the fall of the Four central committee radicals, it was the militia, and not the police which put down the "Tien An Mien" square riots in which the first organized opposition to the Four became visible (Ting Wang, 1978).

If the handling of ordinary "street" crime had been somewhat consolidated in a new working relationship between the courts, police, and mass organizations, the handling of political conflicts was still very much undecided and at issue. The 1975 Constitution was in part an attempt to build "massline" principles into bureaucratic procedures, but the whole previous history of the legal agencies indicates that "self-regulation" has not prevented the drift towards elitism and rigidity.

The rather disappointing history of citizen-professional collaboration in the work of the "People's Supervisory Committees" would also point to the need for a continuing direct mass role in overviewing and guiding local officials and administrators. The Revolutionary Committees which controlled schools, factories, and local government through the early 1970s provided this line of popular influence, through the "three-in-one" combination of P.L.A., Party, and mass organizations in leadership triumvirates. Likewise, the infrastructure of committees, mass meetings, and criticism/self-criticism sessions which compromised "ongoing rectification" helped to keep the egalitarian principles of the Cultural Revolution alive in the day-to-day operations of schools and work centers (Hinton, 1969). All of these measures, as well as the May 7th Schools, were designed to maintain revolutionary standards for government and social relations (Pfeffer, 1972).

The problem with these measures is that China has neither the fiscal nor personnel resources available to permit a thorough reorganization of leadership and must for its survival continue to rely on a considerable degree of centralization. The citizen activists in policy-making bodies were often unqualified by education or experience, and in a country like China the gaps between specialist and citizen are often enormous. To the extent that the demands of citizens in the rectification process of administrative councils were unrealistic they served only to alienate intellectuals and officials. Finally, it is clear that the new reforms were gradually bureaucratized and removed from the effective influence of either the public or the revolutionary principles of the Cultural Revolution. Thus, for example, the May 7th Schools lost their cutting edge as a disruptive and challenging experience with semi-penal overtones, to become a more relaxed and routine part of bureaucratic training by the mid-1970s (Tiewes, 1974).

Recognizing these difficulties and the continuing existence of wide social inequalities even after the Cultural Revolution, the radicals were reluctant to entrust the political and legal future of the country to even a reformed set of laws and bureaucracies. Despite the urgings of the resurgent conservatives in the early-1970s, the leftists continued to drag their feet on codification. The law schools were typically the last departments to reopen in the nation's universities after the Cultural Revolution. Legal officials lingered at May 7th Schools and anti-professionalism was still part of their language in official interviews (Cohen, 1973; Hao Hsuang Lu, 1975; Lambe, 1974).

Most important and most controversial was the leftist insistence that "mass campaigns" remain as a part of the political vocabulary and an option for mass participation. While the campaigns were not recognized in the 1974 Constitution, few officials dared speak of China's history or its current situation without a compulsory bow to the advances brought about by the Cultural Revolution and earlier campaigns. The radicals also insisted upon the "continuing rectification" process through public challenge and demonstration. As one left advocate (Hsiang Sih,) argued in a prominent legal journal:

> The masses, through the method of great blooming and contending, the writing of wall posters, the presentation of facts and the discussion of reasons advance the people's democracy . . . the democratic debate on the part of the masses not only is the correct method for handling contradictions among the people, but it is also the method to solidify and educate the people to wage struggle against the enemy. It can thus be seen that the mass movement has tremendous vitality in the correct application of jurisdiction. The rightist fallacy that "mass movements undermine the legal system" is entirely baseless and a malicious slander. Such a fallacy only proves that they are afraid of the mass movement.

Challenges such as these reasserted both the *theoretical* basis of popular justice, i.e., principles of "continuing revolution" and Mao's writings on the correct handling of contradictions"; and the *practical* outlets for mass action beyond the limits of the legal bureaucracies. It is significant that the person chosen by the Central Committee to succeed Mao Tse Tung as Premier in 1976 was Hua Kuo feng, a relatively unknown figure whose most important previous experience was as the national chief of the reformed police bureaucracy. Hua has been generally described (Buttlerfield, 1977; Ting Wang, 1978) as a "centrist" in the two line struggle, who like the police force he led tried to steer clear of the political battles continuing after the Cultural Revolution. No such middle ground could be found in politics or in justice.

ATTACK FROM THE RIGHT, AND LAWS AS POLITICAL WEAPONS

It was the uniformed professionals of police unit 4831 who burst into the homes of the four radical leaders to arrest them soon after Mao's death. While defending the Four, Mao's nephew and the commander of the Peking workers militia were killed. The action of this most centrally controlled police unit indicated the formation of a new and repressive centre-right coalition. In planning a counter-attack that never materialized, the radicals counted heavily on the popularly recruited militia; but it remained inactive, neutralized by shock and bereft of leadership (Onate, 1978). Within a few months a national purge had removed or demoted hundreds of radicals at the middle levels of government and party. A national campaign of vilification has continued against the Four, the Cultural Revolution, radical supporters and their ideas. Protest strikes and riots which followed in 1976 to 1978 in Fukien, Kiangsi, and Shanghai were brought to heel by stern police action (Hua Kuo feng, 1979).

Once again justice has become both a central subject and object of political contest. Though the Four and their supporters were arrested without formal legal procedures, the government has moved quickly to fashion a new legal system along lines more thoroughly bureaucratic and professional than ever before. Indeed, the chief claims of the new regime to legitimacy are its commitment to economic modernization and legalization. In distinguishing itself from the radicals and the whole tradition of revolutionary politics, the new elite claim to act in the interests of the Chinese masses,

> Having had enough of a decade of turmoil caused by Lin Piao and the Gang of Four, the people want law and order more than anything else. Democratization and legalization which the Chinese people have long been yearning for, are now gradually becoming a reality. Political democracy protected by the legal system will certainly give a powerful impetus to the early realization of modernization (J.M.J.P. 20 July 1979).

The regime has claimed that the new laws and legal bureaux established or reorganized under their leadership, offer new prospects for freedom and progress in China. They point (Ling Yun, 1978) to the new Constitution of 1978, to the new criminal and civil codes with pride, and cite China as an outstanding example of "human rights".

Closer examination reveals that the new legal system is not an expression of social consensus but of protracted conflict. The new codes are primarily designed to restrict dissent and to guarantee the increasingly unequal property relations. In many cases the penal codes are pointedly written to outlaw precisely those tactics which were used so successfully by the left during the Cultural Revolution. For example the new criminal law enacted in January 1980 stipulates a term of detention or imprisonment up to 3 years for anyone who,

> (1) uses threats or violence to obstruct a state functionary from carrying out his lawful duties, or who
> (2) disturbs public order by any means, or who
> (3) gathers a crowd which seriously disturbs public order at a railroad, bus station, airport, department store, or any public site,
> (4) flagrantly disrupts public order by gathering a crowd to engage in an affray,
> (5) commits acts of vandalism against culturel relics or historic sites protected by the state (*Peking Review*, 17 Aug. 1979).

The Cultural Revolution of course began with student gatherings in public centers and attacks on religious shrines which they considered to be remnants of feudal superstition. The Red Guards later travelled by commandeered trains or buses to carry dissent to other towns, often ending with noisy demonstrations encircling local government or party offices. Another important tactic (*Hung ch'i*, 30 March 1967; J.M.J.P., 16 June 1968) has been the writing and posting of "big character posters" and "wall newspapers" critical of local authorities. These practices are also increasingly restricted and criminalized (*N.Y. Times*, 15, 22, 26 November 1979). Following small protest demonstrations in March 1979 in Peking and Shanghai, the local authorities pronounced almost identical decrees against political dissent. These decrees virtually nullify the guarantees of free individual expression in the 1978 Constitution, as they proclaimed:

> In order to strengthen the Socialist Legal System and protect the people's democratic rights, the Security Bureau with the approval of the municipal committee, issued a notice to the effect that participants in public assemblies and demonstrations must obey the direction of the people's police and that no one is allowed to intercept trains, create disturbances, in government institutions or stir up troubles.
> It is also stipulated that except in designated places, no one is allowed to put up slogans, posters, or wall newspapers on public buildings and the printing and selling of reactionary or pornographic books, journals, and pictures are prohibited.
> . . . owing to the pernicious influence of anarchism of the last ten years and more, some people mistake democracy for absolute individual freedom and they oppose all kinds of discipline and authority. While much of this influence is still in evidence today, many people are not accustomed to exercising their democratic rights or do not know how to use them in a correct way (J.M.J.P., 6 April 1979)

Of course there were more than a few outrages and miscarriages of justice committed by Red Guards, police, and courts in the heat of the Cultural Revolution (Pan, 1968, pp. 130–40), and the new regime has cited this as reason for creating a new "socialist legality" (Buttlerfield, 1977; Hung ch'i, 1 June 1979; Munro, 1977), but the limited and precarious "freedom of expression" allowed by Peking's "Democracy Wall" must be compared with the larger policies of repression (Buttlerfield, 1979; J.M.J.P., 17 Oct. 1979; Matthews, 1979). Most recently, too, another Cultural Revolution practice was slated for elimination as the "National Conference on Judicial Work" convened by the Supreme Court resolved that "slander against a person's character... such as subjecting people to criticism at one public meeting after another and parading them on the streets as a form of public humiliation, must be abolished" (*Peking Review,* 16 1979).

The judges' resolution was followed by inclusion of new prohibitions in the criminal code. The new law is summarized by Peng Zehn (1979) of the Directorate of Legal Affairs for the National People's Congress as follows:

> The Draft Criminal Law stipulates that, whoever insults another person by violent or other means, including the use of "big character posters" or "small character posters" or fabrication of facts to libel another person, to a serious degree, shall be sentenced to imprisonment for not more than 3 years or to detention.
> We must defend the right to criticism and counter-criticism, to refute opposing views in discussion... all of which must be strictly distinguished from libel and insults (Peng Zhen, 1979).

One needs little imagination to guess whom such new laws and proposals are designed to protect. Certainly it is not the ordinary citizens who are likely to be the focus of mass criticism at a public meeting or demonstrations, rallies, and on critical wall posters. The whole history of "mass campaigns" and "ongoing rectification" bears witness that these have been key forms of political dissent and popular justice action mounted against elitist or corrupt officials and intellectuals (Bennett, 1978; Brady, 1974).

Along with codification, the new regime has greatly expanded and professionalized the justice bureaucracies, with a corresponding decline in mass participation. It is highly significant that the government chose Chao Tse Ang, Ching Hua, and Huang Hao Ch'ing to be respectively, the new national chiefs of the courts, police, and revitalized Procurate. All three men had been singled out for criticism and public censure during the Cultural Revolution and all three were removed from lower offices in the legal system. Their sudden "rehabilitation" and promotion is clear indication of new rightist trends in the legal system (Wang Hsiao T'ing, 1978, pp. 59, 60). The law profession was also sharply criticized for its arrogance and elitism in the past and as the Director of a leading legal research institute noted (Lin Heng Yuan, 1979), "To this day many people in our profession have misgivings and are reluctant to return to practice." Evidently their comeback is well underway, with a tremendous expansion of re-opened law schools and training institutes enrolling thousands of new students (Lei jie gonng, 1979).

The legal process has become increasingly formal. Lawyers have replaced the representatives of mass organizations in presenting evidence and arguments at trials. Citizen participation is restricted to a secondary role as "people's assessors." Echoing the views of earlier bureaucrats the current Minister of Justice believes legal decision making to be beyond public capacity, as he argued that (*Peking Review,* 10 Aug. 1979) "... judicial work involves a high degree of thinking and is different from production work in a factory or mine." Along with their elevated status and occupational prominence, justice professionals (along with other officials and intellectuals) have drawn increased salaries and privileges. The previous insistence that judges, lawyers and law students engage in periodic manual labor and political education to combat elitist tendencies has been dropped with the regime's abandonment of the "red and expert" ideals (*Peking Review,* 17 Aug. 1979).

The regulation of government, like social order, is left increasingly to the professionals. The Procurate has been reconstituted and greatly expanded to meet its official role as the overseer of police and courts. While the Procurate is supposed to be responsible to both its own bureaucratic hierarchy and to the various local People's Congress representatives, in fact the Congress is not and never has been sufficiently active to provide such regular guidance. The Procurate proudly announced (Gong Zeng, 1979) that in 1979 its various staff members had reviewed thousands of cases and reversed some 2000 instances of violation of the law by courts or police. The Procurate also received over 270,000 complaints from citizens (*Peking Review*, 17 Aug. 1979). But these numbers are hardly impressive in comparison with the scale of complaints lodged during periods of mass rectification campaigns, and in the past the Procurate has never been sufficiently strong or committed to energetic supervision of the far more powerful police and court bureaucracies (Ginsbergs, 1964). Finally, there is the inherent limitation in the nature of the Procurate's review and its available options for redress of grievances. The Procurate reviews other agencies only in terms of their conformity to specified legal procedures, not the broader and more ambitious dictates of revolutionary principles like the "mass line" (N.P.C., 1978). Such a legalistic review leaves little place for citizen involvement, and the Procurate's action can extend no further than the reversal of individual decisions made by police courts or other bureaux. The procurate is not empowered to consider or correct overall problems of citizen-professional relations or general failings of agencies such as bureaucratic isolation or elitism.

REVISIONIST ECONOMICS, INTERNATIONAL CAPITAL, AND THE ROLE OF LAW

The new legal system serves not only to control dissent and to centralize state power, but it serves also to extend and standardize the Peking regime's modernization strategies. The government has decisively broken with Maoist traditions by reducing worker participation in favor of "expert" management, by relying on increased mate-

rial incentives, encouraging peasant capitalism, by regarding profitability as the central criterion for evaluation of production units, and by inviting large-scale foreign investment by capitalist firms while borrowing from capitalist nations. Each of these turns in policy has been confirmed in new legal statutes and contracts; and the new constitution guarantees against any further redistribution of property. The writing of economic strategies into law helps to reassure both the emerging Chinese economic elite and western investors and creditors. The contrast between the current emphasis on legalism and policies during the Maoist era is illuminating.

It should be remembered that the Chinese Maoists were always reluctant to adopt extensive or finalized legal codes precisely because they were as yet dissatisfied with continuing inequalities and vestiges of capitalism in the society. Wu Tu peng argued during the Great Leap Forward that:

> A time of radical social change is not the time to codify laws . . . Law is the armour of the social system. If, for example, laws pertaining to property had been codified during the cooperative stage of agriculture they would now be quite out of date, since the commune movement has altered the whole basis of ownership (Greene, 1962, p. 187).

Today, in a time of renewed emphasis on material incentives, widened wage gaps, and peasant capitalism, the government has undertaken to finalize property relations (Jinag Hua and Huang Huong Ping, 1979). The erosion of egalitarian commitments was already apparent in the language of the 1975 Constitution, and the Constitution of 1978 further legitimates private production and brakes the process of collectivization in favor of individual incentives (Cohen, 1979, pp. 806-9; N.P.C., 1975; 1978). The new Penal Code was introduced this year by Peng Zhen (1979), with the forthright assertion that:

> One of the major purposes of the criminal law was to defend socialist property owned by the whole people and by the collective and the legitimate

property of individuals, including income savings, houses and other means of livelihood, and means of production such as plots of land, animals and trees owned or used by an individual or family according to law (Peng Zhen, 1979).

The discipline of labor is a central concern of the new legal order. While radicals have tended to rely on political education and the mobilization of energies through mass organizations, the new regime has followed the bureaucratic tradition in creating new regulatory laws and agencies. The new Constitution of 1978 specifies that one of the "duties" of Chinese citizens is "to maintain labor discipline"; and accompanying reports by national officials stress the need for "unity and iron discipline" among workers. This contrasts with the 1975 Constitution which contained no such language and which included, for the first time, the right to strike (N.P.C., 1978). Mao Tse Tung had earlier remarked (Cohen, 1979, p. 833) that "Strikes and boycotts are means of struggle against bureaucracy . . . When the use of struggle by criticism cannot solve the problem, we must allow the strike to be used."

The formal/legal contract has become the new basis of relationships between the central government and local units of production. The individual plant or commune manager is recognized as the sole authority in these contracts which exclude the increasingly passive mass organizations from decision making. The highly paid professional managers are evaluated almost entirely on the basis of profits earned by their enterprises, with little concern for such Maoist goals as egalitarian wage levelling or democratic participation. New laws have also established "work standards" to be enforced by the newly created "Economic Divisions" of intermediate courts. These courts are empowered both to settle labor management disputes through mediation and to punish those who are guilty of "seriously defective or shoddy work, neglect of duty, embezzlement" or other offenses involving heavy economic losses or breaches of authority (*Peking Review*, 10 Aug. 1979). The tone of these policies

and the direction for the future is unmistakable in the official announcement of new labor legislation in 1977:

> Rules and regulations ought never to be eliminated. Moreover, with the development of production and technology rules and regulations must become stricter and people must follow them more precisely. This is the law of nature (Peking Radio as quoted in Bettleheim, 1978).

China's growing alliance with capitalist nations and her blooming partnerships with multinational corporations are also formalized. The legal contract has become the new standard of measurement for production and new laws guarantee foreign investors sizeable advantages, subject to only limited controls by the Chinese government. A corporation need only invest a minimal capital share of 25% to qualify for 2 years initial tax exemption and partial tax refunds for later reinvestment. The lack of any limits above 25% means that a multinational could legally take 100% of the profits produced from the use of Chinese labor and materials. Legal guarantees against nationalization imply that multinational exploitation of the country could become a permanent feature. The economic plans developed by the new leadership lay heavy stress on the importation of western technology and capital investment; yet, there is no mention of potential social and political contradictions. We are thus confronted with the astonishing prospect of a socialist government committed to enforcement of increasingly strict labor regulations to ensure the profits and production of foreign controlled capitalist firms.

In considering the politics and motivations of the new legal order it would be unfair to ignore China's imperative need for stability and central direction of what is still a backward and precarious economy. Likewise it is certain that the intellectuals and professionals need some reassurance and encouragement after the shock of criticism and sanction in the Cultural Revolution. There is nothing inherently repressive about disciplinary regulations or necessarily exploitive about limited foreign investment. Certainly, too, the "cult of Mao" contributed to immaturity and adventurism among many of the radical young cadres and activists. The excesses of the Cultural Revolution and China's historic xenophobia did require constructive criticism and correction; perhaps in the form of new codes and a stabilized legal system.

What has occurred is far more than that. The most important principles of Maoist thought and the most progressive reform policies have been overturned. The elimination of revolutionary committees and the weakening of mass organizations leaves the bureaucracy without an effective popular counterweight. The rewriting of history and the practical rejection of revolutionary ideologies such as the "mass line" and the "continuing revolution" has weakened the theoretical base of popular activism and reform even as its organizational means have been eliminated. The intimidation and purge of radical cadres from the national to the local level further releases the established elite from the constraints of challenge and criticism. All of the political and legal changes are paralleled by increased inequality resulting from the emphasis on material incentives, hierarchical rigidity, and limited rural capitalism. China is not merely facing a problem of ideological conservatism, but the threatened emergence of a new and exploitive ruling class. While this is not yet an accomplished fact, it cannot be reversed by moderate means of criticism/ self-criticism and elite re-education.

LEGITIMIZING THE NEW STATE AND THE PROMISE OF "INDIVIDUAL RIGHTS"

The revisionist leadership hopes that the new legal system will both strengthen their popular legitimacy and their effective powers. They have organized a national "mass campaign" of their own design which features public readings of the new laws and lectures by legal professionals (Ye Jiang Ying, 1979). The laws and accompanying lectures have for months dominated the newspaper columns, airways, and public speeches (Hua Kuo feng, 1978; *Hung ch'i,* 4 May 1979). Yet there is much in these laws which contradicts public needs. Not only do the new laws cement existing social inequalities and power relations, but they strengthen new alliances, especially those which conservative officials would make with the intellectual class and the capitalist nations. The laws and the re-established justice agencies have undertaken to repress political dissent and to enforce labor discipline. Yet new economic policies can only lead to greater domestic dissatisfaction. The current emphasis on professionalism and formality in justice agencies and procedures is paralleled by the increased centralization of decision making and the decline of citizen participation in both peace-keeping and political expression.

The change from revolutionary to revisionist policies is perhaps crystallized in the new concept of freedom advanced in the 1978 Constitution and the regime's official statements. The notion of freedom implicit in popular justice and the Maoist tradition is a clearly social one, measured in the velocity of egalitarian change and the responsiveness of government to the public community. This rebellious and restless definition of freedom has been carried on the banners of the Long March, the Great Leap Forward, and the Cultural Revolution. It was present still even in the compromise Constitution of 1975 which contained the following passage:

> Article 13: Speaking out freely, airing views fully, holding great debates and writing big character posters are new forms of carrying on socialist revolution created by the masses of the people. The state shall ensure to the masses the right to use these forms to create a political situation in which there are both centralism and democracy, both discipline and freedom, both unity of will and personal ease of mind and liveliness, and so help consolidate the leadership of the Communist Party of China over the state and consolidate the dictatorship of the proletariat (N.P.C., 1975, p. 17).

The new leadership has promised the people "individual rights" protected with new guarantees for free expression and due process under law (Li Bo yon, 1979). Thus far, the record indicates that these guarantees are hardly binding in the case of serious dissent. However, even in its idealized form this kind of freedom is bourgeois in theory, and sterile in practice. It fragments liberty into pieces of personal rights and privilege and makes government answerable only to its own laws and regulatory bodies rather than to mass action and revolutionary principles. This notion of freedom is borrowed directly from the class societies of capitalism or from revisionist socialism (as in the U.S.S.R.).

The alternative revolutionary conception measures freedom in social terms: in the extent of "community control" the people exercise over social institutions and in the movement toward equality in social relations and material conditions. The limits of liberty are not set in law, but in the dialectical interface of community organizations, Party, and state. This more ambitious dimension of freedom is increasingly circumscribed by the present Hua Kuo feng regime. The abolition of "revolutionary committees" and of "ongoing rectification" has reduced public influence and led to a decline in mass participation. The widening of wage gaps, tightening up of school admissions. and rigidification of hierarchies in government and production, means a lowering of horizons for most workers and peasants. The flavored intellectuals and the conservative bureaucrats have buried the radical opposition at the national level; and seem now determined to bury Maoist principles with the Chairman himself. The Constitution of 1978 is intended as the tombstone for the "continuing revolution" and the invigorated justice bureaucracies are its pallbearers. But social contradictions are not so easily laid away as even the greatest of heroes.

REFLECTION ON THE ROLE OF LAW AND IMPLICATIONS FOR CHINA'S FUTURE

While I have argued that China is now on the road to revisionism and a new sort of ruling-class dominion, the present situation is still subject to change. For one thing, the conservative officials have not yet fully integrated the intellectual class into political leadership and class alliance. For another, there is yet a simmering of dissent and leftist sentiments remaining especially from the Great Leap and the Cultural Revolution. The revisionist leadership has promised to raise living standards substantially in the next few years; and failure to do this could lead to a drop in popular support expressed either in lower productivity of resentful workers or in a renewed mobilization of criticism and rectification from the left.

Given the entrenched position of the new regime and the confirmation of present policies and power relations in law, it would doubtless take a massive upheaval on the scale of the Cultural Revolution to reverse present trends. The problem, from the left's view, is that such events have always been initiated and coordinated from the national level, to be then energized and implemented by the local cadres and activists. No such left leadership now exists at the national level. There are, however, certainly lines of division between the centrists, such as Hua Kuo feng and rightists, such as Teng Hsiaso ping. The police, P.L.A., and some of the middle level party cadres are generally counted today as aligned with the center, while the intellectual class and large parts of the bureaucracy (including the courts and Procurate) could be expected to support the more conservative policies led by Teng. Should the revisionist policies fail to bear fruit in terms of domestic production and living standards, it is possible that the center elite might lead the lower level left cadres in a renewal of rectification.

The sudden reversals in this China's "Season of Startling Alliance" have shocked alike many friends and foes of Maoist China. But only those first illusioned by political caricatures can easily be dis-illusioned by subsequent political events. The seeds of conflict have long been present in the contradictions of the Chinese political economy. These recent events underscore the volatile and complex nature of the transformation to socialism. Certainly the final outcome of a revolution is not determined by the initial seizure of power. Milovan Djilas (1962) has well described the evolution of revisionism and the "new class" in the Soviet Union; and Mao Tse Tung (1956) warned of this possibility in China even before the Great Leap Forward. As Sweezy and Bettleheim so correctly observed:

> Without revolutionary enthusiasm and mass participation, centralized planning becomes increasingly authoritarian and rigid with resulting multiplication of economic difficulties and failures. In an attempt to solve these increasingly serious problems the rulers turn to capitalist techniques, vesting increasing power within the economic enterprises in managements and relying for their guidance and control more and more on the impersonal pressures of the market. Under these circumstances, the juridical form of state property becomes increasingly empty and the real power over the means of production, which is the essence of the ownership concept, gravitates into the hands of the managerial elite (Sweezy and Bettleheim, 1971, p. 29).

The new Peking leaders and their appreciative supporters in the West would now hope that the "anarchic" era of mass mobilization, political conflict and social experiment is past. The Chinese state should now pursue "modernization" with single minded zeal and by almost any means necessary. One can appreciate their impatience to reach industrial parity after China's long history of humiliation and threat at the hands of the West and, most recently, of the U.S.S.R. However, the reformulation of national purpose ignores the social and moral aspect of socialist transformation and measures development only in steel tonnage and transport mileage. The dangers of this sort of narrowness and expedience have been well recognized and described, not only by the defeated Maoist radicals, but also by other socialist nations emerging in the Third World. Che Guevara in particular, pointedly rejected this falsely "practical" path to modernization for Cuba, insisting:

> There is still a long stretch to be covered in the construction of an economic base, and the tempta-

tion to take the beaten path of material interest as the lever of accelerated development is very great. There is the danger of not seeing the forest because of the trees. Pursuing the wild idea of trying to realize socialism with the worn out weapons left by capitalism (the market place as the basic economic cell, profit making, individual material incentives, and so forth), one can arrive at a dead end. And one arrives there after having travelled a long distance with so many forked roads where it is difficult to perceive the moment when the wrong path was taken. Meanwhile the adapted economic base has undermined the development of consciousness. To construct communism simultaneously with the material base of our society, we must create a new man (Bonachea and Valdes, 1969, p. 256).

The Peking leadership has deliberately disregarded such observations and also the weight of China's own revolutionary traditions, in choosing the downhill path to modernization. Nothing so clearly expresses their determination as their haste in writing new political and economic principles into law.

The new legal order has been erected as both girder and façade for the revisionist state, its stratified social relations, and expedient development strategies. New prohibitions against political dissent loom behind the official propaganda attack on Maoist ideas and the Gang of Four, even on Mao himself. State bureaucracies have been invested with sole regulatory power over administration and peace-keeping, while citizens' organizations are disbanded or reduced to auxiliary roles. The managerial elite is freed of obligation to Maoist ethics and granted increased power under legal contract arrangements which equate success only with profitability. The increasingly uneven distribution of wealth is guaranteed against redistribution by new statutes, even as foreign investments and the exploitation of Chinese labor and resources is protected by new laws and judicial bodies.

In formulating a critique of the new Chinese legal order one returns to Marxist critiques of capitalist law and finds much that is sadly relevant. The layering of law as a protective and regulating armour upon an increasingly unequal and undemocratic social order has been described as a central feature of developed capitalism. Marx's own commentary is brief but cogent:

> It is furthermore clear that here as always it is in the interests of the ruling section of society to sanction the existing order as law and to legally establish its limits through usage and tradition . . . and such regulation and order are themselves indispensable elements of any mode of production, if it is to assume social stability and independence from mere chaos and arbitrariness (Marx, 1972, p. 793).

The Soviet theorist Pashukanis (1978) described the capitalist state's reliance on formal law as an expression of social alienation born of class conflict. The state serves as the (falsely) neutral arbiter of conflict, and laws define the obligation and duties of citizens whose sense of shared community is too weak to support social order on a more informal or organic basis. Pashukanis demonstrated that increasing reliance on law and formal administration was a feature of developing capitalism; but he recognized that law would continue as a diminishing part of the political vocabulary during the period of socialist transition so long as social isolation and fragmented consciousness remained.

Clearly the experience of the Soviet Union and recent events in China indicate that social isolation can not only continue, but even deepen if expedience sets the course of socialist transition and if "new class" elites form to undermine egalitarian reform and democratic participation in decision making. The state and its legal apparatus does not wither; but rather it is the revolutionary forms and organs of popular participation which become hollow and ultimately bureaucratic. Such has been the recent fate of the Revolutionary Committees, the rural communes, and the various student, worker, and urban community organizations in China. The Peking leadership's increasing reliance on law is necessary, then, not only to suppress radical dissent, but also to regulate the domestic market economy, protect property relations, and win public

acceptance. Moreover, law must also provide some sort of framework of social obligation to replace the universals of Maoist ethics and the self-correcting dynamics of voluntary "self-reliant" mass associations.

The closing argument here should not be construed as a condemnation of all law or as blanket praise for popular spontaneity and community autonomy. Such an anarchist position would be totally neglectful of China's pressing need to coordinate closely her meagre technical and capital resources. Moreover, law can serve revolutionary ends even as it now sets the course of revisionism; and China provides an excellent example of the former. The early land reform statutes and marriage laws of the 1940s and 1950s were instruments of radical social change. The relations of property and marriage specified in those laws were far in advance of existing conditions and the laws both legitimated and accelerated the collectivization of land, reduction of class inequality, and improvement in women's position. The state threw its full weight behind these laws; but the mass organizations of peasants and women were also mobilized and strengthened through their direct role in the enforcement of the laws (see Hinton, 1967; Meijer, 1971, pp. 85–157). The new legal order now under construction in China owes nothing to these revolutionary legal traditions. It remains to be seen what it owes to the masses of Chinese working people as opposed to the looming power of an elitist "new class."

REFERENCES

Bennett, G. (1977) Mass campaigns and social control. In *Development and Social Control* (Oskenburg, O., Ed.). Random House: New York.

Bettleheim, C. (1970) Letter of resignation. In *China Since Mao*. Monthly Review Press: New York.

Bettleheim, C. (1970) The Great Leap Backward. In *China Since Mao*. Monthly Review Press: New York.

Bonachea, R. & Valdés, N. (1969) *Che: Selected Works*. MIT Press: Cambridge.

Brady, J. (1974) *Popular Justice: Conflict and Commu-*

nity in the Chinese Legal System. Unpublished doctoral dissertation. University of California: Berkeley.

Brady, J. (1977a) Dialectics of justice policy in the People's Republic of China. *Contemporary Crisis* **1.**

Brady, J. (1977b) Political economy and justice policy in the United States and China. *Journal of Political Repression* **4.**

Bridgham, P. (1968) Mao's cultural revolution in 1967. *China Quarterly* **34.**

Bridgham, P. (1971) The Lin Piao Affair. *China Quarterly* **49.**

Buttlerfield, F. (1976) Peking publishes abuses of rights. *N.Y. Times* 28 Feb.

Buttlerfield, F. (1977) Behind the scenes power figures. *N.Y. Times* 23 Sept.

Butterfield, F. (1978) China to drop revolutionary units. *N.Y. Times* 6 March.

Buttlerfield, F. (1979) Another dissident on trial in Peking. *N.Y. Times* 13 Oct.

Casella, A. (1973) Naniwan May 7th School. *China Quarterly* **53.**

Cheng Shih yi (1976) Open door education. *Peking Review* 2 Jan.

Chi, B. (1979) Crime and punishment in China, *N.Y. Times* 7 Oct.

Cohen J. (1972) Drafting mediation rules for Chinese cites. *Studies in Chinese Law.* **13,** Harvard E. Asian Research Series.

Cohen, J. (1973a) Chinese law at the crossroads. *China Quarterly* **53.**

Cohen, J. (1973b) Notes on legal education in China. *Harvard Law School Alumnii Bulletin* Feb.

Cohen, J. (1979) China's changing constitution. *China Quarterly* **76.**

Diao, R. (1970) The impact of the cultural revolution on the Chinese economic elite. *China Quarterly* **42.**

Dittmar, L. (1973) The structural evolution of criticism-self criticism. *China Quarterly* **56.**

Djilas, M. (1962) *The New Class.* Unpublished Conference Paper, New York.

Donnithone, A. (1966) Centralized Economic control in China. China Conference, Chicago, May.

Dutt, G. (1970) *China's Cultural Revolution.* Asia Publishing House: New York.

Edwards, R. (1977) Reflections on crime and punishment in China. *Columbia Journal of Transnational Law*

Ginsbergs, G. & Stankhe, A. (1964) The people's procurate in China. *China Quarterly* **34.**

Gong, Z. (1979) People's new democratic legal system. *Hung ch'i* 2 Feb.

Gray, J. (1970) The economics of Maoism. *China After the Cultural Revolution.* (Atomic Scientists, Eds). Vintage: New York.

Greene, F. (1962) *China.* Ballantine Books: New York.

Hinton, H. (1969) Communist China's Domestic Scene. Institute for Defense Analysis: Arlington, Va.

Hinton, W. (1972) *Hundred Day War.* Monthly Review Press: New York.

Hinton, W. (1967) *Fanshen.* Monthly Review Press: New York.

Hsia, A. (1972) *The Chinese Cultural Revolution.* Seabury Press: New York.

Hsiang Shih (1969) New problems in the realm of legal studies. *chen fa yen chiu in Chinese Law and Government* **1.**

Hsu, I. C. (1964) The reorganization of higher education. *China Quarterly* **19.**

Institute of Political and Legal Research (IPLR) Central People's Judicial Cadre School (1958) Lectures on General Principles of Criminal Law. Peking.

Jinag, H. & Huang, H. (1979) Reports on the People's democratic legal system. National People's Congress. *Hung ch'i* 26 June.

Lambe, W. (1974) Interview with Chinese legal officials. *China Quarterly* **54.**

Lee, H. Y. (1978) *The Politics of the Chinese Cultural Revolution.* University of California Press: Berkeley.

Leng, S. C. (1967) *Justice in Communist China.* Oceana Publications: New York.

Li Bo yon (1979) Report on Organic Law of People's Court and the new socialist legal system. *Hung ch'i* 6 March.

Li Hong Rin (1979) What sort of socialism should we uphold? *Peking Review* 5 June.

Li Victor (1973) Criminal law and penology. *Academy of Political Science Proceedings* March.

Lie Jie Gonng (1979) Report on the criminal code. *Peking Review* 20 July.

Lieken, R. (1979) Comments on China since Mao. *Monthly Review* **3.**

Lin Heng Yuan (1979) Advance the People's new democratic legal system. *Peking Review* 20 July.

Liu Shao chi (1956) Speech before the Eighth Party Congress. *Documents of the Eighth Party Congress.* Peking.

Lubman, S. (1969) Form and function in the Chinese criminal process. *Columbia Law Review* **69.**

Lubman, S. (1977) Mao and mediation. *California Law Review* **55.**

Marx, K. (1972) *Capital,* vol. III. Lawrence and Wishart: London.

Malden, W. (1965) A new class structure emerging in China? *China Quarterly* **22.**

Mao Tse Tung (1943) Some questions concerning methods of leadership. In *Selected Works.* Foreign Language Press: Peking.

Mao Tse Tung (1957) On the correct handling of contradictions among the people. In *Selected Works.* Foreign Language Press: Peking.

Mao Tse Tung (1970) Red and expert. In *Mao Papers.* (J. Chen, Ed.). Oxford University Press: New York.

Matthews, J. (1979) Chinese dissident gets 5 year term. *Boston Globe* 7 Oct.

Meijer, M. (1971) *Marriage Law and Policy in the People's Republic of China.* Hong Kong University Press: Hong Kong.

Monthly Review Editors (1979) New theories for old. *Monthly Review* **31.**

Munro, R. (1977) China, for want of a formal legal code. *New York Times* 12 Oct.

MacDougall, C. (1977) Chinese economy in 1976. *China Quarterly* **60.**

MacFarqhar, R. (1974) *The Origins of the Cultural Revolution.* Columbia University Press: New York.

Nee, V. (1973) Revolution and bureaucracy: Shanghai. In *China's Uninterrupted Revolution* (Nee & Peck, Eds). Pantheon: New York.

Onate, A. (1978) Hua Kuo feng and the arrest of the Gang of Four. *China Quarterly* **75.**

Pan, S. & de Juegher, R. (1968) *Peking's Red Guards.* Twin Circle Publications: New York.

Pashukanis, E. B. (1978) *Law and Marxism.* Ink Links: London.

Peng Zhen (1979) Report on the draft criminal code. *Peking Review* 13 July.

Pepper, Z. (1977) Education and changes after the fall of the Gang of Four. *China Quarterly* **72.**

Pfeffer, R. (1972) Serving the people and continuing the revolution. *China Quarterly* **52.**

Pfeffer, R. (1975) Leaders and masses. *Academy of Political Science Proceedings* **34.**

Pincus, F. (1979) Higher education and socialist transformation in China since 1970. *Review of Radical Political Economics* **IX.**

Riskin, C. (1972) Maoism and motivation. In *China's Uninterrupted Revolution.* (Nee & Peck, Eds). Pantheon: New York.

Ruge, G. (1976) Interviews with Chinese legal officials. *China Quarterly* **57.**

Salaff, J. (1975) Urban social structure in the wake of the cultural revolution. *China Quarterly* **29.**

Schram, S. (1963) Urban rural income differences in Communist China. *China Quarterly* **36.**

Schram, S. (1971) Mao tse Tung and the permanent revolution. *China Quarterly* **46.**

Schurmann, F. (1966) *Ideology and Organization in Communist China.* University of California: Berkeley.

Selden, M. (1969) *The Yenan Way.* Doubleday: New York.

Shang Zhe (1979) Persistently carry forward socialist democracy. *Hung ch'i* 1 June.

Stankhe, A. (1966) The background and evolution of party policy in the drafting of legal codes. *American Journal of Comparative Law* **15.**

Sun Yeh fang (1979) Report on modernization in agriculture. *Peking Review* 4 Sept.

Sweezy, P. & Bettleheim, C. (1971) *On the Transition to Socialism.* Monthly Review Press: New York.

Teng Hsiao ping (1978) Speech at National Education Conference. *Peking Review* 5 May.

Terrill, R. (1978) *The Future of China After Mao.* Dell: Philadelphia.

Tiewes, F. (1974) China before and after the Cultural Revolution. *China Quarterly* **58.**

Ting Wang (1978) A concise biography of Hua Kuo feng. *Chinese Law and Government* **1.**

Townsend, J. (1974) *Politics in China.* University of California Press: Berkeley.

Tung Pi Wu (1956) Report to Eighth Party Congress. *Documents of Eighth Party Congress.* Foreign Languages Press: Peking.

Wang Hsiao t'ing (1978) An evaluation and analysis of China's revised constitution. *Chinese Law and Government* **9.**

Whiting, A. (1976) As quoted in *N.Y. Times* 17 Oct.

Whyte, L. (1974) Inequality and stratification in China. *China Quarterly* **64.**

Yan yi (1979) Observe and safeguard Party rules. *Hung ch'i* 13 April.

Ye Jian Ying (1979) Report to National People's Congress, *Peking Review* 20 July.

Hung ch'i (Red Flag) is the chief theoretical journal of the Chinese Communist Party, published in Peking and translated by the U.S. Joint Publications Research Service.

Peking Review is a weekly news summary published in Peking (abbreviated P.R.).

Jen Min Jih Pao (abbreviated J.M.J.P.) is the official news daily of the Chinese Communist Party, published in Peking and translated by the Survey of China Mainland Press.

National People's Congress (abbreviated N.P.C.) has published the various national constitutions referred to in text of article.

POPULAR JUSTICE, DUAL POWER AND SOCIALIST STRATEGY

BOAVENTURA de SOUSA SANTOS

It is almost a commonplace to say that there is no Marxist theory *of* law, though it is less commonly acknowledged that there are a few Marxist theories *against* law, the most famous one being Pashukanis'.[1] The reason usually invoked for this theoretical deficit has been that neither Marx nor Engels devoted more than scattered and sketchy (non-systematic) references to the question of law in capitalist society.[2] It seems to me, however, that in view of the mutual implications of theoretical and strategic issues in Marxism, the *material* reason of this theoretical deficit has to be found in the fact that neither of the dominant strategies in the working-class movement up until now has necessitated a Marxist theory of law. Leaving aside for the moment the problems related to the distinction between reform and revolution, we can *grosso modo* identify two main strategies: the revolutionary (insurrectionary) strategy, the most coherent and global formulation of which is Lenin's, was the official line of the Third International particularly until 1934/35 (the beginning of the Popular Front period); the reformist strategy, for which Eduard Bernstein provided the most eloquent theoretical reconstruction, corresponded to the practice of the parties of the Second International till its collapse in 1914 and became the official line of the socialist movement after the split of the working-class movement between the socialists and the communists in 1922–3.

The revolutionary strategy aims at destroying the capitalist state by means of a global confrontation that may include violence, substituting for it the dictatorship of the proletariat, a new state form created in the struggle by the working class

---

[1] To a certain extent, the same can be said about the capitalist state in spite of the vast bibliography on the topic produced in the last two decades. Althusser, a major influence in the new Marxist studies on the state, has recently asserted that "there does not *really* exist any Marxist theory of the state" (quoted by G. Therbonn, "The Travail of Latin American Democracy," *New Left Review*, 113-114, 72). Among the most important contributions to this discussion in the last decade see N. Poulantzas, *Pouvoir Politique et Classes Sociales de L'Etat Capitaliste* Paris, 1968; C. Offe, *Strukturprobleme des Kapitalistischen Staates,* Frankfurt 1972; E. Altvater, "Zu einigen Problemen des Staatsinterventionismus," *Prokla* 3, 1; R. Miliband, *The State in Capitalist Society*, London, 1973; J O'Connor, *The Fiscal Crisis of the State,* New York, 1973; P. Anderson, *Lineages of the Absolutist State,* London, 1974; J. Hirsch, *Staatsapparat und Reproduktion des Kapitals,* Frankfurt, 1974; A. Negri, *La Forma Stato,* Milan, 1977; G. Therborn, *What Does the Ruling Class Do When It Rules?* London, 1978; E. O. Wright, *Class Crisis and the State,* London, 1978; On the important debate on the capitalist state in West Germany see V. Brandes et al. (Eds.), *Handbuch 5 Staat,* Frankfurt, 1977; a perspective of the same debate in a more accessible language in J. Holloway and S. Picciotto, *State and Capital. A Marxist Debate,* London, 1978. A not less important debate on the state in Latin America in *Revista Mexicana de Sociologia* 1-2/77.

[2] Though Marx did not produce a theory of the state, as he intended to, the references to law can be found in almost all of his texts from the first contributions to the *Rheinische Zeitung* to the *Critique of the Gotha Programme.* There have been some attempts to systematize this vast material. One of the first is U. Cerroni, *Marx e il Diritto,* Roma, 1962, and one of the last is M. Cain and A. Hunt, *Marx and Engels on Law,* London, 1979.

Source: From 1979 National Deviancy Conference/ Conference of Socialist-Economists, *Capitalism and the Rule of Law* Bob Fine, Richard Kinsey, John Lea, Sol Picciotto, and Jock Young, eds., (London: Hutchinson, 1979), pp. 151–163. Reprinted by permission.

and adequate to the performance of the tasks of the transitional period before communism. Law does not play any important role within this strategy. As an instrument of capitalist domination bourgeois law has to be fought against as much as the bourgeois state. Indeed the third condition of admission to the Communist International stated that "the communists can have no confidence in bourgeois law." In view of this there is no need to theorize in detail the possible use of legality by the working class; on the contrary, the Marxist theory of law, if one is produced at all, must reveal the negativity of law *vis-à-vis* the revolutionary movement. In this sense the Marxist theory of law becomes a Marxist theory against law. The best example is Pashukanis's general theory of law, no matter how crucial his insights may be for the elaboration of a Marxist theory of law adequate to our current strategic needs.[3]

Unlike the revolutionary strategy, the reformist strategy is based on the extensive use of law, since the gradual transformation of the capitalist state into a socialist state is to be achieved by means of social reforms brought about within the established constitutional framework. But the use of law presupposes a sophisticated Marxist theory of law only if and when the gradual transformation of the state is conceived of as a gradual destruction of the capitalist state form and the gradual emergence of a new socialist state form. However, the reformist strategy in practice has tended to *forget* its strategic goal—i.e. the transformation and destruction of the capitalist state—concentrating rather on social reforms, which in the end have, in fact, stabilized the capitalist state. In view of this practice, the use of law, far from presupposing a Marxist theory of law, is most adequately guided by the bourgeois

theories of law which, with their vast, rich, and sophisticated body of legal thought, always reproduce the capitalist state. The impasse of the Marxist theory of law is best illustrated by the work of Karl Renner.[4] Renner's Marxist critique of the law of property ends up in the apologetic view of the state stabilizing changes in the capitalist law of property at the beginning of the twentieth century.

To my mind a sophisticated Marxist theory of law is only needed by a working-class strategy based on the supersession of the reform/revolution dichotomy as historically known. This implies the non-bourgeois use of bourgeois legality and the creation and expansion of instances of alternative socialist legality. Though embryonic, hesitant, and reversible, there are signs of a strategic reorientation in this direction throughout Europe, both West and East, since the early 1960s. Such reorientation is related to three main factors. First, the profound changes in the process of capitalist accumulation and in the structure of the capitalist state after the Second World War. Second, the horrifying experience of fascism and the consequent relegitimation of the democratic rule in general. Third, the ever more visible degenerative features of state socialism in the USSR and the states under its influence and the consequent re-evaluation of the rather ambiguous role of the USSR in the European working-class movement since the foundation of the Third International, particularly after Stalin's takeover.

The theoretocal foundation for such strategic reorientation in the field of law and the state must be based upon three preliminary tasks. First, to eliminate some time-honoured pseudo-theoretical constructs such as the topographic

[3]E. Pashukanis, *Law and Marxism. A General Theory*, London, 1978. The radical critique of bourgeois legality in Pashukanis does not lead to any alternative legality. Indeed, given the close connection between the legal form and the abstract principle of equality implicit in commodity production and exchange, there is no room for proletarian legality even in the transitional period before the whithering away of the state and law.

[4]K. Renner, *The Institutions of Private Law and their Social Function*, London, 1949. However the left wing of the Austro-Marxism, and particularly Otto Bauer, offered an original and important contribution to a theory of law and of the relationship between law and revolution, a contribution that has been silenced or ignored up until now. The recent rediscovery of Otto Bauer in the socialist movement of Western Europe may lead to important theoretical and strategic developments.

metaphor (base/superstructure) and replace it by a more analytical, more consciously materialistic model of determination, which will also have to be more sensitive to strategy and tactics.[5] Second, it must accept the challenge to re-read, re-think, and re-evaluate the period of the European working-class movement between 1890 and 1923, more or less the period of the Second International and the founding years of the Third International, in the course of which the most profound, rich, open-ended debate within Marxism took place. The names of four people emerge, amongst others, as of crucial importance for our theoretical undertakings, particularly in their least well-known (rarely translated?) works. I mean Karl Kautsky, Karl Korsch, Rosa Luxemburg and Eduard Bernstein; especially the last two.[6] It may be surprising, even shocking that these two names are thus brought together, given the widely known fact that they belonged to opposite wings of the German social democracy. Eighty years later, however, we must read and evaluate them in view of our struggles, not theirs. Besides, no matter how much did actually separate them, they did share some important views: the intimate link between democracy and socialist struggle (starting inside the working-class party) and the global democratization of social and political life in socialist society.

Finally, the third preliminary task consists in reanalysing concrete revolutionary struggles, some of which are of the insurrectionary type, and in considering the empirical concepts emerging from them in view of their possible use, in transformed versions and under very different conditions, in future struggles. In this essay I will concentrate on this last task, using as an example the experiences of dual power in some modern revolutions from the Russian revolution in 1917 to the Portuguese revolution in 1974–5. I will start by commenting on Lenin's and Trotsky's conceptualizations of dual power. I will then explore some possible lines of theoretical reconstruction of the concept of dual power with specific focus on law and judicial action. Finally I will refer to some strategic and tactical uses of dual power in law and justice, both in revolutionary and non-revolutionary situations.

THE DISCUSSION OF DUAL POWER IN LENIN AND TROTSKY

For Lenin dual power is "the striking feature" of the Russian revolution: "it is the main peculiarity of our revolution, a peculiarity urgently requiring the most thoughtful analysis.[7] It consists

> in the fact that side by side with the Provisional Government, the government of the *bourgeoisie*, there has developed *another* government, weak

---

[5]The concept of structural causality developed by the Althusserian school is a significant theoretical progress, but it is still too abstract to serve as a reliable guide in regional analyses, particularly in the field of law. The analytical objective is to distinguish among the different modes of juridicity. In my own research I have reached the conclusion that the three structural components of capitalist legality are *rhetoric, bureaucracy,* and *violence* and that these components are articulated in specific ways (*quantitative covariation, geopolitical combination,* and *structural interpenetration*). The relative weight of the different components and their relative positions in the different articulations vary across the different fields of law and these variations account for the different modes of juridicity. See B. de Sousa Santos, "Law and Community: The Changing Nature of State Power in Late Capitalism," *International Journal of Sociology of Law,* 8, 379ff. (1980).

[6]K. Kautsky, *Der Parlamentarismus die Volksgesetzgeöung und die Sozialdemokratie,* Stuttgart, 1893; *Patriotismus und Sozialdemokratie,* Leipzig, 1907; *Nationalität und Internationalität,* 1908; *National Staat, Imperialistischer Staat und Staatenbund,* Nurmberg, 1915; *Von der Demokratie zur Staats-Sklaverei. Eine Ausseinandersetzung mit Trotzki,* Berlin, 1921; K. Korsch, *Was ist Sozialisierung?,* Hanover, 1919; *Quintessenz des Marxismus,* Jena, 1922; *Arbeitsrecht fur Betriebsräte,* Berlin, 1922; *Marxismus und Philosophie,* Leipzig, 1923, *Der Weg der Komintern,* Berlin, 1926; *Die Materialistische Geschichtsauffassung,* Leipzig, 1929; R. Luxemburg, *Gesammelte Werke,* 5 volumes, Berlin, 1972; E. Bernstein, *Die Voraussetzungen des Sozialismus und die Aufgaben der Sozialdemokratie,* 1898; *Zur Geschichte und Theorie des Sozialismus,* 1901; and in general his contributions to periodicals, particularly to *Sozialistische Monatshefte* after 1900.

[7]Lenin, *Selected Works in Three Volumes,* Vol. 2 (Moscow, 1960). On dual power in the Russian Revolution see, besides Trotsky quoted below, M. Ferro, *La Revolution de 1917,* Paris, 1967; O. Anweiler, *Die Rätebewegung in Russland 1905–1921,* Leiden, 1958.

and embryonic as yet, but undoubtedly and actually existing and growing government—the Soviets of Workers' and Soldiers' Deputies.

To the question of the class composition of this other government, Lenin answers that "it consists of the proletariat and the peasantry (clad in army uniform)." As to the political nature of this government Lenin goes on to say:

> It is a revolutionary dictatorship, i.e., a power based on outright revolutionary seizure, on the direct initiative of the masses from below and *not on a law* enacted by a centralized state power. It is an entirely different power from that generally existing in parliamentary bourgeois-democratic republics of the usual type still prevailing in the advanced countries of Europe and America. This circumstance is often forgotten, often not given enough thought, yet it is the crux of the matter. *This* power is of *the same type* as the Paris Commune of 1871. Its fundamental characteristics are:
> 1) The source of power is not a law previously discussed and enacted by parliament, but the direct initiative of the people from below, in their localities—outright "seizure," to use a current expression;
> 2) The direct arming of the whole people in place of the police and the army, which are institutions separated from the people and set against the people; order in the state under such a power is maintained by the armed workers and peasants *themselves*, by the armed people *itself*;
> 3) Officials and bureaucrats are either similarly replaced by the direct rule of the people themselves or at least placed under special control; they not only become elected officials, but are also *subject to recall* at the first demand of the people; they are reduced to the position of single agents; from a privileged group occupying "posts" remunerated on a high "bourgeois" scale, they become workers of a special "branch" and remunerated at a salary *not exceeding* that of a competent worker (Lenin 1960), p. 50).

Writing in April, Lenin acknowledges that the soviets are an embryonic and incipient proletarian state form. Moreover, owing to the influence of petit-bourgeois elements (Mensheviks and Social Revolutionaries) in the soviets, the latter,

having entered into an agreement to support the Provisional Government, are in fact "voluntarily surrendering its own supremacy to the bourgeoisie." These extremely peculiar circumstances of the Russian revolution, "unparalleled in history," have led to the *"interlocking of two dictatorships:* the dictatorship of the bourgeoisie and the dictatorship of the proletariat and the peasantry." But

> there is not the slightest doubt that such an "interlocking" cannot last long. Two powers cannot exist in a state. One of them is bound to disappear. . . . The dual power merely expresses a *transitional* phase in the development of the revolution, when it has gone farther than the ordinary bourgeois-democratic revolution, but has *not yet reached* a "pure" dictatorship of the proletariat and the peasantry (Lenin, 1960a, pp. 58–9).

Trotsky's characterization of dual power is simultaneously broader and more optimistic. Unlike Lenin, Trotsky sees the situation of dual power as a "distinct condition of social crisis, by no means peculiar to the Russian revolution of 1917, although there most clearly marked out."[8] After specifying that there is no question of dual power where the ruling class power is divided between two of its factions such as the German Junkers and the bourgeoisie (whether in the Hohenzollern form or the republic). Trotsky adds that the dual power

> does not presuppose—generally speaking, indeed, it excludes—the possibility of a division of the power into two equal halves or indeed any formal equilibrium of forces whatever. It is not a constitutional, but a revolutionary fact. It implies that a destruction of the social equilibrium has already split the state superstructure. It arises where the hostile classes are already each relying upon essentially incompatible governmental organization—the one outlived, the other in process of formation—which jostle against each other at every step in the sphere of government. The amount of power which falls to each of these struggling classes in such a situation is

[8]Trotsky, *The Basic Writings of Trotsky*, New York, 1963, p. 101.

determined by the correlation of forces in the course of the struggle (Trotsky 1963, p. 103).

The situation of dual power may lead to a civil war, in which case the duality of power assumes a territorial expression and thus becomes even more visible. "But before the competing classes and parties will go to that extreme . . . they may feel compelled for quite a long time to endure, and even to sanction a two power system." Trotsky then illustrates the situation of dual power with references to the English, French, German, and Russian revolutions. As to the Russian revolution the peculiarity of its dual power lies in that, contrary to the previous revolutions, "we see the official democracy consciously and intentionally creating a two power system, dodging with all its might the transfer of power into its own hands." (Trotsky 1963, p. 107). Thus dual power starts in a concealed form and comes to the surface only when the bolsheviks displace the compromisers at the head of the soviet. Trotsky concludes that

> in the immeasurably greater maturity of the Russian proletariat in comparison with the town masses of the older revolutions, lies the basic peculiarity of the Russian revolution. This first led to the paradox of a half-spectral double government, and afterwards prevented the real one from being resolved in favour of the bourgeoisie.

The differences between Trotsky and Lenin on the question of dual power may probably be traced back to the different contexts of their writing: on the one side, a political statement written in 1917 and on the spot; on the other side, an historical analysis written between 1930 and 1932 in Prinkipo island. In any case their writings have much in common and reveal the following general features of dual power:

1. It occurs in a revolutionary crisis, in a situation of intense class struggle in which the question of the radical transformation of society becomes a "practical," "realistic," political question;

2. There is a plurality of centres of political power arising from contradictions between competing classes and not from divisions within any of the classes in the struggle;

3. the source of legitimacy of the emerging (proletarian) class power is not law issued by a centralized government but rather "revolutionary legality" or, as Lenin puts it, "outright revolutionary seizure on direct initiative of the masses from below." This initiative may be so "direct" that it may even surprise the "professional revolutionaries" for, as Lenin (1960, p. 50) candidly confesses, "we must know, for instance, how to supplement and amend our old Bolshevik "formulas" for, as it proved, they were sound in general, but their concrete realization turned out to be different. *Nobody* hitherto thought, or could have thought, of dual power."

4. The differences in social support and institutional development between the two polar powers may be more or less notorious and are always changing;

5. the powers in conflict find themselves in a situation of global confrontation or, at least, they tend to such a situation, since in the initial stages insufficient class consciousness or other factors may lead the emerging power to compromises and concessions;

6. the two powers represent not only contradictory class interests, but also contradictory state forms, a parliamentary democracy versus a Paris Commune type of government;

7. the situation of dual power is always an unstable one, because the division of power it entails tends to be resolved in favour of one of the classes in the struggle.

Trotsky's conversion of dual power into a universal dimension of a revolutionary situation has contributed to a fuller understanding of other twentieth century revolutions: in Germany 1917-23[9], in Spain 1936-9[10] and in various

---

[9]P. Broué, *Revolution en Allemagne (1917-1923)*, Paris, 1971.

[10]P. Broué and E. Témime, *La Revolution et la Guerre d'Espagne*, Paris, 1961.

countries in Latin America[11]. It is now imperative that we revise the concept of dual power so as to enrich its analytical content and adapt it to the strategic prospects of socialist revolution in Europe today. With this in mind I propose now to discuss the issue of dual power in the context of the Portuguese revolution 1974–5.

POPULAR JUSTICE IN THE CONTEXT OF DUAL POWERLESSNESS IN PORTUGAL

This is not the place to give a full account of the Portuguese revolution. It is even highly probable that the historians of the future will deny the status of a true revolution to the Portuguese events of 1974–5 as they have done with the German revolution of November 1918 (Broué 1971, p. 161).

The Portuguese revolution began as a military revolt led by a sizeable group of democratic and anti-fascist young officers, who were eager to put an end to the colonial war. In relation to the political project at home the programme of the Movement of the Armed Forces (MFA) was straightforward in spite of its generalities: immediate destruction of the fascist features of the state apparatus; elections for a constitutional assembly where parliamentary democracy would be restored; political pluralism and autonomy of working-class organizations; an anti-monopolist economic policy aiming at a more equitable distribution of wealth. Concerning the colonial question, however, the programme was rather ambiguous. It called for a political settlement in a large Portuguese space. Such ambiguity was the inevitable consequence of the fact that the young officers had felt compelled to compromise with Spinola who, excepting Costa Gomes, was the only general who had had conflicts with Caetano's regime. To compromise was then considered important, not only to minimize the possibility of resistance by some military units loyal to the old regime, but also to avoid any attempt at

a unilateral declaration of independence by the white population in the colonies, particularly in Angola.

Spinola clearly represented the interests of monopoly capital while the young officers of the MFA were granted from the start a tremendous popular support by the working class and large sectors of the petit-bourgeoisie. This popular mobilization (economic *and political* strikes broke out throughout the country) was instrumental in bringing about Spinola's total defeat, as well as the neutralization of the rightist elements inside the MFA and the political radicalization of its more leftist elements. This fact plus the firm rejection by the leading liberation movements of any Spinola-type solution for the colonial question were the main preconditions for what would become the most remarkable decolonization process of modern times—a decolonization process almost totally free from neocolonialist features.

The qualitative changes in the political process took place after March 1975 when Portuguese society underwent a revolutionary crisis: extensive nationalization of the industry; total nationalization of the banking and insurance system land seizures in Alentejo; house occupations in large cities; workers' councils; self-management in industrial and commercial enterprises abandoned by their former owners; cooperatives in industry, commerce, and agriculture; neighbourhood associations; people's clinics; and cultural dynamization in the most backward parts of the country. None of these measures, taken individually, challenged the capitalist foundations of society or the class nature of state power. However, all these measures taken together—along with the internal dynamics of working-class mobilization and of popular initiative, the generalized paralysis of the state apparatus and the developing conflict within the armed forces—did indeed bring about a revolutionary crisis. But on no occasion was there a situation of dual power conceived of as a situation of "global confrontation" between "two dictatorships." Although a full analysis of this fact is still to be made it seems to me that one of the

---

[11]Zavaleta Mercado, *El Poder Dual en America Latina*, Mexico, 1974.

major causative factors lies in the very nature of the events that led to the revolutionary crisis. It all started as a *military* revolt, that is, a revolt from above, originating within the state apparatus itself. The aim was to destroy the fascist state power but indeed only the most explicitly fascist features of the state were destroyed, such as the political police, political courts and prisons, the one-party system, and paramilitary fascist militias. The state apparatus was otherwise kept intact, with its fifty-year heritage of authoritarian ideology, recruitment, training, and practice. Though under popular pressure there were some purges of personnel in public administration and industry, they were rather limited in number, often opportunistic and, in some crucial sectors of the state apparatus, such as the administration of justice, virtually non-existent. In any case, purges were always restricted to personnel and never reached the structures of the state power. As to the two branches of the repressive state apparatus—the police (PSP and GNR) and the armed forces—the situation was even more striking. Since the police offered no resistance to the young officers of the MFA, there was no need to dismantle or even restructure the organization; only the top officers were replaced. As to the armed forces, there is no question but that they were shaken to their roots; but precisely because the revolt originated in their ranks and the political process was kept under military leadership, the armed forces felt globally re-legitimized and postponed any profound internal restructuring. This explains, among other things, why the soldiers' committees appeared very late in the process and without internal dynamics.

In sum, the state apparatus, once cleansed of its distinctly fascist features, did not collapse. It rather suffered a generalized paralysis. Because the political events had started inside it, it was 'relatively easy' to bring about the paralysis of the bourgeois state power. In this sense there was no bourgeois rule. But neither, and for similar reasons, was there a proletarian rule. In this connection the role played by the big working-class parties (PS and PCP) must be briefly mentioned.

Having gained considerable influence in the state apparatus and inside the armed forces after March 1975, the PCP, the only political organization worth the name, looked rather suspiciously on the spontaneous mobilization and creative organizations of the working class, both at the point of production and at the point of reproduction. Under the mystifying argument that the enemy had already been destroyed by the nationalization of monopoly capital and that the sector of the MFA then in power would, if supported, carry out the class interests of the proletariat, the PCP always favoured policies inside the state apparatus and rejected as adventuristic the idea of revolutionary legality and of popular power. The socialist party, of recent formation and heterogeneous composition, resented the influence of the communists in the state apparatus and rejected as authoritarian any political form but parliamentary democracy. Drawing its support from the bourgeoisie, sectors of the petit-bourgeoisie and of the working class, who resented the power politics and the arrogance of the communists, the socialist party soon became the opposition party *par excellence*. As in Germany in 1918, the socialists became the leading party in a broad coalition of bourgeois and conservative political forces which, as the recent developments reveal, subsequently managed to subalternize them.

It may be said that the same process that had quite rapidly obtained the suspension or neutralization of bourgeois rule, had at the same time prevented proletarian rule from emerging in its own name. This was less a situation of dual power than a situation of dual powerlessness, as I would characterize it; a situation which was resolved in favour of bourgeois rule in November 1975. The Portuguese revolution shows, indeed, as one of its striking features, that the bourgeois state may undergo a generalized paralysis for an extended period of time without coming to a collapse. On the contrary, it remains intact as a kind of reserve state only to be reactivated if and as soon as the relations of forces change in its favour.

Within the global situation of dual powerlessness I have just described, restricted forms of dual power emerged in specific areas of social life and in specific sectors of the state apparatus. One of such situations of dual power took place in the judicial apparatus and assumed the form of popular justice. I have elsewhere described and analysed in detail the major instances of popular justice in Portugal between March and November 1975.[12] The most publicized case, though not the most characteristic one, was the Diogo case. José Diogo, a rural worker in Alentejo, was accused of having murdered a big landowner, his former *patrão* and for many years president of the municipality. In view of the increasing popular solidarity for Diogo the case was transferred from the local court to the Lisbon court, since "the emotional climate around the case," in the state attorney's words, did not allow for an "independent and orderly" administration of justice. From the Lisbon court, and for the same reasons, the case was again transferred, this time to Tomar, a small town some 100 kilometres north of Lisbon. A big political rally was held there on the day of the trial, and close to one thousand people jammed the area in front of the court-house. For reasons that were not clear, Diogo was not brought to the court, and the "official" trial was postponed. Thereupon José Diogo was tried, on the steps of the state court-house, by a self-appointed popular jury of industrial and rural workers. After many people spoke up, particularly amongst the rural workers, denouncing the despotic rule of large landowners in Alentejo as well as the oppressive conditions under which the rural proletariat were forced to live, the *latifundiário* was "posthumously condemned" by the jury "for having oppressed and exploited" the people of Alentejo; at the same time, after considering the extreme conditions under which José Diogo had acted, the same jury acquitted him; his action, however, being an individual action, could not be considered, nor justified, as a revolutionary action. This was a highly confused situation: José Diogo, though in preventive detention, could not be brought to court; on the other hand, against previous rulings, bail was granted and raised in a few hours.

Most of the other popular courts dealt with housing problems. The best known of these cases was the Maria Rodrigues case. Maria Rodrigues was illegally occupying a house. Suit was brought against her by her landlady and she was to be tried in November 1975. The secretariat of the revolutionary residents' commissions, acting in her name, boycotted the trial and organized a popular jury composed of twenty-eight delegates of several residents' commissions. This popular jury met in the inner courtyard of the state court-house and, after long hours of discussion on the housing question, Maria Rodrigues was granted the right to stay in the house she had occupied. Vigilance committees were then organized to prevent any attempt at eviction by the police.

All these cases are very embryonic, poorly-organized forms of popular justice, hence of dual power in the judicial area. Nevertheless they point to a proletarian revolutionary legality and legal form. The normative boundaries of the cases are transformed so that the class content of the dispute—always mystified by bourgeois legality—becomes apparent. The object of the dispute is thus immensely expanded and the gap—characteristic of bourgeois legal process—between the "real" dispute and the processed dispute is eliminated. Moreover, the class relations in the dispute are inverted. The popular jury, organized on the basis of class position rather than abstract citizenship, assumes itself as the justice of the oppressed classes; accordingly, the defendant in the state court becomes the plaintiff in the popular court and vice versa. The effect of isolation—also characteristic of bourgeois justice—disappears since both parties come to court not as abstract individuals but rather as class members. The trial form is retained but not only the jury structure is changed but also the rules defining the relevant issues are completely subverted. The actions of José Diogo

[12]B. de Sousa Santos, "Law and Revolution in Portugal: The Experiences of Popular Justice in Portugal after the 25th of April, 1974," R. Abel, *The Politics of Informal Justice*, New York, 1981.

and Maria Rodrigues are contextualized in the history of class struggle in Alentejo and in urban ghettos respectively, and are evaluated differently in the light of their different meaning in that struggle. There is no strict distinction between substantive and procedural issues; the question of the fairness of the trial is mediated by the recognition that the dispute as brought to court is the tip of the iceberg, a small detail of a much broader class struggle in which the class enemy can never be presumed not guilty. There is neither a professional monopolization of the legal process nor technical expropriation of legal language and discourse.

Since these restricted instances of dual power, as many others in other areas of social life (industry, education, prisons, etc.), were taking place in a situation of global dual powerlessness, they were always fragmentary actions and as such they could not be reproduced in a cumulative way. As there was no unified revolutionary strategy to bring about proletarian rule in its own name, the dual power initiatives could not grow into a global confrontation with bourgeois state power. State power was paralysed but virtually undivided. This explains why the state judicial apparatus never lost control of either the Diogo or Rodrigues cases. Indeed, after 25 November, 1975, when the conditions for active bourgeois rule were restored, the two cases were tried and both defendants were found guilty. And though I will not go into that here, it is highly debatable whether the specific instances of popular justice in the specific conditions of the Portuguese revolution played a positive or a negative role.

ANOTHER ALTERNATIVE LEGALITY: SQUATTER SETTLEMENTS IN RIO

The cases of popular justice in the Portuguese revolution makes a two-fold contribution to revolutionary strategy. First, they show that in order to eliminate the historical aberrations involving the idea of popular justice, the latter must be conceptualized as dual power in the judicial function, as working-class justice versus bourgeois-class jus-

tice. Second, they illustrate one of the possible ways in which the concept of dual power must be transformed in order to increase its analytical and strategic value. Once the specific conditions of the revolutionary crisis do not permit a global confrontation with the old state power, it may be possible and correct to create restricted or sectionalized forms of dual power to operate in specific areas of social life or in specific sectors of state action.

It is, however, possible to think of other ways in which the concept of dual power may be transformed to fit the complex diversity and dynamics of the socialist struggle in our time. In the cases presented so far the dual power takes place in a revolutionary crisis and, though in a sectionalized version, it embodies a situation in which antagonistic powers confront each other, that is, a situation of inter-class conflict. It is conceivable, however, to use the concept of dual power—in a weakened but nonetheless valuable form—in non-revolutionary situations, embodying complementary or parallel, rather than confrontational, powers and in which, on the surface at least, intra-class conflicts are dealt with. I will try to demonstrate such a possibility—restricted for the present purposes to dual power in law and justice—by referring to the judicial functions performed by residents' associations in squatter settlements throughout Latin America and elsewhere, and presenting as an example the case of the residents' association in a squatter settlement in Rio (Brazil), which I have studied extensively.[13]

Pasargada, as in my study I call this *favela*, is a large old squatter settlement in Rio. The land which the founders of the settlement first occupied in the early 1930s was at the time privately owned and is now state property. For some years the community has been electing a residents' association (RA) formally in charge of representing the community interests before the various state agencies, particularly in relation to

[13]B. de Sousa Santos, *Law Against Law: Legal Reasoning in Pasargada Law*, Cuernavaca, 1974; "The Law of the Oppressed: The Construction and Reproduction of Legality in Pasargada," *Law and Society Review*, 12(H77), pp. 5-126.

public services and facilities, and of promoting peaceful interaction inside the *favela*. My research, however, has revealed that beyond these functions—which are of course poorly performed, given the over-exploitation of the masses, the repressive legislation and the fascist political rule in today's Brazil—the residents' association has gradually become a legal forum, an instrument of dispute prevention and dispute settlement inside Pasargada. In this capacity the RA performs two kinds of functions: ratification of legal relationships and settlement of disputes arising from them. The legal relationships usually originate in contracts (sales, leases, etc.) involving property and property rights to land, shacks, houses and parts of houses and shacks, but may also consist of relationships of a public-law type involving the rights of the community as a whole *vis-à-vis* its individual members.

When, for instance, residents want to draft a contract they may come to the RA to see the *presidente*. Usually they are accompanied by relatives, friends or neighbours, some of whom will serve as witnesses. The parties explain their intentions to the *presidente,* who raises questions about the nature of the contract and its object until he is satisfied. Then the contract is written down and filed. The RA's intervention, which I call ratification, is a very subtle and complex process by means of which the legal relationship between the parties is provided with an autonomous source of security. When a dispute breaks out between two neighbours, the RA may be called upon to settle it, in which case a process is set in motion leading to the discussion of the case by the parties and neighbours in a hearing presided over by the *presidente*.

I have analysed in detail the normative and rhetorical structures of these legal processes, which I have called Pasargada law, and which cover a very intense and complex legal interaction outside the state legal system. In Pasargada, the state legal system is called the asphalt law. Pasargada law is obviously valid only inside the community, since from the point of view of state legality all the transactions based upon land illegally occupied have no legal validity. Pasargada's normative structure is thus based on the *inversion of the basic norm (grundnorm)* of property by means of which the legal status of Pasargada land is consequently inverted: from illegal occupation into legal possession. Once this inversion takes place the property norms of the asphalt law can be selectively borrowed by Pasargada law and applied inside the community. Indeed the principle of private property and the legal consequences it entails are as respected in Pasargada law as in Brazilian official law. Legal discourse in Pasargada relies on a very rich and elaborate legal rhetoric and I would suggest that the studies of legal rhetoric in Western philosophy, particularly in German legal philosophy, have a great deal to say to Pasargadian legal reasoning.[14] Comparing Pasargada legal reasoning with the prevalent legal reasoning in modern capitalist state justice it can probably be shown that in a given legal apparatus the wealth of legal rhetoric tends to increase as the amount of coercive powers decreases, and vice-versa. And indeed Pasargada law is a very embryonic and precarious form of legality and the RA coexists with other power centres in the community. It is also a very accessible, participatory, and non-professionalized legal setting. The distinction between procedural and substantive questions is not rigidly established and mediation is the dominant model of dispute settlement.

However precarious, Pasargada law represents an alternative legality to the bourgeois state legality and, as such, it also represents the exercise of an alternative form of power, however weak. Since Pasargada law does not claim validity or enforcement outside the community and merely aims at solving intra-class conflicts, the two legal powers are not in confrontation. They are rather parallel or even complementary. In this weakened form the concept of dual power could, I suggest, be applied to the unequal relation be-

[14]One of the main scientific interests of the works quoted in footnote 13 consists of the sociological analysis of legal rhetoric that has been traditionally a monopoly of legal philosophers.

tween Pasargada law and asphalt law. The objection might be raised that this is an illegitimate extension of the concept of dual power since Pasargada law merely prolongs the state law and is probably highly functional for the latter's overall objectives of domination. Though I partially grant that, I would like to counter-argue with three remarks.

First, by producing an alternative legality, Pasargada law attempts to neutralize or to counteract the fact that in capitalist societies (at least in peripheral ones) the working classes have no access, as proprietors, to social relations based on property, because their rights are declared to be illegal by the official legal system. It should be borne in mind that though in terms of their surface structure the conflicts dealt with by Pasargada law are created, discussed, and solved as intra-class conflicts, in terms of their deep structure, however, they are reflexive expressions of a much broader inter-class conflict. And this duality is ever present in Pasargada law, since the security of legal relations is a guarantee of the internal development of the community. Indeed the greater the internal development of the community the lesser the likelihood that the bourgeois interests in urban land speculation will pressure the state to remove the community to the outskirts of the city.

Second, Pasargada law centres around a community-based *elected* organization, the Residents' Association. Despite the limitations of the electoral process, Pasargada law thus offers an alternative democratic administration of justice, all the more remarkable because it takes place at the fringes of a fascist state. It performs, if no other, an educative function and potentially at least may contribute to raise the class consciousness of the urban working class living in squatter settlements.

Third, Pasargada law is not part of a revolutionary strategy nor does it take place in a revolutionary situation. On the contrary it operates under very difficult conditions of struggle. And in view of such conditions it may be argued that a complementary or parallel dual power is the necessary prehistory of a confrontational dual power.

CONCLUSION

I have explored in this essay some possible ways of expanding the concept of dual power with specific reference to the judicial functions of the state apparatus. I do not claim to have been exhaustive. On the contrary, I am fully aware that between the two extreme instances analyzed here—popular courts and Pasargada law—there are an infinite number of intermediate cases. As an example I would only mention the neighbourhood courts organized in Santiago squatter settlements during the Allende government and with his support. Considering the reciprocal implications of theoretical and strategic questions in Marxism, the conceptual work must take into account the ever changing conditions of socialist struggle in Europe today, both West and East, both in central and peripherial countries. Whenever the global overthrow of the class state is out of the question a realistic socialist strategy must start from the redefinition of the state itself. The state's non-monolithic and contradictory structure must be studied in detail; the modes of determination that are specific to each of its sectors must be closely analysed; strategies of dual power must then be organized in those sectors where conditions are most favourable.

This strategic orientation does not presuppose the rejection of bourgeois democratic legality and parliamentary democracy wherever they exist. It rather presupposes the possibility of a non-bourgeois use of bourgeois democratic legal and political forms. In the present conditions in South Europe, particularly in Portugal, it seems that it is up to the working class to defend bourgeois democratic legality and parliamentary democracy and to put these bourgeois forms to a non-bourgeois use. Such use involves an unequal struggle but given the contradictory nature of those forms such inequality is itself dynamic and a source of new conditions of struggle. The strategic objective is to raise the contradictions in specific sectors of state action to the point at which bourgeois legal and political forms and instruments become un-reproductive of class domination beyond the limits of controllable dysfunctionality. This is a strategy of maximum risk, as any revolutionary strategy should be.

REFERENCES

Broué, P. (1971), *Revolution en allemagne 1917 –23,* ed. De Minuit.

Lenin, V. I. (1960), ''The Dual Power,'' in V. I. Lenin, *Selected Works,* 3 vols. (Moscow: Progress Publishers, 1960), Vol. 2, pp. 50 –2.

Trotsky, L. (1969), ''Fascism, Stalinism and the United Front,'' *International Socialism,* no. 38/39 (1969), pp. 2 –70.

Wright, E. D. (1978), *Class, Crisis and the State* (London: New Left Books, 1978).

INDEX

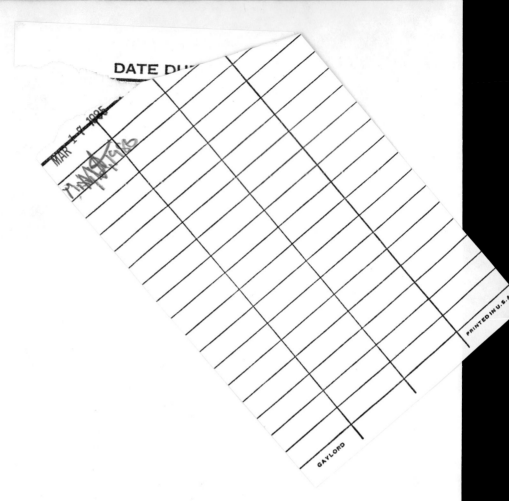
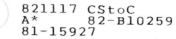